GRAPHIC DESIGN, TRANSLATED

LE LANGAGE DU GRAPHISME

GRAFIK DESIGN ÜBERSETZT

IL LINGUAGGIO DELLA GRAFICA

EL LENGUAJE DEL DISEÑO GRÁFICO

ROCKPORT

First published in the United States of America by
Rockport Publishers, a member of
Quayside Publishing Group
100 Cummings Center
Suite 406-L
Beverly, Massachusetts 01915-6101
Telephone: (978) 282-9590
Fax: (978) 283-2742
www.rockpub.com

Library of Congress Cataloging-in-Publication Data

Wolf, Peter J.
  Graphic design, translated : a visual directory of terms for global design / Peter J. Wolf.
      p. cm.
  Includes bibliographical references and index.
  ISBN-13: 978-1-59253-595-8
  ISBN-10: 1-59253-595-X
  1. Graphic arts—Dictionaries—Polyglot. 2. Printing—Dictionaries—Polyglot. 3. Dictionaries,
Polyglot. I. Title. II. Title: Visual dictionary of terms for global design.
  NC997.W65 2010
  741.603—dc22

                                                                                    2009039499

ISBN-13: 978-1-59253-595-8
ISBN-10: 1-59253-595-X

10 9 8 7 6 5 4 3 2 1

Design: Traffic Design Consultants
Cover Design: Traffic Design Consultants
Book Layout: Megan Jones Design

Printed in China

GRAPHIC DESIGN, TRANSLATED

ENGLISH

LE LANGAGE DU GRAPHISME

FRANÇAIS

DEUTSCH

IL LINGUAGGIO DELLA GRAFICA

ITALIANO

EL LENGUAJE DEL DISEÑO GRÁFICO

ESPAÑOL

ROCKPORT PUBLISHERS

Acknowledgments

It is some kind of injustice that most books—certainly one of this size—are attributed to an individual; such projects are necessarily collaborative.

And I am deeply indebted to the team of talented people responsible for this book's conception, design, and production. (Sadly, I will never meet most of them, this being one of those twenty-first century, Internet-enabled teams referred to in the introduction.)

Thanks, first of all, to the many contributing artists, designers, photographers, printers, educators, archivists, and collectors, without whom such a project would be simply impossible. More than once, some kind soul (often somebody I've never met) diverted his or her attention from far more pressing matters to send me images, fill out forms, answer questions, etc. I look forward to working with these people again in the future (perhaps—though it's a remarkably old-fashioned notion—even meeting in person one day).

The crew at Lux Coffee bar were, whether they knew it or not, also an integral part of the team. In addition to keeping my caffeine and glucose levels sufficiently elevated, they provided an environment conducive to working—be it email correspondence, face-to-face meetings, or the writing itself.

Thanks also to Laurel, for her generous recommendation, which set me off on a great adventure. And to Emily, for trusting me—a "recovering engineer"—with such an undertaking. And to Donna, for her experience, skills, and, most of all, patience. And finally to Kate, for her unwavering faith and constant encouragement, and for showing me that it's okay—not always, maybe, but sometimes—to leap without looking.

—Peter J. Wolf

Table of Contents

Introduction

For centuries now, graphic design has been used to celebrate national identities. Aspects of a country's values and self-image (as well as its design sensibility) are displayed daily in its currency, postage stamps, and all manner of official documents and communications.

Such examples are intended largely for domestic consumption, however. For "branding" a nation globally, visual communication efforts are focused outward—and few opportunities compare to the Olympic Games. Their sophisticated identity systems become forever associated not just with a particular time, but also a particular place. Otl Aicher's highly systematic approach to the graphics for the 1972 Games in Munich, to take just one example, is considered by many to be quintessential German design, reflecting the rich legacies of the Bauhaus and the Ulm School. More recently, the branding of the 2008 Summer Games in China presented a carefully crafted image of the country to the rest of the world, using the Games as a "global coming out party."[1]

Yet the history of graphic design is one of transcending international borders, too. During the fifteenth century, following the invention of the printing press, ideas about typography and illustration filtered quickly from Germany into the rest of Europe—just in time for the Italian Renaissance, a period of great innovation in typeface and book design. Nineteenth-century Victorian design, a response to the excesses of the Industrial Revolution, was adopted widely—especially by advertisers—across Europe and America. And the twentieth century saw the powerful influences of the Bauhaus and the International Typographic Style spread far beyond their origins in Western Europe, with an unprecedented reach across the globe.

International borders are defined not just by geographical and physical barriers, however, but also by culture and language. It was precisely these barriers that the Austrian philosopher Otto Neurath, along with his wife Marie Reidemeister and illustrator Gerd Arntz, sought to overcome with their Isotype (International System of Typographic Picture Education) system of pictograms. First developed during the 1920s—the First World War having brought international issues suddenly into sharp focus—the goal of Isotype was nothing less than "a world language without words."[2] The extensive Isotype system, with approximately 4,000 illustrations credited to Arntz alone, eventually spread throughout Europe to North America and beyond—transcending cultural and language barriers, and paving the way for the information graphics with which designers and the general public are now so familiar.

Today, of course, such transcendence is easier than ever; international design teams routinely collaborate using little more than a fluid network of Web-cruising laptops (often via increasingly ubiquitous wireless connections). And thanks to the

---

1 Quelch, John. "How Olympics Branding Is Shaping China," 2008. http://blogs.harvardbusiness.org
2 Meggs, Philip B. & Purvis, Alston W., *Meggs' History of Graphic Design*. Fourth ed. Hoboken, NJ: John Wiley & Sons, 2006.

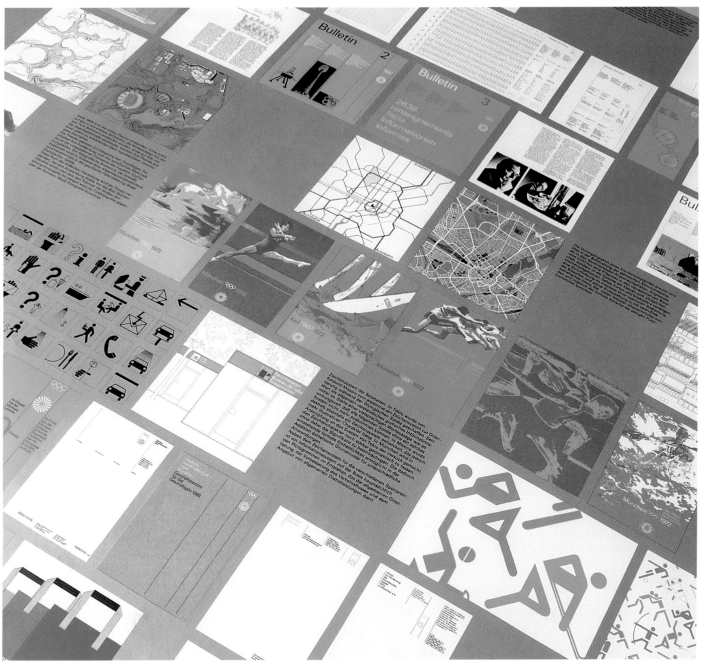

Examples of the extensive identity system developed by Otl Aicher for the 1972 Munich Olympics

Collection of Joe Miller; Photography: Joe Miller

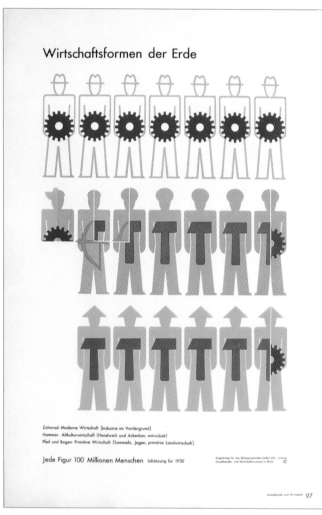

Wirtschaftsformen der Erde

Zahnrad: Moderne Wirtschaft (Industrie im Vordergrund)
Hammer: Altkulturwirtschaft (Handwerk und Ackerbau entwickelt)
Pfeil und Bogen: Primitive Wirtschaft (Sammeln, Jagen, primitive Landwirtschaft)

Jede Figur 100 Millionen Menschen Schätzung für 1930

"The World Economy," from *Gesellschaft* und *Wirtschaft* (Society and Economy),
a portfolio of 100 large format information charts published in 1930
Courtesy of the Otto and Marie Neurath Isotype Collection, University of Reading

numerous social media applications the Internet has made possible, the latest "great idea" in graphic design makes its way into—and around—the world in a matter of hours. Online portfolios, accessible 24/7 from practically anywhere, have become standard tools for promoting one's work. Location simply doesn't mean what it used to; in an era of nearly instantaneous global access to news, culture, the arts, and more, the world seems very small.

In the "flat" world proposed by Thomas Friedman's 2005 bestseller,[3] global communication is lightning-fast and dirt-cheap—and growing more so all the time. Email, seen just a couple years ago as the pinnacle of twenty-first-century correspondence, is being overshadowed today by Facebook and Twitter (which may themselves be overshadowed by something else just making its way into the world at the time of this writing). All of which increases our dependency on language. While it is true that contemporary life is rich with symbols, icons, and pictograms to a degree Neurath could only have dreamed of—not to mention the countless instant messaging-style abbreviations that have become both commonplace and universal—a "world language without words" remains out of reach.

Graphic Design, Translated is a compilation of more than two hundred of the most common terms in visual communication design, culled from a broad range of categories: design history, printing and paper,

3 Friedman, Thomas L. *The World Is Flat: A Brief History of the Twenty-first Century*. New York: Farrar, Straus and Giroux, 2005.

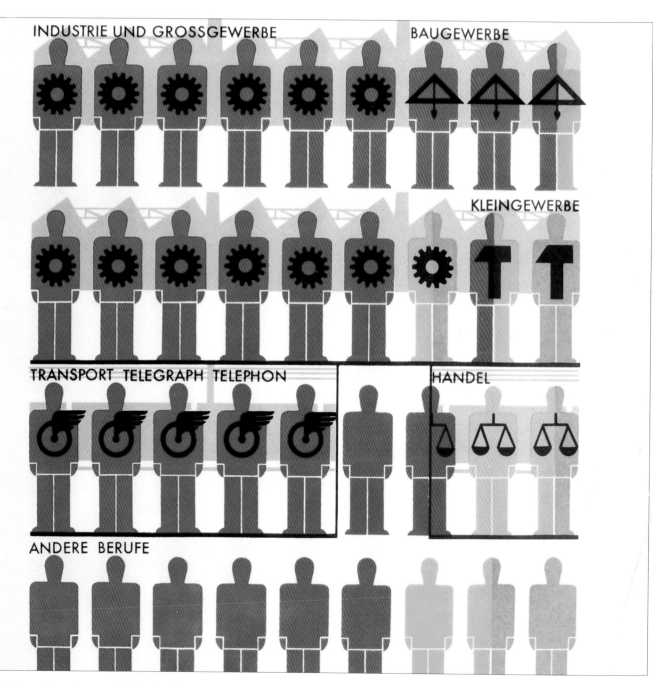

"Industry and Large Commercial," from *Gesellschaft* und *Wirtschaft* (Society and Economy), a portfolio of 100 large format information charts published in 1930

typography, digital technology, and design practice. Naturally, such an undertaking can never be fully comprehensive. Nor can it go into great detail about any one topic. The intent is to provide a brief introduction—for students, practitioners, clients, and others—to those terms that may be unfamiliar, and to revisit others whose meanings have grown foggy with frequent use (or misuse).

Some of the descriptions included are quite straightforward. *Baseline* or *x-height*, for example, require little more than a simple illustration and caption—though even here, the subtler point of *visual alignment* must also be introduced for a comprehensive understanding. Other descriptions are necessarily more subjective, perhaps even a little philosophical. After all, what one designer considers "balanced" may,

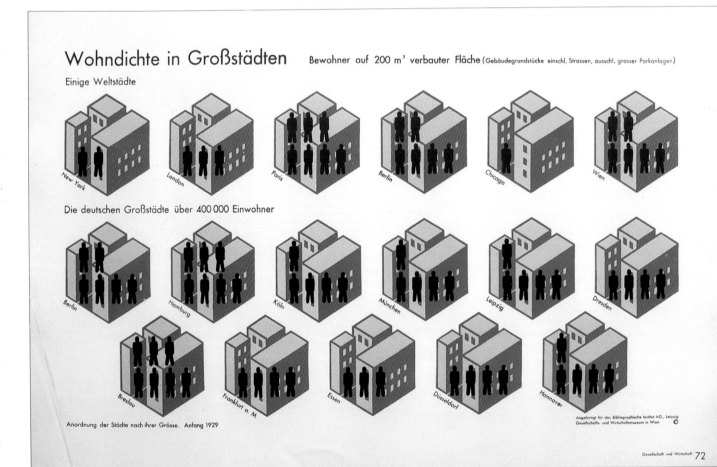

"Residents in Großstädten," from *Gesellschaft* und *Wirtschaft* (Society and Economy), a portfolio of 100 large format information charts published in 1930
Courtesy of the Otto and Marie Neurath Isotype Collection, University of Reading

to another designer, appear too safe—even boring. And the client may have a different understanding altogether. In such cases the descriptions are intended not to be the "final word," but rather points of departure—common ground from which conversations might begin.

These days, such conversations—among designers, but also beyond the graphic design community—occur with ever-increasing frequency and span borders both real and virtual. There is great value, then, in a reference book that can facilitate global communication, which is why this book is presented in five languages and illustrated with examples from around the globe. By taking such an approach, *Graphic Design, Translated* continues the rich tradition of graphic design transcending international borders and languages.

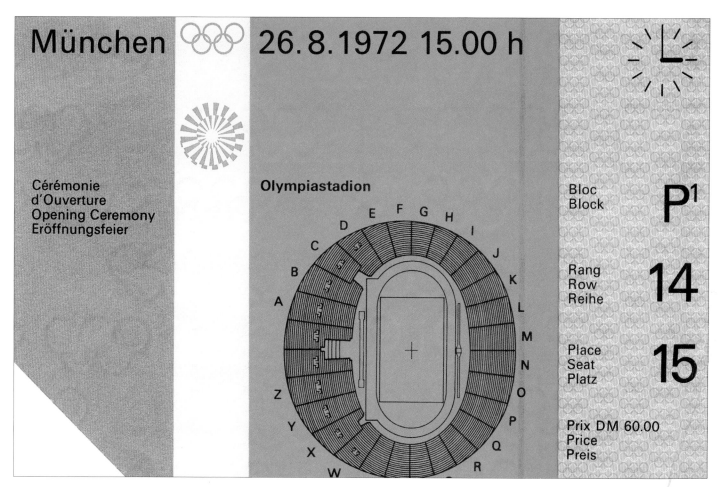

Announcement for *Spiele: Otl Aicher's Olympic Graphic Design*, a 2009 exhibition at San Francisco Museum of Modern Art, designed by Joe Miller

Collection of Joe Miller; Photography: Joe Miller

How To Use This Book

The two hundred-plus terms in this book are listed alphabetically for easy reference. Along with each term's description is a visual representation of the element, technology, or concept being explained.

In some cases, such as the entries for *apostrophe* and *leading*, the corresponding illustrations are intended to be direct and unambiguous; the text is supplemental to the images. For other entries, however, the imagery serves as just one among many valid examples of the term described. Obviously, there is no single solution or best choice for illustrating these more conceptual terms, such as *balance* and *white space*. In such cases, then, the work shown may require some "unpacking" on the part of the reader.

So much of visual communication design is dependent upon relationships. The relationship of figure to ground, for example, or positive and negative space. Rhythm and balance exist within a particular context; each is understood only in terms of its surroundings. Typography, too, is driven largely by relationships. Letter spacing, leading—even ligatures—are meant to harmonize such relationships.

It should come as no surprise, then that many of the terms included in *Graphic Design, Translated* are cross-referenced with other, related terms described elsewhere in the book. These are indicated with **bold** type. *Italic* type is used to highlight industry terminology that, while important for a thorough understanding of the subject, is beyond the scope of this book.

Although all descriptions have been fully translated, some terms have not. Some of the terms, such as *RGB*, obviously require no translation and are therefore listed under the same spelling in each section of the book. There are also some terms that do not have equivalent words in other languages. In those cases, readers will be directed to a related or similar term. For instance, there is no German word for *caliper*, but there is a German word for *ream*, the term that most closely corresponds to *caliper*. So, under *caliper*, next to the German reference, readers will be directed to *ream*.

Translated terms are indicated at the end of each description, along with the corresponding page numbers for those terms. Each language section is alphabetical according to that language for easy reference. There is also an index in the back of the book to find page numbers corresponding to specific terms in any language.

Pronunciation Guide

The following guide is meant to help readers with proper pronunciation in English; however, we discovered while translating this book that several foreign language dictionaries do not use such guides because the words are so literal.

ə	pencil	h	hollow	r	red
ər	learn	i	tip	s	select
a	hand	ir	clear	sh	show
ā	paper	ī	website	t	tool
ä	option	j	edge	th	thick
är	sharpen	k	craft	t̲h	feather
au̇	mouse	l	yellow	ü	tool
b	box	m	map	u̇	book
ch	chip	n	network	u̇r	contour
d	dot	ŋ	ink	v	vision
e	pen	ō	open	w	web
er	wear	ȯ	draw	y	yellow
ē	see	ȯi	choice	z	zip
f	fill	ȯr	pour	zh	visual
g	green	p	paper		

Languages Table of Contents

ENGLISH⁰

A B C D E F G H I J K L M N O P Q R S T U V W X Y Z

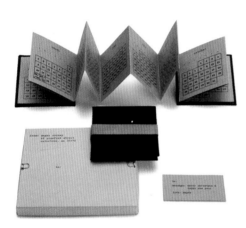

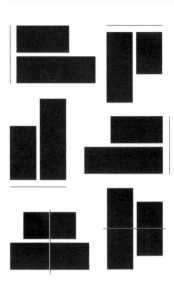

ACCORDION FOLD
\ə-ˈkȯr-dē-ən fōld\, *n*

Alternating folds made to a sheet of paper such that each of the *panels* (of which there are six or more) bends in a direction opposite to its adjacent panels. Two folds in this manner yield a six-panel (or six-page) accordion (three panels on each side of the sheet); three folds make an eight-panel accordion, and so on. Also called *concertina*.

Fr: PLI ACCORDÉON
Ger: LEPORELLO
It: PIEGHEVOLE A FISARMONICA
Sp: PLEGADO EN ACORDEÓN

Design: Megan Jones, www.meganjonesdesign.com

ALIASING
\ˈā-lē-ə-siŋ\, *n*

ANTI-ALIASING
\ˈan-tī-ˈā-lē-ə-siŋ\, n

Aliasing occurs when the **resolution** of a **bitmap** image is exceeded by that of the device used to display or print it. An image with a resolution of 72 *samples per inch* (or spi), for example, will exhibit aliasing when printed full-size at 300 *dots per inch* (dpi), resulting in a noticeable "stair-step" pattern. Anti-aliasing is a technique employed by digital image-editing software for minimizing the distortion caused by aliasing. This is accomplished through a slight blurring of the image, which softens the sharp edges of the stair steps. Although some quality is sacrificed in the process, it is often preferable to aliasing.

Fr: CRÉNELAGE, ANTICRÉNELAGE
Ger: ALIAS EFFEKT, ANTIALIASING
It: ALIASING/ANTI-ALIASING
Sp: SOLAPAMIENTO/ANTISOLAPAMIENTO

Design: Donna S. Atwood, www.atwooddesign.com

ALIGNMENT
\ə-ˈlīn-mənt\, *n*

Alignment refers to the arrangement of multiple design elements, such as images and **type**, relative to one another. Elements are often aligned such that their edges (left, right, upper, or lower) or centerlines (horizontal or vertical) correspond to a common reference line, which is often part of a **grid**. Alignment can also refer to the arrangement of type within a block of type. See also **flush-left**, **flush-right**, **centered type**, and **justified type**.

Fr: ALIGNEMENT
Ger: AXIALITÄT
It: ALLINEAMENTO
Sp: ALINEACIÓN

Design: Donna S. Atwood, www.atwooddesign.com

A BCDEFGHIJKLMNOPQRSTUVWXYZ

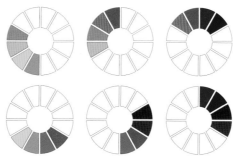

ALL CAPS
\ȯl ˈkaps\, *n*

Another name for **type** set exclusively in capital or *uppercase* letters, so called because the metal type used to print them was stored in the printer's upper drawers (or *cases*) whereas the more commonly used *lowercase* letters were stored in the more convenient lower drawers. Uppercase letters are also known as *majuscules*; lowercase letters are *minuscules*.

Fr: TOUT EN CAPITALES
Ger: VERSALIEN
It: TUTTE MAIUSCOLE
Sp: ALL CAPS

Art Direction: Brian Adducci; **Design:** Michelle Hyster; **Copy:** Russ Stark; **Printing:** Studio On Fire; **Firm:** Capsule, www.capsule.us

ANALOGOUS COLORS
\ə-ˈna-lə-gəs kə-lərs\, *n*

Two or more **colors** that are adjacent to one another on the **color wheel** (e.g., green, yellow-green, and yellow). Because analogous colors are closely "related" to one another, using two or three of them together generally lends a design a harmonious look.

Fr: COULEURS ANALOGUES
Ger: ANALOGE FARBEN
It: COLORI ANALOGHI
Sp: COLORES ANÁLOGOS

Design: Donna S. Atwood, www.atwooddesign.com

ANIMATION
\a-nə-ˈmā-shən\, *n*

A series of digital images displayed in a specific sequence so that a sense of continuous motion is created. Animated *GIF*s are often used for relatively simple Web design animation, whereas more complex animations are created by way of sophisticated software application, such as Adobe's Flash®.

Fr: ANIMATION
Ger: ANIMATION
It: ANIMAZIONE/I
Sp: ANIMACIÓN

Design: Donna S. Atwood, www.atwooddesign.com

A B C D E F G H I J K L M N O P Q R S T U V W X Y Z

'

(Apostrophe)

'

(Typewriter apostrophe)

/

(Prime)

APOSTROPHE
\ə-ˈpäs-trə-(ˌ)fē\, *n*

In the English language, apostrophes generally serve two functions: to mark omissions (e.g., '80s to indicate the 1980s) and to indicate the possessive forms of nouns (e.g., the cat's toy) and many pronouns (e.g., everybody's problem). Proper usage can be confusing because the same punctuation mark is also used as a single **quotation mark**. Apostrophes have a shape that curves or angles downward and to the left, and should not be confused with the straight apostrophe associated with typewriters, or the prime symbol used to denote units of measure (e.g., 2' to indicate 2 feet) and in mathematical notation.

Fr: APOSTROPHE
Ger: APOSTROPH
It: APOSTROFO
Sp: APÓSTROFO

AQUEOUS COATING
\ˈā-kwē-əs, a- kō-tiŋ\, *n*

A water-based coating applied to an entire sheet of paper, following printing, to produce an overall sheen (e.g., glossy or matte) and protect the underlying ink from scuffing and moisture. Uncoated papers tend to absorb ink, thereby softening the look of printed images, whereas coated papers prevent ink from being absorbed, thus allowing images to remain crisp. Aqueous coatings are typically used for printed materials that receive extensive handling, such as magazines and brochures. Other coatings, such as **varnishes**, are used for similar purposes to produce a variety of coated papers.

Fr: PELLICULAGE AQUEUX
Ger: DRUCKLACK
It: RIVESTIMENTO AD ACQUA
Sp: REVESTIMIENTO ACUOSO

ART DECO
\ärt de-(ˌ)kō\, *n*

A style that combined the decorative tendencies of **Art Nouveau** with the spare geometric forms and abstraction of **Modernism**, Art Deco was popular during the 1920s and 1930s in the United States and throughout much of Europe. Blending a wide range of influences, including Aztec and Native American art, Egyptian ziggurats, **Cubism**, and more, the Art Deco style was celebrated in architecture, interior and product design, and graphic design. Bold graphics were often combined with equally bold, stylized **type**.

Fr: ART DÉCO
Ger: ART DÉCO
It: ART DÉCO
Sp: ART DECÓ

A BCDEFGHIJKLMNOPQRSTUVWXYZ

ave nothing
in your house that
you do not know to
be useful or believe
to be beautiful.

WILLIAM MORRIS

Typography

ART NOUVEAU
\ärt nü-ˈvō\, *n*

A highly decorative style of architecture and design prevalent throughout much of Europe between the 1880s and the outbreak of World War I, and for a short time in the United States. Art Nouveau, as the name implies, aimed to create an entirely new aesthetic, rejecting the chaotic clutter of the **Victorian** era in favor of organic, curvaceous forms. Popular motifs included plants and animals (especially birds), as well female figures, often depicted with a level of abstraction far greater than was common in Victorian graphics.

Fr: ART NOUVEAU
Ger: JUGENDSTIL
It: ART NOUVEAU
Sp: ART NOUVEAU

Design: Donna S. Atwood, www.atwooddesign.com

ARTS AND CRAFTS
\ärts ən(d) ˈkrafts\, *n*

A reform movement begun in England in the late nineteenth century as a reaction to the Industrial Revolution and its emphasis on mass production at the expense of aesthetics. In graphic design, the Arts and Crafts movement was epitomized in the books of William Morris. Although his use of decorative capitals, *Gothic* typefaces, and heavy **layouts** recall printed works from centuries earlier, Morris's emphasis on reuniting design and production activities set the stage for twentieth-century **Modernism**.

Fr: ARTS & CRAFTS
Ger: ARTS AND CRAFTS
It: ARTS AND CRAFTS
Sp: ARTS AND CRAFTS

Design: Donna S. Atwood, www.atwooddesign.com

ASCENDER
\ə-ˈsen-dər\, *n*

Any portion of a *lowercase* letterform that extends above the **x-height** of a given typeface to the *ascent line*. The relative size and weight of ascenders varies by **typeface**; those with larger x-heights tend to have more subtle ascenders, while those with smaller x-heights tend to have more prominent ascenders. See also **descender** and **x-height**.

Fr: ASCENDANTE
Ger: OBERLÄNGE
It: TRATTO ASCENDENTE
Sp: ASCENDENTE

Design: Donna S. Atwood, www.atwooddesign.com

A B C D E F G H I J K L M N O P Q R S T U V W X Y Z

ASYMMETRY
\ā-ˈsi-mə-trē\, *n*

The organization of design elements such that they are distributed unevenly with respect to a layout's primary horizontal and vertical axes. Asymmetry can also be used to describe a **spread** in which the **facing pages** are not mirror images of each other. Effective asymmetrical **layouts** achieve **balance** through the careful interplay of **positive space** and **negative space**, and tend to be more dynamic than symmetrical layouts. See also **symmetry** and **eye flow**.

Fr: ASYMÉTRIE
Ger: ASYMMETRIE
It: ASIMMETRIA
Sp: ASIMETRÍA

Design: Mike Joyce, Stereotype Design, www.stereotype-design.com

BACK MATTER
See **end matter**.

BALANCE
\ˈba-lən(t)s\, *n*

The visual relationship among design elements within a particular context. A **layout** is said to have balance when the shapes, proportions, **textures**, **colors**, and **values** of each element work to create a sense of visual harmony. Balanced layouts need not be conservative, however. In fact, the sensitive designer can use balance to activate spaces throughout an entire layout, thereby creating a more engaging experience for the audience.

Fr: ÉQUILIBRE
Ger: BALANCE (AUSGEWOGENHEIT)
It: BILANCIAMENTO
Sp: EQUILIBRIO

Design/Photography: Skolos-Wedell, www.skolos-wedell.com

BARREL FOLD
\ˈber-əl fōld\, *n*

Alternating parallel folds made to a sheet of paper so that the resulting series of panels fold in, or "rolls up," on one another. In order for each panel to nest properly, outer panels are progressively wider (measured from fold-to-fold or edge-to-fold) than adjacent panels closer to the interior. Also called *roll fold*. See also **accordion fold**.

Fr: PLI ROULÉ
Ger: WICKELFALZ
It: PIEGHEVOLE A PORTAFOGLIO
Sp: DOBLADO TIPO ROLLO

Art Direction: Tracy Holdeman; **Design:** Casey Zimmerman; **Firm:** Insight Design Communications, www.insightdesign.com

A **B** C D E F G H I J K L M N O P Q R S T U V W X Y Z

Typography

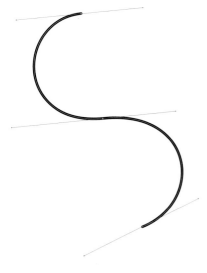

BASELINE
\ˈbās-ˌlīn\, *n*

A reference line used for the proper horizontal **alignment** of type. The lower edges of *uppercase* letters and those *lowercase* letters having no **descenders** rest along the baseline, or very nearly so. In fact, only the flat-based lowercase letters, such as *h* and *i*, sit properly on the baseline. Those with rounded bases, such as *o* and *u*, actually drop slightly below the baseline. The resulting "optical illusion" illustrates the importance of **visual alignment** over precision alignment when it comes to fine **typography**.

Fr: LIGNE DE BASE
Ger: GRUNDLINIE (SCHRIFTLINIE)
It: LINEA DI BASE
Sp: LÍNEA DE BASE

BAUHAUS
\ˈbau̇-ˌhau̇s\, *n*

A highly influential school of art, architecture, and design that operated in Germany from 1919 until 1933. The graphic design produced by the Bauhaus was distinctive for its unadorned, geometric appearance resulting from the school's emphasis on functionality. **Layouts** employed **sans serif** type almost exclusively, often organized with heavy **rules** and strict **grids**, as well as photography and **photomontage**. Black, white, and gray dominated the Bauhaus **color palette**, although **primary colors** were frequently used as accents.

Fr: BAUHAUS
Ger: BAUHAUS
It: BAUHAUS
Sp: BAUHAUS

BÉZIER CURVE
\ˈbāz-ˈyā ˈkərv\, *n*

A mathematical approximation of a continuous curve, defined by its two anchor points (one at each end) and any number of control points along it. The **paths** used by most graphic design software applications are made up of multiple Bézier curves, which is why they can be enlarged indefinitely. Bézier curves can also be used in **animation**, as tools for controlling motion.

Fr: COURBE DE BÉZIER
Ger: BÉZIERKURVE
It: CURVA DI BÉZIER
Sp: CURVA DE BÉZIER

Design: Donna S. Atwood, www.atwooddesign.com

A **B** C D E F G H I J K L M N O P Q R S T U V W X Y Z

BINDING
\ˈbīn-diŋ\, *n*

Any one of several methods used to hold together the pages of a book, magazine, brochure, or other multiple-page print publication. Some, such as ring binding and plastic comb binding, use fasteners placed through a series of holes in each page, and as such, are not permanent. Permanent binding methods include **case binding**, **perfect binding**, and **saddle-stitch binding**, among others.

Fr: RELIURE
Ger: EINBAND
It: RILEGATURA
Sp: ENCUADERNACIÓN

Prisma Graphic Corporation, www.prismagraphic.com

BITMAP
\ˈbit-ˌmap\, *n*

At its most fundamental level, a bitmap is the rectangular grid of points (or samples) that make up a digital image, such as a photograph or **letterform**. Each sample is associated with a particular **color** and location within the bitmap grid. The more *samples per inch* (spi), the higher the bitmap's **resolution**. Because there are a fixed number of samples in a bitmap image (unlike with **vector graphics**), they cannot be displayed or printed at resolutions beyond that of the particular output device without having **aliasing** occur. Also called *raster graphics*.

Fr: IMAGE MATRICIELLE
Ger: BITMAP
It: BITMAP
Sp: MAPA DE BITS

the keena gift show announcement
✻✻✻
the usual time, the usual place... you know the dates

✦ ✦ ✦

KEENA ~ SAN FRANCISCO
2400 fulton street
san francisco, california 94118
415-831-8809

KEENA ~ CHICAGO
1629 north ashland
chicago, illinois 60622
773-328-8804

KEENA ~ NEW YORK
416 west 13th street no.7
new york, new york 10014
212-206-6238

BLACKLETTER
\blak-ˈle-tər\, *n*

A classification of ornate **typefaces** that originated in the middle of the fifteenth century. Blackletter (or Black Letter) was first developed by German printers to imitate the handwriting commonly used by scribes of the period. Often used interchangeably with other terms, such as Fraktur, Textura, Old English, and Gothic, that describe similarly ornate typefaces. Adding to the confusion, *Gothic* can be used to describe either the ornate typeface suggested by Blackletter or the early **sans serif** typefaces, which have little in common with Blackletter.

Fr: GOTHIQUE
Ger: FRAKTUR (SCHRIFTEN)
It: BLACKLETTER
Sp: LETRA GÓTICA

Design: Goodesign, www.goodesignny.com

A **B** C D E F G H I J K L M N O P Q R S T U V W X Y Z

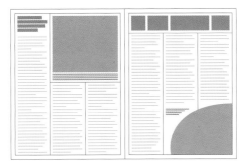

Garamond

Garamond Bold

TRAJAN

TRAJAN BOLD

BLEED
\blēd\, *n*

The portion of a design element, such as a printed image, line of type, field of **color**, etc., that extends beyond the actual page size. Trim marks are used to indicate the actual page size; anything printed outside of these marks will "bleed" off the page. The size required for a bleed will depend upon the accuracy of the printing press and the trimming equipment.

Fr: FONDS PERDUS
Ger: BESCHNITT
It: STAMPA AL VIVO
Sp: IMPRIMIR "A SANGRE"

Design: Kate Benjamin, www.moderncat.net

BODY COPY
\ˈbä-dē ˈkä-pē\, *n*

A term traditionally used to refer to the primary text within a book, brochure, or other publication. Used in this context, the body copy (or *body text*) excludes **front matter** and **back matter**, titles, **headlines**, **subheads**, and the like. *Body copy* can also refer to the main text of a website.

Fr: CORPS DU TEXTE
Ger: FLIESSTEXT
It: CORPO DEL TESTO
Sp: CUERPO DE TEXTO

Design: Donna S. Atwood, www.atwooddesign.com

BOLD/BOLDFACE
\ˈbōl(d)/ˈbōl(d)-ˌfās\, *n*

A **typeface** in which **letterforms** have heavier *stroke weights* than those used for the "regular" version of the same typeface. Desktop publishing applications typically offer a tool that "toggles" bold type, which merely thickens the stroke of the current typeface. True bold type, on the other hand, is designed to be proportional to other "members" of the same type family, resulting in an appealing "family resemblance" when printed.

Fr: GRAS, CARACTÈRES GRAS
Ger: FETT (SCHRIFTEN)
It: GRASSETTO
Sp: NEGRITA

A **B** C D E F G H I J K L M N O P Q R S T U V W X Y Z

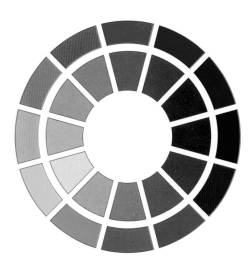

BORDER
\bȯr-dər\, *n*

A frame surrounding a photo, an illustration, a text block, or another design element that creates a transition between the element and the rest of the **layout**. Frames can be simple, a rectangle or a circle of thin line weight, for example, or highly ornate. Heavier, more detailed frames tend to deemphasize the image within, calling attention to the frame itself, whereas lighter, simpler frames help the image within stand out against its background.

Fr: BORDURE
Ger: RAHMEN
It: BORDO/I
Sp: BORDE

Art Direction/Design: Gaby Brink, www.tomorrowpartners.com, and Joel Templin, Hatch Design, www.hatchsf.com

BRANDING
\bran-diŋ\, *v*

The strategic differentiation of one "offering" (product, service, interaction, experience, etc.) from its competitors. In visual terms, the brand often begins with a **logo** or *logotype*, which is used to anchor the *brand promise*—a set of expectations associated with a particular offering. An effective *brand identity* involves, among other things, a comprehensive and consistent visual language (logo, **typeface**, **color palette**, and other visual cues). Contemporary brand strategies generally go well beyond traditional print and television advertising to include websites, blogs, and other evolving forms of *social media*.

Fr: STRATÉGIE DE MARQUE
Ger: MARKENBILDUNG
It: BRANDING
Sp: BRANDING

Creative Direction: Peter Shikany; **Design:** Marc Simpson, Judy Smith; **Illustration:** Jeff Jones; **Firm:** P.S. Studios, www.psstudios.com

BRIGHTNESS
\brīt-nes\, *n*

The relative lightness or darkness of a **color**, also called **value** or *tone*. Colors with similar brightness levels will appear nearly indistinguishable in a black-and-white photocopy. See also **color wheel**.

Fr: LUMINOSITÉ
Ger: LEUCHTDICHTE
It: LUMINOSITÀ
Sp: BRILLO

Design: Donna S. Atwood, www.atwooddesign.com

A B C D E F G H I J K L M N O P Q R S T U V W X Y Z

BULLET
\ˈbu̇-lət\, *n*

A typographic character (•) used most commonly to designate items in a list (called, not surprisingly, a *bulleted list*), although bullets are also sometimes used to separate short, sequential lines of **type**, such as an address on a letterhead. In either case, a space should be used between the bullet and the type. Bullets are generally included with **symbol** and **dingbat fonts**. See also **hanging punctuation**.

Fr: PUCE
Ger: AUFZÄHLUNGSPUNKT
It: PUNTO ELENCO
Sp: BOLO

CALIPER
See **ream**.

CALLIGRAPHY
\kə-ˈli-grə-fē\, *n*

Derived from the Greek *kalli* and *graphos*, calligraphy means "beautiful writing." It is an artistic form of handwriting, typically done with traditional tools, such as a nib or paintbrush, and distinctive for its flowing **letterforms** of varying stroke thickness.

Fr: CALLIGRAPHIE
Ger: KALLIGRAPHIE
     (SCHÖNSCHREIBKUNST)
It: CALLIGRAFIA
Sp: CALIGRAFÍA

Design: Teri Kahan, Richard Stumpf; **Firm:** Teri Kahan Design, www.terikahandesign.com

CALLOUT
\ˈkȯl-ˌau̇t\, *n*

A brief passage of text, often accompanied by a **line** and/or an arrow, used as a label to identify various key parts of a photo, illustration, or other type of artwork used in a **layout**. The term is also used for referring to portions of the text that are pulled out of the main text and given special emphasis, perhaps by way of a different **typeface**, **color**, size, etc. See also **caption** and **pull quote**.

Fr: CHIFFRES RÉFÉRENCES
Ger: HINWEIS
It: CALLOUT
Sp: LLAMADA

Art Direction/Design: Michael Ulrich, *STEP Inside Design*, Volume 24, Number 3

A B **C** D E F G H I J K L M N O P Q R S T U V W X Y Z

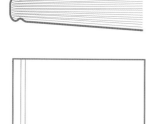

Typography

CAP HEIGHT
\ˈkap hīt\, *n*

The distance from the **baseline** to the upper edges of the *uppercase* letters, which lie along the *ascent line*. Cap heights vary even among **typefaces** of the same **point** size. See also **small capitals**.

Fr: HAUTEUR DE CAPITALE
Ger: VERSALHÖHE
It: ALTEZZA DELLA MAIUSCOLA
Sp: ALTURA DE LAS MAYÚSCULAS

CAPTION
\ˈkap-shən\, *n*

A brief passage of text used to describe or explain a photo, an illustration, a chart, or another visual element. Captions are generally placed above, below, or beside the artwork, separate from the **body copy**. See also **callout**.

Fr: LÉGENDE
Ger: BILDUNTERSCHRIFT
It: DIDASCALIA
Sp: PIE DE FOTO

Creative Direction: Peter Shikany, Judy Smith;
Firm: P.S. Studios, www.psstudios.com

CASE BINDING
\ˈkās ˈbīn-diŋ\, *n*

A form of permanent **binding** commonly used for hardcover books. First, **signatures** are sewn together at the spine, using thread. The *book block* is then glued along the spine, trimmed on the other three sides, and glued to the cover.

Fr: RELIURE CARTONNÉE
Ger: BUCHEINBAND
It: CARTONATURA
Sp: ENCUADERNACIÓN EN TAPA DURA

A B **C** D E F G H I J K L M N O P Q R S T U V W X Y Z

CENTERED TYPE/TEXT
\ˈsen-tərd ˈtīp/ˈtekst\, *n*

Successive lines of **type** aligned such that each line's midpoint lies along a common reference line. Because centered type demands a somewhat unnatural reading pattern, it is generally reserved for business cards, invitations, and other materials with relatively little type. See also **alignment**.

Fr: TEXTE CENTRÉ
Ger: MITTELACHSSATZ
It: TESTO/CARATTERI CENTRATI
Sp: TEXTO O TIPO CENTRADO

Creative Direction: Peter Shikany, Judy Smith; **Firm:** P.S. Studios, www.psstudios.com

A B C D E F G H I J K L M N O P Q R S T U V W X Y Z

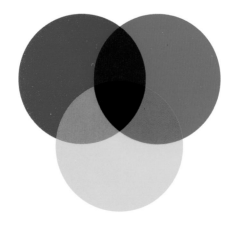

CHANNELS
\'cha-nəlz\, *n*

The digital information corresponding to the relative quantities of the three (for **RGB**) or four (for **CMYK**) **primary colors** used to represent color images. Each channel is like a **grayscale** image in which the **values** of gray have been replaced with values of a single primary color. The final color image is created, either on-screen or in print, by combining all channels of a given **color model**.

Fr: CANAUX
Ger: FARBKANÄLE
It: CANALI
Sp: CANAL

Design: Donna S. Atwood, www.atwooddesign.com

CHROMA
See **saturation**.

CLIP ART
\'klip ärt\, *n*

Illustrations, available in either print or digital format, for use in graphic **layouts**. Popular for years due to its availability, variety, and copyright-free designation. See also **stock photography/images**.

Fr: CLIPART
Ger: CLIPART
It: CLIP ART
Sp: CLIP ART

Courtesy of Dover Publications, Inc., www.doverpublications.com

CMYK

Abbreviation for cyan, magenta, yellow, and black, the ink colors used in **four-color process** printing. When combined in pairs, the *subtractive primary* colors cyan, magenta, and yellow reproduce the *additive primary* colors red, green, and blue, which correspond to the three different types of light receptors in the human eye. In theory, the three subtractive primaries combine to produce black; in practice, however, the result is not rich enough to produce a full range of tones for color printing, which is why black is included separately. Also called *process colors*.

Fr: CMJN
Ger: CMYK
It: CMYK
Sp: CMYK

Design: Kate Benjamin, www.moderncat.net

COATED PAPER
See **aqueous coating**.

A B **C** D E F G H I J K L M N O P Q R S T U V W X Y Z

COLLAGE
\kə-ˈläzh\, *n*

A technique used to create an original artwork by assembling paper, fabric, photography, or other media on a board or canvas, often in unexpected ways. The name is derived from the French *coller*, meaning "to stick." Collages can also be created digitally by "sticking" any number of digital elements, often scanned images of textural, three-dimensional objects, together in the same spirit of bricolage. See also **photomontage**.

Fr: COLLAGE
Ger: KOLLAGE
It: COLLAGE
Sp: COLLAGE

Design: Sean Adams; **Firm:** AdamsMorioka, www.adamsmorioka.com

COLOR
\ˈkə-lər\, *n*

The different wavelengths of light perceived by the human eye. Objects are perceived as having a particular color as a result of their ability to absorb, reflect, or transmit different wavelengths of light. The three basic properties of color are **hue**, **saturation** (or **chroma**), and **brightness** (also called **value** or *tone*). Color is also used by typographers when referring to the overall lightness or darkness of a page of **type**, or that of one paragraph relative to another. See also **color wheel**.

Fr: COULEUR
Ger: FARBE
It: COLORE/I
Sp: COLOR

Design: Hayes Henderson; **Illustration:** Henderson, William Hackley; **Firm:** HendersonBromsteadArt, www.hendersonbromsteadart.com

COLOR CORRECTION
\ˈkə-lər kə-ˈrek-shən\, *v*

The process of modifying the **color** in a digital photograph or scanned image either to achieve a more accurate representation of the original subject or to match the color range (or *gamut*) of the printing technology being used.

Fr: CORRECTION DES COULEURS
Ger: FARBKORREKTUR
It: CORREZIONE DEI COLORI
Sp: CORRECCIÓN DE COLOR

Design: Donna S. Atwood, www.atwooddesign.com

A B **C** D E F G H I J K L M N O P Q R S T U V W X Y Z

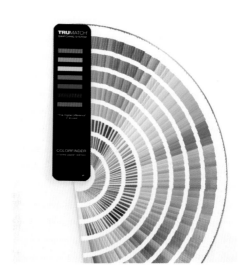

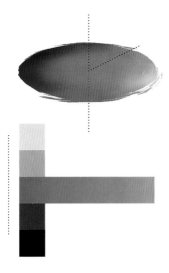

COLOR-MATCHING SYSTEM
\ˈkə-lər ˈma-chiŋ ˈsis-təm\, *n*

Any one of a handful of standard references, typically available as **color** charts or color swatches, each with a corresponding numeric designation, used for the precise specification of color. Designers use these designations to ensure that the colors intended for a particular project are "translated" correctly during the printing phase. For precise color matching, it is important to know which color-matching system(s) a printing service supports.

Fr: SYSTÈME D'ASSORTIMENT DES COULEURS
Ger: FARBKENNZEICHNUNGSSYSTEM
It: SISTEMA DI COMBINAZIONE DEI COLORI
Sp: SISTEMA DE AJUSTE DEL COLOR

Swatch compliments of Trumatch, www.trumatch.com

COLOR MODEL
\ˈkə-lər ˈmä-dəl\, *n*

A system by which **color** is defined absolutely (i.e., independent of the device used to display or print it) by way of just a few color components that, when adjusted, can be used to create a broad spectrum of color. **RGB** and **CMYK** are two common color models, although others exist as well. HSB, for example, uses color characteristics associated with the traditional color wheel: **hue**, **saturation**, and **brightness** (as shown here via the Munsell color system). The LAB color model is based on the coordinates used in *colorimetry*. Color model is often confused with **color space**, which is the range of color produced by a particular display or printing device within a specific color model.

Fr: MODÈLE COLORIMÉTRIQUE
Ger: FARBMODELL
It: MODELLO DI COLORE
Sp: MODELO DE COLOR

Design: Timothy Samara, tsamara_designer@hotmail.com

COLOR PALETTE
\ˈkə-lər ˈpa-lət\, *n*

A set of colors defined either by a particular media, such as the 216-color Web-safe color palette, or by a designer or an artist, for a specific project. Custom color palettes are often created using the relationships illustrated by the **color wheel**.

Fr: PALETTE DES COULEURS
Ger: FARBPALETTE
It: PALETTE DI COLORI
Sp: PALETA DE COLORES

Design: Donna S. Atwood, www.atwooddesign.com

COLOR SPACE
See **color model**.

A B **C** D E F G H I J K L M N O P Q R S T U V W X Y Z

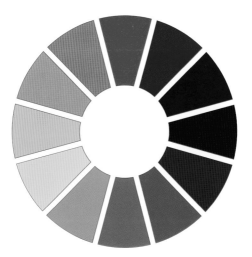

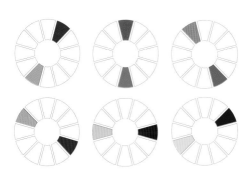

COLOR WHEEL
\ˈkə-lər ˈhwēl\, *n*

The **color** spectrum represented as segments of a circle. The most common color wheel, used for mixing pigments, has as its foundation the **primary colors** red, yellow, and blue, equally spaced along the circumference. Red, yellow, and blue are pure colors; they cannot be created by combining other colors. By mixing them together in various proportions, however, all other colors on the color wheel can be made. Other color wheels are used to illustrate similar relationships within other color systems, such as the **RGB** model used to display screen graphics. See also **analogous colors**, **complementary colors**, **primary colors**, **secondary colors**, and **tertiary colors**.

Fr: ROUE CHROMATIQUE
Ger: FARBKREIS
It: RUOTA DEI COLORI
Sp: RUEDA DE COLORES

Design: Donna S. Atwood, www.atwooddesign.com

COLUMN
\kä-ləm\, *n*

As the areas of a page **layout** where text is placed, columns often form the basic building blocks of a layout's **grid**. For text-heavy layouts, two or more columns are frequently used. Tall rectangular columns are perhaps the most common, but various other styles can be found as well.

Fr: COLONNE
Ger: SATZSPALTE
It: COLONNE
Sp: COLUMNA

Creative Direction: Vince Frost; **Firm:** Frost Design, www.frostdesign.com.au

COMPLEMENTARY COLORS
\käm-plə-ˈmen-t(ə-)rē ˈkə-lərz\, *n*

Colors that are opposite each other on the **color wheel**, as, for example, red and green are on the pigment color wheel. Also called *contrasting* colors. Using complementary colors together in a design can be overwhelming. More common is a *split complementary* scheme, in which one color is used together with the two colors that flank its complement on the color wheel.

Fr: COULEURS COMPLÉMENTAIRES
Ger: KOMPLEMENTÄRFARBEN
It: COLORI COMPLEMENTARI
Sp: COLORES COMPLEMENTARIOS

Design: Donna S. Atwood, www.atwooddesign.com

A B **C** D E F G H I J K L M N O P Q R S T U V W X Y Z

Futura

Futura condensed

American Typewriter

American Typewriter condensed

COMPOSITE
\käm-ˈpä-zət\, *n*

An image created by combining other images or elements of other images. Unlike **collage**, which refers to an overall work of art, or **photomontage**, which refers to the combination specifically of photographic elements, *composite* typically refers to a single photograph or illustration within a larger creative work.

Fr: IMAGE COMPOSITE
Ger: BILDMONTAGE (COMPOSING)
It: COMPOSITE
Sp: FOTOCOMPOSICIÓN

Art Direction/Illustration/Design: Breet Yasko;
Creative Direction: James Nesbitt and Bernard Uy;
Firm: Wall to Wall Studios, www.walltowall.com

COMPOSITION
\käm-pə-ˈzi-shən\, *n*

A generic term used to describe the organization of design elements in a **layout**, the effectiveness of which is often expressed in rather abstract terms, such as **balance**, **contrast**, *flow*, and so forth. *Composition* can also be used as a noun, when referring to a layout of different elements.

Fr: COMPOSITION
Ger: KOMPOSITION
It: COMPOSIZIONE
Sp: COMPOSICIÓN

Design: Timothy Samara,
tsamara_designer@hotmail.com

CONDENSED TYPE
\kən-ˈden(t)st ˈtīp\, *n*

A **typeface** in which each **letterform** is narrower than the "regular" versions of the same typeface. In addition, each letter is set closer to adjacent letters, thus allowing for greater amounts of **type** to fit into a given space. Because the resulting **readability** suffers somewhat, condensed type is generally reserved for titles, **display type**, or other applications in which the passages of text are brief.

Fr: CONDENSÉ
Ger: SCHMALE SCHRIFT
It: CARATTERI CONDENSATI
Sp: LETRA CONDENSADA

A B **C** D E F G H I J K L M N O P Q R S T U V W X Y Z

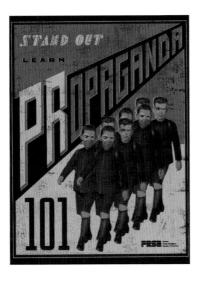

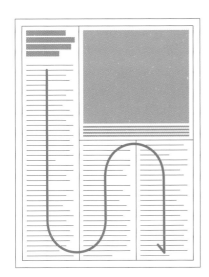

CONSTRUCTIVISM
\kən-ˈstrək-ti-ˌvi-zəm\, *n*

A Russian movement of the 1920s that integrated avant-garde art and design (especially the influences of **Cubism** and **Futurism**) with pro-Revolution political leanings. Key visual characteristics included abstract, geometric forms and **bold** type, **layouts** that broke with horizontal/vertical conventions, and a **color palette** often limited to red, black, and white. **Collage** and **photomontage**, techniques borrowed from **Dada**, were also used to create powerful visual communication design.

Fr: CONSTRUCTIVISME
Ger: KONSTRUKTIVISMUS
It: COSTRUTTIVISMO
Sp: CONSTRUCTIVISMO

Art Direction: Tracy Holdeman; **Design:** Lea Carmichael; **Firm:** Insight Design Communications, www.insightdesign.com

CONTRAST
\ˈkän-trast\, *n*

At its most basic level, contrast is nothing more than the difference between two design elements. Large **type**, for example, can be used to contrast with small type; the greater the difference in type size, the greater the contrast. Used effectively, contrast can create visually interesting **layouts**. **Textures**, **colors**, shapes, *line weights*, and other elements can be used to create contrast. See also **balance**, **complementary colors**, and **figure-ground**.

Fr: CONTRASTE
Ger: KONTRAST
It: CONTRASTO
Sp: CONTRASTE

Design: Noreen Morioka; **Firm:** AdamsMorioka, www.adamsmorioka.com

COPYFITTING
\ˈkä-pē ˈfit-tiŋ\, *v*

The typographic process of adjusting the **point size** and **leading** of **type** so that it fits into a defined area or across a specified number of pages. Calculations can be used to provide estimates, or the process can be done in an iterative fashion, using page-layout software, until the correct fit is achieved.

Fr: CALIBRAGE
Ger: TEXTEINPASSUNG
It: AGGIUSTAMENTO DEL TESTO
Sp: AJUSTE DEL ORIGINAL

Design: Donna S. Atwood, www.atwooddesign.com

A B **C** D E F G H I J K L M N O P Q R S T U V W X Y Z

Typography

COUNTER
\ˈkau̇n-tər\, *n*

The space enclosed, either completely (as in the letter *o*) or partially (as in the letter *c*), within a **letterform**. *Counter* is also sometimes used in a more general sense, referring to the space between neighboring letterforms. See also **negative space**.

Fr: CONTREPOINÇON
Ger: PUNZE
It: OCCHIELLO
Sp: CONTRAFORMA

CROP
\ˈkräp\, *v*

To trim a photograph or other piece of artwork through either digital or mechanical means, removing any unwanted portions around its outer edges. Cropping is done to precisely frame the contents of a photograph, or to match the size and proportions of an image to the space allotted for it within a given **layout**. The small lines used to frame the artwork for cropping are called *crop marks*.

Fr: RECADRER
Ger: AUSSCHNITT
It: CROP
Sp: RECORTAR

CUBISM
\ˈkyü-ˌbi-zəm\, *n*

An early twentieth-century (roughly 1907–1920) avant-garde European art movement in which objects, including the human figure, were often abstracted into geometric shapes. Multiple perspectives were presented simultaneously, and three dimensions reduced to two, challenging conventional rules of perspective dating back to the Renaissance. Soon, graphic design would reflect similar experimental approaches to spatial **composition** and geometric abstraction.

Fr: CUBISME
Ger: KUBISMUS
It: CUBISMO
Sp: CUBISMO

Design: Cristiano Siqueira Ilustração & Design, www.crisvector.com

Typography

DADA
\ˈdä-(ˌ)dä\, *n*

An artistic movement that began in Zurich, Switzerland, and spread across Europe as a reaction against World War I. Dada challenged a number of traditional beliefs, including those concerning art, morality, and religion, with its provocative, even nonsensical, visuals (though in Germany the Dadaists' work took on a darker and more political tone, as Hitler rose to power in the 1930s). Dadaist graphics suggested a broad range of influences, including the organizational approaches of **Constructivism** and **De Stijl**, and the raw energy of **collage** and **photomontage**, a technique that the Dadaists claimed to invent.

Fr: DADA
Ger: DADAISMUS
It: DADA
Sp: DADA

Design: Donna S. Atwood, www.atwooddesign.com

DE STIJL
\də-ˈstī(-ə)l\, *n*

An early twentieth-century (1917–1931) Dutch art and design movement concerned with expressing universal laws through a purely objective visual language. **Colors** were limited to neutrals (black, white, gray) and the **primaries** red, blue, and yellow, while forms were restricted mostly to squares and rectangles arranged asymmetrically along horizontals and verticals. **Sans serif** type was used almost exclusively, and was often combined with blocky, hand-drawn **display type**.

Fr: DE STIJL
Ger: DE STIJL
It: DE STIJL
Sp: DE STIJL

DEBOSS
See **emboss**.

DESCENDER
\di-ˈsen-dər\, *n*

Any portion of a *lowercase* **letterform** that extends below the **baseline**. As with **ascenders**, the relative size and weight of descenders varies by typeface. See also **ascender**.

Fr: DESCENDANTE
Ger: UNTERLÄNGE
It: TRATTO DISCENDENTE
Sp: DESCENDENTE

Design: Donna S. Atwood, www.atwooddesign.com

A B C **D** E F G H I J K L M N O P Q R S T U V W X Y Z

(Monotype Sorts)

(Webdings)

(Zapf Dingbats)

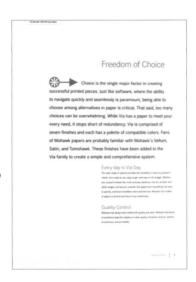

DIE CUT
\\ˈdī ˈkət\, *n*

A process by which precise cuts are made in a printed sheet of paper. These cuts can be functional, such as pocket folders and tab-and-slot style packaging, or decorative, such as "windows" that reveal images and edge treatments. In some cases, the functional and the decorative are combined. See also **kiss die cut** and **laser cut**.

Fr: DÉCOUPE
Ger: STANZSCHNITT
It: FUSTELLA
Sp: TROQUELADO

Creative Direction: Clifton Alexander; **Art Direction:** Chase Wilson; **Firm:** Reactor, www.yourreactor.com

DINGBATS
\\ˈdiŋ-ˌbats\, *n*

A broad range of special typographic characters, including **symbols** (e.g., mathematical, punctuation marks, etc.), **bullets** (e.g., circles, stars, etc.), various graphic ornaments, and more.

Fr: DINGBATS
Ger: DINGBATS
It: DINGBATS
Sp: DINGBATS

DISPLAY TYPE
\\di-ˈsplā ˈtīp\, *n*

Type set in a **point size** larger than the surrounding type in order to distinguish it from the main text, such as that used in titles and **headlines**.

Fr: CARACTÈRES DE TITRE
Ger: AUSZEICHNUNGSSCHRIFT
It: CARATTERI DI VISUALIZZAZIONE
Sp: TIPO TITULAR

Design: Sean Adams, Chris Taillon; **Firm:** AdamsMorioka, www.adamsmorioka.com

A B C **D** E F G H I J K L M N O P Q R S T U V W X Y Z

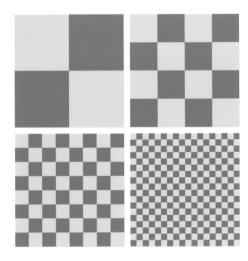

D rop caps provide a paragraph with a dramatic entrance, and indicate to the reader the beginning of a new section of text.

DITHER
\ˈdi-thər\, *v*

A method of approximating the true **colors** of a digital image using only those colors available in a given **color palette**. When a color digital image is converted to web-safe colors, for example, a specific set of 216 different colors (the *Web-safe color palette*) is used to approximate the colors of the original image. This is done by way of a "patchwork" of **pixels** in the case of computer monitors, or dots in the case of digital printers. A patchwork of blue and yellow pixels/dots could be used to approximate green, for instance. Although some detail is sacrificed in the process, dithering can be useful for smoothing out the unwanted jagged edges that can appear along adjacent fields of color. See also **posterization**.

Fr: TRAMAGE ALÉATOIRE
Ger: DITHERING
It: RETINO
Sp: DIFUMINADO

Design: Donna S. Atwood, www.atwooddesign.com

DROP CAPITAL/CAP
\ˈdräp ˈka-pə-təl/ˈkap\, *n*

An *uppercase* letter used as the initial letter of the first word in a paragraph, set in a **point size** larger than the surrounding type so that it extends into the text below. For additional impact, drop caps may be set in a **typeface** much different from that used for the **body copy**. They are specified in terms of how many lines of type they occupy. A three-line drop cap, for example, occupies the first, second, and third lines of a paragraph. See also **initial capital/cap** and **standing capital/cap**.

Fr: LETTRINE
Ger: HÄNGENDE INITIALE
It: CAPOLETTERA
Sp: MAYÚSCULA CAÍDA

DUOTONE
\ˈdü-(ˌ)ō̩tōn\, *n*

A **grayscale** image printed using two **colors** of ink rather than one. Although black often remains the primary ink, two non-black inks can also be used. Using black as the primary ink and a shade of gray as the secondary ink results in a tonal variation more closely approximating that of black-and-white photography. Using a non-neutral color as the secondary ink, or using two non-neutral colors together, allows for many interesting visual effects, from the subtle to the dramatic. **Tritones** are grayscale images printed with three colors.

Fr: SIMILI DEUX TONS
Ger: DUPLEX
It: BICROMIA
Sp: BITONO

Design: Timothy Samara,
tsamara_designer@hotmail.com

A B C D **E** F G H I J K L M N O P Q R S T U V W X Y Z

EGYPTIAN
\i-ˈjip-shən\, *n*

Any one of a number of *slab serif* **typefaces**. Their overall heavy appearance and minimal variation in *stroke weight* make them more suitable for posters, advertising, and headlines than for use in **body copy**.

Fr: ÉGYPTIENNE
Ger: EGYPTIENNE
It: CARATTERI EGIZIANI
Sp: EGIPCIO

Design: Mike Joyce, Stereotype Design, www.stereotype-design.com

---

This is an ellipsis…whereas this is a series of periods...

ELLIPSIS
\i-ˈlip-səs\, *n*

A punctuation mark formed by a series of three periods, used to indicate that parts of a text have been omitted, for instance, when portions of a direct quotation are used rather than the entire quotation, or the quotation is incomplete (at the end of a sentence, when a thought trails off). Each **typeface** has its own ellipsis character. Using this character rather than a series of three periods eliminates the risk of having the series split apart at a **line break**. On the other hand, precise spacing can be achieved only by using individual periods. Many style manuals recommend a space before and after each ellipsis, treating it as if it were a word, but typographers often prefer the look of an ellipsis without these spaces.

Fr: POINTS DE SUSPENSION
Ger: ELLIPSE (AUSLASSUNGSPUNKTE)
It: PUNTI DI SOSPENSIONE
Sp: PUNTOS SUSPENSIVOS

Typography

EM
\ˈem\, *n*

A relative unit of measure equal to the size of **type** being used, specified in **points**. For 12-point type, one em is equal to 12 points; for 10-point type, one em is equal to 10 points, and so on. More precisely, an em corresponds to the height (or *body*) of the cast metal blocks used for the *relief printing* of type. An *em-quad* is a cast metal spacer that measures 1 em in height and 1 em in width, and is used to create an **em space**. But, although all bodies of the same point size are the same height, the heights of the **letterforms** themselves vary considerably by **typeface**. So the em is only vaguely related to the actual size of type for a specific **font**. And the relationship is even less clear where digital type is concerned, there being no physical referent at all. See also **em dash**, **em space**, and **pica**.

Fr: CADRATIN
Ger: GEVIERT
It: EM
Sp: CUADRATÍN

A B C D **E** F G H I J K L M N O P Q R S T U V W X Y Z

Typography Typography

Em dash — Em   space

EM DASH
\em ˌdash\, *n*

A dash the length of one **em** used to create a pause in a line of text, especially to set off a parenthetical phrase. When it comes to using a space before and after an em dash, practices vary, although most publications prefer to go without. See also **en dash** and **hyphen**.

Fr:	TIRET CADRATIN
Ger:	GEVIERTSTRICH
It:	LINEETTA EM
Sp:	RAYA

EM SPACE
\em ˌspās\, *n*

A space the width of one **em** within a line of **type**. Digital **fonts** include the em space as a special character of a fixed width, unlike the spaces created by using the space bar, which will vary as the software composes each line of type.

Fr:	ESPACE CADRATIN
Ger:	GEVIERTABSTAND
It:	SPAZIO EM
Sp:	ESPACIO DE CUADRATÍN

EMBOSS
\im-ˈbäs\, *n*

Creating an impression in paper by pressing it between two metal dies, one raised and the other recessed. When the impression is raised above the surface of the paper, it is called an *emboss*; when the impression is below the paper's surface, it is called a *deboss*. Medium-weight papers, especially those with textured finishes, tend to work best. Printed images and **foil stamps** are often used as embellishments, although they are not required. Embossing done without them is called *blind embossing*.

Fr:	GAUFRAGE
Ger:	PRÄGUNG
It:	GOFFRATURA
Sp:	GOFRAR

Design: Igor Brezhnev, www.igorbrezhnev.com;
Production: Impact Printing Services; **Photo:** Natasha Mishano

A B C D **E** F G H I J K L M N O P Q R S T U V W X Y Z

Em

En

EN
\ˈen\, *n*

A typographic unit of measure half of an **em** in width. See also **en dash** and **en space**.

Fr: DEMI-CADRATIN
Ger: HALBGEVIERT
It: EN
Sp: MEDIO CUADRATÍN

Typography

—

EN DASH
\ˈen ˌdash\, *n*

A dash the width of one en used in place of the words *to* (e.g., 2:00–3:00) and *through* (e.g., Monday–Friday). As with the **em** dash, practices vary regarding the use of spaces before and after an en dash. Designers and typographers sometimes prefer to use the spaces, which they can then carefully adjust by way of **kerning**. See also **em dash** and **hyphen**.

Fr: TIRET DEMI-CADRATIN
Ger: DIVIS
It: LINEETTA EN
Sp: SEMIRRAYA

Typography

En space

EN SPACE
\ˈen ˌspās\, *n*

A space the width of one **en** within a line of **type**. As with the **em space**, digital **fonts** include the en space as a special character. Because it is of a fixed width, an en space remains unchanged as the software composes each line of type, unlike the variable spaces created using the space bar.

Fr: ESPACE DEMI-CADRATIN
Ger: HALBGEVIERTABSTAND
It: SPAZIO EN
Sp: ESPACIO DE MEDIO CUADRATÍN

A B C D **E** F G H I J K L M N O P Q R S T U V W X Y Z

ABCDEFGHIJKLMNOPQRSTUVWXYZ
0123456789 ⅛¼⅜½⅝¾⅞⅓⅔
ffffiffiflfflffjct ABCDEFGHIJ
LMNOPQRSTUVWXYZ

END MATTER
\end ˈma-tər\, *n*

Sections of a book that follow the main text, such as appendices, bibliographies, glossaries, notes, and so forth. Also called *back matter*. See also **front matter**.

Fr: PARTIES ANNEXES
Ger: ANHANG
It: PAGINE FINALI
Sp: PÁGINAS FINALES

EXPERT SET
\ek-ˌspərt ˈset\, *n*

A set of "nonstandard" typographic characters, such as **small caps**, **old-style numerals**, **ligatures**, and more, for a particular **typeface**. Critical to fine **typography**, expert sets were once purchased separately from basic fonts, but are now generally included with *OpenType* digital fonts. Also called *alternate fonts*.

Fr: CARACTÈRES ÉTENDUS
Ger: EXPERTENSATZ
It: EXPERT SET
Sp: SET EXPERTO

EYE FLOW
\ˈī ˈflō\, *n*

The path that one's eyes follow as they view a photograph or **layout**. Eye flow is influenced by a number of factors, including **color**, **balance**, **contrast**, and more. Effective designs take advantage of anticipated eye flow; wayfinding signs, for example, need to be simple and direct, while posters often engage viewers with complex eye flow. See also **focal point**.

Fr: CIRCULATION DU REGARD
Ger: BLICKPFADBEWEGUNG
It: FLUSSO VISIVO
Sp: LÍNEA DE ORIENTACIÓN

Design: Timothy Samara,
tsamara_designer@hotmail.com

A B C D E **F** G H I J K L M N O P Q R S T U V W X Y Z

FACING PAGES

\ˈfā-siŋ ˈpā-jəz\, *n*

The left-hand and right-hand pages of a **spread**. **Layout** applications such as Adobe InDesign® allow designers to create documents in either a single-sided format or as facing pages. See also **recto/verso**.

Fr: PAGES EN REGARD
Ger: DOPPELSEITEN
It: PAGINE AFFIANCATE
Sp: PÁGINAS ENFRENTADAS

Creative Direction: Sean Adams, Noreen Morioka; **Design:** Volker Dürre;
Firm: AdamsMorioka, www.adamsmorioka.com

A B C D E **F** G H I J K L M N O P Q R S T U V W X Y Z

FIGURE-GROUND
\ˈfi-gyər-ˈgrau̇nd\, *adj*

An aspect of visual perception based on the relationship between a form, such as a figure, an object, a geometric shape, or a **letterform**, and its surroundings: A form is distinguishable only when set against a background different from itself. By carefully manipulating this inherent relationship, designers can create compelling visuals from even the most basic forms. This can be especially important in the design of **logos**, where much content needs to be distilled into a relatively simple, easily identified mark. Stable figure-ground relationships tend to have an easily identified **focal point** and a harmonious feel, whereas ambiguous figure-ground relationships challenge viewers' perceptions. Used appropriately, each can be very effective. See also **positive space** and **negative space**.

Fr: DESSIN EN GRISÉ
Ger: FORMFLÄCHENGESTALTUNG
It: FIGURA-SFONDO
Sp: RELACIÓN FIGURA-FONDO

Design: Niklaus Troxler; **Firm:** Niklaus Troxler Design, www.troxlerart.ch

FLUSH-LEFT
\fləsh ˈleft\, *adj*

FLUSH-RIGHT
\fləsh ˈrīt\, adj

Successive lines of type that are flush-left begin at points along a common reference line. Also called *left-aligned* or *rag right*. Successive lines of type that are flush-right end at points along a common reference line. Also called *right-aligned* or *rag left*.

Fr: FER À GAUCHE, FER À DROITE
Ger: LINKSBÜNDIG, RECHTSBÜNDIG
It: ALLINEAMENTO A SINISTRA E
     ALLINEAMENTO A DESTRA
Sp: BANDERA A LA IZQUIERDA/BANDERA
     A LA DERECHA

FOCAL POINT
\ˈfō-kəl ˈpȯint\, *n*

The design element in a **layout** that first draws a viewer's attention; the area from which **eye flow** begins. Focal points can be created through a variety of means, among them **color**, **scale**, and **composition**. Advertising, in particular, often benefits from having a single, unambiguous focal point.

Fr: POINT CENTRAL
Ger: FOKUS
It: PUNTO FOCALE
Sp: PUNTO FOCAL

Design: Timothy Samara, tsamara_designer@hotmail.com

A B C D E **F** G H I J K L M N O P Q R S T U V W X Y Z

FOIL STAMPING
\ˈfȯi(-ə)l ˈstam-piŋ\, *v*

A process by which a thin plastic film is fused to paper by way of a heated die, often used to emphasize **logos**, illustrations, **type**, or other design elements. The plastic film is available in a wide range of **colors** and sheens, as well as metallic finishes. Opaque film can be used to apply a light color to a dark background; translucent film can be used to simulate **varnish**. Also called *foil block* or *hot foil stamp*.

Fr: DORURE
Ger: FOLIENPRÄGUNG
It: STAMPA A LAMINA DI PLASTICA
Sp: ESTAMPADO METÁLICO

Design: Adam Head; **Firm:** Fuse, www.fuse-design.co.uk

FONT
\ˈfänt\, *n*

A font typically includes *uppercase* and *lowercase* letters, as well as numerals and punctuation marks, although many *OpenType* fonts also include special characters once the domain of **expert sets**. For cast metal and wood type, fonts are size-specific; digital type, on the other hand, can be reduced or enlarged with the click of a mouse. Although *font* and *typeface* are often used interchangeably, there is a clear distinction: *Typeface* refers to the overall design of a set of characters; *fonts* are the means of production, either physical or digital.

Fr: FONTE
Ger: SCHRIFTSATZ
It: FONT
Sp: FUENTE

Design: Elias Roustom; **Firm:** EM Letterpress, www.emletterpress.com

FOR POSITION ONLY (FPO)
\ˈfər pə ˈzi-shən ˈōn-lē\, *adj*

A term used to describe an image of inferior quality, often a low-resolution version of the image to be used in the final version of the image to be used in the final version of the **layout**, that serves as a placeholder in a layout. By designating such images "FPO," their limited function is immediately understood by other members of the design team.

Fr: IMAGE DE PLACEMENT
Ger: PLATZHALTER
It: FOR POSITION ONLY (FPO)
Sp: FPO (SÓLO PARA REFERENCIA DE POSICIÓN)

Design: Donna S. Atwood, www.atwooddesign.com

FORM-COUNTERFORM
See **positive space** and **negative space**.

A B C D E **F G** H I J K L M N O P Q R S T U V W X Y Z

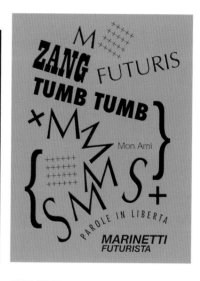

FOUR-COLOR PROCESS
\ˈfȯr ˈkə-lər ˈprä-ˌses\, *n*

A printing technique whereby the full spectrum of **color** is approximated by using individual *halftone screens*, called *color separations*, for each of the four **process colors**: cyan, magenta, yellow, and black. Each color is printed as a pattern of small dots of varying size and density. Because the four process colors, combined in pairs, produce the *additive primary* colors (red, green, and blue) that correspond to the three different types of light receptors in the human eye, the overall effect of "full color" is quite convincing. See also **CMYK** and **halftone**.

Fr: QUADRICHROMIE
Ger: VIERFARBDRUCK
It: PROCESSO A QUATTRO COLORI
Sp: CUATRICOMÍA

Design: Donna S. Atwood, www.atwooddesign.com

FRONT MATTER
\ˈfrənt ˈma-tər\, *n*

Sections of a book that precede the main text, such as the title page, *frontispiece* (illustration or other artwork on the page opposite the title page), table of contents, lists of figures and tables, foreword, and the like. See also **end matter**.

Fr: PAGES LIMINAIRES
Ger: TITELEI
It: PAGINE INIZIALI
Sp: PÁGINAS PRELIMINARES

FUTURISM
\ˈfyü-chə-ˌri-zəm\, *n*

A radical European art movement, based largely in Italy, during the early part of the twentieth century (approximately 1909–1930). Futurism sought to integrate the speed and noise of the "machine age" into art and design. **Collage** and **photomontage** were used to express this energy, as were techniques suggesting cinematic motion. Futurism's greatest influence on graphic design, however, was its use of **type** for its visual impact. Multiple **typefaces** in a wide range of sizes, sometimes set at odd angles or even distorted, were often used in a single **layout**, with **bold** and *italic* type suggesting points of particular emphasis.

Fr: FUTURISME
Ger: FUTURISMUS
It: FUTURISMO
Sp: FUTURISMO

Design: Donna S. Atwood, www.atwooddesign.com

GALLEY PROOF
See **proof**.

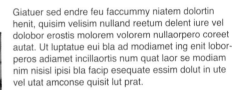

ABCDEF**G**HIJKLMNOPQRSTUVWXYZ

Giatuer sed endre feu faccummy niatem dolortin henit, quisim velisim nulland reetum delent iure vel dolobor erostis molorem volorem nullaorpero coreet autat. Ut luptatue eui bla ad modiamet ing enit loborperos adiamet incillaortis num quat laor se modiam nim nisisl ipisi bla facip esequate essim dolut in ute vel utat amconse quisit lut prat.

Irit, vulluptat vel delese magniam, cor sequam ing ex enit at wis adiamet, conse tem init luptatuerat, corper at, vel etum zzriure magnim nullut adit alismolobore tionsequat.

GRADIENT
\ˈgrā-dē-ənt\, *n*

The gradual blending of one **color** into another, or from white or black into a fully **saturated** color, generally in even gradations. Gradients are often used to fill parts of illustrations, backgrounds, or **outline type**.

Fr: DÉGRADÉ
Ger: VERLAUF
It: GRADIENTE/I
Sp: DEGRADADO

Design: Donna S. Atwood, www.atwooddesign.com

GRAYSCALE
\ˈgrā-ˌskāl\, *n*

An image comprised of varying shades of gray, white, and black. Color photographs can be converted to grayscale images digitally by way of software applications that translate the **value** of each dot to its gray equivalent, resulting in an image that simulates black-and-white photography. See also **monochromatic**.

Fr: ÉCHELLE DE GRIS
Ger: GRAUSTUFENBILD
It: SCALA DEI GRIGI
Sp: ESCALA DE GRISES

GREEKING
\ˈgrē-kiŋ\, *v*

The insertion of nonsensical, or "dummy," text as a placeholder during the **layout** process. The term is also used for describing the way some page-layout applications use gray bars to represent lines of **type** too small to be rendered clearly for a given display or view. Also called *Lorem Ipsum*.

Fr: FAUX TEXTE
Ger: BLINDTEXT
Sp: GREEKING

A B C D E F **G** H I J K L M N O P Q R S T U V W X Y Z

GRID
\ˈgrid\, *n*

A network made up of intersecting lines, most often running horizontally and vertically. Grids are used to organize design elements and provide a consistent structure to **layouts**. Especially useful for large projects, they can permit designers to work efficiently, virtually eliminating arbitrary decisions. On the other hand, grids are often criticized for stifling creativity or critical thinking. Used effectively, grids serve as "scaffolding," providing an underlying support structure that allows the designer more freedom, not less.

Fr: GRILLE
Ger: RASTER (SATZSPIEGEL)
It: GRIGLIA
Sp: CUADRÍCULA

Creative Direction: Sean Adams, Noreen Morioka;
Design: Sean Adams; **Firm:** AdamsMorioka,
www.adamsmorioka.com

A B C D E F **G H** I J K L M N O P Q R S T U V W X Y Z

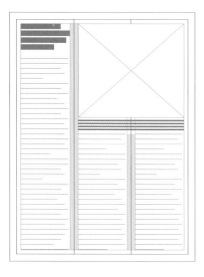

That is the great American story: young people just like you, following their passions, determined to meet the times on their own terms. They weren't doing it for the money. Their titles weren't fancy: ex-slave, minister, student, citizen. But they changed the course of history—and so can you.

That is the great American story: young people just like you, following their passions, determined to meet the times on their own terms. They weren't doing it for the money. Their titles weren't fancy: ex-slave, minister, student, citizen. But they changed the course of history—and so can you.

That is the great American story: young people just like you, following their passions, determined to meet the times on their own terms. They weren't doing it for the money. Their titles weren't fancy: ex-slave, minister, student, citizen. But they changed the course of history—and so can you.

That is the great American story: young people just like you, following their passions, determined to meet the times on their own terms. They weren't doing it for the money. Their titles weren't fancy: ex-slave, minister, student, citizen. But they changed the course of history—and so can you.

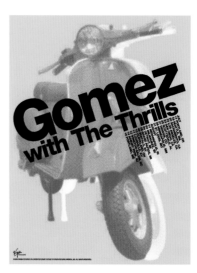

GUTTER
\\ˈgə-tər\\, *n*

The space between two **columns** of **type**, or, more generally, between any two columns in a **layout**. Sometimes also used to describe the narrow strip of a page nearest its **binding** edge, or the area where two such strips meet in a **spread**.

Fr: GOUTTIÈRE
Ger: SPALTENABSTAND
It: MARGINE INTERNO
Sp: MEDIANIL

Design: Donna S. Atwood, www.atwooddesign.com

H&J

Abbreviation for *Hyphenation & Justification*, the process by which software applications fill lines with **type**. Regardless of whether a block of text is aligned **flush-left**, **flush-right**, **justified**, or **centered**, the software automatically fills each line across the entire length of its **measure** with a combination of characters and spaces. This is called *justification* (a term commonly used to describe only those lines of type that completely fill their measure). *Hyphenation* refers to the breaking of words in such a way that each line of type can be more completely filled. Advanced page-layout applications allow for a number of H&J parameters to be adjusted, thereby giving the designer the flexibility necessary to create fine **typography**. See also **justified type**.

Fr: C&J
Ger: SILBENTRENNUNG & BLOCKSATZ (S&B)
It: H&J
Sp: H&J

HALFTONE
\\ˈhaf-ˌtōn\\, *n*

A **grayscale** image in which the full tonal range has been converted into a grid of tiny black dots, or *halftone screens*. Darker areas of the image are represented by patches of larger dots than those used to represent lighter areas of the image. Halftones corresponding to each **channel** are combined to simulate the full spectrum of visible **color** in **four-color process** printing. The same principle can also be scaled-up, using halftones to create interesting visual effects.

Fr: SIMILI
Ger: HALBTON
It: MEZZITONI
Sp: MEDIO TONO

Design: Mike Joyce; **Firm:** Stereotype Design, www.stereotype-design.com

A B C D E F G **H** I J K L M N O P Q R S T U V W X Y Z

"Four score and seven years
ago our fathers brought forth…"

"Four score and seven years
ago our fathers brought forth…"

• The Gettysburg Address

•The Gettysburg Address

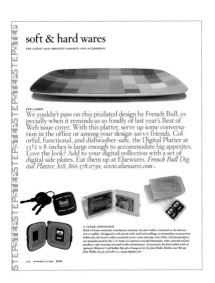

HANGING PUNCTUATION
\ˈhaŋ-iŋ ˌpəŋk-chə-ˈwā-shən\, *n*

Punctuation marks that are set slightly outside of a block of **type** in order to improve **visual alignment**. Opening **quotation marks** and **bullets** are sometimes set so that they lean into the left **margin**, while closing quotation marks and **hyphens** can be set into the right margin. Hanging punctuation requires a delicate touch, as the goal is to create clean **typography**, not to draw attention to specific elements. Non-punctuation characters are also sometimes set beyond the bounds of a given block of type in the pursuit of visual alignment, as when a footnote or citation reference mark is included in a column of decimal-aligned numbers. These are called *hanging characters*.

Fr: PONCTUATION MARGINALE
Ger: SATZKANTENAUSGLEICH
It: PUNTEGGIATURA ESTERNA
Sp: PUNTUACIÓN VOLADA

HEADING
\ˈhe-diŋ\, *n*

A typographical device used to break a lengthy text into its major sections, as when chapter headings are used in a book, or section headings in a brochure or report. Headings are frequently **typeset** with **all caps** or a combination of caps and **small caps**, often in **bold**. **Subheads** are used to further break up a text according to its organizational structure.

Fr: TITRE
Ger: ÜBERSCHRIFT
It: TESTATINA
Sp: TÍTULO

Art Direction/Design: Michael Ulrich, *STEP Inside Design*, Volume 22, Number 5

HEADLINE
\ˈhed-ˌlīn\, *n*

A term generally associated with journalism and advertising, used to describe a very short passage of text that appears before the **body copy**, suggesting something about its nature. Because headlines "set the stage" for the text, they are typically set in much larger **type**, perhaps of a different **typeface** than that used for the body. **All caps**, or a combination of standard and **small caps**, are frequently used for headlines, especially in newspapers.

Fr: CHAPEAU
Ger: SCHLAGZEILE
It: TITOLO
Sp: TITULAR

Creative Direction: Michael Fallone; **Design Direction:** Doug Bartow; **Design:** Susan Merrick; **Firm:** id29, www.id29.com

ABCDEFG**H**IJKLMNOPQRSTUVWXYZ

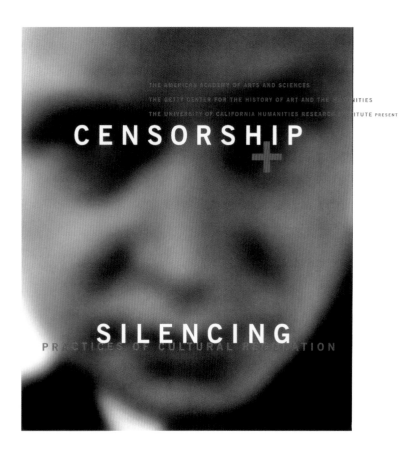

HIERARCHY
\ˈhī-(ə-)ˌrär-kē\, *n*

A discernable order expressed through variations in **scale**, placement, **value**, **color**, and any number of other visual cues. **Headings** and **subheads**, for example, create order throughout lengthy publications. By arranging elements in a hierarchical manner, designers guide viewers/readers through a business card, brochure, poster, book, or other creative work, revealing each element in a deliberate, thoughtful way. "Flat" hierarchies, by contrast, tend to be less interesting and/or confusing.

Fr: HIÉRARCHIE
Ger: HIERARCHIE
It: GERARCHIA TIPOGRAFICA
Sp: JERARQUÍA

Creative Direction/Design: Sean Adams;
Firm: AdamsMorioka, www.adamsmorioka.com

A B C D E F G **H I** J K L M N O P Q R S T U V W X Y Z

(Hyphen)

(En dash)

(Em dash)

HUE
\ˈhyü\, *n*

The basic characteristic of a **color**, corresponding to its particular wavelength in the light spectrum, used to distinguish one color from another. Hue relates to the relative position of a particular color along the circumference of a **color wheel**.

Fr: TEINTE
Ger: FARBTON
It: TONALITÀ
Sp: MATIZ

Design: Donna S. Atwood, www.atwooddesign.com

HYPHEN
\ˈhī-fən\, *n*

A punctuation mark often confused with the **en dash** and **em dash**, the hyphen is shorter in length than either of the other two marks and serves a different purpose. In English, the hyphen is used to indicate the two parts of a word broken across a **line break**, and to create compound words, such as *three-quarters*, *fixed-rate mortgage*, and *Asian-American*.

Fr: TRAIT D'UNION
Ger: TRENNSTRICH
It: TRATTINO
Sp: GUIÓN

HYPHENATION
See **H&J**.

ICON
\ˈī-ˌkän\, *n*

A graphical sign that looks like what it signifies. The printer icon on a computer screen, for example, looks like a printer, even if it is a generic one. Other examples include the cigarette graphic used on No Smoking signs, and the suitcase icon used for airport baggage claim signage. In both cases, the icons look like what they represent, which is what makes them easily recognizable, even across language and cultural barriers. See also **symbol** and **pictogram**.

Fr: ICÔNE
Ger: BILDZEICHEN
It: ICONA
Sp: ICONO

A B C D E F G H **I** J K L M N O P Q R S T U V W X Y Z

IDENTITY
\ī-ˈden-tə-tē\, *n*

The "personality" of a company, expressed visually (both internally and externally) through its distinctive **branding**. An *identity package* typically includes **logos** and/or *logotypes*, particular **color palettes** (often specified by way of a **color-matching system**), standardized **layouts** for documents and packaging, and the guidelines governing how each element is to be used in order to maintain consistency throughout the company. Large corporations may have several brands that share common visual elements, thereby connecting each brand to a larger corporate identity system.

Fr: IDENTITÉ
Ger: FIRMENERSCHEINUNGSBILD
It: IDENTITÀ
Sp: IDENTIDAD

Creative Direction: Sean Adams, Noreen Morioka;
Design: Monica Schlaug; **Firm:** AdamsMorioka,
www.adamsmorioka.com

Back

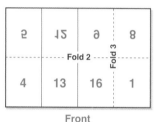

Front

IMPOSITION
\ˌim-pə-ˈzi-shən\, *v*

The careful arrangement of multiple pages of a publication for printing on large sheets of paper. Imposition ensures that the pages will be properly oriented and in the correct sequence once they are printed, folded into **signatures**, and bound. This can be done manually, although today it is more often done by way of software applications. See also **pagination**.

Fr: IMPOSITION
Ger: AUSSCHIESSEN
It: IMPOSIZIONE TIPOGRAFICA
Sp: IMPOSICIÓN

First-line indent

This generation, your generation, is the one that must find a path back to prosperity and decide how we respond to a global economy that left millions behind even before the most recent crisis hit — an economy where greed and short-term thinking were too often rewarded at the expense…

Running indent

This generation, your generation, is the one that must find a path back to prosperity and decide how we respond to a global economy that left millions behind even before the most recent crisis hit — an economy where greed and short-term thinking were too often rewarded at the expense …

Hanging indent

This generation, your generation, is the one that must find a path back to prosperity and decide how we respond to a global economy that left millions behind even before the most recent crisis hit — an economy where greed and short-term thinking were too often rewarded at the expense…

Indent on character

• This generation, your generation, is the one that must find a path back to prosperity and decide how we respond to a global economy that left millions behind even before the most recent crisis hit — an economy where greed and short-term thinking were too often rewarded at the expense…

INDENT
\in-ˈdent\, *n*

An adjustment made to the **margins** of one or more lines of **type**. Indents are most commonly used to indicate the beginning of a new paragraph, where the margin of the first line is noticeably larger than subsequent lines of type. *Hanging indents* are used to increase the margins of all lines following the first line in a paragraph. *Running indents* can be used to alter the left and/or right margins of multiple lines of type, as when wrapping around an illustration or photograph. *Indents on a point/character* are used when setting the margins to correspond to a specific point or character on a previous line of type.

Fr: COMPOSITION EN ALINÉA
Ger: ZEILENEINZUG
It: RIENTRO
Sp: SANGRÍA

A B C D E F G H I J K L M N O P Q R S T U V W X Y Z

Within the phantasmagorical sculptural world of Jessica Joslin, a rose is not a rose, despite poetic assertions of Lost Generation writer Gertrude Stein to the contrary. It may look like a rose, perhaps even feel and smell like a rose, but chances are excellent that, in Joslin's universe, any such floral form would be composed of a variety of puzzle-like parts that have little to do with the traditional worlds of botany or flora.

myth and magic
AN INTRODUCTION TO THE WORK OF JESSICA JOSLIN

Kathleen Vanesian

The artfully imagined skeletal macrocosm that sculptor Jessica Joslin has constructed over the past 16 years teems with elusive three-dimensional mammalian, avian and insect forms. Many of these animals are articulated and movable. They are all painstakingly created from a complex assortment of disparate objects that Joslin has collected from the worlds of nature and of man. The artist baptizes each of her intricately fabricated offspring with whimsical, often mythological, names, including some directly appropriated from her own family's genealogical chart. Not surprisingly, Joslin collects names as obsessively as she does the other detritus and artifacts that fill the small Chicago studio space she has shared with her husband, mentor and sounding board, painter Jared Joslin, for the last fifteen years.

Animal skulls, bird and fish bones, feathers plucked from another millennium's millinery masterpieces, orphaned electric and gas lamps, once fashionable furs harvested from what the artist terms "grandma collars," antique silverware, jewelry findings, arcane industrial hardware, Oddfellow ritual regalia, glass eyes — these and many more esoteric items are cannibalized, recycled and reconfigured by the artist into her unearthly menagerie of preternatural specimens. With consummate craftsmanship, Joslin reaches into this wildly diverse bag of ingredients to magically conjure eerily life-like skeletal sculptures, highly evocative of real members of the *animalia* kingdom, which she often places within theatrical or historical contexts — all with a wry gothic edge.

As pointed out by psychoanalyst Werner Muensterberger, a contemporary artist's collections frequently provide animation and inspiration for his art, or may even sway his barely conscious susceptibilities, long before the artist himself is fully aware of the source.[2] There is no question that this is the case for Joslin, who, along with her husband, admits to being an inveterate collector of just about anything intriguing to her, or potentially reducible into useful component parts.

"As you can imagine, I have quite a few bones of all kinds and many boxes of things like antique car horns and musical instruments...." notes the artist. "There's a wall [in the studio] lined with hundreds of tiny

MARCO, 2006

INITIAL CAPITAL/CAP
\i-'ni-shəl 'ka-pə-təl/'kap\, *n*

A decorative *uppercase* letter used as the initial letter of a paragraph's first word, generally set in a size larger than the surrounding **type**. Initial caps may also be of a different **typeface** and/or printed in a different **color** to create additional visual interest. Among the many variations commonly used are **drop caps** and **standing caps**. As with **swashes**, initial caps should be used sparingly, even in lengthy publications.

Fr: INITIALE
Ger: INITIALE
It: LETTERA MAIUSCOLA INIZIALE
Sp: MAYÚSCULA INICIAL

Design: Peter Shikany, Judy Smith; **Firm:** P.S. Studios, www.psstudios.com

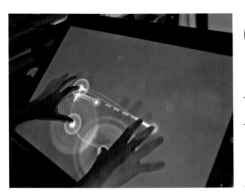

Caslon

Caslon Italic

Palatino

Palatino Italic

INTERACTION DESIGN
\ˌin-tər-ˈak-shən di-ˈzīn\, *n*

The practice of describing, defining, and creating the elements of a product, a system, or an organization with which a person might interact. The most common examples generally involve complex technological interfaces, such as those used for websites and portable electronic devices, although even simple interactions require thoughtful design consideration. The handle of a coffee cup, for example, is often designed for easy, intuitive use, although this is not always the case. Interaction designers are frequently involved in various forms of user research, applying methodologies from other disciplines, such as cognitive psychology and anthropology, among others.

Fr: DESIGN NUMÉRIQUE
Ger: INTERAKTIVES DESIGN
It: DESIGN INTERATTIVO
Sp: DISEÑO INTERACTIVO

Prototouch by wirmachenbunt (Engler/Fuchs), 2007,
www.wirmachenbunt.de

ITALIC
\ə-ˈta-lik, i-, ī-\, *n*

A **typeface** that is inclined to the right, frequently used for emphasis within a passage of text. Italic type was first developed in Italy around 1500 as a means to fit more type onto a single page, thereby reducing the size of printed books. True italics are sets of **letterforms** distinct from the **typeface** upon which they are based. **Oblique type** also slants to the right, but its letterforms remain largely unchanged from those of the "regular" typeface upon which it is based.

Fr: ITALIQUE
Ger: KURSIV
It: CORSIVO
Sp: CURSIVA

JUSTIFIED TYPE/TEXT
\ˈjəs-tə-ˌfīd ˈtīp/ˈtekst\, *n*

A term commonly used to describe successive lines of **type** that begin at points along one common imaginary reference line and end at points along another. Technically, all lines of type are justified, meaning that each line is filled across the entire length of its **measure** with a combination of characters and spaces; the difference lies in where the spaces are placed. Nevertheless, justified type has become ubiquitous for referring to cases in which all spaces are located between words, pushing the type out to both ends of the measure. This kind of justification, especially across a short measure, can sometimes lead to distracting gaps, called **rivers**, that "flow through" a block of type. See also **alignment** and **H&J**.

Fr: TEXTE JUSTIFIÉ
Ger: BLOCKSATZ
It: TESTO/CARATTERI GIUSTIFICATI
Sp: JUSTIFICACIÓN

Design: Mike Joyce; **Firm:** Stereotype Design,
www.stereotype-design.com

ABCDEFGHIJ **KL** MNOPQRSTUVWXYZ

Palatino

−19   −37   +7

Palatino

−76   0   +11   −25

KERNING
\ˈkər-niŋ\, *v*

Adjusting the space between two adjacent characters to create a visually appealing **rhythm**. When certain characters, such as *T* and *o*, are set together, the interaction of their shapes creates a distracting gap. Kerning is used to tighten the spacing, resulting in a more natural look. *Kerning pairs* are commonly used pairs of letters that require kerning for proper spacing (a task generally handled automatically by software applications, though not always to the satisfaction of designers and typographers).

Fr: CRÉNAGE
Ger: UNTERSCHNEIDEN
It: CRENATURA
Sp: KERNING

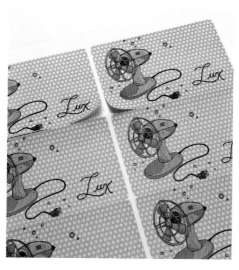

KISS DIE CUT
\ˈkis ˈdī ˈkət\, *n*

A version of the **die cut** process used for stickers and decals. Cuts are made in a printed sheet of paper without cutting into its backing, thereby allowing the stickers or decals to be removed from the backing.

Fr: DÉCOUPE PAR EFFLEUREMENT
Ger: ANSTANZUNG
It: ADESIVO CON FUSTELLA
Sp: TROQUELADO DE MEDIO CORTE

Design: Sammy Black,
www.luxcoffee.com/art/sammyblack/art/htm

LASER CUT
\ˈlā-zər ˈkət\, *v*

A process by which a computer-guided high-powered laser is used to etch into or cut through sheets of paper, wood, plastics, and even some metals. Laser cutting is very precise, accommodating a greater level of intricate detail than can conventional **die cutting**. And because there is no metal die involved, laser cutting can be less costly and more expedient than die cutting for very small production runs. Costs can increase dramatically, however, for extremely detailed work or when working with "difficult" materials, such as those that are easily scorched or melted, very thick, and so forth.

Fr: DÉCOUPE AU LASER
Ger: LASERSCHNITT
It: TAGLIO AL LASER
Sp: CORTE LÁSER

Design/Photography: Mario Trejo, www.mariotrejo.com

A B C D E F G H I J K **L** M N O P Q R S T U V W X Y Z

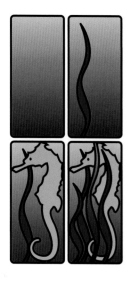

LAYER
\ˈlā-ər\, *n*

A feature of digital imaging software that treats different design elements as if they exist on transparent sheets, thereby allowing for the editing, combining, and manipulation of specific parts of an image without affecting others. The final image is the result of "stacking" layers in a particular sequence.

Fr: CALQUE
Ger: EBENE
It: LIVELLO
Sp: CAPA

Design: Donna S. Atwood, www.atwooddesign.com

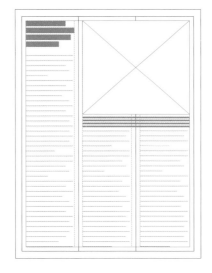

LAYOUT
\ˈlā-ˌaůt\, *n*

A preliminary step in the design process involving the organization of various design elements, such as **type**, photographs, and illustrations, in such a way that the expected outcome can be understood. Can also be used to describe the overall organization of a completed design. Layouts for books, brochures, reports, and other documents containing multiple pages are often organized by way of **grids**.

Fr: MAQUETTE
Ger: LAYOUT
It: LAYOUT
Sp: MAQUETACIÓN

Design: Donna S. Atwood, www.atwooddesign.com

Leading equal to
1 × point size

Leading equal to
1¼ × point size

Leading equal to
1½ × point size

LEADING
\ˈle-diŋ\, *n*

The distance between successive lines of **type**, measured from baseline to **baseline** and specified in **points**. The name comes from the strips of lead used for spacing lines of cast metal type. Unlike metal type, digital type can be set with *negative leading*, which means that the point size of the type exceeds the point size of the leading. Although **readability** suffers, negative leading can be used to create dramatic effects for advertising graphics, posters, and the like.

Fr: INTERLIGNAGE
Ger: DURCHSCHUSS (ZEILENABSTAND)
It: INTERLINEA
Sp: INTERLINEADO

A B C D E F G H I J K **L** M N O P Q R S T U V W X Y Z

LEGIBILITY: HOW EASILY LETTERFORMS AND WORDS CAN BE DECIPHERED

Legibility: how easily letterforms and words can be deciphered

Legibility: how easily letterforms and words can be deciphered

LEGIBILITY

\ˌle-jə-ˈbi-lə-tē\, *n*

A qualitative measure of how easily **letterforms** and words can be deciphered by the reader/viewer. Illegible texts are also unreadable; however, legibility does not ensure **readability**, the ease with which one proceeds through a passage of carefully set **typography**. The need for legibility depends largely on the context: posters and book jackets, for example, often employ **type** that borders on the illegible but is quite engaging. If the same type were used for wayfinding signage or an annual report, the results would be disastrous.

Fr: LISIBILITÉ
Ger: LESERLICHKEIT
It: LEGGIBILITÀ
Sp: LEGIBILIDAD TIPOGRÁFICA

Tracking = 0

This generation, your generation, is the one that must find a path back to prosperity and decide how we respond to a global economy that left millions behind even before the most recent crisis hit — an economy where greed and short-term thinking were too often rewarded at the expense of fairness, and diligence, and an honest day's work.

Tracking = -20

This generation, your generation, is the one that must find a path back to prosperity and decide how we respond to a global economy that left millions behind even before the most recent crisis hit — an economy where greed and short-term thinking were too often rewarded at the expense of fairness, and diligence, and an honest day's work.

LETTER SPACING

\ˈle-tər ˈspā-siŋ\, *n*

The overall spacing between characters within a body of text. Letter spacing is of particular concern when using **justified type** because of its propensity for distracting gaps between words, especially where the **measure** is short. Often confused with *letterspacing*, the process of increasing the spaces between the characters of **display type** in order to create visual interest. See also **tracking**.

Fr: INTERLETTRAGE
Ger: SPATIONIEREN
It: SPAZIO LETTERA
Sp: INTERLETRAJE

LETTERFORM

\ˈle-tər-ˈform\, *n*

The shape of an individual character, whether or not it's actually a letter. The common elements shared among a collection of letterforms are what make up a **typeface**. *Type anatomy* can be described by way of an extensive vocabulary that includes terms such as **serif**, **ascender**, **descender**, and many more.

Fr: DESSIN D'UNE LETTRE
Ger: SCHRIFTCHARAKTER
It: GLIFO/I
Sp: LETRA

Design: Stephanie Horn, www.stephanie-horn.com

A B C D E F G H I J K **L** M N O P Q R S T U V W X Y Z

Mar / 08   Sun Mon Tue Wed Thu Fri Sat
                                             1

LETTERPRESS
\ˈle-tər-ˌpres\, *n*

A process of *relief printing* that dates back to fifteenth-century Germany and the invention of the printing press. Blocks of **type** and illustrative elements, created in "reverse" so that their images read correctly when transferred to the paper, are locked into place on the press. Their surfaces are covered with ink and they are pressed evenly against the paper. Once done with cast metal and wooden type, letterpress work today typically incorporates a polymer plate created from a digital file.

Fr: IMPRESSION TYPOGRAPHIQUE
Ger: HOCHDRUCK
It: RILIEVOGRAFIA
Sp: IMPRESIÓN TIPOGRÁFICA

Design: Studio on Fire, www.studioonfire.com

A B C D E F G H I J K **L** M N O P Q R S T U V W X Y Z

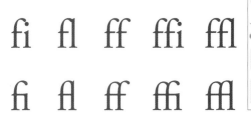

… and discipline, qualitative research can help designers understand the patterns of behavior as well as …

… understand the patterns of behavior as well as the patterns of thinking that underlie people's daily lives—exactly the sort of information designers need to …

… hours Wednesdays 11:00–1:00 & Thursdays 11:00–12:00, or by appointment …

… this can have an unintentional effect on the answers/results you get back …

LIGATURE
\\li-gǝ-ˌchu̇r\\, *n*

Two, sometimes three, **letterforms** combined by using the shared elements of each. Ligatures are typically used to prevent unsightly "collisions" of letterforms, as when the letter *i* follows the letter *f*. If these two letters are set as individual characters, the dot from the *i* will come very close to, or, depending on the **typeface**, even overlap the top of the *f*. By replacing the two characters with a single ligature, a clean, more legible line of **type** results. Ligatures, which can be traced back to ancient handwritten manuscripts, were used from the earliest days of cast metal type but fell out of favor during the *phototype* era. Most digital **fonts**, however, include a range of ligatures.

Fr: LIGATURE
Ger: LIGATUR
It: LEGATURA
Sp: LIGADURA

LINE
\\līn\\, *n*

A series of points, either straight or describing one or more curves. Unlike in geometry, where lines have negligible thickness, lines used by graphic designers may be thin or thick, and need not be consistent over their entire length. They can also be broken or fragmented. Thick lines take on the properties of planes (flat surfaces), and these three elements, point, line, and plane, form the basis for the creation of all forms used in graphic design. See also **rules**.

Fr: LIGNE
Ger: LINIENGESTALTUNG
It: LINEA/E
Sp: LÍNEA

Design: MacFadden & Thorpe,
www.macfaddenandthorpe.com

LINE BREAK
\\līn ˌbrāk\\, *n*

A term used when referring to how and where one line of **type** ends before continuing onto the next line. Layout applications typically break lines of type after a space between words, or following a **hyphen**, an **em dash**, or an **en dash**, although such automatic settings can often be adjusted. In addition, a *soft return* can be used to break a line, thereby beginning a new line of type without starting a new paragraph (which likely has specific characteristics, such as **indents**, associated with it). See also **H&J** and **text wrapping**.

Fr: SAUT DE LIGNE
Ger: ZEILENUMBRUCH
It: INTERRUZIONE DI LINEA
Sp: SALTO DE LÍNEA

A B C D E F G H I J K **L** M N O P Q R S T U V W X Y Z

These things are true. They have been the quiet force of progress throughout our history.

What is demanded then is a return to these truths. What is required of us now is a new era of responsibility — a recognition, on the part of every American, that we have duties to ourselves, our nation and the world, duties that we do not grudgingly accept but rather seize gladly, firm in the knowledge that there is nothing so satisfying to the spirit, so defining of our character than giving our all to a difficult task.

Lining: 0123456789

Paper

Stone or plate

LINE LENGTH
\ˈlīn ˌleŋ(k)th\, *n*

The distance across an individual line of **type**. Line length is often confused with **measure**, the width of the **column** itself. However, when type is set flush-left (or *rag-right*), for example, the lines of type only rarely fill the full measure. The same is true of **flush-left** and **centered type**. Only in cases of **justified type** does the line length correspond to the measure.

Fr: LONGUEUR DE LIGNE
Ger: ZEILENLÄNGE
It: LUNGHEZZA DI RIGA
Sp: LONGITUD DE LÍNEA

LINING NUMERALS/FIGURES
\ˈlī-niŋ ˈnüm-rəlz/ˈfi-gyərz\, *n*

Sets of numerals having the same (or nearly the same) height as a **typeface's** *uppercase* letters. Because they also have a constant character width and rest along the **baseline**, they are often used in tables, where their alignment can be visually appealing. See also **old-style numerals/figures**.

Fr: CHIFFRES ARABES
Ger: MAJUSKELZIFFERN
        (TABELLENZIFFERN)
It: NUMERI E LETTERE DI
ALLINEAMENTO
Sp: NÚMEROS DE CAJA ALTA

LITHOGRAPHY
\li-ˈthä-grə-fē\, *n*

A printing process in which ink is applied to a smooth stone or metal plate, from which it is then transferred onto paper. The name comes from the Greek *lithos*, meaning "stone," and *grapho*, meaning "to write." In lithography, an oil-based medium, such as crayon, is used to mark on the stone or metal, defining the areas where the ink, which is water-based, will be either accepted or rejected. Unmarked areas of the plate "hold" the ink and transfer it to the paper, whereas oily areas repel the ink and thereby become the background of the final printed image. See also **offset lithography**.

Fr: LITHOGRAPHIE
Ger: LITHOGRAFIE
It: LITOGRAFIA
Sp: LITOGRAFÍA

Design: Donna S. Atwood, www.atwooddesign.com

A B C D E F G H I J K **L M** N O P Q R S T U V W X Y Z

LOGO
\lō-(ˌ)gō\, *n*

A graphical sign used, typically for commercial reasons, as part of an organization's **branding**. Logos represent the values and personality of an organization. They must be memorable and instantly recognizable, and distinctive from those of competitors. Given these challenges, it is not surprising that companies will often use a successful logo for many, many years. A *logotype* is a specific set of **letterforms**, typically spelling out an organization's name or acronym, the details of which (**color**, **typeface**, **letter spacing**, etc.) are unique and an integral part of the organization's brand.

Fr: LOGO
Ger: LOGO
It: LOGO
Sp: LOGO

Logo used with permission of Best Friends Animal Society. All rights reserved.

LOREM IPSUM
See **greeking**.

MAKEREADY
\māk-ˌre-dē\, *n*

The process by which the printing press, as well as any finishing, folding, or **binding** equipment, are prepared for a particular print run. *Makeready* is also used to describe the sheets of paper used, often repeatedly, as "test cases" during this process. Such sheets are sometimes also treated as artworks in their own right.

Fr: MACULE
Ger: DRUCKEINRICHTUNG
It: AVVIAMENTO MACCHINA
Sp: ARREGLO

Design: Yee-Haw Industries, www.yeehawindustries.com

MARGIN
\mär-jən\, *n*

The areas along the four edges of a page that typically frame the **body copy** and/or images of a particular **layout**. Elements such as page numbers, footnotes, and **captions** are often printed in the margins. The margins that lie along the spine of a bound publication are sometimes also called the **gutter**.

Fr: MARGES
Ger: SEITENRAND
It: MARGINE/I
Sp: MARGEN

Design: Donna S. Atwood, www.atwooddesign.com

A B C D E F G H I J K L **M** N O P Q R S T U V W X Y Z

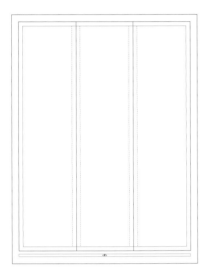

These things are true. They have been the quiet force of progress throughout our history.

What is demanded then is a return to these truths. What is required of us now is a new era of responsibility — a recognition, on the part of every American, that we have duties to ourselves, our nation and the world, duties that we do not grudgingly accept but rather seize gladly, firm in the knowledge that there is nothing so satisfying to the spirit, so defining of our character than giving our all to a difficult task.

Typography

MASTER PAGE
\\mas-tər ˈpāj\, *n*

A template used by page-layout applications to ensure consistent placement of the **grid**, text **columns**, page numbers, and other common **layout** elements throughout a document. Multiple master pages can be used within a single document, each one corresponding to a different section or layout style. Page numbering is typically done automatically when using master pages.

Fr: PAGE TYPE
Ger: MUSTERSEITE
It: PAGINA MASTRO
Sp: PÁGINA MAESTRA

Design: Donna S. Atwood, www.atwooddesign.com

MEAN LINE
\\mēn ˈlīn\, *n*

A reference line used for the proper horizontal **alignment** of type, corresponding to the **x-height** of a given **typeface**. The upper edges of those *lowercase* letters having no **ascenders** lie along the mean line, or very nearly so. In fact, only the flat-topped lowercase letters, such as *u* and *x*, end at the mean line. Those with rounded tops, such as *a* and *o*, actually extend slightly beyond the mean line. A similar "optical illusion" is used along the **baseline**; both cases illustrate the importance of **visual alignment** over precision alignment when it comes to fine **typography**.

Fr: LIGNE DE TÊTE
Ger: X-LINIE (MITTELLINIE)
It: LINEA MEDIANA
Sp: LÍNEA MEDIA

MEASURE
\\me-zhər\, *n*

A term used to describe the width of a block of type, traditionally measured in **points**, **picas**, or **ems**, although millimeters and **pixels** are also used in some contexts. The optimum measure with regard to **legibility** is generally considered to be 52 to 78 characters (the equivalent of two to three alphabets), including spaces, although factors such as **leading**, **letter spacing**, and the **typeface** itself must also be considered. See also **line length**.

Fr: MESURE
Ger: SATZBREITE
It: GIUSTEZZA
Sp: ANCHO

ABCDEFGHIJKL **M** NOPQRSTUVWXYZ

BRIGHT IDEA
You can do something very good for Solectron, our community and our world. It's this simple. If you're not using the lights, your computer or production machinery, and it won't adversely affect our business or operations, then please switch it off. Energy efficiency is good business. Now that's simple and brilliant.

SOLECTRON®

METAPHOR
\ˈme-tə-ˌfȯr\, *n*

The description or expression of one subject by way of another. In graphic design, metaphors can include textual components, as when a line of clever copy links an image to a seemingly unrelated concept. A photo of a dense, foreboding jungle, for example, may be combined with the line, "Shopping for auto insurance?" The idea that "it's a jungle out there" comes across without ever stating so directly. Purely visual metaphors draw upon the generally accepted associations of one or more images, transferring them to another. This is often done by way of *fused images*, created by "fusing" two or more images in order to facilitate such a transfer of meaning. The images of a pen and a gun, for example, might be combined to suggest the power of the written word.

Fr: MÉTAPHORE
Ger: METAPHER
It: METAFORA
Sp: METÁFORA

Art Direction/Design: Gaby Brink, www.tomorrowpartners.com, and Joel Templin, Hatch Design, www.hatchsf.com

A B C D E F G H I J K L **M** N O P Q R S T U V W X Y Z

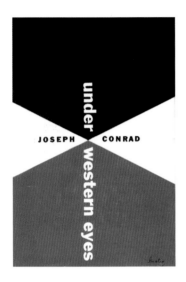

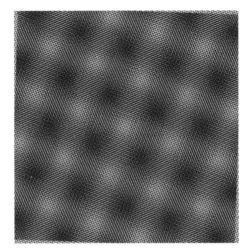

MODERNISM
\\mä-dər-ˌni-zəm\\, *n*

More a collection of movements than a single movement, Modernism first took root around 1907 with **Cubism** and its rejection of natural forms in favor of abstraction. In the subsequent hundred-plus years, Modernist design has been interpreted and reinterpreted around the world, taking on a great range of diverse forms, some more closely aligned with its mythology (e.g., strict use of **grids**, **sans serif** type, generous **white space**, etc.) than others. For every "rule" of Modernism, countless exceptions exist. Nevertheless, common threads can be found, among them an emphasis on functional visual communication and a forward-looking, often optimistic spirit.

Fr: MODERNISME
Ger: MODERNE
It: MODERNISMO
Sp: MODERNISMO

Design: Alvin Lustig, www.alvinlustig.com
Photo courtesy of Elaine Lustig Cohen

MOIRÉ
\\mȯ-ˈrā\\, *n*

An undesirable effect that can occur when the *halftone screens* used in **four-color** printing are aligned in such a way that a discernable pattern emerges. To prevent moiré, the screens are rotated at specific angles relative to one another, resulting in tiny **CMYK** rosettes, which are rarely noticeable in the final printing. Moiré can also occur when a printed image is digitally scanned without applying the *descreening* feature. See also **halftone**.

Fr: MOIRÉ
Ger: MOIRÉ-EFFEKT
It: EFFETTO MOIRÉ
Sp: MOARÉ

MONOCHROMATIC
\\mä-nə-krō-ˈma-tik\\, *adj*

Having a **color palette** comprised of *shades* and **tints** of a single **hue**. In monochromatic images, tonal variation is represented by way of differences in **saturation** and **brightness**. **Grayscale** images are monochromatic images with a color palette comprised of grays, white, and black.

Fr: MONOCHROMATIQUE
Ger: MONOCHROMATISCH (EINFARBIG)
It: MONOCROMATICO
Sp: MONOCROMÁTICO

A B C D E F G H I J K L **M N** O P Q R S T U V W X Y Z

Courier
Lucida Sans Typewriter

MONOSPACED
\ˈmä-(ˌ)nō-ˈspāst\, *n*

A term used to describe a **typeface** in which each character is of the same width. The resulting **type** is reminiscent of that produced by typewriters. See also **proportional**.

Fr: CARACTÈRES À CHASSE CONSTANTE
Ger: DICKTENGLEICH
     (NICHTPROPORTIONALE SCHRIFT)
It: MONOSPAZIO
Sp: MONOESPACIADA

MONTAGE
See **collage** and **photomontage**.

MULTIMEDIA
\ˈməl-tē-ˈmē-dē-ə\, *adj*

A term used to describe media in which content is delivered in more than one way. A single website, for example, may integrate text (including hypertext) and still images, as well as streaming audio and video, all on the same subject. The term can also be used to describe devices that support multimedia content and delivery, or for devices, such as video games, that allow for interactive user experiences.

Fr: MULTIMÉDIA
Ger: MULTIMEDIA
It: MULTIMEDIA
Sp: MULTIMEDIA

Design: Kate Benjamin, www.moderncat.net

NEGATIVE SPACE
\ˈne-gə-tiv ˈspās\, *n*

Generally used to describe a void created from the relationship of two or more design elements and the associated **positive space**. Negative space is frequently used to describe aspects of large **layouts**, but can also be used to describe elements of **typography**, where **letterforms** generate relationships of negative and positive space with neighboring letterforms. **Logos**, because they are generally small, are often designed with careful attention paid to the relationship of negative and positive space. See also **figure-ground** and **white space**.

Fr: ESPACE NÉGATIF
Ger: FREIE FLÄCHE
It: SPAZIO NEGATIVO
Sp: ESPACIO NEGATIVO

Creative Direction: Michael Fallone; **Design Direction:** Doug Bartow; **Design:** Susan Merrick; **Firm:** id29, www.id29.com

A B C D E F G H I J K L M N **O** P Q R S T U V W X Y Z

Futura
Futura Oblique

Helvetica Neue
Helvetica Neue Oblique

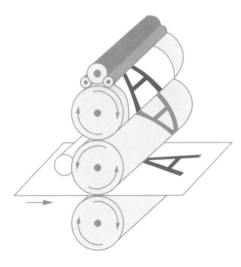

Old-style: 0123456789

OBLIQUE
\ō-'blēk\, *n*

Sans serif type that is inclined to the right, comprised of **letterforms** very similar to those of the "normal" **typeface** upon which it is based. **Italic** type is also inclined to the right, but its letterforms have been completely redrawn and are often quite different from those upon which they are based.

Fr: OBLIQUE
Ger: SCHRÄG
It: CARATTERI OBLIQUE
Sp: OBLICUA

OFFSET LITHOGRAPHY
\'òf-ˌset li-'thä-grə-fē\, *n*

A printing process based on the principles of **lithography**, in which an inked image is first transferred, or *offset*, to a rubber *blanket* before being applied to a printing surface. One set of rollers is used to apply the ink to the plate, while another set rolls the blanket over it, thereby transferring the ink to the blanket. High quality and economies of scale have helped make offset lithography, sometimes called *offset printing*, the most common form of commercial printing.

Fr: LITHOGRAPHIE OFFSET
Ger: OFFSETDRUCK
It: LITOGRAFIA OFFSET
Sp: LITOGRAFÍA OFFSET

OLD-STYLE NUMERALS/FIGURES
\'ōld-ˌstī(-ə)l 'nüm-rəlz/'fi-gyərz\, *n*

Sets of numerals having proportions comparable to a **typeface's** *lowercase* letters. As with the use of **small caps**, old-style numerals are often used within a line of type because they are less obtrusive than **lining numerals**.

Fr: CHIFFRES SUSPENDUS
Ger: MEDIÄVALZIFFERN
It: NUMERI E LETTERE IN STILE ANTICO
Sp: NÚMEROS ELZEVIRIANOS

OPTICAL ALIGNMENT
See **visual alignment**.

A B C D E F G H I J K L M N **O** P Q R S T U V W X Y Z

So, first of all, let me assert my firm belief that the only thing we have to fear is fear itself — nameless, unreasoning, unjustified terror which paralyzes needed efforts to convert retreat into advance. In every dark hour of our national life, a leadership of frankness and of vigor has met with that understanding and support of the people themselves which is essential to victory. And I am convinced that you will again give that support to leadership in these critical days.

In such a spirit on my part and on yours we face our common difficulties. They concern, thank God, only material things. Values have shrunk to fantastic levels; taxes have risen; our ability to pay has fallen; government of all kinds is faced by serious curtailment of income; the means of exchange are frozen in the currents of trade; the withered leaves of industrial enterprise lie on every side; farmers find no markets for their produce; and the savings of many years in thousands of families are gone. More important, a host of unemployed citizens face the grim problem of existence, and an equally great number toil with little return. Only a foolish optimist can

deny the dark realities of the moment.

And yet our distress comes from no failure of substance. We are stricken by no plague of locusts. Compared with the perils which our forefathers conquered, because they believed and were not afraid, we have still much to be thankful for. Nature still offers her bounty and human efforts have multiplied it. Plenty is at our doorstep, but a generous use of it languishes in the very sight of the supply.

ORPHAN
\ˈȯr-fən\, *n*

One or two lines of a paragraph that are separated from the main paragraph, set either at the bottom (if they begin the paragraph) or top (if they end the paragraph) of a **column** of text. Orphans can be avoided through several techniques, the most common of which are **letter spacing** and **hyphenation**. See also **widow**.

Fr: ORPHELINE
Ger: SCHUSTERJUNGE
It: ORFANO
Sp: HUÉRFANA

OUTLINE TYPE
\ˈaůt-ˌlīn ˈtīp\, *n*

A **typeface** in which characters are designed as outlined forms rather than as a collection of solid strokes. Outlines can also be created for typefaces not available in outline versions by using software applications such as Adobe Illustrator®. The resulting **Bézier curves** can be scaled up or down without loss of sharpness; however, the type's correct proportions will be lost in the process.

Fr: CARACTÈRES AU FIL
Ger: KONTURSCHRIFT
It: CARATTERI CONTORNATI
Sp: LETRA PERFILADA

Design: Eric Kass; **Firm:** Funnel, www.funnel.tv

OVERPRINTING
\ˈō-vər-ˈprin-tiŋ\, *n*

The blending of inks printed on top of each other in such a way that a new **color** results. In most cases when two design elements overlap, only the color of the "upper" element is printed; its color *knocks out* that of anything "below." When overprinting is done, on the other hand, the two or more colors of ink are combined to form another color. In this example, yellow was applied to the entire piece, followed by magenta, applied to all but the yellow type, and finally cyan, to the areas without type.

Fr: SURIMPRESSION
Ger: ÜBERDRUCKEN
It: SOVRASTAMPA
Sp: SOBREIMPRESIÓN

Design: Andrew Weed, andrew.weed@asu.edu;
Lithography: Prisma Graphic Corporation

A B C D E F G H I J K L M N O **P** Q R S T U V W X Y Z

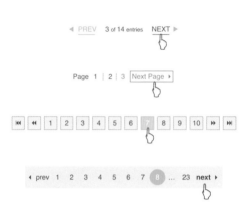

PACKAGING DESIGN
\ˈpa-ˌki-jiŋ di-ˈzīn\, *n*

From the perspective of a graphic designer, package design involves the creation of enclosures that protect and showcase products during their distribution, storage, sales, and use stages. **Logos**, *logotypes*, and other visual (and tactile) elements of **branding** play a critical role in package design, although aesthetic considerations may be just the beginning. Other factors include safety (as in child-resistant pill bottles), economics (taking into account the number of boxes that will fit into a standard shipping container), and ease of use (allowing the end user to open the package in such a way that the experience will be a pleasurable one), to name just a few.

Fr: DESIGN DE PACKAGING
Ger: VERPACKUNGSDESIGN
It: PACKAGING DESIGN
Sp: DISEÑO DE EMBALAJE

Art Director: Brian Adducci; **Design:** Dan Baggenstoss; **Firm:** Capsule, www.capsule.us

PAGINATION
\ˌpa-jə-ˈnā-shən\, *n*

The numbering of pages so as to indicate their proper sequence in a book or other printed publication. More generally, pagination can be used when referring simply to the total number of pages in a given publication. And recently the term has taken on yet another meaning, as when it is used to describe the way information is organized, and navigation is conducted, on Web pages. Blogs, for example, may be paginated in such a way that only the first paragraph or two of a post is displayed on the main page, or so that no more than ten comments appear following the original post to which they refer. See also **imposition**.

Fr: PAGINATION
Ger: PAGINIERUNG
It: IMPAGINAZIONE
Sp: PAGINACIÓN

PANTONE MATCHING SYSTEM (PMS)
See **color-matching system**.

PAPER SIZES
See **sheet sizes**.

PATH
\ˈpath\, *n*

A series of **Bézier curves**, or *vectors*, used by graphic design software to describe the shapes of various design elements, including **type**. Because they are vectors, paths can be enlarged dramatically without sacrificing **resolution**. User-defined paths are commonly used to "cut out" a specific part of one digital photo and place it into another, as when a person is "Photoshopped" into or out of a photo.

Fr: CHEMIN
Ger: PFAD
It: PERCORSO/I
Sp: TRAZADO

Design: Donna S. Atwood, www.atwooddesign.com

A B C D E F G H I J K L M N O **P** Q R S T U V W X Y Z

PERFECT BINDING
\ˈpər-fikt ˈbīn-diŋ\, *n*

A form of permanent **binding** commonly used for paperback books, in which **signatures** are *gathered* (assembled in sequence), ground along their bound edges, and attached by a flexible adhesive to the book's one-page cover, thereby forming its spine.

Fr: RELIURE SANS COUTURE
Ger: KLEBEBINDUNG
It: RILEGATURA PERFETTA
Sp: ENCUADERNACIÓN A LA AMERICANA

PHOTOMONTAGE
\ˈfō-(ˌ)tō\ -män-ˈtäzh\, *n*

A term used to describe the process of creating a photographic **composition** by combining elements from several other photographs. The result, which is also called *photomontage*, or *montage*, is produced by way of cutting and pasting, either in the literal sense or by using digital image-editing software. Photomontages created manually are sometimes photographed upon completion, thereby giving the impression of it being a "straight" photograph. See also **collage**.

Fr: PHOTOMONTAGE
Ger: FOTOMONTAGE
It: FOTOMONTAGGIO
Sp: FOTOMONTAJE

Design/Photography: Joe Miller, www.joemillersco.com

Inch

Picas

PICA
\ˈpī-kə\, *n*

An absolute typographic unit of measure equal to 12 **points**. Six American picas are equal to 0.9936 inch, whereas six *PostScript* picas are equal to one inch exactly. A *pica em* is a space one pica, or one-sixth of an inch, in width.

Fr: POINT PICA
Ger: PICA
It: PICA
Sp: PICA

A B C D E F G H I J K L M N O **P** Q R S T U V W X Y Z

PICTOGRAM
\ˈpik-tə-ˌgram\, *n*

An **icon** or a **symbol** used in such a way that its meaning is immediately understood regardless of language or cultural barriers. Effective pictograms are part of a standardized system of pictograms, governed by numerous conventions and guidelines, as when an entire collection is created for the Olympic Games or in the case of internationally recognized traffic signs. Pictograms rely on context for their interpretation. The Baggage Claim signs used in many airports, for example, are merely icons until they are placed in the context of an airport or other transit terminal. The same icon could be used, for example, on a website where suitcases are sold. There, although its iconic meaning would remain the same, its meaning as a pictogram would be quite different.

Fr: PICTOGRAMME
Ger: PIKTOGRAMM
It: PITTOGRAMMA
Sp: PICTOGRAMA

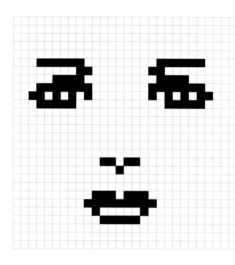

PIXEL
\ˈpik-səl\, *n*

The basic element used by many types of digital displays to represent images. In fact, the name *pixel* is derived from the combination of *picture* and *element*. Pixels are arranged on a two-dimensional grid, each pixel being a sample of the corresponding point in the original image. Image **resolution** is a function of the grid's density. For displays that employ the **RGB** color system, the color displayed by each pixel is a result of the numerical values of red, green, and blue assigned to it.

Fr: PIXEL
Ger: PIXEL (BILDPUNKT)
It: PIXEL
Sp: PÍXEL

Design: Donna S. Atwood, www.atwooddesign.com

48-point
36-point
24-point
18-point
14-point
12-point
10-point
8-point

POINT/POINT SIZE
\ˈpȯint/ˈpȯint ˈsīz\, *n*

A point is an absolute unit of measure in **typography**. An American point is equal to 0.0138 inch; a *PostScript* point is equal to 0.0139 inch. Point size refers to the size of **type**, as measured in points. However, although the point is an absolute measure, the actual size of type for a given point size will vary by **typeface**. This is because the point size was originally determined not by the size of the characters themselves but by the metal blocks on which they were cast. For digital type, the relationship between point size and character size is even less straightforward. See also **pica**.

Fr: CORPS
Ger: PUNKT/PUNKTGRÖSSE
It: PUNTO/I/DIMENSIONI DEL PUNTO
Sp: PUNTO/TAMAÑO DE PUNTO

A B C D E F G H I J K L M N O **P** Q R S T U V W X Y Z

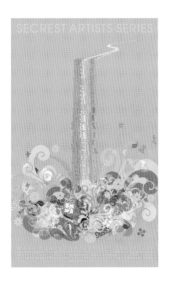

POSITIVE SPACE
\ˈpä-zə-tiv ˈspās\, *n*

A generic term used to describe the area(s) of a layout or individual design element(s) where forms exist (the resulting voids are referred to as **negative space**). Although positive space is often used to describe aspects of entire **layouts**, it can also be used to describe aspects of **typography**, where **letterforms** generate relationships of positive and negative space with neighboring letterforms. **Logos**, because they are generally small, are often designed with careful attention paid to the relationship between positive and negative space. See also **negative space, figure-ground**, and **white space**.

Fr: ESPACE POSITIF
Ger: GESTALTETE FLÄCHE
It: SPAZIO POSITIVO
Sp: ESPACIO POSITIVO

Art Direction: Hayes Henderson; **Design/Illustration:** Joel Bowers; **Firm:** HendersonBromsteadArt, www.hendersonbromsteadart.com

POSTERIZATION
\ˌpōs-tə-rə-ˈzā-shən\, *n*

An effect that occurs when the range of **colors** (or grays) available is insufficient to reproduce, either on-screen or in print, an image that contains areas of gradual tonal change. This can happen when, for example, an image is converted to a 256-color *GIF* for use as a simple Web graphic. Posterization can also be done deliberately using image-editing software to convert continuous tones into a limited number of discrete color fields, thereby creating interesting visual effects similar to those seen in traditional graphic posters.

Fr: POSTERISATION
Ger: POSTERISATION
It: POSTERIZZAZIONE
Sp: POSTERIZACIÓN

Design: Donna S. Atwood, www.atwooddesign.com

POST-MODERNISM
\ˌpōs(t)-ˈmä-dər-ˌni-zəm\, *n*

Largely a reaction against the often-dogmatic approach of **Modernism**, Post-Modernism began to take shape during the 1960s and rose to international prominence in the 1980s. Where the Modernists had largely rejected the past, the Post-Modernists celebrated historical styles and their decorative tendencies, reinterpreting and combining them in unexpected, often playful ways. Visual characteristics included *letterspaced* **typography**, the seemingly random placement of elements, intricate **collage**, pastel **color palettes**, and much more.

Fr: POSTMODERNISME
Ger: POSTMODERNE
It: POST-MODERNISMO
Sp: POSTMODERNISMO

Design: William Longhauser Design, www.longhauser.com; **Client:** The Goldie Paley Gallery, 1983

A B C D E F G H I J K L M N O **P** Q R S T U V W X Y Z

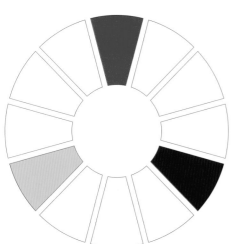

Times
Palatino
Futura

PRIMARY COLORS
\ˈprī-ˌmer-ē ˈkə-lərz\, *n*

Colors that form the key reference points of a given **color wheel**, equally spaced along its circumference. In the traditional color wheel, used for mixing pigments, the primaries are red, blue, and yellow. However, other color wheels are based on the *subtractive primaries* cyan, magenta, and yellow, and the *additive primaries* red, green, and blue. See also **CMYK** and **RGB**.

Fr: COULEURS PRIMAIRES
Ger: PRIMÄRFARBEN
It: COLORI PRIMARI
Sp: COLORES PRIMARIOS

Design: Donna S. Atwood, www.atwooddesign.com

PROCESS COLORS
See **CMYK** and **four-color process**.

PROOF
\ˈprüf\, *n*

A general term used when referring to a preliminary version of a book, report, brochure, or other document intended for publication. Proofs serve a variety of purposes, from copyediting and proofreading to the promotional, as when a book proof is sent to reviewers in advance of its publication. Traditionally a collection of unbound and untrimmed pages, electronic proofs are now becoming increasingly common. When cast metal **type** was still in common use, the initial **typesetting** was done in metal trays prior to being set on the press itself. Because these trays were called *galleys*, the resulting prints were called *galley proofs*, a term still used by some when referring to early proofs. *Contract proofs* are used to confirm details such as **color** just prior to printing.

Fr: ÉPREUVES
Ger: KORREKTURABZUG
It: BOZZA/E
Sp: PRUEBA

Design/Photography: Mario Trejo, www.mariotrejo.com

PROPORTIONAL
\prə-ˈpȯr-shnəl\, *n*

A term used to describe a **typeface** in which the width of each character is unique, unlike **monospaced** typefaces, in which all characters are of the same width.

Fr: CARACTÈRES À CHASSE VARIABLE
Ger: PROPORTIONALSCHRIFT
It: PROPORZIONALE
Sp: PROPORCIONAL

A B C D E F G H I J K L M N O **P** Q R S T U V W X Y Z

"I AM ON CONSTANT ALERT; I FEEL LIKE PAVLOV'S DOG WAITING FOR A BELL — OR AN ELECTRICAL SHOCK."

20–25 years old. We stand outside in the chill wind. The alarm continues to blare, raking my eardrums. The smokers light up. I move further away from the crowd to avoid the press of bodies. Lieutenants stride purposefully through the crowd into the building.

Ten minutes pass. No order to leave the area. Relief. Today will not be a shakedown. Today I will not have to spend hours reorganizing my pitiful few possessions. I might still get something accomplished before work. The Lieutenant walks out the door screaming, "You must stand behind the yellow line!"

13

PULL QUOTE
\ˈpu̇l ˈkwōt\, *n*

A quotation excerpted from an article or other text, placed outside of its original context (but typically on the same page) and set in such a way that it attracts the attention of readers. Pull quotes are often set in a much larger, perhaps even different, **typeface** than the **body copy**. Further differentiation can be achieved by way of **color**, ornaments, **borders**, and more.

Fr: EXERGUE
Ger: HERVORGEHOBENES ZITAT
It: CITAZIONE ESTERNA
Sp: SUMARIO

Design: Firebelly Design, www.firebellydesign.com

A B C D E F G H I J K L M N O P **Q R** S T U V W X Y Z

"

(Typographic quotes)

"

(Typewriter quotes)

QUOTATION MARKS
\kwō-'tā-shən 'märks\, *n*

Punctuation marks that serve a variety of purposes, such as indicating speech or a direct quotation within a block of text, or to suggest ironic or unusual usage of a word or phrase (e.g., The "simple" application took 30 minutes to complete). Typographic quotes, sometimes called *smart quotes*, are shaped differently from typewriter-style quotes (often referred to as *dumb quotes* or *neutral quotes*) and the double prime symbol used to denote inches and in mathematical notation. In the United States, double quotation marks are the standard; in other parts of the world, single quotation marks serve the same purpose. See also **apostrophe**.

Fr: GUILLEMETS
Ger: ANFÜHRUNGSSTRICHE
It: VIRGOLETTE
Sp: COMILLAS

That is the great American story: ▮ young people just like you, following ▮ their passions, determined to meet the ▮ times on their own terms. They weren't doing it for the money. Their titles ▮ weren't fancy: ex-slave, minister, ▮ student, citizen. But they changed the ▮ course of history — and so can you. ▮

RAG
\rag\, *n*

The irregular shape created between a block of text and the adjacent margin as a result of uneven **line lengths**. For **flush-left type**, the rag is along the right **margin**, while for **flush-right type**, the rag is along the left margin. **Justified type** has no rag. In order to ensure **readability**, typographers and designers strive for a rather random-looking rag, avoiding visual distractions that come from geometric or overly rhythmic rags.

Fr: DRAPEAU
Ger: FLATTERSATZ
It: BANDIERA
Sp: BANDERA

RASTER GRAPHICS
See **bitmap**.

Now we are engaged in a great civil war, testing whether that nation, or any nation, so conceived and so dedicated, can long endure. We are met on a great battlefield of that war. We have come to dedicate a portion of that field, as a final resting place for those who here gave their lives that that nation might live. It is altogether fitting and proper that we should do this.

Now we are engaged in a great civil war, testing whether that nation, or any nation, so conceived and so dedicated, can long endure. We are met on a great battlefield of that war. We have come to dedicate a portion of that field, as a final resting place for those who here gave their lives that that nation might live. It is altogether fitting and proper that we should do this.

Now we are engaged in a great civil war, testing whether that nation, or any nation, so conceived and so dedicated, can long endure. We are met on a great battlefield of that war. We have come to dedicate a portion of that field, as a final resting place for those who here gave their lives that that nation might live. It is altogether fitting and proper that we should do this.

READABILITY
\rē-də-'bi-lə-tē\, *n*

A qualitative measure of how pleasurable a particular passage of text is to read, based on its **typography**. Often confused with **legibility**, which has to do with typographic *clarity*. In order to be readable, a line of **type** must first be legible; however, distinguishing one **letterform** or word from another does not automatically result in readability. A novel set in **condensed type**, for example, might be perfectly legible but nevertheless unreadable. Readable typography is a function of numerous factors, including type size, **letter spacing**, **leading**, and, of course, the **typeface** itself.

Ger: LESBARKEIT
Sp: LEGIBILIDAD LINGÜÍSTICA

A B C D E F G H I J K L M N O P Q **R** S T U V W X Y Z

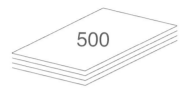

Paper Grade	Basic Size
Bond, ledger, writing	17″ × 22″
Uncoated book, text	25″ × 38″
Coated book	25″ × 38″
Cover	20″ × 26″
Bristol	22 ½″ × 28 ½″
Kraft, tag, newsprint	24″ × 36″

REAM
\ˈrēm\, *n*

A ream of paper is made up of 500 sheets of a given paper grade at its basic size. Although there are many different standard **sheet sizes**, the basic size is determined solely by the grade of paper. Bond, ledger, and writing stock, for example, have a basic size of 17 × 22 inches; cover stock, on the other hand, has a basic size of 20 × 26 inches. *Basis weight* or *ream weight*, then, refers to the weight of one ream of paper. In the United States, basis weight is specified in pounds, typically using the abbreviation #. Because the basis weight is a function of the paper's basic size, two grades of paper having the same basis weight may feel quite different in terms of their individual thickness and weight. A 28# bond, for example, is about the same thickness as a 70# text stock. The thickness of a sheet of paper, or *stock*, is its *caliper*. Paper with lower caliper values tend to have lower weight than higher caliper papers. The term *bulk* is used to quantify a paper's caliper relative to its weight.

Fr: RAME
Ger: RIES
It: RISMA
Sp: RESMA

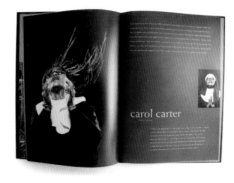

RECTO/VERSO
\ˈrek-(ˌ)tō/ˈvər-(ˌ)sō\, *n*

A term used when referring to the right- and left-hand pages of a set of **facing pages**. The right-hand page is referred to as the *recto*; the left-hand page is referred to as the *verso*. Strictly speaking, however, the terms refer to opposite sides of the same page, *recto* being the front and *verso* being the back.

Fr: RECTO VERSO
Ger: RECHTE/LINKE SEITE (VORDER-/ RÜCKSEITE)
It: RECTO/VERSO
Sp: RECTO/VERSO

Design: Peter Shikany, Judy Smith; **Photography:** Troy Aossey; **Firm:** P.S. Studios, www.psstudios.com

Proper Registration   Misregistration

REGISTRATION
\ˌre-jə-ˈstrā-shən\, *n*

The precise alignment of all layers of ink printed on a given job. Ideally, each successive application of ink is aligned with the previous application; different **colors** overlap or meet exactly as they were intended. In practice, however, there can be some variation, called *misregistration*, resulting from the paper stretching, for example, or by a problem with the press. Many issues related to misregistration can be mitigated by **trapping** or **overprinting**.

Fr: REPÉRAGE
Ger: REGISTERHALTIGKEIT
It: REGISTRO
Sp: REGISTRO

72 dpi   150 dpi   300 dpi

RESOLUTION
\re-zə-ˈlü-shən\, *n*

The relative quality of a digital image in terms of the number of samples per unit of measure. The various terms used to describe the resolution of digital graphics are often used interchangeably. *DPI*, or *dots per inch*, is a relative measure of a printing device's quality. For example, 300-dpi printers are capable of printing 300 dots side-by-side in the space of one inch. *PPI*, on the other hand, is an abbreviation for *pixels per inch*, which is used to quantify the resolution of a computer monitor or other digital display. And finally, *LPI*, or *lines per inch*, is a measure of a **halftone's** frequency. Although the "lines" are actually rows of tiny dots, they appear as lines when they are printed side-by-side. The greater the screen frequency, the more detailed the image will be when printed. Newspapers use screens of 65 to 85 lpi, while art books require finer screens, in some cases 300 lpi.

Fr: RÉSOLUTION
Ger: AUFLÖSUNG
It: RISOLUZIONE
Sp: RESOLUCIÓN

REVERSE/REVERSE OUT
\ri-ˈvərs/ri-ˈvərs ˈaůt\, *n*

A term used to describe **type** that is created by applying ink to the areas around and within each character, rather than to the strokes themselves. As a result, the type is the **color** of the stock being used, not the ink. The same effect can be achieved on computer monitors by matching the color of the type to the background color, and setting the type against a field of a different color. The weight of light-colored type, especially when small to begin with, appears to diminish when set against a dark background, so a slightly larger and heavier **typeface** is often required to maintain **legibility**.

Fr: INVERSION
Ger: NEGATIVE SCHRIFT
It: REVERSE/REVERSE OUT
Sp: TIPO EN NEGATIVO

Design: Firebelly Design, www.firebellydesign.com

RGB

Abbreviation for red, green, and blue, the three colors used to display graphics on computer monitors and other digital devices. Red, green, and blue are called the *additive primaries*; combined together in equal proportions, they form white light. They also correspond to the three different types of light receptors in the human eye. See also **CMYK**.

Fr: RVB
Ger: RGB
It: RGB
Sp: RGB

Design: Donna S. Atwood, www.atwooddesign.com

A B C D E F G H I J K L M N O P Q **R** S T U V W X Y Z

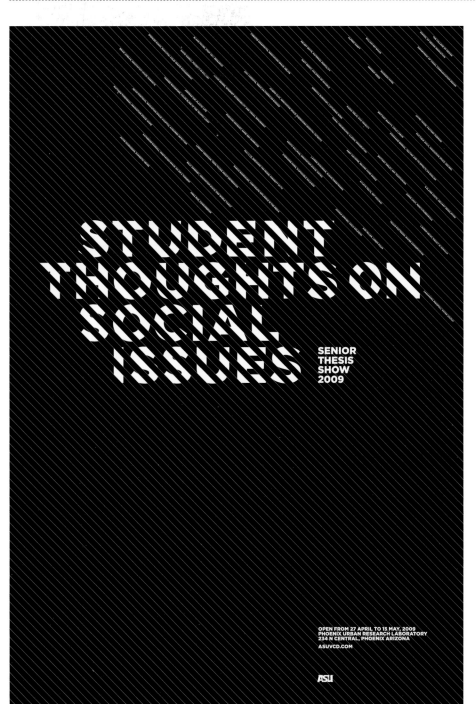

RHYTHM
\'ri-thəm\, *n*

Visual repetition created through underlying structural patterns within and among various design elements, such as **type**, **lines**, and shapes. A single line of type, for example, might have a particular rhythm by way of its many vertical strokes, created through careful **letter spacing**. Posters and book covers often use geometric patterns to create a stable rhythm against which surprising elements can then be played up. And on an even larger scale, **grids** can be used to provide a gentle rhythm throughout a lengthy publication, carrying the reader along.

Fr: RYTHME
Ger: RHYTHMUS
It: RITMO
Sp: RITMO

Design: Tanner Woodford, www.tannerwoodford.com

A B C D E F G H I J K L M N O P Q **R** S T U V W X Y Z

Thank you, President Crow, for that generous introduction, and for your inspired leadership here at ASU. And I want to thank the entire ASU community for the honor of attaching my name to a scholarship program that will help open the doors of higher education to students from every background. That is the core mission of this school; it is a core mission of my presidency; and I hope this program will serve as a model for universities across this country.

Now, before I begin, I'd like to clear the air about that little controversy everyone was talking about a few weeks back. I have to tell you, I really thought it was much ado about nothing, although I think we all learned an important lesson. I learned to never again pick another team over the Sun Devils in my NCAA bracket. And your university President and Board of Regents will soon learn all about being audited by the IRS.

In all seriousness, I come here not to dispute the suggestion that I haven't yet achieved enough in my life. I come to embrace it; to heartily concur; to affirm that one's title, even a title like President, says very little about how well one's life has been led – and that no matter how much you've done, or how successful you've been, there's always more to do, more to learn, more to achieve.

And I want to say to you today, graduates, that despite having achieved a remarkable milestone, one that you and your families are rightfully proud of, you too cannot rest on your laurels. Your body of work is yet to come.

Baskerville

Caslon

Garamond

Times New Roman

RIVERS
\ˈri-vərz\, *n*

The visually distracting vertical gaps that can appear in a block of text as a result of the unintentional vertical alignment of spaces between words. Rivers tend to occur in blocks of **justified type** because of the often-unnatural software-generated word spacing. The best way to eliminate or reduce the impact of rivers is to *rewrap* the lines of type by way of **tracking** and/or **hyphenation**. See also **H&J** and **text wrapping**.

Fr: LÉZARDES
Ger: GIESSBÄCHLEIN
It: CANALETTI
Sp: CALLE

Design: Donna S. Atwood, www.atwooddesign.com

ROMAN TYPE
\rō-ˈmän ˈtīp\, *n*

Used to refer to a broad range of **typefaces** having **serifs** and origins dating to fifteenth-century Italy. *Roman* is also used more generally to describe the "regular" version of a typeface with or without serfis, as opposed to the **bold** and **italic** versions, for example, of the same typeface.

Fr: CARACTÈRES ROMAINS
Ger: ANTIQUA
It: CARATTERI ROMAN
Sp: REDONDA

RULE
\ˈrül\, *n*

A **line** used as a typographic device to separate one element of a **layout** from another, organizing the space and creating a sense of **hierarchy**. The weight of a rule is typically specified in **points**.

Fr: FILET
Ger: LINIE
It: FILETTO TIPOGRAFICO
Sp: FILETE

A B C D E F G H I J K L M N O P Q R **S** T U V W X Y Z

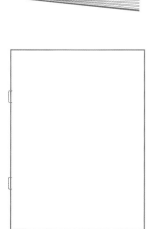

Impact

Gill Sans

LITHOS

Optima

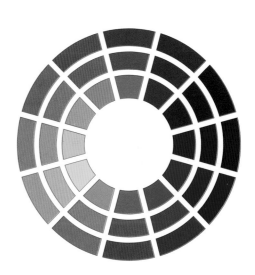

SADDLE-STITCH BINDING
\sa-dəl-ˌstich ˈbīn-diŋ\, *n*

A form of permanent **binding** commonly used for brochures and some magazines, in which **signatures** and the cover are nested together along a common spine, secured by way of wire staples, and then trimmed.

Fr: PIQÛRE MÉTALLIQUE À CHEVAL
Ger: DRAHTHEFTUNG
It: GRAFFETTATURA
Sp: ENCUADERNACIÓN A CABALLETE

SANS SERIF
\san-ˈser-əf\, *n*

A term used to refer to any number of **typefaces** lacking **serifs**, the small strokes at the ends of a character's main strokes. Compared to many serif typefaces, sans serif typefaces typically have less contrast between their thin and thick strokes, if any, which can improve the **readability** of **type** intended to be read on a computer screen.

Fr: CARACTÈRES SANS EMPATTEMENTS
Ger: SERIFENLOS
It: CARATTERI SENZA GRAZIE
Sp: PALO SECO

SATURATION
\ˌsa-chə-ˈrā-shən\, *n*

The purity of a **color** relative to the amount of gray it contains. Pure **hues** are fully saturated and appear vivid. As saturation levels are decreased, a color becomes increasingly muted, despite remaining the same hue. Desaturation can be accomplished by adding gray to a hue (resulting in a *tone*) or by mixing in a smaller portion of its **complementary color** (resulting in a *shade*).

Fr: SATURATION
Ger: SÄTTIGUNG
It: SATURAZIONE
Sp: SATURACIÓN

Design: Donna S. Atwood, www.atwooddesign.com

A B C D E F G H I J K L M N O P Q R **S** T U V W X Y Z

SCALE

\ˈskāl\, *n*

The perceived size or weight of one design element relative to others in the same **layout**. Scale can come down to easily measured differences, as when larger **type** is used to indicate which parts of a text are of greater importance. Often, however, differences in scale are far subtler. Objects with dissimilar shapes, for example, tend to convey a different scale even when they measure the same area, geometrically. Shape and **color** also influence the scale of an element, as does context; the scale of an object is a function of its surroundings.

Fr: ÉCHELLE
Ger: GRÖSSENVERHÄLTNIS
It: SCALA
Sp: ESCALA

Design: Stephanie Horn, www.stephanie-horn.com

A B C D E F G H I J K L M N O P Q R **S** T U V W X Y Z

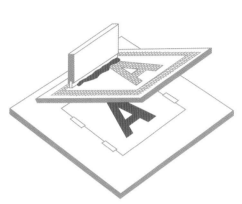

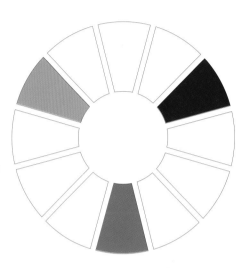

SCREEN PRINTING
\\'skrēn ˈprin-tiŋ\\, *v*

A printing process in which ink is forced through a fine mesh screen and onto the surface of the material to be printed, such as paper or fabric. A stencil, created either by using another material or by sealing the surface of the mesh itself, is used to determine which areas of the surface will be inked. The most common use of screen printing is for clothing production, but the process is also used for printing on irregular surfaces. Also called *silk screening*.

Fr: SÉRIGRAPHIE
Ger: SIEBDRUCK
It: SERIGRAFIA
Sp: SERIGRAFÍA

SCRIPT TYPE
\\'skript ˈtīp\\, *n*

Any one of a number of **typefaces** designed to imitate handwriting. Although script typefaces can lend an elegant, somewhat personal touch to a block of text, they should generally be used sparingly and only in the appropriate context. Invitations and announcements, for example, often use script **type** very effectively. Long passages of text set in script, on the other hand, tend to wear on the reader.

Fr: CURSIVE
Ger: SCHREIBSCHRIFT
It: CARATTERI INFORMALI
Sp: SCRIPT TYPE

Design: Eric Kass; **Firm:** Funnel, www.funnel.tv

SECONDARY COLORS
\\'se-kən-ˌder-ē ˈkə-lərz\\, *n*

Colors (orange, purple, or green) created by mixing equal parts of two **primary colors**. Orange, for example, is created by mixing together equal parts of red and yellow. See also **color wheel** and **tertiary colors**.

Fr: COULEURS SECONDAIRES
Ger: SEKUNDÄRFARBEN
It: COLORI SECONDARI
Sp: COLORES SECUNDARIOS

Design: Donna S. Atwood, www.atwooddesign.com

A B C D E F G H I J K L M N O P Q R **S** T U V W X Y Z

Caslon

Playbill

Georgia

Didot

SERIF
\ˈser-əf\, *n*

A small stroke at the end of a character's main strokes. *Serif* is also commonly used when referring to a broad range of **typefaces** with serifs (though they are more correctly called *seriffed* typefaces), so as to distinguish them from an equally broad category of those without, called **sans serif** typefaces. Serifs aid in reading **type**, especially at small sizes, in part because they allow the eye to quickly distinguish one **letterform** from another. Serifs originated in ancient Rome, although the details are the subject of debate: Some suggest that they originated with stone masons, who used them to "clean up" the strokes of their chiseled type, while others suggest they were flourishes created by the paintbrushes used to mark out the letterforms prior to cutting. See also **sans serif**.

Fr: EMPATTEMENT
Ger: SERIFE
It: CARATTERI CON GRAZIE
Sp: SERIFA

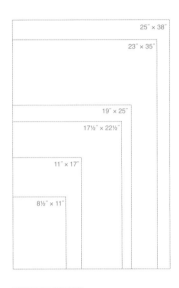

SHEET SIZES
\ˈshēt ˈsīz-əz\, *n*

In North America, standard sheet sizes are specified in such a way that multiple 8½ × 11-inch sheets can be produced from them with a minimal amount of waste. A 23 × 35-inch sheet, for example, could be used to produce a sixteen-page **signature** 8½ × 11 inches in size after trimming. Outside of North America, the International Standards Organization (ISO) has established sheet sizes based on one square meter.

Fr: FORMAT DE FEUILLE
Ger: BOGENGRÖßEN
It: FORMATI DEI FOGLI
Sp: TAMAÑO DE HOJA

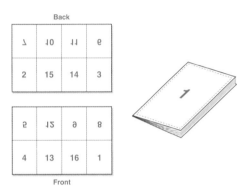

SIGNATURE
\ˈsig-nə-ˌchu̇r\, *n*

A collection of pages printed on both sides of a large sheet of paper that, once folded and trimmed, will be in the proper orientation and sequence for **binding**. See also **imposition**.

Fr: CAHIER
Ger: BOGENMONTAGE
It: SEGNATURA
Sp: PLIEGO

The CMYK color space…

The CMYK color space…

S tanding caps serve the same purpose as drop caps — indicating the beginning of a new section of text — but extend upward rather than downward.

SMALL CAPITALS/CAPS
\\'smȯl 'ka-pə-təlz/'kaps\\, *n*

Uppercase letters having proportions and *stroke weight* that make them compatible with a **typeface's** *lowercase* letters. Small caps are used within a line of type for the same reason **lining numerals** are used: because they are less obtrusive than the alternative. When referring to an acronym in mid-sentence, for example, a string of capital letters would be distracting. Another advantage of small caps is that their proportions allow for **legibility** even at small sizes.

Fr: PETITES CAPITALES
Ger: KAPITÄLCHEN
It: MAIUSCOLETTI
Sp: VERSALITA

SPREAD
\\'spred\\, *n*

Any two **facing pages** of a bound publication. The term *two-page spread*, although commonly used, is actually redundant. See also **recto/verso**.

Fr: DOUBLE PAGE
Sp: DOBLE PÁGINA

Art Direction/Design: Michael Ulrich, *STEP Inside Design*, Volume 22, Number 5

STANDING CAPITAL/CAP
\\'stan-diŋ 'ka-pə-təlz/'kaps\\, *n*

An *uppercase* letter used as the initial letter of the first word in a paragraph, set in a **point size** larger than the surrounding type but along the same **baseline**. For additional impact, standing caps may be set in a **typeface** much different from that used for the **body copy**. See also **initial capital/cap** and **drop capital/cap**.

Fr: GRANDE CAPITALE
Ger: STEHENDE INITIALE
It: STANDING CAP
Sp: CAPITULAR

A B C D E F G H I J K L M N O P Q R **S** T U V W X Y Z

$$4Na + O_2 \rightarrow 2Na_2O$$

STOCK PHOTOGRAPHY/IMAGES
\ˈstäk fə-ˈtä-grə-fē/ˈi-mi-jəz\, *n*

Photographs and/or illustrations available, via a licensing agreement, for specific uses. Using such images is much less expensive than hiring a photographer, although some creative control is sacrificed in the process. In addition, the designer and client can never be sure how the same image might be used elsewhere by others; there is no exclusive arrangement with the provider. Today, several online collections of stock photography and illustrations allow for easy searching, payment, and downloading.

Fr: BANQUE D'IMAGES
Ger: STOCK FOTOS (BILDARCHIV)
It: BANCA IMMAGINI
Sp: BANCO DE IMÁGENES Y
    FOTOGRAFÍAS

Design: Donna S. Atwood, www.atwooddesign.com

SUBHEAD
\ˈsəb-ˌhed\, *n*

A lower-level **heading** used to break a lengthy text into sections, revealing its organizational structure and providing cues about its **hierarchy**. The way a publication's subheads are **typeset**, including its size, **color**, **typeface**, and placement, should reflect the degree to which one level is similar to or different from those "above" and "below" it in the overall hierarchy. If *level-A subheads* are used for the names of major cities, for example, and *level-B subheads* have to do with different categories of census data, it would be reasonable for the two subheads to look quite different from one another. If, on the other hand, the level-B subheads were used for the names of nearby suburbs, the difference in their appearance might be subtler.

Fr: INTERTITRE
Ger: UNTERTITEL
It: SOTTOTITOLO
Sp: SUBTÍTULO

SUBSCRIPT
\ˈsəb-ˌskript\, *n*

A character set in a size smaller than the main text, generally centered along the **baseline**. Subscripts, also called *inferiors*, are often used in mathematical notation and various scientific expressions. Subscripts created from scaled-down versions of a **typeface's** standard characters will have a *stroke weight* lighter than the surrounding **type**, which can be distracting. As a rule, therefore, typographers and designers prefer to use a **font's** special subscript characters whenever they are available.

Fr: INDICE
Ger: TIEFGESTELLTE SCHRIFTZEICHEN
It: PEDICE/I
Sp: SUBÍNDICE

ABCDEFGHIJKLMNOPQR**S**TUVWXYZ

Several recent studies^{3}…

$$\tfrac{3}{4} \times \tfrac{1}{2} = \tfrac{3}{8}$$

$$A^2 + B^2 = C^2$$

Tuesday, July 4th

SUPERSCRIPT
\ˈsü-pər-ˌskript\, *n*

As with **subscripts**, superscripts are specially scaled characters smaller than the main text with which they are set. However, the place-ment of superscripts, also called *superiors*, depends upon their purpose. As numerals to indicate footnotes or the numerator of a fraction, superscripts are top-aligned along the *ascent line*. In mathematical or scientific expressions, they are center-aligned instead. *Lowercase* letters are also sometimes used as top-aligned superscripts, but rarely in English. The English *ordinals* commonly used to indicate dates (e.g., 4th of July) are often set as superscripts, although they are more properly set as standard lowercase letters.

Fr: EXPOSANT
Ger: HOCHGESTELLTE SCHRIFTZEICHEN
It: APICE/I
Sp: SUPERÍNDICE

SURREALISM
\sə-ˈrē-ə-ˌli-zəm\, *n*

A European art movement of the 1920s and 1930s concerned with intuition, dreams, and the unconscious mind, often expressed through surprising or unsettling juxtaposi-tions, optical illusions, and obvious violations of the laws of physics. Graphic design-ers found inspiration not only in the many techniques used by the Surrealists but also in their experimental approach to depicting three-dimensional space.

Fr: SURRÉALISME
Ger: SURREALISMUS
It: SURREALISMO
Sp: SURREALISMO

Design: Donna S. Atwood, www.atwooddesign.com

*A*nd so my fellow Americans: ask not what your country can do for you—ask what you can do for your country.

SWASH CHARACTERS
\ˈswäsh ˈker-ik-tərz\, *n*

Highly decorative characters with extended strokes, often capitals slanted to the right. As capitals, swash characters are typically used as the initial letter of the first word in a paragraph, often set in a **point size** larger than the surrounding **type**. As *lowercase* letters, swashes are generally used at the opposite end of the paragraph: for the final letter in the final word of a sentence. Although swashes can give a block of text a sense of elegance, they should be used sparingly. A line of type set all in swashes, for example, is both distracting and illegible. See also **initial capital/cap**.

Fr: LETTRE ITALIQUE ORNÉE
Ger: ZIERBUCHSTABEN
It: CARATTERI SWASH
Sp: LETRA DE FANTASÍA

A B C D E F G H I J K L M N O P Q R **S T** U V W X Y Z

SYMBOL
\\'sim-bəl\\, *n*

A graphical sign that represents something other than what is shown. In many cultures, for example, a simple illustration of a heart, especially in red, is used to symbolize affection or love. The sign does not look like love; indeed, it scarcely looks like an actual heart. But because the meaning is more or less universally agreed upon, this symbol can be used to communicate effectively. Similarly, a red cross carries a meaning understood across many language and cultural barriers, but only because its meaning is first agreed upon by those using it. See also **icon** and **pictogram**.

Fr: SYMBOLE
Ger: SYMBOL
It: SIMBOLO
Sp: SÍMBOLO

SYMMETRY
\\'si-mə-trē\\, *n*

The even distribution of elements along a particular axis, often vertically or horizontally oriented. Symmetrical layouts are organized so that elements are more or less evenly distributed top-to-bottom and/or left-to-right, and therefore tend to be more conservative, conveying greater stability than asymmetrical **layouts**. See also **asymmetry**, **balance**, and **eye flow**.

Fr: SYMÉTRIE
Ger: SYMMETRIE
It: SIMMETRIA
Sp: SIMETRÍA

Art Direction: Hayes Henderson; **Design/Illustration:** Kris Hendershott; **Firm:** HendersonBromsteadArt,; www.hendersonbromsteadart.com

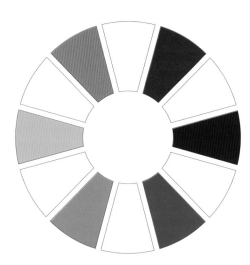

TERTIARY COLORS
\\'tər-shē-ˌer-ē ˈkə-lərz\\, *n*

Colors created through the combination of one **primary** and one **secondary** color. Red-orange, for example, results from mixing red (a primary color) and orange (a secondary color created by mixing equal parts of the primaries red and yellow). See also **color wheel**.

Fr: COULEURS TERTIAIRES
Ger: TERTIÄRFARBEN
It: COLORI TERZIARI
Sp: COLORES TERCIARIOS

Design: Donna S. Atwood, www.atwooddesign.com

A B C D E F G H I J K L M N O P Q R S **T** U V W X Y Z

That is the great American story: young people just like you, following their passions, determined to meet the times on their own terms. They weren't doing it for the money. Their titles weren't fancy: ex-slave, minister, student, citizen. But they changed the course of history — and so can you.

TEXT WRAPPING
\ˈtekst ˈra-piŋ\, *n*

A term used in a generic sense to describe the way in which one line of **type** ends and continues automatically on the subsequent line. Editing a line of type will often cause several other neighboring lines to *rewrap*. More specifically, the term is used to describe how lines of type can be made to "wrap" around other design elements, such as photos and illustrations. See also **H&J**.

Fr: RETOUR À LA LIGNE AUTOMATIQUE
Ger: TEXTUMBRUCH
It: INVIO A CAPO AUTOMATICO
Sp: AJUSTE DE TEXTO

TEXTURE
\ˈteks-chər\, *n*

The perceived tactile quality of a design element or **layout**. Although texture is typically used to describe three-dimensional attributes, such as a paper's surface, it is also used when referring to those same qualities conveyed or suggested in two-dimensional design work. Various patterns and **gradients**, for example, can lend a sense of texture, especially when set in **contrast** to smooth, uniform elements. Certain printing techniques, such as *block printing*, also provide texture. Even a page of **type**, with its strong vertical and horizontal **rhythms**, has a certain texture to it, determined by how the type is set. When such texture is relatively even across a page or layout, the type has what typographers call "good **color**."

Fr: TEXTURE
Ger: STRUKTUR
It: TEXTURE
Sp: TEXTURA

Design: Eric Kass; **Firm:** Funnel, www.funnel.tv

THUMBNAIL
\ˈthəm-ˌnāl\, *n*

A term used to describe a small, often low-quality, sketch used to convey a concept quickly. Thumbnails are used during the early stages of a project as an integral part of the design process; often, the final design emerges through the generation of many increasingly refined thumbnails. The term can also be used to refer to smaller, low-**resolution** images that serve as placeholders for their high-resolution versions. An online image gallery, for example, might display dozens of thumbnails on a single webpage for easy viewing and quick *page loading*. This has become such common practice that the very presence of thumbnails often suggests to users that high-resolution versions exist, and are likely just a click away.

Fr: CRAYONNAGE
Ger: DAUMENNAGELSKIZZE
It: THUMBNAIL
Sp: MINIATURA

Art Direction: Tracy Holdeman; **Design:** Casey Zimmerman; **Firm:** Insight Design Communications, www.insightdesign.com

A B C D E F G H I J K L M N O P Q R S **T** U V W X Y Z

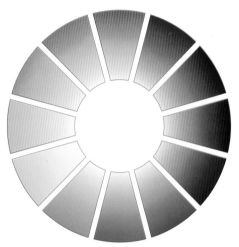

Design: Donna S. Atwood, www.atwooddesign.com

Tracking
(Tracking = -50)

Tracking
(Tracking = 0)

Tracking
(Tracking = +50)

Misregistration with
no trap

Trap: 100%M, 40%C
(size exaggerated)

TINT
\'tint\, *n*

A term used to describe a **color** created by adjusting its **brightness** by adding white to it. Darkening a color's brightness by adding black results in a shade of that hue. *Tint* is also used when referring to the *density of dots* on the halftone screens used in four-color printing. An area of the cyan screen covered 60 percent with dots is said to be a *60 percent tint*.

Fr: COULEUR DE FOND
Ger: TÖNUNG
It: TINTA
Sp: TINTE

TRACKING
\'tra-kiŋ\, *n*

A measure of how tightly or loosely a line of **type** is set. Increasing the tracking increases the overall spacing of the type by increasing the spaces between characters proportionally. Decreasing the tracking has the reverse effect. **Letter spacing** refers broadly to the spacing between characters; tracking quantifies it.

Fr: APPROCHE DE GROUPE
Ger: SPERREN
It: TRACKING
Sp: TRACKING

TRAPPING
\'tra-piŋ\, *n*

A technique used to prevent gaps between areas of **color** when **registration** is imperfect. If, for example, magenta **type** were printed against a background of pure cyan, any *misregistration* would result in a gap between the type and the background, exposing the unprinted paper beneath. A *trap* is a very thin line of color, in this case a combination of magenta and cyan, created around an object to prevent such gaps. There are several types of traps; which one is most suitable for a given printing situation depends on several factors, and in most cases, is best handled by the printer. See also **registration**.

Fr: GROSSI-MAIGRI
Ger: ÜBERFÜLLUNG
It: TRAPPING
Sp: REVENTADO

TRITONE
See **duotone**.

A B C D E F G H I J K L M N O P Q R S **T** U V W X Y Z

TYPE

\tīp\, *n*

A term used to describe characters arranged in a deliberate manner so that they can be read in either a printed or an on-screen format. Also commonly used when referring to the **fonts** used to produce type, as in "Cast metal type was stored in cases …" See also **typesetting** and **typography**.

Fr: CARACTÈRES
Ger: SCHRIFT
It: SEQUENZA DI CARATTERI
Sp: TIPO

Creative Direction: Michael Fallone; **Design Direction:** Doug Bartow; **Design:** Bryan Kahrs; **Firm:** id29, www.id29.com

A B C D E F G H I J K L M N O P Q R S **T** U V W X Y Z

Bernhard Modern Std
(Serif)

Eurostile
(Sans serif)

Edwardian Script
(Script)

Blackmoor
(Blackletter)

Helvetica Neue

Helvetica Neue Light

Helvetica Neue Ultralight

Helvetica Neue Ultralight Italic

Helvetica Neue Italic

Helvetica Neue Bold Italic

Helvetica Neue Bold Italic

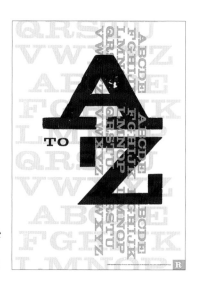

TYPE CLASSIFICATION
\ˈtīp ˌkla-sə-fə-ˈkā-shən\, *n*

Any one of various systems used to categorize **typefaces** based upon their shared visual characteristics, such as the presence or lack of **serifs**, similarity to handwriting, and so on. Because many typefaces can fit into more than one category, such classification systems are best understood as broad generalizations rather than rigid definitions.

Fr: CLASSIFICATION TYPOGRAPHIQUE
Ger: SCHRIFTKLASSIFIKATION
It: CLASSIFICAZIONE DEI CARATTERI
Sp: CLASIFICACIÓN TIPOGRÁFICA

TYPE FAMILY
\ˈtīp ˈfam-lē\, *n*

The variations of a particular **typeface**, such as **bold**, **italic**, **condensed**, *extended*, and so forth. The broad range of "family members" available is largely a consequence of the nineteenth century's advertising boom and the subsequent demand for distinctive **typography**. See also **expert set**.

Fr: FAMILLE DE CARACTÈRES
Ger: SCHRIFTFAMILIE
It: FAMIGLIA DI CARATTERI
Sp: FAMILIA TIPOGRÁFICA

TYPEFACE
\ˈtīp-ˌfās\, *n*

A character set that shares obvious design characteristics, such as *stroke weight*, proportions, presence or lack of **serifs**, and so forth. A typeface typically includes letters (often *uppercase* and *lowercase*), numerals, and a wide range of **symbols** (typographical, mathematical, etc.). *Typeface* and **font** are often mistakenly used interchangeably. *Typeface* refers to the overall design of the characters; fonts are the means of production, whether mechanical, photomechanical, or digital.

Fr: POLICE
Ger: SCHRIFTTYPE
It: CARATTERE/I
Sp: TIPO DE LETRA

Design: Rowan Moore-Seifred; **Firm:** DoubleMRanch Design, www.doublemranch.com

A B C D E F G H I J K L M N O P Q R S **T U** V W X Y Z

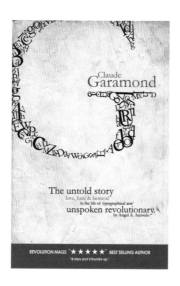

TYPESETTING
\ˈtīp-ˌse-tiŋ\, *v*

The arrangement of characters for the purpose of printing and/or reading on-screen. For centuries, typesetting was done using cast metal or wood **type** that was set on the printing press. The Linotype machine, which came into commercial use in 1886, increased the efficiency of cast metal typesetting considerably by casting "lines of type," called *slugs*. *Phototype*, a technique by which **fonts** moved from cast metal onto sheets of film, became the dominant form of typesetting during the 1960s and remained so into the 1980s, when it began to be replaced with digital type.

Fr: COMPOSITION TYPOGRAPHIQUE
Ger: SETZEN
It: COMPOSIZIONE TIPOGRAFICA
Sp: COMPOSICIÓN TIPOGRÁFICA

Design: Lauren Hecht, www.laurenhecht.com

TYPOGRAPHY
\tī-ˈpä-grə-fē\, *n*

A term used to describe the art and science of **typesetting**, as well as the resulting work. Typographers concern themselves with a great range of issues, from the broad, such as the **readability** of a text, to the finest details, such as **kerning** and the aesthetics of **letterforms**. Although digital technology makes it easier than ever to create fine typography, it is perhaps no more common than it was in the days of cast metal type or *phototype*, when typographers were forced to contemplate every detail.

Fr: TYPOGRAPHIE
Ger: TYPOGRAFIE
It: TIPOGRAFIA
Sp: TIPOGRAFÍA

Design: Angel A. Acevedo, www.angelaacevedo.com

ULTRAVIOLET COATING
\ˌəl-trə-ˈvī-(ə-)lət ˈkō-tiŋ\, *n*

A process in which a liquid polymer is applied to paper, either while the work is on the printing press or as a separate process immediately following the printing, and dried by way of ultraviolet lighting. Compared to **aqueous coatings**, ultraviolet (or UV) coatings offer greater protection against scuffs and other damage due to handling, but are prone to cracking along sharp creases. UV coatings are applied to specific areas of a printed piece as *spot varnishes*, or as *flood varnishes*, covering the entire page. See also **varnish**.

Fr: VERNIS UV
Ger: UV-LACK
It: FINITURA A ULTRAVIOLETTI
Sp: REVESTIMIENTO ULTRAVIOLETA

Design: Tim Jarvis; **Firm:** The Profission Partnership, www.profission.com

VALUE
See **brightness**.

ABCDEFGHIJKLMNOPQRSTU**V**WXYZ

VARNISH
\ˈvär-nish\, *n*

A clear coating applied to paper as part of the printing process, generally done after all inks have been printed. As with other coatings, varnishes provide some protection against handling, but are more often used for their aesthetic benefits, as they provide various sheens ranging from dull to high gloss. Varnishes applied to specific areas are called *spot varnishes*; those that are applied to entire pages are called *flood varnishes*.

Fr: VERNIS
Ger: LACKIERUNG
It: VERNICE
Sp: BARNIZ

ABCDEFGHIJKLMNOPQRSTU **V** WXYZ

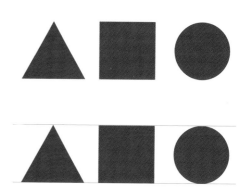

VECTOR GRAPHIC
\\ˈvek-tər ˈgra-fik\, *n*

A digital image created by way of mathematically defined shapes, as opposed to the arrays of samples used in **bitmaps**. This property allows vector graphics to be enlarged dramatically without sacrificing **resolution**. Bitmaps, on the other hand, can achieve a level of detail and subtle tonal variation not possible with vector graphics. See also **Bézier curve**.

Fr: IMAGES VECTORIELLES
Ger: VEKTORGRAFIK
It: GRAFICA VETTORIALE
Sp: GRÁFICO VECTORIAL

Design: Donna S. Atwood, www.atwooddesign.com

VERSO
See **recto/verso**.

VICTORIAN
\\vik-ˈtȯr-ē-ən\, *adj*

A decorative, often ostentatious style of architecture and design that began in England and became immensely popular throughout much of Europe and America between approximately 1820 and 1900. Named after England's Queen Victoria, Victorian design was a response to the Industrial Revolution and the excess that accompanied the shift from craft to mass production. Advances in technology largely outpaced the skills of designers and typographers, and the result was often a chaotic hodgepodge of different styles from different periods. During the first half of the Victorian era, ill-proportioned, heavy-stroke type, called *Fat Face*, was often used alongside crudely drawn illustrations; several different sizes and styles of **type** were employed in a single, overcrowded **layout**. Toward the end of the period, however, a lighter, more sophisticated touch began to emerge.

Fr: STYLE VICTORIEN
Ger: VIKTORIANISCHER STIL
It: STILE VITTORIANO
Sp: VICTORIANO

VISUAL ALIGNMENT
\\ˈvi-zhə-wəl ə-ˈlīn-mənt\, *n*

Aligning **type** or other design elements according to what looks properly **aligned** rather than exact measurements. This is especially important when the forms being aligned are of different shapes. Aligning a circle, an equilateral triangle, and a square, all of the same height, along the same horizontal line, for example, results in an optical illusion. The square appears to be taller than either of the other shapes, while the circle appears to be smaller than either the square or the triangle.

Fr: ALIGNEMENT VISUEL
Ger: OPTISCHE AUSRICHTUNG
It: ALLINEAMENTO VISIVO
Sp: ALINEACIÓN VISUAL

A B C D E F G H I J K L M N O P Q R S T U V **W X** Y Z

So, first of all, let me assert my firm belief that the only thing we have to fear is fear itself — nameless, unreasoning, unjustified terror which paralyzes needed efforts to convert retreat into advance. In every dark hour of our national life, a leadership of frankness and of vigor has met with that understanding and support of the people themselves which is essential to victory. And I am convinced that you will again give that support to leadership in these critical days.

Typography

WHITE SPACE
\'whīt ˈspās\, *n*

A generic term used to describe those areas of a **layout** left "blank," whether or not they are actually white in **color**. However, white space is as integral to a successful design as the design elements it contains; it is active, not passive. Indeed, the effective use of white space creates structure and maintains a sense of **rhythm** and **balance** throughout a layout in much the same way that the interplay of **positive space** and **negative space** energizes the relationships among design elements. See also **grid**.

Fr: BLANCS
Ger: WEISSRAUM
It: SPAZIO BIANCO
Sp: ESPACIO BLANCO

Design/Photography: Mario Trejo, www.mariotrejo.com

WIDOW
\'wi-(ˌ)dō\, *n*

A very short final line of a paragraph, often a single word, that creates the appearance of a space between paragraphs when one doesn't exist. As with **orphans**, widows can be avoided through several techniques, the most common of which are **letter spacing** and **hyphenation**. See also **H&J** and **text wrapping**.

Fr: VEUVE
Ger: WITWE
It: VEDOVA
Sp: VIUDA

X-HEIGHT
\'eks-ˌhīt\, *n*

For a given **typeface**, the height of the *lowercase* letters that have neither **ascenders** nor **descenders**. Measured in **points**, x-height is the distance between the **baseline** and the *mean line*. At small point sizes, typefaces with large x-heights generally provide greater **readability** than comparable typefaces with smaller x-heights.

Fr: HAUTEUR D'X
Ger: X-HÖHE
It: ALTEZZA DELLA X
Sp: ALTURA X

FRANÇAIS

A B C D E F G H I J K L M N O P Q R S T U V W X Y Z

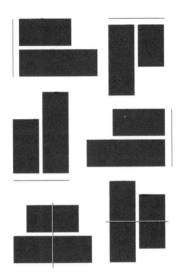

ALIGNEMENT

Disposition de tous les éléments graphiques – images et **typographie,** par exemple – de façon cohérente les uns par rapport aux autres. Ces éléments sont le plus souvent alignés de sorte que leurs côtés (gauche, droit, haut ou bas) ou leurs axes (horizontal ou vertical) soient disposés sur une même ligne de référence faisant, en principe, partie de la **grille.** Ce terme peut également faire référence à un agencement typographique au sein d'un bloc de texte. Voir aussi **fer à gauche, fer à droite, texte centré** et **texte justifié.**

Ang: ALIGNMENT
All: AXIALITÄT
Ital: ALLINEAMENTO
Esp: ALINEACIÓN

Design : Donna S. Atwood, www.atwooddesign.com

ALIGNEMENT OPTIQUE
Voir **alignement visuel.**

ALIGNEMENT VISUEL

Alignement de texte ou de tout autre élément graphique à l'œil plutôt que selon des mesures précises. Ceci est particulièrement important lorsqu'il s'agit d'aligner des formes différentes. En effet, quand on aligne, par exemple, horizontalement un cercle, un triangle équilatéral et un carré de même hauteur, on crée une illusion d'optique : le carré semble plus grand que les deux autres formes, alors que le cercle paraît plus petit.

Ang: VISUAL ALIGNMENT
All: OPTISCHE AUSRICHTUNG
Ital: ALLINEAMENTO VISIVO
Esp: ALINEACIÓN VISUAL

Affiche « La cantatrice chauve »
Design : Malte Martin, www.atelier-malte-martin.net

ANIMATION

Série d'images agencées en une séquence spécifique afin de faire naître une sensation de mouvement continu. Les gifs animés, par exemple, sont souvent utilisés pour des animations Web assez simples, alors que les créations plus complexes font appel à des logiciels sophistiqués, comme Adobe Flash®.

Ang: ANIMATION
All: ANIMATION
Ital: ANIMAZIONE/I
Esp: ANIMACIÓN

Folioscope « Roller »
Design : Akinori Oishi, www.aki-air.com

A BCDEFGHIJKLMNOPQRSTUVWXYZ

Double page extraite de l'ouvrage *Affiches, paroles publiques,* de Diego Zaccaria édité aux éditions Textuel

’

Apostrophe

'

Apostrophe droite

Approche = 0

Lorem ipsum dolor sit amet, consectetuer adipiscing elit. Sed non risus. Suspendisse lectus tortor, dignissim sit amet, adipiscing nec, ultricies sed, dolor. Cras elementum ultrices diam. Maecenas ligula massa, varius a, semper congue, euismod non, mi. Proin porttitor, orci nec nonummy molestie, enim est eleifend mi, non fermentum diam nisl sit amet erat. Duis semper.

Approche = -20

Lorem ipsum dolor sit amet, consectetuer adipiscing elit. Sed non risus. Suspendisse lectus tortor, dignissim sit amet, adipiscing nec, ultricies sed, dolor. Cras elementum ultrices diam. Maecenas ligula massa, varius a, semper congue, euismod non, mi. Proin porttitor, orci nec nonummy molestie, enim est eleifend mi, non fermentum diam nisl sit amet erat. Duis semper.

ANNEXES

Partie d'un ouvrage suivant le texte principal et qui comprend généralement l'appendice, la bibliographie, le glossaire, les notes, etc. Voir aussi **pages liminaires.**

Ang: BACK MATTER
Ital: NOTE CONCLUSIVE
Esp: PAGINAS REFERENCIALES

APOSTROPHE

L'apostrophe est un signe de ponctuation typographique s'apparentant à une virgule placée en hauteur. Elle marque l'élision des voyelles finales de certains mots suivis par un « h » muet, par exemple : l'homme, l'hôpital. La conjonction de « si » et du pronom « il » s'écrira toujours « s'il ». Il ne faut pas confondre une apostrophe droite tracée par une barre verticale droite, « ' », qui se trouve être une contrainte des claviers d'ordinateurs, avec l'apostrophe typographique, courbe « ' ».

Ang: APOSTROPHE
All: APOSTROPH
Ital: APOSTROFO
Esp: APÓSTROFO

APPROCHE DE GROUPE

Augmentation ou diminution de l'espace situé entre les lettres d'une ligne de texte. En augmentant proportionnellement l'espace entre chaque **caractère,** on augmente l'espacement général du texte, et inversement. On parle aussi d'**interlettrage.**

Ang: TRACKING
All: SPERREN
Ital: TRACKING
Esp: TRACKING

A BCDEFGHIJKLMNOPQRSTUVWXYZ

ART DÉCO

Mouvement artistique qui combine les formes décoratives de l'**Art nouveau** avec la géométrie sobre et l'abstraction du **modernisme.** Le style Art déco fut très populaire durant les années 1920-1930 aux États-Unis et à travers une grande partie de l'Europe. Entrecroisant une vaste palette d'influences, comme l'art aztèque, l'art naïf américain, les ziggourats égyptiennes, le **cubisme,** etc., l'Art déco fut extrêmement influent en architecture, design produit et d'intérieur, tout comme en design graphique. Des images fortes étaient le plus souvent combinées avec de la **typographie** tout aussi stylisée et imposante.

Ang: ART DECO
All: ART DÉCO
Ital: ART DÉCO
Esp: ART DECÓ

Couverture de la collection « ¾ Polar »,
éditions Les Allusifs
Directeur de création : Louis Gagnon; **Directeur artistique :** David Guarnieri;
Design : Paprika, www.paprika.com

A B C D E F G H I J K L M N O P Q R S T U V W X Y Z

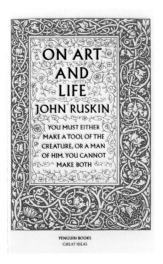

Typographie

ART NOUVEAU

Style d'architecture et de design extrêmement décoratif, prégnant à travers une large partie de l'Europe entre les années 1880 et le début de la Première Guerre mondiale, et durant une courte période aux États-Unis. Comme son nom l'indique, ce mouvement cherchait à créer une esthétique radicalement nouvelle, en opposition au désordre chaotique du **style victorien** privilégiant des formes organiques et galbées. Des motifs populaires, comme des plantes et des animaux (surtout des oiseaux), ainsi que des figures féminines, étaient souvent représentées avec un degré d'abstraction nettement plus ingénieux que celui des arts décoratifs victoriens.

Ang: ART NOUVEAU
All: JUGENDSTIL
Ital: ART NOUVEAU
Esp: ART NOUVEAU

Affiche pour le cycle de conférences
Oxbridge/Académie de France
Design et direction artistique : Catherine Guiral,
www.cathguiral.com

ARTS & CRAFTS

Mouvement artistique réformateur apparu en Angleterre à la fin du XIXᵉ siècle en réaction à l'importance apportée par la révolution industrielle à la production de masse ausc dépens de l'esthétique. En design graphique, le mouvement Arts & Crafts fut résumé dans le livre de William Morris. Si son utilisation de **lettrines**, de **typographies** gothiques et de **maquettes** chargées, rappelle les imprimés des siècles passés, l'attachement de William Morris à la réunion du design et des activités de production ouvrit la voie au **modernisme** du XXᵉ siècle.

Ang: ARTS AND CRAFTS
All: ARTS AND CRAFTS
Ital: ARTS AND CRAFTS
Esp: ARTS AND CRAFTS

Penguin Books Great Ideas, n° 15. *On Art and Life*
Design : David Pearson, d'après William Morris,
www.davidpearsondesign.com

ASCENDANTE

Partie d'une lettre *bas-de-casse* qui s'étend au-dessus de la **hauteur d'x** jusqu'à la **ligne de base.** La taille et l'épaisseur des ascendantes (aussi appelées « hampes ») varient d'une **typographie** à l'autre. En effet, selon la taille de la hauteur d'x, l'aspect des ascendantes sera plus ou moins subtil. Voir aussi **descendantes** et **hauteur d'x.**

Ang: ASCENDER
All: OBERLÄNGE
Ital: TRATTO ASCENDENTE
Esp: ASCENDENTE

A B CDEFGHIJKLMNOPQRSTUVWXYZ

ASYMÉTRIE

Disposition irrégulière des éléments graphiques d'une mise en pages, restant néanmoins structurés par les axes horizontaux et verticaux dominants. L'asymétrie décrit également une **double page** dont les **pages en regard** ne sont pas des reflets fidèles de l'une et de l'autre. Une **maquette** asymétrique est équilibrée lorsque les **espaces positifs** et **négatifs** interagissent efficacement. Cette **composition** s'avère souvent plus dynamique qu'une grille symétrique. Voir aussi **symétrie** et **circulation du regard.**

Ang: ASYMMETRY
All: ASYMMETRIE
Ital: ASIMMETRIA
Esp: ASIMETRÍA

Affiche « Air Poster »
Design : Toko Design, www.toko.nu

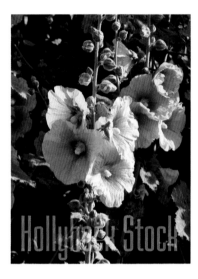

BANQUE D'IMAGES

Photographies et/ou illustrations disponibles pour un usage spécifique, uniquement via un contrat de licence. L'utilisation de telles images est nettement plus économique que lorsqu'on fait appel à un photographe professionnel, mais elles restent néanmoins vides de toute démarche créative personnelle. Sans compter le fait que, les licences d'utilisation n'étant pas exclusives, le graphiste et le commanditaire ne peuvent s'assurer que l'image qu'ils ont choisie ne sera pas ensuite utilisée par d'autres. De nombreuses banques d'images existent aujourd'hui, permettant d'effectuer des recherches, de payer et de télécharger les images très simplement.

Ang: STOCK PHOTOGRAPHY/IMAGES
All: STOCK FOTOS (BILDARCHIV)
Ital: BANCA IMMAGINI
Esp: BANCO DE IMÁGENES Y
     FOTOGRAFÍAS

Design : Donna S. Atwood, www.atwooddesign.com

BAUHAUS

École d'art, d'architecture et de design extrêmement influente, opérant en Allemagne de 1919 à 1933. L'emphase de l'école pour le fonctionnalisme se perçoit dans ses productions graphiques géométriques et sans fioritures. La quasi-totalité des **mises en pages** utilisent de la **typographie** sans **empattements,** composée avec des **filets** massifs et selon une **grille** stricte, des photographies et des **photomontages.** Si le noir, le blanc et le gris constituent la **palette de couleurs** principale du Bauhaus, les **couleurs primaires** étaient souvent utilisées pour accentuer la composition.

Ang: BAUHAUS
All: BAUHAUS
Ital: BAUHAUS
Esp: BAUHAUS

Lettre d'amour prête à cocher conçue en hommage à László Moholy-Nagy, avec des citations de films de Casavettes et de Woody Allen
Design : Muriel Paris et Vanina Gallo, www.murielparis.com

ABCDEFGHIJKLMNOPQRSTUVWXYZ

BLANCS

Terme désignant les zones d'une **mise en pages** laissées « blanches », c'est-à-dire exemptes de tous éléments graphiques. Les blancs sont des zones actives tout aussi importantes à l'harmonie d'une **maquette** que les éléments graphiques qui la composent. Ils structurent la page tout en amenant du **rythme** et un **équilibre,** de la même façon que les **espaces positifs** et **négatifs** dynamisent, par leur interaction, la relation entre les différents éléments graphiques. Voir aussi **grille.**

Ang: WHITE SPACE
All: WEISSRAUM
Ital: SPAZIO BIANCO
Esp: ESPACIO BLANCO

Affiche « Art More Precious Than Gold » (L'art est plus précieux que l'or) célébrant la première acquisition du Museum of Modern Art de Varsovie
Design : Ludovic Balland, Typography Cabinet, www.ludovic-balland.ch

BORDURE

Cadre créant une transition entre un élément graphique – photographie, illustration, bloc de texte, etc. – et le reste de la **mise en pages.** Il peut être basique, par exemple un **filet** maigre en forme de rectangle ou de cercle, ou très ornemental. Un cadre chargé aura tendance à détourner l'attention de l'image qu'il contient et à en diminuer ainsi l'impact, alors qu'un cadre plus simple et fin contribuera à détacher une image du fond.

Ang: BORDER
All: RAHMEN
Ital: BORDO/I
Esp: BORDE

Programme annuel 2008-2009 du Centre Chorégraphique national de Tours
Design : Atelier Müesli, www.ateliermuesli.com

Lorem ipsum dolor sit amet, consectetuer adipiscing elit. Sed non risus. Suspendisse lectus tortor, dignissim sit amet, adipiscing nec, ultricies sed, dolor. Cras elementum ultrices diam. Maecenas ligula massa, varius a, semper congue, euismod non, mi. Proin porttitor, orci nec nonummy molestie, enim est eleifend mi, non fermentum diam nisl sit amet erat.

Lorem ipsum dolor sit amet, consectetuer adipiscing elit. Sed non risus. Suspendisse lectus tortor, dignissim sit amet, adipiscing nec, ultricies sed, dolor. Cras elementum ultrices diam. Maecenas ligula massa, varius a, semper congue, euismod non, mi. Proin porttitor, orci nec nonummy molestie, enim est eleifend mi, non fermentum diam nisl sit amet erat.

Lorem ipsum dolor sit amet, consectetuer adipiscing elit. Sed non risus. Suspendisse lectus tortor, dignissim sit amet, adipiscing nec, ultricies sed, dolor. Cras elementum ultrices diam. Maecenas ligula massa, varius a, semper congue, euismod non, mi. Proin porttitor, orci nec nonummy molestie, enim est eleifend mi, non fermentum diam nisl sit amet erat.

Lorem ipsum dolor sit amet, consectetuer adipiscing elit. Sed non risus. Suspendisse lectus tortor, dignissim sit amet, adipiscing nec, ultricies sed, dolor. Cras elementum ultrices diam. Maecenas ligula massa, varius a, semper congue, euismod non, mi. Proin porttitor, orci nec nonummy molestie, enim est eleifend mi, non fermentum diam nisl sit amet erat.

C&J

Abréviation de *césure* et *justification*, procédé à partir duquel les logiciels vont disposer les **caractères** sur une **ligne.** Selon qu'un bloc de texte est en **fer à gauche, fer à droite, justifié** ou **centré,** le logiciel remplira de façon automatique chaque ligne sur toute sa **mesure** en combinant les lettres et les espaces. On parle alors de « justification » (terme couramment utilisé pour décrire les lignes de texte qui s'étendent sur l'intégralité de leur mesure). Le terme « césure » fait référence aux **coupures de mots** effectuées afin de faire tenir plus de texte sur une ligne. Les logiciels de **mise en pages** permettent d'ajuster un certain nombre de paramètres de C&J afin que le graphiste puisse disposer de la flexibilité nécessaire à une **composition typographique** précise. Voir aussi **texte justifié.**

Ang: H&J
All: SILBENTRENNUNG & BLOCKSATZ (S&B)
Ital: H&J
Esp: H&J

A B **C** D E F G H I J K L M N O P Q R S T U V W X Y Z

Verso

Recto

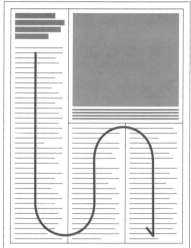

Typographie

CADRATIN

Unité de mesure relative qui équivaut au **corps** du **caractère** en points. Pour une **typographie** en corps 12, un cadratin est égal à 12 points et, de la même façon, pour une typographie en corps 10, un cadratin équivaut à 10 points, et ainsi de suite.
On peut dire de façon plus précise qu'un cadratin correspond à la taille (ou corps) du bloc typographique en métal utilisé pour le procédé d'*impression en relief.* C'est une espace « carrée » qui équivaut à un cadratin de largeur sur un cadratin de hauteur, on parle d'**espace cadratin.** Alors que tous les corps d'une taille spécifique sont de même hauteur, les hauteurs des caractères varient beaucoup d'une typo à l'autre. Ainsi, le cadratin n'a qu'un rapport ténu à la taille réelle des caractères d'une typo donnée. Et lorsque la typo est numérique, le rapport est encore moins évident, faute de référent physique. Voir aussi **tiret cadratin, espace cadratin,** et **point pica.**

Ang: EM
All: GEVIERT
Ital: EM
Esp: CUADRATÍN

CAHIER

Pages imprimées de chaque côté d'une feuille d'impression qui, une fois pliées et massicotées, sont assemblées selon une certaine orientation et séquence afin d'être ensuite reliées. Voir aussi **imposition.**

Ang: SIGNATURE
All: BOGENMONTAGE
Ital: SEGNATURA
Esp: PLIEGO

CALIBRAGE

Procédé typographique permettant d'ajuster la taille de **corps** et l'**interlignage** d'un texte afin de le faire rentrer dans un espace donné ou un nombre de pages spécifique. Certains calculs permettent d'établir des estimations mais, plus fréquemment, le procédé s'effectue directement à l'aide d'un logiciel de **mise en pages,** jusqu'à ce que le bon ajustement soit trouvé.

Ang: COPYFITTING
All: TEXTEINPASSUNG
Ital: AGGIUSTAMENTO DEL TESTO
Esp: AJUSTE DEL ORIGINAL

Design : Donna S. Atwood, www.atwooddesign.com

A B **C** D E F G H I J K L M N O P Q R S T U V W X Y Z

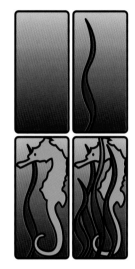

CALLIGRAPHIE

Du grec *kallos* (« beau ») et *graphein* (« écrire »), la calligraphie signifie littéralement « belle écriture ». C'est une façon artistique de dessiner des **caractères** d'écriture, traditionnellement réalisée avec des outils comme une plume ou un pinceau, remarquable par ses lettres gracieuses et les variations d'épaisseur des fûts des lettres.

Ang: CALLIGRAPHY
All: KALLIGRAPHIE
 (SCHÖNSCHREIBKUNST)
Ital: CALLIGRAFIA
Esp: CALIGRAFÍA

« Click me, Read me, Buy me, Love me »
Design : Marian Bantjes, www.bantjes.com

CALQUE

En infographie, les calques sont un ensemble de couches empilées les unes au-dessus des autres, dont chacune contient une partie des éléments constituant l'ensemble. Chacun de ces éléments peut ainsi être travaillé indépendamment des autres. Le résultat final est obtenu par la superposition de tous les calques dans un certain ordre.

Ang: LAYER
All: EBENE
Ital: LIVELLO
Esp: CAPA

Design : Donna S. Atwood, www.atwooddesign.com

CANAUX

Information numérique correspondant aux quantités relatives des trois **(RVB)** ou quatre **(CMJN) couleurs primaires** utilisées pour représenter les images en couleur. Chaque canal est comme une image en niveaux de gris dans laquelle les **valeurs** de gris ont été remplacées par les valeurs d'une seule couleur primaire. La couleur finale est obtenue, que ce soit à l'écran ou à l'impression, par une combinaison de tous les canaux selon un certain **modèle colorimétrique.**

Ang: CHANNELS
All: FARBKANÄLE
Ital: CANALI
Esp: CANAL

Design : Donna S. Atwood, www.atwooddesign.com

A B **C** D E F G H I J K L M N O P Q R S T U V W X Y Z

Times

Palatino

Futura

Courier
Lucida Sans Typewriter

CARACTÈRES

Terme désignant de façon générale une variante d'un signe typographique destiné à l'impression ou à une lecture à l'écran. À l'origine, un caractère était une pièce en plomb, sur laquelle était dessinée une lettre à l'envers et en relief, permettant l'impression. Voir aussi **composition typographique** et **typographie.**

Ang: TYPE
All: SCHRIFT
Ital: SEQUENZA DI CARATTERI
Esp: TIPO

Le Zinzolin, caractère de titrage d'après le Polyphème de Deberny & Peignot
Design : Muriel Paris assisté d'Alex Singer, www.murielparis.com

CARACTÈRES À CHASSE CONSTANTE

Typographie dont tous les **caractères** ont la même largeur, elle est semblable à celle des machines à écrire. Voir aussi **caractères à chasse variable.**

Ang: MONOSPACED
All: DICKTENGLEICH
        (NICHTPROPORTIONALE SCHRIFT)
Ital: MONOSPAZIO
Esp: MONOESPACIADA

CARACTÈRES À CHASSE VARIABLE

Typographie dont chaque **caractère** a une largeur spécifique, contrairement aux **caractères à chasse constante.**

Ang: PROPORTIONAL
All: PROPORTIONALSCHRIFT
Ital: PROPORZIONALE
Esp: PROPORCIONAL

A **C** D E F G H I J K L M N O P Q R S T U V W X Y Z

CARACTÈRES AU FIL

Typographie dont les **caractères** ne sont représentés que par leurs contours plutôt que par des fûts pleins. Des logiciels comme Adobe Illustrator® permettent de créer de tels caractères lorsque ceux-ci ne sont pas disponibles dans une **famille de caractères** donnée. La **courbe de Bézier** que l'on obtient peut ensuite être agrandie ou réduite, sans que la netteté soit mise à mal. Par contre, les proportions de la lettre seront endommagées par ce procédé.

Ang: OUTLINE TYPE
All: KONTURSCHRIFT
Ital: CARATTERI CONTORNATI
Esp: LETRA PERFILADA

Affiche pour les conférences Bitjmer Nites à l'Apple Center d'Amsterdam
Design : Adriaan Mellegers et Alfons Hooikaas (Planet Earth), www.adriaanmellegers.com

A B **C** D E F G H I J K L M N O P Q R S T U V W X Y Z

ABCDEFGHIJKLMNOPQRSTUVWXYZ
0123456789 ⅛¼⅜½⅝¾⅞⅓⅔
ffffifflfflflffßæ *ABCDEFGHIJ LMNOPQRSTUVWXYZ*

Baskerville

Caslon

Garamond

Times New Roman

CARACTÈRES DE TITRE

Caractères composés dans une taille de **corps** plus grande que celle du texte courant afin de les démarquer ; utilisés par exemple pour les **titres** ou les titres courants.

Ang: DISPLAY TYPE
All: AUSZEICHNUNGSSCHRIFT
Ital: CARATTERI DI VISUALIZZAZIONE
Esp: TIPO TITULAR

Magazine *Mood*
Design : Akatre, www.akatre.com

CARACTÈRES ÉTENDUS

Ensemble de **caractères** typographiques non courants, comme les **petites capitales,** les **chiffres suspendus,** les **ligatures,** etc., propres à une **fonte.** Auparavant, les caractères étendus s'obtenaient séparément des caractères de base, mais ils sont aujourd'hui généralement inclus avec les fontes numériques OpenType. On parle aussi de *caractères auxiliaires*.

Ang: EXPERT SET
All: EXPERTENSATZ
Ital: EXPERT SET
Esp: SET EXPERTO

CARACTÈRES ROMAINS

Qualificatif utilisé pour définir une vaste série de **caractères** avec **empattements** utilisés au xvᵉ siècle en Italie. On parle aussi de caractères romains pour décrire la version normale d'une **typographie** – en opposition à l'**italique** – avec ou sans empattements.

Ang: ROMAN TYPE
All: ANTIQUA
Ital: CARATTERI ROMAN
Esp: REDONDA

A **B** C D E F G H I J K L M N O P Q R S T U V W X Y Z

Impact

Gill Sans

LITHOS

Optima

CARACTÈRES SANS EMPATTEMENTS

Terme désignant les **typographies** sans **empattements** – extrémités latérales en pied et en tête d'une lettre. Elles se distinguent des typographies avec empattements notamment par le fait que le **contraste** entre leurs fûts fins et épais est assez faible, quand il y en a un. Ces **caractères** sont à privilégier pour optimiser la **lisibilitéo** à l'écran.

Ang: SANS SERIF
All: SERIFENLOS
Ital: CARATTERI SENZA GRAZIE
Esp: PALO SECO

CHAPEAU

Terme souvent associé au journalisme, le chapeau est un passage de texte très court qui se situe avant le **corps du texte** dont l'objet est d'éveiller la curiosité du lecteur. Étant donné que les chapeaux servent parfois à résumer le texte, ils sont la plupart du temps composés dans un **corps** plus grand, parfois même dans une autre **typographie** que celle utilisée pour le texte courant. On trouve aussi des chapeaux **tout en capitales,** ou avec une combinaison de **caractères** standards et de **petites capitales,** surtout dans la presse quotidienne.

Ang: HEADLINE
All: SCHLAGZEILE
Ital: TITOLO
Esp: TITULAR

Double page extraite de l'ouvrage *Danse Noire Banche Amérique,* édition du CND, 2009
Design : Agnès Dahan, www.agnesdahan.net

CHEMIN

Série de **courbes de Bézier**, ou vecteurs**,** utilisées par les logiciels d'infographie pour décrire les formes de différents éléments graphiques, y compris la **typographie**. Ils peuvent être considérablement agrandis sans affecter la **résolution.** Les chemins définis par les utilisateurs peuvent, par exemple, servir à découper une partie d'une photographie numérique pour la mettre ailleurs, notamment quand une personne est sortie de sa photo originelle pour être placée dans une autre.

Ang: PATH
All: PFAD
Ital: PERCORSO/I
Esp: TRAZADO

Design : Donna S. Atwood, www.atwooddesign.com

ABCDEFGHIJKLMNOPQRSTUVWXYZ

Chiffres arabes :
0123456789

CHIFFRES ARABES

Jeu de chiffres ayant une hauteur identique, ou approchante, à celle des lettres capitales d'une **famille de caractères.** Ils sont souvent utilisés dans les tableaux car ils ont une chasse constante et s'appuient tous sur la **ligne de base,** leur alignement est donc visuellement attrayant. Voir aussi **chiffres suspendus.**

Ang: LINING NUMERALS/FIGURES
All: MAJUSKELZIFFERN
 (TABELLENZIFFERN)
Ital: NUMERI E LETTERE DI
 ALLINEAMENTO
Esp: NÚMEROS DE CAJA ALTA

CHIFFRES RÉFÉRENCES

Portion de texte accompagnée d'une ligne et/ou d'une flèche, servant de légende à différentes parties—une photo, illustration, ou tout autre type de travail présenté dans une **mise en pages.** Voir aussi **légende** et **exergue.**

Ang: CALLOUT
All: HINWEIS
Ital: CALLOUT
Esp: LLAMADA

Plan des expositions des Rencontres d'Arles 2009
Design : Michel Bouvet

Chiffres suspendus :
0123456789

CHIFFRES SUSPENDUS

Ensemble de chiffres ayant des proportions comparables à celles des *bas-de-casse* d'une **typographie.** De la même façon que les **petites capitales,** les chiffres suspendus sont employés au sein d'une ligne de texte car ils sont moins encombrants que les **chiffres arabes.**

Ang: OLD-STYLE NUMERALS/FIGURES
All: MEDIÄVALZIFFERN
Ital: NUMERI E LETTERE IN STILE ANTICO
Esp: NÚMEROS ELZEVIRIANOS

CIRCULATION DU REGARD

Chemin suivi par le regard au sein d'une photographie ou d'une **mise en pages.** La circulation du regard est influencée par divers facteurs, comme la **couleur,** l'**équilibre,** le **contraste,** etc. Les créations graphiques efficaces anticipent ce paramètre. Ainsi, les panneaux de signalisation se doivent d'être simples et directs, alors que les affiches proposent souvent au regard du spectateur un cheminement plus complexe. Voir aussi **point central.**

Ang: EYE FLOW
All: BLICKPFADBEWEGUNG
Ital: FLUSSO VISIVO
Esp: LÍNEA DE ORIENTACIÓN

Affiche pour le Festival de poésie contemporaine à Caen « La poésie/nuit »
Design : Tom Henni, www.tomhenni.fr

A B **C** D E F G H I J K L M N O P Q R S T U V W X Y Z

Bernhard Modern Std
Avec empattements

Eurostile
Sans empattements

Cursive

Gothique

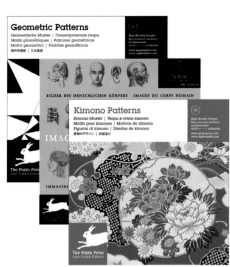

CLASSIFICATION TYPOGRAPHIQUE

Système utilisé pour classer les **typographies** en fonction de leurs aspects communs : la présence ou non d'**empattements,** la ressemblance à la typographie manuscrite, etc. Étant donné que de nombreuses typographies peuvent être à la fois intégrées à l'une ou à l'autre de ces catégories, il est préférable de considérer cette classification comme une vaste généralisation plutôt que comme un système rigide.

Ang: TYPE CLASSIFICATION
All: SCHRIFTKLASSIFIKATION
Ital: CLASSIFICAZIONE DEI CARATTERI
Esp: CLASIFICACIÓN TIPOGRÁFICA

CLIPART

Illustrations conçues pour être intégrées à des **mises en pages,** disponibles aussi bien en format imprimé qu'en numérique. Elles connurent une grande popularité grâce à leur disponibilité, leur variété et leur licence libre. Voir aussi **banque d'images.**

Ang: CLIP ART
All: CLIPART
Ital: CLIP ART
Esp: CLIP ART

Couvertures de livres *Images of the Human Body, Geometric Patterns* et *Kimono Patterns,* publiés par Pepin Press, www.pepinpress.com

CMJN

Abréviation employée pour les encres utilisées en **quadrichromie** : cyan, magenta, jaune et noir. Lorsque l'on mélange deux des *primaires soustractives* que sont le cyan, le magenta et le jaune, on obtient des *primaires additives* : le rouge, le vert et le bleu. Celles-ci correspondent aux trois différents types de capteurs de lumière de l'œil humain. En théorie, si on associe les trois primaires soustractives on peut produire du noir, mais, en pratique, le résultat n'est pas assez riche pour créer une gamme complète de *tons* pour l'impression en **couleur,** c'est pourquoi on ajoute la composante noire en supplément. On parle aussi d'**encres primaires.**

Ang: CMYK
All: CMYK
Ital: CMYK
Esp: CMYK

Design : Kate Benjamin, www.moderncat.net

A B **C** D E F G H I J K L M N O P Q R S T U V W X Y Z

COLLAGE

Technique d'assemblage, souvent
déroutante, de papiers, matériaux,
photographies, etc., permettant de créer
des compositions originales. Les collages
peuvent aussi être réalisés sur ordinateur
en assemblant autant d'éléments numériques
que souhaité, par exemple des scans de
textures, d'objets en trois dimensions,
toujours dans un certain esprit de bricolage.
Voir aussi **photomontage.**

Ang: COLLAGE
All: KOLLAGE
Ital: COLLAGE
Esp: COLLAGE

Affiche pour le festival « We Love in Cité »
Design : Pierre Vanni, www.pierrevanni.com

COLONNE

Les colonnes forment le plus souvent, au
sein de la **mise en pages,** l'élément de base
d'une **grille.** Dans les **maquettes** comportant
une quantité importante de texte, on utilise
fréquemment deux colonnes, voire plus.
Si une grande variété de factures peut être
trouvée, les colonnes hautes et rectangulaires
restent cependant les plus courantes.

Ang: COLUMN
All: SATZSPALTE
Ital: COLONNE
Esp: COLUMNA

Double page extraite de l'ouvrage *Horst Faas : 50 ans
de photojournalisme,* éditions du Chêne/Hachette, 2008
Design : Agnès Dahan, www.agnesdahan.net

COMPOSITION

Terme utilisé pour décrire la disposition des
éléments graphiques au sein d'une **mise en
pages,** son efficacité est décrite de manière
plus ou moins subjective avec des termes
comme **équilibre, contraste, circulation du
regard,** etc. Le terme « composition » peut
également définir une mise en pages.

Ang: COMPOSITION
All: KOMPOSITION
Ital: COMPOSIZIONE
Esp: COMPOSICIÓN

Couverture du livre *Sous-culture : le sens du style,*
de Dick Hebdige pour la collection « Zones » des
éditions La Découverte
Design : deValence, www.devalence.net

A B **C** D E F G H I J K L M N O P Q R S T U V W X Y Z

Composition en alinéa

Lorem ipsum dolor sit amet, consectetuer adipiscing elit. Sed non risus. Suspendisse lectus tortor, dignissim sit amet, adipiscing nec, ultricies sed, dolor. Cras elementum ultrices diam. Maecenas ligula massa, varius a, semper congue, euismod non, mi. Proin porttitor, orci nec nonummy molestie, enim est eleifend mi, non fermentum diam nisl sit amet erat.

Habillage

Lorem ipsum dolor sit amet, consectetuer adipiscing elit. Sed non risus. Suspendisse lectus tortor, dignissim sit amet, adipiscing nec, ultricies sed, dolor. Cras elementum ultrices diam. Maecenas ligula massa, varius a, semper congue, euismod non, mi. Proin porttitor, orci nec nonummy molestie, enim est eleifend mi, non fermentum diam nisl sit amet erat.

Composition en sommaire

Lorem ipsum dolor sit amet, consectetuer adipiscing elit. Sed non risus. Suspendisse lectus tortor, dignissim sit amet, adipiscing nec, ultricies sed, dolor. Cras elementum ultrices diam. Maecenas ligula massa, varius a, semper congue, euismod non, mi. Proin porttitor, orci nec nonummy molestie, enim est eleifend mi, non fermentum diam nisl sit amet erat.

Alignement sur un point

• Lorem ipsum dolor sit amet, consectetuer adipiscing elit. Sed non risus. Suspendisse lectus tortor, dignissim sit amet, adipiscing nec, ultricies sed, dolor. Cras elementum ultrices diam. Maecenas ligula massa, varius a, semper congue, euismod non, mi. Proin porttitor, orci nec nonummy molestie, enim est eleifend mi, non fermentum diam nisl sit amet erat.

COMPOSITION EN ALINÉA

Réglage des **marges** d'une ou de plusieurs **lignes** de texte. Ce type de présentation est habituellement utilisé pour indiquer un nouveau paragraphe. Une *composition en sommaire* est un bloc de texte avec la première ligne au fer à gauche et les suivantes avec alinéa. Un *habillage* peut être utilisé afin d'ajuster les marges gauche et/ou droite de plusieurs lignes de texte, par exemple pour envelopper une illustration ou une photographie. L'*alignement sur un point* est utilisé pour que les marges des lignes suivantes s'alignent sur un point ou un **caractère** spécifique situé sur la ligne précédente.

Ang: INDENT
All: ZEILENEINZUG
Ital: RIENTRO
Esp: SANGRÍA

COMPOSITION TYPOGRAPHIQUE

Agencement de **caractères** pour l'impression et/ou la lecture à l'écran. Durant des siècles, la composition se faisait à l'aide de caractères en plomb qu'un *compositeur* agençait dans une presse. L'invention de la Linotype en 1886 révolutionna ce procédé de composition en permettant de composer une **ligne** de texte complète en un seul bloc de plomb. La *phototypie* est un procédé de reproduction à l'encre grasse où un film est reporté sur une plaque de verre recouverte de gélatine. Elle fut prédominante entre les années 1960 et 1980.

Ang: TYPESETTING
All: SETZEN
Ital: COMPOSIZIONE TIPOGRAFICA
Esp: COMPOSICIÓN TIPOGRÁFICA

Affiche « I Love Távora »
Design : R2 (Lizá Ramalho + Artur Rebelo), www.r2design.pt

Helvetica
Helvetica condensed

Clarendon
Clarendon condensed

CONDENSÉ

Au sein d'une **famille de caractères**, se dit des lettres plus étroites que la version regular. Chaque lettre a également un **interlettrage** réduit de sorte qu'elle va se placer plus près des lettres adjacentes, ce qui permet de faire tenir beaucoup de texte dans un espace donné. Dans la mesure où la **lisibilité** en pâtit quelque peu, les **typographies** condensées sont habituellement réservées aux **titres**, à l'affichage, ou à toute application avec peu de texte.

Ang: CONDENSED TYPE
All: SCHMALE SCHRIFT
Ital: CARATTERI CONDENSATI
Esp: LETRA CONDENSADA

A B **C** D E F G H I J K L M N O P Q R S T U V W X Y Z

BCQ a e g

CONSTRUCTIVISME

Mouvement russe des années 1920 intégrant l'art d'avant-garde et le design (tout particulièrement les influences du **cubisme** et du **futurisme**) avec les tendances politiques prorévolutionnaires. Les éléments visuels caractéristiques sont des formes abstraites, géométriques, des **caractères gras,** des **mises en pages** coupant court aux conventions horizontal/vertical, et une **palette de couleurs** souvent limitée au rouge, au noir et au blanc. Les **collages** et **photomontages,** techniques empruntées au **dada,** étaient aussi utilisés pour communiquer visuellement de façon très forte.

Ang: CONSTRUCTIVISM
All: KONSTRUKTIVISMUS
Ital: COSTRUTTIVISMO
Esp: CONSTRUCTIVISMO

Affiche « ZTHollandia »
Design : Toko Design, www.toko.nu

CONTRASTE

Le contraste est ni plus ni moins la différence entre deux éléments graphiques. Une **typographie** très large peut, par exemple, être utilisée pour contraster avec une typographie plus petite ; plus la différence de **corps** est importante, plus le contraste sera fort. Lorsqu'il est utilisé à bon escient, le contraste peut aboutir à des **mises en pages** très intéressantes. **Textures, couleurs,** formes, épaisseur des lignes, etc., peuvent être employées pour créer du contraste. Voir aussi **équilibre, couleurs complémentaires** et **dessin en grisé.**

Ang: CONTRAST
All: KONTRAST
Ital: CONTRASTO
Esp: CONTRASTE

Affiche pour la Fête de la musique 2008
Design : Fanette Mellier, www.fanettemellier.com

CONTREPOINÇON

Espace blanc, totalement (comme dans la lettre « o ») ou partiellement (comme dans la lettre « c ») enclos à l'intérieur de la panse d'un **caractère.** Voir aussi **espace négatif.**

Ang: COUNTER
All: PUNZE
Ital: OCCHIELLO
Esp: CONTRAFORMA

A **C** D E F G H I J K L M N O P Q R S T U V W X Y Z

48-point
36-point
24-point
18-point
14-point
12-point
10-point
8-point

CORPS

Le corps est exprimé en points, l'unité de mesure principale de la **typographie.** Celle-ci est aujourd'hui standardisée : un **point pica** équivaut à 1/72 de l'inch, le pouce anglo-saxon, ou 0,351 millimètre. Issu des anciens **caractères** en plomb, le corps était autrefois déterminé par la hauteur physique de la pièce elle-même. Ainsi, le corps étant une valeur absolue, la taille réelle d'une lettre dans un certain corps variera en fonction des **familles de caractères.** Cette relation entre corps et taille de caractère est encore moins évidente pour les **typographies** numériques. Voir aussi **point pica.**

Ang: POINT/POINT SIZE
All: PUNKT/PUNKTGRÖSSE
Ital: PUNTO/I/DIMENSIONI DEL PUNTO
Esp: PUNTO/TAMAÑO DE PUNTO

CORPS DU TEXTE

Terme employé pour désigner la partie essentielle du texte dans un livre, une brochure ou toute autre publication.
Il exclut les **pages liminaires,** les **annexes,** les **titres,** les titres courants, les **intertitres,** etc. Le corps du texte peut également définir le texte principal d'un site Internet.

Ang: BODY COPY
All: FLIESSTEXT
Ital: CORPO DEL TESTO
Esp: CUERPO DE TEXTO

Design : Donna S. Atwood, www.atwooddesign.com

CORRECTION DES COULEURS

Procédé consistant à régler l'ensemble ou une partie des **couleurs** d'une photographie numérique ou d'une image scannée afin de représenter le plus fidèlement possible le sujet original, ou de coller au plus près de la gamme des couleurs (ou *gamut*) de la technique d'impression utilisée.

Ang: COLOR CORRECTION
All: FARBKORREKTUR
Ital: CORREZIONE DEI COLORI
Esp: CORRECCIÓN DE COLOR

Design : Donna S. Atwood, www.atwooddesign.com

A **C** D E F G H I J K L M N O P Q R S T U V W X Y Z

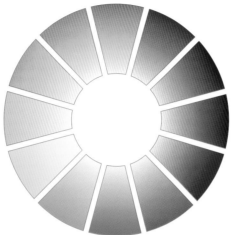

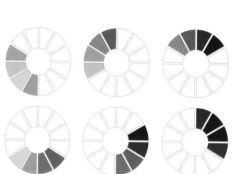

COULEUR

Sensation produite par la stimulation de la rétine par des ondes lumineuses de longueurs variables. Les objets sont perçus comme ayant des couleurs spécifiques en raison de leur capacité à absorber, réfléchir et transmettre différentes ondes lumineuses. Les trois propriétés de la couleur sont la **teinte,** la **saturation** (ou *chromie*) et la **luminosité** (on parle aussi de **valeur** ou de *ton*). Les typographes parlent également de la couleur d'une page de texte, ou d'un paragraphe par rapport à un autre, pour définir la luminosité ou l'obscurité globale. Voir aussi **roue chromatique.**

Ang: COLOR
All: FARBE
Ital: COLORE/I
Esp: COLOR

Production d'une série d'ouvrages traitant du processus de fabrication du livre
Design : Alexandre Chapus, www.achapus.com

COULEUR DE FOND

Couleur dont la **luminosité** a été accrue par l'addition de blanc. On diminue la luminosité d'une couleur en y ajoutant du noir, on obtient alors une *nuance* de cette **teinte.**

Ang: TINT
All: TÖNUNG
Ital: TINTA
Esp: TINTE

Design : Donna S. Atwood, www.atwooddesign.com

COULEURS ANALOGUES

Deux **couleurs,** ou plus, qui sont adjacentes à une autre sur la **roue chromatique** (par exemple, vert, jaune-vert et jaune). Ainsi, lorsque l'on associe des couleurs analogues au sein d'une **composition,** celle-ci gagne en harmonie.

Ang: ANALOGOUS COLORS
All: ANALOGE FARBEN
Ital: COLORI ANALOGHI
Esp: COLORES ANÁLOGOS

Design : Donna S. Atwood, www.atwooddesign.com

A **C** D E F G H I J K L M N O P Q R S T U V W X Y Z

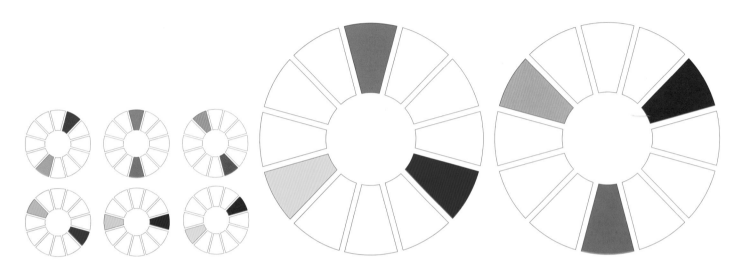

COULEURS COMPLÉMENTAIRES

Couleurs opposées sur la **roue chromatique,** comme le rouge et le vert. On parle aussi de *couleurs contrastées*. Le fait d'associer des couleurs complémentaires dans une **composition** se révèle la plupart du temps spectaculaire. On trouve souvent un *schéma analogue-complémentaire* qui associe une couleur avec les deux couleurs qui entourent sa complémentaire sur la roue chromatique.

Ang: COMPLEMENTARY COLORS
All: KOMPLEMENTÄRFARBEN
Ital: COLORI COMPLEMENTARI
Esp: COLORES COMPLEMENTARIOS

Design : Donna S. Atwood, www.atwooddesign.com

COULEURS PRIMAIRES

Couleurs réparties équitablement autour de la circonférence de la **roue chromatique** et formant ses éléments de référence. Sur la roue chromatique traditionnelle, utilisée pour mélanger les couleurs, les couleurs primaires sont le rouge, le bleu et le jaune. D'autres roues chromatiques existent, fondées à partir des *couleurs primaires soustractives,* que sont le cyan, le magenta et le jaune, et des *couleurs primaires additives,* que sont le rouge, le vert et le bleu. Voir aussi **CMJN** et **RVB.**

Ang: PRIMARY COLORS
All: PRIMÄRFARBEN
Ital: COLORI PRIMARI
Esp: COLORES PRIMARIOS

Design : Donna S. Atwood, www.atwooddesign.com

COULEURS SECONDAIRES

Couleurs (orange, violet et vert) obtenues par le mélange de deux **couleurs primaires** dans des proportions égales. Par exemple, en mélangeant du rouge et du jaune, on obtient de l'orange. Voir aussi **roue chromatique** et **couleurs tertiaires.**

Ang: SECONDARY COLORS
All: SEKUNDÄRFARBEN
Ital: COLORI SECONDARI
Esp: COLORES SECUNDARIOS

Design : Donna S. Atwood, www.atwooddesign.com

A B **C** D E F G H I J K L M N O P Q R S T U V W X Y Z

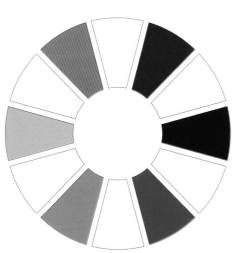

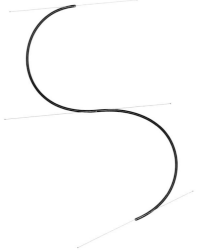

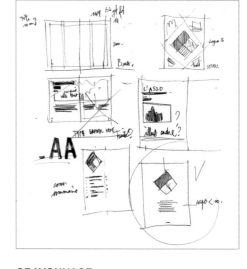

COULEURS TERTIAIRES

Couleurs obtenues par le mélange d'une **couleur primaire** et d'une **couleur secondaire.** Par exemple, le rouge-orange s'obtient en mélangeant du rouge (couleur primaire) et du orange (couleur secondaire créée en mélangeant dans des proportions égales les couleurs primaires rouge et jaune). Voir aussi **roue chromatique.**

Ang: TERTIARY COLORS
All: TERTIÄRFARBEN
Ital: COLORI TERZIARI
Esp: COLORES TERCIARIOS

Design : Donna S. Atwood, www.atwooddesign.com

COUPURE DE MOTS
Voir **C&J.**

COURBE DE BÉZIER

Approximation mathématique d'une courbe continue calculée à partir de ses deux points de contrôle (situés à l'une et l'autre extrémité) et autant de points supplémentaires que nécessaire. Les **chemins** utilisés par la majorité des logiciels de design graphique sont constitués d'une multitude de courbes de Bézier, ce qui leur permet d'être agrandies indéfiniment. Elles sont également utilisées en **animation** comme un outil de contrôle du mouvement.

Ang: BÉZIER CURVE
All: BÉZIERKURVE
Ital: CURVA DI BÉZIER
Esp: CURVA DE BÉZIER

Design : Donna S. Atwood, www.atwooddesign.com

CRAYONNAGE

Esquisse sommaire destinée à véhiculer rapidement un concept. Les crayonnages, qui servent généralement durant les premières étapes d'un projet, font partie intégrante du processus de design. En effet, la création finale émerge très souvent d'une accumulation de plusieurs esquisses s'affinant progressivement. Le terme peut aussi définir des vignettes en basse **résolution** servant de substitut à leurs versions en haute définition. Par exemple, les **banques d'images** en ligne exposent sur une seule et même page des douzaines de vignettes afin que le chargement et l'affichage s'effectuent rapidement. Cette pratique est aujourd'hui tellement courante que la seule présence de vignettes induit que leur version en haute définition est disponible en quelques clics.

Ang: THUMBNAIL
All: DAUMENNAGELSKIZZE
Ital: THUMBNAIL
Esp: MINIATURA

A B **C** D E F G H I J K L M N O P Q R S T U V W X Y Z

Helvetica

−34   −15   +7   -6
Helvetica g g
−31   0   +18 −9

CRÉNAGE

Ajustement de l'espace entre les lettres afin de créer un **rythme** visuellement attrayant. La juxtaposition de certaines lettres, comme le « T » et le « o », génère un espacement maladroit. Le crénage permet de régler cet espacement afin d'obtenir un effet plus naturel. Si certains logiciels se chargent automatiquement de cette tâche, ce n'est pas toujours pour plaire aux graphistes et typographes.

Ang: KERNING
All: UNTERSCHNEIDEN
Ital: CRENATURA
Esp: KERNING

CRÉNELAGE, ANTICRÉNELAGE

Le crénelage (ou aliasing) est un phénomène qui se produit quand la **résolution** d'une **image matricielle** est trop petite par rapport à la technique employée pour l'afficher ou l'imprimer. Par exemple, une image dans une résolution de 72 **dpi** (*dot per inch*) sera crénelée si elle est imprimée à taille réelle en 300 dpi et aura une apparence dentelée (ou en « marches d'escalier »). L'anticrénelage (ou lissage) est une méthode employée par certains logiciels d'affichage d'images numériques pour pallier cet effet de distorsion. Le procédé consiste à flouter légèrement l'image afin d'adoucir l'aspect en marches d'escalier de certains éléments graphiques. Cela induit une légère perte de qualité, mais reste néanmoins préférable au crénelage. Voir aussi **résolution.**

Ang: ALIASING, ANTI-ALIASING
All: ALIAS EFFEKT, ANTIALIASING
Ital: ALIASING/ANTI-ALIASING
Esp: SOLAPAMIENTO/ANTISOLAPAMIENTO

CUBISME

Courant artistique européen d'avant-garde, du début du xxᵉ siècle (1907-1920), transcrivant les objets, y compris la figure humaine, en des formes géométriques abstraites. Les partisans de ce courant utilisaient la vision simultanée de multiples perspectives, réduisaient en deux dimensions des éléments en trois dimensions, et défiaient les règles conventionnelles de la perspective remontant à la Renaissance. Le graphisme expérimentera ensuite de la même façon la composition de l'espace et l'abstraction géométrique.

Ang: CUBISM
All: KUBISMUS
Ital: CUBISMO
Esp: CUBISMO

Illustration du groupe Zoot Woman pour le festival de musique Iceland Airwaves
Design : Siggi Eggertsson, www.vanillusaft.com

A B **C D** E F G H I J K L M N O P Q R S T U V W X Y Z

CURSIVE

Typographies imitant l'écriture manuscrite. Elles ajoutent parfois une touche élégante et personnelle à un texte, mais il convient de ne pas en abuser et surtout de les utiliser dans un contexte approprié. Par exemple, sur une invitation ou un faire-part, les cursives peuvent trouver leur place. Par contre, appliquée à un long bloc de texte, une cursive s'avère pénible pour le lecteur.

Ang: SCRIPT TYPE
All: SCHREIBSCHRIFT
Ital: CARATTERI INFORMALI
Esp: SCRIPT TYPE

Design : Underware, Liza Display Pro, www.underware.nl

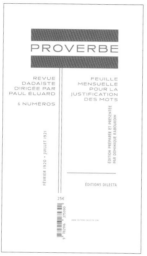

DADA

Mouvement artistique qui débuta à Zurich, en Suisse, et s'étendit dans toute l'Europe en réaction à la Première Guerre mondiale. Dada se caractérise par une remise en cause de toutes les croyances traditionnelles, qu'elles soient artistiques, morales ou religieuses, par la création d'images provocantes et absurdes. Toutefois, en Allemagne, le travail des membres de dada prit un ton plus sombre et politisé à la suite de la prise du pouvoir par Hitler dans les années 1930. On trouve un vaste champ d'influences dans les créations graphiques des dadaïstes, comme les méthodes de composition propres au **constructivisme** et à **De Stijl,** et l'énergie brute que l'on trouve dans les techniques du **collage** et du **photomontage,** technique d'ailleurs revendiquées par les dadaïstes.

Ang: DADA
All: DADAISMUS
Ital: DADA
Esp: DADA

Proverbe, Éditions Dilecta
Design typographique : © Jean-Baptiste Levée, 2008, www.opto.fr

DE STIJL

Mouvement artistique allemand du début du xxe siècle (1917-1931) dont les préoccupations majeures étaient de construire des lois universelles fondées sur un langage visuel purement objectif. Les **couleurs** se limitaient aux couleurs neutres (noir, blanc et gris) et aux **couleurs primaires** (rouge, bleu et jaune), et les formes, à des carrés et des rectangles composés horizontalement et verticalement de façon asymétrique. Des **caractères sans empattements** étaient utilisés de façon quasi systématique et étaient parfois associés à des agglomérats de **caractères de titre** dessinés à la main.

Ang: DE STIJL
All: DE STIJL
Ital: DE STIJL
Esp: DE STIJL

Affiche pour une exposition au MAC/VAL, Musée d'art contemporain du Val-de-Marne
Design : Atelier ter Bekke & Behage, www.terbekke-behage.com

Festival de danse et des arts multiples de Marseille

14

17 juin > 11 juillet 2009

DÉCOUPE

Procédé permettant d'effectuer des découpes précises dans une feuille de papier imprimée. Celles-ci peuvent être fonctionnelles (par exemple sur des pochettes ou des emballages), décoratives (comme des ouvertures sur des images ou des traitements particuliers des bords), ou bien les deux. Voir aussi **découpe par effleurement** et **découpe au laser.**

Ang: DIE CUT
All: STANZSCHNITT
Ital: FUSTELLA
Esp: TROQUELADO

Catalogue du Festival de Marseille F/D/Am/M* 2009
Design : Jean-Claude Chianale,
www.jeanclaude-design.com

A B C **D** E F G H I J K L M N O P Q R S T U V W X Y Z

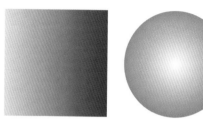

DÉCOUPE AU LASER

Procédé à partir duquel un laser guidé
par un ordinateur vient graver ou découper
du papier, du bois, du plastique et même
quelques métaux. Du fait de sa très haute
précision, la découpe au laser permet de
réaliser des détails plus complexes que le
procédé de **découpe** classique. D'autre part,
ce procédé est plus économique et rapide
sur de très petites quantités car les matrices
en métal ne sont plus utilisées. Par contre,
dès qu'il s'agit d'un travail de découpe
extrêmement précis ou bien lorsque le
support est délicat, par exemple s'il brûle
ou fond facilement, s'il est très épais, etc.,
les coûts augmentent de façon exponentielle.

Ang: LASER CUT
All: LASERSCHNITT
Ital: TAGLIO AL LASER
Esp: CORTE LÁSER

Design : Richard Niessen et Esther de Vries,
www.niessendevries.nl

DÉCOUPE PAR EFFLEUREMENT

Opération similaire à la **découpe** utilisée
pour les autocollants et les décalcomanies.
Les découpes sont effectuées sur une feuille
de papier imprimée sans passer à travers
le dos afin que les autocollants ou les
décalcomanies puissent s'en détacher.

Ang: KISS DIE CUT
All: ANSTANZUNG
Ital: ADESIVO CON FUSTELLA
Esp: TROQUELADO DE MEDIO CORTE

Programme pour le Théâtre de Vevey 2006-2007
Design : Welcometo.as, Adam Machacek,
Sébastien Bohner, www.welcometo.as

DÉGRADÉ

Transition progressive d'une **couleur**
à une autre, ou du blanc (ou du noir) vers
une couleur saturée, généralement par
une progression régulière. Les dégradés
servent souvent à remplir certaines parties
d'une illustration, d'un arrière-plan ou d'un
caractère au fil.

Ang: GRADIENT
All: VERLAUF
Ital: GRADIENTE/I
Esp: DEGRADADO

Design : Donna S. Atwood, www.atwooddesign.com

A B C **D** E F G H I J K L M N O P Q R S T U V W X Y Z

Cadratin

Demi-cadratin

Typographie

DEMI-CADRATIN

Mesure typographique qui correspond
à la moitié de la largeur d'un **cadratin.**
Voir aussi **tiret demi-cadratin** et **espace
demi-cadratin.**

Ang: EN
All: HALBGEVIERT
Ital: EN
Esp: MEDIO CUADRATÍN

DESCENDANTE

Partie des lettres *bas-de-casse* qui s'étend
au-dessous de la **ligne de base.** Tout comme
les **ascendantes,** la taille et l'épaisseur des
descendantes varient selon les **familles
de caractères.** Voir aussi **ascendantes.**

Ang: DESCENDER
All: UNTERLÄNGE
Ital: TRATTO DISCENDENTE
Esp: DESCENDENTE

DESIGN DE PACKAGING

Le design de packaging consiste à créer
un emballage qui va protéger et présenter
un produit, de la distribution au stockage,
en passant par sa mise en vente et son
utilisation. Si les **logos,** et tout un ensemble
d'éléments visuels et tactiles faisant partie
de la **stratégie de la marque,** jouent un rôle
déterminant, ces considérations esthétiques
ne sont pourtant que les prémices du design
de packaging. D'autres facteurs doivent aussi
être pris en compte, en matière de sécurité
(boîtes de médicaments impossibles à
ouvrir par des enfants), d'économie (nombre
de cartons par conteneur) et de facilité
d'utilisation (impression agréable à l'ouverture
pour l'utilisateur final), pour n'en citer que
quelques-uns.

Ang: PACKAGING DESIGN
All: VERPACKUNGSDESIGN
Ital: PACKAGING DESIGN
Esp: DISEÑO DE EMBALAJE

Derby, marque premier prix des supermarchés
Delhaize, 1996-2000
Design : © Donuts, A. Franssen – O. Vandervliet –
N. Wathelet, www.donuts.be

DESIGN NUMÉRIQUE

Le design numérique est une activité de conception de produits, de services ou de systèmes intégrant des technologies qui permettent de créer une relation entre des humains et des systèmes techniques. Les exemples les plus couramment cités intègrent des interfaces technologiques très complexes – sites Internet, appareils électroniques portatifs –, alors que l'interaction la plus basique qui soit requiert un design réfléchi. Un distributeur de billets, un titre de transport électronique, une application iPhone, par exemple, doivent être conçus pour être maniés avec aisance et assurer ainsi une expérience agréable et intuitive à l'utilisateur. Les designers interactifs sont souvent amenés à étudier les comportements des utilisateurs, en appliquant des méthodologies propres à d'autres disciplines, comme la psychologie cognitive ou l'anthropologie.

Ang: INTERACTION DESIGN
All: INTERAKTIVES DESIGN
Ital: DESIGN INTERATTIVO
Esp: DISEÑO INTERACTIVO

Design numérique et innovation
Design : nodesign.net, www.nodesign.net

A B C **D** E F G H I J K L M N O P Q R S T U V W X Y Z

DESSIN D'UNE LETTRE

Forme d'un **caractère** (qu'il s'agisse ou non d'une lettre). Les éléments qu'une série de caractères ont en commun constituent la spécificité d'une **famille de caractères.** Le vocabulaire permettant de qualifier l'*anatomie des caractères* est très vaste, il comprend des termes tels qu'**empattement, ascendante, descendante,** etc.

Ang: LETTERFORM
All: SCHRIFTCHARAKTER
Ital: GLIFO/I
Esp: LETRA

Design : Stephanie Horn, www.stephanie-horn.com

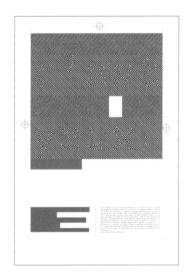

DESSIN EN GRISÉ

Principe de la perception visuelle, basé sur la relation entre une forme et ce qui l'entoure. Une forme ne peut se distinguer que si elle est placée sur un arrière-plan dont elle se détache. Une maîtrise réfléchie de cette relation intrinsèque amène certains designers graphiques à créer des visuels fascinants, même à partir de formes très basiques. Ceci s'avère déterminant pour la création de **logos,** censés contenir beaucoup d'informations en un signe simple et facilement identifiable. Un dessin en grisé stable devrait avoir un **point central** évident et dégager une sensation d'harmonie, alors qu'un dessin en grisé ambigu met au défi la perception du spectateur, les deux s'avérant tout aussi efficaces. Voir aussi **espace positif** et **espace négatif.**

Ang: FIGURE-GROUND
All: FORMFLÄCHENGESTALTUNG
Ital: FIGURA-SFONDO
Esp: RELACIÓN FIGURA-FONDO

Affiche extraite d'une série conçue pour l'exposition « Impressions françaises » Festival de Chaumont, 2007
Design : Vanina Pinter, Vincent Perrottet, William Jean et Étienne Hervy

African Ornaments One

Webdings

Zapf Dingbats

DINGBATS

Vaste gamme de **caractères** spéciaux comprenant les **symboles** (par exemple, les symboles mathématiques, la ponctuation, les signes, etc.), les **puces** (cercles, étoiles, etc.), divers ornements graphiques, et bien d'autres encore.

Ang: DINGBATS
All: DINGBATS
Ital: DINGBATS
Esp: DINGBATS

A B C **D** E F G H I J K L M N O P Q R S T U V W X Y Z

DORURE

Procédé permettant d'appliquer sur du papier une mince couche de film plastique à l'aide d'une matrice chauffée. Il sert, la plupart du temps, à attirer l'attention sur des **logos,** des illustrations, des **caractères,** ou tout autre composant graphique. Le film plastique est décliné en une vaste gamme de **couleurs,** de brillances et de finis métalliques. Un film opaque pourra servir à rehausser un arrière-plan plutôt sombre ; un film transparent pourra, quant à lui, simuler un **vernis.** On parle aussi de *dorure industrielle* ou de *dorure à chaud.*

Ang: FOIL STAMPING
All: FOLIENPRÄGUNG
Ital: STAMPA A LAMINA DI PLASTICA
Esp: ESTAMPADO METÁLICO

Carte de visite de l'atelier Akatre
Design : Akatre, www.akatre.com

DOUBLE PAGE

Pages en regard au sein d'une publication reliée. Voir aussi **recto verso.**

Ang: SPREAD
Esp: DOBLE PÁGINA

Double page extraite du livre *Unfinished Trajectories*
Design : R2 Design, www.r2design.pt

DPI (DOTS PER INCH)
Voir **résolution.**

DRAPEAU

Terme utilisé pour décrire un texte non justifié. Le drapeau d'un texte **en fer à gauche** se situe le long de la **marge** droite, et inversement pour un texte **en fer à droite.** Plutôt que de donner une forme trop géométrique ou rythmée à un drapeau, engendrant des distractions visuelles, les typographes et les graphistes privilégient un drapeau n'ayant pas une forme précise afin d'assurer une **lisibilité** maximale.

Ang: RAG
All: FLATTERSATZ
Ital: BANDIERA
Esp: BANDERA

The New York Times Op-Ed, « All you do is just sit down », 1992
Direction artistique/Designer : Mirko Ilić, www.mirkoilic.com ; **Illustrateur :** Milan Trenc

ABC**D** **E** FGHIJKLMNOPQRSTUVWXYZ

Pop Typography

ÉCHELLE

Taille perçue d'un élément graphique par rapport aux autres, au sein d'une **mise en pages.** Cela peut tenir à des différences minimes, comme lorsqu'une portion de texte est composée dans un **corps** plus grand que celui du texte courant, afin de signifier son importance. Néanmoins, les différences d'échelle sont souvent beaucoup plus subtiles. Par exemple, des objets ayant des formes différentes mais occupant la même superficie amènent une différence d'échelle. En effet, tout comme le contexte dans lequel se situe un élément, sa forme et sa **couleur** influent sur son échelle.

Ang: SCALE
All: GRÖSSENVERHÄLTNIS
Ital: SCALA
Esp: ESCALA

« The Year in Culture 2006 », couverture pour le *New York Times*
Design : Post Typography, www.posttypography.com

A B C D **E** F G H I J K L M N O P Q R S T U V W X Y Z

Caslon

Playbill

CAIRO
Tutenkhamon
Curse of the Mummies

Georgia

Didot

ÉCHELLE DE GRIS

Une image en niveaux de gris est composée de différentes nuances de gris, de blanc et de noir. Les photographies en **couleur** peuvent être converties en niveaux de gris par le biais de logiciels basculant les **valeurs** de chaque point en sa valeur de gris équivalente, ce qui donnera une image simulant une photographie en noir et blanc. Voir aussi **monochromatique.**

Ang: GRAYSCALE
All: GRAUSTUFENBILD
Ital: SCALA DEI GRIGI
Esp: ESCALA DE GRISES

ÉGYPTIENNE

Famille de caractères à **empattements** rectangulaires. Ils conviennent mieux pour les affiches, les publicités et les titres courants que pour le **corps du texte,** car leur allure est assez massive et l'épaisseur de leurs fûts ne varie quasiment pas.

Ang: EGYPTIAN
All: EGYPTIENNE
Ital: CARATTERI EGIZIANI
Esp: EGIPCIO

Design : House Industries, Neutraslab, www.houseind.com

EMPATTEMENT

Terminaison d'un **caractère** typographique. Ce terme sert également à la classification des **familles de caractères,** à empattements ou sans. Les **typographies** à empattements sont plus agréables pour le *texte de labeur,* surtout dans une petite force de **corps,** car elles permettent de distinguer facilement un caractère d'un autre. Voir aussi **caractères sans empattements.**

Ang: SERIF
All: SERIFE
Ital: CARATTERI CON GRAZIE
Esp: SERIFA

ENCRES PRIMAIRES
Voir **CMJN** et **quadrichromie.**

ÉPAISSEUR (DU PAPIER)
Voir **rame.**

ÉPREUVES EN PLACARD
Voir **épreuves.**

A B C D **E** F G H I J K L M N O P Q R S T U V W X Y Z

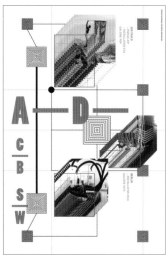

Typographie
Espace cadratin

ÉPREUVES

Terme générique utilisé pour parler des versions préliminaires d'un livre, d'un rapport annuel, d'une brochure ou de tout autre document avant sa publication. Les épreuves servent à différents stades du projet, notamment au moment de la révision, de la correction ou même de la promotion, par exemple quand un livre est envoyé aux critiques avant sa parution. Avant l'avènement de l'informatique, les épreuves étaient essentiellement des sorties papier brutes ; aujourd'hui, les épreuves numériques sont de plus en plus courantes. Les *épreuves certifiées* permettent de s'assurer du rendu exact des **couleurs** à l'impression.

Ang: PROOF
All: KORREKTURABZUG
Ital: BOZZA/E
Esp: PRUEBA

« Mémento des signes de correction typographique », extrait du livre *Typoésie,* de Jérôme Peignot, Imprimerie nationale, Paris, 1993

ÉQUILIBRE

Accord visuel entre les différents éléments graphiques composant un imprimé. On dit d'une **mise en pages** qu'elle est équilibrée lorsque les formes, proportions, matières, **couleurs** et **valeurs,** participent à la création d'une harmonie visuelle. Réaliser une mise en pages équilibrée requiert de la part du graphiste un certain respect de la tradition. En effet, en équilibrant sa **composition,** il pourra en dynamiser les différents espaces, et ainsi créer une expérience engageante pour le public.

Ang: BALANCE
All: BALANCE (AUSGEWOGENHEIT)
Ital: BILANCIAMENTO
Esp: EQUILIBRIO

Affiche pour l'Association des Designeurs
Design : Brice Domingues, www.bricedomingues.com

ESPACE CADRATIN

Espace égale à un **cadratin** au sein d'une ligne de texte. Contrairement aux espaces créées en utilisant la barre d'espace du clavier (espaces à chasse variable), qui varieront à mesure que chaque ligne de texte est composée, l'espace cadratin a une chasse fixe.

Ang: EM SPACE
All: GEVIERTABSTAND
Ital: SPAZIO EM
Esp: ESPACIO DE CUADRATÍN

ESPACE COLORIMÉTRIQUE
Voir **modèle colorimétrique.**

A B C D **E** F G H I J K L M N O P Q R S T U V W X Y Z

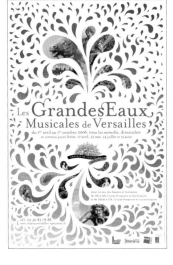

Typographie
Espace demi-cadratin

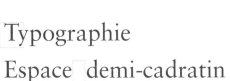

ESPACE DEMI-CADRATIN

Espace égale à un **demi-cadratin** au sein d'une ligne de texte. D'une chasse fixe, une espace demi-cadratin ne changera pas au fur et à mesure de la **composition** du texte, à l'inverse des espaces créées avec la barre d'espace.

Ang: EN SPACE
All: HALBGEVIERTABSTAND
Ital: SPAZIO EN
Esp: ESPACIO DE MEDIO CUADRATÍN

ESPACE NÉGATIF

Terme utilisé pour décrire l'arrière-plan et toute zone autour d'un **espace positif.** S'il est souvent employé pour décrire les caractéristiques d'une **mise en pages,** ce terme s'applique aussi bien à la **typographie,** notamment lorsque le **dessin d'une lettre** entraîne une relation d'espace positif et négatif avec les lettres avoisinantes. Une attention particulière doit être portée à cette relation lors de la conception des **logos,** car ceux-ci sont souvent présentés dans un format réduit. Voir aussi **espace positif, dessin en grisé** et **blancs.**

Ang: NEGATIVE SPACE
All: FREIE FLÄCHE
Ital: SPAZIO NEGATIVO
Esp: ESPACIO NEGATIVO

Kiblind XXIII+, couverture du hors-série *Kiblind,* n° 23+, novembre 2008
Design : Superscript[2], www.super-script.com

ESPACE POSITIF

Terme désignant les zones d'une création graphique occupées par des éléments (l'arrière-plan et le reste de l'image étant qualifiés d'**espace négatif**). S'il est souvent employé pour décrire les caractéristiques d'une **mise en pages,** ce terme s'applique aussi à la **typographie,** notamment lorsque le **dessin d'une lettre** entraîne une relation d'espace positif et négatif avec les lettres avoisinantes. Une attention particulière doit être portée à cette relation lors de la conception des **logos,** car ceux-ci sont souvent présentés dans un format réduit. Voir aussi **espace négatif, dessin en grisé** et **blancs.**

Ang: POSITIVE SPACE
All: GESTALTETE FLÄCHE
Ital: SPAZIO POSITIVO
Esp: ESPACIO POSITIVO

Affiche pour le Spectacle des grandes eaux musicales du château de Versailles, 2006
Design : Polymago, © photo De Givry, N'Daye, www.polymago.fr

A B C D **E F** G H I J K L M N O P Q R S T U V W X Y Z

$$\tfrac{3}{4} \times \tfrac{1}{2} = \tfrac{3}{8}$$

$$A^2 + B^2 = C^2$$

Helvetica Neue

Helvetica Neue Light

Helvetica Neue Ultralight

Helvetica Neue Ultralight Italic

Helvetica Neue Italic

Helvetica Neue Bold Italic

Helvetica Neue Bold Italic

EXERGUE

Citation extraite d'un article, ou d'un texte (souvent située sur la même page), et composée de façon à capter l'attention du lecteur. Ainsi, les exergues sont souvent dans un **corps** beaucoup plus grand que le texte courant, parfois même dans une autre **typographie.** L'utilisation d'une **couleur,** d'ornements, de **bordures,** etc., pourra aussi venir renforcer cette différentiation.

Ang: PULL QUOTE
All: HERVORGEHOBENES ZITAT
Ital: CITAZIONE ESTERNA
Esp: SUMARIO

Double page extraite de *L'opéra au xxᵉ siècle,* éditons Textuel, 2007
Design : Helmo, www.helmo.fr

EXPOSANT

De la même façon que les **indices,** les exposants sont des **caractères** plus petits que ceux du texte dans lequel ils se trouvent. Le placement d'un exposant va dépendre de l'usage dont il fait l'objet. Ainsi, l'exposant servant d'appel de note ou de numérateur aura son sommet aligné sur la ligne des hauteurs de capitales, alors que dans des formules mathématiques ou scientifiques, il est centré sur cette même ligne. On peut également placer en exposant certaines *bas-de-casse,* par exemple pour des abréviations (1ᵉʳ, 2ᵉ, xxᵉ siècle, etc.).

Ang: SUPERSCRIPT
All: HOCHGESTELLTE SCHRIFTZEICHEN
Ital: APICE/I
Esp: SUPERÍNDICE

FAMILLE DE CARACTÈRES

Toutes les déclinaisons d'une **typographie,** par exemple, **gras, italique, condensé,** étendu, etc. La variété de déclinaisons que l'on connaît aujourd'hui est en partie liée à l'avènement de la publicité, au xixᵉ siècle, qui a fait naître une grande demande pour des typographies originales. Voir aussi **caractères étendus.**

Ang: TYPE FAMILY
All: SCHRIFTFAMILIE
Ital: FAMIGLIA DI CARATTERI
Esp: FAMILIA TIPOGRÁFICA

A B C D E **F** G H I J K L M N O P Q R S T U V W X Y Z

Lorem ipsum dolor sit amet, consectetuer adipiscing elit. Sed non risus. Suspendisse lectus tortor, dignissim sit amet, adipiscing nec, ultricies sed, dolor. Cras elementum ultrices diam. Maecenas ligula massa, varius a, semper congue, euismod non, mi. Proin porttitor, orci nec nonummy molestie, enim est eleifend mi, non fermentum diam nisl sit amet erat. Duis semper.

Duis arcu massa, scelerisque vitae, consequat in, pretium a, enim. Pellentesque congue. Ut in risus volutpat libero pharetra tempor. Cras vestibulum bibendum augue. Praesent egestas leo in pede. Praesent blandit odio eu enim. Pellentesque sed dui ut augue blandit sodales. Vestibulum ante ipsum primis in faucibus orci luctus et ultrices posuere cubilia Curae; Aliquam nibh. Mauris ac mauris sed pede pellentesque fermentum. Maecenas adipiscing ante non diam sodales hendrerit.

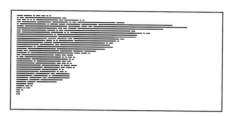

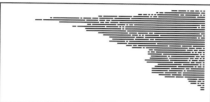

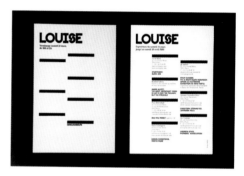

FAUX TEXTE

Texte sans valeur sémantique, permettant de remplir la **mise en pages** en l'absence du texte définitif afin d'effectuer un **calibrage** par exemple. On parle aussi de **Lorem ipsum.**

Ang: GREEKING
All: BLINDTEXT
Esp: GREEKING

FER À GAUCHE, FER À DROITE

Des lignes de texte successives ferrées à gauche et démarrant toutes à partir de la même ligne de référence. On parle aussi d'*alignement à gauche* ou de *drapeau à droite*. Des lignes successives de texte ferré à droite et se terminant toutes sur la même ligne de référence. On parle aussi d'*alignement à droite* ou de *drapeau à gauche*.

Ang: FLUSH-LEFT, FLUSH-RIGHT
All: LINKSBÜNDIG, RECHTSBÜNDIG
Ital: ALLINEAMENTO A SINISTRA E
      ALLINEAMENTO A DESTRA
Esp: BANDERA A LA IZQUIERDA/BANDERA
      A LA DERECHA

Left-Aligned, Right-Aligned
Design : Angela Detanico, Rafael Lain, www.detanicolain.com

FILET

Ligne utilisée pour séparer un élément d'un autre au sein d'une **mise en pages** de façon à organiser l'espace et créer une **hiérarchie.** La largeur d'un **filet** est définie en points.

Ang: RULE
All: LINIE
Ital: FILETTO TIPOGRAFICO
Esp: FILETE

Carton d'invitation du regroupement de galeries Louise 13
Design : Akatre, www.akatre.com

A B C D E **F** G H I J K L M N O P Q R S T U V W X Y Z

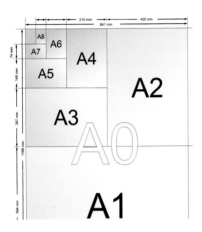

FONDS PERDUS

Partie des éléments de la **composition** graphique, comme une image, une ligne de texte, un aplat de **couleur,** etc., qui s'étend au-delà du format fini de la page. Les traits de coupe permettent de signaler cette zone où tout ce qui est imprimé « débordera » hors de la page. La taille requise pour les fonds perdus dépend de la précision à la fois de la machine à imprimer et du matériel de massicotage, mais elle est, en général, de 5 mm.

Ang: BLEED
All: BESCHNITT
Ital: STAMPA AL VIVO
Esp: IMPRIMIR "A SANGRE"

Détail d'un support de communication pour lux*
Design : Helmo, www.helmo.fr

FONTE

Source physique ou numérique permettant de produire des **caractères.** Aujourd'hui, la plupart des fontes OpenType comprennent des caractères spéciaux, autrefois réservés aux **caractères étendus.** Pour les **caractères** en plomb, la taille des fontes est fixe, contrairement aux caractères numériques dont la taille peut être modifiée d'un simple clic. Si les termes « fonte » et « **police** » sont souvent utilisés indifféremment, il existe une réelle nuance entre les deux. Une police est l'intégralité d'une **famille de caractères** dans sa conception, alors qu'une **fonte** est un jeu de **caractères** dans sa mise en œuvre, physique ou numérique.

Ang: FONT
All: SCHRIFTSATZ
Ital: FONT
Esp: FUENTE

Recto du spécimen de la typographie Replica, distribuée par la fonderie Lineto, www.lineto.com
Design : Norm, www.norm.to ; **Photographie :** Daniela Droz

FORMAT DE FEUILLE
Voir **format de papier.**

FORMAT DE PAPIER

En Europe, les formats de papier standards sont régis par la norme internationale ISO 216. Elle définit trois séries de formats de papier : A, B et C. Le format de référence pour la série A est le A0, d'une surface d'un mètre carré. Le rapport largeur-hauteur de ces formats est constant. Ainsi, le format A1 correspond à la moitié d'une feuille A0, le A2 à la moitié d'une feuille A1, le A3 à la moitié d'un A2, le A4 (format très courant) à la moitié d'un A3, et ainsi de suite. Le format de papier américain est dérivé de formats de papier traditionnels.

Ang: PAPER SIZES
All: PAPIERGRÖSSEN
Ital: FORMATI DI CARTA
Esp: TAMAÑO DE PAPEL

FORME, CONTRE-FORME
Voir **espace positif** et **espace négatif.**

ABCDE **FG** HIJKLMNOPQRSTUVWXYZ

FUTURISME

Le futurisme est un mouvement artistique radical, œuvrant essentiellement en Italie au début du XXe siècle (1909-1930). Ses créations exaltaient l'ère de la machine et en particulier la vitesse et le bruit. Le **collage,** le **photomontage** et toute technique suggérant le mouvement cinématographique, étaient utilisés pour exprimer cette énergie. Le graphisme ne garde néanmoins comme influence majeure du futurisme que la force visuelle de son utilisation des **caractères.** De nombreuses **familles de caractères** dans une grande variété de tailles, parfois composées selon des angles étranges voire déformés, étaient convoquées au sein d'une même **mise en pages** ; l'usage de caractères **gras** et **italiques** indiquant les informations d'importance.

Ang: FUTURISM
All: FUTURISMUS
Ital: FUTURISMO
Esp: FUTURISMO

Pochette de l'album *Movement,* du groupe New Order, 1981, d'après Fortunato Depero, couverture de *Depero futurista,* 1932
Design : Peter Saville

GAUFRAGE

Impression du papier obtenue en le pressant entre deux matrices en métal, l'une surélevée, l'autre en retrait. On parle de gaufrage lorsque l'impression est surélevée par rapport à la surface du papier, lorsque, au contraire, l'impression est en retrait, on parle d'*impression en creux*. Ce procédé fonctionne particulièrement bien avec du papier texturé dans un grammage assez fort. Si elles ne sont pas toujours indispensables, les images gaufrées ou la **dorure** sont surtout employées pour leur aspect décoratif. On parlee de *gaufrage à froid* lorsqu'il n'y a ni encre ni autre traitement.

Ang: EMBOSS
All: PRÄGUNG
Ital: GOFFRATURA
Esp: GOFRAR

Packaging pour la Compagnie de Provence
Design : Stéphan Muntaner, c-ktre@wanadoo.fr

GOTHIQUE

Classification des **caractères** ornementaux apparus au milieu du XVe siècle. Dans un premier temps, les gothiques furent travaillées par les imprimeurs allemands dans le but d'imiter l'écriture manuscrite couramment utilisée par les scribes à cette époque. Elles sont désignées alternativement par d'autres termes, comme fractures, latines ou anglaises, chacun définissant des caractères ornementaux. Pour ajouter un peu plus à cette confusion, l'appellation « gothique » peut être utilisée pour désigner aussi bien les caractères ornementaux que les plus récents **caractères sans empattements,** malgré une totale absence de ressemblance.

Ang: BLACKLETTER
All: FRAKTUR (SCHRIFTEN)
Ital: BLACKLETTER
Esp: LETRA GÓTICA

Fonte Bastard Katakana, 2002
Design : barnbrook design/virusfonts, www.barnbrook.net

A B C D E F **G** H I J K L M N O P Q R S T U V W X Y Z

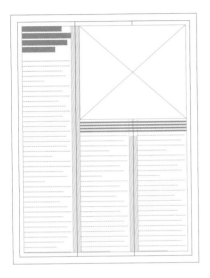

GOUTTIÈRE

Espace entre deux **colonnes** de texte, ou autre, au sein d'une **mise en pages.** Ce terme sert aussi parfois à décrire la bande étroite située près de la zone de **reliure** sur une page, ou les deux bandes formées par la **double page.**

Ang: GUTTER
All: SPALTENABSTAND
Ital: MARGINE INTERNO
Esp: MEDIANIL

Design : Donna S. Atwood, www.atwooddesign.com

N om donné aux lettres capitales pour les différencier des petites capitales.

GRANDES CAPITALES

Nom donné aux lettres capitales pour les différencier des **petites capitales.** À l'origine, le terme *haut-de-casse* était employé, faisant référence à l'emplacement des **caractères** en plomb dans la casse : les lettres capitales étaient rangées dans les cassetins d'en haut et les lettres minuscules, dans les cassetins d'en bas, d'où l'appellation « *bas-de-casse* » encore utilisée aujourd'hui. Voir aussi **initiale** et **lettrine.**

Ang: STANDING CAPITAL/CAP
All: STEHENDE INITIALE
Ital: STANDING CAP
Esp: CAPITULAR

GRAPHIQUE MATRICIEL
Voir **image matricielle.**

Sabon

Sabon Bold

Rockwell

Rockwell Bold

GRAS, CARACTÈRES GRAS

Caractère typographique dont le tracé est plus épais que celui du caractère normal. Les logiciels de PAO (publication assistée par ordinateur) proposent tous un outil permettant de basculer un caractère en gras, en ne faisant que grossir le fût des lettres. Toutefois, un véritable caractère gras a été dessiné de façon proportionnelle aux autres graisses de sa **famille de caractères** afin d'avoir un rendu homogène une fois imprimé.

Ang: BOLD/BOLDFACE
All: FETT (SCHRIFTEN)
Ital: GRASSETTO
Esp: NEGRITA

A B C D E F **G** H I J K L M N O P Q R S T U V W X Y Z

Problème de repérage
sans grossi-maigri

Grossi-maigri : 100% M, 40% C
(taille accrue exagérément)

« Guillemets »
"Guillemets anglais"
"Guillemets droits"

GRILLE

Réseau de lignes horizontales et verticales
qui s'entrecroisent pour former une grille
servant de structure à la **mise en pages** et
permettant d'organiser les différents éléments
graphiques qui la composent. Elle s'avère
particulièrement utile pour les travaux longs,
permettant ainsi aux graphistes de travailler
efficacement en mettant de côté l'arbitraire.
Les grilles se voient parfois critiquées sous
prétexte qu'elles brideraient la créativité
et la pensée critique. Toutefois, si elles sont
utilisées avec intelligence, elles servent
d'une certaine manière d'« échafaudage »
en fournissant une structure sous-jacente
sur laquelle le graphiste peut se reposer
et ainsi donner libre cours à sa créativité.

Ang: GRID
All: RASTER (SATZSPIEGEL)
Ital: GRIGLIA
Esp: CUADRÍCULA

Catalogue de l'exposition « Life in a Glass House »,
Stedelijk Museum CS, Amsterdam
Design : Coup, Erica Terpstra et Peter van den
Hoogen, www.coup.nl

GROSSI-MAIGRI

Technique consistant à prévoir la
superposition de **couleurs** voisines afin de
pallier les éventuels problèmes de **repérage.**
Un mauvais repérage provoquera un espace
blanc indésirable entre deux zones de
couleurs adjacentes, par exemple, si on
imprime du texte en magenta sur un fond
cyan, laissant ainsi apparaître le papier.
On peut éviter ce type de problème en
superposant légèrement les deux couleurs
(généralement la couleur la plus claire, qui
est « grossie », déborde sur la couleur la
plus sombre, « maigrie »). De nombreuses
variantes de grossi-maigri existent, et
déterminer celle qui convient le mieux pour
un produit imprimé donné, dépend de
plusieurs facteurs. Toutefois, cette opération
est, en principe, du ressort de l'imprimeur.
Voir aussi **repérage.**

Ang: TRAPPING
All: ÜBERFÜLLUNG
Ital: TRAPPING
Esp: REVENTADO

GUILLEMETS

Signe de ponctuation que l'on emploie
par paire pour signifier, notamment, une
citation au sein d'un texte ou pour suggérer
l'utilisation ironique ou détournée d'un mot
ou d'une phrase (par exemple : L'application
a pris « seulement » trente minutes pour
exécuter une commande). En français, les
guillemets sont aussi appelés *chevrons* en
raison de leur forme. Voir aussi **apostrophe.**

Ang: QUOTATION MARKS
All: ANFÜHRUNGSSTRICHE
Ital: VIRGOLETTE
Esp: COMILLAS

ABCDEFG**H**IJKLMNOPQRSTUVWXYZ

TypographieTypographie

HAUTEUR D'X

Hauteur des lettres *bas-de-casse* d'une **typographie** n'ayant ni **ascendantes** ni **descendantes.** On la mesure en points, de la **ligne de base** jusqu'à la **ligne de tête.** Les typographies dont la hauteur d'x est élevée offrent une meilleure **lisibilité,** lorsqu'elles sont composées dans un petit **corps,** que celles ayant une faible hauteur d'x.

Ang: X-HEIGHT
All:　X-HÖHE
Ital:　ALTEZZA DELLA X
Esp: ALTURA X

HAUTEUR DE CAPITALE

Distance entre la **ligne de base** et l'extrémité supérieure des capitales. Les hauteurs de capitales varient dans un même **corps** selon les **familles de caractères.** Voir aussi **petites capitales.**

Ang: CAP HEIGHT
All:　VERSALHÖHE
Ital:　ALTEZZA DELLA MAIUSCOLA
Esp: ALTURA DE LAS MAYÚSCULAS

HIÉRARCHIE

Organisation distinctive par le biais de variations d'**échelle,** de placement, de **valeur,** de **couleur** et de nombreux autres paramètres. Les **titres** et les **intertitres,** par exemple, permettent d'ordonner des ouvrages longs. En hiérarchisant ainsi les éléments, les graphistes guident le lecteur à travers une carte de visite, une brochure, une affiche, un livre ou toute autre création, en révélant chaque élément dans un ordre bien précis. À l'inverse, une hiérarchie inexpressive perturbera ce cheminement.

Ang: HIERARCHY
All:　HIERARCHIE
Ital:　GERARCHIA TIPOGRAFICA
Esp: JERARQUÍA

Affiche pour l'exposition « Sandberg Nu » (Sandberg maintenant) au Stedelijk Museum CS (SMCS), Amsterdam, 2004
Design : Experimental Jetset, www.experimentaljetset.nl

A B C D E F G H **I** J K L M N O P Q R S T U V W X Y Z

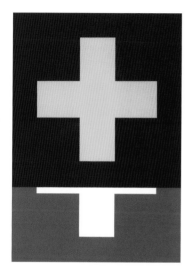

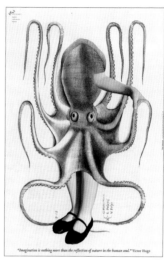

ICÔNE

Signe graphique s'apparentant à ce qu'il signifie ; par exemple, l'icône de l'imprimante sur un écran d'ordinateur ressemble à une imprimante. On trouve de nombreux autres exemples, comme le signe de la cigarette utilisé sur les panneaux d'interdiction de fumer, ou celui de la valise que l'on trouve dans les aéroports pour indiquer la zone de contrôle des bagages. Dans tous les cas, les icônes prennent les traits de ce qu'ils indiquent, les rendant ainsi aisément identifiables, quelles que soient la langue ou la barrière culturelle. Voir aussi **symbole** et **pictogramme.**

Ang: ICON
All: BILDZEICHEN
Ital: ICONA
Esp: ICONO

Affiche en faveur de l'entrée de la Suisse en Europe, projet personnel, 1996
Design : Niklaus Troxler, www.troxlerart.ch

IDENTITÉ

La « personnalité » d'une entreprise exprimée visuellement, en interne et en externe, à travers une **stratégie de marque** distinctive. Une *charte* comprend habituellement un **logo,** une **palette de couleurs** spécifique (la majeure partie du temps définie par un **système d'assortiment des couleurs**), une **mise en pages** type pour les documents et les packagings, et un cahier des charges régissant la disposition de n'importe quel élément, afin de conserver une cohérence à tous les niveaux de l'entreprise. Les grandes entreprises ont parfois différentes marques ayant toutes en commun des éléments visuels afin que chacune soit apparentée à la maison mère.

Ang: IDENTITY
All: FIRMENERSCHEINUNGSBILD
Ital: IDENTITÀ
Esp: IDENTIDAD

Identité graphique du Centre chorégraphique national de Tours
Design : Atelier Müesli, www.ateliermuesli.com

IMAGE COMPOSITE

Image obtenue par la combinaison d'images ou d'éléments d'autres images. Contrairement au **collage,** qui se réfère à l'intégralité d'une création artistique, ou au **photomontage,** définissant l'association d'éléments photographiques, une image composite définit un agencement spécifique au sein d'un travail de création plus vaste.

Ang: COMPOSITE
All: BILDMONTAGE (COMPOSING)
Ital: COMPOSITE
Esp: FOTOCOMPOSICIÓN

Affiche « Imagination »
Design : Yann Legendre, www.yannlegendre.com

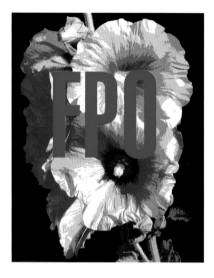

IMAGE DE PLACEMENT

Image basse **résolution** placée dans une **mise en pages** temporairement afin d'indiquer sa position. Cette image est la plupart du temps une version basse définition de l'image haute résolution qui occupera finalement cet espace. Une telle désignation évite toute confusion au sein de l'équipe de graphistes quant à l'utilisation limitée de ces images.

Ang: FOR POSITION ONLY (FPO)
All: PLATZHALTER
Ital: FOR POSITION ONLY (FPO)
Esp: FPO (SÓLO PARA REFERENCIA DE POSICIÓN)

Design : Donna S. Atwood, www.atwooddesign.com

IMAGE MATRICIELLE

Une image matricielle est une image numérique, comme une photographie ou le **dessin d'une lettre,** dans un format de données composé d'une grille de points (ou trame). Chaque point est défini par une **couleur** et une position spécifique au sein de la grille matricielle. Plus il y aura de points par pouce, plus la **résolution** de l'image sera fine. Lorsque l'on affiche ou que l'on imprime une image matricielle dans une taille supérieure à sa taille réelle, cela induit une perte de qualité visible puisqu'elle ne dispose que d'un nombre limité de points (contrairement aux **images vectorielles**). On parle aussi d'*image en mode point*.

Ang: BITMAP
All: BITMAP
Ital: BITMAP
Esp: MAPA DE BITS

Affiche « X'XY – Kataline Patkaï »
Design : © Frédéric Teschner Studio, www.fredericteschner.com

IMAGES VECTORIELLES

Images numériques créées à partir de coordonnées mathématiques, contrairement aux **images matricielles** composées de points. Ces images peuvent être agrandies sans que la **résolution** en soit affectée, mais elles n'offrent pas la même finesse de détails, ni une variation tonale aussi précise que les images matricielles. Voir aussi **courbe de Bézier.**

Ang: VECTOR GRAPHIC
All: VEKTORGRAFIK
Ital: GRAFICA VETTORIALE
Esp: GRÁFICO VECTORIAL

Affiche « Overhead Trafficways »
Design : Roman Bittner, www.apfelzet.de

A B C D E F G H **I** J K L M N O P Q R S T U V W X Y Z

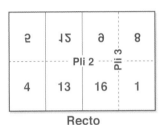

$$4Na + O_2 \rightarrow 2Na_2O$$

IMPOSITION

L'imposition consiste à placer sur une grande feuille de papier les pages d'un ouvrage afin que, une fois imprimées, pliées en **cahiers** et reliées, celles-ci se suivent dans l'ordre de la **pagination.** Cela peut être fait manuellement, même si, aujourd'hui, il est plus fréquent d'utiliser des logiciels spécifiques. Voir aussi **pagination.**

Ang: IMPOSITION
All: AUSSCHIESSEN
Ital: IMPOSIZIONE TIPOGRAFICA
Esp: IMPOSICIÓN

IMPRESSION EN CREUX
Voir **gaufrage.**

IMPRESSION TYPOGRAPHIQUE

Procédé d'*impression en relief* créé au XVe siècle en Allemagne au même moment que la machine à imprimer. Des blocs composés de **caractères** et d'illustrations sont fixés à la presse. Les éléments à imprimer sont dessinés à l'envers afin qu'ils puissent se lire dans le bon sens une fois imprimés. Leur surface est recouverte d'encre puis pressée de façon homogène contre le papier. Les caractères en métal ou en bois, aujourd'hui obsolètes, ont été remplacés par des plaques en polymère créées à partir de fichiers numériques. L'avènement de cette technologie a permis, même sur des applications modestes, de produire une variété de créations inouïe et de redonner une vitalité à un art en déclin.

Ang: LETTERPRESS
All: HOCHDRUCK
Ital: RILIEVOGRAFIA
Esp: IMPRESIÓN TIPOGRÁFICA

Papeterie pour Commissaires
Design : Paprika ; **Directeur de création :** Louis Gagnon ; **Directeur artistique :** David Guarnieri, www.paprika.com

INDICE

Caractère plus petit que le texte principal centré sur la **ligne de base.** Les indices se trouvent surtout dans les annotations mathématiques et les diverses formules scientifiques. Le fait de réduire la taille d'un caractère pour obtenir un indice aura pour effet de diminuer la largeur des fûts et produira donc un effet gênant dû à la différence créée avec les lettres avoisinantes. Ainsi, les typographes et les graphistes préféreront toujours utiliser le caractère conçu à cet effet, si toutefois celui-ci est disponible. Voir aussi **exposant.**

Ang: SUBSCRIPT
All: TIEFGESTELLTE SCHRIFTZEICHEN
Ital: PEDICE/I
Esp: SUBÍNDICE

A B C D E F G H **I** J K L M N O P Q R S T U V W X Y Z

# Interlettrage
Approche = -50

# Interlettrage
Approche = 0

# Interlettrage
Approche = +50

L'interlignage équivaut à 1 x la force de corps

L'interlignage équivaut à 1¼ x la force de corps

L'interlignage équivaut à 1½ x la force de corps

INITIALE

Lettre capitale décorative appliquée à l'initiale du premier mot d'un paragraphe, souvent dans une taille de **corps** plus grande que le reste du texte. Les initiales sont parfois imprimées dans une **typographie** et/ou dans une **couleur** différentes afin de créer une spécificité visuelle supplémentaire. Les initiales, tout comme les **lettres italiques ornées,** doivent être utilisées avec parcimonie, même dans les ouvrages longs.

Ang: INITIAL CAPITAL/CAP
All: INITIALE
Ital: LETTERA MAIUSCOLA INIZIALE
Esp: MAYÚSCULA INICIAL

Couvertures pour la collection « L'Arc », éditions Inculte
Design : Yann Legendre, www.yannlegendre.com

INTERLETTRAGE

Espacement global entre des **caractères** d'un même **corps.** Lorsque le texte est justifié, l'interlettrage est un point sur lequel il convient d'être particulièrement vigilant car ce type de **composition** à tendance à créer des **lézardes** disgracieuses entre les mots, surtout quand la **mesure** est petite. Voir aussi **crénage.**

Ang: LETTER SPACING
All: SPATIONIEREN
Ital: SPAZIO LETTERA
Esp: INTERLETRAJE

INTERLIGNAGE

Distance en points entre les **lignes de base** de deux lignes successives de **caractères.** Contrairement à la **composition** au plomb, les caractères numériques peuvent supporter un *interlignage négatif,* c'est-à-dire que la taille en points des caractères est supérieure à celle de l'interlignage. Si la **lisibilité** est mise à mal par un tel agencement, cela peut parfois créer des effets saisissants au sein de compositions publicitaires ou d'affiches.

Ang: LEADING
All: DURCHSCHUSS (ZEILENABSTAND)
Ital: INTERLINEA
Esp: INTERLINEADO

A B C D E F G H **I** J K L M N O P Q R S T U V W X Y Z

**LE NEW DANCE GROUP
ENTRE EN SCÈNE**

Caslon

Caslon Italic

Palatino

Palatino Italic

INTERTITRE

Niveau de **titre** intermédiaire permettant d'aérer un texte long en le morcelant en courtes sections, révélant ainsi sa structure et sa **hiérarchie**. La **composition** d'un intertitre (sa **typographie,** son **corps,** sa **couleur,** son placement…) doit indiquer son niveau au sein des différents intertitres hiérarchisant l'intégralité du texte. Par exemple, si l'*intertitre de niveau A* est utilisé pour des noms de grandes villes et l'*intertitre de niveau B* pour des catégories de données démographiques, il serait juste que ces deux niveaux se distinguent bien l'un de l'autre. Par contre, si l'*intertitre de niveau B* sert à indiquer des noms de banlieues proches, on pourra les différencier de façon plus subtile.

Ang: SUBHEAD
All: UNTERTITEL
Ital: SOTTOTITOLO
Esp: SUBTÍTULO

Double page extraite de l'ouvrage *Dance is a weapon,* éditions du CND, 2008
Design : Agnès Dahan, www.agnesdahan.net

INVERSION

Impression de lettres blanches sur un fond de **couleur.** La « couleur » du texte est en fait obtenue par l'impression de toutes les zones autour du **caractère,** et non du caractère lui-même. Sa couleur est donc celle du papier, et non celle d'une encre. On peut obtenir le même effet sur les écrans d'ordinateurs en assortissant la couleur du texte avec celle du fond, puis en le plaçant sur un aplat de couleur différent. Lorsqu'une **typographie** fine composée dans un petit **corps** est ainsi entourée d'une couleur sombre, on perd en **lisibilité.** Il vaut donc mieux privilégier dans ce cas une typographie légèrement plus large et grasse.

Ang: REVERSE/REVERSE OUT
All: NEGATIVE SCHRIFT
Ital: REVERSE/REVERSE OUT
Esp: TIPO EN NEGATIVO

Affiche pour la pièce *Les noces de Figaro,* au théâtre municipal de Berne
Design : Flag, www.flag.cc

ITALIQUE

Caractère typographique, légèrement incliné vers la droite, utilisé pour attirer l'attention sur un passage de texte. L'italique a été développé en Italie, vers 1500, afin de placer plus de texte sur une même page et ainsi réduire la taille des livres imprimés. Les vraies italiques ont un dessin différent du caractère dont elles sont issues. Les **obliques** penchent aussi vers la droite, mais leur forme est assez peu différente de la version romaine.

Ang: ITALIC
All: KURSIV
Ital: CORSIVO
Esp: CURSIVA

A B C D E F G H I J K **L** M N O P Q R S T U V W X Y Z

Sur les quais de Seine, à l'époque des Ballets de Paris, 1953.
Photo Serge Lido.

LÉGENDE

Texte servant à décrire ou à expliquer une photographie, une illustration, un schéma ou tout autre élément visuel. Les légendes sont généralement placées au-dessus, au-dessous ou à côté de l'image, séparées du **corps du texte**. Voir aussi **chiffres références**.

Ang: CAPTION
All: BILDUNTERSCHRIFT
Ital: DIDASCALIA
Esp: PIE DE FOTO

Double page extraite de l'ouvrage *Violette Verdy,* édition du CND, collection « Parcours d'artistes », 2008
Design : Agnès Dahan, www.agnesdahan.net

A B C D E F G H I J K **L** M N O P Q R S T U V W X Y Z

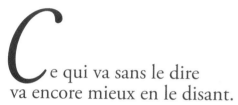

*C*e qui va sans le dire
va encore mieux en le disant.

Talleyrand-Périgord Charles Maurice, prince de

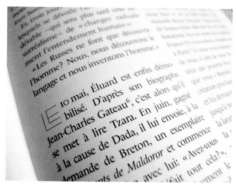

Lorem ipsum dolor sit amet, consectetuer adipiscing elit. Sed non risus. Suspendisse lectus tortor, dignissim sit amet, adipiscing nec, ultricies sed, dolor. Cras elementum ultrices diam. Maecenas ligula massa, varius a, semper congue, euismod non, mi. Proin porttitor, orci nec nonummy molestie, enim est eleifend mi, non fermentum diam nisl sit amet erat. Duis semper. Duis arcu massa, scelerisque vitae, consequat in, pretium a, enim. Pellentesque congue. Ut in risus volutpat libero pharetra tempor. Cras vestibulum bibendum augue. Praesent egestas leo in pede. Praesent blandit odio eu enim. Pellentesque sed dui ut augue blandit sodales. Vestibulum ante ipsum primis in faucibus orci luctus et ultrices posuere cubilia Curae. Aliquam nibh. Mauris ac mauris sed pede pellentesque fermentum. Maecenas adipiscing ante non diam sodales hendrerit.

LETTRE ITALIQUE ORNÉE

Caractère italique décoratif avec des tracés étendus. Elles sont surtout utilisées en guise de **lettrine** et composées dans un **corps** plus grand que le texte courant. On peut aussi les trouver, en *bas-de-casse,* au dernier mot d'une phrase à la toute fin d'un paragraphe. Si ces caractères donnent une certaine élégance à un bloc de texte, il convient d'en user sporadiquement car, appliqués à une ligne entière, ils peuvent vite devenir gênants, voire illisibles. Voir aussi **initiale.**

Ang: SWASH CHARACTERS
All: ZIERBUCHSTABEN
Ital: CARATTERI SWASH
Esp: LETRA DE FANTASÍA

LETTRINE

Capitale initiale du premier mot d'un paragraphe, imprimée dans un **corps** supérieur à celui des autres mots du texte, de sorte que la lettre s'étende dans le texte situé en dessous. Pour un impact visuel maximal, les lettrines peuvent être composées dans une **typographie** très éloignée de celle du **corps du texte.** Elles se définissent en fonction du nombre de lignes qu'elles occupent. Ainsi, une lettrine de trois lignes occupe les trois premières lignes d'un paragraphe. Voir aussi **initiale** et **grandes capitales.**

Ang: DROP CAPITAL/CAP
All: HÄNGENDE INITIALE
Ital: CAPOLETTERA
Esp: MAYÚSCULA CAÍDA

Détail d'une page du livre *Proverbe,* Éditions Dilecta
Design typographique : © Jean-Baptiste Levée, 2008, www.opto.fr

LÉZARDES

Alignement horizontal accidentel d'espaces mots sur plusieurs lignes consécutives, créant une ligne blanche décelable à l'œil. Un **texte justifié** aura souvent tendance à présenter des lézardes, car les logiciels règlent l'approche par défaut. Le **crénage** et/ou les **coupures de mots** permettent de travailler les lignes de texte de façon à réduire, ou éliminer, ces lézardes. Voir aussi **C&J** et **retour à la ligne automatique.**

Ang: RIVERS
All: GIESSBÄCHLEIN
Ital: CANALETTI
Esp: CALLE

ABCDEFGHIJK**L**MNOPQRSTUVWXYZ

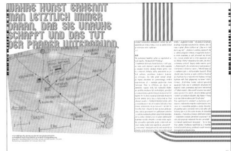

Typographie

LIGATURE

Deux, voire trois, lettres liées les unes aux autres. Elles servent notamment à éviter que certaines lettres s'entrechoquent, par exemple lorsque la lettre « i » suit la lettre « f ». Si ces deux **caractères** sont composés de façon individuelle, le point du « i » se posera très près du sommet du « f », et pourra même le chevaucher selon les **familles de caractères.** En remplaçant ces deux lettres par leur ligature, la lecture de la ligne de texte gagnera en **lisibilité.** Les ligatures, descendantes des anciens écrits des scribes, sont utilisées depuis les premiers jours de l'impression au plomb, mais connurent un désintérêt à l'ère de la *phototypie.* Néanmoins, la plupart des **fontes** numériques comprennent aujourd'hui une série de ligatures.

Ang: LIGATURE
All: LIGATUR
Ital: LEGATURA
Esp: LIGADURA

La Ligature Pananatomique présente toutes les caractéristiques anatomiques de l'alphabet latin
Design : © Jack Usine, 2007, www.usine.name

LIGNE

Série de points formant une droite ou une courbe. Alors que l'épaisseur des lignes en géométrie est sans importance, les graphistes utilisent des lignes fines ou larges, qui ne doivent pas nécessairement avoir une même épaisseur sur toute la longueur. Elles peuvent être brisées ou fragmentées. Les lignes épaisses ont les mêmes caractéristiques que les surfaces planes. Le point, la ligne et la surface plane sont à la base de toutes les formes utilisées en design graphique.

Ang: LINE
All: LINIENGESTALTUNG
Ital: LINEA/E
Esp: LÍNEA

Double page extraite de l'un des quatre livres autoédités à l'occasion du quarantième anniversaire de la révolution étudiante allemande en 1969, du Printemps de Prague et des vingt ans de la chute du mur de Berlin, en 1989
Design : Formdusche, www.formdusche.de

LIGNE DE BASE

Ligne de référence horizontale servant à l'**alignement** des **caractères.** La plupart des lettres capitales et *bas-de-casse* n'ayant pas de **descendantes** reposent sur celle-ci. Les caractères ayant une base arrondie – comme le « o » ou le « u » – débordent très légèrement en dessous de la ligne de base, a contrario des lettres avec une assise droite – comme le « h » ou le « i ». Cette illusion d'optique démontre l'importance de l'**alignement visuel** lorsqu'il est question de **typographie.**

Ang: BASELINE
All: GRUNDLINIE (SCHRIFTLINIE)
Ital: LINEA DI BASE
Esp: LÍNEA DE BASE

A B C D E F G H I J K **L** M N O P Q R S T U V W X Y Z

Typographie

LIGNE DE TÊTE

Ligne de référence utilisée pour l'**alignement** horizontal d'un texte, correspondant à la **hauteur d'x** d'une **typographie** donnée. La partie supérieure des lettres *bas-de-casse* n'ayant pas d'**ascendantes** s'appuie contre la ligne de tête. Contrairement aux *bas-de-casse* ayant un sommet arrondi, le « a » et le « o » par exemple, qui débordent très légèrement au-delà de la ligne de tête, les lettres dont le sommet est plat, comme les lettres « u » et « x », s'y alignent parfaitement. Cette « illusion d'optique » se produit également le long de la **ligne de base.** Cela illustre l'importance d'un **alignement visuel** extrêmement précis quand il s'agit de créer une **composition typographique** élégante.

Ang: MEAN LINE
All: X-LINIE (MITTELLINIE)
Ital: LINEA MEDIANA
Esp: LÍNEA MEDIA

LISIBILITÉ : AISANCE DE LECTURE D'UN TEXTE

Lisibilité : Aisance de lecture d'un texte

Lisibilité : Aisance de lecture d'un texte

LISIBILITÉ

Estimation de la facilité de lecture d'un texte en fonction de la qualité des **caractères** dans lesquels il est composé. Contrairement à la langue anglaise, le français ne fait pas de distinction entre *legibility,* facilité de lecture due à la **typographie,** et *readability,* clarté et simplicité du style. La nécessité d'une bonne lisibilité dépend grandement du contexte. Ainsi, les affiches et les couvertures de livres, par exemple, utilisent parfois des typographies qui se jouent de la lisibilité mais qui sont non moins engageantes pour le lecteur. Par contre, si de telles **compositions** étaient utilisées pour la signalisation ou un rapport annuel, cela aurait un effet plutôt désastreux.

Ang: LEGIBILITY
All: LESERLICHKEIT
Ital: LEGGIBILITÀ
Esp: LEGIBILIDAD TIPOGRÁFICA

Papier

Pierre ou plaque

LITHOGRAPHIE

Procédé d'impression à partir duquel l'encre est appliquée sur une pierre lisse ou une plaque de métal puis transférée directement sur le papier. Le terme vient de la combinaison des mots grecs *lithos,* « pierre », et *graphos,* « écrire ». Les zones non imprimables sont délimitées par un corps gras afin que l'encre, à base d'eau, se dépose partout ailleurs. Les zones qui ne sont pas marquées « capturent » ainsi l'encre et la transfèrent sur le papier, alors que les zones huileuses rejettent l'encre et forment donc le fond de l'image imprimée. Voir aussi **lithographie offset.**

Ang: LITHOGRAPHY
All: LITHOGRAFIE
Ital: LITOGRAFIA
Esp: LITOGRAFÍA

A B C D E F G H I J K **L** M N O P Q R S T U V W X Y Z

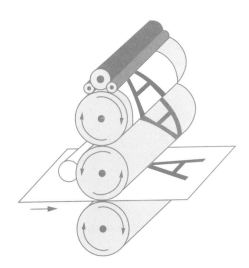

SIXPACK FRANCE

LITHOGRAPHIE OFFSET

Procédé d'impression fondé sur les mêmes principes que la **lithographie,** selon lequel l'encre est d'abord transférée sur un *blanchet* en caoutchouc avant d'être imprimée sur le support à imprimer. Un jeu de cylindres sert à appliquer l'encre sur la plaque, pendant qu'un autre se charge de faire tourner le blanchet, transférant ainsi l'encre sur le blanchet. Un accroissement de la qualité ainsi que des économies d'échelle significatives ont fait de la lithographie offset, souvent appelé uniquement « offset », la technique d'impression la plus courante dans le domaine commercial.

Ang: OFFSET LITHOGRAPHY
All:　OFFSETDRUCK
Ital:　LITOGRAFIA OFFSET
Esp: LITOGRAFÍA OFFSET

LOGO

Signe graphique utilisé, spécifiquement à des fins commerciales, au sein de la **stratégie de marque** d'une entreprise. Créer un logo efficace s'avère être bien plus complexe que son élégante simplicité ne pourrait le laisser penser. Un logo doit être à la fois simple, afin d'être identifié même lorsqu'il est imprimé ou affiché en petit format, et riche en termes de sémantique, car il représente les valeurs et la personnalité d'une entreprise. Il doit être mémorisable, instantanément reconnaissable et différent de celui de ses concurrents. Compte tenu de tous ces défis à relever, il n'est pas étonnant que les entreprises utilisent un logo efficient durant de très nombreuses années. Un *logotype* est un assemblage spécifique de lettres composant le nom, ou l'acronyme, d'une entreprise et dont l'agencement original (**couleur, typographie, interlettrage,** etc.) fait partie intégrante de son identité.

Ang: LOGO
All:　LOGO
Ital:　LOGO
Esp: LOGO

LONGUEUR DE LIGNE

Distance d'une ligne de **caractères.** La longueur d'une ligne est souvent confondue avec la **mesure,** qui est en fait la largeur d'une colonne de texte. Toutefois, lorsque le texte est, par exemple, en **fer à gauche** (ou *en drapeau à droite*), les lignes n'emplissent que rarement toute la mesure ; de même lorsque le texte est en **fer à droite** ou centré. La longueur de ligne est identique à la mesure uniquement lorsque le texte est justifié.

Ang: LINE LENGTH
All:　ZEILENLÄNGE
Ital:　LUNGHEZZA DI RIGA
Esp: LONGITUD DE LÍNEA

LOREM IPSUM
Voir **faux texte.**

LPI
Voir **résolution.**

Design : Akroe pour Sixpack France, www.akroe.net

A B C D E F G H I J K **L M** N O P Q R S T U V W X Y Z

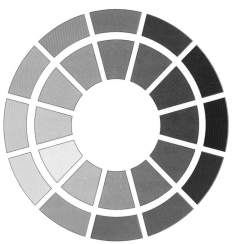

LUMINOSITÉ

Luminosité ou obscurité relative d'une **couleur** ; on parle aussi de **valeur** ou de *ton*. Sur une photocopie en noir et blanc, des couleurs d'une même luminosité seront quasiment indissociables. Voir aussi **roue chromatique.**

Ang: BRIGHTNESS
All: LEUCHTDICHTE
Ital: LUMINOSITÀ
Esp: BRILLO

Design : Donna S. Atwood, www.atwooddesign.com

MACULE

Procédé qui consiste à préparer une machine à imprimer, de même que l'équipement utilisé pour les finitions, le pliage, ou la **reliure,** pour une nouvelle impression. Ce terme est également utilisé pour qualifier les feuilles de papier utilisées pour les essais durant ce processus.

Ang: MAKEREADY
All: DRUCKEINRICHTUNG
Ital: AVVIAMENTO MACCHINA
Esp: ARREGLO

Affiches dans l'atelier de l'artiste
Design : Vincent Perrottet, www.vincentperrottet.com

MAQUETTE

Étape préliminaire dans le processus de création permettant d'organiser les divers éléments graphiques, comme la **typographie,** les photographies, les illustrations, de telle sorte que le résultat final puisse être appréhendé. Ce terme qualifie également l'ensemble de l'organisation d'une création graphique. Les maquettes de livres, de brochures, de rapports annuels et de tout autre document contenant plusieurs pages, sont organisées selon des **grilles.**

Ang: LAYOUT
All: LAYOUT
Ital: LAYOUT
Esp: MAQUETACIÓN

Design : Donna S. Atwood, www.atwooddesign.com

A B C D E F G H I J K L **M** N O P Q R S T U V W X Y Z

1. Les mots imprimés sont vus et non lus.
2. Les concepts sont communiqués par des mots conventionnels et façonnés en lettres de l'alphabet.
3. Les concepts devraient être exprimés avec un minimum d'économie – optiquement et non phonétiquement.
4. La mise en pages du texte, régie par les lois de la mécanique typographique, doit refléter le rythme du contenu.
5. Les clichés doivent être utilisés dans la mise en pages selon la nouvelle théorie visuelle : la *réalité supernaturaliste de l'œil perfectionné.*
6. Les pages en séquence continue – le livre cinématographique.
7. À livre nouveau, auteur nouveau ; encriers et plumes d'oies désuets.
8. La page imprimée n'est conditionnée ni par l'espace ni par le temps. Il faut dépasser la page imprimée et le nombre infini de livres.
El Lissitzky
Extrait de *Merz 4,* 1923.

MARGES

Zones situées le long des quatre bords d'une page entourant habituellement le **corps du texte** et/ou les images d'une **mise en pages** donnée. Les éléments comme les folios, les notes de bas de page et les **légendes,** sont souvent placés dans les marges. Les marges situées le long du dos d'un ouvrage relié sont aussi appelées « **gouttières** ».

Ang: MARGIN
All: SEITENRAND
Ital: MARGINE/I
Esp: MARGEN

Design : Donna S. Atwood, www.atwooddesign.com

MESURE

Terme utilisé pour décrire la largeur d'un bloc de texte, habituellement mesurée en **points picas** ou **cadratins,** parfois en millimètres et en **pixels** selon les contextes. Il est admis que la mesure optimale pour assurer une bonne **lisibilité** est de 52 à 78 **caractères** (soit deux ou trois alphabets), espaces compris. Toutefois, la **typographie** utilisée et l'**interlettrage** peuvent faire varier cette moyenne. Voir aussi **longueur de ligne.**

Ang: MEASURE
All: SATZBREITE
Ital: GIUSTEZZA
Esp: ANCHO

MÉTAPHORE

Figure de style consistant à signifier une chose par une autre. En design graphique, elle peut comprendre des éléments textuels : un texte qui met en rapport une image avec des concepts qui n'ont a priori aucun lien. La photographie d'une jungle dense et menaçante, associée à cette phrase : « Vous recherchez une police d'assurance ? », afin d'insinuer l'idée que le « monde est une jungle »… Une métaphore purement visuelle repose sur des associations communément admises entre une ou plusieurs images, en transférant le sens de l'une à l'autre. Cela est souvent réalisé en fusionnant les images afin de faciliter l'acceptation d'un rapport de ressemblance entre deux réalités distinctes. Ainsi, la combinaison entre l'image d'un stylo et celle d'une arme pourra suggérer la puissance de l'écriture.

Ang: METAPHOR
All: METAPHER
Ital: METAFORA
Esp: METÁFORA

Affiche pour un concert de Ted Leo + Pharmacists
Design : Jason Munn / The Small Stakes,
www.thesmallstakes.com

A B C D E F G H I J K L **M** N O P Q R S T U V W X Y Z

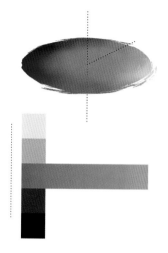

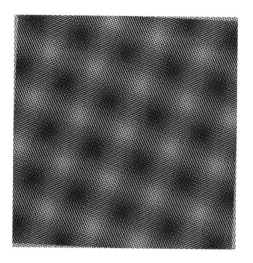

MODÈLE COLORIMÉTRIQUE

Système de description des **couleurs** à partir de quelques composantes couleurs qui, une fois réglées, peuvent être utilisées pour produire un vaste spectre chromatique. Les modes RVB et CMJN sont les plus courants, mais il en existe d'autres. Le mode HSB utilise les caractéristiques des couleurs associées à la traditionnelle **roue chromatique : teinte, saturation** et **luminosité.** Le modèle LAB se fonde sur les coordonnées utilisées en *colorimétrie*. Le modèle colorimétrique est souvent confondu avec l'espace colorimétrique, qui est l'étendue des couleurs produit par un procédé d'affichage ou d'impression spécifique au sein d'un modèle colorimétrique donné.

Ang: COLOR MODEL
All: FARBMODELL
Ital: MODELLO DI COLORE
Esp: MODELO DE COLOR

Design : Timothy Samara,
tsamara_designer@hotmail.com

MODERNISME

Plus qu'un seul et unique courant artistique, le modernisme, apparu dans les années 1900, prend racine dans le **cubisme** et son rejet des formes naturelles en faveur de l'abstraction. Durant le siècle qui a suivi son apparition, le modernisme a été réinventé de très nombreuses fois, endossant ainsi une vaste panoplie de formes plus ou moins éloignées de ses racines (par exemple, l'utilisation stricte de **grilles,** de **typographies** sans empattements ou des **blancs** généreux). S'il existe un bon nombre d'exceptions à toutes ces « règles » instituées par le modernisme, certaines lignes de forces peuvent être identifiées, comme une communication visuelle fonctionnelle et un esprit optimiste tourné vers l'avenir.

Ang: MODERNISM
All: MODERNE
Ital: MODERNISMO
Esp: MODERNISMO

Grid-It! Notepads, The Royal College of Art, 2005
Design : Astrid Stavro, www.astridstavro.com ;
Photographe : Mauricio Salinas

MOIRÉ

Motif indésirable qui peut apparaître lors de la superposition des *trames de simili* en **quadrichromie.** Cette anomalie peut être évitée en donnant des orientations convenables aux différentes trames utilisées, afin d'obtenir une très petite rosette des **couleurs CMJN,** rarement visible sur le produit imprimé. Un moiré peut également apparaître lorsque l'on scanne une image déjà imprimée sans lui appliquer l'option « détramage ».

Ang: MOIRÉ
All: MOIRÉ-EFFEKT
Ital: EFFETTO MOIRÉ
Esp: MOARÉ

A B C D E F G H I J K L **M** N **O** P Q R S T U V W X Y Z

Futura
Futura Oblique

Helvetica Neue
Helvetica Neue Oblique

MONOCHROMATIQUE

Palette de couleurs constituée des *tons* et des **couleurs de fonds** d'une même **teinte.** Les variations de tonalités au sein d'une image monochromatique sont représentées par des différences de **saturation** et de **luminosité.** Les images en **échelles de gris** sont des images monochromatiques avec une palette de couleurs composée de gris, de blancs et de noirs.

Ang: MONOCHROMATIC
All: MONOCHROMATISCH (EINFARBIG)
Ital: MONOCROMATICO
Esp: MONOCROMÁTICO

MONTAGE
Voir **collage** et **photomontage.**

MULTIMÉDIA

Technologie permettant de délivrer du contenu, à l'intérieur d'une même application, de plusieurs façons différentes. Par exemple, un site Internet pourra intégrer, sur une même plateforme et sur un même sujet, aussi bien du texte (y compris de l'hypertexte), des images fixes, que de la lecture audio en transit et des vidéos. Ce terme est aussi utilisé pour décrire les appareils acceptant et délivrant un contenu multimédia ou pour les dispositifs offrant une expérience interactive aux utilisateurs, les jeux vidéo notamment.

Ang: MULTIMEDIA
All: MULTIMEDIA
Ital: MULTIMEDIA
Esp: MULTIMEDIA

Site Internet de la revue *étapes:,*
www.etapes.com
Design : Pyramyd NTCV

OBLIQUE

Typographie sans empattements inclinée vers la droite, dont le dessin est très proche des **caractères** romains dont elle est issue. Une typographie **italique** est également inclinée vers la droite, mais les caractères ont été complètement redessinés et sont souvent assez différents de ceux à partir desquels ils ont été conçus.

Ang: OBLIQUE
All: SCHRÄG
Ital: CARATTERI OBLIQUE
Esp: OBLICUA

A B C D E F G H I J K L M N **O P** Q R S T U V W X Y Z

Lorem ipsum dolor sit amet, consectetuer adipiscing elit. Sed non risus.
Suspendisse lectus tortor, dignissim sit
amet, adipiscing nec, ultricies sed, dolor.
Cras elementum ultrices diam. Maecenas
ligula massa, varius a, semper congue,
euismod non, mi. Proin porttitor, orci
nec nonummy molestie, enim est eleifend
mi, non fermentum diam nisl sit amet
erat. Duis semper. Duis arcu massa,
scelerisque vitae, consequat in, pretium
a, enim. Pellentesque congue. Ut in risus
volutpat libero pharetra tempor. Cras
vestibulum bibendum augue. Praesent
egestas leo in pede. Praesent blandit odio
eu enim. Pellentesque sed dui ut augue
blandit sodales. Vestibulum ante ipsum
primis in faucibus orci luctus et ultrices
posuere cubilia Curae; Aliquam nibh.
Mauris ac mauris sed pede pellentesque
fermentum. Maecenas adipiscing ante

non diam sodales hendrerit.

Ut velit mauris, egestas sed, gravida nec,
ornare ut, mi. Aenean at orci vel massa
suscipit pulvinar. Nulla sollicitudin.
Fusce varius, ligula non tempus aliquam,
nunc turpis ullamcorper nibh, in tempus
sapien eros vitae ligula. Pellentesque
rhoncus nunc et augue. Integer id felis.
Curabitur aliquet pellentesque diam.
Integer quis metus vitae elit lobortis
egestas. Lorem ipsum dolor sit amet,
consectetuer adipiscing elit. Morbi vel
erat non mauris convallis vehicula. Nulla
et sapien. Integer tortor tellus, aliquam
faucibus, convallis id, congue eu, quam.
Mauris ullamcorper felis vitae erat. Proin
feugiat, augue non elementum posuere,
metus purus iaculis lectus, et tristique
ligula justo vitae magna.

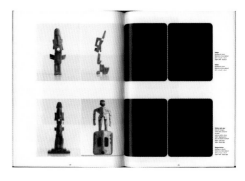

ORPHELINE

Une ligne (voire deux) séparée du paragraphe
principal et située en haut d'une **colonne**
de texte. Une orpheline peut être évitée en
réglant divers paramètres, les plus courants
étant l'**interlettrage** et les **coupures de
mots.** Voir aussi **veuve.**

Ang: ORPHAN
All: SCHUSTERJUNGE
Ital: ORFANO
Esp: HUÉRFANA

PAGE TYPE

Gabarit défini au sein des logiciels de
mise en pages afin d'assurer un placement
identique tout au long du document des
grilles, des **colonnes** de texte, des folios,
et de tout autre élément typique d'une
maquette. Plusieurs pages types peuvent
être utilisées au sein d'un même document,
chacune correspondant à une section ou
un style de mise en pages différent. Utiliser
des pages types permet d'automatiser
le foliotage.

Ang: MASTER PAGE
All: MUSTERSEITE
Ital: PAGINA MASTRO
Esp: PÁGINA MAESTRA

Design : Donna S. Atwood, www.atwooddesign.com

PAGES EN REGARD

Désigne, au sein d'une **double page,** les
pages de gauche et de droite. Les logiciels
de **mise en pages** tels qu'Adobe InDesign®
permettent aux graphistes de créer des
documents soit d'une seule page soit avec
des pages en regard. Voir aussi **recto verso.**

Ang: FACING PAGES
All: DOPPELSEITEN
Ital: PAGINE AFFIANCATE
Esp: PÁGINAS ENFRENTADAS

Double page extraite du catalogue pour le musée Ziem
Design : Les Graphistes Associés

A B C D E F G H I J K L M N O **P** Q R S T U V W X Y Z

PAGES LIMINAIRES

Dans un ouvrage, il s'agit de la partie qui précède le texte principal, comme la page de **titre,** le *frontispice* (illustration ou gravure placée en regard de la page de titre), table des matières, liste des illustrations et tableaux, une préface, etc. Voir aussi **parties annexes.**

Ang: FRONT MATTER
All: TITELEI
Ital: PAGINE INIZIALI
Esp: PÁGINAS PRELIMINARES

Double page extraite de l'ouvrage *Travaux en cours,* éditions Pyramyd, 2006
www.editions-pyramyd.com

A B C D E F G H I J K L M N O **P** Q R S T U V W X Y Z

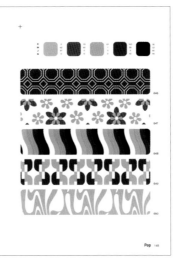

PAGINATION

Action de numéroter des pages afin d'indiquer leur exact enchaînement au sein d'un livre ou de toute autre publication imprimée. Ce terme désigne aussi, plus couramment, le nombre de pages total d'une publication. Il s'est vu attribuer récemment une nouvelle signification, afin de décrire la façon dont l'information est organisée au sein des pages Web. Les blogs peuvent, par exemple, être paginés afin qu'un ou deux paragraphes d'un post soient visibles sur la page principale et que seuls les dix premiers commentaires s'affichent. Voir aussi **imposition.**

Ang: PAGINATION
All: PAGINIERUNG
Ital: IMPAGINAZIONE
Esp: PAGINACIÓN

Ink IV, Laboratoire typographique, mai 2009
Superscript[2], ESA Lorient, magazine *Ink,*
www.super-script.com

PALETTE DE COULEURS

Ensemble de **couleurs** définies soit par un média donné, comme la palette de 216 couleurs garanties pour le Web, soit par un designer ou un artiste pour un projet donné. Les palettes de couleurs sont habituellement composées en fonction des relations illustrées au sein de la **roue chromatique.**

Ang: COLOR PALETTE
All: FARBPALETTE
Ital: PALETTE DI COLORI
Esp: PALETA DE COLORES

Page extraite de l'ouvrage *Couleurs + motifs 2,* éditions Pyramyd, 2009
www.editions-pyramyd.com

PAPIER COUCHÉ
Voir **pelliculage aqueux.**

PARTIES ANNEXES
Voir **annexes.**

PELLICULAGE AQUEUX

Pelliculage à base d'eau appliqué sur l'intégralité d'une feuille de papier, après l'impression, afin de produire une patine uniforme (par exemple, brillant ou mat) et protéger l'encre sous-jacente des éraflures et de l'humidité. Les *papiers non couchés* absorbent davantage l'encre, affadissant ainsi la **couleur** des images imprimées, alors que le **papier couché** permet aux images de rester éclatantes en évitant l'absorption de l'encre. Le pelliculage aqueux est caractéristique des imprimés énormément manipulés, comme des magazines et des brochures. D'autres types de traitements de surface, comme les **vernis,** peuvent être utilisés dans le même but.

Ang: AQUEOUS COATING
All: DRUCKLACK
Ital: RIVESTIMENTO AD ACQUA
Esp: REVESTIMIENTO ACUOSO

Useful Photography #008
Design : KesselsKramer Publishing,
www.kesselskramerpublishing.com

ABCDEFGHIJKLMN O **P** QRSTUVWXYZ

L'espace colorimétrique CMJN

L'espace colorimétrique CMJN

PETITES CAPITALES

Capitales dont les proportions et la largeur des fûts font qu'elles s'harmonisent avec les *bas-de-casse*. Tout comme les **chiffres suspendus,** les petites capitales sont plus discrètes que leurs versions alternatives. Par exemple, on privilégiera l'usage des petites capitales pour les noms d'auteurs dans une bibliographie. D'autre part, un autre avantage des petites capitales est le fait qu'elles restent lisibles même dans un petit **corps.**

Ang: SMALL CAPITALS/CAPS
All:　KAPITÄLCHEN
Ital:　MAIUSCOLETTI
Esp:　VERSALITA

PHOTOMONTAGE

Technique selon laquelle une image est obtenue par l'assemblage de photographies ou d'éléments empruntés à diverses photographies. Un photomontage peut se faire soit en découpant et en collant des images manuellement, soit en utilisant un logiciel de traitement photographique. Lorsque le photomontage est effectué à la main, on peut ensuite le photographier en complément afin de lui donner l'aspect d'une « véritable » photo. On parle aussi bien de photomontage que de **montage.** Voir aussi **collage.**

Ang:　PHOTOMONTAGE
All:　FOTOMONTAGE
Ital:　FOTOMONTAGGIO
Esp:　FOTOMONTAJE

Carte de vœux pour le ballet Preljocaj
Design : Stéphan Muntaner, c-ktre@wanadoo.fr

PICTOGRAMME

Icône, ou **symbole,** utilisé de telle manière que son sens est compris instantanément quelles que soient la langue ou la barrière culturelle. Les pictogrammes efficaces correspondent à une désignation codée et définie par un grand nombre de conventions, comme pour les Jeux olympiques ou les panneaux signalétiques internationaux. Le contexte est important lors de l'interprétation d'un pictogramme, car s'il reste une icône identifiable, son sens peut en être radicalement modifié. Par exemple, si le signe indiquant la zone de récupération des bagages dans un aéroport se trouve placé hors contexte, il ne devient rien d'autre que le symbole d'une valise et pourrait alors être utilisé, par exemple, sur un site de vente en ligne d'articles de voyages.

Ang:　PICTOGRAM
All:　PIKTOGRAMM
Ital:　PITTOGRAMMA
Esp:　PICTOGRAMA

Souriant blanc, enseigne lumineuse, The White Hotel, Bruxelles, 2008
Design : Le Club des chevreuils ;
Photographie : Guillaume Bokiau

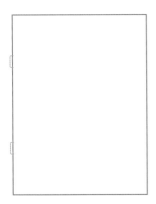

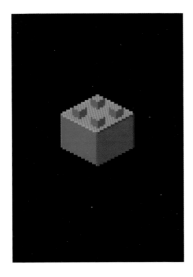

PIQÛRE MÉTALLIQUE À CHEVAL

Forme de **reliure** solide habituellement utilisée pour les brochures et certains magazines. Les **cahiers,** et parfois la couverture, sont encartés les uns dans les autres puis maintenus par des agrafes métalliques insérées dans le pli du dos pour ensuite être massicotés.

Ang: SADDLE-STITCH BINDING
All: DRAHTHEFTUNG
Ital: GRAFFETTATURA
Esp: ENCUADERNACIÓN A CABALLETE

PIXEL

Unité de base en système informatique utilisée pour mesurer une image numérique. Son nom provient de l'expression anglaise *picture element,* c'est-à-dire « élément d'image ». Les pixels sont contenus dans une grille à deux dimensions qui forme l'image finale et dont va dépendre la **résolution** de l'image. Sur les écrans utilisant le **RVB,** la **couleur** de chaque pixel est constituée de valeurs numériques de rouge, vert et bleu.

Ang: PIXEL
All: PIXEL (BILDPUNKT)
Ital: PIXEL
Esp: PÍXEL

Design : Patrick Lindsay, www.lindsay.fr

PLI ACCORDÉON

Série de plis parallèles exécutés tour à tour dans une feuille de papier de sorte que chaque *volet* aille dans le sens opposé de celui qui lui est contigu. Deux plis effectués de cette manière produisent un accordéon en six volets, ou six pages (trois volets de chaque côté de la feuille) ; trois plis donnent un accordéon de huit volets, et ainsi de suite. On parle aussi de *leporello*.

Ang: ACCORDION FOLD
All: LEPORELLO
Ital: PIEGHEVOLE A FISARMONICA
Esp: PLEGADO EN ACORDEÓN

Livre *Marseille, panorama polaire,* édité à l'occasion du festival Laterna Magica 2008 par Fotokino, www.fotokino.org
Design : Jochen Gerner

A B C D E F G H I J K L M N O **P** Q R S T U V W X Y Z

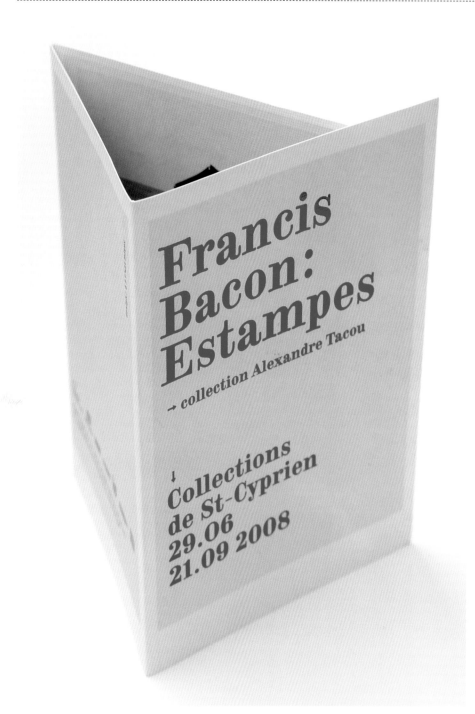

Francis
Bacon:
Estampes
→ collection Alexandre Tacou

↓ Collections
de St-Cyprien
29.06
21.09 2008

PLI ROULÉ

Plis parallèles d'une feuille de papier exécutés de façon à ce que les volets se rabattent, ou « s'enroulent », les uns sur les autres. Les volets intérieurs auront une largeur (du pli au pli, ou du pli au bord) qui diminuera progressivement afin qu'ils se nichent correctement l'un dans l'autre. Voir aussi **pli accordéon.**

Ang: BARREL FOLD
All: WICKELFALZ
Ital: PIEGHEVOLE A PORTAFOGLIO
Esp: DOBLADO TIPO ROLLO

Invitation réalisée pour l'exposition « Francis Bacon : Estampes » pour les collections de Saint-Cyprien
Design : à 2 c'est mieux, www.a2cestmieux.fr

Points

Picas

Ceci est une ellipse… et non une série de trois points…

POINT CENTRAL

Dans une **mise en pages,** premier élément qui va attirer l'œil et à partir duquel la **circulation du regard** va commencer. Un point central peut être créé par de nombreux moyens, comme la **couleur,** l'**échelle** et la **composition.** La publicité tire souvent avantage d'un seul et unique point central manifeste.

Ang: FOCAL POINT
All: FOKUS
Ital: PUNTO FOCALE
Esp: PUNTO FOCAL

Affiche pour une série d'expositions de la collection de photographies du collectif néerlandais Ondertussen.in
Design : t' Brandt Weer, www.tbrandtweer.nl ;
Photographie : Geertjan Cornelissen, www.versebeeldwaren.nl

POINT PICA

Le point pica est une mesure typographique anglo-saxonne qui correspond à la division en 72 parties de l'inch (le pouce anglais). Un point pica équivaut à 0,35 millimètre et à 0,93 point Didot.

Ang: PICA
All: PICA
Ital: PICA
Esp: PICA

POINTS DE SUSPENSION

Signe de ponctuation composé d'une série de trois points, utilisé pour indiquer, par exemple, qu'une partie du texte a été supprimée, qu'une citation n'est pas utilisée dans son intégralité ou que l'expression de la pensée est incomplète. Chaque **famille de caractères** a son propre glyphe de points de suspension. Utiliser ce **caractère** plutôt qu'une série de trois points finaux évite de courir le risque qu'ils se scindent lors d'un **saut de ligne.** Les points de suspension sont toujours collés au mot qui précède et sont suivis d'une espace.

Ang: ELLIPSIS
All: ELLIPSE (AUSLASSUNGSPUNKTE)
Ital: PUNTI DI SOSPENSIONE
Esp: PUNTOS SUSPENSIVOS

A B C D E F G H I J K L M N O **P** Q R S T U V W X Y Z

« Un coup de dés jamais
n'abolira le hasard… »

« Un coup de dés jamais
n'abolira le hasard… »

• Stéphane Mallarmé

• Stéphane Mallarmé

POLICE

Série de **caractères** présentant des
caractéristiques communes, telles que
l'épaisseur des fûts, les proportions, la
présence **d'empattements** ou non, etc.
Une police comprend généralement des
lettres (*bas-de-casse* et capitales), des
chiffres et une vaste gamme de **symboles**
(typographiques, mathématiques…). Les
termes « police » et « **fonte** » sont souvent
utilisés comme synonymes alors qu'il existe
bel et bien une distinction. Une police est
l'intégralité d'une **famille de caractères** dans
sa conception, alors qu'une fonte est un jeu
de caractères dans sa mise en œuvre, qu'elle
soit physique ou numérique.

Ang: TYPEFACE
All: SCHRIFTTYPE
Ital: CARATTERE/I
Esp: TIPO DE LETRA

Site Internet de Lineto, www.lineto.com
Typographie : Akkurat, designée par Laurent Brunner
en 2004

PONCTUATION MARGINALE

Signes de ponctuation placés très
légèrement hors des blocs de texte afin
d'améliorer l'**alignement visuel**. L'utilisation
de ponctuation marginale nécessite une
certaine finesse, le but étant d'aboutir
à une **composition typographique** précise
qui n'attire pas l'attention sur un élément
spécifique. Les **caractères** ne relevant pas
de la ponctuation sont aussi parfois situés
en dehors des limites d'un bloc de texte
de façon à respecter un certain **alignement
visuel,** comme lorsque les appels de note
sont placés dans une colonne de chiffres
alignés sur les décimales. On entend aussi
parfois parler de *caractères suspendus*.

Ang: HANGING PUNCTUATION
All: SATZKANTENAUSGLEICH
Ital: PUNTEGGIATURA ESTERNA
Esp: PUNTUACIÓN VOLADA

POSTERISATION

La posterisation apparaît lorsque, dans une
image, une gradation continue de **couleurs**
(ou de gris) est remplacée par un nombre plus
réduit de couleurs. Des coupures abruptes de
couleurs en résultent, comme sur les affiches
anciennes. Cela peut se produire notamment
lorsqu'une image est convertie pour une
utilisation Web en 256 couleurs. Certains
logiciels permettent de créer délibérément
cet effet en convertissant des *tons* continus
en un nombre limité de couleurs, générant
ainsi d'intéressants effets visuels.

Ang: POSTERIZATION
All: POSTERISATION
Ital: POSTERIZZAZIONE
Esp: POSTERIZACIÓN

Design : Donna S. Atwood, www.atwooddesign.com

A B C D E F G H I J K L M N O **P Q** R S T U V W X Y Z

POSTMODERNISME

Le postmodernisme est un mouvement artistique des années 1960 qui a acquis une renommée internationale dans les années 1980. Il engage une rupture avec les conventions dogmatiques du **modernisme,** et tout particulièrement avec le fait de rejeter le passé. Le postmodernisme célèbre ainsi les styles décoratifs du passé en les réinterprétant et en les combinant de façon inattendue et parfois burlesque. Les caractéristiques stylistiques de ce mouvement sont les **caractères** interlettrés, la disposition a priori aléatoire des éléments, les **collages** complexes ou une **palette de couleurs** pastel.

Ang: POST-MODERNISM
All: POSTMODERNE
Ital: POST-MODERNISMO
Esp: POSTMODERNISMO

Affiche n° 5 de la série « Man and environment » pour le centre culturel De Beyerd, Breda, 1984
Design : Jan van Toorn

PPI
Voir **résolution.**

PUCE

Signe typographique (•) pouvant être utilisé devant les éléments d'une énumération pour les mettre en valeur (on parle alors de *liste non numérotée*). Les puces servent aussi parfois à séparer de courtes lignes de **caractères,** par exemple des adresses sur du papier à en-tête. Une espace devra toujours être placée entre la puce et le caractère qui le suit. On la trouve généralement classée avec les **symboles** et les **dingbats.** Voir aussi **ponctuation marginale.**

Ang: BULLET
All: AUFZÄHLUNGSPUNKT
Ital: PUNTO ELENCO
Esp: BOLO

Page extraite du livre l'*Oulipo,* publié par culturesfrances
Design : SpMillot, spmillot@me.com

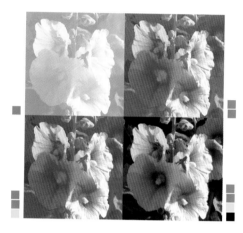

QUADRICHROMIE

Technique d'impression simulant, dans son intégralité, le spectre des **couleurs** par l'utilisation de **similis** individuels – on parle aussi de *séparation des couleurs* – pour chacune des **encres primaires** : cyan, magenta, jaune et noir. Chaque couleur est imprimée sous la forme de petits points de taille et de densité différentes. Le rendu de la couleur ainsi obtenue est réellement convaincant étant donné que, lorsqu'on additionne chacune des quatre encres primaires par paires, on produit les *couleurs primaires additives* – que sont le rouge, le vert et le bleu – qui correspondent aux trois différents capteurs de lumière de l'œil humain. Voir aussi **CMJN** et **simili.**

Ang: FOUR-COLOR PROCESS
All: VIERFARBDRUCK
Ital: PROCESSO A QUATTRO COLORI
Esp: CUATRICOMÍA

Design : Donna S. Atwood, www.atwooddesign.com

A B C D E F G H I J K L M N O P Q **R** S T U V W X Y Z

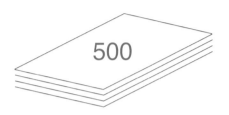

Type de papier	Formats courants
Travaux commerciaux	43,2 x 55,8 cm (17 x 22 pouces)
Livres, non-couchés	63,5 x 96,5 cm (25 x 38 pouces)
Livres, couchés	63,5 x 96,5 cm (25 x 38 pouces)
Couverture	50,8 x 66 cm (20 x 26 pouces)
Bristol	57,15 x 72,4 (22 ½ x 28 ½ pouces)
Kraft, étiquette, journal	60,9 x 91,4 cm (24 x 36 pouces)

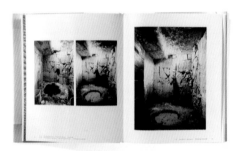

RAME

Unité papetière correspondant à 500 feuilles de papier coupé à son format de base. S'il existe de nombreux standards, le format de base est toujours déterminé par la qualité du papier. Le *grammage* indique le poids au mètre carré d'une rame de papier (g/m^2). Ainsi, deux papiers de qualités différentes mais d'un grammage égal paraîtront différents en matière d'**épaisseur** et de poids. Le terme « bouffant » sert à désigner le rapport entre la mesure de cinq feuilles (mesurées ensemble) par le grammage.

Ang: REAM
All: RIES
Ital: RISMA
Esp: RESMA

RECADRER

Ôter d'une photographie, ou de toute autre création artistique, par des techniques numériques ou mécaniques, des parties non désirées en partant des bords extérieurs. On recadre une image soit pour centrer l'attention sur un élément soit pour la mettre aux dimensions requises pour une **mise en pages** donnée. On appelle *repères de coupe* les marques utilisées pour signaler la zone de recadrage.

Ang: CROP
All: AUSSCHNITT
Ital: CROP
Esp: RECORTAR

RECTO VERSO

Ce terme est utilisé pour définir, au sein de **pages en regard,** les pages de droite et de gauche ; celle de droite étant le recto et celle de gauche, le verso. Il s'agit en fait, plus précisément, des côtés opposés d'une même feuille, le recto étant alors la face et le verso, l'arrière.

Ang: RECTO/VERSO
All: RECHTE/LINKE SEITE (VORDER-/ RÜCKSEITE)
Ital: RECTO/VERSO
Esp: RECTO/VERSO

Double page extraite du catalogue de l'exposition « Gregor Schneider »
Design : R2 (Lizá Ramalho et Artur Rebelo), www.r2design.pt

A B C D E F G H I J K L M N O P Q **R** S T U V W X Y Z

RELIURE

Technique de finition permettant d'assembler les pages d'un livre, d'un magazine, d'une brochure ou de toute autre publication comportant plusieurs pages. Les reliures à spirales ou à anneaux plastiques – utilisant un système de fixation placé dans une série de trous effectués dans chacune des pages – sont assez fragiles. Les **reliures cartonnées, sans coutures** et les **piqûres métalliques à cheval** sont quelques-unes des reliures les plus résistantes.

Ang: BINDING
All: EINBAND
Ital: RILEGATURA
Esp: ENCUADERNACIÓN

Imprimerie Deux-Ponts
Photographie : Audrey Laurent

A B C D E F G H I J K L M N O P Q **R** S T U V W X Y Z

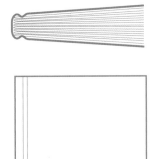

RELIURE CARTONNÉE

Type de **reliure** solide fréquemment utilisée pour les livres reliés. On commence par assembler les **cahiers** en les cousant l'un à l'autre au niveau du dos. De la colle est ensuite appliquée le long du dos du *corps de l'ouvrage,* on massicote les trois autres côtés, puis on fixe la couverture.

Ang: CASE BINDING
All: BUCHEINBAND
Ital: CARTONATURA
Esp: ENCUADERNACIÓN EN TAPA DURA

RELIURE SANS COUTURE

Technique de **reliure** utilisée pour les livres brochés. Le dos des **cahiers** assemblés est coupé puis collé à une couverture fabriquée séparément, formant ainsi le dos du livre.

Ang: PERFECT BINDING
All: KLEBEBINDUNG
Ital: RILEGATURA PERFETTA
Esp: ENCUADERNACIÓN A LA AMERICANA

Repérage   Problème
correct   de repérage

REPÉRAGE

Alignement précis des **couleurs.** Idéalement, chaque couche successive d'encre devrait s'aligner avec la précédente. Néanmoins, en pratique, certaines variations peuvent apparaître, par exemple, à cause d'un problème de papier ou de presse. On dit alors que les couleurs ne sont pas au registre. Des techniques comme le **grossi-maigri** ou la **surimpression** peuvent minimiser ce genre de désagréments.

Ang: REGISTRATION
All: REGISTERHALTIGKEIT
Ital: REGISTRO
Esp: REGISTRO

A B C D E F G H I J K L M N O P Q **R** S T U V W X Y Z

72 dpi   150 dpi   300 dpi

Lorem ipsum dolor sit amet, consectetuer adipiscing elit. Sed non risus. Suspendisse lectus tortor, dignissim sit amet, adipiscing nec, ultricies sed, dolor. Cras elementum ultrices diam. Maecenas ligula massa, varius a, semper congue, euismod non, mi.

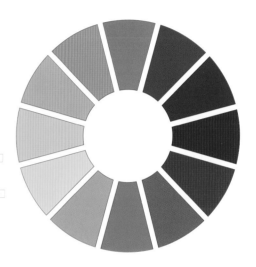

RÉSOLUTION

La résolution d'une image se réfère à sa qualité relative en fonction du nombre de **pixels** par unité de longueur. La résolution d'impression d'une imprimante se définit en ppp (points par pouce), on utilise aussi le terme anglais **dpi** (*dot per inch*) ; les imprimantes 300 dpi peuvent imprimer 300 points par pouce. L'unité de mesure **ppi** (*pixels per inch*), à ne pas confondre avec les ppp, est utilisée pour définir la résolution système des d'affichage (écrans). Enfin, l'unité **lpi** (*lines per inch*) définit la finesse d'une trame. Bien qu'il s'agisse de rangées de minuscules points, on parle de « **lignes** », car elles en donnent l'illusion une fois imprimées. Plus la linéature de la trame est élevée, plus les détails seront fins une fois l'image imprimée. Les journaux sont imprimés avec une linéature de trame de 65 lpi à 85 lpi, alors que les magazines de mode en utilisent une de 133 lpi à 150 lpi.

Ang: RESOLUTION
All: AUFLÖSUNG
Ital: RISOLUZIONE
Esp: RESOLUCIÓN

Design : Donna S. Atwood, www.atwooddesign.com

RETOUR À LA LIGNE AUTOMATIQUE

Terme utilisé pour décrire le fait qu'une ligne de texte se reporte automatiquement à la suivante en fin de ligne. Le fait d'arranger une ligne de texte aura souvent un impact sur les lignes avoisinantes, qu'il faudra à leur tour ajuster. Voir aussi **C&J.**

Ang: TEXT WRAPPING
All: TEXTUMBRUCH
Ital: INVIO A CAPO AUTOMATICO
Esp: AJUSTE DE TEXTO

ROUE CHROMATIQUE

Spectre des **couleurs** représenté sous forme de segments d'un cercle. La plus courante, utilisée pour mélanger des pigments, a pour fondement les **couleurs primaires** rouge, jaune et bleu, placées uniformément autour de la circonférence. Rouge, jaune et bleu sont des couleurs pures dans le sens où elles ne peuvent pas être obtenues par la combinaison d'autres couleurs. Par contre, lorsqu'on mélange celles-ci selon différentes proportions, on peut obtenir toutes les autres couleurs de la roue. D'autres roues chromatiques sont utilisées pour démontrer des relations similaires au sein d'autres systèmes colorimétriques, comme le modèle **RVB** utilisé pour afficher des images sur un écran. Voir aussi **couleurs analogues, couleurs complémentaires, couleurs primaires, couleurs secondaires** et **couleurs tertiaires.**

Ang: COLOR WHEEL
All: FARBKREIS
Ital: RUOTA DEI COLORI
Esp: RUEDA DE COLORES

Design : Donna S. Atwood, www.atwooddesign.com

A B C D E F G H I J K L M N O P Q **R S** T U V W X Y Z

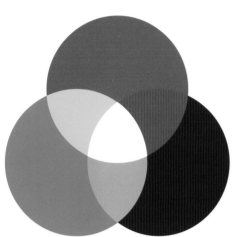

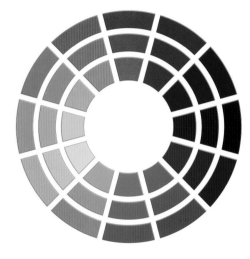

RVB

Abréviation de rouge, vert, bleu, les trois **couleurs** utilisées par les moniteurs et autres écrans numériques pour afficher des éléments. En mélangeant ces trois couleurs, aussi appelées *couleurs primaires additives,* en proportions égales, on obtient de la lumière blanche. Elles correspondent également aux trois différents capteurs de lumière présents dans l'œil humain. Voir aussi **CMJN.**

Ang: RGB
All: RGB
Ital: RGB
Esp: RGB

Design : Donna S. Atwood, www.atwooddesign.com

RYTHME

Répétition d'éléments graphiques, comme de la **typographie,** des **lignes** et des formes, créant un motif structurant. Par exemple, on peut donner un certain rythme à une ligne de texte en travaillant avec précision l'**interlettrage.** Les affiches et les couvertures de livres combinent souvent des motifs géométriques, installant une certaine stabilité, avec des éléments plus inattendus. Par ailleurs, les **grilles,** en instaurant un rythme au sein de longues publications, permettent au lecteur de s'orienter.

Ang: RHYTHM
All: RHYTHMUS
Ital: RITMO
Esp: RITMO

Affiche pour un concert du Bass Drum Bone, 2007
Design : Niklaus Troxler, www.troxlerart.ch

SATURATION

Pureté d'une **couleur** en fonction du gris qu'elle contient. Une **teinte** hautement saturée a une couleur très intense. Plus la saturation diminue, plus la couleur deviendra fade, tout en restant dans la même teinte. On peut désaturer une couleur en y ajoutant du gris (on obtient alors un *ton*) ou en la mélangeant avec une plus petite quantité de sa complémentaire (on obtient alors une *nuance*). Voir aussi **couleur.**

Ang: SATURATION
All: SÄTTIGUNG
Ital: SATURAZIONE
Esp: SATURACIÓN

Design : Donna S. Atwood, www.atwooddesign.com

SATURATION DE LA COULEUR
Voir **saturation.**

A B C D E F G H I J K L M N O P Q R **S** T U V W X Y Z

… et la rigueur, la recherche pertinente peut aider les graphistes à comprendre les différents types de comportements…

… comprendre les différents types de comportements, ainsi que les modes de pensées qui sous-tendent la vie quotidienne des gens – typiquement le genre d'informations dont un graphiste a besoin afin de …

… horaires : les mercredis de 11h-13h et les jeudis de 11h-12h, ou par rendez-vous…

… ceci pourra jouer inconsciemment sur les réponses/résultats de votre enquête…

SAUT DE LIGNE

Terme désignant l'endroit où une ligne de texte se termine, le texte reprenant sur la ligne suivante. Si ce paramètre peut être ajusté, les logiciels de **mise en pages** brisent automatiquement les lignes après une espace entre deux mots ou à la suite d'un **trait d'union.** Placer un *retour à la ligne forcé* à la fin d'une ligne évitera que le bloc de texte suivant prenne les caractéristiques d'un nouveau paragraphe (par exemple, un alinéa). Voir aussi **C&J** et **retour à la ligne automatique.**

Ang: LINE BREAK
All: ZEILENUMBRUCH
Ital: INTERRUZIONE DI LINEA
Esp: SALTO DE LÍNEA

SÉRIGRAPHIE

Procédé d'impression qui utilise un écran formé de mailles. L'encrage est effectué à travers les mailles non obstruées, directement sur la surface à imprimer. Un pochoir peut également être fait dans un autre matériau que celui de l'écran. Aujourd'hui, la sérigraphie est surtout utilisée par l'industrie vestimentaire, mais elle sert également à l'impression de surfaces irrégulières.

Ang: SCREEN PRINTING
All: SIEBDRUCK
Ital: SERIGRAFIA
Esp: SERIGRAFÍA

SIMILI

Image en niveaux de gris dont chaque ton a été converti au moyen de points tramés noirs de différentes grosseurs. Les zones les plus sombres de l'image sont représentées par des points de trame plus grands que ceux utilisés pour les zones plus claires. En **quadrichromie,** les similis correspondant à chaque **canal** sont combinés afin de simuler l'intégralité du spectre des **couleurs** visibles.

Ang: HALFTONE
All: HALBTON
Ital: MEZZITONI
Esp: MEDIO TONO

Proposition de couverture refusée par le Centre Pompidou
Design : Susanna Shannon et Catherine Houbard, design dept. ; **Photographie du catalogue :** Loren Leport, www.susannashannon.com

A B C D E F G H I J K L M N O P Q R **S** T U V W X Y Z

SIMILI DEUX TONS

Image en niveaux de gris imprimée en deux couleurs ou en deux couches d'une même couleur. Si, en général, le noir reste l'encre principale, deux encres autres que le noir peuvent être utilisées. Pour une photographie en noir et blanc, imprimer un premier passage d'encre noire puis un second avec une *nuance* de gris donnera un meilleur rendu des *tons*. Utiliser une couleur non neutre lors du second passage, ou bien associer deux couleurs non neutres, permet de créer de surprenants effets visuels, du subtil au dramatique. Les similis trois tons sont des images en niveaux de gris imprimées en trois couleurs.

Ang: DUOTONE
All: DUPLEX
Ital: BICROMIA
Esp: BITONO

Affiche pour une pièce de théâtre au Centre dramatique national Orléans/Loiret/Centre, France
Design : Laboratoires CCCP = Dr. Pêche + Melle Rose ;
Concept : Dr. Pêche ; **Photographie :** Melle Rose,
www.laboratoires-cccp.org, www.schizoide.org

ABCDEFGHIJKLMNOPQR**S**TUVWXYZ

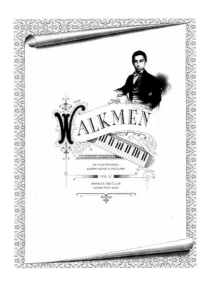

STRATÉGIE DE MARQUE

Stratégie de différenciation d'une offre (produit, service, interactions, expériences, etc.) vis-à-vis de ses concurrents. Dans un premier temps, une marque se constitue souvent d'un **logo,** afin d'ancrer la *promesse de la marque* (ensemble d'attentes associées à un certain type d'offre). Une *identité de marque* efficace inclut notamment une charte visuelle détaillée et cohérente (logo, **typographie, palette de couleurs,** et tout autre signe visuel associé). Les stratégies des marques contemporaines s'étendent généralement bien au-delà des médias traditionnels, que sont l'imprimé et la télévision, pour inclure les sites Internet, les blogs et toutes les nouvelles formes de *médias sociaux.*

Ang: BRANDING
All: MARKENBILDUNG
Ital: BRANDING
Esp: BRANDING

Sacs postaux Royal TNT post, développement d'une identité de marque, 2007
Design : Studio Dumbar, www.studiodumbar.com

STYLE VICTORIEN

Courant stylistique anglais très populaire entre les années 1820 et 1900. L'époque victorienne se caractérise par un style très décoratif, voire ostentatoire. Il s'est établi en réaction à la révolution industrielle et aux excès accompagnant le passage de l'artisanat à la production manufacturée. Les typographes et les designers furent vite distancés par les avancées technologiques, le résultat fut un pot-pourri chaotique de styles issus de différentes périodes. Durant la première période de cette ère, il était courant de voir des illustrations assez brutes associées à des Normandes, **caractères** extra-gras aux grands **contrastes** entre les pleins et les déliés. Différents **corps** et styles de **typographies** étaient employés au sein de **mises en pages** saturées. Vers la fin de ce courant, un style plus clair est apparu.

Ang: VICTORIAN
All: VIKTORIANISCHER STIL
Ital: STILE VITTORIANO
Esp: VICTORIANO

Affiche pour un concert du groupe The Walmen
Design : Jason Munn / The Small Stakes, www.thesmallstakes.com

SURIMPRESSION

Superposition de **couleurs** faisant apparaître une nouvelle couleur. La plupart du temps, lorsque deux éléments se superposent, seule la couleur de celui qui se trouve au dessus est imprimée. On dit alors qu'elle *défonce* celle qui se trouve au-dessous. On ne peut vraiment parler de surimpression que lorsque deux encres, ou plus, sont combinées pour aboutir à une nouvelle couleur.

Ang: OVERPRINTING
All: ÜBERDRUCKEN
Ital: SOVRASTAMPA
Esp: SOBREIMPRESIÓN

Pochette de CD pour « The Elephant in the Room: 3 Commissions », de Mira Calix, Warp Records, 2008
Design : Niall Sweeney, Nigel at Pony, www.ponybox.co.uk

A B C D E F G H I J K L M N O P Q R **S** T U V W X Y Z

SURRÉALISME

Courant artistique majeur en Europe dans les années 1920-1930. Les préoccupations principales des tenants du surréalisme étaient l'intuition, les rêves et l'inconscient, qu'ils exprimaient à travers des juxtapositions étonnantes et déboussolantes, des illusions d'optique ainsi que des transgressions évidentes des lois de la physique. Certains graphistes puisent leur inspiration non seulement dans les nombreuses techniques employées par les surréalistes, mais aussi dans la manière expérimentale qu'ils avaient de représenter l'espace en trois dimensions.

Ang: SURREALISM
All: SURREALISMUS
Ital: SURREALISMO
Esp: SURREALISMO

Affiche pour l'exposition « Lumière d'affiches »,
Chaumont, 2007
Design : © Grégoire Romanet, gregoire.romanet.free.fr

A B C D E F G H I J K L M N O P Q R **S** T U V W X Y Z

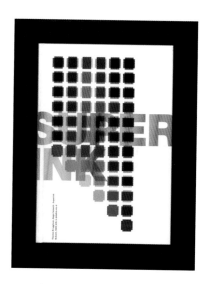

SYMBOLE

Signe graphique qui représente quelque chose d'une façon différente de ce qu'il est en réalité. Par exemple, dans de nombreuses cultures, le symbole du cœur est utilisé pour représenter l'affection ou l'amour (surtout lorsqu'il est en rouge), alors que celui-ci ne ressemble pas à l'amour en tant que tel, de même qu'il ne s'apparente guère à un véritable cœur. Néanmoins, compte tenu du fait que sa signification est universellement admise, il peut être employé pour communiquer efficacement. De la même façon que le symbole de la Croix-Rouge a une même acception quelles que soient la langue ou la barrière culturelle, car son sens a été admis dans un premier temps. Voir aussi **icône** et **pictogramme.**

Ang: SYMBOL
All: SYMBOL
Ital: SIMBOLO
Esp: SÍMBOLO

Design : Fabrice Praeger, studio002.com > « portraits » > menu déroulant > fabrice praeger

SYMÉTRIE

Distribution d'éléments de la même façon de part et d'autre d'un axe, le plus souvent vertical ou horizontal. Les **mises en pages** symétriques sont construites de telle sorte que les éléments sont distribués de façon plus ou moins harmonieuse de bas en haut et de gauche à droite. Ces **grilles** sont donc d'une certaine façon conservatrices car elles installent une plus grande stabilité qu'une grille asymétrique. Voir aussi **asymétrie, équilibre** et **circulation du regard.**

Ang: SYMMETRY
All: SYMMETRIE
Ital: SIMMETRIA
Esp: SIMETRÍA

Affiche-calendrier, avril 2003, pour le restaurant londonien Momo
Design : Ich&Kar, www.ichetkar.com

SYSTÈME D'ASSORTIMENT DES COULEURS

Désigne toute référence standard disponible sous forme de charte **couleur** ou d'échantillon. Ces références ont toutes des valeurs numériques correspondantes, ce qui permet de définir avec précision la couleur utilisée. Les graphistes utilisent ces modèles afin de s'assurer que les couleurs choisies pour un projet donné seront correctement reproduites à l'impression. Afin de garantir cette reproduction fidèle des couleurs, il est important de connaître les types de systèmes d'assortiment des couleurs assurés par l'imprimeur.

Ang: COLOR-MATCHING SYSTEM
All: FARBKENNZEICHNUNGSSYSTEM
Ital: SISTEMA DI COMBINAZIONE DEI COLORI
Esp: SISTEMA DE AJUSTE DEL COLOR

Superink
Éditeur : Brikett Verlag Zürich AG ; **Auteurs :** Thomas Bruggisser et Christine Moser, www.brikett.ch

SYSTÈME D'ASSORTIMENT DES COULEURS PANTONE®
Voir **système d'assortiment des couleurs.**

A B C D E F G H I J K L M N O P Q R S **T** U V W X Y Z

Lorem ipsum dolor sit amet, consectetuer adipiscing elit. Sed non risus. Suspendisse lectus tortor, dignissim sit amet, adipiscing nec, ultricies sed, dolor. Cras elementum ultrices diam. Maecenas ligula massa, varius a, semper congue, euismod non, mi. Proin porttitor, orci nec nonummy molestie, enim est eleifend mi, non fermentum diam nisl sit amet erat. Duis semper. Duis arcu massa, scelerisque vitae, consequat in, pretium a, enim. Pellentesque congue. Ut in risus volutpat libero pharetra tempor. Cras vestibulum bibendum augue. Praesent egestas leo in pede. Praesent blandit odio eu enim. Pellentesque sed dui ut augue blandit sodales. Vestibulum ante ipsum primis in faucibus orci luctus et ultrices posuere cubilia Curae. Aliquam nibh. Mauris ac mauris sed pede pellentesque fermentum. Maecenas adipiscing ante non diam sodales hendrerit.

TEINTE

Une des caractéristiques fondamentales de la **couleur,** qui correspond à sa longueur d'ondes dans le spectre de la lumière, utilisé pour différencier une couleur d'une autre. La teinte est en rapport avec la position d'une couleur sur la circonférence de la **roue chromatique.**

Ang: HUE
All: FARBTON
Ital: TONALITÀ
Esp: MATIZ

Design : Donna S. Atwood, www.atwooddesign.com

TEXTE CENTRÉ

Lignes successives de **caractères** alignées de façon que le milieu de chaque phrase s'aligne sur une même ligne de référence. Une **composition typographique** centrée présente un sens de lecture inhabituel, elle est donc généralement réservée aux cartes de visite, invitations et tout autre type de support contenant assez peu de texte. Voir aussi **alignement.**

Ang: CENTERED TYPE/TEXT
All: MITTELACHSSATZ
Ital: TESTO/CARATTERI CENTRATI
Esp: TEXTO O TIPO CENTRADO

Invitation composée dans la police de caractères Ordinaire, avec ses variantes : Ordinaire-c'est-l'heure, Ordinaire-grasse-matinée et Ordinaire-lève-tôt
Design : David Poullard

TEXTE JUSTIFIÉ

Lignes successives de texte alignées à la fois à gauche et à droite sur une ligne de référence imaginaire. Un texte justifié s'étend sur l'intégralité de la **mesure** d'une **ligne.** Justifier un texte peut parfois produire des **lézardes,** surtout lorsque la **mesure** de la ligne de texte est courte. Voir aussi **alignement** et **C&J.**

Ang: JUSTIFIED TYPE/TEXT
All: BLOCKSATZ
Ital: TESTO/CARATTERI GIUSTIFICATI
Esp: JUSTIFICACIÓN

A B C D E F G H I J K L M N O P Q R S **T** U V W X Y Z

Typographie

Tiret cadratin —

Typographie

Tiret demi-cadratin –

TEXTURE

Propriété tactile perçue d'un élément graphique ou d'une **mise en pages.** Bien qu'on parle surtout de texture pour décrire des éléments en trois dimensions, comme la surface d'un papier, ce terme peut aussi être utilisé pour décrire une création en deux dimensions. Par exemple, des motifs et des **dégradés** différents peuvent amener une impression de texture, surtout quand on crée un **contraste** avec des éléments lisses et uniformes. Certaines techniques d'impression, comme l'impression sur bois, donnent aussi de la texture. Même une page de texte, avec ses **rythmes** verticaux et horizontaux affirmés, a une certaine texture, selon la façon dont celle-ci est composée. On dit alors que le texte a une « belle couleur ».

Ang: TEXTURE
All: STRUKTUR
Ital: TEXTURE
Esp: TEXTURA

Affiche « Entrevues »
Design et photographie : Pierre-Emm Meunier,
pierre.emm@gmail.com

TIRET CADRATIN

Tiret dont la largeur est égale à un **cadratin,** utilisé notamment pour mettre en évidence une portion de texte ou dans les dialogues. Concernant l'usage des espaces avant et après un tiret cadratin, il est courant, en français, d'en mettre. Voir aussi **tiret demi-cadratin** et **trait d'union.**

Ang: EM DASH
All: Geviertstrich
Ital: LINEETTA EM
Esp: RAYA

TIRET DEMI-CADRATIN

Tiret dont la largeur est égale à un **demi-cadratin,** utilisé pour les énumérations, les dialogues et les incises. Tout comme le **tiret cadratin,** le tiret demi-cadratin est précédé et suivi d'une espace en français. Voir aussi **tiret cadratin** et **trait d'union.**

Ang: EN DASH
All: DIVIS
Ital: LINEETTA EN
Esp: SEMIRRAYA

A B C D E F G H I J K L M N O P Q R S **T** U V W X Y Z

Trait d'union

Tiret demi-cadratin

Tiret cadratin

TITRE

Artifice typographique permettant de décomposer un texte long en grandes parties, à la manière des titres de chapitres dans un livre, ou titres de rubriques dans une brochure ou un rapport. Les titres sont souvent composés **tout en capitales** ou en combinant des capitales et des **petites capitales,** souvent en **caractères gras.** Les **intertitres** servent ensuite à décomposer le texte selon sa structure interne.

Ang: HEADING
All: ÜBERSCHRIFT
Ital: TESTATINA
Esp: TÍTULO

Livret d'exposition pour le MAC/VAL, Musée d'art contemporain du Val-de-Marne
Design : Akatre, www.akatre.com

TOUT EN CAPITALES

Texte composé exclusivement en capitales aussi appelées *haut-de-casse* ; cette appellation tire son origine des tiroirs (ou casses) dans lesquels l'imprimeur rangeait autrefois ses **caractères** en plomb, les capitales étaient placées dans les casses supérieures et les *bas-de-casse,* que l'on utilisait plus souvent, dans les tiroirs inférieurs, plus faciles d'accès. On parle aussi de *majuscules* et de *minuscules*.

Ang: ALL CAPS
All: VERSALIEN
Ital: TUTTE MAIUSCOLE
Esp: ALL CAPS

Dépliant pour le Salon du livre 2009, éditions Galaade
Design : Hey Ho, www.heyho.fr

TRAIT D'UNION

Signe de ponctuation dont la longueur est plus courte que celle du **tiret demi-cadratin** et du **tiret cadratin.** Il est souvent confondu avec ceux-ci malgré un usage distinct. Un trait d'union sert à indiquer une **coupure de mot** en bout de ligne, à créer des mots composés, comme un trois-quarts, un arc-en-ciel et un sourd-muet.

Ang: HYPHEN
All: TRENNSTRICH
Ital: TRATTINO
Esp: GUIÓN

A B C D E F G H I J K L M N O P Q R S **T U V** W X Y Z

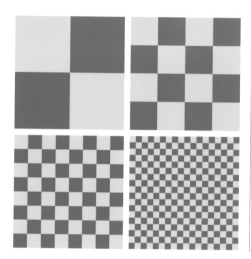

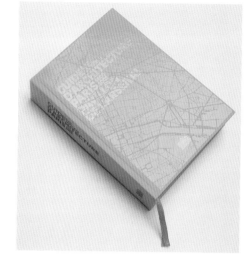

TRAMAGE ALÉATOIRE

Technique utilisée pour simuler les **couleurs** d'une image numérique en n'utilisant que les couleurs disponibles dans une **palette de couleurs** donnée. Lorsque, par exemple, une image numérique en couleur est convertie en couleur Web-safe, une palette de 216 couleurs garanties pour le Web est utilisée pour simuler la couleur de l'image originale. Ceci est possible grâce à un patchwork de **pixels** sur un écran d'ordinateur, ou de points pour une imprimante numérique. Par exemple, un patchwork de pixels, ou de points, rouge et jaune peut être utilisé pour simuler de l'orange. Si on perd des détails par ce procédé, le tramage aléatoire reste néanmoins efficace pour lisser les contours dentelés indésirables qui peuvent apparaître entre différentes zones de couleur. Voir aussi **posterisation.**

Ang: DITHER
All: DITHERING
Ital: RETINO
Esp: DIFUMINADO

Design : Donna S. Atwood, www.atwooddesign.com

TYPOGRAPHIE

Art de la **composition typographique.** Les typographes considèrent un grand nombre de paramètres, du plus général, comme la **lisibilité,** au plus précis, comme le **crénage.** Les technologies numériques rendent cette discipline plus accessible que jamais, mais non moins commune qu'à l'âge de la **composition** au plomb ou de la *phototypie,* lorsque les typographes s'attardaient méticuleusement sur chaque détail.

Ang: TYPOGRAPHY
All: TYPOGRAFIE
Ital: TIPOGRAFIA
Esp: TIPOGRAFÍA

Affiche pour l'exposition « My Home » au Vitra Design Museum
Design : Ludovic Balland, Typography Cabinet, www.ludovic-balland.ch

VALEUR
Voir **luminosité.**

VERNIS

Pellicule transparente appliquée sur une feuille de papier imprimée. L'application d'un vernis permet à la fois de protéger les imprimés, mais également de leur donner une finition soignée. Une grande variété de brillances est disponible, du vernis mat à l'ultrabrillant.

Ang: VARNISH
All: LACKIERUNG
Ital: VERNICE
Esp: BARNIZ

Guide d'Architecture Paris 1900-2008,
éditions du Pavillon de l'Arsenal
Design : Benoît Santiard avec la collaboration de Frédéric Tacer, www.bsantiard.com

A B C D E F G H I J K L M N O P Q R S T U **V** W X Y Z

VERNIS UV

Couche de polymère liquide appliquée sur une feuille de papier, soit grâce à un dernier passage après les différentes encres, soit hors ligne, mais toujours immédiatement après l'impression. Elle est ensuite séchée par une exposition à une lumière ultraviolette (UV). Un vernis UV offre une meilleure résistance à l'abrasion, et autres dommages liés à la manipulation, qu'un **pelliculage aqueux,** mais est plus enclin aux craquelures le long de plis anguleux. Les vernis UV peuvent être appliqués seulement sur certaines zones du support imprimé, on parle alors de *vernis sélectif*. Voir aussi **vernis.**

Ang: ULTRAVIOLET COATING
All: UV-LACK
Ital: FINITURA A ULTRAVIOLETTI
Esp: REVESTIMIENTO ULTRAVIOLETA

Détail d'une affiche pour le festival de danse
Météores, 2009
Design : Stéphan Muntaner, c-ktre@wanadoo.fr

VERSO
Voir **recto verso.**

Lorem ipsum dolor sit amet, consectetuer adipiscing elit. Sed non risus. Suspendisse lectus tortor, dignissim sit amet, adipiscing nec, ultricies sed, dolor. Cras elementum ultrices diam. Maecenas ligula massa, varius a, semper congue, euismod non, mi. Proin porttitor, orci nec nonummy molestie, enim est eleifend mi, non fermentum diam nisl sit amet erat. Duis semper.

Duis arcu massa, scelerisque vitae, consequat in,

pretium a, enim. Pellentesque congue. Ut in risus volutpat libero pharetra tempor. Cras vestibulum bibendum augue. Praesent egestas leo in pede. Praesent blandit odio eu enim. Pellentesque sed dui ut augue blandit sodales.

Vestibulum ante ipsum primis in faucibus orci luctus et ultrices posuere cubilia Curae. Aliquam nibh. Mauris ac mauris sed pede pellentesque fermentum. Maecenas adipiscing ante non diam sodales hendrerit.

VEUVE

Il s'agit de la première ligne, voire les deux premières, séparée du paragraphe principal et située en bas d'une **colonne** de texte. Les veuves peuvent être évitées, tout comme les **orphelines,** par un certain nombre de techniques, dont les plus courantes sont l'**interlettrage** et les **coupures de mots.** Voir aussi **C&J** et **retour à la ligne automatique.**

Ang: WIDOW
All: WITWE
Ital: VEDOVA
Esp: VIUDA

DEUTSCH

A B C D E F G H I J K L M N O P Q R S T U V W X Y Z

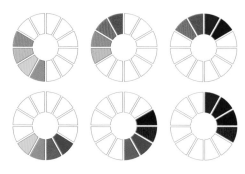

„Trinkst Du Deinen Kaffee mit Milch und Zucker?" fragte er sie.

Der umstrittene Artikel stammte aus der „Morgenpost".

…und für diese „Heldentat" möchtest Du auch noch belohnt werden?"

ALIAS-EFFEKT, ANTIALIASING

Der Alias-Effekt tritt auf, wenn die **Auflösung** eines Bildes im **Bitmap**-Format geringer ist als die des darstellenden Geräts (z. B. Bildschirm) oder Druckers. Bei einem Bild mit einer Auflösung von 72 *spi* – „samples per inch" (Bildpunkte pro Zoll) – tritt der Alias-Effekt z. B. auf, wenn es in Originalgröße mit 300 „dots per inch" (Druckpunkte pro Zoll) – kurz *dpi* – gedruckt wird. Daraus resultieren sichtbar verpixelte Ränder, die an Treppenstufen erinnern.

Antialiasing ist ein von digitalen Bildbearbeitungsprogrammen angewandtes Verfahren zur Minimierung der durch den Alias-Effekt verursachten Bildverzerrung. Das wird durch eine geringfügige Reduzierung der Bildschärfe erreicht, wodurch die groben Kanten der „Treppenstufen" verwischen. Trotz der geringfügigen Qualitätseinbußen, die hierdurch entstehen, ist die Anwendung von Antialiasing oft durchaus sinnvoll.

En: ALIASING, ANTI-ALIASING
Fr: CRÉNELAGE, ANTICRÉNELAGE
It: ALIASING/ANTI-ALIASING
Spa: SOLAPAMIENTO/ANTISOLAPAMIENTO

ANALOGE FARBEN

Zwei oder mehr **Farben**, die auf dem **Farbkreis** aneinandergrenzen (z. B. Grün, Gelbgrün und Gelb). Da analoge Farben eng miteinander verwandt sind, verleihen sie – richtig eingesetzt – dem Design einen harmonischen Anblick.

En: ANALOGOUS COLORS
Fr: COULEURS ANALOGUES
It: COLORI ANALOGHI
Spa: COLORES ANÁLOGOS

Design: Donna S. Atwood, www.atwooddesign.com

ANFÜHRUNGSSTRICHE

Ein Satzzeichen, das verschiedene Bedeutungen haben kann. Sie markieren einerseits indirekte Rede, Werktitel, Namen von Publikationen oder wörtliche Zitate innerhalb eines Textes. Andererseits signalisieren sie auch die ironische Bedeutung eines Wortes (z. B.: Es sind „nur" 1000 km). (Siehe auch **Apostroph**.)

En: QUOTATION MARKS
Fr: GUILLEMETS
It: VIRGOLETTE
Spa: COMILLAS

A B C D E F G H I J K L M N O P Q R S T U V W X Y Z

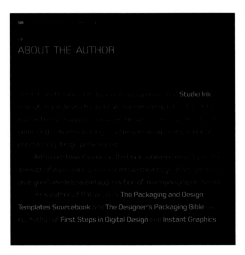

ANHANG

Teile eines Buches, die nach dem Haupttext
angelegt sind, wie Anlagen, Quellenver-
zeichnisse, *Nomenklatur*, Anmerkungen usw.
(Siehe auch **Titelei**.)

En: END MATTER
Fr: PARTIES ANNEXES
It: PAGINE FINALI
Spa: PÁGINAS FINALES

ANIMATION

Eine Reihe digitaler Bilder, die in einer
bestimmten Abfolge angezeigt werden,
sodass der Eindruck von fortlaufender
Bewegung erzeugt wird. Für relativ simple Webdesignanimationen werden häufig
animierte *GIFs* verwendet, wohingegen kom-
plexere Animationen mithilfe technisch hoch
entwickelter Software wie z. B. Adobe Flash®
erstellt werden.

En: ANIMATION
Fr: ANIMATION
It: ANIMAZIONE/I
Spa: ANIMACIÓN

Design: Grafikstudio Steinert,
www.grafikstudio-steinert.com

ANSTANZUNG

Eine Form der Stanzung, die für Aufkleber
und Klebedekore benutzt wird. Ein bedrucktes Blatt Papier wird gestanzt, ohne die
Rückseite durchzutrennen, sodass Aufkleber
und Klebedekore vom Untergrund gelöst
werden können.

En: KISS DIE CUT
Fr: DÉCOUPE PAR EFFLEUREMENT
It: ADESIVO CON FUSTELLA
Spa: TROQUELADO DE MEDIO CORTE

Design: Jan Kruse, Carolin Rauen; **Firma:** Ligalux
GmbH, www.ligalux.de

A B C D E F G H I J K L M N O P Q R S T U V W X Y Z

Caslon
Bodoni
Hoefler
Times

ANTIQUA

Bezeichnet eine Vielzahl von Schriftarten und -bildern mit Serifen, die aus dem Italien des 15. Jahrhunderts stammen. Mit Antiqua wird – im Gegensatz zum **fetten** oder **kursiven** – auch das „normale" Bild einer Schriftart mit oder ohne **Serifen** beschrieben.

En: ROMAN TYPE
Fr: CARACTÈRES ROMAINS
It: CARATTERI ROMAN
Spa: REDONDA

Auslassungszeichen:
Wie geht's? – Wie geht es?
D'dorf – Düsseldorf
Genitiv-s:
Dennis' Freund Kai –
Kai, der Freund von Dennis

APOSTROPH

In der deutschen Sprache haben Apostrophe zwei Funktionen: Zum einen kennzeichnen sie Auslassungen (z. B. '80er = 1980er oder „Wie geht's?" = „Wie geht es?"), zum anderen bilden sie den Genitiv eines Eigennamens, wenn dieser im Singular schon auf -s (z. B. Marcus' Kneipe) endet. Apostrophe haben eine rückläufig linksgebogene Form und sind nicht mit Anführungszeichen zu verwechseln.

En: APOSTROPHE
Fr: APOSTROPHE
It: APOSTROFO
Spa: APÓSTROFO

ART DÉCO

Eine Stilrichtung, die die dekorativen Elemente des **Jugendstils** mit den geometrischen Formen und der Abstraktion des **Modernismus** kombiniert. Art déco war in den USA und in großen Teilen Europas während der 1920er und 1930er Jahre beliebt. Aufgrund verschiedenster Einflüsse, wie aztekischer und indianischer Kunst, ägyptischer *Zikkurate*, dem **Kubismus** und vielen mehr, entfaltete sich der Art-déco-Stil sowohl in Architektur, Innenraumgestaltung und Produktdesign als auch im Grafikdesign. Schwungvolle Grafiken wurden oft mit ähnlich stilisierter und fettgedruckter **Schrift** kombiniert.

En: ART DECO
Fr: ART DÉCO
It: ART DÉCO
Spa: ART DECÓ

A B C D E F G H I J K L M N O P Q R S T U V W X Y Z

ARTS AND CRAFTS

Diese Reformbewegung, die im England des späten 19. Jahrhunderts ihre Anfänge hatte, verstand sich als eine Reaktion auf die industrielle Revolution und die damit einhergehende Entwicklung der Massenproduktion auf Kosten ästhetischer Aspekte. Im Grafikdesign wurde die Arts-and-Crafts-Bewegung in den Büchern von *William Morris* eingeführt. Obwohl er verzierte Buchstaben, gotische Schriftarten und weitere Designelemente vergangener Jahrhunderte benutzte, betonte Morris die Wiederzusammenführung von Design und Produktion und bereitete den Weg für die **Moderne** des 20. Jahrhunderts.

En: ARTS AND CRAFTS
Fr: ARTS & CRAFTS
It: ARTS AND CRAFTS
Spa: ARTS AND CRAFTS

Abb.: William Morris, Artichoke Wallpaper

ASYMMETRIE

Die ungleichmäßige Anordnung von Designelementen in Bezug auf die horizontale und vertikale Achse des **Layouts**. Asymmetrie kann auch Doppelseiten beschreiben, deren Satzspiegel sich nicht gleicht. Effektive asymmetrische **Layouts** erzielen eine **Balance** durch das sorgfältige Zusammenspiel von positivem und negativem Raum und wirken dadurch oft dynamischer als symmetrische **Layouts**. (Siehe auch **Symmetrie** oder **Blickbewegung**.)

En: ASYMMETRY
Fr: ASYMÉTRIE
It: ASIMMETRIA
Spa: ASIMETRÍA

Design: Grafikstudio Steinert,
www.grafikstudio-steinert.com

AUFLÖSUNG

Die relative Qualität eines digitalen Bildes, die in der Anzahl von Punkten pro Maßeinheit angegeben wird. Die verschiedenen Begriffe zur Beschreibung der Auflösung digitaler Grafiken werden oft synonymisch verwendet. *Dpi* – „dots per inch" (Bildpunkte pro Zoll) – ist die relative Maßeinheit für die Qualität von Druckern. 300-dpi-Drucker z. B. können 300 Druckpunkte nebeneinander auf einem Zoll drucken. *Ppi* hingegen ist die Abkürzung für „pixels per inch" (Pixel pro Zoll), was die Auflösung eines Computerbildschirms oder anderen Anzeigegeräts angibt. *Lpi* – „lines per inch" (Zeilen pro Zoll) – ist schließlich die Maßeinheit für eine Halbtonfrequenz. Obwohl „lines" (Zeilen) eigentlich Reihen kleiner Punkte sind, erscheinen sie als Zeilen, wenn diese nebeneinander gedruckt werden. Je größer die Rasterfrequenz, desto detaillierter wird das Bild gedruckt. Zeitungen verwenden **Raster** von 65–85 *lpi*, Hochglanzmagazine benötigen 133–150 *lpi* und Kunstbücher sogar bis zu 300 *lpi*.

En: RESOLUTION
Fr: RÉSOLUTION
It: RISOLUZIONE
Spa: RESOLUCIÓN

A B C D E F G H I J K L M N O P Q R S T U V W X Y Z

RHEINISCHER SAU

REZEPT
(für 4 Personen)

ZUTATEN:
· 1 kg Rinderbraten

FÜR DIE MARINADE:
· ¾ Liter Wein, rot, kräftig
· ½ Liter Himbeeressig
· 2 Zwiebeln, grob zerkleinert
· 1 Möhre, grob zerkleinert
· 10 Wacholderbeeren
· 5 Körner Piment
· 5 Gewürznelken
· 2 Lorbeerblätter
· 1 EL Salz

ZUBEREITUNG MAF

Alle Zutaten für die N
nuten köcheln lasser
lassen. Den Rinderbr₂
bedeckt ist. Sorgfältig
und die nächsten dre

SAUERBRATEN:

Nach drei bis vier Tag
nehmen. Die Marinad
Den Braten abtupfen
anbraten. Die Zwiebe
salzen und schön brä

Rückseite

⅃	10	11	6
2	15	14	3

Falz 1

2	12	6	8
4	13	16	1

Falz 2 / Falz 1

Vorderseite

AUFZÄHLUNGSPUNKT

Ein Schriftzeichen (•), das meist benutzt wird, um einzelne Punkte innerhalb einer Liste (Aufzählung) untereinander aufzuführen und kenntlich zu machen. Zwischen einem Aufzählungspunkt und dem nachfolgenden Text sollte in jedem Fall ein Zwischenraum gelassen werden. Außerdem sind Aufzählungspunkte Bestandteile von **Symbol**- und **Dingbats**-Schriftarten. (Siehe auch **Satzkantenangleich**.)

En: BULLET
Fr: PUCE
It: PUNTO ELENCO
Spa: BOLO

AUSSCHIESSEN

Die sorgfältige Gliederung mehrerer Seiten einer Publikation, die auf große Papierbögen gedruckt werden. Das Ausschießen stellt sicher, dass die einzelnen Seiten in der richtigen Abfolge angeordnet sind, wenn sie gedruckt, gefaltet und gebunden werden. Das kann von Hand gemacht werden, wobei es heutzutage üblicherweise von Softwareanwendungen übernommen wird. (Siehe auch **Paginierung**.)

En: IMPOSITION
Fr: IMPOSITION
It: IMPOSIZIONE TIPOGRAFICA
Spa: IMPOSICIÓN

AUSSCHNITT

Der Prozess, bei dem ein Foto oder eine Illustration entweder digital oder mechanisch so zugeschnitten wird, dass unerwünschte Teile wegfallen. Dies tut man, um einen genauen Ausschnitt eines Fotos zu erhalten oder um die Größe und Proportionen eines Bildes einzuhalten, die innerhalb eines **Layouts** dafür zur Verfügung stehen. Die schmalen Linien, die den Ausschnitt markieren, werden *Schnittmarken* genannt.

En: CROP
Fr: RECADRER
It: CROP
Spa: RECORTAR

A B C D E F G H I J K L M N O P Q R S T U V W X Y Z

AUSZEICHNUNGSSCHRIFT

Schrift, die in einem größeren Schriftgrad gesetzt wird als der übrige Text, sodass sie sich vom Haupttext abhebt, so wie z. B. bei Titeln oder **Überschriften** üblich.

En: DISPLAY TYPE
Fr: CARACTÈRES DE TITRE
It: CARATTERI DI VISUALIZZAZIONE
Spa: TIPO TITULAR

Foto: VOX/Twentieth Century Fox; **Design:** Sixpack Werbeagentur GmbH, www.sixpack.de

AXIALITÄT

Axialität oder Ausrichtung bezieht sich auf die Anordnung mehrerer Designelemente wie Fotos oder Text zueinander. Elemente sind oft so aufgereiht, dass ihre Kanten (links, rechts, oben, unten) oder Mittelachsen (horizontal, vertikal) eine Referenzlinie bilden, die häufig Teil des Seitenlayouts ist. Axialität kann sich auch auf die Anordnung von Schrift innerhalb eines Textblocks beziehen. (Siehe auch **Linksbündig**, **Rechtsbündig**, **Mittelachssatz** und **Blocksatz**.)

En: ALIGNMENT
Fr: ALIGNEMENT
It: ALLINEAMENTO
Spa: ALINEACIÓN

Design: Raphael Pohland, Simone Pohland; **Firma:** stilradar, www.stilradar.de

BALANCE (AUSGEWOGENHEIT)

Das optische Zusammenspiel verschiedener Designelemente innerhalb eines bestimmten Bereichs. Man spricht bei einem **Layout** dann von Ausgeglichenheit, wenn die Formen, Proportionen, Strukturen, **Farben** und Größen aller Elemente so zusammengestellt sind, dass eine optische Harmonie entsteht. Ausgeglichene **Layouts** müssen jedoch nicht konservativ sein. Der feinfühlige Designer kann vielmehr durch eine Ausgeglichenheit im Gesamtlayout sogar eine noch größere Aufmerksamkeit des Betrachters erreichen.

En: BALANCE
Fr: ÉQUILIBRE
It: BILANCIAMENTO
Spa: EQUILIBRIO

Design: Alexander Dahlmann; **Firma:** red cell Werbeagentur GmbH, www.redcell.de

A **B** C D E F G H I J K L M N O P Q R S T U V W X Y Z

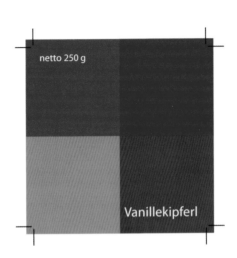

BAUHAUS

Eine sehr einflussreiche Bildungsstätte für Kunst, Architektur und Design, die von 1919 bis 1933 in Deutschland bestand. Charakteristisch für die Art des Grafikdesigns, das das Bauhaus hervorbrachte, waren schlichte, geometrische Formen, die vom Schwerpunkt auf Funktionalität herrührten. Bei **Layouts**, Fotografien und **Fotomontagen** setzte man fast ausschließlich auf Schriftarten ohne Serifen, meist an schweren **Linien** und strengen Satzspiegeln ausgerichtet. Schwarz, Weiß und Grau waren die vorherrschenden Farben des Bauhauses, wobei **Primärfarben** häufig zum Einsatz kamen, um Akzente zu setzen.

En: BAUHAUS
Fr: BAUHAUS
It: BAUHAUS
Spa: BAUHAUS

Design: Michael Thiele, Martin Schonhoff;
Firma: Die Transformer, www.dietransformer.de

BESCHNITT

Der Teil eines Designelements wie Bild, Zeile, Farbfläche etc. der über den Rand der eigentlichen Seitengröße weiterläuft. *Schnittmarken*, die die Schnittlinien andeuten, werden verwendet, um die wirkliche Seitengröße anzuzeigen; alle Elemente, die über die tatsächliche Seitengröße hinausgehen, werden „angeschnitten". Die erforderliche Größe der Schnittfläche hängt von der Genauigkeit der Druckpresse und des Schnittwerkzeugs ab.

En: BLEED
Fr: FONDS PERDUS
It: STAMPA AL VIVO
Spa: IMPRIMIR "A SANGRE"

BÉZIERKURVE

Eine mathematische Annäherung an eine fortlaufende Kurve, die durch ihre zwei Ankerpunkte (an jedem Ende) und eine beliebige Zahl an Punkten definiert wird, die sie beschreibt. Die von Grafikdesignprogrammen am meisten genutzten **Pfade** setzen sich aus mehreren Bézierkurven zusammen. Das ist der Grund, warum man sie unbegrenzt vergrößern kann. Bézierkurven können auch bei **Animationen** verwendet werden, um Bewegungen zu kontrollieren.

En: BÉZIER CURVE
Fr: COURBE DE BÉZIER
It: CURVA DI BÉZIER
Spa: CURVA DE BÉZIER

Design: Donna S. Atwood,
www.atwooddesign.com

BILDMONTAGE (COMPOSING)

Ein Bild, das aus anderen Bildern oder Elementen anderer Bilder
elektronisch zusammengesetzt ist. Nicht zu verwechseln mit dem
Begriff **Kollage**, der ein Gesamtkunstwerk beschreibt, oder mit **Fotomontage**, der sich – wie der Name schon sagt – ausschließlich auf
die Zusammenstellung fotografischer Elemente bezieht, verwendet
man den Begriff „Composing" meist für ein Foto oder eine Illustration
innerhalb einer größeren gestalteten Arbeit.

En: COMPOSITE
Fr: IMAGE COMPOSITE
It: COMPOSITE
Spa: FOTOCOMPOSICIÓN

Design: Michael Thiele; **Firma:** Die Transformer, www.dietransformer.de

A B C D E F G H I J K L M N O P Q R S T U V W X Y Z

BILDUNTERSCHRIFT

Eine kurze Textpassage, die ein Foto, eine Illustration, Tabelle oder ein anderes visuelles Element beschreibt oder erklärt. Bildunterschriften werden grundsätzlich über, unter oder neben der Bebilderung – also separat vom **Fließtext** – platziert. (Siehe auch **Hinweis**.)

En: CAPTION
Fr: LÉGENDE
It: DIDASCALIA
Spa: PIE DE FOTO

Design: Raphael Pohland, Simone Pohland;
Firma: stilradar, www.stilradar.de

BILDZEICHEN

Ein grafisches Zeichen, das nach dem aussieht, wofür es steht. Das Druckersymbol auf dem Computerbildschirm z. B. sieht aus wie ein einfacher, allgemeiner Drucker. Andere Beispiele sind die Zigarette im Rauchen-verboten-Zeichen oder der Koffer, der an Flughäfen für das Gepäckband steht. In beiden Fällen geben die **Symbole** das wieder, was sie bedeuten sollen, weshalb sie auch trotz sprachlicher und kultureller Barrieren leicht verständlich sind. (Siehe auch **Symbol** und **Piktogramm**.)

En: ICON
Fr: ICÔNE
It: ICONA
Spa: ICONO

Design: Helge Rieder, Oliver Henn; **Firma:** 804©
Graphic Design, www.achtnullvier.com

BITMAP

In seiner Grundbedeutung ist ein Bitmap das rechtwinklige **Raster** von Punkten oder Flächen, die zusammen ein digitales Bild – wie z. B. ein Foto oder ein Schriftbild – ergeben. Jede Fläche hat eine bestimmte **Farbe** und einen bestimmten Platz innerhalb des Bitmap-Rasters. Je mehr Flächen pro Zoll (*spi*, samples per inch) – also Bildpunkte auf eine bestimmte Fläche – entfallen, desto höher ist die Auflösung des Bitmaps. Aufgrund der Tatsache, dass ein Bitmap eine feste Anzahl von Flächen beinhaltet (anders als bei **Vektorgrafiken**), tritt bei einer Darstellung, die über die **Auflösung** des Ausgabegeräts hinausgeht, der **Alias-Effekt** auf. Ein anderes Wort für Bitmap ist auch *Rastergrafik*.

En: BITMAP
Fr: IMAGE MATRICIELLE
It: BITMAP
Spa: MAPA DE BITS

A **B** C D E F G H I J K L M N O P Q R S T U V W X Y Z

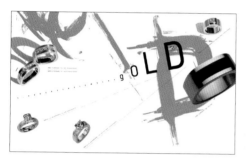

Lorem ipsum dolor sit amet, consectetuer sadipscing elitr, sed diam nonumy eirmod tempor invidunt ut labore et dolore magna aliquyam erat, sed diam voluptua. At vero eos et accusam et justo duo dolores et ea rebum. Stet clita kasd gubergren, no sea takimata sanctus est Lorem ipsum dolor sit amet. Lorem ipsum dolor sit amet, consetetur sadipscing elitr, sed diam nonumy eirmod tempor invidunt ut labore et dolore magna aliquyam erat, sed diam voluptua.

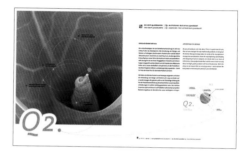

BLICKBEWEGUNG

Das Bewegungsmuster der Augen beim Betrachten eines Fotos oder **Layouts**. Der Blickpfad wird von mehreren Faktoren wie **Farbe**, Ausgeglichenheit, **Kontrast**, etc. beeinflusst. Effektive Designs profitieren von voraussagbaren Augenbewegungsmustern; Wegweiser z. B. müssen einfach und direkt sein, wohingegen Poster den Betrachter mit komplexeren Augenbewegungen beschäftigen. (Siehe auch **Fokus**.)

En: EYE FLOW
Fr: CIRCULATION DU REGARD
It: FLUSSO VISIVO
Spa: LÍNEA DE ORIENTACIÓN

Design: Raphael Pohland, Simone Pohland;
Firma: stilradar, www.stilradar.de

BLINDTEXT

Ein Text, der nichts bedeuten soll, sondern als Platzhalter in einem noch zu bearbeitenden **Layout** dient. Der Begriff wird auch für die grauen Balken verwendet, die manche Layoutanwendungen anstelle von Textzeilen darstellen, die zu klein sind, um auf einem Bildschirm deutlich angezeigt zu werden. Auch *Lorem Ipsum* genannt.

En: GREEKING
Fr: FAUX TEXTE
Spa: GREEKING

BLOCKSATZ

Ein Begriff, mit dem fortlaufende Textzeilen beschrieben werden, die an einer imaginären Referenzlinie beginnen und an einer weiteren enden. Prinzipiell sind alle Texte bündig ausgerichtet, sodass die gesamte Zeile durch Schriftzeichen (z. B. Wörter, Zahlen) und Zwischenräume ausgefüllt ist; sie unterscheiden sich nur in der Wahl der Zwischenräume und ihrer Position. Der Blocksatz steht hierbei für den Fall, in dem die Zwischenräume nur zwischen den Wörtern und nicht am Zeilenende auftreten. Diese Art der **Ausrichtung** kann – vor allem bei kurzen Absätzen – zu verwirrenden Lücken führen, die man auch **Gießbächlein** nennt, weil sie – wie ein Bach – durch den Text fließen. (Siehe auch **Axialität** und **S&B**.)

En: JUSTIFIED TYPE/TEXT
Fr: TEXTE JUSTIFIÉ
It: TESTO/CARATTERI GIUSTIFICATI
Spa: JUSTIFICACIÓN

Design: Raphael Pohland, Simone Pohland;
Firma: stilradar, www.stilradar.de

A **B** C D E F G H I J K L M N O P Q R S T U V W X Y Z

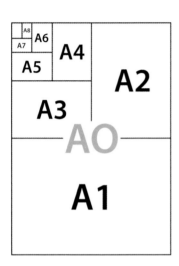

BOGENGRÖSSEN

In Deutschland wurden die Papierformate 1922 durch das Deutsche Institut für Normung e. V. (*DIN*) in der *DIN-Norm 476* mit der Vorzugsreihe A festgelegt. Alle *A-Formate* weisen ein Seitenverhältnis von der Seitenlänge zur Diagonallänge eines Quadrats (~ 1:414) auf. Das ermöglicht es, einen *DIN-A0*-Papierbogen (= 1 m²) ohne Verlust zu teilen. Das Verhältnis von Breite zu Höhe beträgt damit ca. 5:7.

DIN-A-Formate (Breite x Höhe) in Millimetern:
DIN A0 = 841 mm x 1189 mm
DIN A1 = 594 mm x 841 mm
DIN A2 = 420 mm x 594 mm
DIN A3 = 297 mm x 420 mm
DIN A4 = 210 mm x 297 mm
(Deutsches Briefformat)
DIN A5 = 148 mm x 210 mm
DIN A6 = 105 mm x 148 mm
DIN A7 = 74 mm x 105 mm
DIN A8 = 52 mm x 74 mm

En: SHEET SIZES
Fr: FORMAT DE FEUILLE
It: FORMATI DEI FOGLI
Spa: TAMAÑO DE HOJA

BOGENMONTAGE

Eine Sammlung von Seiten, die beidseitig auf einen großen Papierbogen gedruckt sind. Die Seiten werden so angeordnet, dass sich beim Falzen und Schneiden die richtige Reihenfolge für das Einbinden ergibt. (Siehe auch **Ausschießen**.)

En: SIGNATURE
Fr: CAHIER
It: SEGNATURA
Spa: PLIEGO

BUCHEINBAND

Ein Einband, der üblicherweise für fest gebundene Bücher verwendet wird. Hierbei werden zunächst die Seiten mit Faden am Buchrücken zusammengenäht. Der Buchblock wird dann als erstes entlang des Buchrückens verleimt, an den drei übrigen Seiten angepasst und schließlich mit dem Buchdeckel verklebt.

En: CASE BINDING
Fr: RELIURE CARTONNÉE
It: CARTONATURA
Spa: ENCUADERNACIÓN EN TAPA DURA

Design: Claudia Fischer-Appelt, Martina Massong;
Firma: Ligalux GmbH, www.ligalux.de

A B **C D** E F G H I J K L M N O P Q R S T U V W X Y Z

CLIPART

Illustrationen für die Gestaltung von **Layouts**, die sowohl gedruckt als auch im digitalen Format verfügbar sind. Aufgrund ihrer leichten Verfügbarkeit, großen Vielfalt und der Tatsache, dass sie nicht durch *Urheberrechte* geschützt sind, sind sie sehr beliebt. (Siehe auch **Stock-Fotos**.)

En: CLIP ART
Fr: CLIPART
It: CLIP ART
Spa: CLIP ART

Design: Matthias Frey; **Firma:** Q Kreativgesellschaft mbH, www.q-home.de

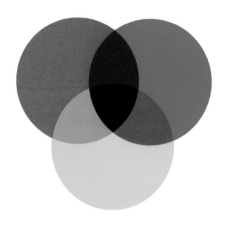

CMYK

Abkürzung für Cyan, Magenta, Gelb und Schwarz, die Farben, die im **Vierfarbdruck** verwendet werden. Wenn sie in Paaren kombiniert werden, reproduzieren die *subtraktiven* Grundfarben Cyan, Magenta, Gelb und Schwarz die *additiven Grundfarben* Rot, Grün und Blau, die den drei verschiedenen Typen der *Lichtrezeptoren* des menschlichen Auges entsprechen. Theoretisch produzieren die drei *subtraktiven* Farben zusammen ein Schwarz, das Ergebnis ist aber nicht satt genug, um die gesamte **Farbpalette** für den **Vierfarbdruck** zu produzieren, weshalb Schwarz separat hinzugefügt wird. Auch *Prozessfarben* genannt.

En: CMYK
Fr: CMJN
It: CMYK
Spa: CMYK

Design: Kate Benjamin, www.moderncat.net

DADAISMUS

Eine Kunstbewegung, die in Zürich (Schweiz) ihren Ursprung nahm und sich als Reaktion gegen den 1. Weltkrieg in ganz Europa ausbreitete. Der Dadaismus stellte mit seinen provokanten bis unsinnigen Darstellungen eine Reihe traditioneller Ansichten bezüglich Kunst, Moral und Religion infrage (allerdings wurden dadaistische Werke in Deutschland düsterer und weitaus politischer, als Hitler in den 1930er Jahren die Macht ergriff). Dadaistische Grafiken weisen verschiedene Einflüsse wie z. B. die strukturierten Leitbilder aus dem **Konstruktivismus** und dem De Stijl auf und verbinden sie etwa mit der Aussagekraft von **Kollagen** und **Fotomontagen** – Techniken, die der Dadaismus als seine eigenen Erfindungen beansprucht.

En: DADA
Fr: DADA
It: DADA
Spa: DADA

Design: Donna S. Atwood, www.atwooddesign.com

A B C **D** E F G H I J K L M N O P Q R S T U V W X Y Z

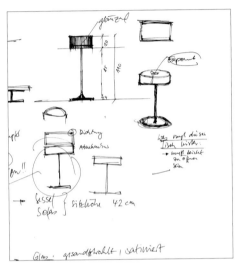

DAUMENNAGELSKIZZE

Ein Begriff, der eine kleine Abbildung oft geringer Qualität beschreibt, die schnell ein Konzept vermittelt. Daumennagelskizzen (engl.: „thumbnail") werden in den ersten Phasen eines Projekts als wesentlicher Bestandteil des Designprozesses verwendet; oft entwickelt sich das finale Design aus der Erstellung vieler stark verfeinerter Daumennagelskizzen. Der Begriff kann auch für kleine, niedrigauflösende Bilder stehen, die als **Platzhalter** ihrer hochauflösenden Version dienen. Online-Bildergalerien z. B. zeigen oft jede Menge Miniaturbilder auf einer einzigen Website an, um eine Übersicht zu schaffen und die Ladezeit zu verringern. Es ist üblich, dass ein Miniaturbild dem Anwender anzeigt, dass hochauflösende Versionen existieren und nur einen Klick entfernt sind.

En: THUMBNAIL
Fr: CRAYONNAGE
It: THUMBNAIL
Spa: MINIATURA

Design: Helge Rieder, Oliver Henn; **Firma:** 804©
Graphic Design, www.achtnullvier.com

DE STIJL

Eine niederländische Kunst- und Designbewegung aus dem frühen 20. Jahrhundert (1917–1931), die allbekannte Gesetzmäßigkeiten durch eine völlig objektive Bildsprache ausdrückte. Bei den **Farben** beschränkte man sich auf neutrale **Farben** (Schwarz, Weiß, Grau) und die **Primärfarben** Rot, Blau und Gelb. Bei den Formen hielt man sich fast ausschließlich an Quadrate und Rechtecke, die entlang der Horizontal- und Vertikalachsen asymmetrisch angeordnet wurden. Es wurde praktisch nur **serifenlose Schrift** verwendet, die häufig mit blockiger handgeschriebener **Auszeichnungsschrift** kombiniert wurde.

En: DE STIJL
Fr: DE STIJL
It: DE STIJL
Spa: DE STIJL

Design: Jan Kruse, Tobias Heidmeier; **Firma:** Ligalux GmbH, www.ligalux.de

Courier
Lucida Sans Typewriter

DICKTENGLEICH (NICHTPROPORTIONALE SCHRIFT)

Ein Begriff, der ein Schriftbild beschreibt, in dem jedes Schriftzeichen dieselbe Breite hat. Das entstehende Bild erinnert an Schreibmaschinenschrift. (Siehe auch **Proportionalschrift**.)

En: MONOSPACED
Fr: CARACTÈRES À CHASSE CONSTANTE
It: MONOSPAZIO
Spa: MONOESPACIADA

ABCD**D**EFGHIJKLMNOPQRSTUVWXYZ

(Monotype Sorts)

(Webdings)

(Zapf Dingbats)

A–Z
10:00–13:00 Uhr
28°–30° Celsius

DINGBATS

Eine große Auswahl besonderer typografischer Schriftzeichen, die u. a. **Symbole** (z. B. mathematische Interpunktionszeichen), Aufzählungszeichen (z. B. Kreise, Sternchen etc.), grafische Ornamente und viele weitere enthält.

En: DINGBATS
Fr: DINGBATS
It: DINGBATS
Spa: DINGBATS

DITHERING

Ein Verfahren, um sich den originalen **Farben** eines digitalen Bildes nur mithilfe der Farben einer vorgegebenen **Farbpalette** anzunähern. Wenn z. B. ein digitales Bild in sog. internettaugliche **Farben** konvertiert wird, wird eine bestimmte Gruppe von 216 verschiedenen Farben (die internettaugliche **Farbpalette**) genutzt, um die Farben des Originals möglichst genau darzustellen. Das wird mithilfe eines „Patchwork" von **Pixeln** bei Computermonitoren und Druckpunkten bei digitalen Druckern erreicht. Ein Patchwork von roten und gelben **Pixeln**/Druckpunkten z. B. könnte Orange darstellen. Obwohl diese Methode Qualitätseinbußen zur Folge hat, kann das Dithering sinnvoll sein, um die zackigen Kanten zu glätten, die entlang benachbarter Farbfelder auftreten können. (Siehe auch **Posterisation**.)

En: DITHER
Fr: TRAMAGE ALÉATOIRE
It: RETINO
Spa: DIFUMINADO

Design: Donna S. Atwood,
www.atwooddesign.com

DIVIS

Ein Strich von der Länge eines Halbgevierts, der das Wort „bis" ersetzt (z. B. 14:00–15:00 oder Montag–Freitag). Wie auch beim **Geviertstrich** gibt es keine Vorgaben für das Setzen von Zwischenräumen vor und hinter einem Divis. Designer und Typografen setzen teilweise Zwischenräume, die sie dann durch **Unterschneiden** anpassen. (Siehe auch **Geviertstrich** und **Trennstrich**.)

En: EN DASH
Fr: TIRET DEMI-CADRATIN
It: LINEETTA EN
Spa: SEMIRRAYA

A B C **D** E F G H I J K L M N O P Q R S T U V W X Y Z

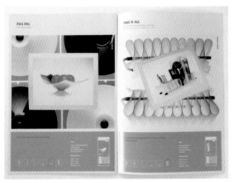

DOPPELSEITEN

Die linke und rechte Seite eines Buches, einer Zeitung, einer Broschüre etc. Computerprogramme zur Erstellung von **Layouts** wie Adobe InDesign® geben Designern die Möglichkeit, Dokumente entweder im Ein-Seiten-Format oder als Doppelseite zu erstellen. (Siehe auch **Rechte/Linke Seite**.)

En: FACING PAGES
Fr: PAGES EN REGARD
It: PAGINE AFFIANCATE
Spa: PÁGINAS ENFRENTADAS

Design: Raphael Pohland, Simone Pohland;
Firma: stilradar, www.stilradar.de

DRAHTHEFTUNG

Eine Art der Bindung, die üblicherweise für Broschüren und bei einigen Magazinen verwendet wird. Die Druckbögen und das Cover werden am gemeinsamen Rücken verschachtelt, mit Heftklammern zusammengehalten und schließlich zugeschnitten.

En: SADDLE-STITCH BINDING
Fr: PIQÛRE MÉTALLIQUE À CHEVAL
It: GRAFFETTATURA
Spa: ENCUADERNACIÓN A CABALLETE

Design: Helge Rieder, Oliver Henn; **Firma:** 804©
Graphic Design, www.achtnullvier.com

DRUCKEINRICHTUNG

Der Vorgang, bei dem die Druckpresse sowie die Geräte zum Lackieren, Falten oder Binden für einen bestimmten Druckvorgang vorbereitet werden. Der Begriff *Makulatur* wird benutzt, um die Papierbögen zu beschreiben, die während dieses Prozesses – oft wiederholt – als Testbögen dienen.

En: MAKEREADY
Fr: MACULE
It: AVVIAMENTO MACCHINA
Spa: ARREGLO

Design: Yee-Haw Industries,
www.yeehawindustries.com

DRUCKFARBEN
Siehe **CMYK** und **Vierfarbdruck**.

ABC**D**EFGHIJKLMNOPQRSTUVWXYZ

DRUCKLACK

Eine Beschichtung auf Wasserbasis, mit der ein schon bedrucktes Blatt Papier überzogen wird, um einen Schimmer (z. B. glänzend oder matt) zu erzeugen und die darunterliegende Tinte vor Verschleiß und Nässe zu schützen. Unbeschichtete Papiere neigen dazu, Tinte aufzunehmen, wodurch gedruckte Bilder verblassen, wohingegen beschichtete Papiere Tinte vor Absorption schützen, wodurch die Farben „frisch" bleiben. Wasserhaltige Beschichtungen werden üblicherweise für gedruckte Materialien wie Magazine und Broschüren genutzt, die stark strapaziert werden.

En: AQUEOUS COATING
Fr: PELLICULAGE AQUEUX
It: RIVESTIMENTO AD ACQUA
Spa: REVESTIMIENTO ACUOSO

Design: Helge Rieder, Oliver Henn; **Firma:** 804© Graphic Design, www.achtnullvier.com

A B C **D E** F G H I J K L M N O P Q R S T U V W X Y Z

DUPLEX

Ein **Graustufenbild**, das mit zwei statt einer **Farbe** gedruckt wird. Obwohl Schwarz oft die primäre Farbe ist, können auch zwei andere Farben verwendet werden. Wenn man mit Schwarz als primärer **Farbe** und einem Grauton als sekundärer **Farbe** druckt, erzielt man mit diesen Tonvarianten ein Resultat, das der original Schwarz-Weiß-Fotografie sehr nahe kommt. Mit einer nicht-neutralen Farbe als Zweitfarbe oder zwei nicht-neutralen **Farben** erzielt man viele interessante Effekte, von zart bis dramatisch. *Triplex* sind **Graustufenbilder,** in drei Farben gedruckt.

En: DUOTONE
Fr: SIMILI DEUX TONS
It: BICROMIA
Spa: BITONO

Lorem ipsum dolor sit amet, consectetuer sadipscing elitr, sed diam nonumy eirmod tempor invidunt ut labore et dolore magna aliquyam erat, sed diam voluptua.

Text 18 pt, Zeilenabstand 18 pt

Lorem ipsum dolor sit amet, consectetuer sadipscing elitr, sed diam nonumy eirmod tempor invidunt ut labore et dolore magna aliquyam erat, sed diam voluptua.

Text 18 pt, Zeilenabstand 24 pt, 6 pt Durchschuss

DURCHSCHUSS UND ZEILENABSTAND

Zeilenabstand ist der in Punkt angegebene Abstand zwischen den Grundlinien aufein-anderfolgender Textzeilen. **Durchschuss** ist der Abstand der Unterlänge der oberen Zeile zur Oberlänge der folgenden Zeile. Anders als beim Bleisatzdruck kann digitale Schrift mit einem negativen Durchschuss gesetzt werden. Das heißt, dass der Schriftgrad (in Punkt) den Zeilenabstand (in Punkt) über-steigt. Obwohl die **Lesbarkeit** darunter leidet, kann ein negativer Durchschuss be-eindruckende Effekte bei Werbegrafik-en, Postern etc. erzielen.

En: LEADING
Fr: INTERLIGNAGE
It: INTERLINEA
Spa: INTERLINEADO

EBENE

Ein *Feature* digitaler Bilderstellungssoftware, das verschiedene Designelemente so behan-delt, als existierten sie auf durchsichtigen Bögen, was dem Designer die Möglichkeit gibt, sie zu editieren, zu kombinieren und bestimmte Teile eines Bildes zu verändern, ohne dass sich dies auf die übrigen Elemente auswirkt. Das finale Bild ist das Ergebnis der Schichtung aller verwendeten Ebenen in einer bestimmten Reihenfolge.

En: LAYER
Fr: CALQUE
It: LIVELLO
Spa: CAPA

Design: Donna S. Atwood,
www.atwooddesign.com

A B C D **E** F G H I J K L M N O P Q R S T U V W X Y Z

Dies sind Auslassungs-
punkte… und dies sind
drei individuelle Punkte...

EGYPTIENNE

Sammelbegriff für serifenbetonte Linear-
Antiqua. Aufgrund ihrer wuchtigen Erschei-
nung und der nur geringen Unterschiede der
Linienstärke der einzelnen Buchstaben sind
sie für Poster, Werbetexte und Überschriften
besser geeignet als für die Anwendung im
Fließtext.

En: EGYPTIAN
Fr: ÉGYPTIENNE
It: CARATTERI EGIZIANI
Spa: EGIPCIO

Design: Alexander Dahlmann; **Firma:** red cell
Werbeagentur GmbH, www.redcell.de

EINBAND

Sammelbegriff für die verschiedenen Verfahren, die Seiten eines Buches, Magazins,
einer Broschüre oder sonstiger mehrseitiger
gedruckter Publikationen zusammenzuhal-
ten. Manche davon wie z. B. die *Ring-* oder
Spiralbindung verwenden Halterungen, die
durch Löcher in jeder Seite befestigt werden
und daher wieder auflösbar sind. Dauerhafte
Bindeverfahren sind u. a. ein fester Einband,
eine **Klebebindung** oder die **Drahtheftung**.

En: BINDING
Fr: RELIURE
It: RILEGATURA
Spa: ENCUADERNACIÓN

Design: Helge Rieder, Oliver Henn; **Firma:** 804©
Graphic Design, www.achtnullvier.com

ELLIPSE (AUSLASSUNGSPUNKTE)

Ein Satzzeichen, das aus einer Reihe von drei
Punkten besteht, die anzeigen, dass Teile
eines Textes weggelassen worden sind –
wenn z. B. Teile eines Zitats, aber nicht das
komplette Zitat verwendet werden oder wenn
ein Satz unvollständig ist (sich am Ende eines
Satzes der Gedanke verliert). Jedes Schriftbild hat dafür sein eigenes Zeichen. Das
Verwenden dieses Satzzeichens anstatt einer
Reihe von drei Punkten vermeidet das Risiko,
dass sich die Punkte am Ende einer Zeile
trennen. Andererseits kann das genaue Aus-
richten der Punktabstände nur erzielt werden,
wenn individuelle Punkte verwendet werden. Viele Stilhandbücher empfehlen einen
Abstand vor und nach jeder Ellipse, als ob
diese ein Wort wäre, aber Typografen bevor-
zugen oft die Ellipse ohne diese Abstände.

En: ELLIPSIS
Fr: POINTS DE SUSPENSION
It: PUNTI DI SOSPENSIONE
Spa: PUNTOS SUSPENSIVOS

A B C D **E F** G H I J K L M N O P Q R S T U V W X Y Z

ABCDEFGHIJKLMNOPQRSTUVWXYZ
0123456789 ⅛¼⅜½⅝¾⅞⅓⅔
ﬀﬁﬃﬄﬂﬅﬆ *ABCDEFGHIJ*
LMNOPQRSTUVWXYZ

EXPERTENSATZ

Eine Reihe von typografischen Zeichen
– neben den Standardzeichen – , wie **Kapitälchen**, altertümliche Ziffern, **Ligaturen** etc.,
einer bestimmten **Schrift**. Für die *Mikrotypografie* mussten Expertensätze früher
gesondert von Grundschriften angeschafft
werden, wohingegen die meisten digitalen
Schriften sie heute schon enthalten.

En: EXPERT SET
Fr: CARACTÈRES ÉTENDUS
It: EXPERT SET
Spa: SET EXPERTO

FARBE

Die unterschiedlich langen Lichtwellen, die
das menschliche Auge wahrnimmt. Objekte
werden in bestimmten Farben erkannt, weil
sie verschieden lange Lichtwellen absorbieren, reflektieren oder übermitteln. Die drei
Grundbestandteile einer Farbe sind der **Farbton**, die **Sättigung** und ihre **Leuchtdichte**
(auch *Farbwert* genannt). Der Begriff Farbe
wird von Typografen auch im Zusammenhang
mit der Gesamthelligkeit bzw. -dunkelheit
einer Textseite oder eines Absatzes im Vergleich zu einem anderen verwendet. (Siehe
auch **Farbkreis**.)

En: COLOR
Fr: COULEUR
It: COLORE/I
Spa: COLOR

Design: Harald Haas; **Firma:** red cell Werbeagentur
GmbH, www.redcell.de

FARBKANÄLE

Die digitalen Informationen bezüglich der relativen Anteile der drei (**RGB**) oder vier (**CMYK**)
Grundfarben, die Farbbilder darstellen. Jeder
Kanal fungiert wie ein **Graustufenbild**, in
dem die grauen *Farbwerte* durch Farbwerte
einer Grundfarbe ersetzt wurden. Das finale
Bild wird – sowohl auf dem Bildschirm als
auch im Druck – durch die Zusammenführung
aller Kanäle eines bestimmten **Farbmodells**
erzeugt.

En: CHANNELS
Fr: CANAUX
It: CANALI
Spa: CANAL

Design: Donna S. Atwood,
www.atwooddesign.com

A B C D E **F** G H I J K L M N O P Q R S T U V W X Y Z

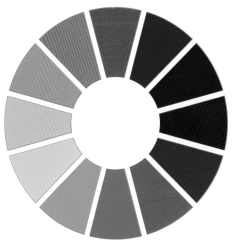

FARBKENNZEICHNUNGSSYSTEM

Farbskalensysteme, die es meist in Form von Farbfächern oder Farbkarten gibt, die mit Ziffern gekennzeichnet sind, und die zur präzisen Festlegung einer **Farbe** dienen. Designer können anhand der Nummer sicherstellen, dass die für ein bestimmtes Projekt gewählte **Farbe** während des Drucks auch korrekt übertragen wird. Für genaue Farbübereinstimmung ist es von großer Wichtigkeit zu wissen, welche(s) Farbübereinstimmungssystem(e) eine Druckerei verwendet.

En: COLOR-MATCHING SYSTEM
Fr: SYSTÈME D'ASSORTIMENT DES COULEURS
It: SISTEMA DI COMBINAZIONE DEI COLORI
Spa: SISTEMA DE AJUSTE DEL COLOR

Design: Helge Rieder, Oliver Henn; **Firma:** 804©
Graphic Design, www.achtnullvier.com

FARBKORREKTUR

Der Prozess, **Farben** eines Digitalfotos oder eines eingescannten Bildes so zu verändern, dass sie dem Original genauer entsprechen. Wird auch angewandt, um das Farbspektrum bzw. die Farbskala der verwendeten Drucktechnik anzupassen.

En: COLOR CORRECTION
Fr: CORRECTION DES COULEURS
It: CORREZIONE DEI COLORI
Spa: CORRECCIÓN DE COLOR

FARBKREIS

Das Farbspektrum in kreisförmiger Darstellung. Der gebräuchlichste Farbkreis, der für das Mischen von Farbpigmenten verwendet wird, hat als Basis die Grundfarben Rot, Gelb und Blau, die in gleichmäßigen Abständen auf dem Kreis verteilt sind. Rot, Gelb und Blau sind reine **Farben**; sie können nicht durch das Mischen von anderen **Farben** erzielt werden. Sie ergeben jedoch in verschiedenen Anteilen zusammengemischt alle weiteren **Farben** des Farbkreises. Andere Farbkreise werden benutzt, um ähnliche Beziehungen innerhalb anderer Farbsysteme wie z. B. dem **RGB**-Modell zu demonstrieren, mit dessen Hilfe Grafiken am Bildschirm angezeigt werden. (Siehe auch **Analoge Farben**, **Komplementärfarben**, **Sekundärfarben** und **Tertiärfarben**.)

En: COLOR WHEEL
Fr: ROUE CHROMATIQUE
It: RUOTA DEI COLORI
Spa: RUEDA DE COLORES

Design: Donna S. Atwood,
www.atwooddesign.com

A B C D E **F** G H I J K L M N O P Q R S T U V W X Y Z

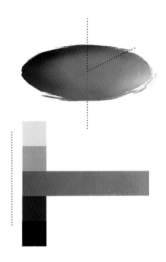

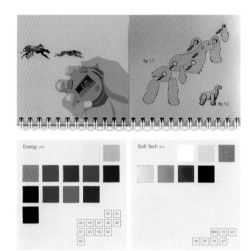

FARBMODELL

Ein System, das **Farbe** nur durch einzelne Farbkomponenten genauestens definiert, die richtig abgestimmt ein breites Farbspektrum bilden können. Die beiden gängigsten Farbmodelle sind **RGB** und **CMYK**, daneben existieren verschiedene andere. *HSB* beispielsweise verwendet Farbcharakteristiken, die an die klassischen Bestandteile des Farbkreises angelehnt sind: **Farbton**, **Sättigung** und **Leuchtdichte**. Das *LAB*-Farbmodell hingegen orientiert sich an den Koordinaten der Farbmessung. Das Farbmodell wird häufig mit dem *Farbraum* verwechselt, der wiederum den Farbbereich beschreibt, den ein bestimmtes Ausgabegerät innerhalb eines bestimmten Farbmodells darstellen kann. Z. B. benutzen ein Tintenstrahldrucker und ein gewerblicher Drucker beide das **CMYK**-Farbmodell; der Bereich von CMYK-Farben, steht für einen spezifischen Farbraum innerhalb des größeren CMYK-Farbmodells.

En: COLOR MODEL
Fr: MODÈLE COLORIMÉTRIQUE
It: MODELLO DI COLORE
Spa: MODELO DE COLOR

Design: Timothy Samara, tsamara_designer@hotmail.com

FARBPALETTE

Eine Auswahl an **Farben**, die entweder von einem Computer (z. B. die internettaugliche *216-color-Farbpalette*) oder von einem Designer bzw. Künstler für ein bestimmtes Projekt festgelegt wird. Farbpaletten werden häufig mithilfe der auf dem **Farbkreis** anschaulich dargestellten Farbbeziehungen erstellt.

En: COLOR PALETTE
Fr: PALETTE DES COULEURS
It: PALETTE DI COLORI
Spa: PALETA DE COLORES

Design: Matthias Frey; **Firma:** Q Kreativgesellschaft mbH, www.q-home.de

FARBRAUM
Siehe **Farbmodell**.

FARBTON

Die Grundcharakteristik einer **Farbe** entsprechend ihrer spezifischen Wellenlänge im Lichtspektrum, die dazu dient, eine **Farbe** von einer anderen zu unterscheiden. Der Farbton hängt mit der relativen Position einer Farbe auf dem **Farbkreis** zusammen.

En: HUE
Fr: TEINTE
It: TONALITÀ
Spa: MATIZ

Design: Donna S. Atwood,
www.atwooddesign.com

A B C D E **F** G H I J K L M N O P Q R S T U V W X Y Z

Frutiger
Frutiger Fett
Bodoni
Bodoni Fett

FETT (SCHRIFTEN)

Ein Schriftbild, in dem die Buchstaben
aus breiteren Konturen bestehen als in der
„normalen" Version derselben Schriftart.
Desktop-Publishing-Programme beinhalten
für gewöhnlich ein Werkzeug, das auf eine
fette Schriftversion umstellt, wodurch die
Konturen dieser **Schrift** lediglich etwas dicker
werden. Korrekte fette **Schriften**, die aus
einem **Schriftsatz** stammen, sind allerdings
so gestaltet, dass sie sich proportional und
stimmig in ihre **Schriftfamilien** einreihen.

En: BOLD/BOLDFACE
Fr: GRAS, CARACTÈRES GRAS
It: GRASSETTO
Spa: NEGRITA

FIRMENERSCHEINUNGSBILD

Die „Persönlichkeit" einer Firma, die visuell
(sowohl intern als auch nach außen) durch
ihre spezifische Markenkennzeichnung
dargestellt wird. Das Erscheinungsbild setzt
sich typischerweise aus **Logos**, Schriftzügen, bestimmten **Farbpaletten** (oft durch ein
Farbkennzeichnungssystem festgelegt),
einheitliche **Layouts** für Dokumente und
Verpackungen und Richtlinien zusammen, die
vorgeben, wie welche Elemente einzusetzen
sind, um die Kontinuität innerhalb einer Firma
zu gewährleisten. Große Unternehmen können
mehrere Marken besitzen, die gemeinsame
optische Elemente verwenden, wodurch diese
Marken wiederum Teil eines größeren, überge-
ordneten Firmenerscheinungsbildes sind.

En: IDENTITY
Fr: IDENTITÉ
It: IDENTITÀ
Spa: IDENTIDAD

Design: Helge Rieder, Oliver Henn; **Firma:** 804©
Graphic Design, www.achtnullvier.com

Donec quam felis, ultricies nec,
pellentesque eu, pretium quis,
sem. Nulla consequat massavar
quis enim. Donec pede justo,
fringilla vel, aliquet nec, vulputate eget, arcu. In enim justo,
rhoncus ut, imperdiet a, venenatis vitae, justo. Nullam dictum
felis eu pede mollis pretium.
Integer tincidunt. Cras dapibus.

FLATTERSATZ

Die unregelmäßige Kontur zwischen einem
Textblock und dessen **Seitenrändern** als
Ergebnis unterschiedlicher **Zeilenlängen**. Bei
linksbündigem Text befindet sich der Flattersatz entlang des rechten Seitenrands; bei
rechtsbündigem Text entsprechend entlang
des linken Seitenrands. Text im **Blocksatz**
weist keinen Flattersatz auf. Um die **Lesbarkeit** zu gewährleisten und zur Vermeidung
optischer Ablenkung durch geometrische
oder übermäßig rhythmische Flattersätze,
bemühen sich Typografen und Designer meist
um einen ausgeglichen wirkenden Flattersatz.

En: RAG
Fr: DRAPEAU
It: BANDIERA
Spa: BANDERA

A B C D E **F** G H I J K L M N O P Q R S T U V W X Y Z

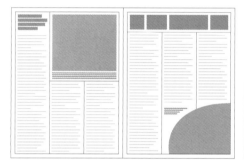

FLIESSTEXT

Ein Begriff, der den Haupttext innerhalb eines Buches, einer Broschüre oder anderer Veröffentlichungen bezeichnet. In diesem Kontext umfasst der Fließtext weder die **Titelei**, noch **Anhang**, **Überschriften**, **Untertitel** und dergleichen. Der Begriff Fließtext kann sich aber auch auf den Haupttext einer Website beziehen.

En: BODY COPY
Fr: CORPS DU TEXTE
It: CORPO DEL TESTO
Spa: CUERPO DE TEXTO

Design: Donna S. Atwood,
www.atwooddesign.com

FOKUS

Das Designelement innerhalb eines **Lay-outs**, das als erstes die Aufmerksamkeit des Betrachters bekommt; der Punkt, an dem das Augenbewegungsmuster beginnt. Blick-punkte können mithilfe verschiedener Mittel wie z. B. **Farbe**, **Größenverhältnisse** oder **Kompositionen** gesetzt werden. Besonders die Werbung profitiert von allein stehenden und eindeutigen Blickpunkten.

En: FOCAL POINT
Fr: POINT CENTRAL
It: PUNTO FOCALE
Spa: PUNTO FOCAL

Design: Michael Thiele, Martin Schonhoff;
Firma: Die Transformer, www.dietransformer.de

FOLIENPRÄGUNG

Ein Verfahren, bei dem mithilfe eines erhitzten Prägewerkzeugs ein dünner Plastikfilm auf einen Papierbogen aufgetragen wird, meist, um **Logos**, Illustrationen, **Schrift** oder andere Designelemente hervorzuheben. Diese Folie ist in einer Vielzahl von **Farben** und Glanzstu-fen erhältlich sowie als Metallicfolie. Mithilfe deckender Folien kann auch helle **Farbe** auf einen dunklen Hintergrund aufgetragen werden; durchsichtige Folien simulieren einen *Lackeffekt*. Auch *Heißfolienprägung* genannt.

En: FOIL STAMPING
Fr: DORURE
It: STAMPA A LAMINA DI PLASTICA
Spa: ESTAMPADO METÁLICO

Design: Matthias Frey; **Firma:** Q Kreativgesellschaft
mbH, www.q-home.de

A B C D E **F** G H I J K L M N O P Q R S T U V W X Y Z

FORMFLÄCHENGESTALTUNG

Ein Aspekt der visuellen Wahrnehmung,
der auf der Beziehung zwischen einer Form
– einer Zahl, eines Objekts, einer geometrischen Form oder einem Buchstaben – und
der umgebung basiert: Eine Form ist nur
auf einem Hintergrund wahrnehmbar, wenn
sie sich von diesem unterscheidet. Durch
das sorgfältige Manipulieren der Elemente
können Designer erstaunliche **Layouts** mit
einfachsten Formen kreieren. Das kann auch
besonders wichtig beim Gestalten von **Logos**
sein, wo viel Inhalt zu einer relativ simplen,
einfach zu identifizierenden Form reduziert
werden muss. Gute Flächengestaltungen
haben einen einfach zu identifizierenden
Schwerpunkt und wirken harmonisch,
während unklare **Kompositionen** die Wahrnehmung des Betrachters herausfordern.
(Siehe auch **Freie Fläche**
und **Gestaltete Fläche**.)

En: FIGURE-GROUND
Fr: DESSIN EN GRISÉ
It: FIGURA-SFONDO
Spa: RELACIÓN FIGURA-FONDO

Design: Fauxpas Grafik, www.fauxpas.ch

A B C D E **F** G H I J K L M N O P Q R S T U V W X Y Z

FOTOMONTAGE

Ein Begriff, der den Prozess beschreibt, bei dem eine fotografische **Komposition** mittels der Zusammenstellung mehrerer Elemente anderer Fotos erstellt wird. Die fertige Fotomontage entsteht durch Ausschneiden und Aufkleben bzw. Einfügen, entweder im wörtlichen Sinn oder mithilfe digitaler Bildbearbeitungssoftware. Handgemachte Fotomontagen werden manchmal nach ihrer Fertigstellung abfotografiert, sodass der Eindruck entsteht, es handele sich dabei um ein einziges „echtes" Foto. (Siehe auch **Kollage**.)

En: PHOTOMONTAGE
Fr: PHOTOMONTAGE
It: FOTOMONTAGGIO
Spa: FOTOMONTAJE

Design: Harald Haas; **Firma:** red cell Werbeagentur GmbH, www.redcell.de

FRAKTUR (SCHRIFTEN)

Kunstvolle **Schriften**, die in der Mitte des 15. Jahrhunderts entstanden sind. Frakturschriften wurden zuerst von deutschen Druckern entwickelt, die die Handschriften der damaligen Schriftgelehrten imitierten. Häufig verwendete andere Begriffe sind *Textura*, *Old English* oder *Gotische Schrift*, die ähnlich verzierte Schriftbilder bezeichnen. Mit *Gotischen Schriften* bezeichnet man sowohl verzierte Frakturschriften als auch frühe **serifenlose** Schriften, die wenig mit der Frakturschrift gemeinsam haben.

En: BLACKLETTER
Fr: GOTHIQUE
It: BLACKLETTER
Spa: LETRA GÓTICA

Design: Matthias Frey; **Firma:** Q Kreativgesellschaft mbH, www.q-home.de

FREIE FLÄCHE

Im Allgemeinen beschreibt der Begriff die Lücken, die durch die Anordnung zweier oder mehrerer Designelemente innerhalb der sog. **gestalteten Fläche** entstehen. Häufig wird dieser Ausdruck im Zusammenhang mit großen **Layouts** verwendet, kann sich aber auch auf Elemente der **Typografie** beziehen. Hier entstehen durch die einzelnen Buchstabensätze Bereiche freier sowie **gestalteter Fläche**. Bei **Logos** achtet man – aufgrund der Tatsache, dass sie meist nur von kleiner Größe sind – sorgfältig auf das Verhältnis zwischen freier und gestalteter Fläche. (Siehe auch **Formflächengestaltung** und **Weißraum**.)

En: NEGATIVE SPACE
Fr: ESPACE NÉGATIF
It: SPAZIO NEGATIVO
Spa: ESPACIO NEGATIVO

Design: Grafikstudio Steinert, www.grafikstudio-steinert.com

A B C D E **F G** H I J K L M N O P Q R S T U V W X Y Z

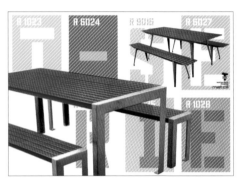

1	½	¼
Geviert	Halbgeviert (Divis)	Viertelgeviert

FUTURISMUS

Eine radikale Kunstbewegung in Europa, die – ausgehend von Italien – im ersten Teil des 20. Jahrhunderts entstand (ca. 1909–1930). Der Futurismus versuchte, die Geschwindigkeit und den Lärm des Maschinenzeitalters in Kunst und Design zu integrieren. **Kollagen** und **Fotomontagen** sollten – als Techniken zur Andeutung filmischer Bewegung – diese Energie darstellen. Den größten Einfluss des Futurismus auf das Grafikdesign stellte jedoch die Verwendung von optisch beeindruckenden Schriftzügen dar. Verschiedene Schriftbilder in einer Vielzahl von Schriftgraden – teilweise in skurrilen Winkeln oder gänzlich verzerrt gesetzt – fanden innerhalb eines **Layouts** Platz, wobei **fette** und **kursive Schrift** Schwerpunkte anzeigte.

En: FUTURISM
Fr: FUTURISME
It: FUTURISMO
Spa: FUTURISMO

GESTALTETE FLÄCHE

Ein allgemeiner Begriff, der die Flächen eines **Layouts** oder Designelements beschreibt, die komplett ausgestaltet sind (die entstehenden Lücken werden als **freie Flächen** bezeichnet). Obwohl man mit gestalteter Fläche oft Elemente kompletter **Layouts** beschreibt, lässt sich der Begriff auch auf die **Typografie** übertragen, wo Buchstaben mit benachbarten Buchstaben Beziehungen zwischen gestalteter und freier Fläche entstehen lassen. **Logos** werden aufgrund der Tatsache, dass sie meist sehr klein abgebildet werden, mit besonderer Berücksichtigung auf den Zusammenhang zwischen gestalteter und **freier Fläche** erstellt. (Siehe auch **Freie Fläche**, **Formflächengestaltung** und **Weißraum**.)

En: POSITIVE SPACE
Fr: ESPACE POSITIF
It: SPAZIO POSITIVO
Spa: ESPACIO POSITIVO

Design: Fauxpas Grafik, www.fauxpas.ch

GESTRICHENES PAPIER
Siehe **Drucklack**.

GEVIERT

Eine relative Maßeinheit, die sich immer auf den verwendeten Schriftgrad in „points" (Punkten) bezieht. Für den Schriftgrad 12 entspricht ein Geviert 12 Punkten; im Schriftgrad 10 ist ein Geviert 10 Punkte breit usw. Ursprünglich stammt der Begriff aus dem *Bleisatzdruck*, bei dem er die Höhe des Metallblocks eines Buchstabens angibt. Ein Geviertquadrat ist ein Metallblock, der bei einer Höhe und Breite von je einem Geviert als Abstandhalter dient, um einen Geviertabstand zu erzeugen. Obwohl aber alle Metallblöcke gleichen Schriftgrads dieselbe Höhe haben, variieren die Höhen der eigentlichen Buchstaben stark von Schriftbild zu Schriftbild. Daher ist das Geviert nur eine ungefähre Angabe für die tatsächliche Schriftgröße einer bestimmten **Schrift**. Noch ungenauer sind die Angaben für digitale Schrift, da es hier keinerlei materielle Bezugsgrößen gibt. (Siehe auch **Geviertstrich** und **Geviertabstand**.)

En: EM
Fr: CADRATIN
It: EM
Spa: CUADRATÍN

A B C D E F **G** H I J K L M N O P Q R S T U V W X Y Z

Reetue dolore dolent nulputate min ut adio ver iure eu feum nulutpat. Ut lam delenim illaor sequatu mmolore vel in henim velit, vullaore tat. Igna alis am vel doliam doloborem nonummt vero od tis dolesectem nonsecte eugait at wisi.

Si. Lore min utpat. Dui tisit ex eros ercing exer ute faccum et la cor sisl utpatio eui eugiam, secte vullaore min henim dionull utpation vel ut auat inis ea feuis et autpat. Esequis nibh ea commolut ver sendre vulla feuis nisit nullaor tionumsandre vel duiscilit alism odolore cortie faccum zzrit ing etuerci lismod dolutat ilit praesenit veros nullam,

Geviertabstand |— hat die Länge…

GEVIERTABSTAND

Ein Zwischenraum von der Breite eines Gevierts innerhalb einer Textzeile. Digitale Schriftarten enthalten den Geviertabstand als Sonderzeichen mit einer festgelegten Breite, die sich von den Zwischenräumen unterscheidet, die man mithilfe der Leertaste setzt. Letztere variieren nämlich, da die Software jede Textzeile einzeln zusammensetzt.

En: EM SPACE
Fr: ESPACE CADRATIN
It: SPAZIO EM
Spa: ESPACIO DE CUADRATÍN

…und Einschübe — etwa in diesem Beispiel — kann der Gedankenstrich das Komma als Satzzeichen ersetzen.

GEVIERTSTRICH

Ein Strich von der Länge eines **Gevierts**, der innerhalb einer Textzeile eine Pause schafft, meist um einen eingeschobenen Satz einzuleiten. In den meisten Veröffentlichungen wird vor und hinter einem Geviertsrich ein Zwischenraum gelassen.

En: EM DASH
Fr: TIRET CADRATIN
It: LINEETTA EM
Spa: RAYA

GIESSBÄCHLEIN

Die ablenkenden vertikalen Lücken, die in einem Textblock als Folge unkontrollierter Anordnung von Zwischenräumen zwischen Wörtern entstehen können. Gießbächlein treten aufgrund der meist unnatürlichen, von der Software bestimmten Abstände zwischen Wörtern vor allem im **Blocksatz** auf. Die beste Methode zur Vermeidung oder Verminderung dieser „Bäche" ist die Überarbeitung der Textzeilen mittels **Sperrung** und/oder **Silbentrennungen**. (Siehe auch **S&B** und **Textumbruch**.)

En: RIVERS
Fr: LÉZARDES
It: CANALETTI
Spa: CALLE

ABCDEF**G**HIJKLMNOPQRSTUVWXYZ

Schriftlinie

GRAUSTUFENBILD

Ein Bild, das verschiedene Grau-, Weiß- und
Schwarztöne beinhaltet. Farbfotos können
auf digitalem Weg in Graustufenbilder konvertiert werden; das geschieht mithilfe von
Softwareanwendungen, die jeden Farbwert in
seinen entsprechenden Grauton umrechnen,
sodass ein Bild entsteht, das eine Schwarz-
Weiß-Aufnahme simuliert. (Siehe auch
Monochromatisch.)

En: GRAYSCALE
Fr: ÉCHELLE DE GRIS
It: SCALA DEI GRIGI
Spa: ESCALA DE GRISES

GRÖSSENVERHÄLTNIS

Die wahrgenommene Größe oder Gewich-
tung eines Designelements in Relation zu
anderen in demselben **Layout**. Das Größen-
verhältnis kann ganz einfach Unterschiede
aufzeigen, z. B. wenn große **Schrift** genutzt
wird, um anzuzeigen, welche Teile eines
Textes von größerer Wichtigkeit sind. Häufig
sind Unterschiede im Ausmaß jedoch weitaus
subtiler. Objekte mit ungleichen Umrissen
z. B. neigen dazu, unterschiedlich groß zu
wirken, obwohl sie geometrisch gesehen die
gleiche Fläche einnehmen. Form und **Farbe**
beeinflussen ebenso die Wirkung eines Elements wie der Kontext, in dem es steht. Die
Große eines Objekts wird von seinem Umfeld
bestimmt.

En: SCALE
Fr: ÉCHELLE
It: SCALA
Spa: ESCALA

Design: Raphael Pohland, Simone Pohland;
Firma: stilradar, www.stilradar.de

GRUNDLINIE (SCHRIFTLINIE)

Eine Referenzlinie für die korrekte horizontale
Anordnung eines Textes. Die unteren Kanten
von Großbuchstaben und den Kleinbuchstaben, die keine **Unterlänge** haben, liegen auf
oder dicht an der Grundlinie. Eigentlich sind
es sogar nur die Kleinbuchstaben mit flachem
Stand, wie h und i, die genau auf der Grundlinie stehen. Die Buchstaben mit rundem
Stand hingegen, wie o und u, gehen etwas
darüber hinaus. Die entstehende „optische
Täuschung" zeigt die Bedeutung der **optischen Ausrichtung** bei der Feinregulierung
der detaillierten **Typografie**.

En: BASELINE
Fr: LIGNE DE BASE
It: LINEA DI BASE
Spa: LÍNEA DE BASE

A B C D E F G **H** I J K L M N O P Q R S T U V W X Y Z

Begriff für einen Buchstaben, der am Anfang eines Buchkapitels oder am Beginn eines Absatzes steht. Eine Initiale kann sich über mehrere Zeilen erstrecken bzw. ihr Schriftgrad kann um das Vielfache größer sein als der der Grundschrift.

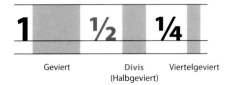

Geviert   Divis   Viertelgeviert
              (Halbgeviert)

Unsere Öffnungszeiten: Mo. Fr. 9⊦–13:00 Uhr und 15:00⊦–18:30 Uhr

HÄNGENDE INITIALE

Der Anfangsbuchstabe des ersten Worts in einem Absatz, der eine größere **Punktgröße** als die anderen Buchstaben des Textes hat und der sich größenmäßig über mehrere Zeilen erstrecken kann. Für zusätzliche Wirkung werden Initialen oft in einer ganz anderen **Schrifttype** als der restliche Text gesetzt. Sie werden nach Anzahl der Zeilen, über die sie sich erstrecken, angegeben. Eine dreizeilige **Initiale** erstreckt sich über die erste, zweite und dritte Zeile des Absatzes. (Siehe auch **Initiale** und **Stehende Initiale**.)

En: DROP CAPITAL/CAP
Fr: LETTRINE
It: CAPOLETTERA
Spa: MAYÚSCULA CAÍDA

HALBGEVIERT

Eine typografische Maßeinheit, die halb so breit ist wie ein **Geviert**. (Siehe auch **Divis** und **Halbgeviertabstand**.)

En: EN
Fr: DEMI-CADRATIN
It: EN
Spa: MEDIO CUADRATÍN

HALBGEVIERTABSTAND

Ein Zwischenraum von der Länge eines Halbgevierts in einer Textzeile. Wie den **Geviertabstand** enthalten digitale **Schriften** den Halbgeviertabstand als Sonderzeichen. Da er eine feste Breite besitzt, bleibt ein Halbgeviertabstand – anders als durch die Leertaste gesetzte Zwischenräume – auch dann unverändert, wenn die Software die Textzeilen zusammensetzt.

En: EN SPACE
Fr: ESPACE DEMI-CADRATIN
It: SPAZIO EN
Spa: ESPACIO DE MEDIO CUADRATÍN

ABCDEFG**H**IJKLMNOPQRSTUVWXYZ

HALBTON

Ein **Graustufenbild**, in dem die gesamte farbliche Bandbreite in ein Gitter kleiner schwarzer Punkte oder Halbtonraster umgewandelt ist. Dunklere Bereiche des Bildes werden durch Flächen größerer Punkte dargestellt, hellere Bereiche mithilfe kleinerer Punkte. Halbtöne, die mit den jeweiligen **Farbkanälen** korrespondieren, werden miteinander kombiniert, um im **Vierfarbdruck** das gesamte Farbspektrum sichtbarer **Farben** zu simulieren. Das gleiche Prinzip kann auch maßstäblich vergrößert werden und so interessante visuelle Effekte erzielen.

En: HALFTONE
Fr: SIMILI
It: MEZZITONI
Spa: MEDIO TONO

Design: Raphael Pohland, Simone Pohland;
Firma: stilradar, www.stilradar.de

A B C D E F G **H** I J K L M N O P Q R S T U V W X Y Z

HERVORGEHOBENES ZITAT

Ein Zitat aus einem Artikel oder einem anderen Text, das außerhalb des ursprünglichen Kontexts (aber für gewöhnlich auf derselben Seite) platziert und so gesetzt wird, dass es die Aufmerksamkeit des Lesers erweckt. Hervorgehobene Zitate werden oft in einer größeren, mitunter etwas anderen **Schrift** gesetzt als der Haupttext. Eine noch deutlichere Abhebung kann durch **Farbe**, dekorative Elemente, **Rahmen** etc. erreicht werden.

En: PULL QUOTE
Fr: EXERGUE
It: CITAZIONE ESTERNA
Spa: SUMARIO

Design: Matthias Frey; **Firma:** Q Kreativgesellschaft mbH, www.q-home.de

HIERARCHIE

Eine erkennbare Ordnung, die durch Unterschiede in der Größe, Position, Ausprägung und **Farbe** sowie bei einigen anderen optischen Hinweisen festgelegt wird. **Überschriften** und **Untertitel** schaffen eine Ordnung innerhalb längerer Publikationen. Durch die Anordnung von Elementen in einer hierarchischen Art und Weise „führt" der Designer den Betrachter/Leser durch den Aufbau einer Visitenkarte, Broschüre, eines Posters, Buches oder einer anderen gestalterischen Arbeit, indem er die einzelnen Elemente nach und nach in einer sinnvollen Reihenfolge erkennen lässt. „Flache" Hierarchien hingegen können langweilig und/oder sogar verwirrend wirken.

En: HIERARCHY
Fr: HIÉRARCHIE
It: GERARCHIA TIPOGRAFICA
Spa: JERARQUÍA

Design: Raphael Pohland, Simone Pohland; **Firma:** stilradar, www.stilradar.de

HINWEIS

Eine oft mit einer **Linie** und/oder einem Pfeil einhergehende Textpassage, die als Beschriftung für wichtige Bereiche eines Fotos, einer Illustration oder einer anderen gestalterischen Arbeit innerhalb eines **Layouts** dient. Der Begriff kann sich auch auf einen Textabschnitt beziehen, der durch die Verwendung eines anderen Schriftbilds, einer anderen **Farbe**, Größe etc. sowohl optisch als auch inhaltlich hervorgehoben wird. (Siehe auch **Bilduntersschrift** und **Hervorgehobenes Zitat**.)

En: CALLOUT
Fr: CHIFFRES RÉFÉRENCES
It: CALLOUT
Spa: LLAMADA

Design: Alexander Dahlmann; **Firma:** red cell Werbeagentur GmbH, www.redcell.de

A B C D E F G **HI** J K L M N O P Q R S T U V W X Y Z

Several recent studies[3]...

$$\tfrac{3}{4} \times \tfrac{1}{2} = \tfrac{3}{8}$$

$$A^2 + B^2 = C^2$$

Tuesday, July 4th

HOCHDRUCK

Erstmals wurde dieses *Reliefdruckverfahren* mit der im 15. Jahrhundert in Deutschland erfundenen Druckpresse angewandt. Textblöcke und Illustrationen werden in Spiegelschrift auf der Presse fixiert, damit sie nach dem Druck auf Papier richtig gelesen werden können. Ihre Oberfläche wird mit Tinte bedeckt und gleichmäßig auf das Papier gedrückt. Benutzte man früher Bleisätze und Holzbuchstaben, verwendet man heute meist eine Polymerplatte, die mittels einer digitalen Datei erstellt wird. Diese neuartige Technologie erlaubt auch bei kleinen Druckvorgängen eine noch nie da gewesene Designvielfalt und ermöglichte einer beinahe vergessenen Kunst ein Revival.

En: LETTERPRESS
Fr: IMPRESSION TYPOGRAPHIQUE
It: RILIEVOGRAFIA
Spa: IMPRESIÓN TIPOGRÁFICA

Design: Helge Rieder, Oliver Henn; **Firma:** 804©
Graphic Design, www.achtnullvier.com

HOCHGESTELLTE SCHRIFTZEICHEN

Wie **tiefgestellte** Buchstaben sind hochgestellte Buchstaben Schriftzeichen, die in einer kleineren Größe gesetzt werden als der Haupttext. Die Anwendung hochgestellter **Schrift** jedoch hängt von ihrem Verwendungszweck ab. Als Zahl zur Markierung einer Fußnote oder als Zähler eines Bruchs werden ihre Kopfteile entlang der *K-Linie* (oberste Kante der Großbuchstaben) ausgerichtet. In mathematischen oder wissenschaftlichen Ausdrücken werden sie dagegen mittig auf der K-*Linie* angeordnet. Kleinbuchstaben werden auch teilweise als an der *K-Linie* ausgerichtete hochgestellte Buchstaben verwendet.

En: SUPERSCRIPT
Fr: EXPOSANT
It: APICE/I
Spa: SUPERÍNDICE

INITIALE

Ein dekorativer Großbuchstabe, der als Anfangsbuchstabe (Initiale) des ersten Wortes eines Absatzes für gewöhnlich in größerem Schriftgrad als der umstehende Text gesetzt wird. Initialen können auch in einer anderen Schriftart gesetzt oder in einer anderen **Farbe** gedruckt werden, um als Blickfang zu dienen. Von vielen Variationen sind die **hängende Initiale** und die **stehende Initiale** die am häufigsten verwendeten. Wie **Zierbuchstaben** sollte auch die Initiale selbst in übermäßig langen Publikationen sparsam eingesetzt werden.

En: INITIAL CAPITAL/CAP
Fr: INITIALE
It: LETTERA MAIUSCOLA INIZIALE
Spa: MAYÚSCULA INICIAL

Design: Peter Shikany, Judy Smith; **Firma:** P.S. Studios, www.psstudios.com

A B C D E F G H **I J K** L M N O P Q R S T U V W X Y Z

INTERACTION DESIGN

Das Beschreiben, Definieren und Erstellen von Elementen eines Produkts, eines Systems oder einer Organisation, mit denen eine Person interagieren kann. Meist entstehen komplexe technische Benutzeroberflächen, zum Beispiel von Websites oder tragbaren Elektrogeräten, aber auch simple Interaktionsmöglichkeiten erfordern ein durchdachtes Design. Der Griff einer Kaffeetasse z. B. sollte für den einfachen, intuitiven Gebrauch gestaltet werden, was aber bei Weitem nicht immer der Fall ist. Designer, die in diesem Bereich tätig sind, setzen bei ihrer Arbeit u. a. auf Benutzererfahrung und Erkenntnisse der Wahrnehmungspsychologie und Anthropologie.

En: INTERACTION DESIGN
Fr: DESIGN NUMÉRIQUE
It: DESIGN INTERATTIVO
Spa: DISEÑO INTERACTIVO

Design: Barski Design, www.barskidesign.com

JUGENDSTIL

Ein zwischen den 1880er Jahren und dem Ausbruch des Ersten Weltkriegs in großen Teilen Europas – und für kurze Zeit auch in den USA – vorherrschender, höchst dekorativer Stil in Architektur und Design. Der Jugendstil, wie seine französische Übersetzung „Art Nouveau" vermuten lässt, versuchte, eine gänzlich neue Ästhetik zu erzeugen. Das chaotische Durcheinander der Viktorianischen Ära sollte durch organische, kurvenreiche Formen abgelöst werden. Beliebte Motive waren Pflanzen und Tiere (vor allem Vögel) sowie der weibliche Körper, oft in einer weitaus abstrakteren Darstellung als es in viktorianischen Bildern noch üblich gewesen war.

En: ART NOUVEAU
Fr: ART NOUVEAU
It: ART NOUVEAU
Spa: ART NOUVEAU

Kochbuchautorinnen: Henriette Davidis und Louise Holle

KALLIGRAFIE (SCHÖNSCHREIBKUNST)

Leitet sich von den griechischen Wörtern „kalli" und „graphos" ab und bedeutet „schönes Schreiben". Sie ist eine kunstvolle Art der Handschrift, bei der man üblicherweise traditionelle Schreibgeräte wie Schreibfeder oder Pinsel gebraucht. Typisch für die Kalligrafie sind fließende, schwungvolle Buchstaben und die unterschiedliche Dicke ihrer Konturen.

En: CALLIGRAPHY
Fr: CALLIGRAPHIE
It: CALLIGRAFIA
Spa: CALIGRAFÍA

Design: Teri Kahan, Richard Stumpf; **Firma:** Teri Kahan Design, www.terikahandesign.com

ABCDEFGHIJ**K**LMNOPQRSTUVWXYZ

In unserer modernen…

In unserer modernen…

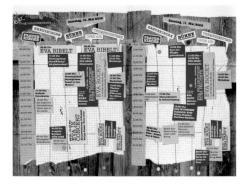

KAPITÄLCHEN

Großbuchstaben mit Proportionen und Konturen, die sich den Kleinbuchstaben eines Schriftbilds anpassen. Kapitälchen werden aus demselben Grund in einer Textzeile benutzt, aus dem gleich große Zahlen benutzt werden: Sie sind weniger aufdringlich als ihre Alternativen. Bei einem Akronym inmitten eines Satzes z. B. wäre eine Aneinanderreihung von Großbuchstaben extrem ablenkend. Ein weiterer Vorteil von Kapitälchen sind ihre Proportionen, die auch in kleinem Schriftgrad eine hohe **Leserlichkeit** gewährleisten.

En: SMALL CAPITALS/CAPS
Fr: PETITES CAPITALES
It: MAIUSCOLETTI
Spa: VERSALITA

KLEBEBINDUNG

Eine üblicherweise für Taschenbücher verwendete Art der Bindung, bei der Druckbögen in der richtigen Reihenfolge zusammengenommen, entlang ihrer Bindungskanten begradigt und beschnitten werden und mittels eines flexiblen Klebemittels an das Buchcover geklebt werden, sodass der Buchrücken entsteht.

En: PERFECT BINDING
Fr: RELIURE SANS COUTURE
It: RILEGATURA PERFETTA
Spa: ENCUADERNACIÓN A LA AMERICANA

KOLLAGE

Eine Technik, eine Darstellung zu erschaffen, indem man Papiere, Stoffe, Fotos oder andere Dinge auf einem Brett oder einer Leinwand, oft in ungewohnter Art und Weise, zusammenfügt. Der Name leitet sich vom französischen „coller" ab, was so viel bedeutet wie „festkleben" oder „befestigen". Kollagen können auch digital erstellt werden, indem man eine Reihe von digitalen Elementen – häufig eingescannte Bilder von dreidimensionalen Objekten mit verschiedenen Oberflächenstrukturen – in der Art einer „Bastelarbeit" zusammenfügt. (Siehe auch **Fotomontage**.)

En: COLLAGE
Fr: COLLAGE
It: COLLAGE
Spa: COLLAGE

Design: Claudia Fischer-Appelt, Jan Kruse, Thomas Kappes, Tobias Heidemeier; **Firma:** Ligalux GmbH, www.ligalux.de

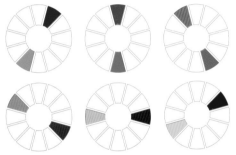

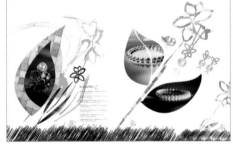

KOMPLEMENTÄRFARBEN

Farben, die sich auf dem **Farbkreis** gegen-überliegen, wie z. B. Rot und Grün auf dem Pigmentfarbkreis. Sie werden auch *Kont-rastfarben* genannt. Die Verwendung von Komplementärfarben in einem Design kann überwältigend wirken. Es ist daher üblicher, ein sog. *Teilkomplementäres Farbschema* anzuwenden, in dem eine Farbe mit den zwei **Farben** kombiniert wird, die auf dem **Farb-kreis** an ihre Komplementärfarbe angrenzen.

En: COMPLEMENTARY COLORS
Fr: COULEURS COMPLÉMENTAIRES
It: COLORI COMPLEMENTARI
Spa: COLORES COMPLEMENTARIOS

Design: Donna S. Atwood,
www.atwooddesign.com

KOMPOSITION

Ein allgemeiner Begriff, der die Anordnung von Designelementen in einem **Layout** beschreibt, deren Wirkung häufig mithilfe abstrakter Begriffe wie **Balance**, **Kontrast**, Linienführung etc. ausgedrückt wird. Kom-position kann auch als Beschreibung für ein **Layout** verwendet werden, das verschiedene Elemente enthält.

En: COMPOSITION
Fr: COMPOSITION
It: COMPOSIZIONE
Spa: COMPOSICIÓN

Design: Raphael Pohland, Simone Pohland;
Firma: stilradar, www.stilradar.de

KONSTRUKTIVISMUS

Eine russische Bewegung in den 1920er Jahren, die sich mit den Zielen der Revo-lution identifizierte und Avantgardekunst und-design (vor allem Einflüsse von **Kubis-mus** und **Futurismus**) mit dieser politischen Haltung verband. Charakteristisch für den Konstruktivismus waren abstrakte, geome-trische Formen, **fette Schriften**, **Layouts**, die mit den horizontalen/vertikalen Richtlinien brachen, sowie eine **Farbpalette**, die häufig auf Rot, Schwarz und Weiß beschränkt war. **Kollagen** und **Fotomontagen** – Techniken aus dem **Dadaismus** – wurden ebenfalls genutzt, um ausdrucksstarkes Kommunikati-onsdesign zu gestalten.

En: CONSTRUCTIVISM
Fr: CONSTRUCTIVISME
It: COSTRUTTIVISMO
Spa: CONSTRUCTIVISMO

Design: Fauxpas Grafik, www.fauxpas.ch

A B C D E F G H I J **K** L M N O P Q R S T U V W X Y Z

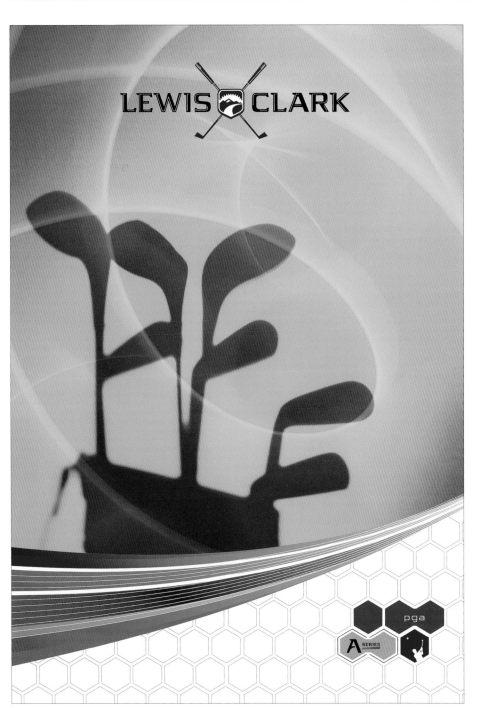

KONTRAST

Ganz allgemein gesagt ist der Kontrast nichts weiter als der Unterschied zwischen zwei Designelementen. Große **Schrift** z. B. kann als Kontrast zu kleiner **Schrift** verwendet werden; je größer der Unterschied der Schriftgrößen, desto größer ist der Kontrast. Richtig eingesetzt kann man **Layouts** mithilfe von Kontrasten optisch sehr interessant und ansprechend gestalten. Strukturen, **Farben**, Formen, **Linien** und andere Elemente können kontrastieren. (Siehe auch **Balance, Komplementärfarben** und **Formflächengestaltung**.)

En: CONTRAST
Fr: CONTRASTE
It: CONTRASTO
Spa: CONTRASTE

Design: Raphael Pohland, Simone Pohland;
Firma: stilradar, www.stilradar.de

A B C D E F G H I J **K** L M N O P Q R S T U V W X Y Z

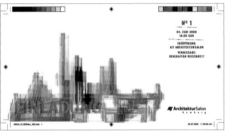

KONTURSCHRIFT

Ein Schriftbild, in dem die Schriftzeichen als Umrisse und nicht als ausgefüllte Formen gestaltet werden. Konturen können mithilfe von Softwareanwendungen wie z. B. dem Adobe Illustrator® auch für Schriftarten erstellt werden, die es nicht als Konturschriften gibt. Die entstehenden **Bézierkurven** könnten vergrößert/verkleinert werden, ohne dass sie an Schärfe verlieren; allerdings ändern sich bei diesem Prozess die ursprünglichen Proportionen der **Schrift**.

En: OUTLINE TYPE
Fr: CARACTÈRES AU FIL
It: CARATTERI CONTORNATI
Spa: LETRA PERFILADA

Design: Raphael Pohland, Simone Pohland;
Firma: stilradar, www.stilradar.de

KORREKTURABZUG

Ein allgemeiner Begriff, der die vorläufige Fassung eines Buches, Berichts, einer Broschüre oder eines anderen zu veröffentlichenden Dokuments beschreibt. Korrekturabzüge dienen verschiedenen Zwecken vom *Redigieren* und Korrekturlesen bis hin zu Werbezwecken, wenn Kritiker ein Buch z. B. schon vor seiner Veröffentlichung erhalten. Ursprünglich nur eine Sammlung ungebundener und nicht zugeschnittener Seiten werden elektronische Korrekturabzüge heutzutage immer gebräuchlicher. Im Zusammenhang mit Korrekturabzügen ist auch der Begriff des *Andrucks* geläufig, der einen Vordruck beschreibt, der zum Abgleichen letzter Details, z. B. der **Farbe**, vor dem Druck dient.

En: PROOF
Fr: ÉPREUVES
It: BOZZA/E
Spa: PRUEBA

Design: Raphael Pohland, Simone Pohland;
Firma: stilradar, www.stilradar.de

KORREKTURFAHNE
Siehe **Korrekturabzug**.

KUBISMUS

Eine avantgardistische Kunstbewegung des frühen 20. Jahrhunderts (ca. 1907–1920) in Europa, in der Objekte – auch die menschliche Gestalt – oft abstrakt und in geometrischen Formen dargestellt wurden. Es wurden gleichzeitig mehrere Perspektiven dargestellt und drei Dimensionen auf zwei reduziert. Man hielt sich also nicht mehr an die konventionellen Vorgaben, die für die perspektivische Darstellung seit der *Renaissance* galten. Nur kurze Zeit später gab es im Grafikdesign ähnliche Annäherungsversuche an räumliche Kompositionen und geometrische Abstraktion.

En: CUBISM
Fr: CUBISME
It: CUBISMO
Spa: CUBISMO

Abb.: Juan Gris, Mann im Café, 1914

A B C D E F G H I J **K L** M N O P Q R S T U V W X Y Z

Frutiger
Frutiger Kursiv
Bodoni
Bodoni Kursiv

KURSIV

Ein Schriftbild, das sich nach rechts neigt und innerhalb einer Textpassage meist dazu gebraucht wird, Schwerpunkte zu setzen. Kursive **Schrift** wurde erstmalig um 1500 in Italien verwendet, um mehr Text auf einer einzelnen Seite unterzubringen, um wiederum die Dicke gedruckter Bücher zu verringern. Echte kursive **Schriften** bestehen aus Buchstaben, die sich von der Schriftart, auf der sie basieren, unterscheiden. **Schrägschrift** neigt sich auch nach rechts, aber ihre Buchstaben bleiben im Vergleich zu ihrer Ausgangsschriftart weitgehend unverändert.

En: ITALIC
Fr: ITALIQUE
It: CORSIVO
Spa: CURSIVA

LACKIERUNG

Eine durchsichtige Beschichtung, die als Teil des Druckprozesses üblicherweise dann auf den Papierbogen aufgetragen wird, wenn die Farbe gedruckt ist. Wie andere Beschichtungen bietet auch eine Lackierung Schutz vor Verschleißerscheinungen, hat dabei aber den Vorteil, dass sie verschiedene Glanzeffekte – von matt bis hochglänzend – erzeugen kann. Lackierungen, die nur an bestimmten Stellen aufgetragen werden, nennt man *Teillackierung*; die Lackierungen, die die ganze Seite bedecken, entsprechend *Gesamtlackierung*.

En: VARNISH
Fr: VERNIS
It: VERNICE
Spa: BARNIZ

Design: Helge Rieder, Oliver Henn; **Firma:** 804© Graphic Design, www.achtnullvier.com

LASERSCHNITT

Ein Verfahren, bei dem Papierbögen, Holz, Plastik und sogar einige Metalle mithilfe eines computergesteuerten Hochleistungslasers an- oder durchgeschnitten werden. Laserschnitte sind sehr präzise und gewähren ein deutlich höheres Detaillevel als ein gewöhnlicher **Stanzschnitt**. Und da sie keine metallene Stanzform benötigt, ist diese Methodik für kleine Produktionsläufe günstiger und durchaus angebracht. Bei extremer Detailarbeit oder der Verarbeitung „komplizierter", z. B. leicht brennbarer/schmelzender oder sehr dicker Materialien können die Kosten jedoch dramatisch zunehmen.

En: LASER CUT
Fr: DÉCOUPE AU LASER
It: TAGLIO AL LASER
Spa: CORTE LÁSER

Design: Helge Rieder, Oliver Henn; **Firma:** 804© Graphic Design, www.achtnullvier.com

A B C D E F G H I J K **L** M N O P Q R S T U V W X Y Z

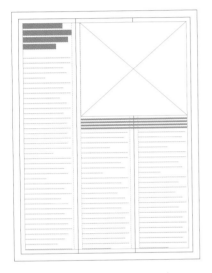

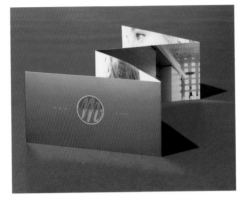

Steht eine strenge konzeptionelle Planung der Kreativität im Weg? Bedeutet Ordnung und Homogenität auch Langeweile und Eintönigkeit? Gerade Corporate Design und dessen erfolgreiche Implementierung wird durch ein wechselseitiges Spannungverhältnis von Reglementierung und gestalterischen Freiraum definiert.

Steht eine strenge konzeptionelle Planung der Kreativität im Weg? Bedeutet Ordnung und Homogenität auch Langeweile und Eintönigkeit? Gerade Corporate Design und dessen erfolgreiche Implementierung wird durch ein wechselseitiges Spannungverhältnis von Reglementierung und gestalterischen Freiraum definiert.

LAYOUT

Ein vorbereitender Schritt innerhalb des Designprozesses, der die Anordnung verschiedener Designelemente wie **Schrift**, Fotos und Illustrationen so darstellt, dass das gewünschte Ergebnis nachvollzogen werden kann. Der Begriff kann auch die Gesamtgestaltung eines fertigen Designs beschreiben. **Layouts** für Bücher, Broschüren, Berichte und andere mehrseitige Dokumente werden oft mithilfe von *Satzspiegeln* erstellt.

En: LAYOUT
Fr: MAQUETTE
It: LAYOUT
Spa: MAQUETACIÓN

Design: Donna S. Atwood,
www.atwooddesign.com

LEPORELLO

Wechselnde Parallelfalzungen eines Papierbogens, bei denen die Seiten (von denen es sechs oder mehr gibt) in gegenläufigen Richtungen, also zickzackartig gefalzt werden. Zwei Falzungen dieser Art ergeben ein 6-Seiten-Leporello (drei Vorderseiten und drei Rückseiten); drei Falzungen ergeben ein 8-Seiten-Leporello usw. Auch *Concertina-* oder *Ziehharmonikafalzung* genannt.

En: ACCORDION FOLD
Fr: PLI ACCORDÉON
It: PIEGHEVOLE A FISARMONICA
Spa: PLEGADO EN ACORDEÓN

Design: Grafikstudio Steinert,
www.grafikstudio-steinert.com

LESBARKEIT

Ein qualitatives Maß dafür, wie angenehm eine Textpassage aufgrund ihrer **Typografie** zu lesen ist. Wird häufig mit der **Leserlichkeit** verwechselt, die sich ausschließlich auf typografische Übersichtlichkeit bezieht. Um lesbar zu sein, muss eine Textzeile leserlich sein; dass man einen Buchstaben oder ein Wort von einem anderen unterscheiden kann, gewährleistet jedoch nicht automatisch eine gute Lesbarkeit. Ein in schmaler **Schrift** gesetzter Roman z. B. kann sehr leserlich und gleichzeitig nicht leicht lesbar sein. Gut lesbare **Typografie** ergibt sich aus dem Zusammenspiel mehrerer Faktoren wie Schriftgröße, **Spationierung**, Zeilenabstand und natürlich dem Schriftbild selbst.

En: READABILITY
Spa: LEGIBILIDAD LINGÜÍSTICA

A B C D E F G H I J K **L** M N O P Q R S T U V W X Y Z

LEGIBILITY: HOW EASILY LETTERFORMS AND WORDS CAN BE DECIPHERED

Legibility: how easily letterforms and words can be deciphered

Legibility: how easily letterforms and words can be deciphered

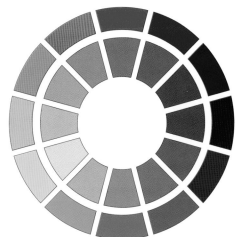

fi fl ff ffi ffl
fi fl ff ffi ffl

LESERLICHKEIT

Ein qualitativer Maßstab dafür, wie einfach Buchstaben und Wörter für den Betrachter/ Leser zu entschlüsseln sind. Unleserliche Texte sind auch unlesbar; Leserlichkeit stellt aber nicht unbedingt eine **Lesbarkeit** sicher, die Leichtigkeit, mit der man durch eine Passage sorgfältig gesetzter **Typografie** voranschreitet. Wie wichtig die Leserlichkeit ist, hängt meist vom Kontext ab. Für Poster und Buchcover z. B. wird häufig **Schrift** gewählt, die an der Grenze zum Unleserlichen ist, aber gleichzeitig Aufmerksamkeit erregt. Andererseits wäre es für den Leser unzumutbar, wenn eine solche Schrift für Wegweiser oder Geschäftsberichte verwendet würde.

En: LEGIBILITY
Fr: LISIBILITÉ
It: LEGGIBILITÀ
Spa: LEGIBILIDAD TIPOGRÁFICA

LEUCHTDICHTE

Die relative Helligkeit oder Dunkelheit einer **Farbe**, die auch als *Farbwert* oder *Farbtiefe* bezeichnet wird. **Farben** ähnlicher Leuchtdichte sind in einer Schwarz-Weiß-Kopie kaum voneinander zu unterscheiden. (Siehe auch **Farbkreis**.)

En: BRIGHTNESS
Fr: LUMINOSITÉ
It: LUMINOSITÀ
Spa: BRILLO

Design: Donna S. Atwood, www.atwooddesign.com

LIGATUR

Zwei, manchmal drei, Buchstaben, die mittels ihrer gemeinsamen Elemente kombiniert werden. Ligaturen dienen meist dazu, unansehnliche „Kollisionen" von Buchstaben zu vermeiden, wie sie z. B. auftreten, wenn der Buchstabe i auf den Buchstaben f folgt. Wenn diese beiden Buchstaben als einzelne Schriftzeichen gesetzt werden, kommt der i-Punkt des i dem Kopfteil des f sehr nahe oder – abhängig von der Schriftart – überlappt ihn sogar. Wenn man die beiden Buchstaben durch eine Ligatur ersetzt, entsteht eine reine, deutlich leserlichere Textzeile. Ligaturen, die schon in antiken Manuskripten Verwendung fanden, wurden auch von Beginn an im *Bleisatzdruck* eingesetzt. Ihre Beliebtheit sank jedoch in Zeiten der *Phototypie*. Die meisten digitalen **Schriften** beinhalten aber eine Auswahl an Ligaturen.

En: LIGATURE
Fr: LIGATURE
It: LEGATURA
Spa: LIGADURA

A B C D E F G H I J K **L** M N O P Q R S T U V W X Y Z

>> MORE SAVETY. MORE FUN.
LET'S MINI.

LINIE

Eine Linie dient als typografisches Hilfsmittel zur Trennung von Elementen innerhalb eines **Layouts**. Mit ihrer Hilfe kann eine Fläche eingeteilt werden, um den Eindruck einer Rangordnung zu vermitteln. Die Größe einer Linie wird üblicherweise in **Punkten** angegeben.

En: RULE
Fr: FILET
It: FILETTO TIPOGRAFICO
Spa: FILETE

Design: Helge Rieder, Oliver Henn; **Firma:** 804© Graphic Design, www.achtnullvier.com

LINIENGESTALTUNG

Eine entweder gerade oder gebogene Reihe von **Punkten**. Anders als in der *Geometrie*, in der die Dicke von **Linien** nebensächlich ist, können von Designern verwendete Linien dünn oder dick sein und müssen nicht über ihre gesamte Länge einheitlich bleiben. Sie können auch unterbrochen oder aufgeteilt sein. Dicke **Linien** nehmen die Eigenschaften einer **Ebene** (flache Oberfläche) an. Die drei Elemente **Punkt**, **Linie** und **Ebene** bilden im Grafikdesign die Basis für die Erschaffung sämtlicher Formen. (Siehe auch **Linie**.)

En: LINE
Fr: LIGNE
It: LINEA/E
Spa: LÍNEA

Design: Grafikstudio Steinert, www.grafikstudio-steinert.com

LINKSBÜNDIG, RECHTSBÜNDIG

Aufeinanderfolgende Zeilen, die links entlang einer gemeinsamen Bezugslinie beginnen, nennt man linksbündig und rechts flatternd. Aufeinanderfolgende Zeilen, die rechts entlang einer gemeinsamen Bezugslinie beginnen, nennt man rechtsbündig und links flatternd.

En: FLUSH-LEFT, FLUSH-RIGHT
Fr: FER À GAUCHE, FER À DROITE
It: ALLINEAMENTO A SINISTRA E ALLINEAMENTO A DESTRA
Spa: BANDERA A LA IZQUIERDA/BANDERA A LA DERECHA

Design: Matthias Frey; **Firma:** Q Kreativgesellschaft mbH, www.q-home.de

Paper

Stone or plate

Zahlen 0123456789

LITHOGRAFIE

Ein Druckvorgang, bei dem die Tinte auf eine glatte Stein- oder Metallplatte aufgetragen und dann auf das Papier übertragen wird. Der Name leitet sich von den griechischen Begriffen „lithos" (Stein) und „grapho" (schreiben) ab. Bei der Lithografie werden auf dem Stein oder dem Metall mithilfe eines ölbasierten Mittels wie z. B. Fettkreide die Bereiche markiert, auf denen die wasserbasierte Tinte haftet bzw. nicht haftet. Nicht bearbeitete Flächen der Platte „halten" die Tinte und übertragen sie auf das Papier, wohingegen die öligen Flächen die Tinte abperlen lassen und somit den Hintergrund des gedruckten Bildes ergeben. (Siehe auch **Offsetdruck**.)

En: LITHOGRAPHY
Fr: LITHOGRAPHIE
It: LITOGRAFIA
Spa: LITOGRAFÍA

Design: Donna S. Atwood,
www.atwooddesign.com

LOGO

Ein grafisches Zeichen, das als Teil der Markenbildung eines Unternehmens dient. Effektive Logos sind weitaus schwieriger zu erschaffen, als ihre elegante Einfachheit oft vermuten lässt. Logos müssen einfach genug sein, dass sie auch klein gedruckt noch deutlich erkennbar sind, und dabei trotzdem enorm viel aussagen; Logos stehen für die Werte und Persönlichkeit einer Firma. Sie müssen einprägsam sein, einen hohen Wiedererkennungswert haben und sich von denen der Wettbewerber abheben. In Anbetracht dieser Ansprüche wird ein erfolgreiches Logo über viele, viele Jahre genutzt. Ein Firmenschriftzug stellt den Firmennamen oder seine Abkürzung in einem Schriftbild dar, dessen Details einzigartig und Bestandteil einer Marke sind.

En: LOGO
Fr: LOGO
It: LOGO
Spa: LOGO

Design: Michael Thiele, Martin Schonhoff;
Firma: Die Transformer, www.dietransformer.de

LOREM IPSUM
Siehe **Blindtext**.

MAJUSKELZIFFERN (TABELLENZIFFERN)

Eine Reihe von Zahlen, die die gleiche (oder annähernd gleiche) Höhe haben wie Großbuchstaben einer Schriftart. Da sie auch eine konstante Breite haben und auf der **Grundlinie** liegen, werden sie häufig in Tabellen verwendet, da ihre Anordnung hier optisch ansprechend sein kann. (Siehe auch **Mediävalziffern**.)

En: LINING NUMERALS/FIGURES
Fr: CHIFFRES ARABES
It: NUMERI E LETTERE DI ALLINEAMENTO
Spa: NÚMEROS DE CAJA ALTA

A B C D E F G H I J K L **M** N O P Q R S T U V W X Y Z

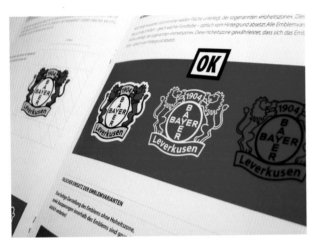

MARKENBILDUNG (BRANDING)

Die strategische Abgrenzung eines Angebots (Produkt, Dienstleistung, Interaktion, Erfahrung etc.) von dem der Konkurrenz. Auf visueller Ebene beginnt eine Marke oft mit einem **Logo**, das dazu dient, das Markenversprechen zu verankern. Voraussetzung für eine erfolgreiche Markenidentität ist unter anderem eine globale und einheitliche Bildsprache (**Logo**, **Schrifttype**, Hausfarben sowie weitere visuelle Hinweise). Markenstrategien gehen heute meist weit über die traditionelle Print- und Fernsehwerbung hinaus und berücksichtigen auch Websites, *Blogs* und andere sich entwickelnde Soziale Medien.

En: BRANDING
Fr: STRATÉGIE DE MARQUE
It: BRANDING
Spa: BRANDING

Design: Helge Rieder, Oliver Henn; **Firma:** 804© Graphic Design, www.achtnullvier.com

A B C D E F G H I J K L **M** N O P Q R S T U V W X Y Z

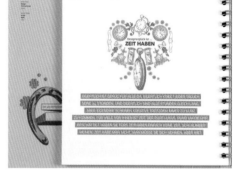

Mediävalziffer 0123456789

MEDIÄVALZIFFERN

Ziffern mit Proportionen, die mit den Klein-buchstaben eines Schriftbilds vergleichbar sind. Wie **Kapitälchen** werden Mediävalzif-fern oft in Textzeilen benutzt, da sie weniger ablenken als arabische Ziffern.

En: OLD-STYLE NUMERALS/FIGURES
Fr: CHIFFRES SUSPENDUS
It: NUMERI E LETTERE IN STILE ANTICO
Spa: NÚMEROS ELZEVIRIANOS

METAPHER

Die Be- oder Umschreibung einer Sache mittels einer anderen. Im Grafikdesign können Metaphern textliche Komponenten enthalten, z. B. wenn eine Textzeile ein Bild auf humor-volle bis ironische Art und Weise mit einem scheinbar völlig anderen Leitbild verbindet. Ein Foto eines dichten, düsteren Dschungels z. B. könnte mit der Zeile „Auf der Suche nach einer Autoversicherung?" verbunden werden. Der Begriff des „undurchschaubaren Versicherungsdschungels" wird so darge-stellt, ohne dass er konkret geäußert wird. Rein optische Metaphern greifen auf allge-meingültige Assoziationen mit einem oder mehreren Bildern zurück, damit der Sinn klar wird. Das wird häufig mithilfe „verschmolze-ner" Bilder gewährleistet, einer Verbindung zweier oder mehrerer Bilder zur Vereinfa-chung der Verständlichkeit.

En: METAPHOR
Fr: MÉTAPHORE
It: METAFORA
Spa: METÁFORA

Design: Harald Haas; **Firma:** red cell Werbeagentur GmbH, www.redcell.de

MITTELACHSSATZ

Fortlaufende Textzeilen, die so ausgerichtet sind, dass die Mittelpunkte der Zeilen auf einer gemeinsamen Referenzlinie liegen. Da der Mittelachssatz beim Lesen sehr unna-türlich wirkt, wird er im Allgemeinen nur bei Visitenkarten, Einladungen und anderen Dokumenten eingesetzt, die nur wenig Text beinhalten. (Siehe auch **Axialität**.)

En: CENTERED TYPE/TEXT
Fr: TEXTE CENTRÉ
It: TESTO/CARATTERI CENTRATI
Spa: TEXTO O TIPO CENTRADO

Design: Matthias Frey; **Firma:** Q Kreativgesellschaft mbH, www.q-home.de

A B C D E F G H I J K L **M** N O P Q R S T U V W X Y Z

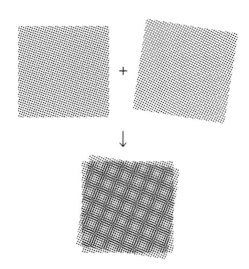

MODERNE

Der Begriff Moderne vereint eine Vielzahl unterschiedlicher Bewegungen. Ihre Anfänge werden oft im um 1907 entstandenen **Kubismus** und seinem Drang nach Abstraktion und der damit einhergehenden Ablehnung natürlicher Formen verortet. In den darauffolgenden 100 Jahren bediente sich das Design der Moderne einer großen Menge verschiedener Formen und wurde auf der ganzen Welt immer wieder neu erfunden und interpretiert. Der klassischen Vorstellung von Modernität entsprechen sicher viele dieser Interpretationen (z. B. konsequente Anwendung von *Satzspiegeln*, **serifenlose Schrift**, große Freiflächen), andererseits gibt es für jede „Regel" in der Moderne unzählige Ausnahmen. Nichtsdestotrotz gibt es auch Konstanten wie den Schwerpunkt auf funktionellem optischem Kommunikationsdesign und den fortschrittlichen, optimistischen Geist.

En: MODERNISM
Fr: MODERNISME
It: MODERNISMO
Spa: MODERNISMO

Design: Martin Schonhoff; **Firma:** Die Transformer, www.dietransformer.de

MOIRÉ-EFFEKT

Ein unerwünschter Effekt, der auftreten kann, wenn Halbtonraster beim **Vierfarbdruck** so angeordnet werden, dass erkennbare „Muster" entstehen. Um ein Moiré-Muster zu vermeiden, rotieren die Raster in solchen Winkeln zueinander, dass kleine **CMYK**-Rosetten entstehen, die im finalen Druck kaum zu erkennen sind. Ein Moiré-Muster kann auch dann entstehen, wenn ein gedrucktes Bild eingescannt wird, ohne dass es entrastert wird.

En: MOIRÉ
Fr: MOIRÉ
It: EFFETTO MOIRÉ
Spa: MOARÉ

MONOCHROMATISCH (EINFARBIG)

Die Verwendung einer **Farbpalette**, die nur Abstufungen und -tönungen eines einzigen **Farbtons** enthält. In monochromatischen Bildern werden farbliche Unterschiede durch Unterschiede in **Sättigung** und **Leuchtdichte** dargestellt. **Graustufenbilder** sind monochromatische Bilder mit einer **Farbpalette** aus Grautönen, Weiß und Schwarz.

En: MONOCHROMATIC
Fr: MONOCHROMATIQUE
It: MONOCROMATICO
Spa: MONOCROMÁTICO

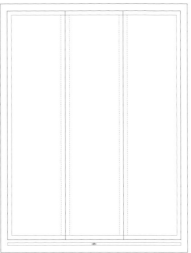

MULTIMEDIA

Beschreibt Medien, die Inhalte in mehr als einer Darstellungsweise übertragen. Eine einzelne Website z. B. kann zu ein und demselben Thema gleichzeitig Texte (auch Hypertext), Bilder sowie *Audio-* und *Video-streams* enthalten. Der Begriff kann sich auch auf Geräte, die Multimediainhalte und -verbreitung ermöglichen, und interaktive Videospiele beziehen.

En: MULTIMEDIA
Fr: MULTIMÉDIA
It: MULTIMEDIA
Spa: MULTIMEDIA

Design: Kate Benjamin,
www.moderncat.net

MUSTERSEITE

Die Vorlage, die von Seitenlayout-Programmen verwendet wird, um die einheitliche Anordnung des *Satzspiegels*, der Spalten, Seitenzahlen und anderer gebräuchlicher Layoutelemente für ein Dokument zu gewährleisten. Innerhalb eines Dokuments können auch mehrere Musterseiten gebraucht werden, die je einem unterschiedlichen Abschnitt oder Layoutstyle entsprechen. Verwendet man Musterseiten, so wird die Seitennummerierung meist automatisch durchgeführt.

En: MASTER PAGE
Fr: PAGE TYPE
It: PAGINA MASTRO
Spa: PÁGINA MAESTRA

Design: Donna S. Atwood,
www.atwooddesign.com

NEGATIVE SCHRIFT

Ein Begriff, der Text beschreibt, bei dem die Farbe nur außerhalb seiner Schriftkonturen gedruckt wird, also die **Schrift** selbst ausgespart wird. Somit hat der Text dann die **Farbe** des Papiers oder Untergrunds und nicht der Druckfarbe. Derselbe Effekt kann am Computerbildschirm erzielt werden, indem man die Schriftfarbe mit der Hintergrundfarbe gleichsetzt und den Text dann in ein Feld anderer **Farbe** setzt. Klein gesetzter Text in heller **Farbe** scheint auf dunklem Hintergrund zu verschwinden, sodass häufig ein etwas größeres und fetteres Schriftbild nötig ist, um die **Leserlichkeit** zu gewährleisten.

En: REVERSE/REVERSE OUT
Fr: INVERSION
It: REVERSE/REVERSE OUT
Spa: TIPO EN NEGATIVO

Design: Martin Schonhoff; **Firma:** Die Transformer,
www.dietransformer.de

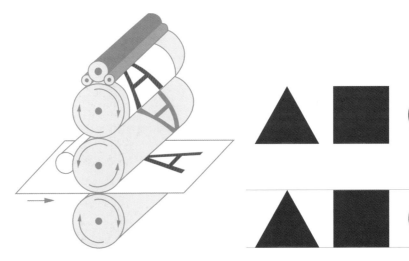

Oberlänge

OBERLÄNGE

Der Teil eines Kleinbuchstabens, der sich von der **x-Linie** bis über die **Versalhöhe** eines bestimmten Schriftbilds erstreckt. Größe und Breite der Oberlänge variieren von Schriftbild zu Schriftbild. Generell gilt: Je größer die **x-Höhe**, desto feiner die Oberlängen. Wird die **x-Höhe** hingegen kleiner, so werden die Oberlängen meist ausgeprägter. (Siehe auch **Unterlänge** und **x-Höhe**.)

En: ASCENDER
Fr: ASCENDANTE
It: TRATTO ASCENDENTE
Spa: ASCENDENTE

OFFSETDRUCK

Ein Druckvorgang, der auf den Prinzipien der *Lithografie* beruht. Hierbei wird ein einge-färbtes Bild zunächst auf ein Gummituch übertragen, bevor es auf die Druckober-fläche aufgetragen wird. Eine Reihe von Walzen trägt dabei die Tinte auf die Platte auf, wonach eine zweite das Tuch darüber rollt, damit es die Tinte aufnimmt. Eine hohe Qualität und große Einsparungen haben dazu geführt, dass der Offsetdruck – auch *Offset-lithografie* – die heutzutage gebräuchlichste Form für den kommerziellen Druck ist.

En: OFFSET LITHOGRAPHY
Fr: LITHOGRAPHIE OFFSET
It: LITOGRAFIA OFFSET
Spa: LITOGRAFÍA OFFSET

OPTISCHE AUSRICHTUNG

Die Ausrichtung von **Schrift** oder ande-ren Designelementen nach ihrer optischen Wirkung und nicht nach exakten Abmessun-gen. Das ist vor allem dann wichtig, wenn Elemente verschiedener Form ausgerichtet werden. Richtet man z. B. einen Kreis, ein gleichseitiges Dreieck und ein Quadrat mit jeweils derselben Höhe entlang derselben Horizontalachse aus, entsteht eine optische Täuschung. Das Quadrat erscheint höher als die anderen Gebilde, wohingegen der Kreis kleiner wirkt als das Quadrat oder das Dreieck.

En: VISUAL ALIGNMENT
Fr: ALIGNEMENT VISUEL
It: ALLINEAMENTO VISIVO
Spa: ALINEACIÓN VISUAL

PAGINIERUNG

Die Nummerierung von Seiten zur Deutlich-
machung ihrer richtigen Reihenfolge in einem
Buch oder einer anderen gedruckten Publikation. Paginierung kann sich im Allgemeinen
aber auch nur auf die Anzahl von Seiten
einer Publikation beziehen. Mittlerweile hat
der Begriff sogar noch eine weitere Verwendung gefunden, nämlich zur Beschreibung
der Anordnung von Informationen auf einer
Website. Blogs z. B. können entweder so
paginiert werden, dass nur die ersten Absätze
eines Beitrags auf der Hauptseite angezeigt
werden, oder so, dass nicht mehr als zehn
Kommentare nach dem ursprünglichen
Beitrag angezeigt werden, auf den sie sich
beziehen. (Siehe auch **Ausschießen**.)

En: PAGINATION
Fr: PAGINATION
It: IMPAGINAZIONE
Spa: PAGINACIÓN

Design: Helge Rieder, Oliver Henn; **Firma:** 804©
Graphic Design, www.achtnullvier.com

PANTONE FARBSYSTEM
Siehe **Farbkennzeichnungssystem**.

PAPIERGRÖSSEN
Siehe auch **Bogengrößen**.

Inch

Picas

PFAD

Eine Abfolge von **Bézierkurven** oder *Vektoren*, die von Grafikdesignsoftware zur Darstellung der Konturen von Designelementen einschließlich **Schrift** verwendet wird. Da *Vektoren* sie beschreiben, können Pfade stark vergrößert werden, ohne dass die **Auflösung** darunter leidet. Benutzerdefinierte Pfade dienen meist dazu, einen bestimmten Teil eines digitalen Fotos „auszuschneiden" und in ein anderes einzufügen.

En: PATH
Fr: CHEMIN
It: PERCORSO/I
Spa: TRAZADO

Design: Donna S. Atwood,
www.atwooddesign.com

PICA

Die kleinste typografische Maßeinheit, die 12 Punkte groß ist. 1 Pica-Punkt entspricht 0,35147 mm. 1 Pica hat entsprechend die Breite von 4,2176 mm.

Umrechnungstabelle:
1 Pica-Point (Pica-Punkt) = 0,35147 mm
1 Pica-Point (Pica-Punkt) = 0,013837 Zoll

1 Pica = 4,2176 mm
1 Pica = 1/6 inch
1 Pica = 12 Pica-Point (Pica-Punkt)

En: PICA
Fr: POINT PICA
It: PICA
Spa: PICA

PIKTOGRAMM

Ein **Bildzeichen** oder **Symbol**, dessen Bedeutung unabhängig von sprachlichen oder kulturellen Barrieren unmissverständlich ist. Effektive Piktogramme sind Teil eines standardisierten Piktogrammsystems, das sich an einer Vielzahl von Konventionen und Richtlinien orientiert, vor allem wenn eine ganze Kollektion erstellt wird wie z. B. für die Olympischen Spiele. Für die Interpretation von Piktogrammen bedarf es eines bestimmten Zusammenhangs. Die Beschilderungen für die Gepäckbänder in vielen Flughäfen z. B. sind lediglich **Symbole**, die im Flughafenkontext verwendet werden. Dasselbe **Symbol** könnte z. B. auch auf einer Website verwendet werden, die Koffer verkauft. Hier wäre – obwohl die bildliche Bedeutung erhalten bliebe – die Bedeutung als Piktogramm eine völlig andere.

En: PICTOGRAM
Fr: PICTOGRAMME
It: PITTOGRAMMA
Spa: PICTOGRAMA

Design: Matthias Frey; **Firma:** Q Kreativgesellschaft mbH, www.q-home.de

ABCDEFGHIJKLMNO**P**QRSTUVWXYZ

PIXEL (BILDPUNKT)

Die Grundkomponente zur Darstellung von Bildern auf einer Vielzahl digitaler Anzeigegeräte. Der Name Pixel setzt sich aus den englischen Begriffen „pictures" – kurz: „pix" – (Bilder) und „element" (Bestandteil) zusammen. Pixel werden auf einem zweidimensionalen **Raster** angeordnet, wobei jeder Pixel das Musterstück des entsprechenden Punktes des Originals ist. Die Bildauflösung ist abhängig von der Rasterdichte. Bei Anwendungen, die das **RGB**-Farbsystem nutzen, besteht die **Farbe**, die jeder einzelne Pixel darstellt, aus numerischen Werten von Rot, Grün und Blau, die ihr zugeordnet sind.

En: PIXEL
Fr: PIXEL
It: PIXEL
Spa: PÍXEL

PLATZHALTER

Ein Bild von geringer Qualität, oft die geringauflösende Version des Bildes, das in der Endfassung eines **Layouts** verwendet wird und als Ersatz im noch zu bearbeitenden **Layout** dient. Werden diese Bilder mit dem Kürzel „FPO" (for position only) gekennzeichnet, so ist ihre Funktion für alle weiteren Mitglieder des Designteams unmissverständlich.

En: FOR POSITION ONLY (FPO)
Fr: IMAGE DE PLACEMENT
It: FOR POSITION ONLY (FPO)
Spa: FPO (SÓLO PARA REFERENCIA DE POSICIÓN)

Design: Donna S. Atwood, www.atwooddesign.com

POSTERISATION

Ein Effekt, der auftritt, wenn die verfügbare Auswahl an **Farben** (oder Grautönen) nicht ausreicht, um ein Bild darzustellen bzw. zu drucken, das Flächen gradueller Farbverläufe enthält. Das kann z. B. passieren, wenn ein Bild in ein 256-Farben-*GIF* für die Verwendung auf einer einfachen Website konvertiert wird. Posterisation kann mithilfe von Bildbearbeitungssoftware auch absichtlich eingesetzt werden, um fortlaufende **Farbtöne** in eine Gruppe einzelner Farbfelder einzuteilen, sodass interessante optische Effekte entstehen, wie sie auf Grafikpostern vorkommen.

En: POSTERIZATION
Fr: POSTERISATION
It: POSTERIZZAZIONE
Spa: POSTERIZACIÓN

A B C D E F G H I J K L M N O **P** Q R S T U V W X Y Z

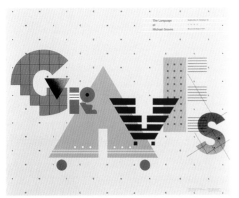

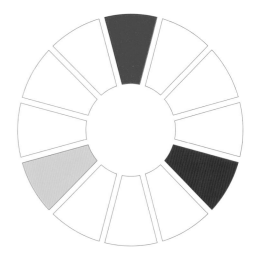

POSTMODERNE

Als Reaktion auf die oft dogmatischen Leitbilder der **Moderne** nahm die Postmoderne während der 1960er Jahre ihren Anfang und erlangte während der 1980er Jahre internationale Bedeutung. Während die Anhänger der **Moderne** die Vergangenheit fast gänzlich vergessen ließen, feierten die Verfechter der Postmoderne historische Stile und ihre dekorativen Züge und interpretierten und kombinierten sie auf unerwartete, oft verspielte Art und Weise neu. Optische Charakteristiken waren gesperrte Schriften, die scheinbar wahllose Anordnung von Elementen, aufwendige **Kollagen**, Pastellfarbpaletten usw.

En: POST-MODERNISM
Fr: POSTMODERNISME
It: POST-MODERNISMO
Spa: POSTMODERNISMO

Design: William Longhauser Design, www.longhauser. com; **Klient:** The Goldie Paley Gallery, 1983

PRÄGUNG

Das Kreieren eines Eindrucks in Papier, indem es zwischen zwei Metallscheiben gepresst wird; auf der einen Scheibe erscheint das Motiv erhoben und auf der anderen Scheibe versunken. Wenn das Motiv auf dem Papier erhoben ist, spricht man von einer Hochprägung, wenn das Motiv in das Papier nach unten gepresst ist, spricht man von einer Tiefprägung. Mittelgewichtige Papiere, vor allem mit strukturierten Oberflächen, eignen sich meist am besten. Gedruckte Bilder und Folien werden häufig als zusätzliche Verzierungen verwendet, aber sie sind nicht erforderlich. Das Prägen ohne ein gedrucktes Bild oder Folie nennt man *Blindprägung*.

En: EMBOSS
Fr: GAUFRAGE
It: GOFFRATURA
Spa: GOFRAR

Design: Matthias Frey; **Firma:** Q Kreativgesellschaft mbH, www.q-home.de

PRIMÄRFARBEN

Farben, die – gleichmäßig angeordnet – die Schlüsselpunkte eines **Farbkreises** bilden. Im traditionellen **Farbkreis**, der zur Vermischung von Farbpigmenten dient, sind die Primärfarben Rot, Blau und Gelb. Andere Farbkreise hingegen basieren auf den subtraktiven Grundfarben Cyan, Magenta und Gelb und den additiven Grundfarben Rot, Grün und Blau. (Siehe auch **CMYK** und **RGB**.)

En: PRIMARY COLORS
Fr: COULEURS PRIMAIRES
It: COLORI PRIMARI
Spa: COLORES PRIMARIOS

Design: Donna S. Atwood, www.atwooddesign.com

Times

Palatino

Futura

48 Punkt
36 Punkt
24 Punkt
18 Punkt
14 Punkt
12 Punkt
10 Punkt
8 Punkt

Typografie

PROPORTIONALSCHRIFT

Ein Begriff, der ein Schriftbild beschreibt, bei der die Breite jedes Schriftzeichens unterschiedlich groß ist – anders als bei **dicktengleichen** Schriftarten, bei denen alle Schriftzeichen dieselbe Breite einnehmen.

En: PROPORTIONAL
Fr: CARACTÈRES À CHASSE VARIABLE
It: PROPORZIONALE
Spa: PROPORCIONAL

PUNKT/PUNKTGRÖSSE

Ein Punkt ist eine absolute Maßeinheit der **Typografie**. Ein Punkt entspricht ca. 0,349 mm. Die Punktgröße bezieht sich auf den in Punkten angegebenen Schriftgrad einer **Schrift**. Obwohl sie eine absolute Maßeinheit ist, variiert die tatsächliche Schriftgröße bei einer bestimmten Punktgröße von Schriftart zu Schriftart. Das hängt damit zusammen, dass die Punktgröße ursprünglich nicht anhand der Schriftzeichengröße festgelegt wurde, sondern anhand der Bleiblöcke, zu denen die Schriftzeichen gegossen wurden. Bei digitaler **Schrift** ist die Beziehung zwischen Punkt- und Schriftzeichengröße sogar noch komplizierter. (Siehe auch **Pica**.)

En: POINT/POINT SIZE
Fr: CORPS
It: PUNTO/DIMENSIONE DEL PUNTO
Spa: TAMAÑO DE PUNTO /PUNTO

PUNZE

Die Fläche, die ein Buchstabe entweder komplett (wie der Buchstabe o) oder teilweise (wie der Buchstabe c) umschließt. Der Begriff kann auch – in einem allgemeineren Sinn – für den Zwischenraum zwischen zwei benachbarten Buchstaben verwendet werden. (Siehe auch **Freie Fläche**.)

En: COUNTER
Fr: CONTREPOINÇON
It: OCCHIELLO
Spa: CONTRAFORMA

ABCDEF**G**HIJKLMNOP**Q****R**STUVWXYZ

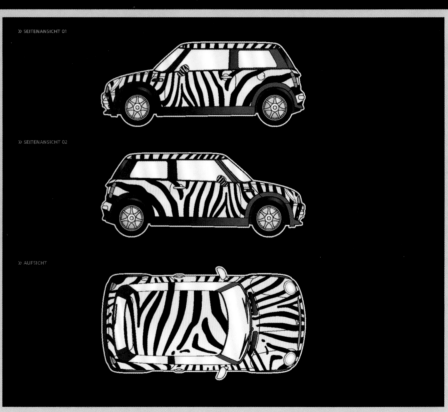

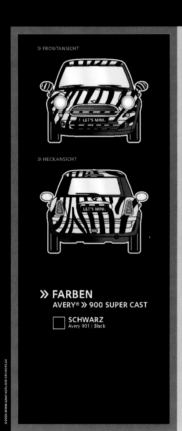

RAHMEN

Die Umrahmung eines Fotos, einer Illustration, eines Textes oder anderer Designelemente, die einen Übergang zwischen diesen Elementen und dem restlichen **Layout** bildet. Rahmen können schlicht – z. B. eine rechteckige oder kreisförmige dünne **Linie** – , aber auch sehr verziert sein. Schwere und detailvollere Rahmen neigen jedoch dazu, von dem Bild, das sie umgeben, abzulenken und die Aufmerksamkeit auf sich zu ziehen. Simple schmale Rahmen hingegen heben das Bild von seinem Hintergrund ab.

En: BORDER
Fr: BORDURE
It: BORDO/I
Spa: BORDE

Design: Grafikstudio Steinert, www.grafikstudio-steinert.com

A B C D E F G H I J K L M N O P Q **R** S T U V W X Y Z

Proper Registration   Misregistration

RASTER (SATZSPIEGEL)

Ein Netzwerk aus meist horizontal und vertikal verlaufenden, sich schneidenden Linien. Satzspiegel werden dazu genutzt, Designelemente auszurichten und einem **Layout** eine gleichmäßige Struktur zu geben. Besonders bei großen Projekten erlauben sie Designern effizientes Arbeiten, da sie willkürliche Entscheidungen praktisch nicht zulassen. Andererseits werden Satzspiegel oft kritisiert, da sie die Kreativität des Designers stark einschränken. Richtig eingesetzt dienen Raster dem Designer jedoch als Basisgerüst, bieten grundlegende Struktur und geben ihm mehr Freiheiten als sie ihm nehmen.

En: GRID
Fr: GRILLE
It: GRIGLIA
Spa: CUADRÍCULA

Design: Raphael Pohland, Simone Pohland;
Firma: stilradar, www.stilradar.de

RASTERGRAFIK
Siehe **Bitmap**.

RECHTE/LINKE SEITE (VORDER-/RÜCKSEITE)

Beschreibt die rechte und linke Seite einer Doppelseite. Die rechte Seite nennt man *Recto*, die linke Seite *Verso*. Wortwörtlich beziehen sich die Begriffe jedoch auf die sich „gegenüberliegenden" Seiten einer Buchseite, wobei *Recto* die Vorder- und *Verso* die Rückseite beschreibt.

En: RECTO/VERSO
Fr: RECTO VERSO
It: RECTO/VERSO
Spa: RECTO/VERSO

Firma: stilradar, www.stilradar.de

REGISTERHALTIGKEIT

Die präzise Zusammenstellung aller Farbschichten, die innerhalb eines bestimmten Druckvorgangs gedruckt werden. Idealerweise ist jede neue Farbschicht auf die vorherige abgestimmt, sodass **Farben** genau da überlappen oder aneinandergrenzen, wo es gewünscht ist. Tatsächlich können dabei aufgrund sog. *Passerfehler* jedoch Unterschiede entstehen, die z. B. mit der Papierspannung oder Problemen mit der Druckpresse zusammenhängen. Viele Probleme der *Passerfehler* können mittels **Überfüllung** oder durch **Überdrucken** gemäßigt werden.

En: REGISTRATION
Fr: REPÉRAGE
It: REGISTRO
Spa: REGISTRO

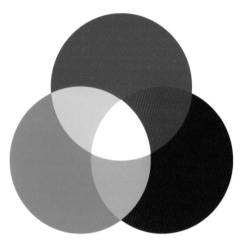

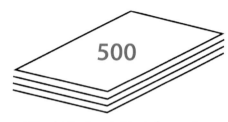

- 1 Ries A4 Papier mit 80 g/m² = 500 Bogen
- 1 Ries (alt) = 480 Bogen Schreibpapier
- 1 Ries = 500 Bogen Druckpapier
- 1 Ries = 20 Buch

RGB

Abkürzung für Rot, Grün und Blau – die drei
Farben, die auf Computerbildschirmen und
anderen digitalen Geräten Grafiken darstellen. Rot, Grün und Blau nennt man auch die
additiven **Primärfarben**; in gleichen Teilen
miteinander kombiniert ergeben sie weißes
Licht. Außerdem sprechen sie jeweils die drei
verschiedenen *Lichtrezeptoren* im menschlichen Auge an. (Siehe auch **CMYK**.)

En: RGB
Fr: RVB
It: RGB
Spa: RGB

Design: Donna S. Atwood,
www.atwooddesign.com

RHYTHMUS

Eine optische Wiederholung, die durch die
zugrunde liegenden Muster innerhalb und
zwischen verschiedenen Designelementen
wie **Schrift**, **Linien** und Umrissen entsteht.
Eine einzelne Textzeile z. B. kann aufgrund
vieler vertikaler Striche einen bestimmten
Rhythmus haben, der durch **Spationieren**
aufgebracht wird. Poster und Buchcover
nutzen oft geometrische Muster, um einen
kontinuierlichen Rhythmus zu schaffen, von
dem sich überraschende Elemente abheben.
Und in größerem Rahmen können *Satzspiegel* dazu dienen, einen sanften Rhythmus
innerhalb einer übermäßig langen Publikation
zu schaffen, der den Leser „führt".

En: RHYTHM
Fr: RYTHME
It: RITMO
Spa: RITMO

Firma: stilradar, www.stilradar.de

RIES

Eine Mengeneinheit für sortengleiche For-
matpapiere (Bogenformate). Der Begriff leitet
sich vom arabischen „rizma" für Bündel bzw.
Paket ab, wo er bereits seit dem siebten
Jahrhundert für das Bündeln von 500 gleich
großen Papierbögen gebräuchlich ist. Wie
viele Papierbögen (Papierblätter) in einem
Ries enthalten sind, ist vom Einzelgewicht der
Papiersorte bzw. des Kartons abhängig. Ein
Ries wiegt in der Regel nicht mehr als
25 Kilogramm.

En: REAM
Fr: RAME
It: RISMA
Spa: RESMA

S&B
Siehe **Silbentrennung & Blocksatz (S&B)**.

A B C D E F G H I J K L M N O P Q R **S** T U V W X Y Z

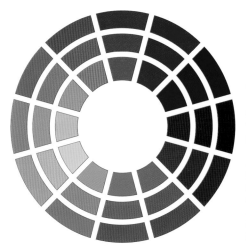

Lorem ipsum dolor sit amet, consectetuer sadipscing elitr, sed diam nonumy eirmod tempor invidunt ut labore et dolore magna aliquyam erat, sed diam voluptua.

At vero eos et accusam et justo duo dolores et ea rebum. Stet clita kasd gubergren, no sea takimata sanctus est Lorem ipsum dolor sit amet. Lorem ipsum dolor sitastor amet, consetetur sadipscing elitr, sed diam nonumy eirmod tempor invidunt ut labore et dolore magna aliquyam erat sed.

„Freundschaft, das ist eine Seele in zwei Körpern." *Aristoteles*

„Freundschaft, das ist eine Seele in zwei Körpern." *Aristoteles*

• 1 Teelöffel Kakao

• 1 Teelöffel Kakao

SÄTTIGUNG

Die Reinheit einer **Farbe** in Relation zu ihrem Grauanteil. Reine **Farbtöne** sind komplett gesättigt und erscheinen klar. Wird der Sättigungsgrad verringert, wirkt eine **Farbe** gedeckter, obwohl es derselbe **Farbton** bleibt. Eine Entsättigung kann durch das Hinzufügen von Grau zu einem Farbton oder das Beimischen einer kleineren Menge seiner **Komplementärfarbe** erreicht werden. (Siehe auch **Farbe**.)

En: SATURATION
Fr: SATURATION
It: SATURAZIONE
Spa: SATURACIÓN

Design: Donna S. Atwood, www.atwooddesign.com

SATZBREITE

Ein Begriff, der die Breite eines Textblocks beschreibt und üblicherweise in **Punkten**, **Pica** oder **Gevierten** angegeben wird, wobei auch Millimeter und **Pixel** in diesem Zusammenhang verwendet werden. Die optimale Satzbreite in Anbetracht der **Leserlichkeit** liegt – Zwischenräume mit einbezogen – zwischen 52–78 Satzzeichen (entspricht einer zwei- bis dreifachen Wiederholung des Alphabets), wobei Faktoren wie Zeilenabstand, **Spationierung** sowie das Schriftbild ebenfalls berücksichtigt werden müssen. (Siehe auch **Zeilenlänge**.)

En: MEASURE
Fr: MESURE
It: GIUSTEZZA
Spa: ANCHO

SATZKANTENAUSGLEICH

Satzzeichen, die geringfügig außerhalb eines Textblocks gesetzt werden, um die optische Ausrichtung zu verbessern. Öffnende **Anführungsstriche** (unten) und Aufzählungszeichen werden oft so gesetzt, dass sie sich dem linken **Seitenrand** zuneigen, wohingegen schließende **Anführungsstriche** (oben) sowie Trenn- und Bindestriche oft bis in den rechten **Seitenrand** reichen. *Überhängende Interpunktion* erfordert Feingefühl, da mit ihrer Hilfe eine saubere **Typografie** entstehen soll. Ziel ist nicht, die überstehenden Elemente hervorzuheben. Auch Schriftzeichen und Ziffern werden für die Optimierung der optischen Ausrichtung bisweilen über die Ränder eines Textblocks hinaus platziert, z. B. dann, wenn Fußnoten oder **Anführungsstriche** in einer Textspalte gesetzt werden müssen, die Dezimalzahlen („Kommazahlen") enthält.

En: HANGING PUNCTUATION
Fr: PONCTUATION MARGINALE
It: PUNTEGGIATURA ESTERNA
Spa: PUNTUACIÓN VOLADA

A B C D E F G H I J K L M N O P Q R **S** T U V W X Y Z

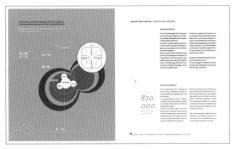

Futura
Futura Schmal
Bodoni
Bodoni Schmal

SATZSPALTE

Die Bereiche eines Seitenlayouts, in denen der Text steht. Textspalten bilden oft die grundlegenden Bausteine eines Satzspiegels. Bei textreichen **Layouts** werden häufig zwei oder drei Spalten verwendet. Lange, rechteckige Spalten werden wohl am häufigsten verwendet, aber man findet auch verschiedene andere Stile.

En: COLUMN
Fr: COLONNE
It: COLONNE
Spa: COLUMNA

Firma: stilradar, www.stilradar.de

SCHLAGZEILE

Ein Begriff, der im Allgemeinen mit Journalismus und Werbung assoziiert wird und eine sehr kurze Textpassage beschreibt, die über dem Haupttext steht und auf dessen Inhalt hinweist. Da Schlagzeilen die Voraussetzungen für den Text schaffen, werden sie gewöhnlicherweise in einem deutlich größeren Schriftgrad – mitunter auch in einer anderen Schriftart – als der Haupttext gesetzt. Die Verwendung von **Versalbuchstaben** oder einer Kombination aus Klein- und Großbuchstaben ist – vor allem in Zeitungen – sehr geläufig.

En: HEADLINE
Fr: CHAPEAU
It: TITOLO
Spa: TITULAR

Design: Jan Kruse, Martina Massong, Martin Schwatio;
Firma: Ligalux GmbH, www.ligalux.de

SCHMALE SCHRIFT

Ein Schriftbild, in dem die Buchstaben schmaler sind als in der normalen Form derselben Schriftart. Zudem stehen die Buchstaben näher aneinander, sodass mehr Text innerhalb einer bestimmten Fläche untergebracht werden kann. Da hierunter allerdings die **Lesbarkeit** leidet, wird schmale Schrift meist nur für **Überschriften**, Slogans oder andere Texte verwendet, die nicht allzu lang sind.

En: CONDENSED TYPE
Fr: CONDENSÉ
It: CARATTERI CONDENSATI
Spa: LETRA CONDENSADA

A B C D E F G H I J K L M N O P Q R **S** T U V W X Y Z

Frutiger
Frutiger Schräg

Bodoni
Bodoni Schräg

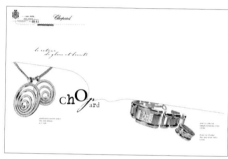

SCHRÄG (OBLIQUE)

Eine **serifenlose Schrift**, die nach rechts geneigt ist und Buchstaben beinhaltet, die denen der „normalen" Schriftart, auf der sie basiert, stark ähneln. **Kursive Schrift** ist auch nach rechts geneigt, aber hier werden die Buchstaben völlig neu dargestellt und unterscheiden sich mitunter von denen, auf denen sie basieren.

En: OBLIQUE
Fr: OBLIQUE
It: CARATTERI OBLIQUE
Spa: OBLICUA

SCHREIBSCHRIFT

Beschreibt alle Schriftbilder, die gestaltet wurden, um Handschrift zu imitieren. Obwohl Schreibschrift einem Textblock einen eleganten bis persönlichen Touch verleihen kann, sollte sie spärlich und nur in einem angemessenen Kontext verwendet werden. In Einladungen und Ankündigungen z. B. kann Schreibschrift effektiv eingesetzt werden. Lange Textpassagen hingegen, die in Schreibschrift gesetzt sind, „ermüden" den Leser.

En: SCRIPT TYPE
Fr: CURSIVE
It: CARATTERI INFORMALI
Spa: SCRIPT TYPE

Design: Michael Thiele; **Firma:** Die Transformer, www.dietransformer.de

SCHRIFT

Ein Begriff, der Schriftzeichen beschreibt, die in einer absichtlichen Reihe angeordnet sind, sodass sie entweder gedruckt oder auf dem Bildschirm gelesen werden können. Der Begriff wird aber auch für den *Bleisatz* verwendet. (Siehe auch **Setzen** und **Typografie**.)

En: TYPE
Fr: CARACTÈRES
It: SEQUENZA DI CARATTERI
Spa: TIPO

Design: Raphael Pohland, Simone Pohland; **Firma:** stilradar, www.stilradar.de

A B C D E F G H I J K L M N O P Q R **S** T U V W X Y Z

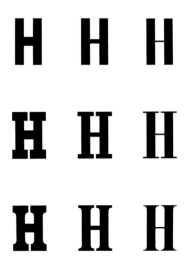

Helvetica Neue

Helvetica Neue Light

Helvetica Neue Ultralight

Helvetica Neue Ultralight Italic

Helvetica Neue Italic

Helvetica Neue Bold Italic

Helvetica Neue Bold Italic

Garamond
(Serif)

Futura
(Sans Serif)

Künstler
(Schreibschrift)

Lucida
(Fraktur)

SCHRIFTCHARAKTER

Die Form eines einzelnen Schriftzeichens (Buchstabe, Ziffer, Satzzeichen etc.). Elemente, die eine Gruppe von Schriftzeichen gemeinsam haben, machen dann das ganze Schriftbild aus. Der Aufbau einer Schrift kann mithilfe komplexer *Terminologie* beschrieben werden, die u. a. die Begriffe **Serifen**, **Ober-** und **Unterlänge** enthält.

En: LETTERFORM
Fr: DESSIN D'UNE LETTRE
It: GLIFO/I
Spa: LETRA

Design: Stephanie Horn,
www.stephanie-horn.com

SCHRIFTFAMILIE

Die Varianten einer bestimmten Schriftart wie **fett**, **kursiv**, **schmal**, breit usw. Die große Vielfalt an „Familienmitgliedern" ist hauptsächlich als Konsequenz des Werbebooms und des daraus resultierenden Bedarfs an extravaganter **Typografie** im 19. Jahrhundert anzusehen. (Siehe auch **Expertensatz**.)

En: TYPE FAMILY
Fr: FAMILLE DE CARACTÈRES
It: FAMIGLIA DI CARATTERI
Spa: FAMILIA TIPOGRÁFICA

SCHRIFTKLASSIFIKATION

Jedes einzelne verschiedener Systeme zur Kategorisierung von Schriftbildern anhand ihrer optischen Gemeinsamkeiten wie **Serifen**, Schreibschriftoptik etc. Da man viele Schriftbilder mehreren Kategorien zuordnen kann, sind solche Systeme der Klassifikation eher als grobe Einteilung denn als strenge Definition zu verstehen.

En: TYPE CLASSIFICATION
Fr: CLASSIFICATION TYPOGRAPHIQUE
It: CLASSIFICAZIONE DEI CARATTERI
Spa: CLASIFICACIÓN TIPOGRÁFICA

SCHRIFTSATZ

Die technische bzw. digitale Quelle für die Erstellung von Text. Ein Schriftsatz enthält Groß- und Kleinbuchstaben sowie Ziffern und Satzeichen. Viele Open-Type-Schriften enthalten seit der Entwicklung der **Expertensätze** auch Sonderzeichen. Bleisatzschriften haben eine spezifische Größe; digitale **Schriften** können per Mausklick verändert werden. Obwohl der Begriff Schriftsatz häufig als Synonym für Schriftbild oder **Schrifttype** verwendet wird, gibt es einen klar definierten Unterschied. Das Schriftbild bezieht sich auf das Design von Satzeichen, wohingegen der Schriftsatz das technische Produktionsmittel beschreibt.

En: FONT
Fr: FONTE
It: FONT
Spa: FUENTE

Design: Helge Rieder, Oliver Henn; **Firma:** 804©
Graphic Design, www.achtnullvier.com

A B C D E F G H I J K L M N O P Q R **S** T U V W X Y Z

Lorem ipsum dolor sit ametivi, consectetuer adipiscing eliberit. Aenean commodo ligula eget dolor. Aenean massa. Cum sociis natoque penatibus et magnis dis parturient montes, nascetur ridiculus mus.

Donec quam felis, ultricies nec, pellentesque eu, pretium quis, sem. Nulla consequat massavar quis enim. Donec pede justo, fringilla vel, aliquet nec, vulputate eget, arcu. In enim justo, rhoncus ut, imperdiet a, venenatis vitae, justo. Nullam dictum felis eu pede mollis pretium. Integer tincidunt. Cras dapibus.

Vivamus elementum.

Aenean vulputate eleifend tellus. Aenean leo ligula, porttitor eu, consequat vitae, eleifend ac, enim. Aliquam lorem ante, dapibus in, viverra quis, feugiat a, tellus. Phasellus viverraarcu nulla ut metus varius laoreet. Quisque rutrum. Aenean illmperdiettiam ultricies nisi velvet augue. Curabitur ullamcorper ultricies nisi. Nam egeteler dui. Etiam rhoncus. Maecenas tempus, tellus eget condimentum rhoncus, semertquam semperit libero, sit amet adipiscing sem neque sed leof ipsum. Nam

SCHRIFTTYPE

Eine Gruppe von Schriftzeichen, die ähnliche Designcharakteristiken wie Konturenbreite, Proportionen, **Serifen** etc. aufweisen. Eine Schrifttype beinhaltet üblicherweise Groß- und Kleinbuchstaben, Ziffern und eine Vielfalt von **Symbolen** (typografische, mathematische etc.). Schrifttype und **Schriftsatz** werden oft fälschlicherweise als Synonyme verwendet. Schrifttype bezieht sich auf das Design der Schriftzeichen; **Schriftsatz** ist das entweder technische, photomechanische oder digitale Produktionsmittel.

En: TYPEFACE
Fr: POLICE
It: CARATTERE/I
Spa: TIPO DE LETRA

Design: Grafikstudio Steinert, www.grafikstudio-steinert.com

SCHUSTERJUNGE

Ein oder zwei Zeilen eines Absatzes, die vom Hauptteil getrennt sind und am unteren (wenn sie den Absatz einleiten) bzw. oberen (wenn sie das Ende des Absatzes bilden) Rand einer Textspalte stehen. Schusterjungen können mittels verschiedener Techniken wie z. B. **Spationieren** und Trennungen vermieden werden. (Siehe auch **Witwe**.)

En: ORPHAN
Fr: ORPHELINE
It: ORFANO
Spa: HUÉRFANA

SEITENRAND

Die Bereiche entlang der vier Außenränder einer Seite, die üblicherweise den Haupttext und/oder Bilder eines bestimmten **Layouts** umrahmen. Elemente wie Seitenzahlen, Fußnoten und die Legende werden oft auf dem Seitenrand gedruckt. Die Ränder, die an der Bindung einer Publikation liegen, werden auch *Bundsteg* genannt.

En: MARGIN
Fr: MARGES
It: MARGINE/I
Spa: MARGEN

Design: Donna S. Atwood, www.atwooddesign.com

ABCDEFGHIJKLMNOPQR**S**TUVWXYZ

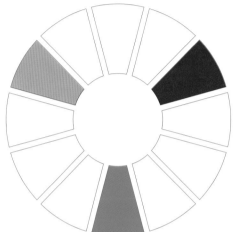

Baskerville
Lomba
Nueva
ROSEWOOD

Frutiger
Futura
Helvetica
Myriad

SEKUNDÄRFARBEN

Farben (Orange, Lila oder Grün), die mithilfe gleicher Anteile zweier **Primärfarben** gemischt werden. Orange z. B. wird aus gleichen Teilen von Rot und Gelb gemischt. (Siehe auch **Farbkreis** und **Tertiärfarben**.)

En: SECONDARY COLORS
Fr: COULEURS SECONDAIRES
It: COLORI SECONDARI
Spa: COLORES SECUNDARIOS

Design: Donna S. Atwood,
www.atwooddesign.com

SERIFE

Ein kleiner Strich am Ende der Hauptkontur eines Schriftzeichens. Mit Serifen kann auch die Vielzahl von Schriftarten bezeichnet werden, die Serifen enthalten, um sie von denen zu unterscheiden, die keine Serifen aufweisen, also **serifenlos** sind. Serifen helfen beim Lesen von Texten vornehmlich kleinen Schriftgrads, da sie dem Auge eine schnelle Unterscheidung der Buchstaben ermöglichen. Serifen stammen aus dem antiken Rom, wobei über ihre genaue Herkunft gestritten wird: Manche sagen, dass Steinmetze so ihre gemeißelten Striche „säuberten", wohingegen andere davon ausgehen, dass sie beim Vorzeichnen der Buchstaben mit dem Pinsel entstanden und dann beim Meißeln mit übernommen wurden. (Siehe auch **Serifenlos**.)

En: SERIF
Fr: EMPATTEMENT
It: CARATTERI CON GRAZIE
Spa: SERIFA

SERIFENLOS

Ein Begriff, der alle Schriftarten ohne **Serifen** beschreibt, die feinen Linien am Ende der Hauptkonturen eines Schriftzeichens. Im Vergleich zu vielen Schriftbildern mit **Serifen** weisen serifenlose Schriftbilder – wenn überhaupt – einen geringeren **Kontrast** zwischen ihren dünnen und dicken Linien auf, was die **Lesbarkeit** von Texten verbessern kann, die am Computerbildschirm gelesen werden.

En: SANS SERIF
Fr: CARACTÈRES SANS EMPATTEMENTS
It: CARATTERI SENZA GRAZIE
Spa: PALO SECO

A B C D E F G H I J K L M N O P Q R **S** T U V W X Y Z

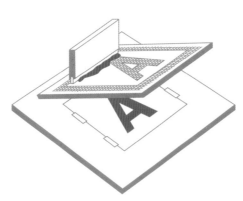

Die Küche ist im besten Sinne rheinisch-deftig. Fleischgerichte stehen dabei im Mittelpunkt, aber auch der Rotkohl wird noch selbst geraspelt und vermutlich kommen auch die Kartoffeln gleich vom Feld nebenan, denn alles schmeckt frisch und nicht nach Systemgastronomie. Zur Spargelsaison gibt es hier wirklich köstlichen Spargel und sensationell ist die Martinsgans im Herbst.

Die Küche ist im besten Sinne rheinisch-deftig. Fleischgerichte stehen dabei im Mittelpunkt, aber auch der Rotkohl wird noch selbst geraspelt und vermutlich kommen auch die Kartoffeln gleich vom Feld nebenan, denn alles schmeckt frisch und nicht nach Systemgastronomie. Zur Spargelsaison gibt es hier wirklich köstlichen Spargel und sensationell ist die Martinsgans im Herbst.

Die Küche ist im besten Sinne rheinisch-deftig. Fleischgerichte stehen dabei im Mittelpunkt, aber auch der Rotkohl wird noch selbst geraspelt und vermutlich kommen auch die Kartoffeln gleich vom Feld nebenan, denn alles schmeckt frisch und nicht nach Systemgastronomie. Zur Spargelsaison gibt es hier wirklich köstlichen Spargel und sensationell ist die Martinsgans im Herbst.

Die Küche ist im besten Sinne rheinisch-deftig. Fleischgerichte stehen dabei im Mittelpunkt, aber auch der Rotkohl wird noch selbst geraspelt und vermutlich kommen auch die Kartoffeln gleich vom Feld nebenan, denn alles schmeckt frisch und nicht nach Systemgastronomie. Zur Spargelsaison gibt es hier wirklich köstlichen Spargel und sensationell ist die Martinsgans im Herbst.

SETZEN

Die Anordnung von Schriftzeichen für den Druck und/oder das Lesen am Bildschirm. Über Jahrhunderte wurde das Setzen mithilfe von *Bleisätzen* ausgeführt, die auf der Druckpresse fixiert wurden. Die *Linotype*-Setzmaschine, die 1886 auf den Markt kam, erhöhte die Effizienz des Bleisatzdrucks, indem sie mithilfe ganzer „Textzeilen" arbeitete, sog. *Setzmaschinenzeilen*. Der *Lichtdruck*, ein Verfahren, bei dem die Schrift nicht mehr aus *Bleisätzen* bestand, sondern auf Spiegelglasplatten gesetzt wurde, wurde die vorherrschende Technik des Setzens während der 1960er bis in die 1980er Jahre; von da an wurde sie allmählich durch digitale **Schrift** ersetzt.

En: TYPESETTING
Fr: COMPOSITION TYPOGRAPHIQUE
It: COMPOSIZIONE TIPOGRAFICA
Spa: COMPOSICIÓN TIPOGRÁFICA

Design: Claudia Fischer-Appelt, Jan Kruse, Thomas Kappes, Tobias Heidemeier; **Firma:** Ligalux GmbH, www.ligalux.de

SIEBDRUCK

Ein Druckverfahren, bei dem die Tinte durch ein feines Sieb auf das zu bedruckende Material wie Papier oder Stoff gedrückt wird. Eine Schablone, die entweder aus einem anderen Material besteht oder durch das teilweise Versiegeln der Sieboberfläche selbst entsteht, dient zur Festlegung der zu bedruckenden Flächen. Der Siebdruck wird überwiegend bei der Textilproduktion verwendet, kann aber auch bei der Bedruckung ungleichmäßiger Oberflächen zum Einsatz kommen.

En: SCREEN PRINTING
Fr: SÉRIGRAPHIE
It: SERIGRAFIA
Spa: SERIGRAFÍA

SILBENTRENNUNG
Siehe **Silbentrennung & Blocksatz (S&B)**.

SILBENTRENNUNG & BLOCKSATZ (S&B)

Ein Verfahren, mit dem Softwareanwendungen Zeilen mit Text füllen. Egal ob ein Text **linksbündig**, **rechtsbündig**, im Blocksatz oder entlang der Mittelachse ausgerichtet ist, füllt die Software den gesamten Raum, der für eine Zeile zur Verfügung steht, mit Schriftzeichen und Zwischenräumen. Diese Ausrichtung nennt man auch Blocksatz (ein Begriff, der üblicherweise nur für Textzeilen benutzt wird, die die gesamte zur Verfügung stehende Fläche ausnutzen). Silbentrennung bezieht sich auf das Trennen von Wörtern, das zur Folge hat, dass eine Textzeile weiter ausgefüllt werden kann. Fortschrittliche Layoutanwendungen geben dem Designer die Möglichkeit, Parameter für die Silbentrennung und Ausrichtung festzulegen, was ihm die für genaue **Typografie** notwendige Flexibilität gibt.

En: H&J
Fr: C&J
It: H&J
Spa: H&J

A B C D E F G H I J K L M N O P Q R **S** T U V W X Y Z

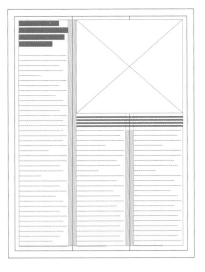

SPALTENABSTAND

Der Zwischenraum zwischen zwei Textspalten oder allgemein zwischen zwei Spalten innerhalb eines **Layouts**. Auch im Zusammenhang mit dem schmalen Streifen einer Seite nahe der Bindung bzw. dem „Bund" einer Doppelseite genutzt. (Siehe auch **Blocksatz**.)

En: GUTTER
Fr: GOUTTIÈRE
It: MARGINE INTERNO
Spa: MEDIANIL

Design: Donna S. Atwood,
www.atwooddesign.com

Buchstabenabstand
(-50 gesperrt)

Buchstabenabstand
(0 gesperrt)

Buchstabenabstand
(+50 gesperrt)

SPATIONIEREN

Die gesamten Abstände zwischen Schriftzeichen innerhalb eines Textes. Das Spationieren ist von besonderer Bedeutung, wenn man den **Blocksatz** verwendet, da hierbei oft verwirrende Lücken zwischen Wörtern entstehen, vor allem dann, wenn die Satzbreite besonders gering ist. Das Spationieren (auch „optischer Schriftweitenausgleich") wird oft mit dem Ausgleichen von **Auszeichnungsschriften** verwechselt, das jedoch das Vergrößern der Abstände zwischen Schriftzeichen beschreibt, um optisch Aufmerksamkeit zu erzielen. (Siehe auch **Sperren**.)

En: LETTER SPACING
Fr: INTERLETTRAGE
It: SPAZIO LETTERA
Spa: INTERLETRAJE

Laufweite: 0

Molor senim zrit esto odignim il utat, quisl ipit velissed et aci blan utate min ulla amer del enim quisim velendipit velis alisi blam nullupt atisit augue verostrud dolore dolessed estionsed tinil utat. Te dolobor perat.

Laufweite: +30

Molor senim zrit esto odignim il utat, quisl ipit velissed et aci blan utate min ulla amer del enim quisim velendipit velis alisi blam nullupt atisit augue verostrud dolore dolessed estionsed tinil utat. Te dolobor perat.

SPERREN

Die enge oder lockere Satzbreite innerhalb einer Textzeile. Vergrößert man die Sperrung, vergrößert man automatisch die Abstände im gesamten Text, da die Zwischenräume zwischen den Schriftzeichen proportional mitwachsen. Eine Verkleinerung der Sperrung hat den gegenteiligen Effekt. **Spationieren** bezieht sich meist auf die Abstände zwischen einzelnen Schriftzeichen; die Sperrung quantifiziert sie.

En: TRACKING
Fr: APPROCHE DE GROUPE
It: TRACKING
Spa: TRACKING

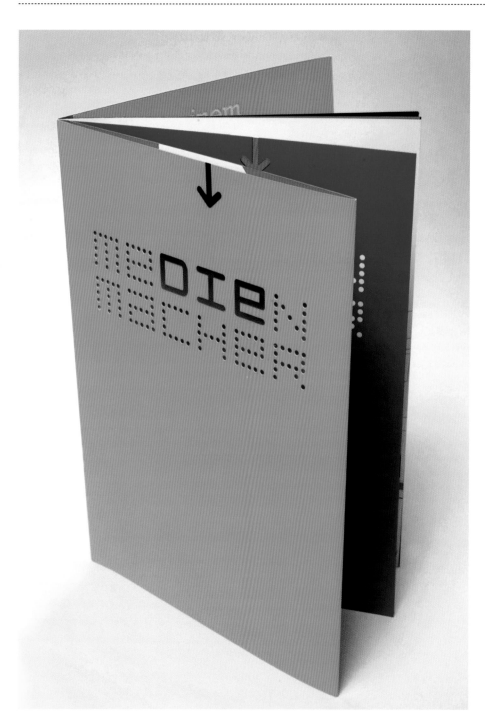

STANZSCHNITT

Ein Prozess, bei dem präzise Schnitte in einen bedruckten Papierbogen gemacht werden. Diese Schnitte können funktionale – wie z. B. bei Sammelmappen mit Einstecktasche oder bei Kartons, die man zusammensteckt – oder dekorative Zwecke erfüllen – z. B. als „Fenster", die Bilder offen legen, oder Randbearbeitungen. Manchmal verbindet man auch das Funktionale mit dem Dekorativen. (Siehe auch **Anstanzung** und **Laserschnitt**.)

En: DIE CUT
Fr: DÉCOUPE
It: FUSTELLA
Spa: TROQUELADO

Design: Michael Thiele, Martin Schonhoff;
Firma: Die Transformer, www.dietransformer.de

A B C D E F G H I J K L M N O P Q R **S** T U V W X Y Z

D ie Initiale entwickelte sich im späten 7. Jahrhundert aus der Buchstabenmalerei in Handschriften und insbesondere aus dem Versal des 9. Jahrhunderts. Ab 1450 adaptierten die deutschen Prototypographen…

STEHENDE INITIALE

Ein Großbuchstabe, der als Anfangsbuchstabe des ersten Wortes in einem Absatz verwendet und in einer größeren **Punktgröße** als der umstehende Text, jedoch auf derselben **Grundlinie** gesetzt wird. Um die Wirkung zu vergrößern, können stehende Initialen auch in einer völlig anderen Schriftart gesetzt werden als der Haupttext. (Siehe auch **Initiale** und **Hängende Initiale**.)

En: STANDING CAPITAL/CAP
Fr: GRANDE CAPITALE
It: STANDING CAP
Spa: CAPITULAR

STOCK-FOTOS (BILDARCHIV)

Fotos und Illustrationen, die mittels einer Lizenzvereinbarung für den spezifischen Gebrauch verfügbar sind. Die Verwendung solcher Bilder ist deutlich günstiger als die Beauftragung eines Fotografen, allerdings geht damit auch ein Teil der Kreativität verloren. Zudem können sich der Designer und der Kunde nie sicher sein, wie und wo das Bild schon zuvor verwendet wurde; es gibt keinen Exklusivnutzungsvertrag mit dem Anbieter. Heutzutage gibt es verschiedenste Online-Archive, in denen Fotos und Illustrationen ganz einfach gesucht, bezahlt und heruntergeladen werden können.

En: STOCK PHOTOGRAPHY/IMAGES
Fr: BANQUE D'IMAGES
It: BANCA IMMAGINI
Spa: BANCO DE IMÁGENES Y
FOTOGRAFÍAS

STRUKTUR

Die wahrgenommene fühlbare Qualität eines Designelements oder **Layouts**. Obwohl der Begriff Struktur normalerweise zur Beschreibung dreidimensionaler Gegebenheiten wie z. B. einer Papieroberfläche gebraucht wird, wird er auch in Bezug auf dieselben Eigenschaften verwendet, wie sie sich in zweidimensionalen Designarbeiten ausdrücken. Verschiedene Muster und Verläufe z. B. können den Eindruck von Struktur erwecken, vor allem wenn sie in **Kontrast** zu weichen, einheitlichen Elementen gesetzt werden. Sogar eine Seite voller Text mit seinen starken vertikalen und horizontalen **Rhythmen** hat eine bestimmte Struktur, die dadurch festgelegt wird, wie der Text gesetzt wird.

En: TEXTURE
Fr: TEXTURE
It: TEXTURE
Spa: TEXTURA

Design: Fauxpas Grafik, www.fauxpas.ch

SURREALISMUS

Eine europäische Kunstbewegung der 1920er und 1930er Jahre, beeinflusst von Gefühlen, Träumen und dem Unterbewusstsein, was oft in überraschenden oder verunsichernden Gegenüberstellungen, optischen Täuschungen und offensichtlichen Verletzungen der physikalischen Gesetze dargestellt wurde. Grafiker ließen sich nicht nur von den vielen Techniken der Surrealisten inspirieren, sondern auch von ihrem experimentellen Versuch, dreidimensionale Räume darzustellen.

En: SURREALISM
Fr: SURRÉALISME
It: SURREALISMO
Spa: SURREALISMO

Design: Matthias Frey; **Firma:** Q Kreativgesellschaft mbH, www.q-home.de

A B C D E F G H I J K L M N O P Q R **S T** U V W X Y Z

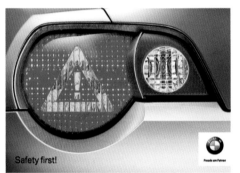

Safety first!

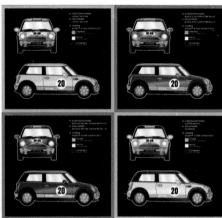

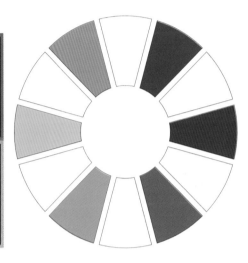

SYMBOL

Ein grafisches Zeichen, das für etwas anderes steht, als was es zeigt. In vielen Kulturen z. B. steht die simple Darstellung eines Herzens – vor allem in Rot – für die Liebe. Das Zeichen sieht nicht wie Liebe aus; eigentlich sieht es auch nicht aus wie ein echtes Herz. Aber da seine Bedeutung mehr oder weniger allgemeingültig ist, dient dieses Symbol der effektiven Kommunikation. Ebenso hat ein rotes Kreuz eine klare Bedeutung, die trotz vieler sprachlicher und kultureller Barrieren verstanden wird; aber nur unter der Voraussetzung, dass eine Vereinbarung derer über die Bedeutung herrscht, die das Symbol verwenden. (Siehe auch **Bildzeichen** und **Piktogramm**.)

En: SYMBOL
Fr: SYMBOLE
It: SIMBOLO
Spa: SÍMBOLO

Design: Grafikstudio Steinert,
www.grafikstudio-steinert.com

SYMMETRIE

Die gleichmäßige Verteilung von Elementen entlang einer bestimmten – oft vertikalen oder horizontalen – Achse. Symmetrische **Layouts** sind so aufgebaut, dass die Elemente von oben nach unten oder links nach rechts mehr oder weniger gleichmäßig verteilt sind, weshalb sie sehr konservativ wirken und größere Ausgeglichenheit vermitteln als asymmetrische **Layouts**. (Siehe auch **Asymmetrie**, **Balance** und **Blickbewegung**.)

En: SYMMETRY
Fr: SYMÉTRIE
It: SIMMETRIA
Spa: SIMETRÍA

Design: Grafikstudio Steinert,
www.grafikstudio-steinert.com

TERTIÄRFARBEN

Farben, die aus einer Kombination einer **Primär-** und einer **Sekundärfarbe** entstehen. Rotorange z. B. entsteht, wenn man Rot (eine **Primärfarbe**) und Orange (eine **Sekundärfarbe**, die aus gleichen Teilen der **Primärfarben** Rot und Gelb besteht) mischt. (Siehe auch **Farbkreis**.)

En: TERTIARY COLORS
Fr: COULEURS TERTIAIRES
It: COLORI TERZIARI
Spa: COLORES TERCIARIOS

Design: Donna S. Atwood,
www.atwooddesign.com

A B C D E F G H I J K L M N O P Q R S **T** U V W X Y Z

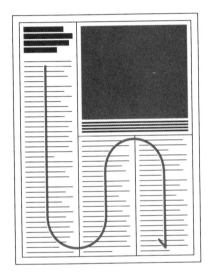

Several recent studies

TEXTEINPASSUNG

Der typografische Prozess, bei dem die Schriftgröße so angepasst wird, dass der Text in eine vorgegebene Fläche passt und sich auf eine bestimmte Anzahl von Seiten verteilt. Dies kann man entweder anhand von Berechnungen ermitteln oder mit einem Seitenlayoutprogramm, mit dem man schrittweise arbeiten kann, bis die gewünschte Einpassung erreicht ist.

En: COPYFITTING
Fr: CALIBRAGE
It: AGGIUSTAMENTO DEL TESTO
Spa: AJUSTE DEL ORIGINAL

Design: Donna S. Atwood,
www.atwooddesign.com

TEXTUMBRUCH

Ein Begriff, der im allgemeinen Sinn die Art und Weise beschreibt, in der eine Textzeile endet und in der nachfolgenden Zeile automatisch weiterläuft. Die Bearbeitung einer Textzeile hat meist eine neue Anordnung der nachfolgenden Zeilen zur Folge. Der Begriff kann sich im Speziellen auch darauf beziehen, wie Textzeilen umbrochen werden, um andere Designelemente wie Fotos und Illustrationen zu umlaufen. (Siehe auch **S&B**.)

En: TEXT WRAPPING
Fr: RETOUR À LA LIGNE AUTOMATIQUE
It: INVIO A CAPO AUTOMATICO
Spa: AJUSTE DE TEXTO

Design: Matthias Frey, Alexander Ginter, Markus Slawik;
Firma: Q Kreativgesellschaft mbH, www.q-home.de

TIEFGESTELLTE SCHRIFTZEICHEN

Schriftzeichen, die in einer kleineren Größe als der Haupttext und mittig auf der **Grundlinie** gesetzt werden. Tiefgestellte Buchstaben werden oft in der mathematischen Darstellung und verschiedenen wissenschaftlichen Ausdrücken verwendet. Tiefgestellte Buchstaben, die mittels der Verkleinerung der Standardbuchstaben einer Schriftart erstellt werden, haben dünnere Konturen als der umstehende Text, was störend sein kann. Daher verwenden Typografen und Designer wenn möglich immer die tiefgestellten Sonderzeichen einer Schrift.

En: SUBSCRIPT
Fr: INDICE
It: PEDICE/I
Spa: SUBÍNDICE

A B C D E F G H I J K L M N O P Q R S **T** U V W X Y Z

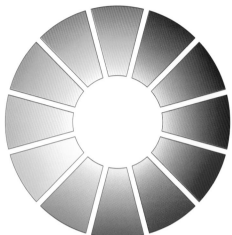

Trennstrich

Divis

Gedankenstrich

TITELEI

Teile eines Buches, die vor dem Haupttext stehen wie z. B. die Titelseite, das *Frontispiz* (eine Illustration oder Ähnliches auf der Gegenseite der Titelseite), ein Inhaltsverzeichnis, eine Begriffsliste, ein Vorwort usw. (Siehe auch **Anhang**.)

En: FRONT MATTER
Fr: PAGES LIMINAIRES
It: PAGINE INIZIALI
Spa: PÁGINAS PRELIMINARES

Design: Helge Rieder, Oliver Henn; **Firma:** 804©
Graphic Design, www.achtnullvier.com

TÖNUNG

Beschreibt einen Farbton, dessen **Leuchtdichte** durch das Hinzufügen von Weiß verändert wird. Das Abdunkeln der **Leuchtdichte** einer **Farbe** durch das Hinzufügen von Schwarz erzeugt eine dunklere Abstufung dieses **Farbtons**. Tönung bezieht sich auch auf die Dichte von Punkten, die beim **Vierfarbdruck** auf ein *Halbtonraster* entfallen. Den Bereich eines *Cyan-Rasters*, der zu 60 Prozent von Punkten bedeckt wird, nennt man eine 60-Prozent-Tönung.

En: TINT
Fr: COULEUR DE FOND
It: TINTA
Spa: TINTE

Design: Donna S. Atwood,
www.atwooddesign.com

TONWERT
Siehe **Leuchtdichte**.

TRENNSTRICH

Ein waagerechter Strich von der Länge eines Viertelgevierts, der im Deutschen meist als Binde-, Trenn- oder Ergänzungsstrich verwendet wird. Als Bindestrich wird er meist zur Gliederung bzw. Verbindung von Wörtern verwendet (z. B. i-Punkt oder römisch-katholisch oder Make-up). Fungiert er hingegen als Trennstrich, so zeigt er die **Silbentrennung** eines Wortes beim Zeilenumbruch an. Außerdem kann er als Ergänzungsstrich dienen (z. B. Haupt- und Nebeneingang).

En: HYPHEN
Fr: TRAIT D'UNION
It: TRATTINO
Spa: GUIÓN

TRIPLEX oder DREITON
Siehe **Duplex**.

A B C D E F G H I J K L M N O P Q R S **T U** V W X Y Z

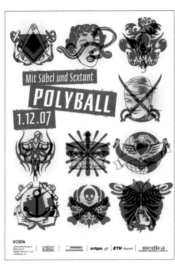

TYPOGRAFIE

Ein Begriff, der die Kunst und Wissenschaft des **Setzens** sowie die daraus entstehenden Werke beschreibt. Typografen beschäftigen sich mit einer Vielzahl von Aufgaben: angefangen von der **Lesbarkeit** eines Textes, bis hin zu den feinsten Details wie z. B. dem Unterschneiden und der Ästhetik der Buchstabenformen. Da digitale Technologien die Erschaffung feiner Typografie immer mehr erleichtern, ist diese Kunst wohl nicht mehr von so großer Bedeutung wie in Zeiten des *Bleisatzes* und *Lichtdrucks*, in denen Typografen jedes Detail berücksichtigen mussten.

En: TYPOGRAPHY
Fr: TYPOGRAPHIE
It: TIPOGRAFIA
Spa: TIPOGRAFÍA

Design: Helge Rieder, Oliver Henn; **Firma:** 804©
Graphic Design, www.achtnullvier.com

ÜBERDRUCKEN

Die Vermischung von übereinander gedruckter Tinte, die eine neue **Farbe** entstehen lässt. In den meisten Fällen, in denen zwei Designelemente überlappen, wird nur die Farbe des „oberen" Elements gedruckt; seine Farbe überdeckt alles Darunterliegende. Beim Überdrucken hingegen werden die zwei oder mehr **Farben** der Tinte so kombiniert, dass eine weitere Farbe entsteht.

En: OVERPRINTING
Fr: SURIMPRESSION
It: SOVRASTAMPA
Spa: SOBREIMPRESIÓN

Design: Fauxpas Grafik, www.fauxpas.ch

ÜBERFÜLLUNG

Eine Technik zur Vermeidung von Lücken zwischen farbigen Bereichen, verursacht durch mangelhafte **Registerhaltigkeit**. Wenn z. B. magentafarbener Text auf einem cyanfarbenen Hintergrund gedruckt wird, führt jeder *Passerfehler* zu einer Lücke zwischen Text und Hintergrund, die unbedrucktes Papier zeigt. Eine Überfüllung ist eine sehr schmale Farblinie bzw. Farbkontur, in diesem Fall in einer Kombination aus Magenta und Cyan, die ein Objekt umschließt, um solchen Lücken vorzubeugen. Es gibt verschiedene Arten von Überfüllungen; welche für den jeweiligen Druckvorgang am sinnvollsten ist, hängt von verschiedenen Faktoren ab. Die Entscheidung sollte deshalb vom Drucker getroffen werden. (Siehe auch **Registerhaltigkeit**.)

En: TRAPPING
Fr: GROSSI-MAIGRI
It: TRAPPING
Spa: REVENTADO

A B C D E F G H I J K L M N O P Q R S T **U** V W X Y Z

VANILLE

VANILLE
-75 -40 +10 +35 -30

Unterlänge

ÜBERSCHRIFT

Ein typografisches Mittel, um einen übermäßig langen Text in seine Hauptabschnitte zu gliedern, wie es Kapitelüberschriften in einem Buch oder Teilüberschriften in einer Broschüre oder einem Bericht tun. Überschriften werden meist in **fetter Schrift** aus **Versalbuchstaben** oder einer Kombination aus **Versalbuchstaben** und **Kapitälchen** gesetzt. **Untertitel** dienen zur weiteren Unterteilung eines Textes entsprechend seines Aufbaus.

En: HEADING
Fr: TITRE
It: TESTATINA
Spa: TÍTULO

Design: Grafikstudio-Steinert,
www.grafikstudio-steinert.com

UNTERLÄNGE

Die Unterlänge ist der Teil eines Kleinbuchstabens, der über die **Grundlinie** hinaus nach unten reicht. Wie bei **Oberlängen** variiert die relative Größe und Ausdehnung von Unterlängen von Schriftart zu Schriftart. Schriften mit größerer **x-Höhe** haben meist weniger Unterlänge, während Schriften mit geringerer **x-Höhe** oft markantere Unterlängen haben. (Siehe auch **Oberlänge** und **x-Höhe**.)

En: DESCENDER
Fr: DESCENDANTE
It: TRATTO DISCENDENTE
Spa: DESCENDENTE

UNTERSCHNEIDEN

Den Zwischenraum zwischen zwei benachbarten Schriftzeichen so wählen, dass eine ansprechende Optik entsteht. Wenn bestimmte Schriftzeichen – wie T und o – nebeneinanderstehen, bilden ihre Umrisse eine störende Lücke. Beim Unterschneiden verringert man den Zwischenraum, sodass ein natürlicheres Bild entsteht. (Häufig haben Textverarbeitungsprogramme eine Automatik dafür, die jedoch nicht immer den Ansprüchen des Designers oder Typografen genügt.)

En: KERNING
Fr: CRÉNAGE
It: CRENATURA
Spa: KERNING

A B C D E F G H I J K L M N O P Q R S T **U V** W X Y Z

UNTERTITEL

Eine Teilüberschrift unter der eigentlichen **Überschrift**, die dazu gebraucht wird, einen längeren Text in Abschnitte zu unterteilen, die seinen Aufbau aufzeigen und Hinweise auf die Rangfolge geben. Die Art und Weise, in der ein Untertitel einer Publikation gesetzt werden sollte (Größe, **Farbe**, Schriftart und Position), sollte berücksichtigen, inwieweit er in der Gesamthierarchie „höher", „tiefer" oder gleichwertig mit anderen einzuordnen ist. Wenn z. B. Rang-A-Untertitel für große Städte verwendet werden und Rang-B-Untertitel sich mit unterschiedlichen Kategorien von Strukturdaten befassen, sollten sich diese zwei Untertitel deutlich voneinander unterscheiden. Wenn jedoch die Rang-B-Untertitel für die Namen nahegelegener Vororte gebraucht werden, sollte der optische Unterschied subtiler sein.

En: SUBHEAD
Fr: INTERTITRE
It: SOTTOTITOLO
Spa: SUBTÍTULO

Design: Raphael Pohland, Simone Pohland;
Firma: stilradar, www.stilradar.de

UV-LACK

Ein Prozess bei dem – entweder bereits während des Drucks oder direkt nach dem Druckvorgang – ein chemisches Mittel auf das Papier aufgetragen und es mit UV-Licht getrocknet wird. Im Vergleich zu einer Wasserbeschichtung bietet die UV-Beschichtung besseren Schutz gegen Abnutzung und Schäden, die einem bedruckten Material durch häufigen Gebrauch zugefügt werden können. Sie ist jedoch anfälliger für Risse, sobald das bedruckte Papier gefaltet oder geknickt wird. UV-Beschichtungen werden entweder nur als Punktbeschichtung an bestimmten Stellen eines bedruckten Materials aufgetragen oder als Gesamtbeschichtung, die das gesamte Blatt bedecken. (Siehe auch **Lackierung**.)

En: ULTRAVIOLET COATING
Fr: VERNIS UV
It: FINITURA A ULTRAVIOLETTI
Spa: REVESTIMIENTO ULTRAVIOLETA

Design: Helge Rieder, Oliver Henn; **Firma:** 804©
Graphic Design, www.achtnullvier.com

VEKTORGRAFIK

Ein digitales Bild, das mithilfe mathematisch definierter Gebilde und nicht wie ein **Bitmap** durch die Anordnung von Punkten erzeugt wird. Aufgrund dieser Tatsache können Vektorgrafiken auch stark vergrößert werden, ohne dass ihre **Auflösung** darunter leidet. **Bitmaps** können dagegen in enorm hohem Detailreichtum und sehr feiner Farbmischung dargestellt werden. (Siehe auch **Bézierkurve**.)

En: VECTOR GRAPHIC
Fr: IMAGES VECTORIELLES
It: GRAFICA VETTORIALE
Spa: GRÁFICO VECTORIAL

Design: Matthias Frey; **Firma:** Q Kreativgesellschaft mbH, www.q-home.de

ABCDEFGHIJKLMNOPQRSTU **V** WXYZ

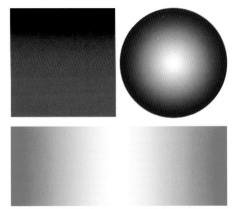

Versalhöhe

VERLAUF

Der fließende Übergang von einer **Farbe** zu einer anderen oder von Weiß bzw. Schwarz zu einer gesättigten **Farbe** in gleichmäßiger Abstufung. Verläufe werden oft zum Ausfüllen bestimmter Teile von Illustrationen, Hintergründen oder **Konturschriften** benutzt.

En: GRADIENT
Fr: DÉGRADÉ
It: GRADIENTE/I
Spa: DEGRADADO

VERPACKUNGSDESIGN

Aus der Sicht eines Grafikdesigners bezeichnet das Verpackungsdesign die Schaffung einer Verpackung, die Produkte während ihrer Lieferung, Lagerung, ihres Verkaufs und ihres Gebrauchs schützt und präsentiert. **Logos**, Schriftzüge und andere optische und fühlbare Elemente der Marke spielen eine wichtige Rolle im Verpackungsdesign, obwohl die künstlerischen Gesichtspunkte nur der Anfang sind. Weitere Faktoren sind Sicherheit (z. B. kindersichere Medikamente), Einsparungen (z. B. die Berücksichtigung der Anzahl an Kisten, die in einen Frachtcontainer passt) oder Benutzerfreundlichkeit (z. B. die Vorgabe, dass der Kunde die Verpackung so öffnen kann, dass er gute Erfahrungen damit macht), um nur einige zu nennen.

En: PACKAGING DESIGN
Fr: DESIGN DE PACKAGING
It: PACKAGING DESIGN
Spa: DISEÑO DE EMBALAJE

Design: Barski Design, www.barskidesign.com

VERSALHÖHE

Der Abstand von der **Grundlinie** bis zu den obersten Kanten von Großbuchstaben, die an der *K-Linie* liegen. Versalhöhen können bei gleichem Schriftgrad unterschiedlicher Schriftarten variieren. (Siehe auch **Kapitälchen**.)

En: CAP HEIGHT
Fr: HAUTEUR DE CAPITALE
It: ALTEZZA DELLA MAIUSCOLA
Spa: ALTURA DE LAS MAYÚSCULAS

A B C D E F G H I J K L M N O P Q R S T U **V** W X Y Z

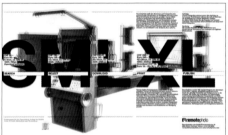

VERSALIEN

Eine andere Bezeichnung für einen Text, der ausschließlich in Großbuchstaben, sog. „uppercase letters", gesetzt wird, die deshalb so heißen, weil die **Bleisätze**, mit denen sie früher gedruckt wurden, meist in den oberen (upper) Schubladen (case) der Druckermeister aufbewahrt wurden. Die wesentlich häufiger benutzten „lowercase letters" (Kleinbuchstaben) hingegen lagerten in den besser zugänglichen unteren (lower) Schubladen. Im Deutschen werden die „uppercase letters" auch mit *Majuskeln* übersetzt; die „lowercase letters" entsprechend mit *Minuskeln*.

En: ALL CAPS
Fr: TOUT EN CAPITALES
It: TUTTE MAIUSCOLE
Spa: ALL CAPS

Design: Jan Kruse, Martin Schwatio; **Firma:** Ligalux GmbH, www.ligalux.de

VIERFARBDRUCK

Ein Druckverfahren, bei dem mithilfe individueller *Halbtonraster* der vier Druckfarben – Cyan, Magenta, Gelb und Schwarz – nahezu das gesamte Farbspektrum abgedeckt wird. Jede **Farbe** wird als Muster kleiner Druckpunkte verschiedener Größe und Dichte gedruckt. Da die vier Druckfarben – je zu zweit kombiniert – die additiven **Primärfarben** (Rot, Grün und Blau) erzeugen, die die drei unterschiedlichen Lichtrezeptoren im menschlichen Auge ansprechen, entsteht ein überzeugender Gesamteindruck „aller **Farben**". (Siehe auch **CMYK** und **Halbton**.)

En: FOUR-COLOR PROCESS
Fr: QUADRICHROMIE
It: PROCESSO A QUATTRO COLORI
Spa: CUATRICOMÍA

Design: Fauxpas Grafik, www.fauxpas.ch

VIKTORIANISCHER STIL

Ein dekorativer, oft pompöser Stil der Architektur und des Designs, der seinen Ursprung in England hatte und sich zwischen 1820 und 1900 in weiten Teilen Europas und Amerikas großer Beliebtheit erfreute. Benannt nach der englischen Königin Victoria war er eine Antwort auf die industrielle Revolution, deren Maßlosigkeit und den Trend weg von der Handarbeit hin zur Massenproduktion. Technologische Fortschritte gaben Designern und Typografen ungeahnte neue Möglichkeiten, was einen großen Mischmasch verschiedener Stilrichtungen aus verschiedenen Epochen zur Folge hatte. Während der ersten Hälfte der Viktorianischen Ära setzte man bei der **Schrift** auf verzerrte Proportionen und breite Konturen, oft in Verbindung mit ganz simplen Illustrationen; verschiedene Schriftgrößen und -arten fanden sich innerhalb ein und desselben überladenen **Layouts**. Gegen Ende dieser Epoche bekam der Stil jedoch einen leichteren und eleganteren Touch.

En: VICTORIAN
Fr: STYLE VICTORIEN
It: STILE VITTORIANO
Spa: VICTORIANO

A B C D E F G H I J K L M N O P Q R S T U V **W** X Y Z

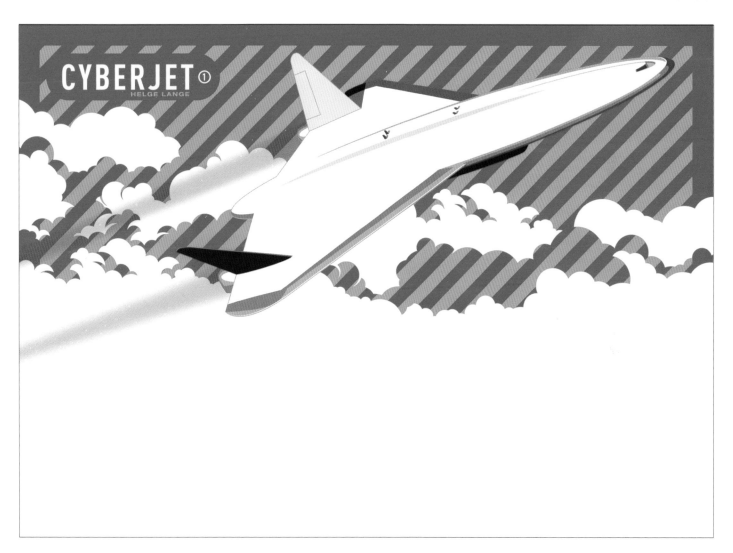

WEISSRAUM

Allgemeine Bezeichnung für die Flächen eines **Layouts**, die leer bleiben, egal ob sie tatsächlich weiß sind oder nicht. Weiße Flächen sind für ein gutes Design jedoch ebenso wichtig wie die Designelemente, die es enthält; sie wirken mit. Die richtige Anwendung weißer Flächen strukturiert ein Design und erhält die Gleichmäßigkeit eines **Layouts**, so wie **gestaltete** und **freie Flächen** eine gewisse Harmonie zwischen Designelementen hervorrufen. (Siehe auch **Raster**.)

En: WHITE SPACE
Fr: BLANCS
It: SPAZIO BIANCO
Spa: ESPACIO BLANCO

Design: Michael Thiele; **Firma:** Die Transformer, www.dietransformer.de

A B C D E F G H I J K L M N O P Q R S T U V **W X** Y Z

Lorem ipsum dolor sit amet, consectetuer adipiscing elit. Aenean commodo ligula eget dolor. Aenean massa. Cumert sociis natoque pentibus et magnis dis parturient montes, nasceturculus mus. Donec quam felis, ultricies nec, pellenteqe eu, pretium quis, sem. Nulla consequat massa quis enim. Donec pede justo, fringilla vel, aliqut nec, vulputate eget, arcu. In enim justo, rhoncus ut, impdiet a, venenatis vitae, justo. Nullam dictum felis eu pede mollis pretium Integer tincidt Cras.

Typografie

WICKELFALZ

Parallelfalzungen an einem Papierbogen, die ohne Richtungswechsel angesetzt werden, sodass sich die einzelnen Seiten ineinander „aufrollen". Damit sich die Seiten richtig miteinander verschachteln, werden sie von außen nach innen stufenweise etwas schmaler. Ein anderer Begriff für den Wickelfalz ist *Rollfalz*. (Siehe auch **Leporello**.)

En: BARREL FOLD
Fr: PLI ROULÉ
It: PIEGHEVOLE A PORTAFOGLIO
Spa: DOBLADO TIPO ROLLO

Kunstdirektor: Tracy Holdeman; **Design:** Casey Zimmerman; **Firma:** Insight Design Communications, www.insightdesign.com

WITWE

Eine sehr kurze letzte Zeile eines Absatzes – oft nur ein einziges Wort–, die den Eindruck eines Zwischenraums zwischen Absätzen erweckt, zwischen denen eigentlich keiner ist. Ebenso wie **Schusterjungen** können Witwen mittels verschiedener Methoden vermieden werden. Die beiden meistverwendeten Techniken hierfür sind das **Sperren** und die **Silbentrennung**. (Siehe auch **S&B** und **Textumbruch**.)

En: WIDOW
Fr: VEUVE
It: VEDOVA
Spa: VIUDA

X-HÖHE

Gibt für ein bestimmtes Schriftbild die Höhe von Kleinbuchstaben an, die weder eine **Ober-** noch eine **Unterlänge** haben. Die x-Höhe beschreibt den Abstand zwischen **Grund-** und **x-Linie** des Schriftbilds. Bei kleinem Schriftgrad sind Schriftarten mit großen x-Höhen besser lesbar als vergleichbare Schriftarten mit kleineren x-Höhen.

En: X-HEIGHT
Fr: HAUTEUR D'X
It: ALTEZZA DELLA X
Spa: ALTURA X

A B C D E F G H I J K L M N O P Q R S T U V W **X** Y **Z**

Erste Zeile Einzug

Lorem ipsum dolor sit amet, consectetuer sadipscing elitr, sed diam nonumy eirmod tempor invidunt ut labore et dolore magna aliquyam erat, sed diam voluptua. At vero eos et accusam et justo duo dolores et ea rebum.

Überhängender Einzug

Lorem ipsum seder dolor sit amet, consectetuer sadipscing elitr, sed diam nonumy eirmod tempor invidunt ut labore et dolore magna aliquyam erat, sed diam voluptua. At vero eos et accusam et justo duo dolores et ea rebum.

Umlaufender Einzug

Lorem ipsum seder dolor sit amet, consectetuer sadipscing elitr, sed diam nonumy eirmod tempor invidunt ut labore et dolore magna aliquyam erat, sed diam voluptua. At vero eos et accusam et justo duo dolores et ea rebum.

Einzug nach Schriftzeichen

· Lorem ipsum seder dolor sit amet, consectetuer sadipscing elitr, sed diam nonumy eirmod tempor invidunt ut labore et dolore magna aliquyam erat, sed diam voluptua. At vero eos et accusam et justo duo elitr dolores et ea rebum.

Nim iril ut aut loreet autat. Periure magnim eros dolorem quat. Tumsan ut nosto odit laor sim eummodiam vent pratuer cidunt atisim irillaortie min ulla alit ing endreet niam, quatie tat, consequisit praesto dolorem zzril.

Cil ulputatumsan ute consenit venim ad ex ea feugait dolobore molutatie delisi. Rud el iustion sequissenim at amcore do estrud tatue tat. Ut vel ullaore rcillute feugait prat at in ut in henibh ea facin etum non eliquam. Tumsan ut

Mittellinie

X-LINIE (MITTELLINIE)

Eine Referenzlinie für die exakte horizontale Ausrichtung von Text, entsprechend der **x-Höhe** einer bestimmten Schriftart. Die oberen Kanten der Kleinbuchstaben, die keine **Oberlänge** aufweisen, liegen auf oder dicht an der x-Linie. Tatsächlich sind es nur die Kleinbuchstaben mit flacher Oberkante, die an der x-Linie enden. Die Buchstaben mit runder Oberkante wie a und o gehen geringfügig über diese Linie hinaus. Eine ähnliche optische Täuschung entsteht an der **Grundlinie**; beide Fälle unterstreichen die Wichtigkeit **optischer Ausrichtung** für genaue **Typografie**.

En: MEAN LINE
Fr: LIGNE DE TÊTE
It: LINEA MEDIANA
Spa: LÍNEA MEDIA

ZEILENEINZUG

Eine Einstellung für die **Seitenränder** innerhalb einer oder mehrerer Textzeilen. Einfache Zeileneinzüge werden meist gesetzt, um den Anfang eines neuen Absatzes anzuzeigen. Der Abstand zwischen Zeilenbeginn und **Seitenrand** ist hier deutlich größer als bei den nachfolgenden Zeilen. Hängende Zeileneinzüge werden dazu genutzt, den Rand aller Zeilen zu vergrößern, die nach der ersten Zeile eines Absatzes folgen. Mithilfe umlaufender Zeileneinzüge kann man den linken und/oder rechten Seitenrand mehrerer Zeilen so verändern, dass sie z. B. eine Illustration oder ein Foto umrahmen („umlaufen"). Zeileneinzüge, die nach einem Schriftzeichen gesetzt werden, dienen dazu, Schriftzeichen mithilfe der **Seitenränder** so anzuordnen, dass sie mit denen einer vorangegangenen Textzeile korrespondieren.

En: INDENT
Fr: COMPOSITION EN ALINÉA
It: RIENTRO
Spa: SANGRÍA

ZEILENLÄNGE

Die Länge einer bestimmten Textzeile. Die Zeilenlänge wird häufig mit der **Satzbreite** verwechselt, der Breite einer ganzen Spalte. Wenn ein Text jedoch z. B. **linksbündig** (oder im **Flattersatz**) gesetzt wird, füllen die Textzeilen nur selten die gesamte Satzbreite. Gleiches gilt auch für **rechtsbündig** und zentriert gesetzte Texte. Nur im **Blocksatz** entspricht die Zeilenlänge der Satzbreite.

En: LINE LENGTH
Fr: LONGUEUR DE LIGNE
It: LUNGHEZZA DI RIGA
Spa: LONGITUD DE LÍNEA

A B C D E F G H I J K L M N O P Q R S T U V W X Y **Z**

Erfolgreiche Markenkommunikation erfordert neben Kreativität, auch Planbarkeit und Systematik…

In unserer modernen Welt der Reizüberflutung scheint vieles austauschbar – die Identität Ihres Unternehmens…

Unsere Öffnungszeiten: Montag–Freitag Freitag 9:00–18:00 Uhr, Samstag 10:00–14:00 Uhr…

ZEILENUMBRUCH

Ein Begriff, der beschreibt, wie und wo eine Textzeile endet, bevor sie in der nächsten Zeile fortgesetzt wird. Layoutanwendungen setzen Zeilenumbrüche üblicherweise bei Zwischenräumen zwischen Wörtern oder nach einem **Trenn-**, **Geviert-** oder **Halbgeviertstrich**, wobei solche automatischen Einstellungen oft angepasst werden können. Außerdem kann man eine Zeile mittels einer sog. „weichen Zeilentrennung" brechen, indem man eine neue Textzeile, nicht aber einen neuen Absatz beginnt (was häufig Einzüge oder andere Effekte verursacht). (Siehe auch **S&B** und **Blocksatz**.)

En: LINE BREAK
Fr: SAUT DE LIGNE
It: INTERRUZIONE DI LINEA
Spa: SALTO DE LÍNEA

Lyrische Texte unterscheiden sich von der Prosa oft durch ihre äußere Form. Im Laufe der Gattungsgeschichte, vor allem im 20. Jahrhundert, verlor dieses Kriterium allerdings weitgehend seine Bedeutung. Lyrische Texte unterscheiden sich dennoch sprachlich-formal von…

ZIERBUCHSTABEN

Höchst dekorative Schriftzeichen – meist nach rechts geneigte Großbuchstaben – mit erweiterten Strichen und Schnörkeln. Als Großbuchstaben werden Zierbuchstaben meist als **Initiale** des ersten Wortes eines Absatzes und in einer größeren **Punktgröße** als der des umstehenden Textes gesetzt. Als Kleinbuchstaben werden sie oft am anderen Ende des Absatzes verwendet: als letzter Buchstabe des letzten Wortes eines Satzes. Obwohl Zierbuchstaben einem Textblock eine gewisse Eleganz verleihen können, sollten sie sparsam verwendet werden. Eine Textzeile, die nur aus Zierbuchstaben besteht z. B., ist nämlich sowohl ablenkend als auch unleserlich. (Siehe auch **Initiale**.)

En: SWASH CHARACTERS
Fr: LETTRE ITALIQUE ORNÉE
It: CARATTERI SWASH
Spa: LETRA DE FANTASÍA

ITALIANO

A BCDEFGHIJKLMNOPQRSTUVWXYZ

ADESIVO CON FUSTELLA

Versione del processo di fustellatura utilizzata per adesivi e decalcomanie. I tagli vengono eseguiti su un foglio di carta stampata senza incidere sulla sua base, permettendo pertanto agli adesivi o alle decalcomanie di essere staccati dal supporto.

Ing: KISS DIE CUT
Fr: DÉCOUPE PAR EFFLEUREMENT
Ted: ANSTANZUNG
Sp: TROQUELADO DE MEDIO CORTE

Agenzia di pubblicità: TECNOSTUDI

AGGIUSTAMENTO DEL TESTO

Processo tipografico di aggiustamento della misura del punto tipografico e dell'**interlinea** dei **caratteri** in modo da farli rientrare in un'area definita o in un certo numero di pagine. Per formulare previsioni si possono utilizzare i calcoli, oppure il processo può essere ripetuto, usando software per l'impaginazione, finché non si ottiene un risultato corretto.

Ing: COPYFITTING
Fr: CALIBRAGE
Ted: TEXTEINPASSUNG
Sp: AJUSTE DEL ORIGINAL

Studio grafico: Latveria Design

ALIASING/ANTI-ALIASING

L'aliasing si verifica quando la **risoluzione** di un'immagine **bitmap** è inferiore rispetto a quella dello strumento usato per mostrarla o stamparla. Un'immagine con risoluzione di 72 spi (*samples per inch*, campioni per pollice) ad es., produrrà un aliasing se stampata a grandezza naturale a 300 dpi (*dots per inch*, punti per pollice), producendo un marcato effetto "a gradino". L'anti-aliasing è la tecnica impiegata da un programma digitale di trattamento delle immagini per minimizzare la distorsione generata dall'aliasing, e si ottiene smussando lievemente l'immagine, in modo da attenuare il "salto" tra i gradini. Sebbene così facendo si sacrifichi qualcosa della qualità, è spesso preferibile all'aliasing.

Ing: ALIASING, ANTI-ALIASING
Fr: CRÉNELAGE, ANTICRÉNELAGE
Ted: ALIAS EFFEKT, ANTIALIASING
Sp: SOLAPAMIENTO/ANTISOLAPAMIENTO

Agenzia di pubblicità: TECNOSTUDI

A BCDEFGHIJKLMNOPQRSTUVWXYZ

ALLINEAMENTO

L'allineamento si riferisce alla disposizione di elementi grafici multipli, come le immagini e i **caratteri**, gli uni rispetto agli altri. Gli elementi sono spesso allineati in modo che le loro estremità (a sinistra, a destra, in basso o in alto) o le linee centrali (orizzontali e verticali) si trovino in corrispondenza di una linea di riferimento comune, che spesso fa parte di una **griglia**. L'allineamento può anche riferirsi alla disposizione dei caratteri all'interno di un blocco di tipi. Vedi anche **allineamento a sinistra** e **a destra**, caratteri centrati e giustificati.

Ing: ALIGNMENT
Fr: ALIGNEMENT
Ted: AXIALITÄT
Sp: ALINEACIÓN

Agenzia di comunicazione e immagine: Brunazzi & Associati, Torino; **Direttori creativi:** Giovanni Brunazzi, Andrea Brunazzi

ALLINEAMENTO A SINISTRA E ALLINEAMENTO A DESTRA

Linee successive di **caratteri**, allineati a sinistra partendo da una comune linea di riferimento, vengono anche chiamate a **bandiera** destra. Linee successive di caratteri allineati a destra, che finiscono su una comune linea di riferimento, vengono anche chiamate a bandiera sinistra.

Ing: FLUSH-LEFT, FLUSH-RIGHT
Fr: FER À GAUCHE, FER À DROITE
Ted: LINKSBÜNDIG, RECHTSBÜNDIG
Sp: BANDERA A LA IZQUIERDA/BANDERA A LA DERECHA

Realizzazione grafica: MP foto&grafica

ALLINEAMENTO VISIVO

Caratteri o altri elementi grafici disposti in modo da farli sembrare correttamente allineati piuttosto che essere il risultato di misurazioni precise. Ciò è particolarmente importante quando le forme allineate sono diverse. Ad esempio, allineando un cerchio, un triangolo equilatero o un quadrato tutti della stessa altezza lungo la medesima linea orizzontale, si produce un'illusione ottica. Il quadrato appare più alto delle altre forme, mentre il cerchio appare più piccolo sia del quadrato, sia del triangolo.

Ing: VISUAL ALIGNMENT
Fr: ALIGNEMENT VISUEL
Ted: OPTISCHE AUSRICHTUNG
Sp: ALINEACIÓN VISUAL

Design: Tassinari/Vetta

A BCDEFGHIJKLMNOPQRSTUVWXYZ

ALTEZZA DELLA MAIUSCOLA

Distanza di una lettera maiuscola dalla **linea di base** al margine superiore, che si dispiega lungo la *linea ascendente*. Le altezze delle maiuscole variano anche all'interno di **caratteri** con punti della stessa misura. Vedi anche **maiuscoletti**.

Ing: CAP HEIGHT
Fr: HAUTEUR DE CAPITALE
Ted: VERSALHÖHE
Sp: ALTURA DE LAS MAYÚSCULAS

Agenzia di pubblicità: TECNOSTUDI

ALTEZZA DELLA X

Dato un certo **carattere**, è l'altezza delle lettere minuscole che non hanno né **tratto ascendente** né **tratto discendente**. Misurata in **punti**, l'altezza della x è la distanza fra la **linea di base** e la **linea mediana**. Nei caratteri con punti di piccole dimensioni, quelli con un'altezza della x elevata offrono una maggiore facilità di lettura rispetto a caratteri equiparabili con altezza della x inferiore.

Ing: X-HEIGHT
Fr: HAUTEUR D'X
Ted: X-HÖHE
Sp: ALTURA X

Studio grafico: Sara Muzio

ANIMAZIONE/I

Serie di immagini digitali disposte secondo una specifica sequenza, così da generare una sensazione di movimento continuo. *GIF*s animati vengono spesso usati per animazioni di web design relativamente semplici, mentre animazioni più complesse vengono solitamente realizzate con software sofisticati, come Adobe's Flash®.

Ing: ANIMATION
Fr: ANIMATION
Ted: ANIMATION
Sp: ANIMACIÓN

Achab Group; **Designer:** Katia Pastrello; **Illustrazioni:** Valentina Tamiazzo; **Copywriter:** Manuela Marassi; **Cliente:** A&T2000 (Udine)

A B C D E F G H I J K L M N O P Q R S T U V W X Y Z

APICE/I

Come i **pedici**, anche gli apici sono caratteri appositamente ridotti in scala inferiore rispetto al testo principale in cui sono collocati. La disposizione degli apici, detti anche *superiori*, dipende comunque dal loro scopo. Per i numeri che rimandano alle note a piè di pagina o per il numeratore di una frazione, gli apici si allineano superiormente lungo la *linea ascendente*. Nelle espressioni matematiche o scientifiche vengono invece allineati al centro. Anche le lettere minuscole si usano a volte come apici, allineandole in alto.

Ing: SUPERSCRIPT
Fr: EXPOSANT
Ted: HOCHGESTELLTE SCHRIFTZEICHEN
Sp: SUPERÍNDICE

Agenzia di pubblicità: TECNOSTUDI

APOSTROFO

L'**apostrofo** (') è un carattere tipografico che si usa nelle lingue scritte in alfabeto latino, come segno di interpunzione e talvolta come segno diacritico. In italiano si usa per indicare l'elisione e il troncamento. Si usa l'apostrofo per indicare l'elisione di una vocale alla fine di una parola, quando la parola successiva inizia con una vocale, e può indicare l'elisione della lettera finale di un verbo all'imperativo, ad esempio: "sta' buono" per "stai buono". Esistono alcune forme come "po'", che è l'apocope di "poco", dove l'apostrofo viene utilizzato per indicare un troncamento (ovvero la caduta della sillaba finale).

Ing: APOSTROPHE
Fr: APOSTROPHE
Ted: APOSTROPH
Sp: APÓSTROFO

Agenzia di comunicazione e immagine: Brunazzi & Associati, Torino; **Direttori creativi:** Giovanni Brunazzi, Andrea Brunazzi

ART DÉCO

Stile che unisce le tendenze decorative dell'Art Nouveau alle sobrie forme geometriche e alle astrazioni del Modernismo, l'Art Déco fu popolare dagli anni Venti agli anni Trenta negli Stati Uniti e in molte parti d'Europa. Mescolando un'ampia gamma di influenze, tra cui l'arte azteca e quella dei nativi americani, gli ziggurat egizi, il Cubismo, e altre ancora, lo stile Art Déco fu celebrato in architettura, nell'arredamento d'interni, nel design di manufatti, così come nella grafica. Immagini dal segno forte furono spesso abbinate a **caratteri** altrettanto appariscenti e stilizzati.

Ing: ART DECO
Fr: ART DÉCO
Ted: ART DÉCO
Sp: ART DECÓ

Courtesy: Archivio Baroni, Milano e archivio Brunazzi & Associati, Torino

A BCDEFGHIJKLMNOPQRSTUVWXYZ

ART NOUVEAU

Stile di architettura e design altamente decorativo, diffusosi prevalentemente in Europa fra il 1880 e la Prima guerra mondiale, e per un breve periodo negli Stati Uniti. L'Art Nouveau, come suggerisce il nome, aspirò a creare un'intera nuova estetica, rifiutando il caotico guazzabuglio dell'era vittoriana a favore di forme organiche e curvilinee. Tra i motivi più diffusi, piante e animali (specialmente uccelli), così come figure femminili, spesso ritratti con un livello di astrazione molto più marcato di quello tipico della grafica vittoriana.

Ing: ART NOUVEAU
Fr: ART NOUVEAU
Ted: JUGENDSTIL
Sp: ART NOUVEAU

Courtesy: Archivio Baroni, Milano e archivio Brunazzi & Associati, Torino

ARTS AND CRAFTS

Movimento riformista sorto in Inghilterra nel tardo XIX secolo come reazione alla Rivoluzione industriale e alla sua tendenza alla produzione di massa a discapito dell'estetica. Nel mondo della grafica il movimento Arts and Crafts raggiunse il culmine con i libri di William Morris. Sebbene l'uso di maiuscole decorative, **caratteri** gotici e **layout** pesanti ricordino i lavori a stampa dei secoli passati, il tentativo di Morris di associare nuovamente le attività del disegno a quelle della produzione preparò il terreno al Modernismo del XX secolo.

Ing: ARTS AND CRAFTS
Fr: ARTS & CRAFTS
Ted: ARTS AND CRAFTS
Sp: ARTS AND CRAFTS

Courtesy: Archivio Baroni, Milano e archivio Brunazzi & Associati, Torino

ASIMMETRIA

Distribuzione irregolare di elementi grafici rispetto agli assi orizzontali e verticali primari del **layout**. L'asimmetria può essere riferita anche a una situazione in cui due **pagine affiancate** non sono speculari l'una all'altra. Layout asimmetrici efficaci raggiungono un equilibrio attraverso un attento **bilanciamento** dello **spazio positivo** e **negativo**, e tendono a essere più dinamici dei layout simmetrici. Vedi anche **simmetria** e **flusso visivo**.

Ing: ASYMMETRY
Fr: ASYMÉTRIE
Ted: ASYMMETRIE
Sp: ASIMETRÍA

Agenzia di comunicazione e immagine: Brunazzi & Associati, Torino; **Direttori creativi:** Giovanni Brunazzi, Andrea Brunazzi

A B CDEFGHIJKLMNOPQRSTUVWXYZ

AVVIAMENTO MACCHINA

Processo in cui la macchina da stampa, nonché le attrezzature per la finitura, la piegatura o la **rilegatura**, vengono preparate per la tiratura. Il termine avviamento viene anche usato per descrivere i fogli di carta usati, spesso ripetutamente, come "test," del processo.

Ing: MAKEREADY
Fr: MACULE
Ted: DRUCKEINRICHTUNG
Sp: ARREGLO

Design: Yee-Haw Industries, www.yeehawindustries .com

BANCA IMMAGINI

Fotografie e/o illustrazioni disponibili, previa licenza, per usi specifici. Utilizzare tali immagini è molto meno dispendioso che ingaggiare un fotografo, sebbene con questo metodo si sacrifichi un po' la creatività, oltre al fatto che il grafico e il cliente non potranno mai essere certi che la stessa immagine non sia usata altrove da altri: non è possibile infatti un accordo esclusivo col fornitore. Oggigiorno, molte collezioni online di banche immagini e di illustrazioni rendono facili la ricerca, il pagamento e il download.

Ing: STOCK PHOTOGRAPHY/IMAGES
Fr: BANQUE D'IMAGES
Ted: STOCK FOTOS (BILDARCHIV)
Sp: BANCO DE IMÁGENES Y
     FOTOGRAFÍAS

Agenzia di pubblicità: TECNOSTUDI

BANDIERA

Spazio irregolare fra un blocco di testo e il **margine** adiacente, prodotto dalle diseguali **lunghezze di righe**. **Caratteri** allineati a sinistra si definiscono anche a bandiera destra (cioè lungo il margine destro), mentre caratteri allineati a destra si definiscono anche a bandiera sinistra (cioè lungo il margine sinistro). I **caratteri** giustificati non sono a bandiera. Per assicurare la **leggibilità**, i tipografi e i grafici cercano di conferire alla bandiera un aspetto apparentemente casuale, evitando le distrazioni visive che possono provenire da bandiere geometriche o eccessivamente ritmate.

Ing: RAG
Fr: DRAPEAU
Ted: FLATTERSATZ
Sp: BANDERA

Realizzazione grafica: MP foto&grafica

A **B** C D E F G H I J K L M N O P Q R S T U V W X Y Z

BAUHAUS

Importante scuola e fonte di ispirazione per arte, architettura e design, che operò in Germania dal 1919 al 1933. La grafica prodotta dal Bauhaus si distinse per il suo aspetto disadorno e geometrico, risultato dell'importanza riservata alla funzionalità. I **layout** utilizzavano quasi esclusivamente **caratteri senza grazie** (sans serif), spesso organizzati secondo regole precise e **griglie** rigide, nonché con fotografie e **fotomontaggi**. Il nero, il bianco e il grigio furono dominanti nella **palette di colori** del Bauhaus, sebbene i **colori primari** fossero spesso usati per conferire maggiore rilievo.

Ing: BAUHAUS
Fr: BAUHAUS
Ted: BAUHAUS
Sp: BAUHAUS

Courtesy: Archivio Baroni, Milano e archivio Brunazzi & Associati, Torino

A **B** C D E F G H I J K L M N O P Q R S T U V W X Y Z

BICROMIA

Immagine realizzata nella **scala dei grigi**, stampata usando due **colori** di inchiostro invece che uno. Sebbene il nero resti l'inchiostro primario, possono essere utilizzati anche due inchiostri non neri. Usando il nero come inchiostro primario e una **tonalità** di grigio come inchiostro secondario, ne risulta una variazione tonale più vicina alla fotografia in bianco e nero. Utilizzando un colore non neutro come inchiostro secondario, o due colori non neutri assieme, si generano effetti visivi molto interessanti, dal più lieve al più intenso. Le **tricromie** sono **scale dei grigi** stampate con tre colori.

Ing: DUOTONE
Fr: SIMILI DEUX TONS
Ted: DUPLEX
Sp: BITONO

Design: Alfredo Carlo

BILANCIAMENTO

È la relazione visiva fra gli elementi grafici all'interno di un contesto particolare. Si ritiene che un **layout** abbia equilibrio quando forme, proporzioni, texture, **colori** e **valori** tonali di ogni elemento interagiscono per ottenere un'armonia visiva. Tuttavia, layout bilanciati non devono per forza essere tradizionali, infatti un grafico attento può usare il bilanciamento per sfruttare spazi all'interno dell'intero layout, e dare luogo a un'esperienza più coinvolgente per l'osservatore.

Ing: BALANCE
Fr: ÉQUILIBRE
Ted: BALANCE (AUSGEWOGENHEIT)
Sp: EQUILIBRIO

Design: Fabrica; **Art director:** Yianni Hill; **Foto:** Yianni Hill; **Direttori creativo:** Omar Vulpinari

BITMAP

Fondamentalmente il bitmap è una griglia rettangolare di **punti** che costituisce un'immagine digitale, come una fotografia o un **glifo**. Ogni punto è associato a un particolare **colore** e collocazione all'interno della **griglia** del bitmap. Maggiori sono gli spi (*samples per inch*, campioni per pollice), e più alto è il grado di **risoluzione** del bitmap. Poiché in un'immagine bitmap si trova un numero fisso di punti (diversamente rispetto ai vettoriali grafici), essi non possono essere visualizzati o stampati a risoluzioni superiori di quelle del dispositivo da cui derivano senza che si produca un **aliasing**. Sono anche chiamati *grafiche raster*.

Ing: BITMAP
Fr: IMAGE MATRICIELLE
Ted: BITMAP
Sp: MAPA DE BITS

Agenzia di comunicazione e immagine: Brunazzi & Associati, Torino; **Direttori creativi:** Giovanni Brunazzi, Andrea Brunazzi

A **B** C D E F G H I J K L M N O P Q R S T U V W X Y Z

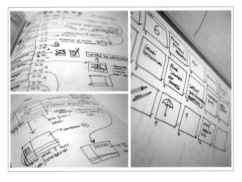

BLACKLETTER

Classificazione di **caratteri** tipografici ornati che ebbe origine alla metà del XV secolo, il Blackletter (o Black Letter) fu sviluppato dagli stampatori tedeschi per imitare la grafia degli scribi del tempo. Spesso si usa in modo intercambiabile con altre **font**, come il Fraktur, il Textura, l'Old English e il Gothic, che descrivono caratteri tipografici ornati simili. Per aumentare la confusione, il Gothic può essere usato per descrivere tanto il carattere ornato suggerito dal Blackletter, quanto i primi **caratteri senza grazie**, che hanno poco in comune con esso.

Ing: BLACKLETTER
Fr: GOTHIQUE
Ted: FRAKTUR (SCHRIFTEN)
Sp: LETRA GÓTICA

Design: Alfredo Carlo

BORDO/I

Cornice intorno a una fotografia, un'illustrazione, un blocco di testo, o altri elementi grafici, che crea una transizione fra l'elemento stesso e il resto del **layout**. Le cornici possono essere semplici – rettangolari o circolari con linee sottili – o assai ornate. Cornici più grosse e più definite tendono a togliere enfasi alle immagini contenute all'interno, richiamando l'attenzione sulla cornice stessa, mentre un bordo più sottile e semplice aiuta l'immagine a stagliarsi rispetto allo sfondo.

Ing: BORDER
Fr: BORDURE
Ted: RAHMEN
Sp: BORDE

Autore: Manuela Marchesan per le MagnificheEditrici

BOZZA/E

Termine generico usato per riferirsi alla versione preliminare di un libro, dépliant, brochure o altro documento destinato alla pubblicazione. Le bozze servono a una grande varietà di fini, dalla correzione e revisione di un testo fino a scopi promozionali, così come per sottoporre un libro ai recensori prima della sua pubblicazione. Quando erano ancora di uso corrente i **caratteri** in metallo fuso, la **composizione tipografica** iniziale veniva disposta su vassoi metallici prima di essere trasferita sulla pressa. Poiché questi vassoi venivano chiamati *in colonna*, le stampe risultanti erano chiamate **bozze in colonna**, termine ancora utilizzato da alcuni per riferirsi alle prime bozze. Le *bozze di stampa* si usano per permettere una valutazione dettagliata prima di procedere alla stampa vera e propria.

Ing: PROOF
Fr: ÉPREUVES
Ted: KORREKTURABZUG
Sp: PRUEBA

Design: Alfredo Carlo

BOZZE IN COLONNA
Vedi **bozze**.

A **B C** D E F G H I J K L M N O P Q R S T U V W X Y Z

BRANDING

Differenziazione strategica di un'"offerta" (prodotto, servizio, interazione, esperienza, ecc.) rispetto alla concorrenza. In termini visivi, il brand (marchio) spesso parte da un **logo** o da un logotipo che serve per ancorare la *brand promise* a una serie di aspettative associate a una particolare offerta. Una *brand identity* efficace richiede, fra le altre cose, un linguaggio visivo (loghi, **caratteri, palette di colori**, e altri segnali) comprensibile e coerente. Le strategie dei brand contemporanei generalmente vanno ben oltre la stampa tradizionale e la pubblicità televisiva, e comprendono siti web, blog e altre forme in evoluzione dei *social media*.

Ing: BRANDING
Fr: STRATÉGIE DE MARQUE
Ted: MARKENBILDUNG
Sp: BRANDING

Design: Armando Chitolina

CALIBRO
Vedi **risma**.

CALLIGRAFIA

Termine che deriva dal greco *kalligraphia*, "bella scrittura". È una forma di scrittura artistica, che si ottiene tipicamente con strumenti tradizionali, come un pennino o un pennello e che si distingue per la fluidità del *lettering* ottenuto con pennellate di diverso spessore.

Ing: CALLIGRAPHY
Fr: CALLIGRAPHIE
Ted: KALLIGRAPHIE
      (SCHÖNSCHREIBKUNST)
Sp: CALIGRAFÍA

Design: Marco Campedelli

CALLOUT

Breve brano di testo, spesso accompagnato da un **linea** e/o da una freccia, che funge da etichetta per identificare le parti chiave di fotografie, illustrazioni, o altre forme artistiche usate nel **layout**. Il termine viene utilizzato anche per riferirsi a brani estrapolati dal testo principale allo scopo di evidenziarli in modo speciale, ad esempio con diversi **caratteri, colori**, dimensioni, ecc. Vedi anche **didascalia** e **citazione esterna**.

Ing: CALLOUT
Fr: CHIFFRES RÉFÉRENCES
Ted: HINWEIS
Sp: LLAMADA

Agenzia di pubblicità: TECNOSTUDI

A B **C** D E F G H I J K L M N O P Q R S T U V W X Y Z

Erano tempi duri a Bologna, tanti soldati lontani da casa si aggiravano per la città, in attesa di ricevere notizie, e tentavano di distrarsi con qualunque pretesto dall'avanzare plumbeo della guerra. A tal fine era stata istituita la Casa del Soldato, un luogo dove i militi si trovavano per trascorrere i momenti di libera uscita, e grazie alle elargizioni della Cassa di Risparmio e di tanti premurosi privati, avevano a disposizione vari generi di conforto: a volte sigari, a volte vino, carta da lettere, cartoline e libri. L'apertura della casa era stata provvidenziale, perché in quei giorni magri i soldati erano stati presi di mira dai truffatori: di tante storie questa ne è solo un esemplare. Il Rossi era un romagnolo di Forlì, accasermato nel 137° Battaglione della milizia territoriale di via San Petronio Vecchio, e non vedeva l'ora di ritornare nella terra d'origine. Si può facilmente immaginare cosa rappresentasse il miraggio di una notizia da parte della famiglia, dei genitori o degli amici. Fu proprio questo l'amo a cui abboccò il giovane, quando un giorno per strada uno strano soggetto lo abbordò. Si sentì chiamare da uno sconosciuto, che gli raccontò di conoscere bene la zona del forlivese e di avere conosciuto sua moglie e i suoi figli. Figuratevi lo stupore del giovane e l'immediata nostalgia da cui fu colto! Per ottenere informazioni tempestò l'uomo con mille domande, e ottenne solo qualche laconica risposta, che andava a parare ben lontano…

«A proposito, tua moglie mi ha detto che tu soffri spesso di dolori. Adesso come stai?». E il Rossi: «Non troppo bene, perché questi maledetti reumatismi, colla stagione che abbiamo, mi danno trafitture acutissime». «Posso giovarti. Torno dal fronte, ove ho servito come ufficiale medico, e ho medicinali che fanno al tuo caso, roba miracolosa, ti assicuro io… Guarirai presto, bene e con spesa limitata. Lo sai, le specialità mediche per i poveri costano sempre troppo, ma io come ufficiale posso avere lo

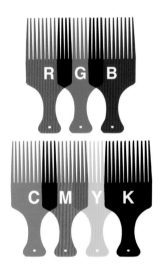

CANALETTI

Spazi verticali visivamente dispersivi che appaiono in un blocco di testo come risultato di un **allineamento** verticale non intenzionale di spazi fra le parole. I canaletti tendono a presentarsi nei blocchi di **caratteri giustificati**, a causa della spaziatura spesso innaturale di parole creata con un software. Il miglior modo per eliminare o ridurne l'impatto è mandando a capo automaticamente le righe di caratteri con il **tracking** e/o la **sillabazione**. Vedi anche **H&J** e **invio a capo automatico**.

Ing: RIVERS
Fr: LÉZARDES
Ted: GIESSBÄCHLEIN
Sp: CALLE

Studio grafico: Sara Muzio

CANALI

Informazioni digitali che corrispondono alle quantità relative dei tre (nell'**RGB**) o dei quattro (nel **CMYK**) **colori primari** usati per rappresentare le immagini a colori. Ogni canale è come un'immagine della **scala dei grigi** in cui i **valori** di grigio sono stati sostituiti con i valori di un singolo colore primario. L'immagine finale viene ottenuta, su schermo o su stampa, combinando tutti i canali di un dato **modello di colore**.

Ing: CHANNELS
Fr: CANAUX
Ted: FARBKANÄLE
Sp: CANAL

Design: Alfredo Carlo

CAPOLETTERA

Lettera maiuscola usata come iniziale della prima parola di un paragrafo, realizzata in un formato più grande rispetto ai **caratteri** vicini, in modo da estendersi nel testo sottostante. Per ottenere un effetto ulteriore, i capilettera si possono realizzare con un carattere molto diverso da quello usato nel **corpo del testo**. Essi vengono definiti in base al numero di righe di caratteri che occupano. Un capolettera di tre righe, ad esempio, occupa la prima, la seconda e la terza riga di un paragrafo. Vedi anche **lettera iniziale maiuscola**.

Ing: DROP CAPITAL/CAP
Fr: LETTRINE
Ted: HÄNGENDE INITIALE
Sp: MAYÚSCULA CAÍDA

Agenzia di comunicazione e immagine: Brunazzi & Associati, Torino; **Direttori creativi:** Giovanni Brunazzi, Andrea Brunazzi

A B **C** D E F G H I J K L M N O P Q R S T U V W X Y Z

CARATTERE/I

Insieme di segni che condividono evidenti caratteristiche grafiche, come il *peso del tratto*, le proporzioni, la presenza o la mancanza di grazie, e così via. Un dato insieme di caratteri solitamente include lettere (quasi sempre maiuscole e minuscole), numeri, e un'ampia gamma di **simboli** (tipografici, matematici, ecc.). Caratteri e **font** vengono spesso erroneamente scambiati: il carattere o *tipo di carattere* si riferisce al disegno complessivo dei caratteri, mentre la font si riferisce al mezzo di produzione dei caratteri, che sia meccanica, fotomeccanica o digitale.

Ing: TYPEFACE
Fr: POLICE
Ted: SCHRIFTTYPE
Sp: TIPO DE LETRA

Foto: MP foto&grafica

CARATTERI CON GRAZIE (SERIF)

La grazia è un piccolo tratto aggiunto alle estremità principali di un **carattere**. Questo termine è anche comunemente usato per riferirsi a un'ampia gamma di caratteri con grazie, chiamati più correttamente *seriffed typefaces*, cioè caratteri serif, per distinguerli da una categoria altrettanto ampia di caratteri chiamati senza grazie (o sans serif). Le grazie aiutano la lettura dei caratteri, specialmente di piccole dimensioni, anche perché permettono all'occhio di distinguere velocemente un **glifo** da un altro. I caratteri con grazie hanno origine nell'antica Roma, sebbene i dettagli siano oggetto di dibattito: alcuni sostengono che siano stati creati dagli scalpellini, che li usavano per "pulire" gli sbaffi dei caratteri cesellati, mentre altri sostengono che fossero ghirigori creati dai pennelli usati per disegnare i glifi prima del taglio. Vedi anche **caratteri senza grazie**.

Ing: SERIF
Fr: EMPATTEMENT
Ted: SERIFE
Sp: SERIFA

Art director: Miguel Sal

CARATTERI CONDENSATI

Caratteri tipografici in cui i **glifi** sono più stretti rispetto alla versione "regolare" degli stessi. Inoltre, ogni glifo viene disposto più vicino a quelli adiacenti, il che permette di inserire un numero maggiore di caratteri in un dato spazio. Poiché la **leggibilità** ne risulta alquanto ridotta, i caratteri condensati sono generalmente riservati a **titoli**, visualizzazioni su monitor, o altre applicazioni in cui le parti di testo sono brevi.

Ing: CONDENSED TYPE
Fr: CONDENSÉ
Ted: SCHMALE SCHRIFT
Sp: LETRA CONDENSADA

Agenzia di comunicazione e immagine: Brunazzi & Associati, Torino; **Direttori creativi:** Giovanni Brunazzi, Andrea Brunazzi

A B **C** D E F G H I J K L M N O P Q R S T U V W X Y Z

CARATTERI CONTORNATI

Caratteri le cui forme sono contornate anziché presentare tratti densi. Le contornature possono essere create anche per caratteri tipografici non disponibili in tali versioni, usando applicazioni software come Adobe Illustrator®. Le **curve di Bézier** che ne derivano si possono ingrandire o ridurre senza perdere la nitidezza; tuttavia questo procedimento può modificare le corrette proporzioni del carattere.

Ing: OUTLINE TYPE
Fr: CARACTÈRES AU FIL
Ted: KONTURSCHRIFT
Sp: LETRA PERFILADA

Design: Emporio Adv

CARATTERI DI VISUALIZZAZIONE

Caratteri con **punti** più grandi dei circostanti per distinguerli dal testo principale, come quelli usati nei **titoli** dei libri e dei giornali.

Ing: DISPLAY TYPE
Fr: CARACTÈRES DE TITRE
Ted: AUSZEICHNUNGSSCHRIFT
Sp: TIPO TITULAR

Design: Emporio Adv

CARATTERI EGIZIANI

Sono quelli che fanno parte dei caratteri *slab serif*. Il loro aspetto complessivamente pesante e una minima variazione nel peso della battuta li rendono più adatti per poster, pubblicità e **titoli** dei giornali piuttosto che per il **corpo del testo**.

Ing: EGYPTIAN
Fr: ÉGYPTIENNE
Ted: EGYPTIENNE
Sp: EGIPCIO

Design: Alfredo Carlo

A B **C** D E F G H I J K L M N O P Q R S T U V W X Y Z

Times New Roman
Times New Roman
Times New Roman

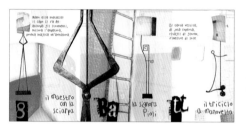

Oblique

Garamond
Garamond
Garamond

CARATTERI INFORMALI

Uno qualsiasi dei tipi di **carattere** utilizzati per imitare la scrittura a mano. Sebbene i caratteri informali, o script, possano conferire un tocco elegante e personale a un blocco di testo, vanno usati con moderazione e solo nel contesto appropriato. Inviti e annunci, ad esempio, spesso utilizzano con efficacia caratteri script. Lunghi passaggi di testo composti con script tendono invece ad affaticare il lettore.

Ing: SCRIPT TYPE
Fr: CURSIVE
Ted: SCHREIBSCHRIFT
Sp: SCRIPT TYPE

Design: Oscar Baroncini per Studio Pirulino

CARATTERI OBLIQUE

Caratteri senza grazie inclinati verso destra, formati da **glifi** molto simili a quelli dei caratteri "regolari" sui quali si basano. Anche il corsivo è inclinato verso destra, ma le sue lettere sono state completamente ridisegnate e spesso sono piuttosto diverse da quelle di partenza.

Ing: OBLIQUE
Fr: OBLIQUE
Ted: SCHRÄG
Sp: OBLICUA

Design: Alfredo Carlo

CARATTERI ROMAN

Termine usato per riferirsi a un'ampia gamma di **caratteri** tipografici che hanno grazie, con origini databili al XV secolo italiano. Il Roman viene anche usato più genericamente per descrivere la versione "regolare" di un carattere con o senza grazie, all'opposto, ad esempio, delle versioni in **grassetto** e in **corsivo** dello stesso tipo.

Ing: ROMAN TYPE
Fr: CARACTÈRES ROMAINS
Ted: ANTIQUA
Sp: REDONDA

Agenzia di pubblicità: TECNOSTUDI

A B **C** D E F G H I J K L M N O P Q R S T U V W X Y Z

CARATTERI SENZA GRAZIE (SANS SERIF)

Termine usato per riferirsi a un qualsiasi tipo di **carattere** privo di grazie (serif), i piccoli tratti aggiunti alle estremità dei tratti principali. Paragonato ai molti **caratteri con grazie**, in quelli senza grazie il contrasto tra i tratti sottili e quelli spessi è solitamente più ridotto, o addirittura assente; ciò può rendere più agevole la comprensione di un tipo di carattere progettato per essere letto sullo schermo di un computer.

Ing: SANS SERIF
Fr: CARACTÈRES SANS EMPATTEMENTS
Ted: SERIFENLOS
Sp: PALO SECO

Courtesy: Archivio Baroni, Milano e archivio Brunazzi & Associati, Torino

CARATTERI SWASH

Caratteri fortemente decorativi dai tratti allungati, spesso maiuscole che tendono obliquamente verso destra. Nella forma di maiuscole, i caratteri swash vengono solitamente usati come lettera iniziale della prima parola di un capoverso, e spesso composti da una misura di **punti** più grande rispetto ai caratteri circostanti. Nella forma di minuscole, i caratteri swash si usano di solito nella parte finale del capoverso, per l'ultima lettera dell'ultima parola di una frase. Nonostante l'eleganza che possono conferire al blocco di testo, vanno adoperati con moderazione. Una riga di caratteri interamente swash può distrarre o essere illeggibile. Vedi anche **lettere maiuscole iniziali**.

Ing: SWASH CHARACTERS
Fr: LETTRE ITALIQUE ORNÉE
Ted: ZIERBUCHSTABEN
Sp: LETRA DE FANTASÍA

Agenzia di pubblicità: TECNOSTUDI

CARTA PATINATA
Vedi **rivestimento ad acqua**.

CARTONATURA

Tipo di **rilegatura** permanente usata di frequente per realizzare le copertine rigide dei libri. Dapprima le **segnature** vengono cucite insieme lungo il dorso usando il filo, poi il corpo del libro viene incollato lungo il dorso, rifilato lungo gli altri tre lati e incollato alla copertina.

Ing: CASE BINDING
Fr: RELIURE CARTONNÉE
Ted: BUCHEINBAND
Sp: ENCUADERNACIÓN EN TAPA DURA

LIZART comunicazione visiva; **Art director:** Simonetta Scala; **Design:** Maria Chinaglia, Simonetta Scala

CHROMA
Vedi **saturazione**.

A B **C** D E F G H I J K L M N O P Q R S T U V W X Y Z

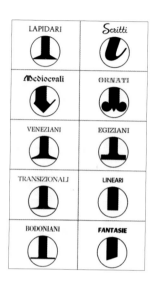

CITAZIONE ESTERNA

Citazione estratta da un articolo o da un altro testo, collocata al di fuori del suo contesto originale (ma solitamente nella stessa pagina) e disposta in modo tale da attirare l'attenzione dei lettori. Le citazioni esterne vengono spesso realizzate con **caratteri** molto più grandi e a volte anche diversi rispetto al **corpo del testo**. Si possono ottenere ulteriori differenziazioni con il **colore**, gli ornamenti, i **bordi** e altro.

Ing: PULL QUOTE
Fr: EXERGUE
Ted: HERVORGEHOBENES ZITAT
Sp: SUMARIO

AD. VENTURE Compagnia di comunicazione
Art director: Franco Mancinelli

CLASSIFICAZIONE DEI CARATTERI

Uno qualsiasi dei vari sistemi utilizzati per classificare i **caratteri** tipografici in base a caratteristiche visive condivise, come la presenza o l'assenza di grazie, somiglianze con la scrittura manuale e così via. Poiché molti caratteri tipografici possono trovarsi in più di una categoria, questi sistemi di classificazione sono da intendersi come parametri generici piuttosto che come definizioni rigide.

Ing: TYPE CLASSIFICATION
Fr: CLASSIFICATION TYPOGRAPHIQUE
Ted: SCHRIFTKLASSIFIKATION
Sp: CLASIFICACIÓN TIPOGRÁFICA

Courtesy: Archivio Baroni, Milano e archivio Brunazzi & Associati, Torino

CLIP ART

Illustrazioni disponibili sia per la stampa sia in forma digitale, per l'uso nei **layout** grafici; sono diffusi da molti anni per la loro facile reperibilità, la varietà e perché sono liberi da copyright. Vedi anche **banca immagini**.

Ing: CLIP ART
Fr: CLIPART
Ted: CLIPART
Sp: CLIP ART

Immagine: MP foto&grafica

A **C** D E F G H I J K L M N O P Q R S T U V W X Y Z

CMYK

Abbreviazione di cyan, magenta, yellow e black (ciano, magenta, giallo e nero), i colori utilizzati nella stampa con **processo a quattro colori**. Combinati in coppie, i colori primari *sottrattivi* ciano, magenta e giallo riproducono i **colori primari** *additivi* rosso, verde e blu, che corrispondono ai tre tipi diversi di ricettori di luce nell'occhio umano. In teoria, i tre primari sottrattivi combinati producono il nero; tuttavia, nella prassi, il risultato non è sufficientemente ricco da produrre una gamma completa di toni per la stampa a colori; per questa ragione, il nero viene incluso separatamente. Sono noti anche come **colori di processo**.

Ing: CMYK
Fr: CMJN
Ted: CMYK
Sp: CMYK

Agenzia di comunicazione e immagine: Brunazzi & Associati, Torino; **Direttori creativi:** Giovanni Brunazzi, Andrea Brunazzi

COLLAGE

Tecnica usata per creare un'opera artistica originale che assembla carta, stoffa, fotografie o altri media su tavola o tela, spesso in modi inconsueti. Il nome deriva dal francese *coller*, che significa "incollare". I collage possono anche essere creati col digitale "incollando" elementi a volontà, spesso immagini scansionate di oggetti tridimensionali con **texture**, secondo lo stesso spirito del bricolage. Vedi anche **fotomontaggio**.

Ing: COLLAGE
Fr: COLLAGE
Ted: KOLLAGE
Sp: COLLAGE

Studio grafico: Latveria Design

COLONNE

In quanto aree del **layout** della pagina in cui viene collocato il testo, le colonne spesso rappresentano gli elementi di base della **griglia** dello stesso. Per layout con forte concentrazione di testo, si usano spesso due o più colonne; quelle alte e rettangolari sono forse le più comuni, ma se ne trovano anche in vari altri stili.

Ing: COLUMN
Fr: COLONNE
Ted: SATZSPALTE
Sp: COLUMNA

Agenzia di pubblicità: TECNOSTUDI

A B **C** D E F G H I J K L M N O P Q R S T U V W X Y Z

COLORE/I

Gli oggetti vengono percepiti dall'occhio umano di un particolare colore a seconda della loro capacità di assorbire, riflettere o trasmettere diverse lunghezze d'onda della luce. Le tre proprietà di base del colore sono la **tonalità**, la **saturazione**, e la **luminosità** (anche chiamata **valore** o tono). Il termine colore viene anche usato dai tipografi per riferirsi alla maggiore o minore luminosità complessiva di una pagina di **caratteri**, o di un paragrafo rispetto a un altro. Vedi anche **ruota dei colori**.

Ing: COLOR
Fr: COULEUR
Ted: FARBE
Sp: COLOR

LIZART comunicazione visiva; **Art director:** Simonetta Scala; **Design:** Maria Chinaglia, Simonetta Scala

ABCDEFGHIJKLMNOPQRSTUVWXYZ

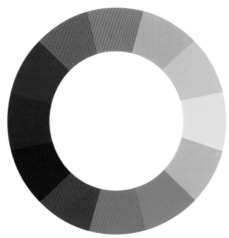

COLORI ANALOGHI

Due o più colori contigui l'uno all'altro nella **ruota dei colori** (ad es. verde, giallo-verde e giallo). Poiché i colori analoghi sono "parenti stretti", usandone due o tre insieme generalmente si ottiene un disegno dall'aspetto armonico.

Ing: ANALOGOUS COLORS
Fr: COULEURS ANALOGUES
Ted: ANALOGE FARBEN
Sp: COLORES ANÁLOGOS

AIPEM Marketing e comunicazione integrata;
Art director: Daria Biasizzo, Luca Pagot; **Copywriter:** Maurizio Clemente; **Account manager:** Andrea Fioritto
Foto: Alessandro Paderni

COLORI COMPLEMENTARI

Colori opposti l'uno all'altro nella **ruota dei colori**, come lo sono, ad esempio, il rosso e il verde nella ruota dei colori dei pigmenti. Sono chiamati anche *colori contrastanti*. Poiché l'abbinamento di colori complementari in uno stesso disegno può risultare fastidioso, è più diffuso l'uso di uno schema complementare scisso, in cui un colore viene usato assieme ai due contigui al suo complementare nella ruota dei colori.

Ing: COMPLEMENTARY COLORS
Fr: COULEURS COMPLÉMENTAIRES
Ted: KOMPLEMENTÄRFARBEN
Sp: COLORES COMPLEMENTARIOS

Design: Alfredo Carlo

COLORI DI PROCESSO
Vedi **CMYK** e **processo a quattro colori**.

COLORI PRIMARI

Colori che costituiscono i punti di riferimento principali di una data **ruota dei colori**, equamente distribuiti lungo la sua circonferenza. Nella tradizionale ruota dei colori, usata per mescolare i pigmenti, i primari sono il rosso, il blu e il giallo. Altre ruote di colori sono basate sui *primari sottrattivi* ciano, magenta e giallo, e sui *primari additivi* rosso, verde e blu. Vedi anche **CMYK**, **colori secondari** e **terziari**.

Ing: PRIMARY COLORS
Fr: COULEURS PRIMAIRES
Ted: PRIMÄRFARBEN
Sp: COLORES PRIMARIOS

LIZART comunicazione visiva; **Art director:** Simonetta Scala; **Design:** Maria Chinaglia, Simonetta Scala

A B **C** D E F G H I J K L M N O P Q R S T U V W X Y Z

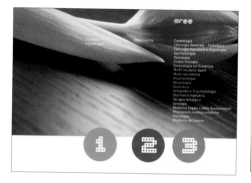

COLORI SECONDARI

Colori (arancione, viola o verde) creati mescolando parti uguali di due **colori primari**. L'arancione, ad esempio, viene creato mescolando insieme parti eguali di rosso e di giallo. Vedi anche **ruota dei colori** e **colori terziari**.

Ing: SECONDARY COLORS
Fr: COULEURS SECONDAIRES
Ted: SEKUNDÄRFARBEN
Sp: COLORES SECUNDARIOS

Design: DSF-DESIGN; **Art director:** Carlo Del Sal-Carlo Facchin; **Cliente:** ABA Bibione

COLORI TERZIARI

Colori generati dalla combinazione di un **colore primario** e di uno **secondario**. Il rosso-arancione, ad esempio, deriva dalla miscela di rosso (colore primario) e arancione (colore secondario creato mescolando eguali parti dei primari rosso e giallo). Vedi anche **ruota dei colori**.

Ing: TERTIARY COLORS
Fr: COULEURS TERTIAIRES
Ted: TERTIÄRFARBEN
Sp: COLORES TERCIARIOS

Design: Armando Chitolina

COMPOSITE

Immagine creata combinando altre immagini o elementi di esse. A differenza del **collage**, che consiste in un lavoro artistico complessivo, o del **fotomontaggio**, che consiste nella combinazione di elementi specificamente fotografici, il termine composite si riferisce in particolare a una fotografia o a un'illustrazione singola all'interno di un lavoro creativo più ampio.

Ing: COMPOSITE
Fr: IMAGE COMPOSITE
Ted: BILDMONTAGE (COMPOSING)
Sp: FOTOCOMPOSICIÓN

Agenzia di pubblicità: TECNOSTUDI

A B **C** D E F G H I J K L M N O P Q R S T U V W X Y Z

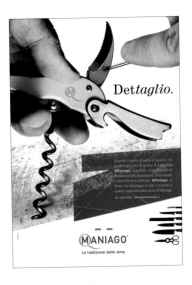

COMPOSIZIONE

Termine generico usato per descrivere l'organizzazione di elementi grafici nel **layout**, l'efficacia della quale viene spesso espressa con termini piuttosto astratti, come **bilanciamento**, **contrasto**, **allineamento**, e così via. La composizione può anche essere usata come sostantivo, quando ci si riferisce a un layout formato da diversi elementi.

Ing: COMPOSITION
Fr: COMPOSITION
Ted: KOMPOSITION
Sp: COMPOSICIÓN

Design: Sintesi

COMPOSIZIONE TIPOGRAFICA

Disposizione di **caratteri** da utilizzare per la stampa e/o per la lettura su schermo. Per secoli la composizione tipografica è stata eseguita usando caratteri in metallo fuso che venivano inseriti nella macchina di stampa. La macchina linotipica, che entrò nell'uso commerciale nel 1886, aumentò considerevolmente l'efficienza della composizione tipografica coi metalli fusi, utilizzando righe di caratteri chiamate *slugs* (lumache). La *fototipia*, una tecnica in cui le **font** metalliche fuse vengono sostituite da fogli di pellicola, divenne la forma dominante di composizione tipografica durante gli anni Sessanta e rimase tale fino agli Ottanta, quando fu rimpiazzata dai caratteri digitali.

Ing: TYPESETTING
Fr: COMPOSITION TYPOGRAPHIQUE
Ted: SETZEN
Sp: COMPOSICIÓN TIPOGRÁFICA

Foto: MP foto&grafica

CONTRASTO

Nel suo significato di base, un contrasto non è niente più che la differenza tra due elementi grafici. Un **carattere** grande ad esempio, può essere utilizzato per contrastare uno piccolo; più grande sarà la differenza nelle dimensioni dei caratteri, maggiore sarà il contrasto, e usato efficacemente può produrre **layout** visivamente interessanti. **Texture**, **colori**, forme, peso delle linee e altri elementi, possono essere usati per creare contrasto. Vedi anche **bilanciamento**, **colori complementari** e **figura-sfondo**.

Ing: CONTRAST
Fr: CONTRASTE
Ted: KONTRAST
Sp: CONTRASTE

Design: Emporio Adv

A B **C** D E F G H I J K L M N O P Q R S T U V W X Y Z

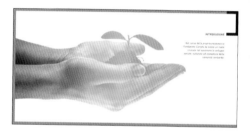

CORPO DEL TESTO

Termine tradizionalmente utilizzato per riferirsi al testo principale all'interno di un libro, di una brochure, o di un'altra pubblicazione. Usato in questo senso, il corpo del testo esclude **pagine iniziali** e **finali**, **titoli**, **sottotitoli**, e simili. Il corpo del testo può anche riferirsi al testo principale di un sito web.

Ing: BODY COPY
Fr: CORPS DU TEXTE
Ted: FLIESSTEXT
Sp: CUERPO DE TEXTO

Agenzia di pubblicità: TECNOSTUDI

CORREZIONE DEI COLORI

Processo di modificazione del colore di una fotografia digitale o di un'immagine scansionata, sia per ottenere una più accurata rappresentazione del soggetto originale, sia per adattarlo alla tabella cromatica (o *gamut*) della tecnica di stampa scelta.

Ing: COLOR CORRECTION
Fr: CORRECTION DES COULEURS
Ted: FARBKORREKTUR
Sp: CORRECCIÓN DE COLOR

Design: LUMEN

CORSIVO

Tipo di **carattere** inclinato verso destra, usato frequentemente per dare enfasi a una parte di un brano di testo. Il carattere corsivo fu sviluppato in Italia attorno al 1500, come modalità per inserire più caratteri in una singola pagina, riducendo pertanto il formato dei libri stampati. I veri caratteri corsivi sono insiemi di **glifi** distinti dai **caratteri** tipografici su cui si basano. Anche il **carattere Oblique** è inclinato verso destra, ma la forma delle sue lettere rimane sostanzialmente inalterata rispetto a quella dei caratteri "regolari" su cui si basa.

Ing: ITALIC
Fr: ITALIQUE
Ted: KURSIV
Sp: CURSIVA

Design: Armando Chitolina

A B **C** D E F G H I J K L M N O P Q R S T U V W X Y Z

COSTRUTTIVISMO

Movimento russo degli anni Venti del Novecento che integrava l'arte d'avanguardia e il design (specialmente le influenze del **Cubismo** e del **Futurismo**) con le tendenze politiche favorevoli alla Rivoluzione. Le caratteristiche visive fondamentali comprendevano forme astratte e geometriche, caratteri in **grassetto**, **layout** che rompevano con le convenzioni di orizzontalità/verticalità, e una **palette di colori** spesso limitata al rosso, nero e bianco. **Collage** e **fotomontaggio**, tecniche prese in prestito dal movimento **Dada**, furono anche usate per dare forza grafica alla comunicazione visiva.

Ing: CONSTRUCTIVISM
Fr: CONSTRUCTIVISME
Ted: KONSTRUKTIVISMUS
Sp: CONSTRUCTIVISMO

Courtesy: Archivio Baroni, Milano e archivio Brunazzi & Associati, Torino

A B **C** D E F G H I J K L M N O P Q R S T U V W X Y Z

Palatino

−19   −37   +7

Palatino

−76   0   +11   −25

CRENATURA

Adattamento dello spazio fra due **caratteri** adiacenti per creare un **ritmo** visivo gradevole. Quando alcuni caratteri, come la *T* e la *o* sono vicini, l'interazione delle loro forme può generare uno spazio inopportuno: la crenatura può essere usata per stringere gli spazi, conferendo un aspetto più omogeneo. Le *coppie di crenatura* sono coppie di lettere usate comunemente che richiedono una crenatura per ottenere spazi corretti (compito di cui si occupano automaticamente le applicazioni software, anche se non sempre con piena soddisfazione di grafici e tipografi).

Ing: KERNING
Fr: CRÉNAGE
Ted: UNTERSCHNEIDEN
Sp: KERNING

CROP

Procedimento con cui si refila una fotografia o altre creazioni artistiche sia con il digitale sia con mezzi meccanici, rimuovendo ogni porzione indesiderata attorno ai **bordi** esterni. Il crop viene eseguito per incorniciare con precisione il contenuto di una fotografia, o per aggiustare le dimensioni e le proporzioni di un'immagine, perché rientri nello spazio assegnatole all'interno di un dato **layout**. Le sottili linee usate per incorniciare la zona da refilare in una creazione artistica si chiamano *crocini*.

Ing: CROP
Fr: RECADRER
Ted: AUSSCHNITT
Sp: RECORTAR

Agenzia di pubblicità: TECNOSTUDI

CUBISMO

Movimento artistico del primo Novecento (1907-1920 circa) in cui oggetti e figure umane furono spesso trasformati in forme geometriche astratte. Prospettive multiple venivano rappresentate simultaneamente e le tre dimensioni furono ridotte a due, sfidando le convenzioni della prospettiva in vigore dal Rinascimento. Ben presto simili sperimentazioni di composizione spaziale e di astrazione geometrica si diffusero anche nella grafica.

Ing: CUBISM
Fr: CUBISME
Ted: KUBISMUS
Sp: CUBISMO

Courtesy: Archivio Baroni, Milano e archivio Brunazzi & Associati, Torino

A B **C D** E F G H I J K L M N O P Q R S T U V W X Y Z

CURVA DI BÉZIER

Approssimazione matematica di una **linea** continua curva, definita dai due **punti** d'ancoraggio (uno a ogni capo) e da un numero qualsiasi di punti di controllo tra di essi. I **percorsi** usati dalla maggior parte delle applicazioni software di grafica sono ottenuti da curve di Bézier multiple, e per questo motivo possono essere ingranditi indefinitamente. Le curve di Bézier possono anche essere usate nell'**animazione**, come strumenti per controllare il movimento.

Ing: BÉZIER CURVE
Fr: COURBE DE BÉZIER
Ted: BÉZIERKURVE
Sp: CURVA DE BÉZIER

Agenzia di pubblicità: TECNOSTUDI

DADA

Movimento artistico che ebbe origine a Zurigo, in Svizzera, e si diffuse in Europa come reazione alla Prima guerra mondiale. Il movimento dadaista sfidò un grande numero di ideali tradizionali, in materia di arte, morale e religione, con immagini provocatorie e a volte strampalate, anche se in Germania la corrente dadaista ha assunto un tono più cupo e politico, quando Hitler salì al potere negli anni Trenta. L'influenza della grafica dadaista fu avvertita in vari ambiti, come nell'approccio razionalista del **Costruttivismo** e del **De Stijl**, e nella rude energia del **collage** e del **fotomontaggio**, tecnica che i dadaisti sostennero di avere inventato.

Ing: DADA
Fr: DADA
Ted: DADAISMUS
Sp: DADA

Courtesy: Archivio Baroni, Milano e archivio Brunazzi & Associati, Torino

DEBOSS
Vedi **goffratura**.

DE STIJL

Movimento artistico e grafico olandese del primo Novecento (1917-1931), che si proponeva di esprimere leggi universali mediante un linguaggio visivo strettamente oggettivo. I **colori** erano limitati ai neutri (nero, bianco e grigio) e ai **primari** rosso, blu e giallo, mentre tra le forme prevalsero soprattutto quadrati e rettangoli disposti asimmetricamente lungo assi orizzontali e verticali. Il **carattere** sans serif (senza grazie) fu usato in modo quasi esclusivo, spesso combinato a **caratteri di visualizzazione** disegnati a mano e squadrati.

Ing: DE STIJL
Fr: DE STIJL
Ted: DE STIJL
Sp: DE STIJL

Courtesy: Archivio Baroni, Milano e archivio Brunazzi & Associati, Torino

A B C **D** E F G H I J K L M N O P Q R S T U V W X Y Z

DESIGN INTERATTIVO

Procedura per descrivere, definire e sviluppare gli elementi di un prodotto, sistema o organizzazione con i quali una persona può interagire. Generalmente gli esempi più comuni coinvolgono complesse interfacce tecnologiche, come quelle usate per i siti web e i dispositivi elettronici portatili, sebbene anche interazioni semplici richiedano considerazioni grafiche ponderate. Il manico di una tazzina da caffè, ad esempio, viene spesso disegnato perché il suo uso sia semplice e intuitivo, anche se ciò non sempre accade. I grafici interattivi svolgono spesso ricerche sugli utenti, anche applicando metodologie provenienti da altre discipline, come la psicologia cognitiva e l'antropologia, fra le altre.

Ing: INTERACTION DESIGN
Fr: DESIGN NUMÉRIQUE
Ted: INTERAKTIVES DESIGN
Sp: DISEÑO INTERACTIVO

Agenzia di pubblicità: TECNOSTUDI

DIDASCALIA

Testo breve usato per descrivere o spiegare foto, illustrazioni, diagrammi o altri elementi visivi. Le didascalie sono generalmente collocate sopra, sotto o accanto all'opera, e separate dal **corpo del testo**. Vedi anche **callout**.

Ing: CAPTION
Fr: LÉGENDE
Ted: BILDUNTERSCHRIFT
Sp: PIE DE FOTO

Design: Teikna; **Art director:** Claudia Neri

DINGBATS

Ampia gamma di **caratteri** tipografici speciali, che comprende **simboli** (ad es., matematici, di interpunzione, ecc.), **punti elenco** (ad es., circoli, stelle, ecc.), vari ornamenti grafici e altro.

Ing: DINGBATS
Fr: DINGBATS
Ted: DINGBATS
Sp: DINGBATS

Design: Alfredo Carlo

A B C D **E** F G H I J K L M N O P Q R S T U V W X Y Z

EFFETTO MOIRÉ

Effetto indesiderato che si produce quando gli *schermi di mezzitoni* usati nella stampa a quattro colori sono allineati in modo tale che ne emerga un pattern percepibile. Per evitare l'effetto moiré, gli schermi vengono ruotati secondo angoli specifici l'uno rispetto all'altro, dando luogo a minuscole rosette **CMYK**, che sono raramente percepibili nella stampa finale. L'effetto moiré può anche apparire quando un'immagine stampata è scansionata digitalmente senza applicare la deretinatura.

Ing: MOIRÉ
Fr: MOIRÉ
Ted: MOIRÉ-EFFEKT
Sp: MOARÉ

Design: Alfredo Carlo

EM

Unità di misura relativa che equivale alla dimensione del corpo del **carattere** usato, specificata in **punti**. Per un carattere di corpo 12, un'em corrisponde a 12 punti; per un carattere di 10 punti, un'em corrisponde a 10 punti, e così via. Più precisamente, un'em corrisponde all'altezza (o corpo) del blocchetto di metallo fuso usato per la *stampa a rilievo* di un carattere. Uno *spaziatore em* è uno spaziatore di metallo fuso che misura 1 em in altezza e 1 em in larghezza, e viene usato per creare uno **spazio em**. Sebbene tutti i corpi con stesso numero di punti (o **font**) abbiano la stessa altezza, l'altezza delle lettere stesse varia marcatamente a seconda del carattere tipografico. Vedi anche **lineetta em**, **spazio em** e **pica em**.

Ing: EM
Fr: CADRATIN
Ted: GEVIERT
Sp: CUADRATÍN

Foto: MP foto&grafica

EN

Unità di misura tipografica, corrispondente a metà della larghezza di un'**em**. Vedi anche **lineetta en** e **spazio en**.

Ing: EN
Fr: DEMI-CADRATIN
Ted: HALBGEVIERT
Sp: MEDIO CUADRATÍN

A B C D **E F** G H I J K L M N O P Q R S T U V W X Y Z

ABCDEFGHIJKLMNOPQRSTUVWXYZ
0123456789 ⅛¼⅜½⅝¾⅞⅓⅔
ffffifflffiflffjĉt *ABCDEFGHIJ*
LMNOPQRSTUVWXYZ

EXPERT SET

Insieme di **caratteri** tipografici "non-standard", come i **maiuscoletti**, i **numeri in stile antico**, le **legature** e altro ancora, per una **font** particolare. Di importanza cruciale per una **composizione tipografica** raffinata, un tempo gli expert set si acquistavano separatamente dalle font di base, mentre oggi sono generalmente inclusi nelle font digitali *OpenType*. Vengono anche chiamate *font alternative*.

Ing: EXPERT SET
Fr: CARACTÈRES ÉTENDUS
Ted: EXPERTENSATZ
Sp: SET EXPERTO

Helvetica Neue

Helvetica Neue Light

Helvetica Neue Ultralight

Helvetica Neue Ultralight Italic

Helvetica Neue Italic

Helvetica Neue Bold Italic

Helvetica Neue Bold Italic

FAMIGLIA DI CARATTERI

Le variazioni di un particolare **carattere** tipografico, come **grassetto**, **corsivo**, **contornato**, **esteso** e così via. La varietà degli elementi disponibili in una stessa famiglia è la conseguenza del boom della pubblicità nel XIX secolo, e della conseguente domanda di una **tipografia** caratterizzata. Vedi anche **expert set**.

Ing: TYPE FAMILY
Fr: FAMILLE DE CARACTÈRES
Ted: SCHRIFTFAMILIE
Sp: FAMILIA TIPOGRÁFICA

FIGURA-SFONDO

Aspetto della percezione visiva basato sulla relazione tra una forma, (figura, oggetto, forma geometrica, **glifo**, ecc.) e ciò che le sta intorno: una forma è distinguibile solo quando si staglia su uno sfondo diverso da essa. Manipolando con cura questa relazione intrinseca, i grafici possono creare immagini affascinanti anche a partire dalle forme più basilari. Ciò può essere particolarmente importante per il design di un **logo**, in cui molti contenuti devono essere distillati in un marchio relativamente semplice e facilmente identificabile. Relazioni stabili di figure-sfondo tendono ad avere un **punto focale** ben distinguibile e a generare una sensazione armoniosa, mentre relazioni ambigue di figure-sfondo mettono alla prova la percezione degli osservatori. Usate appropriatamente, entrambe possono risultare molto efficaci. Vedi anche **spazio positivo** e **spazio negativo**.

Ing: FIGURE-GROUND
Fr: DESSIN EN GRISÉ
Ted: FORMFLÄCHENGESTALTUNG
Sp: RELACIÓN FIGURA-FONDO

Autore: Manuela Marchesan per le MagnificheEditrici

A B C D E **F** G H I J K L M N O P Q R S T U V W X Y Z

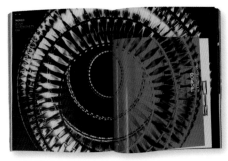

FILETTO TIPOGRAFICO

Linea usata come dispositivo tipografico per separare un elemento di un **layout** da un altro, organizzando lo spazio e dando l'impressione di una **gerarchia tipografica**. Il peso di un filetto tipografico viene solitamente specificato in **punti**.

Ing: RULE
Fr: FILET
Ted: LINIE
Sp: FILETE

Design: Heads Collective

FINITURA A ULTRAVIOLETTI

Processo in cui un polimero liquido viene applicato sulla carta, sia quando il lavoro è nella macchina per la stampa, sia come processo separato immediatamente conseguente a essa, e viene asciugato tramite la luce ultravioletta. Rispetto ai **rivestimenti ad acqua**, i rivestimenti ultravioletti (o UV) offrono una maggiore protezione ai graffi e ad altri danni provocati dalla manipolazione, ma tendono a incrinarsi lungo le pieghe vive. Le finiture UV possono essere applicate su aree specifiche e limitate dello stampato (*vernici spot*) o sull'intera pagina (*vernici coprenti*). Vedi anche **vernici**.

Ing: ULTRAVIOLET COATING
Fr: VERNIS UV
Ted: UV-LACK
Sp: REVESTIMIENTO ULTRAVIOLETA

Design: DESIGNWORK

FLUSSO VISIVO

È il percorso che gli occhi seguono quando osservano una fotografia o un **layout**. Il flusso visivo è influenzato da un gran numero di fattori, fra cui il **colore**, il **bilanciamento**, il **contrasto** e altro ancora. Elementi grafici efficaci sfruttano il flusso visivo previsto: i cartelli stradali, ad esempio, devono essere semplici e diretti, mentre i poster spesso coinvolgono gli osservatori in un flusso visivo complesso. Vedi anche **punto focale**.

Ing: EYE FLOW
Fr: CIRCULATION DU REGARD
Ted: BLICKPFADBEWEGUNG
Sp: LÍNEA DE ORIENTACIÓN

AIPEM Marketing e comunicazione integrata;
Art director: Dino Durigatto, Stefano Mainardis;
Copywriter: Maurizio Clemente; **Account manager:** Paolo Molinaro, Andrea Fioritto; **Foto:** OFF Officine Fotografiche Friulane

ABCDE**F**GHIJKLMNOPQRSTUVWXYZ

FONT

Risorsa fisica o digitale usata per creare i **caratteri**. Una font solitamente comprende lettere maiuscole e minuscole, oltre a numeri e segni di interpunzione, sebbene molte font *OpenType* includano caratteri speciali che una volta si trovavano soltanto negli **expert set**. Nei caratteri in metallo fuso le font hanno una dimensione precisa, mentre quelle digitali possono essere ridotte o ingrandite con un click del mouse. Sebbene font e caratteri siano spesso usati in modo intercambiabile, esiste una chiara distinzione fra i due termini: il carattere tipografico fa riferimento al disegno complessivo dell'insieme dei caratteri, mentre le font sono i mezzi, sia fisici sia digitali, con cui questi ultimi vengono realizzati.

Ing: FONT
Fr: FONTE
Ted: SCHRIFTSATZ
Sp: FUENTE

Design: MEAT graphic collective, Bologna, Italy, www.tastemeat.com

FOR POSITION ONLY (FPO)

Immagine di qualità inferiore, spesso la versione a bassa risoluzione dell'immagine che verrà utilizzata nella versione finale del **layout**, e che funge da "riempiposto". La denominazione FPO data a queste immagini chiarisce immediatamente la funzione limitata agli altri membri del team grafico.

Ing: FOR POSITION ONLY (FPO)
Fr: IMAGE DE PLACEMENT
Ted: PLATZHALTER
Sp: FPO (SÓLO PARA REFERENCIA DE POSICIÓN)

Agenzia di pubblicità: TECNOSTUDI

FORMA-CONTROFORMA
Vedi **spazio positivo** e **spazio negativo**.

FORMATI DEI FOGLI
Vedi **formati di carta**.

FORMATI DI CARTA

I formati di fogli più comunemente usati in tipografia sono il 700x1000 mm (solitamente definito 70x100) e il 640x880 mm (64x88), dai quali vengono ricavati per dimezzamento del lato lungo il 50x70, il 44x64, ecc. In commercio si trovano formati di carta anche maggiori di quelli standard, l'A4 e l'A3, che si utilizzano direttamente nelle stampanti professionali; una volta stampato, il foglio viene piegato e rifilato secondo il formato ISO (International Standards Organization) desiderato.

Ing: PAPER SIZES
Fr: FORMAT DE PAPIER
Ted: PAPIERGRÖSSEN
Sp: TAMAÑO DE PAPEL

Design: Alfredo Carlo

A B C D E **F** G H I J K L M N O P Q R S T U V W X Y Z

FOTOMONTAGGIO

Termine usato per descrivere il processo di creazione di una **composizione** fotografica combinando insieme elementi di altre fotografie. Il risultato, anch'esso chiamato fotomontaggio, si ottiene con tagli e incollaggi, sia in senso letterale sia usando software di trattamento delle immagini. I fotomontaggi creati manualmente spesso vengono fotografati una volta conclusi, dando così l'impressione di una fotografia "classica". I termini fotomontaggio e **montaggio** sono spesso utilizzati in modo intercambiabile. Vedi anche **collage**.

Ing: PHOTOMONTAGE
Fr: PHOTOMONTAGE
Ted: FOTOMONTAGE
Sp: FOTOMONTAJE

Design: Heads Collective

FUSTELLA

Procedimento con cui vengono effettuati tagli precisi su un foglio di carta stampata. Questi tagli possono essere funzionali, come per le carpette con tasche e le buste a incastro, o decorativi, come le "finestre" che rivelano immagini, e le finiture dei **bordi**. In alcuni casi funzionalità e decorazione sono compresenti. Vedi anche **adesivo con fustella** e **taglio al laser**.

Ing: DIE CUT
Fr: DÉCOUPE
Ted: STANZSCHNITT
Sp: TROQUELADO

Studio grafico: Latveria Design

FUTURISMO

Movimento artistico radicale europeo, dei primi decenni del Novecento (circa 1909-1930) con base principale in Italia. Il Futurismo cercò di integrare la velocità e la frenesia dell'"età della macchina" nell'arte e nel design. Per esprimere questa energia vennero impiegati il **collage** e il **fotomontaggio**, e altre tecniche che producevano l'impressione di un movimento cinematico. Il maggior contributo del Futurismo alla grafica fu dato dal particolare utilizzo di vari stili di **caratteri** secondo un'ampia gamma di formati, a volte disposti in modo asimmetrico o persino distorti, e spesso collocati all'interno di un singolo **layout**, in cui **grassetti** e **corsivi** servivano per conferire particolare risalto.

Ing: FUTURISM
Fr: FUTURISME
Ted: FUTURISMUS
Sp: FUTURISMO

Courtesy: Archivio Baroni, Milano e archivio Brunazzi & Associati, Torino

A B C D E F **G** H I J K L M N O P Q R S T U V W X Y Z

Si fa sera nella cattedrale di San Pietro, la chiesa metropolitana di Bologna.

Dopo la funzione tanti fedeli escono e vanno a ritirare l'auto. Stefano Cavina è rimasto dentro alla chiesa e si avvia con passi felpati verso la sagrestia, coperto dal brusio dei fedeli che pregano, nel buio rischiarato solo dalla candele e dai ceri accesi. Si fa notare dal sagrestano, Salvatore Mura, in allerta già da un po' di tempo per via dei furti alle cassette dell'elemosina.

GERARCHIA TIPOGRAFICA

Ordine percettivo espresso mediante variazioni di **scala**, disposizione, **valore**, **colore** e tanti altri segnali visivi. In pubblicazioni ampie, ad es. **titoli** e **sottotitoli** creano ordine. Organizzando i vari elementi secondo una gerarchia, i grafici possono guidare l'osservatore e/o il lettore all'interno di un biglietto da visita, una brochure, un poster, un libro o altre opere creative, mostrando ogni elemento secondo una modalità deliberata e ponderata. Gerarchie "piatte" si rivelano meno interessanti e tendono a confondere.

Ing: HIERARCHY
Fr: HIÉRARCHIE
Ted: HIERARCHIE
Sp: JERARQUÍA

Cliente: Positec Italia srl

GIUSTEZZA

Termine usato per descrivere la larghezza del blocco dei **caratteri**, tradizionalmente misurata in punti, pica o em, anche se in alcuni contesti vengono utilizzati millimetri e pixel. Una giustezza ottimale per una buona leggibilità è generalmente compresa tra i 52 e i 78 caratteri (l'equivalente di 2-3 alfabeti) spazi inclusi, sebbene altri fattori quali l'**interlinea**, gli **spazi lettera** nonché il carattere tipografico stesso debbano essere presi in considerazione. Vedi anche **lunghezza di riga**.

Ing: MEASURE
Fr: MESURE
Ted: SATZBREITE
Sp: ANCHO

Studio grafico: Sara Muzio

GLIFO/I

È la forma di un **carattere** singolo, che sia o meno una lettera. Gli elementi comuni condivisi da una serie di glifi sono quelli che costituiscono un carattere tipografico. L'*anatomia dei caratteri* può essere definita con un lessico molto esteso che comprende termini come grazia, **tratto ascendente**, **tratto discendente** e molti altri.

Ing: LETTERFORM
Fr: DESSIN D'UNE LETTRE
Ted: SCHRIFTCHARAKTER
Sp: LETRA

Design: Tassinari/Vetta

A B C D E F **G** H I J K L M N O P Q R S T U V W X Y Z

GOFFRATURA

Creazione di un'impronta su carta pressando quest'ultima tra due lastre metalliche, una in rilievo e l'altra incassata. Quando la stampa è in rilievo sulla superficie, si chiama goffratura; quando la stampa è sotto la superficie si chiama sotto-rilievo. Le carte di medio peso, specialmente quelle con finiture testurizzate, sono le più adatte. Immagini stampate e stampe a caldo, anche se non sono necessarie, vengono spesso utilizzate come abbellimenti. Una goffratura eseguita senza di esse viene chiamata *goffratura cieca*.

Ing: EMBOSS
Fr: GAUFRAGE
Ted: PRÄGUNG
Sp: GOFRAR

Agenzia di comunicazione e immagine: Brunazzi & Associati, Torino; **Direttori creativi:** Giovanni Brunazzi, Andrea Brunazzi

A B C D E F **G** H I J K L M N O P Q R S T U V W X Y Z

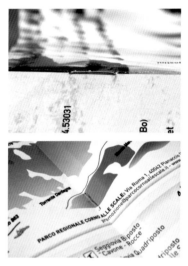

GRADIENTE/I

Fusione graduale di un **colore** in un altro, o del bianco e del nero in un colore completamente **saturo**, generalmente secondo una progressione regolare. I gradienti vengono spesso usati per riempire aree di illustrazioni, sfondi o **caratteri contornati**.

Ing: GRADIENT
Fr: DÉGRADÉ
Ted: VERLAUF
Sp: DEGRADADO

Design: Armando Chitolina

GRAFFETTATURA

Tipo di **rilegatura** permanente usata comunemente per brochure e riviste, dove le **segnature** e la copertina sono sistemate le une dentro le altre in un'unica piega lungo un dorso comune, assicurate con graffette e poi refilate.

Ing: SADDLE-STITCH BINDING
Fr: PIQÛRE MÉTALLIQUE À CHEVAL
Ted: DRAHTHEFTUNG
Sp: ENCUADERNACIÓN A CABALLETE

Design: Alfredo Carlo

GRAFICA VETTORIALE

Immagine digitale creata secondo forme definite matematicamente, all'opposto dell'**allineamento** di campioni usato nei **bitmap**. Questa proprietà permette alle grafiche vettoriali ingrandimenti notevoli senza sacrificare la **risoluzione**. I bitmap, d'altra parte, possono raggiungere un livello di dettagli e di sottili variazioni tonali non attuabili con le grafiche vettoriali. Vedi anche **curva di Bézier**.

Ing: VECTOR GRAPHIC
Fr: IMAGES VECTORIELLES
Ted: VEKTORGRAFIK
Sp: GRÁFICO VECTORIAL

Design: Francesca Ferri per Studio Pirulino

GRAFICHE RASTER
Vedi **bitmap**.

A B C D E F **G H** I J K L M N O P Q R S T U V W X Y Z

GRASSETTO

Carattere in cui il **glifo** ha uno spessore più rilevante rispetto a quelli che vengono usati per la versione regolare dello stesso. Sul desktop delle applicazioni editoriali normalmente si trova uno strumento che abilita il grassetto, ingrossando la **font** del carattere corrente. Il vero grassetto, invece, è disegnato per essere proporzionato agli altri "membri" dello stesso carattere, cosicché quando sono stampati assieme risultano avere una gradevole "aria di famiglia".

Ing: BOLD/BOLDFACE
Fr: GRAS, CARACTÈRES GRAS
Ted: FETT (SCHRIFTEN)
Sp: NEGRITA

Design: Tapiro Camplani + Pescolderung

GRIGLIA

Griglia costituita da linee che si intersecano, molto spesso in senso orizzontale e verticale. Le griglie si utilizzano per organizzare gli elementi grafici e creano una struttura coerente per il **layout**. Si usano soprattutto per i progetti di grande formato e permettono ai grafici di lavorare con efficacia eliminando le decisioni arbitrarie. D'altro lato però le griglie sono spesso criticate perché sacrificano la creatività e il pensiero critico. Usate appropriatamente invece fungono da "impalcature," creando una struttura di supporto che consente ai grafici una libertà maggiore, non minore.

Ing: GRID
Fr: GRILLE
Ted: RASTER (SATZSPIEGEL)
Sp: CUADRÍCULA

Design: Emporio Adv

H&J

Abbreviazione dell'espressione inglese *Hyphenation & Justification* (sillabazione e giustificazione), è il processo con cui applicazioni software riempiono le righe di **caratteri**. Indipendentemente dal fatto che un blocco di testo sia allineato a sinistra o a destra, giustificato o centrato, il software riempie automaticamente l'intera lunghezza della sua misura con una combinazione di caratteri e di spazi. Questa è la giustificazione (termine comunemente usato per descrivere soltanto le righe di caratteri che riempiono completamente la loro misura). La **sillabazione** si riferisce alla divisione delle parole in modo che ogni riga di caratteri possa essere riempita totalmente. Applicazioni avanzate per l'impaginazione permettono di aggiustare un certo numero di parametri H&J, offrendo così al grafico la flessibilità necessaria per creare una **tipografia** raffinata. Vedi anche **caratteri giustificati**.

Ing: H&J
Fr: C&J
Ted: SILBENTRENNUNG & BLOCKSATZ (S&B)
Sp: H&J

Design: AIPEM Marketing e comunicazione integrata

A B C D E F G H **I** J K L M N O P Q R S T U V W X Y Z

ICONA

Segno grafico che assomiglia a ciò che significa. Ad esempio, l'icona della stampante sul desktop di un computer assomiglia a una stampante, anche se in versione generica. Altri esempi possono essere il simbolo grafico di una sigaretta utilizzato nel "divieto di fumare", e l'icona di una valigia usata per indicare l'area per il Recupero bagagli di un aeroporto. In entrambi i casi le icone assomigliano a ciò che rappresentano, il che le rende facilmente riconoscibili, superando barriere linguistiche e culturali. Vedi anche **simboli** e **pittogrammi**.

Ing: ICON
Fr: ICÔNE
Ted: BILDZEICHEN
Sp: ICONO

Cliente: Positec Italia srl

IDENTITÀ

È la "personalità" di un'azienda, espressa visivamente (sia all'interno sia all'esterno) attraverso il suo branding distintivo. Un *identity package* solitamente include **loghi** e/o logotipi, particolari **palette di colori** (spesso specificate con un **sistema di combinazione dei colori**), **layout** standardizzati per documenti e packaging, e linee guida che indicano come usare ogni elemento per mantenere la coerenza dell'immagine aziendale. Grandi aziende possono avere molti marchi che possiedono elementi visivi comuni, collegandosi così a un più ampio sistema di *corporate identity*.

Ing: IDENTITY
Fr: IDENTITÉ
Ted: FIRMENERSCHEINUNGSBILD
Sp: IDENTIDAD

Design: Teikna; **Art director:** Claudia Neri

IMPAGINAZIONE

Numerazione delle pagine che indica la corretta sequenza in un libro o in un altro tipo di pubblicazione stampata. Il termine impaginazione può essere usato più genericamente per indicare il numero totale di pagine di una data pubblicazione e di recente ha assunto anche un altro significato, cioè descrive in che modo un'informazione venga organizzata sulle pagine web. I blog, ad esempio, possono essere impaginati in modo da visualizzare nella pagina principale solo il primo o il secondo paragrafo di un post (messaggio testuale) , o non più di dieci commenti successivamente al post originale cui si riferiscono. Vedi anche **imposizione tipografica**.

Ing: PAGINATION
Fr: PAGINATION
Ted: PAGINIERUNG
Sp: PAGINACIÓN

Design: Omniadvert

Verso

ꞁ	0ꞁ	ꞁꞁ	6
2	15	14	3

Piega 1

ꞁ	15	6	8
4	13	16	1

Piega 2 · Piega 3

Recto

IMPOSIZIONE TIPOGRAFICA

È l'attenta disposizione di molteplici pagine di una pubblicazione per prepararle alla stampa su fogli di carta di grande formato. L'imposizione assicura che le pagine siano orientate correttamente e con una sequenza corretta una volta stampate, piegate in **segnature** e legate. Questa operazione può essere eseguita manualmente, sebbene oggi si ottenga più spesso con le applicazioni software apposite. Vedi anche **impaginazione**.

Ing: IMPOSITION
Fr: IMPOSITION
Ted: AUSSCHIESSEN
Sp: IMPOSICIÓN

Studio grafico: Sara Muzio

INTERLINEA

Distanza tra linee successive di **caratteri**, misurata da una **linea di base** all'altra e specificata mediante **punti**. Diversamente dai caratteri metallici, i caratteri digitali possono essere composti con interlinee negative; ciò significa che la misura del punto del carattere eccede la misura del punto dell'interlinea. Sebbene la **leggibilità** possa soffrirne, le interlinee negative possono essere usate per creare effetti straordinari nella grafica pubblicitaria, nei poster e simili.

Ing: LEADING
Fr: INTERLIGNAGE
Ted: DURCHSCHUSS (ZEILENABSTAND)
Sp: INTERLINEADO

Design: Lunagrafica

INTERRUZIONE DI LINEA

Termine usato per riferirsi a come e quando una riga di **caratteri** finisce prima di continuare in quella successiva. Le applicazioni per i **layout** solitamente interrompono le righe di caratteri dopo uno spazio fra le parole, o dopo un **trattino**, una **lineetta em** o una **lineetta en**, sebbene queste disposizioni automatiche possano spesso essere modificate. In più, un **invio a capo automatico** può essere usato per interrompere la riga, iniziandone una nuova senza iniziare un nuovo paragrafo (che solitamente ha caratteristiche specifiche come il **rientro**. Vedi anche **H&J** e **invio a capo automatico**.

Ing: LINE BREAK
Fr: SAUT DE LIGNE
Ted: ZEILENUMBRUCH
Sp: SALTO DE LÍNEA

Design: DESIGNWORK

A B C D E F G H I J K L M N O P Q R S T U V W X Y Z

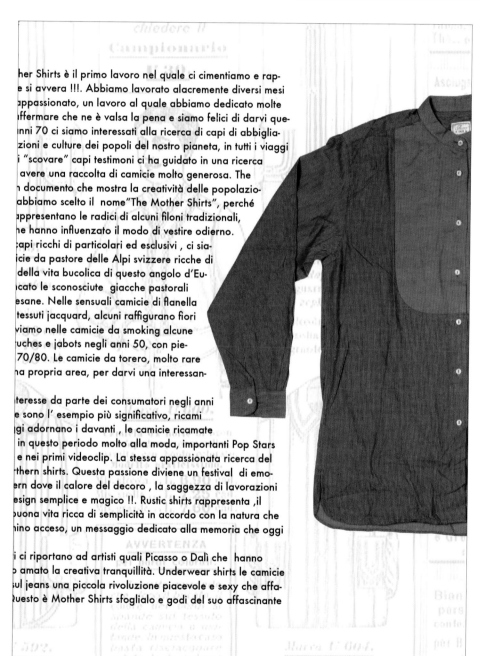

her Shirts è il primo lavoro nel quale ci cimentiamo e rap-
e si avvera !!!. Abbiamo lavorato alacremente diversi mesi
appassionato, un lavoro al quale abbiamo dedicato molte
ffermare che ne è valsa la pena e siamo felici di darvi que-
nni 70 ci siamo interessati alla ricerca di capi di abbiglia-
zioni e culture dei popoli del nostro pianeta, in tutti i viaggi
i "scovare" capi testimoni ci ha guidato in una ricerca
avere una raccolta di camicie molto generosa. The
n documento che mostra la creatività delle popolazio-
abbiamo scelto il nome"The Mother Shirts", perché
appresentano le radici di alcuni filoni tradizionali,
e hanno influenzato il modo di vestire odierno.
api ricchi di particolari ed esclusivi , ci sia-
icie da pastore delle Alpi svizzere ricche di
della vita bucolica di questo angolo d'Eu-
cato le sconosciute giacche pastorali
esane. Nelle sensuali camicie di flanella
tessuti jacquard, alcuni raffigurano fiori
viamo nelle camicie da smoking alcune
uches e jabots negli anni 50, con pie-
70/80. Le camicie da torero, molto rare
na propria area, per darvi una interessan-

teresse da parte dei consumatori negli anni
e sono l' esempio più significativo, ricami
gi adornano i davanti , le camicie ricamate
in questo periodo molto alla moda, importanti Pop Stars
e nei primi videoclip. La stessa appassionata ricerca del
thern shirts. Questa passione diviene un festival di emo-
rn dove il calore del decoro , la saggezza di lavorazioni
esign semplice e magico !!. Rustic shirts rappresenta ,il
uona vita ricca di semplicità in accordo con la natura che
ino acceso, un messaggio dedicato alla memoria che oggi

i ci riportano ad artisti quali Picasso o Dalì che hanno
amato la creativa tranquillità. Underwear shirts le camicie
sul jeans una piccola rivoluzione piacevole e sexy che affa-
Questo è Mother Shirts sfoglialo e godi del suo affascinante

INVIO A CAPO AUTOMATICO

Termine usato in senso generico per descrivere il modo in cui una riga di **caratteri** finisce e riprende automaticamente nella riga succes-siva. La revisione di una riga di caratteri spesso ha l'effetto di modificare il punto in cui una o più righe adiacenti vanno a capo (*rewrap*). In senso più specifico, il termine viene utilizzato per descrivere in che modo alcune righe di caratteri possono "avvolgere" altri elementi grafici, come fotografie e illustrazioni. Vedi anche **H&J**.

Ing: TEXT WRAPPING
Fr: RETOUR À LA LIGNE AUTOMATIQUE
Ted: TEXTUMBRUCH
Sp: AJUSTE DE TEXTO

Realizzazione grafica: MP foto&grafica

A B C D E F G H I J K **L** M N O P Q R S T U V W X Y Z

LAYOUT

Fase preliminare del processo grafico che coinvolge l'organizzazione dei vari elementi del progetto, come i **caratteri**, le fotografie e le illustrazioni, in modo tale che si possa prevederne il risultato finale. Può anche essere usato per descrivere l'organizzazione complessiva di un disegno completo. Layout per libri, brochure, fascicoli e altri documenti che contengono pagine multiple vengono spesso organizzati all'interno di **griglie**.

Ing: LAYOUT
Fr: MAQUETTE
Ted: LAYOUT
Sp: MAQUETACIÓN

Agenzia di comunicazione e immagine: Brunazzi & Associati, Torino; **Direttori creativi:** Giovanni Brunazzi, Andrea Brunazzi

LEGATURA

Due, a volte tre **glifi** combinati usando elementi condivisi di ognuno. Le legature vengono solitamente utilizzate per evitare brutti "scontri" fra le lettere, come quando la lettera *i* segue la lettera *f*. Se queste due lettere sono disposte come **caratteri** singoli, il puntino della *i* sarà molto vicino, o a seconda del carattere usato, persino sovrapposto alla testa della *f*. Sostituire i due caratteri con una singola legatura renderà la riga più leggibile. Le **legature**, che si fanno risalire agli antichi manoscritti, furono usate fin dai primi tempi dei caratteri metallici, ma divennero fuori moda durante l'era della *fototipia*. Oggi la maggior parte delle **font** digitali comprende una gamma di legature.

Ing: LIGATURE
Fr: LIGATURE
Ted: LIGATUR
Sp: LIGADURA

Design: Joele Lucherini per STUDIONO

LEGGIBILITÀ

Vocabolo che si riferisce alla *chiarezza* tipografica. Da non confondere con l'inglese *readibility* che indica il grado di facilità della lettura, basato sulla *qualità* tipografica.

Ing: LEGIBILITY
Fr: LISIBILITÉ
Ted: LESERLICHKEIT
Sp: LEGIBILIDAD TIPOGRÁFICA

Design: Lunagrafica

A B C D E F G H I J K **L** M N O P Q R S T U V W X Y Z

hiou

LETTERA MAIUSCOLA INIZIALE

Lettera maiuscola decorativa usata come lettera iniziale della prima parola di un capoverso, generalmente di dimensione maggiore rispetto ai **caratteri** precedenti e successivi. Le maiuscole iniziali possono anche essere di un carattere tipografico diverso e/o essere stampate con un **colore** differente per aumentare l'impatto visivo. Come per i **caratteri swash**, le maiuscole iniziali devono essere utilizzate con parsimonia, anche nei testi lunghi. Vedi anche **capolettera**.

Ing: INITIAL CAPITAL/CAP
Fr: INITIALE
Ted: INITIALE
Sp: MAYÚSCULA INICIAL

Design: Teikna; **Art director:** Claudia Neri

LINEA/E

Serie di **punti**, sia diritti sia curvilinei. A differenza di quanto accade in geometria, dove le linee hanno uno spessore trascurabile, le linee usate nella grafica possono essere sottili o spesse, e non necessitano di essere uniformi nella loro intera lunghezza, ma possono essere anche spezzate o frammentate. Linee spesse assumono le proprietà dei piani (superfici piatte) e questi tre elementi, punti, linee e piani, sono alla base di tutte le forme utilizzate nella grafica. Vedi anche **filetto tipografico**.

Ing: LINE
Fr: LIGNE
Ted: LINIENGESTALTUNG
Sp: LÍNEA

AIPEM Marketing e comunicazione integrata;
Art director: Daria Biasizzo, Vittoria Turrin; **Copywriter:** Maurizio Clemente; **Account manager:** Carlo Rossi

LINEA DI BASE

Linea di riferimento usata per il corretto **allineamento** orizzontale dei caratteri. I **margini** inferiori delle lettere maiuscole e delle lettere minuscole che non hanno **tratto discendente** si adagiano sulla linea di base, o quasi. Infatti solo le lettere minuscole a base piatta, come la *h* e la *i*, si appoggiano appropriatamente sulla **linea di base**. Quelle con base tonda, quali la *o* o la *u*, scendono invece lievemente sotto la linea di base. La risultante "illusione ottica" mostra l'importanza dell'**allineamento visivo** rispetto all'allineamento di precisione, quando si tratta di **tipografia** raffinata.

Ing: BASELINE
Fr: LIGNE DE BASE
Ted: GRUNDLINIE (SCHRIFTLINIE)
Sp: LÍNEA DE BASE

Agenzia di pubblicità: TECNOSTUDI

A B C D E F G H I J K **L** M N O P Q R S T U V W X Y Z

Tipografia

LINEA MEDIANA

Linea di riferimento utilizzata per un corretto **allineamento** orizzontale dei **caratteri**, corrispondente all'**altezza della x** di un dato carattere tipografico. I bordi superiori delle lettere minuscole senza **tratto ascendente** si trovano lungo la linea mediana o molto vicino a essa. Di fatto solo le lettere minuscole dalla testa piatta, come la *u* e la *x*, finiscono sulla linea mediana. Quelle dalla testa tonda, come la *a* e la *o*, si innalzano invece lieve-mente sopra la linea mediana. Un'illusione ottica simile viene usata lungo la **linea di base**; entrambi i casi illustrano la maggiore importanza dell'**allineamento visivo** rispetto all'allineamento di precisione quando si tratta di **tipografia** raffinata.

Ing: MEAN LINE
Fr: LIGNE DE TÊTE
Ted: X-LINIE (MITTELLINIE)
Sp: LÍNEA MEDIA

Studio grafico: Sara Muzio

Tipografia

lineetta — Em

LINEETTA EM

Si tratta di una lineetta la cui lunghezza **em** viene utilizzata per creare una pausa nella riga di un testo, specialmente per dare rilievo a un inciso. Le consuetudini variano per quanto riguarda l'inserimento di uno spazio prima e dopo una lineetta em, sebbene molti editor preferiscano non usarlo. Vedi anche **lineetta en** e **trattino**.

Ing: EM DASH
Fr: TIRET CADRATIN
Ted: Geviertstrich
Sp: RAYA

Studio grafico: Sara Muzio

Tipografia

LINEETTA EN

Lineetta della larghezza di un'**en** utilizzata in sostituzione delle preposizioni "da... a... " (lunedì – venerdì), "dalle... alle… " (2:00 – 3:00), ecc. Come per la **lineetta em**, le consuetudini riguardo l'uso o meno degli spazi prima e dopo una lineetta en variano; grafici e tipografi a volte preferiscono usarli, calibrandoli successivamente con un'attenta **crenatura**. Vedi anche **lineetta em**.

Ing: EN DASH
Fr: TIRET DEMI-CADRATIN
Ted: DIVIS
Sp: SEMIRRAYA

Studio grafico: Sara Muzio

A B C D E F G H I J K **L** M N O P Q R S T U V W X Y Z

LITOGRAFIA

Processo di stampa in cui l'inchiostro viene applicato su una pietra liscia o su una lamina metallica, dalla quale poi viene trasferito sulla carta. Il nome deriva dal greco *lithos*, "pietra" e *graphia*, "scrittura". Nella litografia, un medium grasso, come un pastello, viene usato per segnare la pietra o il metallo definendo le aree in cui l'inchiostro, che ha una base acquosa, può essere assorbito o respinto. Aree non segnate della superficie "trattengono" l'inchiostro e lo trasferiscono sulla carta, mentre le aree grasse respingono l'inchiostro e diventano lo sfondo per l'immagine finale di stampa. Vedi anche **litografia offset**.

Ing: LITHOGRAPHY
Fr: LITHOGRAPHIE
Ted: LITHOGRAFIE
Sp: LITOGRAFÍA

Courtesy: Archivio Baroni, Milano e archivio Brunazzi & Associati, Torino

LITOGRAFIA OFFSET

Processo di stampa basato sui principi della **litografia**, in cui un'immagine a inchiostro viene trasferita (*offset*) su un telo di caucciù prima di essere applicata sulla superficie stampante. Un set di rulli viene usato per applicare l'inchiostro sulla matrice, mentre un altro set fa scorrere il telo di caucciù sopra di essa, trasferendovi in questo modo l'inchiostro. L'alta qualità e l'economia di scala hanno contribuito a rendere la litografia offset, a volte chiamata anche stampa offset, la forma più diffusa di stampa commerciale.

Ing: OFFSET LITHOGRAPHY
Fr: LITHOGRAPHIE OFFSET
Ted: OFFSETDRUCK
Sp: LITOGRAFÍA OFFSET

Design: Lunagrafica

LIVELLO

Elemento dei software ideato per creare immagini digitali, che tratta i differenti elementi grafici come se fossero collocati su fogli trasparenti, rendendo così possibile il trattamento, la combinazione e la manipolazione di alcune parti specifiche di un'immagine senza incidere sulle altre. L'immagine finale è il risultato di una sovrapposizione di livelli, secondo una particolare sequenza.

Ing: LAYER
Fr: CALQUE
Ted: EBENE
Sp: CAPA

Agenzia di pubblicità: TECNOSTUDI

A B C D E F G H I J K **L** M N O P Q R S T U V W X Y Z

LOGO

Segno grafico utilizzato solitamente per motivi commerciali come parte del **branding** di un'organizzazione. Loghi efficaci sono molto più difficili da creare di quanto la loro elegante semplicità possa suggerire. I loghi devono essere abbastanza semplici per essere riconoscibili persino quando vengono stampati o visualizzati in **scala** ridotta, pur essendo ricchi di contenute rappresentano i valori e l'**identità** di un'organizzazione. Si devono potere ricordare e riconoscere istantaneamente, e distinguersi rispetto a quelli dei concorrenti. Non ci sorprende quindi che le aziende spesso usino per anni e anni uno stesso logo di successo. Un *logotipo* è uno specifico insieme di **glifi** che solitamente compone il nome o la sigla di un'organizzazione, i dettagli dei quali (**colore**, **carattere**, **spazio lettera**, ecc.) sono parte unica e integrante del marchio dell'organizzazione stessa.

Ing: LOGO
Fr: LOGO
Ted: LOGO
Sp: LOGO

Art director: Miguel Sal

LOREM IPSUM

Testo privo di senso o menabò, usato per riempire uno spazio vuoto durante la definizione di un **layout**. Il termine si usa anche per descrivere il modo in cui alcune applicazioni di **impaginazione** usano le barre grigie per rappresentare righe di **caratteri** troppo piccoli per essere leggibili su un display.

Ing: LOREM IPSUM
Fr: LOREM IPSUM
Ted: LOREM IPSUM
Sp: LOREM IPSUM

Agenzia di pubblicità: TECNOSTUDI

LUMINOSITÀ

Grado di maggiore o minore chiarezza di un **colore**, anche chiamata **valore** o **tono**. Colori con livelli simili di luminosità appariranno quasi indistinguibili in una fotocopia in bianco e nero. Vedi anche **ruota dei colori**.

Ing: BRIGHTNESS
Fr: LUMINOSITÉ
Ted: LEUCHTDICHTE
Sp: BRILLO

Design: Omniadvert

A B C D E F G H I J K **L M** N O P Q R S T U V W X Y Z

LUNGHEZZA DI RIGA

Lunghezza di una riga singola di **caratteri**. La lunghezza di riga viene spesso confusa con la **giustezza** tipografica, che è la larghezza della **colonna** stessa. Tuttavia, quando un carattere è allineato a sinistra (o a bandiera destra), ad esempio, le righe dei caratteri solo raramente riempiono l'intera misura. Lo stesso vale per l'**allineamento a destra** e per i caratteri centrati. Soltanto nel caso di caratteri giustificati la lunghezza di una riga corrisponde alla giustezza stessa.

Ing: LINE LENGTH
Fr: LONGUEUR DE LIGNE
Ted: ZEILENLÄNGE
Sp: LONGITUD DE LÍNEA

Design: Tassinari/Vetta

MAIUSCOLETTI

Lettere maiuscole aventi proporzioni e *peso del tratto* che le rendono compatibili con le lettere minuscole di un tipo di **carattere**. I maiuscoletti si usano spesso all'interno di una riga di caratteri per la stessa ragione per cui vengono usati i **numeri di allineamento**, cioè perché siano meno invadenti di quelli alternativi. Quando si cita una sigla nel mezzo di una frase, ad esempio, una stringa di lettere maiuscole potrebbe distrarre. Un altro vantaggio dei maiuscoletti è che le loro proporzioni permettono la **leggibilità** anche di piccoli formati.

Ing: SMALL CAPITALS/CAPS
Fr: PETITES CAPITALES
Ted: KAPITÄLCHEN
Sp: VERSALITA

Agenzia di comunicazione e immagine: Brunazzi & Associati, Torino; **Direttori creativi:** Giovanni Brunazzi, Andrea Brunazzi

MARGINE/I

Aree lungo i quattro lati di una pagina che solitamente incorniciano il **corpo del testo** e/o un particolare **layout**. Elementi come i numeri delle pagine, le note a piè di pagina e le **didascalie**, vengono spesso stampati ai margini. I margini che si trovano lungo il dorso di una pubblicazione rilegata a volte vengono chiamati margini di **rilegatura**.

Ing: MARGIN
Fr: MARGES
Ted: SEITENRAND
Sp: MARGEN

Studio grafico: Latveria Design

ABCDEFGHIJKL **M** NOPQRSTUVWXYZ

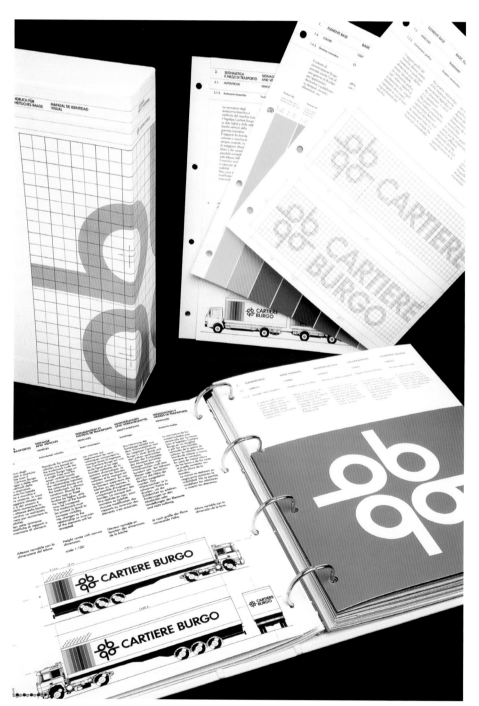

MARGINE INTERNO

Lo spazio fra due **colonne** di **caratteri**, o più genericamente, fra due colonne qualsiasi del **layout**. Il margine interno a volte viene usato per descrivere la stretta striscia di una pagina lungo il bordo della **rilegatura**, o l'area dove due strisce di questo tipo si incontrano tra due **pagine affiancate**.

Ing: GUTTER
Fr: GOUTTIÈRE
Ted: SPALTENABSTAND
Sp: MEDIANIL

Agenzia di comunicazione e immagine: Brunazzi & Associati, Torino; **Direttori creativi:** Giovanni Brunazzi, Andrea Brunazzi

A B C D E F G H I J K L **M** N O P Q R S T U V W X Y Z

METAFORA

Descrizione o espressione di un concetto mediante un altro. Nella grafica le metafore possono comprendere componenti testuali, come quando una frase spiritosa collega un'immagine a un concetto apparentemente non pertinente. Metafore puramente visive sfruttano connotazioni generalmente associate a una o più immagini trasferendole su un'altra. Spesso ciò si attua usando *immagini fuse*, che si ottengono "fondendo" due o più immagini in modo da facilitare un tale trasferimento di significato. Le immagini di una penna e di una pistola, ad esempio, si possono combinare per suggerire il potere della parola scritta.

Ing: METAPHOR
Fr: MÉTAPHORE
Ted: METAPHER
Sp: METÁFORA

Design: Achab Group; **Art director:** Veronica Palasgo; **Illustrazioni:** Lucio Schiavon; **Copywriter:** Ugo Rebeschini; **Cliente:** Comprensorio C6 Val di Non (Trento)

MEZZITONI

Immagine ottenuta con la **scala dei grigi** in cui l'intera gamma tonale è stata convertita in una griglia di minuscoli punti neri, o *schermi di mezzitoni*. Aree più scure dell'immagine vengono rappresentate da macchie di punti più grandi di quelli usati per rappresentare aree più chiare. I mezzitoni corrispondenti a ogni **canale** vengono combinati per simulare l'intero spettro dei colori visibili quando si stampa con **processo a quattro colori**.

Ing: HALFTONE
Fr: SIMILI
Ted: HALBTON
Sp: MEDIO TONO

Design: Joele Lucherini per STUDIONO

MODELLO DI COLORE

Sistema in cui il **colore** viene definito in modo assoluto mediante poche componenti di colore che, quando elaborate, possono essere usate per creare un ampio spettro cromatico. **RGB** e **CMYK** sono i due modelli di colore più noti, sebbene ne esistano anche altri. L'HSB, ad esempio, utilizza caratteristiche cromatiche associate alla tradizionale **ruota dei colori** dei pigmenti: **tonalità**, **saturazione** e **luminosità**. Il modello di colore *LAB color model* si basa sulle coordinate usate nella *colorimetria*. Viene spesso confuso con lo **spazio colore**, che è la gamma di colori prodotta da un particolare visualizzatore o strumento di stampa all'interno di uno specifico modello cromatico. Una stampante a getto d'inchiostro e una stampante professionale usano entrambe il modello di colore CMYK; la gamma di colori CMYK prodotta da ogni stampante rappresenta un particolare **spazio colore** all'interno del più ampio modello di colore CMYK.

Ing: COLOR MODEL
Fr: MODÈLE COLORIMÉTRIQUE
Ted: FARBMODELL
Sp: MODELO DE COLOR

Design: Alfredo Carlo

A B C D E F G H I J K L **M** N O P Q R S T U V W X Y Z

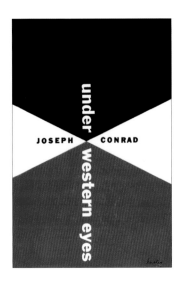

MODERNISMO

Più un insieme di movimenti che un movimento unico, il Modernismo si impose intorno al 1907, assieme al **Cubismo** e al suo rifiuto per le forme naturali a favore dell'astrazione. Nei 100 e più anni a seguire, il design modernista è stato interpretato e reinterpretato in tutto il mondo, assumendo una grande varietà di forme diverse, alcune molto più vicine ai suoi tratti distintivi originali (ad es., un uso rigido di **griglie**, **caratteri senza grazie**, **spazi bianchi** generosi, ecc.) che altre. Per ogni "regola" del Modernismo esistono innumerevoli eccezioni. Ciononostante, si possono trovare fili conduttori comuni, tra cui la preferenza per la comunicazione visiva funzionale e la tendenza a guardare ottimisticamente al futuro.

Ing: MODERNISM
Fr: MODERNISME
Ted: MODERNE
Sp: MODERNISMO

Design: Alvin Lustig, www.alvinlustig.com; **Foto:** Elaine Lustig Cohen

MONOCROMATICO (EFFETTO)

È una **palette di colori** compresa tra le *sfumature* e le **tinte** di una singola **tonalità**. Nelle immagini monocromatiche, la variazione tonale viene rappresentata secondo differenze di **saturazione** e **luminosità**; le immagini comprese nella **scala dei grigi** sono monocromatiche e presentano una palette di colori compresa fra il grigio, il bianco e il nero.

Ing: MONOCHROMATIC
Fr: MONOCHROMATIQUE
Ted: MONOCHROMATISCH (EINFARBIG)
Sp: MONOCROMÁTICO

Design: Heads Collective

MONOSPAZIO

Termine usato per descrivere **caratteri** tutti della stessa larghezza. Il tipo di **caratteri** risultante ricorda quello creato dalle macchine da scrivere. Vedi anche **proporzionale**.

Ing: MONOSPACED
Fr: CARACTÈRES À CHASSE CONSTANTE
Ted: DICKTENGLEICH (NICHTPROPORTIONALE SCHRIFT)
Sp: MONOESPACIADA

Design: Heads Collective

MONTAGGIO
Vedi **collage** e **fotomontaggio**.

Old-style: 0123456789

MULTIMEDIA

Termine usato per descrivere media il cui contenuto viene trasmesso in più di un modo. Un singolo sito web, ad esempio, può integrare testi (e ipertesti) e immagini statiche con materiali audio e video, il tutto vertendo su un unico argomento. Il termine può anche essere usato per descrivere strumenti che supportano i contenuti e la trasmissione dei multimedia, o per dispositivi come i videogiochi con cui gli utenti possono interagire.

Ing: MULTIMEDIA
Fr: MULTIMÉDIA
Ted: MULTIMEDIA
Sp: MULTIMEDIA

Agenzia di pubblicità: TECNOSTUDI

NOTE CONCLUSIVE
Vedi **pagine finali**.

NUMERI E LETTERE DI ALLINEAMENTO

Set di numeri che hanno stessa o simile altezza di una lettera maiuscola di un dato tipo di **carattere**. Poiché possiedono anche larghezza di carattere costante e sono appoggiati lungo la **linea di base**, vengono spesso usati nelle tabelle, dove il loro **allineamento** può essere gradevole a vedersi. Vedi anche **numeri e lettere in stile antico**.

Ing: LINING NUMERALS/FIGURES
Fr: CHIFFRES ARABES
Ted: MAJUSKELZIFFERN
(TABELLENZIFFERN)
Sp: NÚMEROS DE CAJA ALTA

Design: Omniadvert

NUMERI E LETTERE IN STILE ANTICO

Insieme di numeri che hanno proporzioni comparabili alle lettere minuscole di un dato **carattere** tipografico. Come per i **maiuscoletti**, i numeri in stile antico sono spesso usati all'interno di una riga di caratteri poiché meno invadenti dei **numeri di allineamento**.

Ing: OLD-STYLE NUMERALS/FIGURES
Fr: CHIFFRES SUSPENDUS
Ted: MEDIÄVALZIFFERN
Sp: NÚMEROS ELZEVIRIANOS

ABCDEFGHIJKLMN**OP**QRSTUVWXYZ

OCCHIELLO

Spazio chiuso, sia completamente (come nella lettera *o*) sia parzialmente (come nella lettera *c*), all'interno di un **glifo**. A volte viene anche usato più genericamente nel senso di spaziatura, con riferimento allo spazio tra **glifi** vicini. Vedi anche **spazio negativo**.

Ing: COUNTER
Fr: CONTREPOINÇON
Ted: PUNZE
Sp: CONTRAFORMA

Design: Tassinari/Vetta

ORFANO

Una o due righe separate dal paragrafo principale di cui fanno parte, che si trovano in testa (se iniziano il paragrafo) o al piede (se lo concludono) di una **colonna** di testo. Gli orfani possono essere evitati in diversi modi, il più comune è con la spaziatura delle lettere e la **sillabazione**. Vedi anche **vedova**.

Ing: ORPHAN
Fr: ORPHELINE
Ted: SCHUSTERJUNGE
Sp: HUÉRFANA

Agenzia di pubblicità: TECNOSTUDI

PACKAGING DESIGN

Da un punto di vista grafico, il package design (il design di imballaggi) è la creazione di contenitori che proteggono e mettono in mostra i prodotti durante le fasi di distribuzione, immagazzinaggio, vendita e utilizzo. **Loghi** e *logotipi*, assieme ad altri elementi visivi (o tattili) del **branding**, hanno un ruolo centrale nel package design, sebbene le considerazioni estetiche siano solo il primo passo. Altri fattori importanti sono la sicurezza (come i flaconi di pillole a prova di bambini), l'economia (il numero di scatole che un container standard può contenere), e la facilità nell'utilizzo (per rendere agevole l'apertura dell'imballaggio), per citarne alcuni.

Ing: PACKAGING DESIGN
Fr: DESIGN DE PACKAGING
Ted: VERPACKUNGSDESIGN
Sp: DISEÑO DE EMBALAJE

Art director: Fabio Gamberini per D-SIGN

A B C D E F G H I J K L M N O **P** Q R S T U V W X Y Z

PAGINA MASTRO

Matrice usata nelle applicazioni di impaginazione per assicurare in tutto il documento una disposizione uniforme della **griglia**, delle **colonne** di testo, e di altri consueti elementi del **layout**. Pagine mastro multiple possono essere utilizzate all'interno di un documento singolo, ognuna corrispondente a una diversa sezione o stile di layout. Quando si usano pagine mastro, la numerazione delle pagine viene di solito eseguita automaticamente.

Ing: MASTER PAGE
Fr: PAGE TYPE
Ted: MUSTERSEITE
Sp: PÁGINA MAESTRA

Agenzia di comunicazione e immagine: Brunazzi & Associati, Torino; **Direttori creativi:** Giovanni Brunazzi, Andrea Brunazzi

PAGINE AFFIANCATE

Due pagine affiancate qualsiasi di una pubblicazione rilegata. Applicazioni per i **layout** come Adobe InDesign® permettono ai grafici di creare documenti sia su una singola pagina sia su pagine affiancate. Vedi anche **recto/verso**.

Ing: FACING PAGES
Fr: PAGES EN REGARD
Ted: DOPPELSEITEN
Sp: PÁGINAS ENFRENTADAS

Design: Latveria Design

PAGINE FINALI

Sezione di un libro successiva al testo principale, come le appendici, la bibliografia, il glossario, le note e così via. Vedi anche **pagine iniziali**.

Ing: END MATTER
Fr: PARTIES ANNEXES
Ted: ANHANG
Sp: PÁGINAS FINALES

Studio grafico: Sara Muzio

A B C D E F G H I J K L M N O **P** Q R S T U V W X Y Z

PAGINE INIZIALI

Sezione di un libro che precede il testo principale, come ad esempio il frontespizio, l'antiporta (un'illustrazione o decorazione artistica presente nella pagina opposta al frontespizio), l'indice, l'elenco delle immagini e delle tabelle, la prefazione e simili. Vedi anche **pagine finali**.

Ing: FRONT MATTER
Fr: PAGES LIMINAIRES
Ted: TITELEI
Sp: PÁGINAS PRELIMINARES

Design: Armando Chitolina

PALETTE DI COLORI

Insieme di colori definito sia da un medium particolare, come la palette *216-color web-safe*, o da grafici e artisti, per un progetto specifico. Apposite palette di colori spesso vengono create usando le relazioni indicate dalla **ruota dei colori**.

Ing: COLOR PALETTE
Fr: PALETTE DES COULEURS
Ted: FARBPALETTE
Sp: PALETA DE COLORES

LIZART comunicazione visiva; **Art director:** Simonetta Scala; **Designer:** Maria Chinaglia, Simonetta Scala

PANTONE MATCHING SYSTEM (PMS)
Vedi **sistema di abbinamento dei colori**.

PEDICE/I

Insieme di **caratteri** di formato inferiore rispetto a quelli del testo principale, generalmente centrati lungo la **linea di base**. I pedici, detti anche *caratteri deponenti*, vengono spesso utilizzati per le notazioni matematiche e per varie espressioni scientifiche. Pedici creati con scale inferiori di un carattere standard avranno un peso del tratto più leggero del tipo di carattere circostante, il che può generare distrazione. Come regola pertanto, i tipografi e i grafici preferiscono usare i caratteri pedici specifici di una data **font**, quando disponibili.

Ing: SUBSCRIPT
Fr: INDICE
Ted: TIEFGESTELLTE SCHRIFTZEICHEN
Sp: SUBÍNDICE

Agenzia di pubblicità: TECNOSTUDI

A B C D E F G H I J K L M N O **P** Q R S T U V W X Y Z

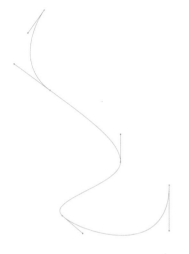

Cm.

Pica

PERCORSO/I

Serie di **curve di Bézier**, o vettoriali, usate dai software grafici per descrivere le forme di vari elementi grafici, inclusi i **caratteri**. Essendo dei vettoriali, i percorsi possono essere molto ingranditi senza sacrificare la **risoluzione**. Percorsi designati dall'utente vengono comunemente utilizzati per "ritagliare" una parte specifica di una fotografia digitale e collocarla su un'altra, come quando si usa Photoshop per inserire una persona all'interno di una fotografia o per eliminarla.

Ing: PATH
Fr: CHEMIN
Ted: PFAD
Sp: TRAZADO

Design: Alfredo Carlo

PICA

Unità di misura tipografica assoluta equivalente a 12 **punti**. Un pica equivale a 0,166 pollici e a 4,233 mm. Un *pica em* è uno spazio pica uno, un sesto di pollice, in larghezza.

Ing: PICA
Fr: POINT PICA
Ted: PICA
Sp: PICA

Studio grafico: Sara Muzio

PIEGHEVOLE A FISARMONICA

Foglio di carta di cui ogni facciata (sei o più) viene piegata in direzione opposta a quella della facciata contigua. Due pieghe eseguite in tale modo producono una fisarmonica di sei facciate, o sei pagine, cioè tre facciate per ogni lato del foglio; tre pieghe creano una fisarmonica con otto facciate, e così via. È anche chiamato *concertina*.

Ing: ACCORDION FOLD
Fr: PLI ACCORDÉON
Ted: LEPORELLO
Sp: PLEGADO EN ACORDEÓN

Autore: Manuela Marchesan per le MagnificheEditrici

A B C D E F G H I J K L M N O **P** Q R S T U V W X Y Z

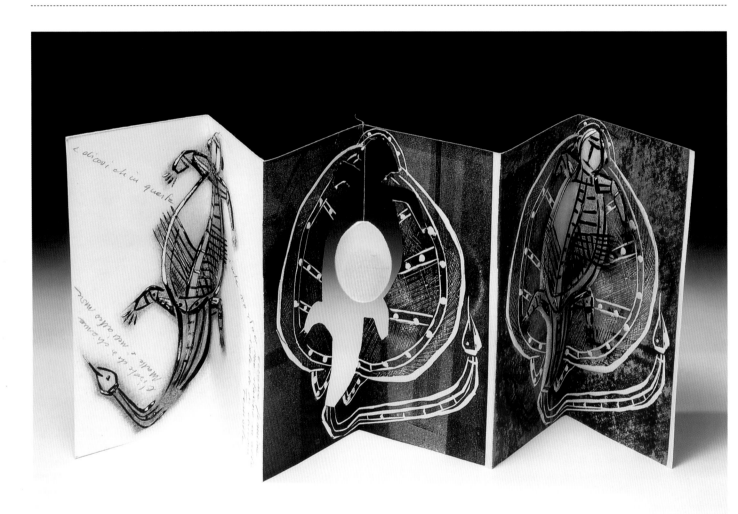

PIEGHEVOLE A PORTAFOGLIO

Pieghe alternate parallele realizzate con un foglio di carta, in modo che la serie di facciate che ne risulta si ripieghi o si "arrotoli" su se stessa. Per far sì che ogni facciata si inserisca bene dentro le altre, quelle esterne sono progressivamente più larghe (misurate da piega a piega o da **margine** a piega) rispetto alle facciate adiacenti più vicine all'interno. Vengono anche chiamate *roll folds*. Vedi anche **pieghevole a fisarmonica**.

Ing: BARREL FOLD
Fr: PLI ROULÉ
Ted: WICKELFALZ
Sp: DOBLADO TIPO ROLLO

Autore: Manuela Marchesan per le MagnificheEditrici

ABCDEFGHIJKLMNO**P**QRSTUVWXYZ

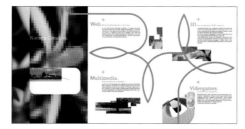

FREE GYM   BODY MACHINE   INDOOR SPORTS   SWIMMING POOL   OUTDOOR SPORTS   KAFÉ RESTAURANT

PITTOGRAMMA

Icona o **simbolo** usato in modo che il suo significato sia immediatamente comprensibile al di là di linguaggi e barriere culturali. Pittogrammi efficaci fanno parte di un sistema standardizzato, che sottostà a numerose convenzioni e linee-guida, come è accaduto ad esempio per i Giochi Olimpici, per i quali è stata creata un'intera collezione, o nel caso dei segnali stradali riconosciuti internazionalmente. L'interpretazione dei pittogrammi si basa sul contesto. Il segnale di Ritiro bagagli utilizzato in molti aeroporti, ad esempio, è una semplice icona finché non viene collocato nel contesto di un aeroporto o di altri luoghi di transito. Si potrebbe usare la stessa icona in un sito web in cui si vendono valige: in questo caso, sebbene il significato come icona rimanga lo stesso, il suo significato come pittogramma sarebbe del tutto diverso.

Ing: PICTOGRAM
Fr: PICTOGRAMME
Ted: PIKTOGRAMM
Sp: PICTOGRAMA

Design: Emporio Adv

PIXEL

Elemento base usato da molti tipi di display digitali per rappresentare le immagini; il nome pixel deriva dalla combinazione di *picture* (quadro, immagine) ed *element* (elemento). I pixel si trovano disposti su una **griglia** bidimensionale, essendo ognuno di essi un campione del **punto** corrispondente nell'immagine originale; la **risoluzione** di un'immagine è una funzione della densità di una **griglia**. Nei display che impiegano il sistema di colori **RGB**, il colore visualizzato da ogni pixel è il risultato del valore numerico di rosso, verde e blu a esso assegnato.

Ing: PIXEL
Fr: PIXEL
Ted: PIXEL (BILDPUNKT)
Sp: PÍXEL

Design: DSF-DESIGN; **Art director:** Carlo Del Sal-Carlo Facchin; **Cliente:** ABA Bibione

POSTERIZZAZIONE

Effetto che si produce quando la gamma dei **colori** (o dei grigi) disponibili è insufficiente per riprodurre sia su schermo sia su stampa un'immagine contenente aree di graduale cambiamento tonale. Ciò accade quando, per esempio, un'immagine viene convertita in *GIF 256-color* per utilizzarla come semplice grafica web. La posterizzazione può anche essere eseguita deliberatamente usando software di trattamento immagini per convertire toni progressivi in un numero limitato di discrete campiture di colore, creando in questo modo interessanti effetti visivi simili a quelli dei tradizionali poster grafici.

Ing: POSTERIZATION
Fr: POSTERISATION
Ted: POSTERISATION
Sp: POSTERIZACIÓN

Foto: MP foto&grafica

A B C D E F G H I J K L M N O **P** Q R S T U V W X Y Z

POST-MODERNISMO

Sorto soprattutto come reazione all'approccio a volte dogmatico del **Modernismo**, il Post-Modernismo prese forma negli anni Sessanta e si impose all'attenzione internazionale negli anni Ottanta. Laddove i modernisti voltarono la schiena in larga misura al passato, i post-modernisti celebrarono gli stili storici e le loro tendenze decorative, reinterpretandoli e combinandoli in modi inaspettati, spesso scherzosi. Tra le caratteristiche visive utilizzate, sono presenti forme tipografiche come la spaziatura delle lettere, una disposizione apparentemente casuale di elementi, **collage** complicati, **palette di colori** pastello e molte altre.

Ing: POST-MODERNISM
Fr: POSTMODERNISME
Ted: POSTMODERNE
Sp: POSTMODERNISMO

Courtesy: Archivio Baroni, Milano e archivio Brunazzi & Associati, Torino

PROCESSO A QUATTRO COLORI

Tecnica di stampa in cui l'intero spettro dei colori viene approssimato usando schermi singoli di **mezzitoni**, anche chiamati *separazioni di colori*, per ognuno dei quattro **colori di processo**: ciano, magenta, giallo e nero. Ogni colore viene stampato come un disegno di piccoli puntini di varia dimensione e densità. Poiché i quattro colori di processo combinati a coppie, producono i *colori primari additivi*, (rosso, verde e blu), che corrispondono ai tre differenti tipi di recettori della luce dell'occhio umano, l'effetto finale di "colore pieno" è assai convincente. Vedi anche **CMYK** e **mezzitoni**.

Ing: FOUR-COLOR PROCESS
Fr: QUADRICHROMIE
Ted: VIERFARBDRUCK
Sp: CUATRICOMÍA

Design: Donna S. Atwood, www.atwooddesign.com

PROPORZIONALE

Termine usato per descrivere un insieme di **caratteri** di cui ognuno ha una larghezza specifica, a differenza di quelli **monospazio**, che possiedono tutti la stessa larghezza.

Ing: PROPORTIONAL
Fr: CARACTÈRES À CHASSE VARIABLE
Ted: PROPORTIONALSCHRIFT
Sp: PROPORCIONAL

Design: Joele Lucherini per STUDIONO

A B C D E F G H I J K L M N O **P** Q R S T U V W X Y Z

"Tanto tempo fa in una landa
 desolata, viveva una piccola..."

" Tanto tempo fa in una landa
 desolata, viveva una piccola..."

• L'indirizzo del Sig. Rossi

• L'indirizzo del Sig. Rossi

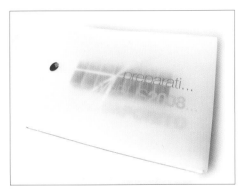

PUNTEGGIATURA ESTERNA

Segni di interpunzione collocati leggermente al di fuori di un blocco di **caratteri**, in modo da migliorare l'**allineamento visivo**. **Virgolette** aperte e **punti elenco** vengono a volte collocati in modo da sporgersi sul **margine** sinistro, mentre virgolette chiuse e **trattini** possono essere collocati sul margine destro. La punteggiatura esterna richiede un tocco delicato, poiché l'obiettivo è ottenere una resa tipografica ordinata, non attirare l'attenzione su ogni elemento specifico. Anche caratteri che non siano d'interpunzione possono essere collocati al di fuori di un dato blocco di caratteri per ottenere l'allineamento visivo, come quando il rimando a una nota a piè di pagina o a una citazione viene inserito in una colonna di numeri allineati decimalmente. Vengono anche chiamati *caratteri esterni*.

Ing: HANGING PUNCTUATION
Fr: PONCTUATION MARGINALE
Ted: SATZKANTENAUSGLEICH
Sp: PUNTUACIÓN VOLADA

Studio grafico: Sara Muzio

PUNTI DI SOSPENSIONE

Segno d'interpunzione formato da una serie di tre **punti**, usato per indicare alcune porzioni di testo che sono state omesse, ad esempio quando parte di una citazione diretta è utilizzata al posto dell'intera citazione, o è incompleta (come un pensiero interrotto alla fine di una frase). Ogni **carattere** possiede specifici punti di sospensione. Usando questo carattere piuttosto che una serie di tre punti si elimina il rischio che la serie si spezzi in corrispondenza di un'**interruzione di linea**. D'altro canto, spazi precisi possono essere realizzati solo adottando punti singoli. Molti manuali di stile raccomandano uno spazio prima e uno dopo i punti di sospensione, considerandoli come se fossero una parola, ma i tipografi spesso preferiscono evitarli.

Ing: ELLIPSIS
Fr: POINTS DE SUSPENSION
Ted: ELLIPSE (AUSLASSUNGSPUNKTE)
Sp: PUNTOS SUSPENSIVOS

Design: Omniadvert

PUNTO ELENCO

Carattere tipografico usato per lo più per evidenziare le voci di un elenco, sebbene a volte venga anche impiegato per separare brevi linee sequenziali di **caratteri**, come un indirizzo in un'intestazione. In entrambi i casi, si deve lasciare uno spazio tra il **punto elenco** e i caratteri. I punti elenco sono generalmente inclusi nelle **font simboli** e **dingbats**. Vedi anche **punteggiatura esterna**.

Ing: BULLET
Fr: PUCE
Ted: AUFZÄHLUNGSPUNKT
Sp: BOLO

Design: Lunagrafica

A B C D E F G H I J K L M N O **P** Q R S T U V W X Y Z

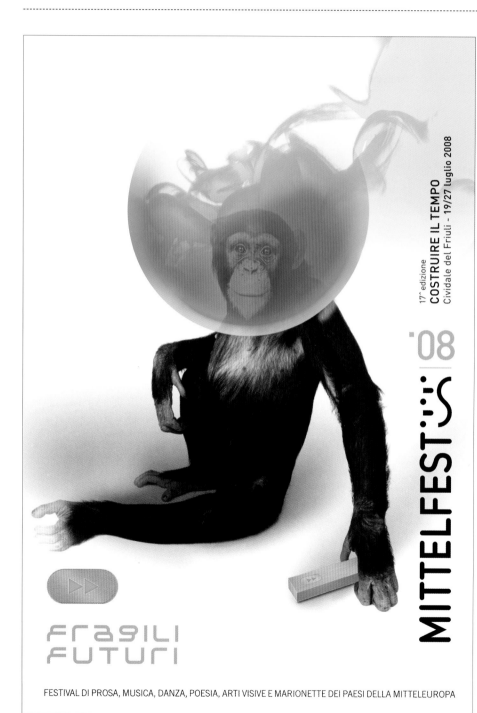

PUNTO FOCALE

Elemento grafico di un **layout** che cattura per primo l'attenzione dell'osservatore: è l'area da cui inizia il **flusso visivo**. I punti focali possono essere creati con una grande varietà di strumenti, tra cui il **colore**, la **scala** e la **composizione**. In particolare la pubblicità trae spesso beneficio dall'avere un unico punto focale non ambiguo.

Ing: FOCAL POINT
Fr: POINT CENTRAL
Ted: FOKUS
Sp: PUNTO FOCAL

Design: SINTESI; **Cliente:** Mittelfest Summer Festival;
Art director: Andrej Pisani

48-point
36-point
24-point
18-point
14-point
12-point
10-point
8-point

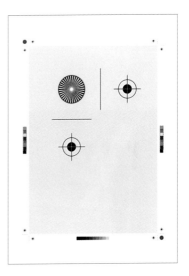

PUNTO/I/DIMENSIONI DEL PUNTO

Nella **tipografia** il punto è un'unità di misura assoluta; un punto di PostScript equivale a 1/72 di pollice, corrispondente a 0,35277 mm. La dimensione del punto si riferisce alla grandezza del tipo di **caratteri**, misurata in punti. Tuttavia, sebbene il punto sia una misura assoluta, le dimensioni reali di un carattere di una data misura di punti varieranno a seconda del carattere in questione. Ciò perché le dimensioni di un punto furono originariamente determinate non dalla misura dei caratteri stessi ma dai blocchi di metallo su cui erano fusi. Nei caratteri digitali, il rapporto fra dimensioni del punto e dimensioni del carattere è ancor più complesso. Vedi anche **pica**.

Ing: POINT/POINT SIZE
Fr: CORPS
Ted: PUNKT/PUNKTGRÖSSE
Sp: PUNTO/TAMAÑO DE PUNTO

Studio grafico: Sara Muzio

RECTO/VERSO

Termine usato per riferirsi al lato destro e sinistro delle pagine di un insieme di **pagine affiancate**. La pagina di destra è chiamata recto, la pagina di sinistra verso. In senso stretto, i termini si riferiscono ai lati opposti della stessa pagina, di cui il recto è il fronte e il verso è il retro.

Ing: RECTO/VERSO
Fr: RECTO VERSO
Ted: RECHTE/LINKE SEITE (VORDER-/ RÜCKSEITE)
Sp: RECTO/VERSO

Design: Teikna; **Art director:** Claudia Neri

REGISTRO

Allineamento preciso di tutti gli strati di inchiostro per un determinato lavoro. Idealmente ogni successiva applicazione di inchiostro viene allineata con l'applicazione precedente; colori differenti si sovrappongono o incontrano esattamente nel punto previsto. Nella pratica può avvenire qualche variazione, chiamata *fuori registro*, risultante ad esempio dalla distensione della carta o da problemi con la macchina da stampa. In molti casi, le conseguenze del fuori registro possono essere attenuate con il **trapping** o la **sovrastampa**.

Ing: REGISTRATION
Fr: REPÉRAGE
Ted: REGISTERHALTIGKEIT
Sp: REGISTRO

Design: Alfredo Carlo

A B C D E F G H I J K L M N O P Q **R** S T U V W X Y Z

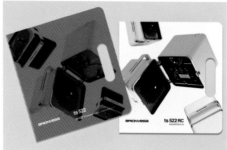

RETINO

Sistema di approssimazione ai **colori** reali di un'immagine digitale che usa i soli colori disponibili di una data palette. Quando un'immagine digitale viene convertita nel sistema *web-safe*, ad esempio, un insieme specifico di 216 colori diversi (la *web-safe color palette*) viene adottato per emulare i colori dell'immagine originale. Ciò si effettua creando una specie di mosaico di **pixel** sullo schermo del computer, o di **punti** nel caso di stampanti digitali. Un mosaico di pixel/punti rossi e gialli può essere utilizzato per ottenere l'arancione, ad esempio. Sebbene alcune sfumature risultino sacrificate da questo procedimento, la retinatura è utile per uniformare bordi dentellati indesiderabili che possono apparire lungo i campi di colore adiacenti. Vedi anche **posterizzazione**.

Ing: DITHER
Fr: TRAMAGE ALÉATOIRE
Ted: DITHERING
Sp: DIFUMINADO

Design: Alfredo Carlo

REVERSE/REVERSE OUT

Termine usato per descrivere **caratteri** stampati prodotti applicando l'inchiostro all'interno e sui contorni di ogni carattere, piuttosto che sui tratti veri e propri. Di conseguenza, il carattere stampato ha il **colore** della carta usata e non dell'inchiostro. Lo stesso effetto si può ottenere sullo schermo del computer rendendo il colore del carattere uguale a quello dello sfondo, e ponendo i caratteri su una campitura di colore diverso. Il peso di un carattere di colore chiaro, specialmente se è piccolo, sembra diminuire quando posto su uno sfondo scuro, cosicché un tipo di carattere più grande e pesante è spesso necessario per ottenere **leggibilità**.

Ing: REVERSE/REVERSE OUT
Fr: INVERSION
Ted: NEGATIVE SCHRIFT
Sp: TIPO EN NEGATIVO

Design: SINTESI; **Cliente:** Brionvega BV Srl;
Art director: Andrej Pisani; **Copywriter:** Rino Lombardi; **Fotografo:** Giuliano Koren

RGB

Abbreviazione di "red, green e blue" (rosso, verde e blu), i tre colori usati per visualizzare elementi grafici sullo schermo dei computer o su altri dispositivi digitali. Il rosso, il verde e il blu sono chiamati *colori additivi primari*: combinati assieme in eguali proporzioni, formano la luce bianca. Essi corrispondono anche ai tre differenti tipi di recettori della luce nell'occhio umano. Vedi anche **CMYK**.

Ing: RGB
Fr: RVB
Ted: RGB
Sp: RGB

Design: Joele Lucherini per STUDIONO

RIENTRO

Aggiustamento del **margine** di una o più righe di **caratteri**. I rientri vengono usati soprattutto per indicare l'inizio di un nuovo paragrafo dove il margine della prima riga è visibilmente più grande delle successive. Rientri esterni si utilizzano per aumentare i margini di tutte le righe che seguono la prima in un paragrafo. Altri tipi di rientri possono essere usati per modificare il margine sinistro e/o destro di righe multiple di caratteri, come quelli che circondano un'illustrazione o una fotografia. Rientri di un punto/carattere si impiegano per disporre i margini in modo che corrispondano a un punto specifico o a un carattere della riga precedente.

Ing: INDENT
Fr: COMPOSITION EN ALINÉA
Ted: ZEILENEINZUG
Sp: SANGRÍA

Agenzia di pubblicità: TECNOSTUDI

RILEGATURA

Uno dei tanti metodi usati per tenere unite le pagine di un libro, rivista, brochure o altre pubblicazioni stampate pagine multiple. Alcune rilegature, come la rilegatura ad anello e quella a pettine, passano attraverso una serie di buchi sulle pagine, e pertanto non sono permanenti. Tra i metodi di rilegatura di questo ultimo tipo si segnalano la **cartonatura**, la *legatura adesiva a doppio ventaglio*, la *pinzatura a sella*.

Ing: BINDING
Fr: RELIURE
Ted: EINBAND
Sp: ENCUADERNACIÓN

Agenzia di comunicazione e immagine: Brunazzi & Associati, Torino; **Direttori creativi:** Giovanni Brunazzi, Andrea Brunazzi

RILEGATURA PERFETTA

Tipo di **rilegatura** permanente usata di frequente per libri tascabili, in cui le **segnature** sono *raccolte* (assemblate in sequenza), molate lungo i bordi rilegati, e incollate con un adesivo alla copertina del libro composta da un unico foglio, formando in questo modo un dorso.

Ing: PERFECT BINDING
Fr: RELIURE SANS COUTURE
Ted: KLEBEBINDUNG
Sp: ENCUADERNACIÓN A LA AMERICANA

Design: Armando Chitolina

A B C D E F G H I J K L M N O P Q **R** S T U V W X Y Z

RILIEVOGRAFIA

Procedimento di *stampa a rilievo* che risale alla Germania del XV secolo e all'invenzione della stampa. Blocchi di **caratteri** ed elementi illustrativi creati "a rovescio" vengono fissati sulla macchina da stampa, affinché la loro immagine si possa leggere correttamente quando trasferita su carta. Le superfici di questi vengono coperte d'inchiostro e pressate contro la carta. La rilievografia un tempo si otteneva con caratteri di metallo fuso e di legno, oggi invece si effettua tramite una placca polimerica creata da un file digitale.

Ing: LETTERPRESS
Fr: IMPRESSION TYPOGRAPHIQUE
Ted: HOCHDRUCK
Sp: IMPRESIÓN TIPOGRÁFICA

Design: Omniadvert

A B C D E F G H I J K L M N O P Q **R** S T U V W X Y Z

RISMA

Una risma è costituita da 500 fogli di una certa qualità di carta nel suo *formato base*. Sebbene esistano molte misure standard, la misura base dei fogli è determinata esclusivamente dalla qualità della carta. In Italia si usano principalmente due formati standard, l'A4 (210x297 mm) e l'A3 (294x420 mm). Il *peso di base* o *peso della risma* si riferisce al peso di una risma di carta. Poiché il peso di base dipende dal formato base della carta, due qualità diverse di carta che hanno lo stesso peso di base possono risultare molto diverse in termini di spessore e peso individuali. Lo spessore di un foglio di carta è il **calibro**. Generalmente parlando, una carta con calibro più basso avrà anche un peso minore di quelle di maggiore calibro. Il termine *grammatura* viene usato per quantificare il calibro della carta rispetto al suo peso.

Ing: REAM
Fr: RAME
Ted: RIES
Sp: RESMA

Designer: Alfredo Carlo

RISOLUZIONE

È la qualità relativa di un'immagine digitale in termini di numero di campioni per unità di misura. I diversi termini utilizzati per descrivere la risoluzione di grafiche digitali sono spesso usati in modo intercambiabile. DPI (o *dots per inch*, punti per pollice), è la misura relativa della qualità di uno strumento per la stampa. Ad esempio, stampanti a 300 dpi possono produrre stampe di 300 **punti** uno accanto all'altro nello spazio di un pollice. PPI è invece l'abbreviazione di *pixel per inch*, usata per quantificare la risoluzione del monitor di un computer o di altri display digitali. Infine, LPI, o *lines per inch*, è la misura della frequenza di un **mezzotono**. Sebbene le "linee" siano in realtà file di minuscoli punti, appaiono come righe quando sono stampate una accanto all'altra. Maggiore è la frequenza dello schermo, maggiormente dettagliata sarà l'immagine stampata.

Ing: RESOLUTION
Fr: RÉSOLUTION
Ted: AUFLÖSUNG
Sp: RESOLUCIÓN

Design: Emporio Adv

RITMO

Ripetizione visiva creata con pattern strutturali sottostanti, all'interno e fra vari elementi grafici, come il tipo di **carattere**, le **linee** e le forme. Una riga singola di caratteri, ad esempio, può avere un ritmo particolare grazie a molti tratti verticali, creati con un'attenta spaziatura delle lettere. Poster e copertine di libri spesso usano pattern geometrici per ottenere un ritmo stabile sul quale fare risaltare elementi inaspettati. Su scala più ampia, si possono utilizzare **griglie** che conferiscono un ritmo regolare e riposante alla lettura di un testo lungo.

Ing: RHYTHM
Fr: RYTHME
Ted: RHYTHMUS
Sp: RITMO

Design: SINTESI; **Cliente:** Brionvega BV Srl; **Art director:** Andrej Pisani; **Copywriter:** Rino Lombardi; **Fotografo:** Giuliano Koren

A B C D E F G H I J K L M N O P Q **R S** T U V W X Y Z

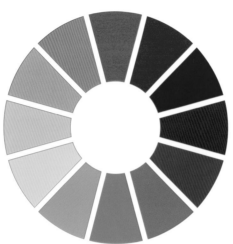

RIVESTIMENTO AD ACQUA

Rivestimento applicato su un intero foglio di carta dopo la stampa, che serve per conferire una patina omogenea (ad es., lucida o opaca) e per proteggere l'inchiostro sottostante da sfregamenti e umidità. La carta non rivestita tende ad assorbire l'inchiostro, dando un aspetto sfuocato alle immagini stampate, mentre la carta rivestita ad acqua evita che l'inchiostro venga assorbito, in modo che le immagini rimangano nitide. I rivestimenti ad acqua vengono usati solitamente per materiali stampati che subiscono una manipolazione intensa, come le riviste e le brochure. Anche le **vernici** si utilizzano per fini simili, offrendo un'ampia varietà di carte rivestite.

Ing: AQUEOUS COATING
Fr: PELLICULAGE AQUEUX
Ted: DRUCKLACK
Sp: REVESTIMIENTO ACUOSO

Design: Omniadvert

RUOTA DEI COLORI

Spettro dei **colori** rappresentati come segmenti di un circolo. La più nota **ruota dei colori**, utilizzata per mescolare i pigmenti, si basa sui **colori primari**, rosso, giallo e blu, equamente distribuiti lungo la sua circonferenza. Il rosso, il giallo e il blu sono colori puri, non si possono infatti ottenere dalla combinazione di altri. Mescolandoli assieme in varie proporzioni invece, si possono creare tutti gli altri colori. Altre ruote vengono usate per illustrare rapporti analoghi all'interno di altri sistemi di colore, come il modello **RGB**, utilizzato per visualizzare grafiche su schermo. Vedi anche **colori analoghi, colori complementari, colori primari, colori secondari** e **colori terziari**.

Ing: COLOR WHEEL
Fr: ROUE CHROMATIQUE
Ted: FARBKREIS
Sp: RUEDA DE COLORES

Design: Donna S. Atwood, www.atwooddesign.com

SATURAZIONE

Purezza di un colore in rapporto alla quantità di grigio che contiene. Le **tonalità** pure sono completamente sature e appaiono brillanti; col decrescere dei livelli di saturazione, un colore risulta sempre più smorzato, pur conservando la stessa tonalità. La de-saturazione può essere ottenuta aggiungendo del colore grigio alla tonalità di base (dando luogo a un tono) o mescolandolo con una porzione più piccola del suo complementare (dando luogo a una *sfumatura*). Viene anche chiamata chroma; vedi **colore**.

Ing: SATURATION
Fr: SATURATION
Ted: SÄTTIGUNG
Sp: SATURACIÓN

Design: AD. VENTURE Compagnia di comunicazione;
Art director: Franco Mancinelli

A B C D E F G H I J K L M N O P Q R **S** T U V W X Y Z

Scala: 10:1

SCALA

La misura o il peso percepito di un elemento grafico in relazione ad altri dello stesso **layout**. La scala può essere semplicemente una questione di differenze misurate, ad esempio quando un **carattere** più grande viene usato per indicare quali parti di un testo sono più importanti. Spesso, comunque, le differenze di scala sono molto sottili. Oggetti con forme dissimili, ad esempio, tendono a dare l'impressione di una scala diversa anche quando ricoprono geometricamente una stessa area. Anche forme e colori influenzano la scala di un elemento, come pure il contesto; la scala di un oggetto è una funzione di ciò che gli sta attorno.

Ing: SCALE
Fr: ÉCHELLE
Ted: GRÖSSENVERHÄLTNIS
Sp: ESCALA

Design: Alfredo Carlo

SCALA DEI GRIGI

Immagine composta da varie sfumature di grigio, di bianco e di nero. Le fotografie a colori possono essere facilmente convertite in immagini digitali della scala dei grigi, mediante applicazioni di software che traducono il valore di ogni punto nel suo equivalente grigio, dando come risultato un'immagine che simula la fotografia in bianco e nero. Vedi anche **monocromatico**.

Ing: GRAYSCALE
Fr: ÉCHELLE DE GRIS
Ted: GRAUSTUFENBILD
Sp: ESCALA DE GRISES

Design: Armando Chitolina

SEGNATURA

Un insieme di pagine stampate su entrambi i lati di un grande foglio di carta che, una volta piegato e refilato, avrà orientamento e sequenza corretti per la **rilegatura**. Vedi anche **imposizione tipografica**.

Ing: SIGNATURE
Fr: CAHIER
Ted: BOGENMONTAGE
Sp: PLIEGO

Studio grafico: Sara Muzio

A B C D E F G H I J K L M N O P Q R **S** T U V W X Y Z

SEQUENZA DI CARATTERI

Termine usato per descrivere i caratteri disposti deliberatamente in modo da poter essere letti sia stampati, sia visualizzati su schermo. Si utilizza anche comunemente per riferirsi alle **font** usate per realizzare i caratteri. Vedi anche **composizione tipografica** e **tipografia**.

Ing: TYPE
Fr: CARACTÈRES
Ted: SCHRIFT
Sp: TIPO

Foto: MP foto&grafica

ABCDEFGHIJKLMNOPQR**S**TUVWXYZ

SERIGRAFIA

Procedimento di stampa in cui l'inchiostro viene fatto passare sulla superficie del materiale che deve essere stampato, come la carta o la stoffa, attraverso una rete a maglia fine. Una matrice, costituita o da un altro materiale o sigillando la superficie della rete stessa, viene usata per determinare quali aree della superficie da stampare riceveranno l'inchiostro. La tecnica serigrafica si utilizza di frequente nell'industria dell'abbigliamento, ma anche per stampare su superfici irregolari.

Ing: SCREEN PRINTING
Fr: SÉRIGRAPHIE
Ted: SIEBDRUCK
Sp: SERIGRAFÍA

Autore: Paola Sapori per le MagnificheEditrici

SILLABAZIONE
Vedi **H&J**.

SIMBOLO

Segno grafico che rappresenta qualcosa di diverso rispetto a ciò che viene mostrato. In molte culture, ad esempio, la semplice raffigurazione di un cuore, rosso in particolare, viene usata per simboleggiare affetto o amore. Questo segno non assomiglia all'amore, e somiglia poco persino a un vero cuore. Ma poiché il suo significato è riconosciuto più o meno universalmente, può essere impiegato per comunicare con efficacia. Allo stesso modo, una croce rossa veicola un significato in grado di superare barriere linguistiche e culturali, ma soltanto perché tra chi ne fa uso vige già un implicito accordo sul suo senso. Vedi anche **icona** e **pittogramma**.

Ing: SYMBOL
Fr: SYMBOLE
Ted: SYMBOL
Sp: SÍMBOLO

AIPEM Marketing e comunicazione integrata;
Art director: Daria Biasizzo, Vittoria Turrin; **Copywriter:** Maurizio Clemente; **Account manager:** Carlo Rossi

SIMMETRIA

Distribuzione regolare di elementi lungo un asse particolare, spesso orientato verticalmente o orizzontalmente. I **layout** simmetrici sono organizzati in modo che gli elementi siano distribuiti più o meno regolarmente dall'alto in basso e/o da sinistra a destra, e perciò tendono a risultare più convenzionali, comunicando un senso di maggiore stabilità rispetto ai layout asimmetrici. Vedi anche **asimmetria**, **bilanciamento** e **flusso visivo**.

Ing: SYMMETRY
Fr: SYMÉTRIE
Ted: SYMMETRIE
Sp: SIMETRÍA

Courtesy: Archivio Baroni, Milano e archivio Brunazzi & Associati, Torino

A B C D E F G H I J K L M N O P Q R **S** T U V W X Y Z

SISTEMA DI COMBINAZIONE DEI COLORI

Uno qualsiasi tra i tanti strumenti standard di riferimento, solitamente disponibile sotto forma di diagramma o di campionario di **colori**, dotato di una destinazione numerica corrispondente usata per specificarli. I grafici usano queste definizioni per assicurarsi che i colori scelti per un particolare progetto siano "tradotti" correttamente durante la fase di stampa. Per ottenere un preciso abbinamento dei colori è importante sapere quale sistema o quali sistemi di combinazione dei colori vengano utilizzati nel servizio di stampa.

Ing: COLOR-MATCHING SYSTEM
Fr: SYSTÈME D'ASSORTIMENT DES COULEURS
Ted: FARBKENNZEICHNUNGSSYSTEM
Sp: SISTEMA DE AJUSTE DEL COLOR

Si ringrazia Trumatch, www.trumatch.com

SOTTOTITOLO

Titolo di livello inferiore usato per spezzare un testo lungo in sezioni, mostrandone la struttura organizzativa e fornendo indizi sulla sua **gerarchia tipografica**. Il modo in cui vengono composti i sottotitoli di una pubblicazione, comprese le dimensioni, il **colore**, i **caratteri**, dovrebbe suggerire quanto un dato livello sia simile o diverso da quelli "sopra" e "sotto" nella gerarchia complessiva. Se *sottotitoli di livello A* vengono utilizzati per i nomi delle città maggiori, ad es., e i *sottotitoli di livello B* riguardano i dati di un censimento, sarebbe auspicabile che i due sottotitoli avessero un aspetto molto diverso. Se, d'altra parte, *sottotitoli di livello B* vengono usati per i nomi di quartieri vicini, la differenza fra il loro aspetto potrebbe essere meno marcata.

Ing: SUBHEAD
Fr: INTERTITRE
Ted: UNTERTITEL
Sp: SUBTÍTULO

Design: Armando Chitolina

SOVRASTAMPA

Fusione di inchiostri stampati sopra ad altri in modo che risulti un nuovo **colore**. Nella maggior parte dei casi, quando due elementi grafici si sovrappongono, solo il colore dell'elemento superiore viene stampato, e il suo colore "annienta" quello sottostante. Quando si esegue una sovrastampa invece, i due o più colori di inchiostro si sommano per formare un altro colore.

Ing: OVERPRINTING
Fr: SURIMPRESSION
Ted: ÜBERDRUCKEN
Sp: SOBREIMPRESIÓN

Design: Joele Lucherini per STUDIONO

A B C D E F G H I J K L M N O P Q R **S** T U V W X Y Z

LINEA DONNA
Linea dermocosmetica termale

Terme di Salsomaggiore

Tipografia spazio ☐ Em

Tipografia spazio ☐ En

SPAZIO BIANCO

Termine generico usato per descrivere aree di un **layout** lasciate "vuote", anche se in realtà non sono di colore bianco. Comunque sia lo spazio bianco è parte integrante di un disegno riuscito nella stessa misura in cui lo sono gli elementi grafici; esso è uno spazio attivo, non passivo. Infatti, l'uso efficace di uno spazio bianco conferisce struttura e mantiene un senso di **ritmo** e **bilanciamento** nel layout, più o meno come l'azione reciproca di uno **spazio positivo** e uno **spazio negativo** dinamizza le relazioni fra gli elementi grafici. Vedi anche **griglia**.

Ing: WHITE SPACE
Fr: BLANCS
Ted: WEISSRAUM
Sp: ESPACIO BLANCO

Agenzia di pubblicità: TECNOSTUDI

SPAZIO COLORE
Vedi **modello di colore**.

SPAZIO EM

Uno spazio della larghezza di un'**em** all'interno di una riga di **caratteri**. Le **font** digitali dispongono di uno spazio em come carattere speciale di larghezza fissa, diversamente dagli spazi creati con la barra spaziatrice, che variano mano a mano che il software compone ogni riga di caratteri.

Ing: EM SPACE
Fr: ESPACE CADRATIN
Ted: GEVIERTABSTAND
Sp: ESPACIO DE CUADRATÍN

Studio grafico: Sara Muzio

SPAZIO EN

Spazio della larghezza di un'**en** all'interno di una riga di **caratteri**. Come per lo **spazio em**, le **font** digitali includono lo spazio en nei caratteri speciali. Poiché è di larghezza fissa, uno spazio en rimane inalterato quando il software compone ogni riga di carattere, diversamente dagli spazi variabili creati con la barra spaziatrice.

Ing: EN SPACE
Fr: ESPACE DEMI-CADRATIN
Ted: HALBGEVIERTABSTAND
Sp: ESPACIO DE MEDIO CUADRATÍN

Studio grafico: Sara Muzio

A B C D E F G H I J K L M N O P Q R **S** T U V W X Y Z

SPAZIO LETTERA

Spazio complessivo tra i **caratteri** all'interno del **corpo del testo**. Lo spazio lettera è particolarmente utile quando si usano **caratteri giustificati**, a causa della loro propensione a creare spazi inopportuni fra le parole, specialmente quando si ha una **giustezza** corta. È spesso confuso con la spaziatura delle lettere, il procedimento che serve per aumentare gli spazi fra caratteri di visualizzazione, accrescendone l'impatto visivo. Vedi anche **tracking**.

Ing: LETTER SPACING
Fr: INTERLETTRAGE
Ted: SPATIONIEREN
Sp: INTERLETRAJE

Design: Armando Chitolina

SPAZIO NEGATIVO

In genere, descrive uno spazio vuoto generato dal rapporto tra due o più elementi grafici e lo **spazio positivo** associato a essi. Spesso lo spazio negativo indica componenti di grandi **layout**, ma può anche servire per descrivere elementi di **tipografia**, quando ad es. alcuni **glifi** producono relazioni di spazi negativi e positivi con quelli vicini. I **loghi**, essendo generalmente piccoli, spesso vengono disegnati ponendo molta attenzione al rapporto fra spazio negativo e positivo. Vedi anche **figure-sfondo** e **spazio bianco**.

Ing: NEGATIVE SPACE
Fr: ESPACE NÉGATIF
Ted: FREIE FLÄCHE
Sp: ESPACIO NEGATIVO

Design: Lunagrafica

SPAZIO POSITIVO

Termine generico usato per descrivere l'area o le aree di un **layout** o di elementi grafici singoli, in cui sono presenti delle forme (le aree vuote invece sono **spazi negativi**). Sebbene lo spazio positivo venga spesso impiegato per definire aspetti di un intero layout, si può usare anche per definire aspetti della **composizione tipografica**, ove alcuni **glifi** producono relazioni di spazi positivi e negativi con i glifi adiacenti. I **loghi**, poiché sono generalmente piccoli, vengono spesso disegnati riservando molta attenzione al rapporto tra spazio positivo e negativo.

Ing: POSITIVE SPACE
Fr: ESPACE POSITIF
Ted: GESTALTETE FLÄCHE
Sp: ESPACIO POSITIVO

Agenzia di pubblicità: TECNOSTUDI

ABCDEFGHIJKLMNOPQR**S**TUVWXYZ

STAMPA A LAMINA DI PLASTICA

Procedimento attraverso cui una sottile lamina di plastica viene fusa sulla carta attraverso una matrice riscaldata; viene spesso utilizzata per dare enfasi a **loghi**, illustrazioni, **caratteri** e altri elementi grafici. La lamina di plastica è disponibile in un'ampia gamma di **colori** e patine, oltre che con finiture metalliche. Una lamina opaca può essere usata per applicare un colore chiaro a uno sfondo scuro; una lamina traslucida può essere adottata per simulare una **vernice**. Viene anche chiamata *stampa a caldo*.

Ing: FOIL STAMPING
Fr: DORURE
Ted: FOLIENPRÄGUNG
Sp: ESTAMPADO METÁLICO

Design: Emporio Adv

STAMPA AL VIVO

Porzione di elemento grafico, come un'immagine stampata, una riga di **caratteri**, un campo di **colore**, ecc., che si estende al di là del formato della pagina. Gli indicatori di refilo vengono usati per indicare la grandezza reale della pagina; qualsiasi elemento stampato al di fuori di questi indicatori sarà refilato dalla pagina. La misura esatta della pagina dipenderà dal grado di precisione della macchina da stampa e della refilatrice.

Ing: BLEED
Fr: FONDS PERDUS
Ted: BESCHNITT
Sp: IMPRIMIR "A SANGRE"

Agenzia di comunicazione e immagine: Brunazzi & Associati, Torino; **Direttori creativi:** Giovanni Brunazzi, Andrea Brunazzi

STANDING CAP

Lettera maiuscola usata come lettera iniziale della prima parola di un capoverso, composta da **punti** di misura superiore a quella dei **caratteri** circostanti, ma appoggiata sulla stessa **linea di base**. Per accrescerne l'effetto, si possono usare maiuscole proprie di un **carattere** molto diverso da quello del **corpo del testo**. Vedi anche **lettere maiuscole iniziali** e **capolettera**.

Ing: STANDING CAPITAL/CAP
Fr: GRANDE CAPITALE
Ted: STEHENDE INITIALE
Sp: CAPITULAR

Design: Alfredo Carlo

A B C D E F G H I J K L M N O P Q R **S T** U V W X Y Z

STILE VITTORIANO

Stile decorativo utilizzato in architettura e nel design, spesso molto ostentato, che ebbe inizio in Inghilterra e conobbe una vasta diffusione in buona parte dell'Europa e dell'America, fra il 1820 e il 1900 circa. Lo stile vittoriano fu una risposta alla Rivoluzione industriale e agli eccessi che derivarono dal passaggio dall'artigianato alla produzione di massa. Designer e tipografi non riuscivano a stare al passo con i progressi della tecnologia, e il risultato fu spesso un caotico guazzabuglio di diversi stili provenienti da epoche diverse. All'inizio dell'era vittoriana, una grafica male proporzionata con **caratteri** dal tratto pesante, chiamati *Fat Face*, fu spesso usata per affiancare illustrazioni eseguite rozzamente. Caratteri di dimensioni e stili diversi furono spesso impiegati in un unico, sovraffollato **layout**. Verso la fine di quel periodo, tuttavia, iniziò a diffondersi un tocco più leggero e sofisticato.

Ing: VICTORIAN
Fr: STYLE VICTORIEN
Ted: VIKTORIANISCHER STIL
Sp: VICTORIANO

Courtesy: Archivio Baroni, Milano e archivio Brunazzi & Associati, Torino

SURREALISMO

Movimento artistico europeo del periodo compreso fra il 1920 e il 1930 incentrato su intuizioni, sogni e inconscio, spesso espressi tramite giustapposizioni sorprendenti o inquietanti, illusioni ottiche, ed evidenti violazioni delle leggi della fisica. I grafici trovarono ispirazione non solo nelle tante tecniche usate dai surrealisti, ma anche nel loro approccio sperimentale nel descrivere lo spazio tridimensionale.

Ing: SURREALISM
Fr: SURRÉALISME
Ted: SURREALISMUS
Sp: SURREALISMO

Courtesy: Archivio Baroni, Milano e archivio Brunazzi & Associati, Torino

TAGLIO AL LASER

Processo attraverso cui un potente laser guidato da un computer viene usato per incidere o tagliare fogli di carta, legno, plastica e persino alcuni metalli. Il taglio al laser è molto preciso, e consente un maggiore livello di complessità dei dettagli rispetto alla convenzionale fustellatura. Poiché non occorre una matrice di metallo, per tirature molto piccole il taglio al laser può risultare più conveniente e più pratico. I costi possono crescere notevolmente, invece, per lavori estremamente dettagliati o se si devono utilizzare materiali "difficili" come quelli che bruciano, fondono facilmente o sono molto spessi.

Ing: LASER CUT
Fr: DÉCOUPE AU LASER
Ted: LASERSCHNITT
Sp: CORTE LÁSER

Design: Omniadvert

A B C D E F G H I J K L M N O P Q R S **T** U V W X Y Z

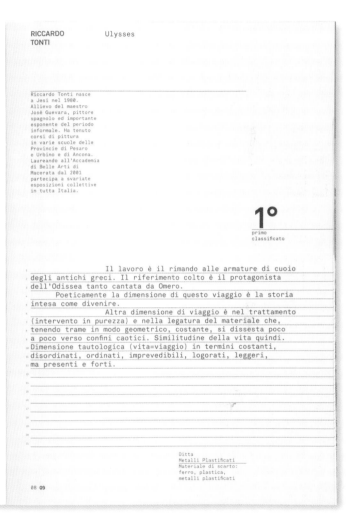

TESTATINA

Dispositivo tipografico utilizzato per dividere un testo lungo nelle sue sezioni principali, come ad esempio i **titoli** dei capitoli di un libro o i titoli dei paragrafi di un dépliant o di un fascicolo. I titoli vengono frequentemente composti con **tutte maiuscole** o con una combinazione di maiuscole e **maiuscoletti**, spesso in **grassetto**. I **sottotitoli** vengono utilizzati per scomporre ulteriormente un testo in base alla sua struttura organizzativa.

Ing: HEADING
Fr: TITRE
Ted: ÜBERSCHRIFT
Sp: TÍTULO

Design: Heads Collective

A B C D E F G H I J K L M N O P Q R S **T** U V W X Y Z

TESTO/CARATTERI CENTRATI

Righe successive di **caratteri** allineati in modo che il punto centrale di ogni riga giaccia su una comune **linea** di riferimento. Poiché i caratteri centrati richiedono una modalità di lettura piuttosto innaturale, sono generalmente riservati a biglietti da visita, inviti e altri materiali contenenti poco testo. Vedi anche **allineamento**.

Ing: CENTERED TYPE/TEXT
Fr: TEXTE CENTRÉ
Ted: MITTELACHSSATZ
Sp: TEXTO O TIPO CENTRADO

Agenzia di pubblicità: TECNOSTUDI

TESTO/CARATTERI GIUSTIFICATI

Termine comunemente usato per descrivere righe successive di **caratteri** che dipartono dai **punti** lungo una **linea** di riferimento immaginaria comune e che finiscono lungo i punti di un'altra. Tecnicamente, tutte le righe dei caratteri sono giustificate, il che significa che ogni riga viene riempita per l'intera lunghezza della sua misura da una combinazione di caratteri e spazi; la differenza consiste nel decidere dove collocare gli spazi. Ciononostante, l'espressione **caratteri giustificati** è ormai utilizzata ovunque per riferirsi ai casi in cui tutti gli spazi sono collocati tra parole, spingendo i caratteri verso entrambe le estremità della misura. Questo tipo di giustificazione, specie quando usato per una misura piccola, può a volte creare spazi inopportuni, chiamati **canaletti**, che "scorrono" lungo un blocco di caratteri. Vedi anche **allineamento** e **H&J**.

Ing: JUSTIFIED TYPE/TEXT
Fr: TEXTE JUSTIFIÉ
Ted: BLOCKSATZ
Sp: JUSTIFICACIÓN

Design: Armando Chitolina

TEXTURE

Qualità tattile percepita di un elemento grafico o di un **layout**. Sebbene la parola texture (trama) descriva in genere attributi tridimensionali, come quelli della superficie della carta, si usa anche per riferirsi a simili qualità rappresentate o suggerite in un lavoro grafico bidimensionale. Vari pattern e **gradienti**, ad es., possono dare l'impressione di una texture, specialmente se posti in contrasto con elementi lisci e uniformi. Anche alcune tecniche di stampa, come la stampa di un blocco, forniscono texture. Persino una pagina di **caratteri**, con forti **ritmi** verticali e orizzontali, ha una certa texture, determinata dalla disposizione dei caratteri stessi; quando questa è relativamente regolare in una pagina o in un layout, il carattere possiede ciò che i tipografi chiamano "buon colore".

Ing: TEXTURE
Fr: TEXTURE
Ted: STRUKTUR
Sp: TEXTURA

Autore: Manuela Marchesan

A B C D E F G H I J K L M N O P Q R S **T** U V W X Y Z

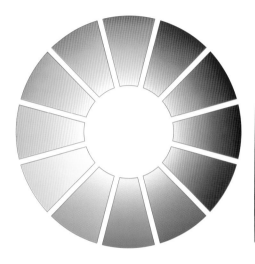

THUMBNAIL (MINIATURA)

Termine adottato per descrivere un piccolo bozzetto, spesso di bassa qualità, usato per comunicare rapidamente un concetto. I thumbnail si utilizzano nei primi stadi di un progetto come parte integrante del processo grafico; spesso il disegno finale emerge dalla produzione di molti thumbnail sempre più raffinati. Il termine può anche essere usato per riferirsi a immagini più piccole e a bassa **risoluzione**, che servono come "riempiposto" delle loro versioni ad alta risoluzione. Una galleria di immagini online, ad esempio, potrebbe mostrare dozzine di thumbnail in una singola pagina web, per permettere una rapida visualizzazione e un veloce caricamento della pagina. Tale pratica è diventata così consueta che la semplice presenza di thumbnail spesso serve a indicare agli utenti l'esistenza di versioni ad alta risoluzione, che possono essere ottenute semplicemente cliccandovi sopra.

Ing: THUMBNAIL
Fr: CRAYONNAGE
Ted: DAUMENNAGELSKIZZE
Sp: MINIATURA

Agenzia di pubblicità: TECNOSTUDI

TINTA

Termine utilizzato per descrivere un **colore** che è stato creato aggiustando la sua **luminosità** grazie all'aggiunta di bianco. Abbassando la luminosità di un colore grazie all'aggiunta di nero, si produce una *sfumatura* della stessa tonalità. Il termine tinta può riferirsi anche alla densità dei punti sugli schermi di **mezzitoni** usati nella stampa a quattro colori. Un'area dello schermo ciano coperto per il 60% con **punti** viene chiamato tinta al 60%.

Ing: TINT
Fr: COULEUR DE FOND
Ted: TÖNUNG
Sp: TINTE

Design: Donna S. Atwood, www.atwooddesign.com

TIPOGRAFIA

Termine usato per descrivere tanto l'arte e la scienza della **composizione tipografica**, quanto il prodotto che ne risulta. I tipografi tengono in considerazione una serie di questioni molto varie, da problemi generali come la facilità di lettura del testo fino ai minimi dettagli, come la **crenatura**. Sebbene la tecnologia digitale renda più facile che mai la realizzazione di una tipografia raffinata, essa forse non è più diffusa di quanto fosse ai tempi dei **caratteri** in metallo fuso o della *fototipia*, quando i tipografi erano costretti a occuparsi di ogni particolare.

Ing: TYPOGRAPHY
Fr: TYPOGRAPHIE
Ted: TYPOGRAFIE
Sp: TIPOGRAFÍA

Design: Armando Chitolina

ABCDEFGHIJKLMNOPQRS**T**UVWXYZ

Keeper of the Couture Flame

In their frothy, sensual, sweet-toothed glamour, Valentino's clothes seem quintessentially Italian – the half-century oeuvre of a maestro whose fashion soul is as Roman as his profile.

The designer's mantra is: "I always wanted to make women beautiful," and his inspiration was that of a provincial boy in the drab post-war period going to the movies with his sister and catching the glory days of Hollywood stars in their silver-screen years.

Like the rest of the Romans, he was fascinated by the shiny, *Dolce Vita* glamour and he gave it classical class. By the time he was touched with the stardust of his own era, dressing the famous who were also his friends, Valentino had become part of the motion picture. Images of the young designer with deep, dark eyes, his models dressed in pristine white, accompanied photographs of his celebrated international clients: Elizabeth Taylor, Sophia Loren and his dear Jackie – Jacqueline Kennedy – who turned to him for her state wardrobe and later for her girlish wedding dress for her marriage to Aristotle Onassis.

But Valentino did not rise, fully formed, like Botticelli's Venus from some mysterious fashion ocean. His famous 'White' collection in Florence in 1968 might have appeared to mark an effortless ascent. But the truth is different: a long and hard-working journey over nearly 20 years to fame and fortune. And a significant mix of French style with his Italian heritage.

Valentino's early years have something in common with the Old Masters of Italian art. For the designer's secret is that he became, at age 17, a humble apprentice – not to an artist, but to the art of haute couture.

Hearing Valentino talk now about the fruitful decade in Paris in the 1950s, when he drew designs on scraps of paper, interviewed with Balenciaga and got a position with Jean Dessès, it seems a world away from today's fashion colleges, runway dramatics and fast, factory-made fashion. The fledgling designer witnessed the high noon of haute couture, as the ideas he had expressed as pencil strokes were transformed via canvas toiles, fine fabrics and fittings into beautiful clothes.

Those French years were also the seedbed of Valentino's fashion style, which grew into that particular Franco-Italian blend of light-handed 'barocco' that is known as Rococo. If you define the essence of Valentino's work, it is also the definition of Rococo: exquisite flourishes developed from a sculpted base. It is evident in the designer's tailoring, when a jacket has a lacy collar or a skirt breaks out into ruffles at the hem. The dresses are pure Rococo with their millefeuille layers and decorative details.

Such finesse does not come easily. Valentino recalls the giddy workload of those formative French years after his parents allowed him to come to Paris and lodged him with friends. He also talks about the gratitude he feels to his parents: his father's support when, to finance the new House of Valentino in Rome in the 1960s, the Garavanis' modest country home was sold. The couturier says he owes to his elegant mother the advice to keep things classy and simple.

Those early years as a studio hand – and his father's example – must have instilled a work ethic that is the essence of Valentino's life. Apart from his beloved couture, for which every silhouette, fabric and embellishment is a personal decision, Giancarlo Giammetti, his partner and friend since they met in 1960, says that 75 per cent of the company's output goes through the maestro's nimble hands.

And what an output! Whereas the great couturiers of the past showed two collections a year to their private clients, Giammetti lists the litany of collections: ready-to-wear, sport, shoes, bags, belts, cruise and pre-season collections. They make up the Valentino empire – further enlarged since the company was bought by Marzotto S.p.A., the Italian conglomerate, in 2002.

TITOLO

Termine generalmente associato al giornalismo e alla pubblicità, impiegato per descrivere un'unità di testo molto breve che appare prima del **corpo del testo**, accennando ai suoi contenuti. Poiché i titoli preparano il terreno al testo, sono solitamente costituiti da **caratteri** molto più grandi, a volte diversi rispetto a quelli usati per il corpo. Lettere **tutte maiuscole** o una combinazione di maiuscole e **maiuscoletti** sono frequentemente utilizzate per i titoli, specialmente nei giornali.

Ing: HEADLINE
Fr: CHAPEAU
Ted: SCHLAGZEILE
Sp: TITULAR

Design: Armando Chitolina

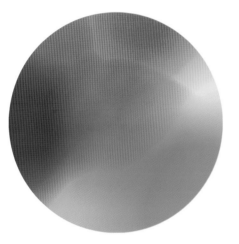

TONALITÀ

Caratteristica basilare di un **colore**, corrispondente alla sua lunghezza di onda nello spettro della luce, che si usa per distinguere un colore dall'altro. La tonalità si riferisce alla posizione relativa di un particolare colore all'interno della **ruota dei colori**.

Ing: HUE
Fr: TEINTE
Ted: FARBTON
Sp: MATIZ

Design: Alfredo Carlo

TRACKING

Termine che indica quanto larga o stretta sia la disposizione di una riga di **caratteri**. Aumentando il tracking si allarga la spaziatura complessiva dei caratteri, e lo spazio tra i caratteri aumenta in modo proporzionale. Diminuendo il tracking si produce l'effetto opposto. Il termine **spazio lettera** si riferisce genericamente allo spazio fra i caratteri; il tracking quantifica la spaziatura.

Ing: TRACKING
Fr: APPROCHE DE GROUPE
Ted: SPERREN
Sp: TRACKING

Agenzia di pubblicità: TECNOSTUDI

TRAPPING

Tecnica usata per prevenire gli spazi fra le aree colorate quando la **registrazione** è imperfetta. Se, ad es., un **carattere** colore magenta fosse stampato su uno sfondo di ciano puro, un eventuale *fuori registro* produrrebbe uno spazio tra i caratteri e lo sfondo, rivelando la carta non stampata sottostante. Un *trap* è una linea di **colore** molto sottile, realizzato attorno a un oggetto per evitare tali vuoti bianchi. Esistono vari tipi di trap: quale sia il più adatto per uno specifico tipo di stampa dipende da molti fattori, e in molti casi è meglio farlo eseguire da chi stampa. Vedi anche **registro**.

Ing: TRAPPING
Fr: GROSSI-MAIGRI
Ted: ÜBERFÜLLUNG
Sp: REVENTADO

Studio grafico: Sara Muzio

A B C D E F G H I J K L M N O P Q R S **T** U V W X Y Z

Per indica-
re che una
parola è
stata spez-
zata e
per crea-
re parole
composte
come

ex–marito
socio-culturale
italo-americano

TRATTINO

Segno di interpunzione spesso confuso con la **lineetta en** e la **lineetta em**, il trattino è più corto degli altri due segni, ha una funzione diversa e normalmente non è preceduto né seguito da spazi. In italiano il trattino viene usato per indicare che una parola è stata spezzata a fine riga oppure per creare parole composte, come ad esempio, "ex-marito", "socio-culturale" o "italo-americano".

Ing: HYPHEN
Fr: TRAIT D'UNION
Ted: TRENNSTRICH
Sp: GUIÓN

Agenzia di pubblicità: TECNOSTUDI

Esempio di

Tratto ascendente

TRATTO ASCENDENTE

Qualsiasi elemento della lettera minuscola che superi l'**altezza della x** di un dato **carattere** tipografico fino alla **linea** (orizzontale) corrispondente all'estremità superiore delle maiuscole. I relativi pesi e dimensioni del tratto ascendente variano a seconda del carattere: quelli con un occhio medio più alto tendono ad avere tratti ascendenti più sottili, quelli con occhio medio più basso tendono ad avere un tratto ascendente più prominente. Vedi anche **tratto discendente** e **altezza della x.**

Ing: ASCENDER
Fr: ASCENDANTE
Ted: OBERLÄNGE
Sp: ASCENDENTE

Agenzia di pubblicità: TECNOSTUDI

Esempio pratico

di

Tratto discendente

TRATTO DISCENDENTE

È la porzione di una lettera minuscola che si estende al di sotto della **linea di base.** Come per il **tratto ascendente**, le dimensioni e il peso del tratto discendente variano a seconda del **carattere** tipografico. Vedi anche **tratto ascendente.**

Ing: DESCENDER
Fr: DESCENDANTE
Ted: UNTERLÄNGE
Sp: DESCENDENTE

Agenzia di pubblicità: TECNOSTUDI

TRICROMIA
Vedi **bicromia.**

A B C D E F G H I J K L M N O P Q R S **T U V** W X Y Z

TUTTE MAIUSCOLE

Altro nome per parti di testo composte esclusivamente di **caratteri** maiuscoli. Sono note anche come lettere maiuscole perché una volta i tipografi conservavano i piombi per stamparle nelle cassette superiori, mentre i caratteri minuscoli, utilizzati più frequentemente, erano chiamati lettere minuscole e conservati nelle più accessibili cassette inferiori.

Ing: ALL CAPS
Fr: TOUT EN CAPITALES
Ted: VERSALIEN
Sp: ALL CAPS

Agenzia di pubblicità: TECNOSTUDI

VALORE
Vedi **luminosità**.

A B C D E F G H I J K L M N O P Q R S T U **V** W X Y Z

...giunti in via degli Alberi, sentirono degli spari alle loro spalle. Si voltarono simultaneamente e videro dietro di loro un uomo che avanzava puntandogli contro una pistola. A tale vista il Gaspari reagì con rapidità: saltando addosso al losco individuo e cercando disperatamente di togliergli l'arma di mano, ingaggiò una violenta colluttazione. Durante questa rissa dall'arma partirono due colpi, che ferirono alla schiena la bella Enrica, la quale rotolò in un fosso laterale della via.

Riportare:
«un discorso o una "citazione diretta" all'interno di un blocco di testo»
O per suggerire un uso "ironico o 'inusuale' di una parola" o di una frase.

VEDOVA

Riga finale molto corta di un paragrafo, spesso una parola singola, che dà l'impressione di uno spazio tra capoversi quando non c'è. Come per gli **orfani**, ci sono molte tecniche per evitare le vedove, le più comuni delle quali sono la spaziatura delle lettere e la **sillabazione**. Vedi anche **H&J** e **invio a capo automatico**.

Ing: WIDOW
Fr: VEUVE
Ted: WITWE
Sp: VIUDA

Studio grafico: Sara Muzio

VERNICE

Rivestimento trasparente applicato sulla carta come parte del processo di stampa, generalmente eseguito dopo che sono stati stampati tutti gli inchiostri. Come anche altri rivestimenti, le vernici proteggono in parte dagli effetti della manipolazione, ma vengono usate soprattutto per i loro vantaggi estetici, poiché offrono varie gamme di lucentezza, dall'opaco al lucidissimo. Vernici applicate su aree specifiche vengono chiamate *vernici spot*, altre applicate su pagine intere sono dette anche *vernici coprenti*.

Ing: VARNISH
Fr: VERNIS
Ted: LACKIERUNG
Sp: BARNIZ

Design: DESIGNWORK

VERSO
Vedi **recto/verso**.

VIRGOLETTE

Le virgolette si utilizzano in una grande varietà di casi come ad esempio per riportare un discorso o una citazione diretta all'interno di un blocco di testo, o per suggerire un uso ironico o inusuale di una parola o di una frase (ad es. "Il programma più 'semplice' ha richiesto 30 minuti per essere completato"). Le virgolette tipografiche, a volte chiamate *virgolette eleganti*, sono diverse da quelle in stile "macchina da scrivere" e dal simbolo **apice** usato per indicare misure e notazioni matematiche. In Italia si utilizzano tre tipi di virgolette, quelle a sergente o caporali (« »), le alte doppie o doppi apici (" "), le alte semplici o apici singoli (' '), utilizzate soprattutto all'interno di una citazione introdotta da doppi apici. Vedi anche **apostrofo**.

Ing: QUOTATION MARKS
Fr: GUILLEMETS
Ted: ANFÜHRUNGSSTRICHE
Sp: COMILLAS

Agenzia di pubblicità: TECNOSTUDI

ESPAÑOL

A B C D E F G H I J K L M N O P Q R S T U V W X Y Z

ESTE ES UN TEXTO AJUSTADO
AL TAMAÑO DEL ÁREA DEFINIDA

ESTE NO
ES
UN TEXTO
AJUSTADO
AL ÁREA
DEFINIDA

AJUSTE DEL ORIGINAL

Proceso tipográfico de ajuste del **tamaño de punto** e **interlineado** de una **tipografía** de manera que encaje en un área definida o a través de un número específico de páginas. Para lograrlo se pueden realizar cálculos para obtener resultados aproximados del ajuste o realizar el proceso de manera iterativa, utilizando un software de maquetación de página hasta conseguir el ajuste deseado.

Ing: COPYFITTING
Fr: CALIBRAGE
Al: TEXTEINPASSUNG
It: AGGIUSTAMENTO DEL TESTO

AJUSTE DE TEXTO

Manera en la que una línea de tipo acaba y continúa en la línea siguiente. La edición de una línea de tipo suele hacer que las líneas siguientes se tengan que *reajustar*. El ajuste de texto es la forma en la que las líneas encajan con otros elementos de diseño, como fotografías o ilustraciones. Véase: *H&J*.

Ing: TEXT WRAPPING
Fr: RETOUR À LA LIGNE AUTOMATIQUE
Al: TEXTUMBRUCH
It: INVIO A CAPO AUTOMATICO

Diseño: Maja Denzer; **Compañía:** Gestaltica, www.gestaltica.de

ALINEACIÓN

Ajuste de los diferentes elementos del diseño, como imágenes y **tipos**, y las relaciones entre unos y otros. Los elementos suelen alinearse de forma que sus bordes (izquierdo, derecho, superior, inferior) o líneas centrales (horizontales o verticales) sigan una línea de referencia común, que suele formar parte de la cuadrícula. La alineación también puede referirse al ajuste de tipos dentro de un bloque tipográfico. Véase: **bandera a la izquierda/a la derecha**, **centrado**, y **justificación**.

Ing: ALIGNMENT
Fr: ALIGNEMENT
Al: AXIALITÄT
It: ALLINEAMENTO

Diseño: Bendita Gloria (Alba Rosell + Santi Fuster); **Compañía:** Bendita Gloria, www.benditagloria.com

ALINEACIÓN ÓPTICA
Véase: **alineación visual**.

A B C D E F G H I J K L M N O P Q R S T U V W X Y Z

Diseño: Rubengarcia-Castro.com 2009; **Compañía:**
RubenGarcia-Castro, www.rubengarcia-castro.com

ALINEACIÓN VISUAL

Alineación de **tipos** u otros elementos de diseño según lo que parece bien alineado, sin seguir medidas exactas. Esta alineación resulta importante cuando los elementos que deben alinearse tienen diferentes formas. Si se **alinea** un círculo, un triángulo equilátero y un cuadrado de la misma altura en la misma línea horizontal se crea una ilusión óptica: el cuadrado parece mayor que las otras dos formas, mientras que el círculo parece más pequeño que el cuadrado o el triángulo.

Ing: VISUAL ALIGNMENT
Fr: ALIGNEMENT VISUEL
Al: OPTISCHE AUSRICHTUNG
It: ALLINEAMENTO VISIVO

ALL CAPS

Conjunto tipográfico formado únicamente por letras de *caja alta*, llamadas así porque el tipo metálico usado para su impresión se guardaba en los cajones (o *cajas*) más altos, mientras que las de *caja baja*, más utilizadas, estaban guardadas en los cajones bajos, más accesibles. Las letras de caja baja también se llaman *minúsculas*.

Ing: ALL CAPS
Fr: TOUT EN CAPITALES
Al: VERSALIEN
It: TUTTE MAIUSCOLE

↕ Altura de las mayúsculas
línea base

ALTURA DE LAS MAYÚSCULAS

Distancia desde la **línea base** hasta el borde superior de las letras *de caja alta*, que se extiende por la *línea ascendente*. La altura de las mayúsculas puede ser diferente entre **tipos** del mismo tamaño de **punto**. Véase: **versalitas**.

Ing: CAP HEIGHT
Fr: HAUTEUR DE CAPITALE
Al: VERSALHÖHE
It: ALTEZZA DELLA MAIUSCOLA

A BCDEFGHIJKLMNOPQRSTUVWXYZ

Tipografía

Y el caso es que cuando transcurrieron los años y le llegó aquel en el que los dioses habían hilado que regresara a su casa de Itaca, ni siquiera entonces estuvo libre de pruebas; ni cuando estuvo ya con los suyos. Todos los dioses se compadecían de él excepto Poseidón, quién se mantuvo siempre rencoroso con el divino Odiseo hasta que llegó a su tierra.

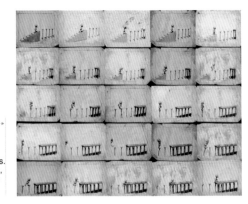

ALTURA X

Altura de las letras de caja baja de un tipo de letra sin **ascendentes** ni **descendentes**. Se mide en puntos y corresponde a la distancia entre la **línea de base** y la *línea media*. En tamaños de punto pequeños, los tipos de letras con altura x alta son más legibles que los que tienen una altura x más baja.

Ing: X-HEIGHT
Fr: HAUTEUR D'X
Al: X-HÖHE
It: ALTEZZA DELLA X

ANCHO

Anchura de un bloque de tipo, medida normalmente en **puntos**, **picas** o **cuadratines**, aunque también en milímetros o píxeles. El ancho óptimo para la **legibilidad tipográfica** suele ser de 52–78 caracteres (el equivalente a 2–3 abecedarios) con espacios incluidos, aunque deben tenerse en cuenta factores como el interlineado, el interletraje o el tamaño de **letra**.

Ing: MEASURE
Fr: MESURE
Al: SATZBREITE
It: GIUSTEZZA

ANIMACIÓN

Técnica en la que una serie de imágenes digitales se exponen en una secuencia específica de manera que se crea un sentido de movimiento continuo. Para las animaciones sencillas de diseño Web se emplean GIF animados, mientras que las animaciones más complejas se crean mediante aplicaciones de software sofisticadas, como Flash® de Adobe.

Ing: ANIMATION
Fr: ANIMATION
Al: ANIMATION
It: ANIMAZIONE/I

Diseño: Dani Fornaguera; **Compañía:** Dani Fornaguera, fornaguera.dani@gmail.com

A B C D E F G H I J K L M N O P Q R S T U V W X Y Z

APÓSTROFO

Signo ortográfico en forma de coma alta, prácticamente en desuso en español excepto para indicar la omisión de una vocal. Se debe evitar su uso por influencia del inglés, en construcciones incorrectas en español.

Ing: APOSTROPHE
Fr: APOSTROPHE
Al: APOSTROPH
It: APOSTROFO

ARREGLO

Proceso de preparación de una imprenta y otros equipos de acabado, plegado o **encuadernación**, necesarios para realizar un trabajo de impresión.

Ing: MAKEREADY
Fr: MACULE
Al: DRUCKEINRICHTUNG
It: AVVIAMENTO MACCHINA

Diseño: Bendita Gloria (Alba Rosell + Santi Fuster);
Compañía: Bendita Gloria, www.benditagloria.com

ART DECÓ

Estilo que combina las tendencias decorativas del **Art Nouveau** con las formas geométricas desnudas y la abstracción del **Modernismo**. El Art Decó se hizo famoso durante los años 1920-1930 en EE.UU. y parte de Europa. Este estilo, que combina una amplia variedad de influencias, desde el arte azteca o el nativo americano, los zigurats egipcios, el **Cubismo**, etc., fue muy utilizado en arquitectura, diseño de interiores y de productos, y también en el diseño gráfico, combinando tipos estilizados con otros en negrita.

Ing: ART DECO
Fr: ART DÉCO
Al: ART DÉCO
It: ART DÉCO

Diseño: 2008 by Bob Staake. All Rights Reserved;
Compañía: Bob Staake, www.bobstaake.com

ART NOUVEAU

Estilo de arquitectura y diseño muy decorativo que se impuso en buena parte de Europa entre 1880 y los primeros años de la Primera Guerra Mundial y que también llegó a EE.UU. El Art Nouveau, como su nombre indica, pretendía crear una nueva estética, rechazando el desorden y el caos de la época victoriana y creando formas orgánicas y curvas. Los principales motivos decorativos eran plantas, animales (especialmente pájaros) y figuras femeninas, a menudo representadas con un nivel de abstracción mucho mayor que el de los gráficos **victorianos**.

Ing: ART NOUVEAU
Fr: ART NOUVEAU
Al: JUGENDSTIL
It: ART NOUVEAU

ARTS AND CRAFTS

Movimiento de reforma iniciado en Inglaterra a finales del siglo XIX como reacción a la Revolución Industrial y a la importancia que se le daba a la producción masificada en sacrificio de la estética. En diseño gráfico, el movimiento de Arts and Crafts se definió en los libros de William Morris. A pesar de que utilizaba iniciales decorativas, tipografías **góticas** y densas **maquetas** de impresión de reminiscencias antiguas, el interés de Morris en unificar las actividades de diseño y producción sentó las bases para el **Modernismo** del siglo XX.

Ing: ARTS AND CRAFTS
Fr: ARTS & CRAFTS
Al: ARTS AND CRAFTS
It: ARTS AND CRAFTS

Diseño: ADRIANNE SCHREINER; **Compañía:** ADRIANNE SCHREINER, a.schreiner@globo.com

ASCENDENTE

Parte de una letra de *caja baja* que sobrepasa la **altura** X de un tipo de letra hasta la *línea ascedente*. El tamaño y peso de los ascendentes dependen del **tipo de letra**: los que tienen una altura X mayor suelen tener ascendentes más sutiles mientras que los que tienen una altura X menor suelen tener ascendentes más vistosos. Véase: **descendente** y **altura X**.

Ing: ASCENDER
Fr: ASCENDANTE
Al: OBERLÄNGE
It: TRATTO ASCENDENTE

Festes de Moros i Cristians
17 al 20 de Juliol
Oliva 2008

ASIMETRÍA

Organización de los elementos de una maqueta para que queden distribuidos de manera irregular con respecto a los ejes horizontal y vertical. Un **desplegable** en el que las **páginas enfrentadas** no sean imágenes especulares puede considerarse asimétrico. Una buena **maqueta** asimétrica consigue el **equilibrio** mediante una cuidadosa interacción de los **espacios positivos** y **negativos**, y suele ser más dinámica que una maqueta simétrica. Véase: **simetría** y **línea de orientación**.

Ing: ASYMMETRY
Fr: ASYMÉTRIE
Al: ASYMMETRIE
It: ASIMMETRIA

Diseño: Jeroni Mira Flanagan; **Compañía:** Jeroni Mira Flanagan, sickokiller@hotmail.com

A **B** C D E F G H I J K L M N O P Q R S T U V W X Y Z

BANCO DE IMÁGENES Y FOTOGRAFÍAS

Imágenes y fotografías disponibles para su utilización mediante un acuerdo de licencia. El uso de estas imágenes es más barato que la contratación de un fotógrafo, aunque se pierde control creativo. Además, ni el diseñador ni el cliente pueden estar seguros de que aquella imagen haya sido utilizada antes, ya que no existe un acuerdo de exclusividad. Actualmente existen muchas colecciones *online* de fácil búsqueda, pago y descarga.

Ing: STOCK PHOTOGRAPHY/IMAGES
Fr: BANQUE D'IMAGES
Al: STOCK FOTOS (BILDARCHIV)
It: BANCA IMMAGINI

Diseño: Maja Denzer; **Compañía:** Gestaltica, www.gestaltica.de

BANDERA

Forma irregular que se crea entre un bloque de texto y el margen adyacente como resultado de **longitudes de línea** diferentes, creando la imagen de una bandera. En la **bandera a la izquierda** el mástil de la bandera queda a la izquierda. Si se usan tipos **justificados** no aparecen banderas. Para asegurar la **legibilidad**, los tipógrafos y diseñadores intentan crear banderas aleatorias, evitando distracciones visuales provocadas por banderas geométricas o demasiado rítmicas.

Ing: RAG
Fr: DRAPEAU
Al: FLATTERSATZ
It: BANDIERA

Diseño: Bendita Gloria (Alba Rosell + Santi Fuster); **Compañía:** Bendita Gloria, www.benditagloria.com

BANDERA A LA IZQUIERDA/BANDERA A LA DERECHA

Se habla de bandera a la izquierda cuando las líneas sucesivas de un texto empiezan en la misma línea de referencia vertical. También se llama *bandera de salida*. Cuando las líneas acaban siguiendo una misma línea de referencia vertical, se habla de bandera a la derecha, o *de entrada*.

Ing: FLUSH-LEFT, FLUSH-RIGHT
Fr: FER À GAUCHE, FER À DROITE
Al: LINKSBÜNDIG, RECHTSBÜNDIG
It: ALLINEAMENTO A SINISTRA E ALLINEAMENTO A DESTRA

A **B** C D E F G H I J K L M N O P Q R S T U V W X Y Z

BARNIZ

Revestimiento transparente aplicado a un papel en el proceso de impresión, normalmente después de la impresión de tintas. Al igual que otros tipos de revestimiento, protegen de la manipulación, aunque suelen usarse principalmente con fines estéticos, ya que proporcionan lustres diferentes, desde el mate hasta el brillante. Cuando el barniz se aplica únicamente a reservas se llama *máscara* y cuando se aplica a la página entera se habla de *cama*.

Ing: VARNISH
Fr: VERNIS
Al: LACKIERUNG
It: VERNICE

Diseño: Maja Denzer; **Compañía:** Gestaltica, www.gestaltica.de

BAUHAUS

Escuela de arte, arquitectura y diseño que funcionó en Alemania desde 1919 hasta 1933. La Bauhaus daba una gran importancia a la funcionalidad, por lo que su diseño gráfico tenía como característica principal la geometría y la ausencia de adornos. Para las maquetas utilizaban casi exclusivamente la tipografía **sans-serif**, que solía estar organizada mediante gruesos filetes y **cuadrículas** muy ordenadas, fotografía y **fotomontajes**. En la **paleta de colores** de la Bauhaus predominaba el blanco, el negro y el gris, aunque también se usaban **colores primarios** como acentos.

Ing: BAUHAUS
Fr: BAUHAUS
Al: BAUHAUS
It: BAUHAUS

BITONO

Imagen en escala de grises impresa usando dos colores de tinta en lugar de uno solo. Se pueden utilizar dos tintas que no sean negras, aunque la negra suele ser la tinta principal. Si se utiliza el negro como tinta principal y un tono de gris como secundaria, el resultado es una variación de tono que se aproxima al efecto de una fotografía en blanco y negro. Si se utiliza un color no neutro como tinta secundaria, o dos colores no neutros, se consiguen efectos visuales muy interesantes, algunos sutiles y otros más radicales. Un **tritono** es una imagen en escala de grises impresa con tres colores de tinta.

Ing: DUOTONE
Fr: SIMILI DEUX TONS
Al: DUPLEX
It: BICROMIA

A **B** C D E F G H I J K L M N O P Q R S T U V W X Y Z

BOLO

Carácter tipográfico (•) utilizado para ordenar términos en una lista, aunque también se utilizan para separar líneas cortas secuenciales de un tipo, como una dirección en una carta. Entre el bolo y el tipo debe colocarse un espacio. Los bolos suelen incluirse dentro de las fuentes de **símbolos** y *dingbat*. Véase: **puntuación volada**.

Ing: BULLET
Fr: PUCE
Al: AUFZÄHLUNGSPUNKT
It: PUNTO ELENCO

BORDE

Marco que rodea una fotografía, ilustración, bloque de texto o cualquier otro elemento de diseño, que crea una transición entre el elemento en cuestión y el resto de la **maqueta**. Los marcos pueden ser sencillos, como un rectángulo o círculo de trazo fino, o muy adornados. Los marcos más gruesos o detallados restan fuerza a la imagen que rodean, atrayendo la atención sobre ellos, mientras que los marcos más finos o sencillos hacen que destaque la imagen sobre el fondo.

Ing: BORDER
Fr: BORDURE
Al: RAHMEN
It: BORDO/I

Diseño: Andi Rivas, S-Pain; **Compañía:** RD2 Art Direction & Contemporary Graphic Design, www.andirivas.com

BRANDING

Diferenciación estratégica de una oferta (producto, servicio, interacción, experiencia, etc.) sobre la de sus competidores. En términos visuales, la primera impresión de la marca suele ser un **logo** o logotipo, que se utiliza para fijar la *promesa de marca*: el conjunto de expectativas asociadas con una oferta. Una buena *identidad de marca* implica, entre otras cosas, un lenguaje visual de conjunto coherente (logo, tipo de letra, **paleta de colores** y otras claves visuales). Las estrategias de marca contemporáneas van más allá de la publicidad tradicional en prensa y televisión para llegar a sitios Web, *blogs* y nuevos medios sociales emergentes.

Ing: BRANDING
Fr: STRATÉGIE DE MARQUE
Al: MARKENBILDUNG
It: BRANDING

Diseño: Rubengarcia-Castro.com 2009; **Compañía:** RubenGarcia-Castro, www.rubengarcia-castro.com

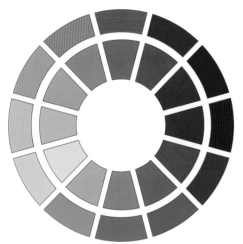

Un río es una corriente natural de agua que fluye con continuidad. Posee un caudal determinado, rara vez constante a lo largo del año, y desemboca en el mar, en un lago o en otro río, en cuyo caso se denomina afluente. La parte final de un río es su desembocadura. Algunas veces terminan en zonas desérticas donde sus aguas se pierden por infiltración y evaporación: es el caso de los ríos alóctonos (llamados así porque sus aguas proceden de otros lugares con clima más húmedo), como el caso del Okavango en el falso delta donde desemboca numerosos uadis (wadi en inglés) del Sáhara y de otros desiertos. Cuando el río es corto y estrecho, recibe el nombre de riacho, riachuelo o arroyo.

BRILLO

Claridad u oscuridad relativas de un color, también denominado **valor** o *tono*. En una fotocopia en blanco y negro, los colores de niveles de claridad similar prácticamente no se distinguen unos de otros. Véase: **rueda de colores**.

Ing: BRIGHTNESS
Fr: LUMINOSITÉ
Al: LEUCHTDICHTE
It: LUMINOSITÀ

Diseño: Donna S. Atwood, www.atwooddesign.com

CALIBRE
Véase: **resma**.

CALIGRAFÍA

Palabra derivada del griego (*kalli y graphos*), que significa "escritura bella". Arte de la escritura a mano, realizada normalmente con herramientas tradicionales como un plumín o un pincel. Se caracteriza por la fluidez de sus letras, de trazos de grosor variable.

Ing: CALLIGRAPHY
Fr: CALLIGRAPHIE
Al: KALLIGRAPHIE
     (SCHÖNSCHREIBKUNST)
It: CALLIGRAFIA

Diseño: Diego Feijóo; **Compañía:** Studio Diego Feijóo, www.dfeijoo.com

CALLE

Espacios verticales que aparecen en un bloque de texto como resultado de una alineación vertical de los espacios entre palabras, lo que provoca una distracción visual. Las calles aparecen con más frecuencia en bloques de texto **justificados** debido al espaciado de palabras poco natural creado por *software*. La mejor manera de eliminar o reducir el impacto de las calles es juntando las líneas de tipo mediante el *tracking* o la **partición silábica**. Véase: ***H&J*** y **ajuste de texto**.

Ing: RIVERS
Fr: LÉZARDES
Al: GIESSBÄCHLEIN
It: CANALETTI

A B **C** D E F G H I J K L M N O P Q R S T U V W X Y Z

CANAL

Información digital correspondiente a las cantidades relativas de los tres (**RGB**) o cuatro (**CMYK**) **colores primarios** utilizados para representar imágenes en color. Cada canal es como una imagen en **escala de grises** en la que los **valores** de gris han sido sustituidos por valores de un color primario único. La imagen en color se crea, tanto en pantalla como impresa, gracias a la combinación de todos los canales de un *modelo de color* determinado.

Ing: CHANNELS
Fr: CANAUX
Al: FARBKANÄLE
It: CANALI

A B **C** D E F G H I J K L M N O P Q R S T U V W X Y Z

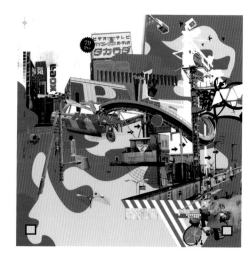

Garamond
Serif

Helvetica
Sans Serif

Edwardian Script Italic
Script

Blackmoor LET
Blackletter

T odo lo que diga será utilizado en su contra.

CAPA

Característica de los *software* de creación de imágenes digitales que trata diferentes elementos del diseño como si existieran en hojas transparentes independientes, permitiendo la edición, combinación y manipulación de partes de una imagen sin afectar a las otras. La imagen final es el resultado de la colocación de capas una encima de otra en un orden determinado.

Ing: LAYER
Fr: CALQUE
Al: EBENE
It: LIVELLO

Diseño: Cless. Belio Magazine; **Compañía:** Cless, www.cless.info

CAPITULAR

Letra de *caja alta* utilizada como letra inicial de la primera palabra de un párrafo, establecida en un tamaño de punto mayor que el resto del tipo pero sobre la misma línea de base. Para distinguirla aún más, se puede escribir en un **tipo de letra** diferente del resto del cuerpo de texto. Véase: **mayúscula inicial** y **mayúscula caída**.

Ing: STANDING CAPITAL/CAP
Fr: GRANDE CAPITALE
Al: STEHENDE INITIALE
It: STANDING CAP

CLASIFICACIÓN TIPOGRÁFICA

Sistema de catalogación de **tipos de letra** según las características visuales que comparten, como la presencia o ausencia de **serifas**, la similitud con la escritura a mano, etc. Estas clasificaciones deben entenderse como generalizaciones muy amplias y no como definiciones estrictas, ya que muchos tipos de letra pueden entrar en más de una clasificación.

Ing: TYPE CLASSIFICATION
Fr: CLASSIFICATION TYPOGRAPHIQUE
Al: SCHRIFTKLASSIFIKATION
It: CLASSIFICAZIONE DEI CARATTERI

CLIP ART

Ilustraciones disponibles tanto en formato digital como impresas, para su uso en **maquetas** gráficas. Durante años han gozado de gran popularidad debido a su disponibilidad, variedad y a la libertad de *copyright*. Véase: **banco de imágenes y fotografías**.

Ing: CLIP ART
Fr: CLIPART
Al: CLIPART
It: CLIP ART

Diseño: Cless; **Compañía:** Cless, www.cless.info

CMYK

Sigla inglesa que corresponde a cian, magenta, amarillo y negro, los colores de tinta utilizados para la **cuatricromía**. En español también puede encontrarse, raramente, el acrónimo traducido CMAN. Cuando se combinan en parejas, los colores *primarios sustractivos* cian, magenta y amarillo, reproducen los colores *primarios aditivos* rojo, verde y azul, que corresponden a los tres tipos diferentes de receptores de luz del ojo humano En teoría, los tres colores primarios sustractivos se combinan para producir el color negro. Sin embargo, en la práctica, el resultado de esta combinación no es suficientemente rico como para producir una gama completa de tonos de impresión de color. Por esa razón, el negro se añade de forma separada. También denominado *colores de proceso*.

Ing: CMYK
Fr: CMJN
Al: CMYK
It: CMYK

Diseño: Kate Benjamin, www.moderncat.net

COLLAGE

Técnica de creación de material gráfico original mediante la mezcla de papel, tela, fotografía, etc., en una tabla o lienzo. El nombre proviene del francés *coller*, que significa "pegar". También pueden crearse *collages* digitales pegando elementos digitales, como imágenes escaneadas de objetos texturados o en tres dimensiones. Véase: **fotomontaje**.

Ing: COLLAGE
Fr: COLLAGE
Al: KOLLAGE
It: COLLAGE

Diseño: Cless; **Compañía:** Cless, www.cless.info

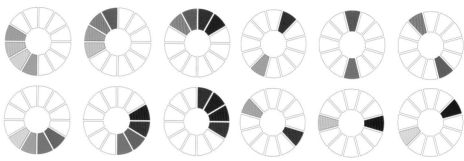

COLOR

Variedad de longitud de onda de la luz que percibe el ojo humano. El color de los objetos se percibe según su capacidad de absorber, reflejar o transmitir diferentes longitudes de onda. Las tres propiedades básicas del color son el **matiz**, la **saturación** (o *croma*) y el **brillo** (también llamado *valor*). Los tipógrafos también llaman *color* a la claridad u oscuridad general de una página de **tipo**, o a la de un párrafo en relación con otro. Véase: **rueda de colores**.

Ing: COLOR
Fr: COULEUR
Al: FARBE
It: COLORE/I

COLORES ANÁLOGOS

Dos o más colores adyacentes en la rueda de colores (p. ej., verde, amarillo-verde y amarillo). El uso de dos o tres colores análogos proporciona un diseño de apariencia armoniosa.

Ing: ANALOGOUS COLORS
Fr: COULEURS ANALOGUES
Al: ANALOGE FARBEN
It: COLORI ANALOGHI

Diseño: Donna S. Atwood, www.atwooddesign.com

COLORES COMPLEMENTARIOS

Colores contrarios en la **rueda de colores**, como el rojo y el verde en la rueda de colores tradicional. También denominados colores *contrastados*. La combinación de colores complementarios en un diseño puede resultar abrumadora. Normalmente se realiza una división del esquema complementario, combinando un color con los dos que flanquean a su complementario dentro de la rueda.

Ing: COMPLEMENTARY COLORS
Fr: COULEURS COMPLÉMENTAIRES
Al: KOMPLEMENTÄRFARBEN
It: COLORI COMPLEMENTARI

Diseño: Donna S. Atwood, www.atwooddesign.com

COLORES DE PROCESO
Véase: **CMYK** y **cuatricromía**.

A B **C** D E F G H I J K L M N O P Q R S T U V W X Y Z

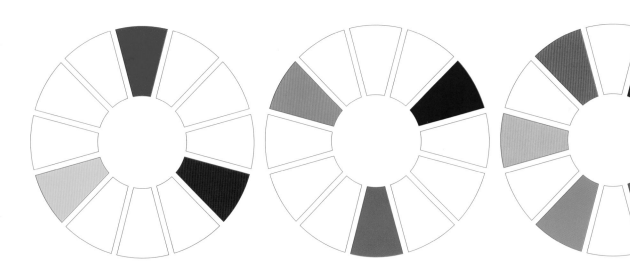

COLORES PRIMARIOS

Colores que forman los puntos clave de refe-rencia de una **rueda de colores**, distribuidos proporcionalmente sobre la circunferencia. En la rueda de colores tradicional, utilizada para la mezcla de pigmentos, los primarios son el rojo, el azul y el amarillo. Otras ruedas de colores se basan en los *colores primarios sustractivos*, cian, magenta y amarillo, o en los *colores primarios aditivos*, rojo, verde y azul. Véase: **CMYK** y **RGB**.

Ing: PRIMARY COLORS
Fr: COULEURS PRIMAIRES
Al: PRIMÄRFARBEN
It: COLORI PRIMARI

Diseño: Donna S. Atwood, www.atwooddesign.com

COLORES SECUNDARIOS

Colores (naranja, morado o verde) crea-dos por la mezcla de partes iguales de dos **colores primarios**. El naranja, por ejemplo, se crea mezclando partes iguales de amarillo y rojo. Véase: **rueda de colores** y **colores terciarios**.

Ing: SECONDARY COLORS
Fr: COULEURS SECONDAIRES
Al: SEKUNDÄRFARBEN
It: COLORI SECONDARI

Diseño: Donna S. Atwood, www.atwooddesign.com

COLORES TERCIARIOS

Colores creados por la combinación de un color **primario** y otro **secundario**. El rojo-anaranjado, por ejemplo, es el resultado de la combinación del rojo (color primario) y el naranja (color secundario creado por la mez-cla equitativa de los primarios rojo y amarillo). Véase: **rueda de colores**.

Ing: TERTIARY COLORS
Fr: COULEURS TERTIAIRES
Al: TERTIÄRFARBEN
It: COLORI TERZIARI

Diseño: Donna S. Atwood, www.atwooddesign.com

Mies van der Rohe y Sanaa

KAZUYO SEJIMA Y RYUE NISHIZAWA

BIEN SABIDO ES QUE LOS ARQUITECTOS SE EXPRESAN MEJOR A TRAVÉS DE SUS EDIFICIOS QUE MEDIANTE SUS PALABRAS. SIN EMBARGO, LOS HAY MÁS DADOS A FILOSOFAR UNA VEZ REALIZADO EL TRABAJO MATERIAL, A EXPONER SU PROPIA TEORÍA. SEGURAMENTE, KAZUYO SEJIMA (IBARAKI, 1956) Y RYUE NISHIZAWA (TOKYO, 1966), AMBOS SOCIOS DESDE 1995 Y CONOCIDOS BAJO EL NOMBRE DE SANAA, NO SE ENCUENTRAN ENTRE ELLOS. LAS ATMÓSFERAS LLENAS DE SIMPLICIDAD Y TRANSPARENCIA QUE HAN CREADO TANTO EN SUS TRABAJOS CONJUNTOS COMO EN SUS CARRERAS POR SEPARADO HABLAN POR ELLOS.

Texto: Marga Casado
Ilustración: Max-o-matic

"Los japoneses somos gente muy indirecta y podemos decir cosas a menudo difíciles de interpretar, a veces somos demasiado educados y por eso no tratamos los asuntos yendo al grano", reflexiona Ryue. ¿Quiere esto decir que su arquitectura también es indirecta y difícil de interpretar? Seguramente sí, aunque uno de sus principales empeños sea la sencillez, el esfuerzo por dejarlo todo a la vista. "Si se ve cómo una columna conecta con el muro, mucho mejor. No queremos esconder nada", aseguran.

Los dos componentes de SANAA han viajado hasta Barcelona para presentar su instalación en el Pabellón Mies van der Rohe, una espiral sinuosa que consigue crear una nueva atmósfera interior casi sin tocar el edificio. Estos arquitectos, pareja personal y profesional, tienen con Mies una relación de admiración. Y se nota. Creando paredes transparentes de material acrílico han querido sobre todo mirar y respetar el trabajo de quien fue "el mejor arquitecto", según Ryue Nishizawa. Tal vez por ello han optado por la serena semi-espiral. "La escogimos porque es una forma muy suave y también porque es la manera más simple de envolver el espacio", destaca Ryue. Su propuesta es mínima aunque de una sutil complejidad, de modo que "en el interior se han producido cambios, pero no se notan desde el exterior y, además, desde dentro sigues viendo los árboles y el espacio que rodea al pabellón", nos cuenta Sejima. La instalación dirige el movimiento del visitante por la diáfana sala obligándole a caminar en círculos, recorriendo más de una vez el mismo lugar hasta llegar a su centro, punto en el que hay que deshacer el camino andado. "Queríamos coger un espacio que admiramos y añadir algo simple que lo transfor-

mara de forma sutil", resume Kazuyo. En el interior, el diálogo entre arquitectos se extiende al mobiliario mediante algunas sillas Rabbit, una edición limitada del 2005 diseñada por SANAA para Neenmann, cuyas líneas simples comparten espacio por un tiempo con la famosa silla Barcelona de Mies van der Rohe, diseñada en 1929 para el pabellón alemán durante la Exposición Internacional.

La instalación de Barcelona, abierta hasta el próximo 18 de enero, nos trae a la memoria algunos aspectos del Glass Pavilion del Museo de Arte de Toledo (Ohio), el primer edificio diseñado por SANAA en Estados Unidos, inaugurado en el 2006. También en aquella ocasión se trataba de un edificio ubicado en un parque. Conservar las vistas de los árboles desde el interior de los arquitectos. La solución fue un único espacio cuyas paredes interiores están formadas por vidrios curvos, de manera que se asegura el contacto visual y la relación fluida entre interior y exterior. El cristal, uno de los materiales favoritos de estos arquitectos japoneses, "permite al espectador poder ver cómo se compenetran y se relacionan los espacios confundidos", algo muy importante en todas sus propuestas.

A este tándem de arquitectos volcados en mostrar lo complejo con sencillez, les interesan las construcciones de líneas simples y claras. Lo demostraron el año pasado con su nueva sede para el New Museum of Contemporary Art de Manhattan, un singular edificio compuesto por varios cubos rectangulares desencajados. Como es habitual en sus trazados, en aquella ocasión buscaron "establecer una relación entre el edificio, el museo, la calle Bowery, la ciudad de

Nueva York". Sejima y Nishizawa no se olvidaron de ofrecer un magnífico mirador sobre las vistas del Lower East Side. Con perfeccionismo japonés ellos insisten en explorar la relación de cada obra con el entorno que la acoge. "Nos gusta trabajar con espacios abiertos y encontrar el modo en que la gente pueda sentir la relación entre ellos y el edificio, y también el edificio en relación con el espacio que lo rodea".

Su proyecto de ampliación del IVAM de Valencia, iniciado en 2003 y actualmente a la espera de empezarse a construir, plantea una comunicación entre la ciudad y el Instituto de Arte Moderno a través de un cubo de acero blanco al que llaman "la piel". Esta cubierta una manzana englobando en su interior el antiguo edificio. Pero no todo son edificios públicos y de gran escala. Como señala Sejima, "no queremos hacer siempre escuelas o museos (precisamente ahora trabajan en dos proyectos en Europa, la sede del Louvre en Lens y una facultad politécnica en Lausana). Queremos variar: las casas pequeñas también tienen su complejidad y los grandes edificios tienen sus retos, y esto es lo que nos gusta, ir moviéndonos entre diferentes escalas". Hace algunos años, una joven pareja con dos niños y una abuela encargó a la arquitecta una vivienda que fuera a la vez "un refugio para la mente" y "un lugar donde disfrutar de los ciruelos floridos del jardín". De este encargo surgió la famosa Casa en un Huerto de Ciruelos de Tokio (2003). Con ella Sejima cuestionó la vigencia de la vivienda convencional proponiendo 17 compartimentaciones distintas en una superficie total que no llegaba a los 80 metros cuadrados, de modo que reducía cada habitación a un mueble o a una acción determi-

nada. Consiguió así redefinir la interrelación entre espacios y ofrecer una experiencia distinta a sus habitantes. "Nuestros proyectos siempre buscan que la gente pueda tener opciones diversas a fin de poder experimentar dentro de ellos", aseguran.

Con la Dior Store de Tokio, la Escuela de Diseño Zollverein en Essen, el Museo de Arte del Siglo XXI en Ishikawa o la Small House de Tokio, Sejima y Nishizawa siguen los pasos marcados por la generación de arquitectos japoneses compuesta por figuras de reconocimiento internacional como Tadao Ando, Arata Isozaki, Kisho Kurokawa o Toyo Ito, con quien Kazuyo empezó su carrera. "Aprendí muchísimo con él, pero al mismo tiempo han pasado tantos años que pienso que ya he cambiado bastante". A la hora de enfrentarse a un nuevo reto arquitectónico, Ryue reconoce que ambos tienen "formas diferentes de ver lo mismo, pero también compartimos muchos puntos de vista. Además, hace mucho tiempo que trabajamos juntos y en ocasiones puedo predecir lo que opinará ella, otras se queda en sólo una predicción", cuenta riéndose. "A veces pensamos cosas completamente diferentes y cuando yo digo sí, él dice no y al revés", confirma Kazuyo. En esos casos, la solución pasa por "discutir y argumentar hasta que uno de los dos se cansa y cede", confiesa Ryue.

www.sanaa.co.jp

12 13

COLUMNA

Área de una **maqueta** de página en la que se coloca el texto. Las columnas suelen formar la base de la **cuadrícula** de una maqueta. En maquetas de mucho texto se utilizan dos o más columnas. Las más utilizadas son altas y rectangulares, aunque existen muchos estilos.

Ing: COLUMN
Fr: COLONNE
Al: SATZSPALTE
It: COLONNE

Diseño: Diseño; **Compañía:** Max-o-matic, www. maxomatic.net

A B **C** D E F G H I J K L M N O P Q R S T U V W X Y Z

COMILLAS

Signo ortográfico con diversas funciones: puede indicar discurso o una cita directa dentro de un bloque de texto, o puede sugerir un uso irónico o impropio de una palabra o frase. En español hay tres tipos de comillas: las latinas (« »), las inglesas (" ") y las simples (' '). Las comillas tipográficas (o estilizadas) son diferentes de las comillas de máquina de escribir (llamadas comillas rectas). Véase: **apóstrofo**.

Ing: QUOTATION MARKS
Fr: GUILLEMETS
Al: ANFÜHRUNGSSTRICHE
It: VIRGOLETTE

COMPOSICIÓN

Término genérico que describe la organización de los elementos de una **maqueta**, cuya efectividad se expresa en términos abstractos, como **equilibrio**, **contraste**, fluidez, etc. También puede referirse a la maquetación de varios elementos.

Ing: COMPOSITION
Fr: COMPOSITION
Al: KOMPOSITION
It: COMPOSIZIONE

Diseño: La Fábrica De Diseño; **Compañía:** La Fábrica De Diseño, www.lafabricadigital.com

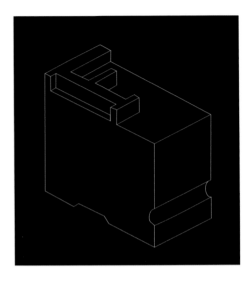

COMPOSICIÓN TIPOGRÁFICA

Disposición de los caracteres para ser impresos o leídos en pantalla. Durante siglos, la composición se realizaba con **tipos** metálicos que se componían en la imprenta. La linotipia, que apareció en 1886, aumentó la eficacia de la composición de tipos metálicos fundiendo "líneas de tipo", llamadas *lingotes*. La *fototipia*, una técnica mediante la cual las fuentes se transferían de los tipos metálicos a película fotográfica, se convirtió en la principal forma de composición tipográfica durante la década de 1960 y hasta la década de 1980, cuando empezaron a usarse tipos digitales.

Ing: TYPESETTING
Fr: COMPOSITION TYPOGRAPHIQUE
Al: SETZEN
It: COMPOSIZIONE TIPOGRAFICA

ABCDEFGHIJKLMNOPQRSTUVWXYZ

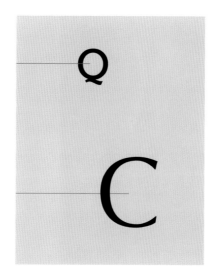

CONSTRUCTIVISMO

Movimiento artístico ruso de los años 1920 que integraba el arte y el diseño de vanguardia (especialmente elementos del Cubismo y el Futurismo) con las tendencias políticas prerrevolucionarias. Sus principales características visuales eran las formas geométricas y abstractas, el uso de la negrita, maquetaciones que rompían con las convenciones horizontal/vertical y una paleta de colores que solía limitarse al rojo, negro y blanco. También se utilizaron las técnicas del *collage* y el **fotomontaje**, tomadas del **Dada**, para crear diseños potentes de comunicación visual.

Ing: CONSTRUCTIVISM
Fr: CONSTRUCTIVISME
Al: KONSTRUKTIVISMUS
It: COSTRUTTIVISMO

Diseño: Pietari Posti, Typography by Underware;
Compañía: Pietari Posti, www.pposti.com

CONTRAFORMA

Espacio cerrado en una **letra**. Puede estar totalmente cerrado, como en la letra *o*, o solo en parte, como en la letra *c*. A veces este término se puede utilizar para indicar el espacio entre dos letras adyacentes. Véase: **espacio negativo**.

Ing: COUNTER
Fr: CONTREPOINÇON
Al: PUNZE
It: OCCHIELLO

CONTRASTE

Diferencia entre dos elementos de diseño. Un **tipo** más grande, por ejemplo, puede ser utilizado para contrastar con un tipo de menor tamaño, consiguiendo un contraste mayor cuanto mayor sea la diferencia de tamaños. Utilizado adecuadamente, el contraste puede crear **maquetas** muy atractivas. Para crear contraste se pueden utilizar elementos como la textura, el color, la forma o el grosor de línea, entre otros. Véase: **equilibrio**, **colores complementarios** y **relación figura-fondo**.

Ing: CONTRAST
Fr: CONTRASTE
Al: KONTRAST
It: CONTRASTO

Diseño: Bendita Gloria (Alba Rosell + Santi Fuster);
Compañía: Bendita Gloria, www.benditagloria.com

A B **C** D E F G H I J K L M N O P Q R S T U V W X Y Z

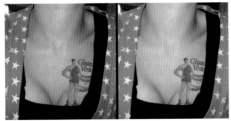

CUADRATÍN **PTO**

CORRECCIÓN DE COLOR

Proceso de modificación del color en una fotografía digital o una imagen escaneada para conseguir una representación más nítida del contenido original o para ajustar la gama de color (o *gamut*) de la tecnología de impresión empleada.

Ing: COLOR CORRECTION
Fr: CORRECTION DES COULEURS
Al: FARBKORREKTUR
It: CORREZIONE DEI COLORI

CORTE LÁSER

Proceso de corte o grabado de papel, madera, plástico y algunos metales mediante un láser de alta potencia dirigido por ordenador. Es un tipo de corte muy preciso, que proporciona un mayor nivel de detalle que el del **troquelado** convencional. Además, como no requiere el uso de piezas metálicas, para los procesos de producción pequeños resulta más económico y conveniente que el troquelado. Sin embargo, el coste puede aumentar considerablemente en trabajos de corte de gran detalle o cuando se trabaja con materiales difíciles, como los que se deshacen o se queman con facilidad, los muy gruesos, etc.

Ing: LASER CUT
Fr: DÉCOUPE AU LASER
Al: LASERSCHNITT
It: TAGLIO AL LASER

Diseño: David López at Campaña; **Compañía:** Campaña, www.suscreativos.com

CROMA
Véase: **saturación**.

CUADRATÍN

Unidad de medida relativa del mismo tamaño que el **tipo** que se va a utilizar, expresada en **puntos**. Para tipos de 12 puntos, un cuadratín mide 12 puntos, para tipos de 10 puntos mide 10, etc. El cuadratín, en realidad, corresponde a la altura (o *cuerpo*) de las piezas metálicas que se utilizan para la impresión de un tipo. Un cuadratín es un espaciador metálico cuadrado de la misma altura y anchura que se usa para crear un **espacio de cuadratín**. Todos los cuerpos del mismo tamaño de punto tienen la misma altura, pero la altura de las **letras** varía considerablemente según el tipo, por lo que el cuadratín está únicamente relacionado vagamente con el tamaño real de tipo para una **fuente** específica. Esta relación se pierde aún más con los tipos digitales, en los que no existe el referente físico. Véase: raya, espacio de cuadratín. Véase: **raya**, **espacio de cuadratín** y **pica**.

Ing: EM
Fr: CADRATIN
Al: GEVIERT
It: EM

A **C** D E F G H I J K L M N O P Q R S T U V W X Y Z

CUADRÍCULA

Red de líneas entrecruzadas, normalmente en dirección horizontal y vertical, utilizada para organizar los elementos de un diseño y dar una estructura lógica a una maqueta. Es una herramienta muy útil para proyectos de gran tamaño, ya que permite a los diseñadores un trabajo más eficiente, evitando decisiones arbitrarias. Su utilización es muy criticada porque inhibe la creatividad y el pensamiento crítico. Sin embargo, utilizada correctamente, una cuadrícula sirve de "andamio" de una maqueta, proporcionando una estructura de apoyo que permite que el diseñador trabaje con mayor libertad, y no al revés.

Ing: GRID
Fr: GRILLE
Al: RASTER (SATZSPIEGEL)
It: GRIGLIA

Diseño: Damià Rotger Miró; **Compañía:** Dúctil, www.ductilct.com

CUATRICROMÍA

Técnica de impresión en el que se realiza una aproximación al espectro completo del color mediante *pantallas de medio tono*, llamadas *separaciones de color*, para cada uno de los cuatro colores de proceso: cian, magenta, amarillo y negro. Cada color se imprime como un patrón de pequeños puntos de tamaño y densidad variables. Como los cuatro **colores de proceso**, al combinarse en parejas, crean los colores primarios aditivos (rojo, amarillo y azul), que corresponden a los tres tipos de receptores de luz que posee el ojo humano, el efecto general de color total es bastante bueno. Véase **CMYK** y **medio tono**.

Ing: FOUR-COLOR PROCESS
Fr: QUADRICHROMIE
Al: VIERFARBDRUCK
It: PROCESSO A QUATTRO COLORI

CUBISMO

Movimiento artístico europeo de vanguardia de principios de siglo XX (entre 1907 y 1920) en el se jugaba con la abstracción geométrica de los objetos y la figura humana. Se presentaban perspectivas múltiples de forma simultánea, en dos dimensiones en vez de en tres, desafiando las leyes de la perspectiva vigentes desde el Renacimiento. Gracias a su influencia, el diseño gráfico empezó a experimentar con la composición espacial y la abstracción geométrica.

Ing: CUBISM
Fr: CUBISME
Al: KUBISMUS
It: CUBISMO

Diseño: Andi Rivas; **Compañía:** RD2 Art Direction & Contemporary Graphic Design, www.andirivas.com

A B **C** D E F G H I J K L M N O P Q R S T U V W X Y Z

CUERPO DE TEXTO

Término tradicionalmente utilizado para denominar el texto principal de un libro, folleto u otra publicación. En este sentido, el cuerpo de texto excluye las **páginas preliminares**, las **referenciales**, los títulos, titulares, **subtítulos**, etc. También puede referirse al texto principal de un sitio web.

Ing: BODY COPY
Fr: CORPS DU TEXTE
Al: FLIESSTEXT
It: CORPO DEL TESTO

Diseño: Max-o-matic; **Compañía:** Max-o-matic, www. maxomatic.net

optima
optima cursiva

GARAMOND

GARAMOND CURSIVA

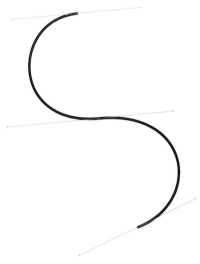

CURSIVA

Letra inclinada a la derecha, utilizada para recalcar una parte de un texto. La cursiva, también llamada *itálica*, se desarrolló en Italia sobre el 1500 para que cupieran más letras en una página y así reducir el tamaño de los libros. Los *True italic* son conjuntos de **letras** distintas del **tipo** en el que se basan. El **tipo oblicuo** también se inclina hacia la derecha, pero las letras prácticamente no se distinguen de las redondas del mismo tipo.

Ing: ITALIC
Fr: ITALIQUE
Al: KURSIV
It: CORSIVO

CURVA DE BÉZIER

Aproximación matemática a una curva continua, definida por sus dos puntos de anclaje (uno a cada extremo) y cualquier número de puntos de control a lo largo de ella. Los **trazados** que utilizan la mayoría de las aplicaciones de software de diseño gráfico están formados por múltiples curvas de Bézier, razón por la cual pueden ampliarse indefinidamente. Las curvas de Bézier también pueden ser utilizadas como herramientas de control de movimiento para la **animación**.

Ing: BÉZIER CURVE
Fr: COURBE DE BÉZIER
Al: BÉZIERKURVE
It: CURVA DI BÉZIER

Diseño: Donna S. Atwood, www.atwooddesign.com

DADA

Movimiento artístico nacido como reacción a la Primera Guerra Mundial. Se inició en Zúrich, Suiza, y después se expandió por el resto de Europa. El Dada cuestionaba muchas creencias tradicionales sobre el arte, la moralidad o la religión, a través de una estética provocativa e incluso absurda (aunque en Alemania, el dadaísmo adquirió un tono más oscuro y politizado cuando Hitler llegó al poder en la década de 1930). Las artes gráficas dadaístas tuvieron una gran influencia, por ejemplo, en el enfoque organizativo del **Constructivismo** o del **De Stijl** y en la energía pura del *collage* o el **fotomontaje**, cuya invención reivindicaron.

Ing: DADA
Fr: DADA
Al: DADAISMUS
It: DADA

Diseño: Cless, INK by Picnic Editorial; **Compañía:** Cless, www.cless.info

A B C **D** E F G H I J K L M N O P Q R S T U V W X Y Z

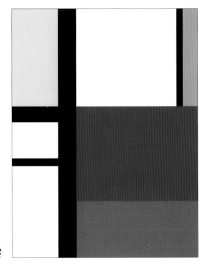

Partes de letras por debajo de la línea base

DEGRADADO

Mezcla gradual de un **color** en otro, o de blanco a negro hasta conseguir un color saturado, generalmente en gradaciones uniformes. Los degradados se usan para llenar partes de ilustraciones, fondos o **tipos abiertos**.

Ing: GRADIENT
Fr: DÉGRADÉ
Al: VERLAUF
It: GRADIENTE/I

Diseño: Maja Denzer & Txell Gràcia; **Compañía:** Gestaltica, www.gestaltica.de

DESCENDENTE

Parte de una **letra** de *caja baja* que sobrepasa la **línea de base** por debajo. Como en el caso de los **ascendentes**, su tamaño y peso relativos varían según el **tipo**. Véase: **ascendente**.

Ing: DESCENDER
Fr: DESCENDANTE
Al: UNTERLÄNGE
It: TRATTO DISCENDENTE

DE STIJL

Movimiento artístico y de diseño nacido en Holanda a principios del siglo XX (1917-1931) que pretendía expresar las leyes universales mediante un lenguaje visual objetivo. El uso de colores se limitaba a los neutros (blanco, negro y gris) y los primarios (rojo, azul y amarillo). Las formas empleadas eran cuadrados y rectángulos colocados de manera asimétrica sobre líneas horizontales y verticales. Utilizaban la tipografía **sans serif**, a menudo combinada con la **titular**.

Ing: DE STIJL
Fr: DE STIJL
Al: DE STIJL
It: DE STIJL

A B C **D** E F G H I J K L M N O P Q R S T U V W X Y Z

Zapt dingbats

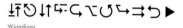
Webdings

Wingdings

IKUSIMAKUSI

DIFUMINADO

Método de aproximación de los colores verdaderos de una imagen digital mediante la utilización de los colores disponibles en una **paleta de colores** determinada. Para convertir una imagen digital en color a colores seguros para web, se utiliza un conjunto específico de 216 colores (la *paleta de colores seguros para Web*) que ajustan los colores de la imagen original. Este proceso se realiza mediante un mosaico, que puede ser de píxeles (para monitores de ordenadores) o de puntos (para impresoras digitales). Por ejemplo, se puede crear un mosaico de píxeles o puntos rojos y amarillos para crear una aproximación al naranja. A pesar de que en el proceso se pierde nitidez, puede ser muy útil para suavizar los bordes dentados que pueden aparecer a lo largo de campos de color adyacentes. Véase: **posterización**.

Ing: DITHER
Fr: TRAMAGE ALÉATOIRE
Al: DITHERING
It: RETINO

Diseño: FAMMILIA; **Compañía:** FAMMILIA, www.fammilia.com

DINGBATS

Gama de caracteres tipográficos especiales, como los **símbolos** (p. ej., signos matemáticos, de puntuación, etc.), **bolos** (p. ej., círculos, estrellas, etc.), diversos adornos gráficos, etc.

Ing: DINGBATS
Fr: DINGBATS
Al: DINGBATS
It: DINGBATS

DISEÑO DE EMBALAJE

Desde el punto de vista de un diseñador gráfico, el diseño de embalaje supone la creación de cajas que protejan y muestren los productos durante las etapas de distribución, almacenaje, venta y uso. Los **logos**, **logotipos** y otros elementos visuales (y táctiles) del *branding*, tienen un papel importantísimo en el diseño de embalajes, aunque las primeras consideraciones pueden ser puramente estéticas. Existen otros factores a tener en cuenta, como la seguridad (en los frascos de medicinas con cierre de seguridad para niños), factores económicos (cálculo del número de cajas que cabrán en un contenedor de transporte) y facilidad de uso (permitiendo que la experiencia de apertura del paquete para el usuario final sea fácil), entre otros.

Ing: PACKAGING DESIGN
Fr: DESIGN DE PACKAGING
Al: VERPACKUNGSDESIGN
It: PACKAGING DESIGN

Diseño: José Jimenez Valladares; Valladares Diseño y Comunicación; **Compañía:** Valladares Diseño y Comunicación, www.valladaresdc.net

A B C **D** E F G H I J K L M N O P Q R S T U V W X Y Z

DISEÑO INTERACTIVO

Práctica de describir, definir y crear elementos de un producto, sistema u organización con los que una persona puede interactuar. Los ejemplos más comunes suelen requerir interfaces tecnológicas complejas, como las de los sitios web o los dispositivos electrónicos portátiles, aunque incluso la interacción más sencilla requiere un diseño muy estudiado. El asa de una taza suele diseñarse para que tenga un uso intuitivo y sencillo. Los profesionales del diseño interactivo tienen que realizar una gran labor de investigación del usuario y aplicar métodos de otras disciplinas, como la psicología cognitiva o la antropología.

Ing: INTERACTION DESIGN
Fr: DESIGN NUMÉRIQUE
Al: INTERAKTIVES DESIGN
It: DESIGN INTERATTIVO

Diseño: Rubengarcia-Castro.com 2009; **Compañía:** RubenGarcia-Castro, www.rubengarcia-castro.com

DOBLADO TIPO ROLLO

Sistema de plegado que consiste en realizar pliegues paralelos alternos sobre una hoja de papel de manera que los paneles resultantes se plieguen o enrollen unos sobre otros. Para que todos los paneles encajen, los exteriores se van haciendo más anchos (medidos de pliegue a pliegue o de borde a pliegue) a medida que se van plegando. Véase: **plegado en acordeón**.

Ing: BARREL FOLD
Fr: PLI ROULÉ
Al: WICKELFALZ
It: PIEGHEVOLE A PORTAFOGLIO

Diseño: Andreas Hidber & Rubén García-Castro; **Compañía:** Andreas Hidber + Rubén García-Castro, www.rubengarcia-castro.com

DOBLE PÁGINA

Páginas enfrentadas de una publicación encuadernada. Véase: **recto/verso**.

Ing: SPREAD
Fr: DOUBLE PAGE

Diseño: Max-o-matic; **Photo:** Meli-k; **Compañía:** Max-o-matic, www. maxomatic.net

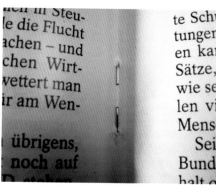

EGIPCIO

Tipo **slab-serif**. Su aspecto robusto y la mínima variación del peso del trazado lo convierten en un tipo adecuado para pósters, anuncios y titulares más que para su uso dentro el **cuerpo de texto**.

Ing: EGYPTIAN
Fr: ÉGYPTIENNE
Al: EGYPTIENNE
It: CARATTERI EGIZIANI

Diseño: ANDREU BALIUS; **Compañía:** TYPEREPUBLIC, www.typerepublic.com

ENCUADERNACIÓN

Método de unión de las páginas de un libro, revista, folleto o cualquier otra publicación impresa con un gran número de páginas. Algunos métodos de encuadernación, como la de anillas o la de canutillo, utilizan grapas que se colocan en una serie de agujeros realizados en cada página y, por tanto, no son permanentes. Los métodos de encuadernación permanente son: **encuadernación en tapa dura**, **a la americana** y **a caballete**.

Ing: BINDING
Fr: RELIURE
Al: EINBAND
It: RILEGATURA

Diseño: Ibán Ramón Rodríguez; **Compañía:** Estudio Ibán ramón, www.ibanramon.com

ENCUADERNACIÓN A CABALLETE

Tipo de **encuadernación** permanente utilizada en folletos y algunas revistas. Los **pliegos** y las cubiertas se unen por el lomo, se grapan y luego se recortan.

Ing: SADDLE-STITCH BINDING
Fr: PIQÛRE MÉTALLIQUE À CHEVAL
Al: DRAHTHEFTUNG
It: GRAFFETTATURA

A B C D **E** F G H I J K L M N O P Q R S T U V W X Y Z

ENCUADERNACIÓN A LA AMERICANA

Tipo de **encuadernación** permanente utilizada para ediciones en rústica en las que los **pliegos** se unen como en un *fruncido* (de manera secuencial), se raspan los bordes por los que se han de encuadernar y se pegan por el lomo a la cubierta, de hoja única, con un adhesivo flexible.

Ing: PERFECT BINDING
Fr: RELIURE SANS COUTURE
Al: KLEBEBINDUNG
It: RILEGATURA PERFETTA

Diseño: F33, www.f33.es

ENCUADERNACIÓN EN TAPA DURA

Método de **encuadernación** permanente, utilizada principalmente para libros de tapa dura. Se realiza mediante el cosido con hilo de los **pliegos** por el lomo, que posteriormente se encola. Una vez realizado esto se recortan los bordes y se le pega una cubierta.

Ing: CASE BINDING
Fr: RELIURE CARTONNÉE
Al: BUCHEINBAND
It: CARTONATURA

Diseño: Bendita Gloria (Alba Rosell + Santi Fuster) in collaboration with AGOrient; **Compañía:** Bendita Gloria, www.benditagloria.com

EQUILIBRIO

Relación visual entre elementos de un diseño dentro de un contexto concreto. Se dice que una **maqueta** está equilibrada cuando la forma, proporción, textura, **color** y **valor** de cada elemento consiguen crear una armonía visual. A pesar de eso, un diseño equilibrado no tiene por qué ser conservador. De hecho, un buen diseñador puede jugar con el equilibrio para activar espacios que cubran todo el diseño, creando una experiencia más enriquecedora para el público.

Ing: BALANCE
Fr: ÉQUILIBRE
Al: BALANCE (AUSGEWOGENHEIT)
It: BILANCIAMENTO

Diseño: RD2 (Andi Rivas) TORO Osborne Spain; **Compañía:** RD2 Art Direction & Contemporary Graphic Design, www.andirivas.com

A B C D **E** F G H I J K L M N O P Q R S T U V W X Y Z

ESCALA

Tamaño o "peso" de un elemento del diseño en relación con los demás dentro de una misma **maqueta**. La escala puede ser fácilmente diferenciada, como cuando se utiliza un **tipo** más grande para indicar qué partes del texto son más importantes, aunque muchas veces las diferencias de escala son muy sutiles. Los objetos de formas diferentes, por ejemplo, suelen transportarse a escalas diferentes aunque ocupen geométricamente una misma área. La forma y el color también influyen en la escala de un elemento, al igual que el contexto; la escala de un objeto depende de su entorno.

Ing: SCALE
Fr: ÉCHELLE
Al: GRÖSSENVERHÄLTNIS
It: SCALA

Diseño: Damià Rotger Miró; **Compañía:** Dúctil, www.ductilct.com

ESCALA DE GRISES

Imagen compuesta por tonos variables de gris, blanco y negro. Las fotografías en color pueden convertirse digitalmente en imágenes en escala de grises mediante aplicaciones de *software* que traducen el **valor** de cada punto a su equivalente en gris, creando una imagen que imita la fotografía en blanco y negro.
Véase: **monocromático**.

Ing: GRAYSCALE
Fr: ÉCHELLE DE GRIS
Al: GRAUSTUFENBILD
It: SCALA DEI GRIGI

Diseño: Damià Rotger Miró, fotoclub f/llum;
Compañía: Dúctil, www.ductilct.com

ESPACIO BLANCO

Áreas de una **maqueta** que quedan en blanco, aunque no sean de color blanco. Estos espacios son tan importantes en un diseño como el resto de elementos de diseño. Son un elemento activo, no pasivo. De hecho, el uso adecuado de los espacios blancos crea una estructura y mantiene el sentido del **ritmo** y el **equilibrio** en una maqueta de la misma manera que los **espacios positivos y negativos** dan energía a las relaciones entre los elementos del diseño.
Véase: **cuadrícula**.

Ing: WHITE SPACE
Fr: BLANCS
Al: WEISSRAUM
It: SPAZIO BIANCO

Diseño: Subcoolture, in collaboration with AA Records;
Compañía: Subcoolture, www.subcoolture.com

ESPACIO CROMÁTICO
Véase: **modelo de color**.

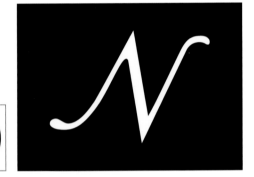

ESPACIO DE CUADRATÍN

Espacio de anchura equivalente a un **cuadratín**. Las **fuentes** digitales incluyen este espacio como carácter especial de anchura fija, a diferencia de los creados mediante la barra espaciadora, que varían según la composición de línea creada por el *software*.

Ing: EM SPACE
Fr: ESPACE CADRATIN
Al: GEVIERTABSTAND
It: SPAZIO EM

ESPACIO DE MEDIO CUADRATÍN

Espacio de anchura equivalente a medio cuadratín. Igual que para el espacio de **cuadratín**, las **fuentes** digitales disponen de un carácter específico. Debido a su anchura fija, el espacio de medio cuadratín permanece invariable en la composición de línea del *software*, mientras que los creados por la barra espaciadora tienen una anchura variable.

Ing: EN SPACE
Fr: ESPACE DEMI-CADRATIN
Al: HALBGEVIERTABSTAND
It: SPAZIO EN

ESPACIO NEGATIVO

Vacío creado por la relación entre dos o más elementos del diseño y el **espacio positivo** al que van asociados. Suele utilizarse para describir aspectos de grandes **maquetas**, pero también se puede utilizar para describir elementos de **tipografía**, donde las **letras** generan relaciones de **espacios positivos** y negativos con las letras vecinas. Los **logos**, como suelen ser de pequeño tamaño, se diseñan teniendo muy en cuenta a la relación entre espacios positivo y negativo. Véase: **relación figura-fondo** y **espacio blanco**.

Ing: NEGATIVE SPACE
Fr: ESPACE NÉGATIF
Al: FREIE FLÄCHE
It: SPAZIO NEGATIVO

A B C D **E F** G H I J K L M N O P Q R S T U V W X Y Z

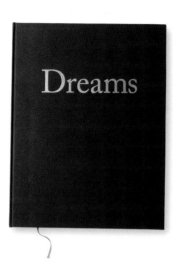

Myriad Pro

Myriad Pro Bold

Myriad Pro Bold Condensed

Myriad Pro Bold Condensed Italic

Myriad Pro Bold Italic

Myriad Pro Condensed

Myriad Pro Condensed Italic

Myriad Pro Italic

Myriad Pro Semibold

Myriad Pro Semibold Italic

ESPACIO POSITIVO

Área o áreas de una maqueta o elementos del diseño individuales en los que hay una forma (los vacíos resultantes se llaman **espacio negativo**). Aunque el espacio positivo se usa mucho para describir aspectos de **maquetaciones** completas, también puede usarse para describir aspectos relacionados con la **tipografía**, donde las letras generan relaciones de espacios positivos y negativos con las letras contiguas. Los **logos**, al ser normalmente de tamaño reducido, suelen diseñarse prestando especial atención a la relación entre espacio positivo y negativo. Véase: **espacio negativo**, **relación figura-fondo** y **espacio blanco**.

Ing: POSITIVE SPACE
Fr: ESPACE POSITIF
Al: GESTALTETE FLÄCHE
It: SPAZIO POSITIVO

ESTAMPADO METÁLICO

Proceso de fundido de una delgada lámina de plástico sobre un papel mediante un dado metálico caliente. Se utiliza para resaltar **logos**, ilustraciones, **tipos** u otros elementos del diseño. Las láminas de plástico pueden ser de muchos colores y lustres e incluso tener acabados metálicos. Se pueden utilizar láminas opacas para aplicar un color suave sobre un fondo oscuro, o láminas translúcidas para imitar un **barniz**. También llamado *estampado en caliente*

Ing: FOIL STAMPING
Fr: DORURE
Al: FOLIENPRÄGUNG
It: STAMPA A LAMINA DI PLASTICA

Diseño: Bisgràfic; **Compañía:** Bisgràfic, www.bisgrafic.com

FAMILIA TIPOGRÁFICA

Variaciones de un **tipo de letra** concreto, como la **negrita**, la **cursiva**, la **condensada**, la expandida, etc. El amplio abanico de "miembros" de una familia es el resultado del *boom* de la publicidad del siglo XIX y la consecuente demanda de tipografías distintivas. Véase: **set experto**.

Ing: TYPE FAMILY
Fr: FAMILLE DE CARACTÈRES
Al: SCHRIFTFAMILIE
It: FAMIGLIA DI CARATTERI

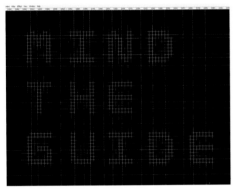

FILETE

Línea que en tipografía se usa para separar un elemento de una **maqueta** de otro, organizando el espacio y creando un sentido de **jerarquía**. El grosor de un filete se expresa en **puntos**.

Ing: RULE
Fr: FILET
Al: LINIE
It: FILETTO TIPOGRAFICO

Diseño: Luis Princep Fabra; **Compañía:** DEFERE, www.defere.com

FORMA-CONTRAFORMA

Véase **espacio positivo** y **espacio negativo**.

FOTOCOMPOSICIÓN

Imagen creada por la combinación de otras imágenes o elementos de otras imágenes. A diferencia del *collage*, que hace referencia a una obra de arte, o del **fotomontaje**, que es únicamente una combinación de elementos fotográficos, la *fotocomposición* hace referencia a una única fotografía o ilustración dentro de una obra creativa más grande.

Ing: COMPOSITE
Fr: IMAGE COMPOSITE
Al: BILDMONTAGE (COMPOSING)
It: COMPOSITE

Diseño: Bendita Gloria (Alba Rosell + Santi Fuster); **Compañía:** Bendita Gloria, www.benditagloria.com

FOTOMONTAJE

Proceso de creación de una **composición** fotográfica mediante la combinación de elementos de diferentes fotografías. El resultado, que también se llama *fotomontaje*, se realiza cortando y pegando, tanto en sentido literal como mediante la utilización de un *software* de edición digital. Los fotomontajes creados a mano a veces se fotografían una vez completados, dando la sensación de ser una fotografía "real". Los términos *fotomontaje y montaje* se usan indistintamente. Véase: *collage*.

Ing: PHOTOMONTAGE
Fr: PHOTOMONTAGE
Al: FOTOMONTAGE
It: FOTOMONTAGGIO

Diseño: Diego Feijóo, Shau Chung Shin; **Compañía:** Studio Diego Feijóo, www.dfeijoo.com

A B C D E **F** G H I J K L M N O P Q R S T U V W X Y Z

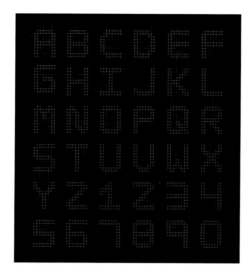

FPO (SÓLO PARA REFERENCIA DE POSICIÓN)

Imagen de calidad inferior, a menudo una versión de la imagen final a menor resolución, que sirve como marcador de posición en una **maqueta**. Las imágenes se marcan como FPO para que todo el equipo de diseño conozca su función.

Ing: FOR POSITION ONLY (FPO)
Fr: IMAGE DE PLACEMENT
Al: PLATZHALTER
It: FOR POSITION ONLY (FPO)

FUENTE

Fuente física o digital que se utiliza para crear **tipos**. Está compuesta por letras de *caja alta* y de *caja baja*, numerales y signos de puntuación, aunque muchos *OpenType* incluyen actualmente caracteres especiales que antiguamente formaban parte de los **set experto**. En los tipos metálicos, las fuentes son de tamaño único, pero los tipos digitales pueden cambiar de tamaño. Fuente y tipo son dos términos que suelen confundirse. Cuando se habla de tipo se hace referencia al diseño global de un conjunto de caracteres, mientras que las fuentes son los medios de producción, ya sean físicos o digitales.

Ing: FONT
Fr: FONTE
Al: SCHRIFTSATZ
It: FONT

Diseño: Luis Princep Fabra; **Compañía:** DEFERE, www.defere.com

FUTURISMO

Movimiento artístico europeo muy radical de la primera parte del siglo XX (1909-1930), desarrollado principalmente en Italia. El futurismo pretendía integrar la velocidad y el ruido de la era de las máquinas en el arte y el diseño. Para expresar esta energía se utilizaban el ***collage***, el **fotomontaje** y otras técnicas que sugerían el movimiento cinemático. La mayor aportación del futurismo al diseño gráfico, sin embargo, fue la utilización de los **tipos** para crear un impacto visual. En una misma **maqueta** se utilizaban múltiples tipos en diferentes tamaños, a veces situados en ángulos extraños o distorsionados. La **negrita** y la **cursiva** creaban acentos de expresión.

Ing: FUTURISM
Fr: FUTURISME
Al: FUTURISMUS
It: FUTURISMO

Diseño: Pietari Posti; **Compañía:** Pietari Posti, www.pposti.com

GOFRAR

Crear una impresión sobre un papel colocándola entre dos cubos metálicos, uno con una marca en positivo y el otro con otra en negativo. La impresión puede ser en relieve o en hueco. Los mejores papeles para crear este efecto son los de gramaje medio, especialmente los de acabados texturados. Muchas veces se utilizan imágenes o **estampados metálicos** como embellecedores. Cuando no se utilizan se llama *gofrado ciego*.

Ing: EMBOSS
Fr: GAUFRAGE
Al: PRÄGUNG
It: GOFFRATURA

Diseño: Damià Rotger Miró; **Compañía:** Dúctil, www.ductilct.com

GRÁFICOS RASTERIZADOS
Véase: **mapa de bits**.

A B C D E F **G** H I J K L M N O P Q R S T U V W X Y Z

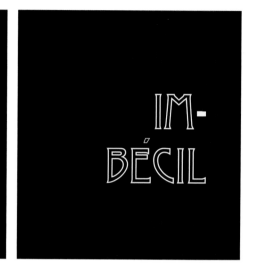

GRÁFICO VECTORIAL

Imagen digital creada mediante formas definidas matemáticamente, en lugar de las colecciones de muestras que se usan en los **mapas de bits**. Esta propiedad permite que los gráficos vectoriales puedan agrandarse sin perder **resolución**. Los mapas de bits, por otra parte, alcanzan unos niveles de detalle y variación de tonos que no alcanzan los gráficos vectoriales. Véase: **curva de Bézier**.

Ing: VECTOR GRAPHIC
Fr: IMAGES VECTORIELLES
Al: VEKTORGRAFIK
It: GRAFICA VETTORIALE

Diseño: Antonio Guzmán; **Compañía:** Domodo estudio, www.domodoestudio.com

GREEKING

Texto sin sentido o monstruo que se utiliza en maquetación como marcador. También hace referencia a la manera en que algunas aplicaciones de maquetación utilizan líneas en gris para representar líneas de **tipo** demasiado pequeñas para ser visualizadas en un dispositivo. También llamado **Lorem Ipsum**.

Ing: GREEKING
Fr: FAUX TEXTE
Al: BLINDTEXT

GUIÓN

Signo ortográfico, que no debe confundirse con la raya o la semirraya, de usos diferentes. En español, el guión se utiliza para la partición silábica a final de línea, para crear palabras compuestas y para unir otras combinaciones gráficas.

Ing: HYPHEN
Fr: TRAIT D'UNION
Al: TRENNSTRICH
It: TRATTINO

A B C D E F G **H I** J K L M N O P Q R S T U V W X Y Z

Este texto está justificado pero no tiene aplicada la par-tición silábica por lo que los bordes están alineados pero   quedan espacios entre   palabras.

¿Que imagen y sonidos se recrean en nuestra mente cuando pensamos en un entorno natural? ¿Árboles, pájaros?

Desde mi punto de vista, la actual concepción del entorno natural, se ha distorsionado hasta el extremo de haber asimilado dicho medio como un espacio más de consumo.

Esto supone notables consecuencias en nuestra interpretación de dicho entorno.

Lo que me llama la atención de este fenómeno es como influye esta interpretación del entorno natural en las creaciones del hombre, como por ejemplo en arquitectura, diseño, ciencia

y arte.

Esta consecuente interpretación constituye uno de los factores que conforman la teoría de la sociedad del simulacro, la primacía de los símbolos sobre las cosas.

Pero, cuando la realidad no es lo que se puede reproducir sino lo reproducido, ¿cómo es su representación?

1. DO NOT TOUCH   2. DO NOT TAKE PICTURES   3. DO NOT RECOGNIZE

H&J

Abreviatura de *Hyphenation & Justification* (partición silábica y justificación), el proceso por el cual las aplicaciones de *software* llenan las líneas con **tipos**. Independientemente de si el texto está **alineado a la derecha**, **a la izquierda**, **justificado** o **centrado**, el *software* llena automáticamente cada línea por toda su extensión con una combinación de caracteres y espacios. Esto se llama *justificación* (término que suele utilizarse únicamente para describir las líneas de tipo que llenan totalmente su extensión). La *partición silábica* es el corte de palabras necesario para que cada línea de tipo quede completa. Las aplicaciones avanzadas de maquetación permiten ajustar varios parámetros de *H&J*, proporcionando al diseñador la flexibilidad necesaria para crear tipografía elegante. Véase: **justificación**.

Ing: H&J
Fr: C&J
Al: SILBENTRENNUNG & BLOCKSATZ
     (S&B)
It: H&J

HUÉRFANA

Una o dos líneas de un párrafo que quedan separadas del párrafo principal en una **columna** de texto, situadas en la parte inferior (si empiezan el párrafo) o en la superior (si lo finalizan). Las huérfanas se pueden evitar mediante diversas técnicas, como el **interletraje** y la **partición silábica**. Véase: **viuda**.
HUÉRFANA

Ing: ORPHAN
Fr: ORPHELINE
Al: SCHUSTERJUNGE
It: ORFANO

ICONO

Signo gráfico que mantiene una relación de semejanza con lo que representa. El icono de impresión de una pantalla de ordenador es una impresora. Otros ejemplos pueden ser el gráfico de un cigarrillo en las señales de *prohibido fumar* y el icono de una maleta utilizado en los aeropuertos para indicar el lugar de recogida de equipajes. Esta relación de semejanza hace que sean fácilmente reconocibles, salvando incluso barreras lingüísticas o culturales. Véase: **símbolo** y **pictograma**.

Ing: ICON
Fr: ICÔNE
Al: BILDZEICHEN
It: ICONA

Diseño: Paz Tornero; **Compañía:** Paz Tornero, paz.tornero@gmail.com

A B C D E F G H **I** J K L M N O P Q R S T U V W X Y Z

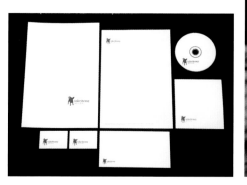

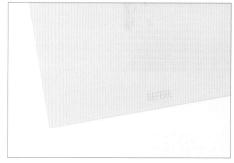

IDENTIDAD

Personalidad de una empresa, expresada de manera visual (tanto interna como externamente) gracias a su ***branding*** distintivo. Dentro del *paquete de identidad* se encuentran **logos**, logotipos, **paletas de colores** (a menudo determinadas por un **sistema de ajuste de color**), **maquetas** estándar para documentos y embalaje y las directrices de uso de cada elemento para mantener la coherencia. Las corporaciones de gran tamaño pueden tener diferentes marcas que comparten elementos visuales comunes, conectando cada una de las marcas con un sistema de identidad corporativo mayor.

Ing: IDENTITY
Fr: IDENTITÉ
Al: FIRMENERSCHEINUNGSBILD
It: IDENTITÀ

Diseño: Ismael Medina/ Sebas Cangiano; **Compañía:** Virgen Extra, www. virgen-extra.com

IMPOSICIÓN

Orden cuidadoso de múltiples páginas de una publicación para su impresión en hojas de gran tamaño. Mediante este proceso se asegura que las páginas estén correctamente orientadas y en el orden adecuado una vez impresas, dobladas en **pliegos** y encuadernadas. Se puede realizar a mano, aunque actualmente se utilizan aplicaciones de *software*. Véase: **paginación**.

Ing: IMPOSITION
Fr: IMPOSITION
Al: AUSSCHIESSEN
It: IMPOSIZIONE TIPOGRAFICA

Diseño: Bendita Gloria (Alba Rosell + Santi Fuster); **Compañía:** Bendita Gloria, www.benditagloria.com

IMPRESIÓN TIPOGRÁFICA

Proceso de *impresión en relieve* nacido en el siglo XV, en Alemania, momento de invención de la imprenta. Se realiza colocando en la imprenta los bloques de **tipo** y las ilustraciones, que se componen en negativo para que se puedan leer correctamente una vez transferidas al papel. Se cubre la superficie con tinta y se imprime sobre un papel. Antiguamente, la impresión se realizaba mediante tipos metálicos o de madera, pero actualmente se lleva a cabo en planchas de polímero creadas a partir de archivos digitales. Las nuevas tecnologías han conseguido que se realicen incluso operaciones de imprenta de tamaños reducidos, produciendo una variedad de diseños sin precedentes, así como la resurrección de un arte que parecía en vías de extinción.

Ing: LETTERPRESS
Fr: IMPRESSION TYPOGRAPHIQUE
Al: HOCHDRUCK
It: RILIEVOGRAFIA

Diseño: Luis Princep Fabra; **Compañía:** DEFERE, www.defere.com

A B C D E F G H **I** J K L M N O P Q R S T U V W X Y Z

ESPACIADO

E S P A C I A D O

Kyjn
Kyjn

INTERLINEADO
NEGATIVO

IMPRIMIR "A SANGRE"

Impresión de un elemento de diseño, como una imagen, una línea de tipo, un campo de color, etc., que sobrepasa el tamaño de página. Las marcas de corte se utilizan para indicar el tamaño real de página; por lo que todo lo que se imprima fuera de estas marcas "sangrará" por fuera de la página. El tamaño necesario para imprimir algo "a sangre" dependerá de la precisión de la impresora y del material de corte.

Ing: BLEED
Fr: FONDS PERDUS
Al: BESCHNITT
It: STAMPA AL VIVO

Diseño: Max-o-matic; **Compañía:** Max-o-matic, www. maxomatic.net

INTERLETRAJE

Espacio general entre caracteres dentro de un cuerpo de texto. El interletraje puede resultar un problema si se utiliza un tipo **justificado**, ya que suele crear huecos entre palabras, especialmente cuando el **ancho** de línea es corto. No debe confundirse con el proceso de aumento del espacio entre los caracteres de un **tipo titular** para crear un mayor interés visual. Véase: ***tracking***.

Ing: LETTER SPACING
Fr: INTERLETTRAGE
Al: SPATIONIEREN
It: SPAZIO LETTERA

INTERLINEADO

Distancia entre líneas de **tipo** sucesivas, medida de **línea de base** a línea de base y expresada en **puntos**. A diferencia de los tipos metálicos, los tipos digitales se pueden ajustar mediante un *interlineado negativo*, lo que significa que el tamaño de punto del tipo es mayor que el tamaño de punto del interlineado. Se utiliza para crear efectos sorprendentes para gráficos publicitarios, pósters, etc., aunque la **legibilidad lingüística** se resiente.

Ing: LEADING
Fr: INTERLIGNAGE
Al: DURCHSCHUSS (ZEILENABSTAND)
It: INTERLINEA

JERARQUÍA

JERARQUÍA

Orden distinguible expresado mediante variaciones de **escala**, ubicación, **valor**, **color** y otras claves visuales. Los **títulos** y **subtítulos**, por ejemplo, crean un orden en las publicaciones largas. Los diseñadores, mediante la disposición jerárquica de los elementos, guían al espectador/lector por la tarjeta de visita, folleto, póster, libro o trabajo creativo, enseñando cada elemento del diseño de forma deliberada. Las jerarquías "planas" resultan menos interesantes y más confusas.

Ing: HIERARCHY
Fr: HIÉRARCHIE
Al: HIERARCHIE
It: GERARCHIA TIPOGRAFICA

Diseño: Ismael Medina/ Sebas Cangiano; **Compañía:** Virgen Extra, www. virgen-extra.com

JUSTIFICACIÓN

Término utilizado para describir líneas de tipo sucesivas que empiezan en un mismo punto, siguiendo una línea de referencia imaginaria y que acaban también en el mismo punto sobre otra línea imaginaria. Técnicamente, todas las líneas de tipo están justificadas, ya que cada línea se completa por toda su extensión con una combinación de caracteres y espacios. La diferencia estriba en la colocación de esos espacios. Este término se utiliza sobre todo para los casos en los que se añaden espacios entre palabras, moviendo el tipo hacia ambos extremos de su **anchura**. Este tipo de justificación, especialmente cuando se realiza en anchuras cortas, puede crear huecos, llamados **calles**, que atraviesan los bloques tipográficos. Véase **alineación** y *H&J*.

Ing: JUSTIFIED TYPE/TEXT
Fr: TEXTE JUSTIFIÉ
Al: BLOCKSATZ
It: TESTO/CARATTERI GIUSTIFICATI

KERNING

Ajuste de los espacios entre dos caracteres adyacentes para crear un **ritmo** visualmente atractivo. Al juntar algunos caracteres, como la *T* y la *o*, la interacción de sus formas crea un hueco. Se utiliza el *kerning* para estrechar este espacio y proporcionar una apariencia más natural. Los pares *kerning* son parejas de letras que requieren de este ajuste para un interletraje adecuado (una tarea que suelen realizar automáticamente las aplicaciones de *software*, pero que proporcionan resultados que no siempre agradan a diseñadores o tipógrafos).

Ing: KERNING
Fr: CRÉNAGE
Al: UNTERSCHNEIDEN
It: CRENATURA

LEGIBILIDAD LINGÜÍSTICA

Medida cualitativa de la facilidad de lectura de un texto, basada en la **tipografía**. Para que sea comprensible, una línea de **tipo** debe ser legible tipográficamente, aunque distinguir una **letra** o palabra de otra no asegura su legibilidad lingüística. Una novela realizada con **tipografía condensada**, por ejemplo, puede tener una alta legibilidad tipográfica pero no lingüística. Una tipografía legible (comprensible) depende de varios factores, como el tamaño de tipo, el **interletraje**, el **interlineado** y, por supuesto, el **tipo de letra**.

Ing: READABILITY
Al: LESBARKEIT

Diseño: ANDREU BALIUS; **Compañía:** TYPEREPUBLIC, www.typerepublic.com

myriad pro

myriad pro condensada

LEGIBLE

LEGIBILIDAD TIPOGRÁFICA

Medida cualitativa de la facilidad de lectura de las **letras** y palabras. La legibilidad tipográfica también influye en la **legibilidad lingüística**, es decir, en la facilidad de leer un texto creado con una **tipografía**. La necesidad de que un texto tenga mayor o menor legibilidad tipográfica depende mucho del contexto: los pósters o las sobrecubiertas, por ejemplo, suelen emplear tipos atractivos pero prácticamente ilegibles. Esos mismos **tipos**, usados para señalizaciones o en un informe anual, darían unos resultados desastrosos.

Ing: LEGIBILITY
Fr: LISIBILITÉ
Al: LESERLICHKEIT
It: LEGGIBILITÀ

LETRA

Signo gráfico. Los elementos comunes de un grupo de letras crean un **tipo de letra**. La *anatomía de tipos* viene descrita por una gran variedad de términos, como **serifa**, **ascendente**, **descendente**, etc.

Ing: LETTERFORM
Fr: DESSIN D'UNE LETTRE
Al: SCHRIFTCHARAKTER
It: GLIFO/I

Diseño: Cless; **Compañía:** Cless, www.cless.info

AMERICAN TYPEWRITE

AMERICAN TYPEWRITE CONDENSADA

LETRA CONDENSADA

Tipo en el que las **letras** son más estrechas que la versión ordinaria de la misma tipografía. Además, se colocan más cerca unas de otras, permitiendo que el espacio se llene con más tipos. Es el tipo más utilizado en títulos, pancartas, etc., en las que los textos son breves, ya que al usarla se reduce la **legibilidad**.

Ing: CONDENSED TYPE
Fr: CONDENSÉ
Al: SCHMALE SCHRIFT
It: CARATTERI CONDENSATI

A B C D E F G H I J K **L** M N O P Q R S T U V W X Y Z

LETRA DE FANTASÍA

Caracteres decorativos con trazos alargados, cuyas mayúsculas suelen inclinarse hacia la derecha. En mayúscula se utilizan como letra inicial de principio de párrafo, a menudo de un tamaño de punto mayor que el resto. En minúscula se usan a final de párrafo, para la letra final de la última palabra de un párrafo. La letra de fantasía puede dar un toque de elegancia a un texto, pero debe usarse con moderación, ya que una línea de texto entera es difícil de leer y distrae. Véase: **mayúscula inicial**.

Ing: SWASH CHARACTERS
Fr: LETTRE ITALIQUE ORNÉE
Al: ZIERBUCHSTABEN
It: CARATTERI SWASH

LETRA GÓTICA

Clase de caracteres decorativos de mediados del siglo XV. Los primeros en desarrollar la letra gótica fueron los impresores alemanes, que querían imitar la escritura a mano de los escribientes de la época. A menudo se llama también gótica a otras letras decorativas, como Fraktur, Textura u Old English. Para añadir más confusión, *Gótico* puede referirse a la letra decorativa pero también a los primeros tipos **sans serif**, que poco tienen que ver con la letra gótica.

Ing: BLACKLETTER
Fr: GOTHIQUE
Al: FRAKTUR (SCHRIFTEN)
It: BLACKLETTER

Diseño: FÈLIX BELLA; **Compañía:** CAMPGRÀFIC EDITORS, S. L., www.campgrafic.com

LETRA PERFILADA

Tipo de letra en la que los caracteres están diseñados como formas perfiladas en lugar de con trazos sólidos. Los perfiles también pueden crearse mediante aplicaciones de *software* como el Adobe Illustrator®. Las **curvas de Bézier** que se crean con estas aplicaciones pueden realizarse a mayor o menor escala sin que se pierda la definición, aunque en el proceso se puede perder la proporción adecuada del tipo.

Ing: OUTLINE TYPE
Fr: CARACTÈRES AU FIL
Al: KONTURSCHRIFT
It: CARATTERI CONTORNATI

Diseño: Ricardo Rousselot; **Compañía:** Grupo Erre, www.rousselot.com

A B C D E F G H I J K **L** M N O P Q R S T U V W X Y Z

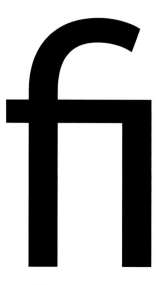

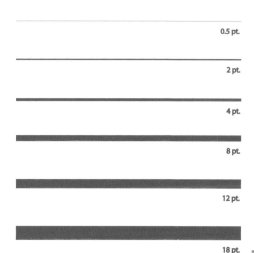

0.5 pt.

2 pt.

4 pt.

8 pt.

12 pt.

18 pt.

LIGADURA

Combinación de dos o tres letras mediante elementos comunes. Se utiliza para evitar colisiones antiestéticas entre **letras**, como en el caso de la *i* detrás de la *f*. Si estas letras se colocan como caracteres separados, el punto de la *i* queda muy cerca, o incluso superpuesto, a la parte superior de la *f*. Al reemplazar los dos caracteres con una ligadura, se consigue una línea de tipo más clara y legible. Las ligaduras, que se remontan a los manuscritos antiguos, se utilizaban desde el inicio de los tipos metálicos, pero desaparecieron en la era del *fototipo*. Casi todas las **fuentes** digitales, sin embargo, incluyen una selección de ligaduras.

Ing: LIGATURE
Fr: LIGATURE
Al: LIGATUR
It: LEGATURA

LÍNEA

Sucesión de puntos colocados en línea recta o creando curvas. A diferencia de las líneas usadas en geometría, en las que el grosor no tiene importancia, las líneas usadas por los diseñadores gráficos pueden ser finas o gruesas y no tienen por qué ser constantes en toda su longitud. Pueden ser líneas rotas o fragmentadas. Las líneas gruesas adoptan las propiedades de los planos (superficies planas). Los tres elementos que forman la base de la creación de cualquier forma del diseño gráfico son el punto, la línea y el plano. Véase: **filete**.

Ing: LINE
Fr: LIGNE
Al: LINIENGESTALTUNG
It: LINEA/E

LÍNEA DE BASE

En tipografía, línea de referencia que se utiliza para la alineación horizontal de los tipos. Las bases de las letras de *caja alta* y las letras de *caja baja* sin **descendentes** se sitúan a lo largo de la línea de base, muy cerca de ella. De hecho, únicamente las letras de caja baja de base plana, como la *h* o la *i*, descansan realmente sobre la línea de base. Las de base redondeada, como la *o* o la *u*, quedan ligeramente por debajo de ella. La ilusión óptica que crea este hecho muestra la importancia de la **alineación visual** por encima de la alineación de precisión cuando se utiliza **tipografía** elegante.

Ing: BASELINE
Fr: LIGNE DE BASE
Al: GRUNDLINIE (SCHRIFTLINIE)
It: LINEA DI BASE

Tipografía

LÍNEA DE ORIENTACIÓN

Línea que debe seguir el ojo para ver una fotografía o diseño. La línea de orientación depende de muchos factores, como el **color**, el **equilibrio**, el **contraste**, etc. Un buen diseño debe saber aprovechar la línea de orientación; los signos de orientación, por ejemplo, deben ser sencillos y directos, mientras que los pósters captan la atención mediante una línea de orientación compleja. Véase: **punto focal**.

Ing: EYE FLOW
Fr: CIRCULATION DU REGARD
Al: BLICKPFADBEWEGUNG
It: FLUSSO VISIVO

Diseño: Cless, Paxanga; **Compañía:** Cless, www.cless.info

LÍNEA MEDIA

Línea de referencia utilizada para conseguir la **alineación** horizontal de un tipo, que corresponde a la **altura X** de un **tipo de letra**. Los bordes superiores de las letras de *caja baja* sin **ascendentes** se apoyan en la línea media o quedan muy cerca de ella. De hecho, únicamente las letras de caja baja de borde plano, como la *u* o la *x*, terminan en la línea media. Las letras con bordes redondeados, como la *a* o la *o*, sobrepasan ligeramente la línea media por arriba. En la línea de base sucede una ilusión óptica similar, lo que también muestra la importancia de la alineación visual sobre la alineación de precisión.

Ing: MEAN LINE
Fr: LIGNE DE TÊTE
Al: X-LINIE (MITTELLINIE)
It: LINEA MEDIANA

LITOGRAFÍA

Proceso de impresión en el que la tinta se transfiere al papel a través de una piedra pulida o una plancha metálica. La palabra procede del griego: *lithos* (piedra) y *grapho* (escribir). Para la realización de litografías se marca la piedra o el metal con un medio de base oleosa, como el crayón, para definir las áreas en las que la tinta (de base acuosa) se absorberá o no. Las zonas sin marcar de la plancha son las que aguantan la tinta, mientras que las marcadas con el crayón la repelen y se convierten en el fondo para la imagen impresa final. Véase: **litografía offset**.

Ing: LITHOGRAPHY
Fr: LITHOGRAPHIE
Al: LITHOGRAFIE
It: LITOGRAFIA

Diseño: JULIEN CANAVEZES; **Compañía:** JULIEN CANAVEZES, www.toyzmachin.com

A B C D E F G H I J K **L** M N O P Q R S T U V W X Y Z

LITOGRAFÍA OFFSET

Proceso de impresión basado en los principios de la litografía, en el que una imagen tintada se transfiere a una sábana de goma antes de ser aplicada a la superficie de impresión. La tinta se aplica en la plancha mediante un conjunto de rodillos y, a la vez, otros rodillos envuelven la plancha con la sábana, transfiriendo la tinta a la sábana. Su gran calidad y menor coste han hecho que este tipo de impresión, también llamada *impresión offset*, se haya convertido en la más utilizada para trabajos de impresión comerciales.

Ing: OFFSET LITHOGRAPHY
Fr: LITHOGRAPHIE OFFSET
Al: OFFSETDRUCK
It: LITOGRAFIA OFFSET

Diseño: JULIEN CANAVEZES; **Compañía:** JULIEN CANAVEZES, www.toyzmachin.com

Esto tiene mala pinta...

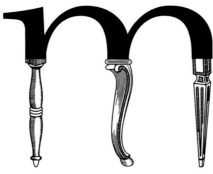

Alicia abrió la puerta y descubrió que daba a un pequeño pasillo, no mucho más grande que una ratonera: se arrodilló y, a través del pasadizo, vio el jardín más bonito que jamás hayáis visto.
¡Cómo deseaba salir de aquella oscura sala y pasearse entre esos lechos de brillantes flores y esas fuentes fresquísimas!, pero no podía ni siquiera sacar la cabeza por la puerta: "Incluso si mi cabeza pasase por aquí", pensó la pobre Alicia, "no serviría de nada sin mis hombros. ¡Oh, ojalá pudiese encogerme como un telescopio! Creo que podría hacerlo, si al menos supiese como empezar".
Porque ya veis, le habían ocurrido tantas cosas extrañas últimamente que Alicia había empezado a pensar que muy pocas cosas eran realmente imposibles.

LLAMADA

Texto breve, a menudo acompañado por una línea o flecha, que se utiliza como etiqueta identificativa de las diferentes partes de una fotografía, ilustración o material gráfico de una maquetación. Una llamada también es aquella porción de texto que se extrae del principal a la que se da un tratamiento especial para distinguirla del resto del texto (cambio de tipo de letra, color, tamaño, etc.) Véase: pie de foto y sumario.

Ing: CALLOUT
Fr: CHIFFRES RÉFÉRENCES
Al: HINWEIS
It: CALLOUT

LOGO

Signo gráfico utilizado para fines comerciales como parte integral del *branding* de una organización. A pesar de la elegante simplicidad que sugiere un logo, es un elemento de difícil creación. Debe ser muy sencillo para ser reconocido incluso en tamaños muy reducidos y a la vez muy rico en contenido, ya que representa los valores y personalidad de una organización. Debe poder ser recordado con facilidad y reconocido al instante, y ser distintivo de sus competidores. Todas estas características necesarias en un logo hacen que muchas empresas utilicen el mismo durante años. Un *logotipo* es un conjunto de **letras** específico que representa el nombre de una organización o acrónimo, cuyos detalles (**color**, **tipo de letra**, **interletraje**, etc.) son únicos y forman parte integral de la marca de una organización.

Ing: LOGO
Fr: LOGO
Al: LOGO
It: LOGO

Diseño: Ismael Medina/ Sebas Cangiano; **Compañía:** Virgen Extra, www. virgen-extra.com

LONGITUD DE LÍNEA

Distancia de un extremo a otro de una línea de **tipo**. Se confunde a menudo con el **ancho de columna**. Cuando se alinea con **bandera a la izquierda**, por ejemplo, las líneas de tipo raramente llenan todo el ancho de línea. Pasa lo mismo cuando la **bandera es a la derecha** o si se usa un tipo **centrado**. El único caso en el que la longitud de línea corresponde al ancho de línea es cuando se utilizan **tipos justificados**.

Ing: LINE LENGTH
Fr: LONGUEUR DE LIGNE
Al: ZEILENLÄNGE
It: LUNGHEZZA DI RIGA

LOREM IPSUM
Véase: *greeking*.

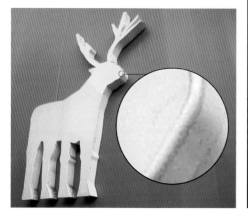

MAPA DE BITS

En un nivel básico, un mapa de bits es una cuadrícula rectangular de puntos (o *muestras*) que crean una imagen digital, como una fotografía o **letra**. Cada muestra se asocia con un **color** concreto y con una ubicación dentro de la cuadrícula. Cuantas más muestras por pulgada (spi) existan, mayor será la **resolución** del mapa de bits. El número de muestras de una imagen de mapa de bits es fijo (a diferencia de los **gráficos vectoriales**), por eso no pueden visualizarse o imprimirse a mayor resolución de la que tenga el dispositivo de salida sin que aparezca el efecto de **solapamiento**. También denominado *gráfico rasterizado*.

Ing: BITMAP
Fr: IMAGE MATRICIELLE
Al: BITMAP
It: BITMAP

MAQUETACIÓN

Fase preliminar en el proceso de diseño en el que se organizan los diferentes elementos, como los **tipos**, fotografías e ilustraciones, para obtener un resultado final que sea fácilmente comprensible. También representa la organización general de un diseño ya finalizado. Las maquetas de libros, folletos, informes o documentos de muchas páginas suelen organizarse mediante **cuadrículas**.

Ing: LAYOUT
Fr: MAQUETTE
Al: LAYOUT
It: LAYOUT

Diseño: Cristina U. Llorente para El Gaviero;
Compañía: Cristina U. Llorente, cris.ull@gmail.com

MARGEN

Área en blanco de los cuatro extremos de una página que enmarcan el **cuerpo de texto** y las imágenes en una **maqueta**. Algunos elementos, como los números de página, las notas al pie o los **pies de foto** a menudo se imprimen en los márgenes. El margen situado a lo largo del lomo del libro de una publicación encuadernada se llama **medianil**.

Ing: MARGIN
Fr: MARGES
Al: SEITENRAND
It: MARGINE/I

A B C D E F G H I J K L **M** N O P Q R S T U V W X Y Z

---

*A*l principio había un árbol con unos frutos morados del tamaño de un melón. Si te acercabas a esperar paciente la caída, pues estaban lo suficiente maduros, encontrabas recompensa en su interior.

*E*l patito feo es un cuento clásico-contemporáneo escrito por Hans Christian Andersen sobre un patito particularmente más grande, torpe y feo que sus hermanitos.

El cuento fue publicado por primera vez el 11 de noviembre de 1843 y fue incluido en la colección de Nuevos Cuentos (*Nye Eventyr*) de Andersen en 1844.

MATIZ

Característica básica de un **color**, que corresponde a su longitud de onda en el espectro de luz y se utiliza para distinguir un color de otro. El matiz es la posición relativa de un color en la circunferencia de la **rueda de colores**.

Ing: HUE
Fr: TEINTE
Al: FARBTON
It: TONALITÀ

Diseño: Donna S. Atwood, www.atwooddesign.com

MAYÚSCULA CAÍDA

Letra de caja alta utilizada como inicial de la primera palabra de un párrafo, fijado en un tamaño de punto mayor que el resto de letras, de manera que se extiende en el texto situado debajo. Para crear un impacto mayor, la mayúscula caída puede ser de un **tipo** diferente del que se use en el **cuerpo de texto**. Están determinadas por las líneas de tipo que pueden ocupar. Por ejemplo, una mayúscula caída tres líneas ocupa la primera, segunda y tercera línea de un párrafo. Véase: **mayúscula inicial** y **capitular**.

Ing: DROP CAPITAL/CAP
Fr: LETTRINE
Al: HÄNGENDE INITIALE
It: CAPOLETTERA

MAYÚSCULA INICIAL

Letra de *caja alta* decorativa utilizada como inicial de la primera palabra de un párrafo, normalmente en tamaño mayor que el resto del texto. A veces se utiliza una tipografía diferente al resto del texto o se imprime en un color diferente para crear un interés visual adicional. Entre las diversas opciones más utilizadas se encuentran las **mayúsculas caídas** y las **capitulares**.

Ing: INITIAL CAPITAL/CAP
Fr: INITIALE
Al: INITIALE
It: LETTERA MAIUSCOLA INIZIALE

MEDIANIL

Espacio entre dos **columnas** de **tipo** o entre pares de columnas de una **maqueta**. También es el espacio estrecho de una página cercano al borde de **encuadernación**, o al área en la que se unen las dos tiras en un **desplegable**.

Ing: GUTTER
Fr: GOUTTIÈRE
Al: SPALTENABSTAND
It: MARGINE INTERNO

Diseño: Ibán Ramón Rodríguez; **Compañía:** Estudio Ibán ramón, www.ibanramon.com

MEDIO CUADRATÍN

Unidad de medida tipográfica correspondiente a la anchura de medio cuadratín.
Véase: **semirraya** y **espacio de medio cuadratín**.

Ing: EN
Fr: DEMI-CADRATIN
Al: HALBGEVIERT
It: EN

MEDIO TONO

Imagen en **escala de grises** en la que la gama de tono total se ha convertido en una póliza de puntos negros minúsculos, o *trama de medio tono*. Las zonas más oscuras de la imagen están representadas por parches de puntos más grandes que los utilizados para representar zonas más claras de la imagen. Para simular el espectro completo de color visible en la **cuatricromía**, se combinan los medios tonos correspondientes a cada **canal**.

Ing: HALFTONE
Fr: SIMILI
Al: HALBTON
It: MEZZITONI

A B C D E F G H I J K L **M** N O P Q R S T U V W X Y Z

METÁFORA

Descripción o expresión de un tema por medio de otro. En el diseño gráfico, las metáforas pueden incluir componentes textuales, como cuando una línea de texto relaciona una imagen con un concepto que no parece estar relacionado. Una foto de una jungla densa y amenazadora puede combinarse con un texto que rece: "¿Busca un seguro para el coche?" La idea de "hay una jungla ahí fuera" se intuye incluso sin el texto. Las metáforas puramente visuales recurren a las asociaciones más aceptadas entre una o más imágenes, transfiriéndolas a otra. Esto suele hacerse mediante imágenes fusionadas, creadas mezclando dos o más imágenes para facilitar la transferencia del significado. Las imágenes de una pluma y un arma, por ejemplo, se pueden unir para sugerir el poder de la palabra escrita.

Ing: METAPHOR
Fr: MÉTAPHORE
Al: METAPHER
It: METAFORA

Diseño: Antonio Guzmán; **Compañía:** Domodo estudio, www.domodoestudio.com

MINIATURA

Boceto o muestra de pequeño tamaño y baja calidad que se utiliza para distinguir con rapidez un concepto. Se utilizan durante las primeras etapas de un proyecto como parte integral del proceso de diseño y, a menudo, el diseño final procede de la generación de miniaturas cada vez más sofisticadas. También puede referirse a imágenes de pequeño tamaño y baja resolución que sirven como marcadores de las versiones de alta resolución. Por ejemplo, una galería de imágenes online puede mostrar un gran número de miniaturas en una página web para una mejor visualización y una *carga de página* más rápida. Esto se ha convertido en algo tan común, que la sola presencia de las miniaturas ya sugiere al usuario que existe una versión en alta resolución a la que se accede con un simple clic.

Ing: THUMBNAIL
Fr: CRAYONNAGE
Al: DAUMENNAGELSKIZZE
It: THUMBNAIL

Diseño: Rubengarcia-Castro.com 2009; **Compañía:** RubenGarcia-Castro, www.rubengarcia-castro.com

MOARÉ

Efecto indeseable que se produce cuando las *tramas de medio tono* que se utilizan en la cuatricromía se alinean de manera que se puede ver un dibujo. Para evitar este efecto se hacen rotar las tramas en ángulos específicos de relación entre unas y otras, con lo que aparecen rosetas **CMYK** que no suelen apreciarse en el trabajo final de impresión. Este efecto también puede aparecer cuando se escanea digitalmente una imagen sin utilizar la opción de *destramado*.

Ing: MOIRÉ
Fr: MOIRÉ
Al: MOIRÉ-EFFEKT
It: EFFETTO MOIRÉ

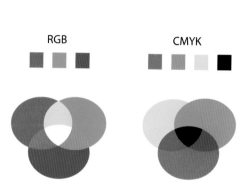

RGB CMYK

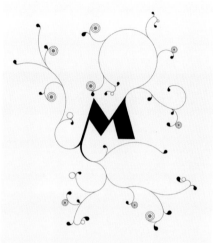

MODELO DE COLOR

Sistema de definición absoluta del **color** (independientemente del dispositivo utilizado para su visualización o impresión) mediante una cantidad mínima de componentes de color que, al ser ajustados, pueden usarse para crear un amplio espectro de color. Existen diversos modelos de color, aunque los más utilizados son el **RGB** y el **CMYK**. El modelo HSB utiliza características de color asociadas con la rueda de colores tradicional: **matiz**, **saturación** y **brillo**. El modelo LAB se basa en las coordenadas que se emplean en *colorimetría*. No debe confundirse con el *espacio cromático*, que es la gama de color producida por un dispositivo de visualización o impresión dentro de un modelo de color específico. Por ejemplo, una impresora de inyección de tinta y una comercial utilizan el modelo de color CMYK, pero la gama de color CMYK que producirá cada impresora representa un espacio cromático específico dentro ese modelo de color específico.

Ing: COLOR MODEL
Fr: MODÈLE COLORIMÉTRIQUE
Al: FARBMODELL
It: MODELLO DI COLORE

MODERNISMO

Conjunto de movimientos artísticos apareci-dos sobre el año 1907 con el **Cubismo** y su rechazo de las formas naturales en favor de la abstracción. Durante los últimos 100 años, el diseño modernista se ha interpretado y reinterpretado por todo el mundo, adoptando una gran variedad de formas, algunas más relacionadas con su mitología (p. ej., uso estricto de **cuadrículas**, tipos **sans serif**, uso generoso del **espacio blanco**, etc.) que otras. Cada "regla" del modernismo tiene innumerables excepciones. Sin embargo, existen varios rasgos comunes, como la importancia de la comunicación visual fun-cional o el espíritu, a menudo optimista, con visión de futuro.

Ing: MODERNISM
Fr: MODERNISME
Al: MODERNE
It: MODERNISMO

Diseño: Damià Rotger Miró y Andreu Moragues Provenzal; **Compañía:** Dúctil, www.ductilct.com

MONOCROMÁTICO

Que tiene una **paleta de colores** compuesta por *tonos* y tintes de un matiz único. En las imágenes monocromas la variación tonal se representa mediante las diferencias de saturación y brillo. Las imágenes en **escala de grises** son imágenes monocromas con una paleta de colores compuesta por grises, blanco y negro.

Ing: MONOCHROMATIC
Fr: MONOCHROMATIQUE
Al: MONOCHROMATISCH (EINFARBIG)
It: MONOCROMATICO

Diseño: Max-o-matic; **Ping Pong Character:** Gastón Caba; **Compañía:** Max-o-matic, www.maxomatic.net

Letter Gothic Std

MONOESPACIADA

Tipo de letra en el que todos los caracteres tienen la misma anchura. El **tipo** resultante se parece al de las máquinas de escribir. Véase: **proporcional**.

Ing: MONOSPACED
Fr: CARACTÈRES À CHASSE CONSTANTE
Al: DICKTENGLEICH
     (NICHTPROPORTIONALE SCHRIFT)
It: MONOSPAZIO

MONTAJE
Véase: *collage* y **fotomontaje**.

MULTIMEDIA

Sistema de comunicación en el que el contenido se presenta de múltiples maneras. Un sitio web, por ejemplo, puede integrar texto (e hipertexto), foto fija y audio y vídeo *streaming* en el mismo lugar. El término multimedia se usa también para definir aquellos dispositivos que pueden mostrar contenidos multimedia o que permiten experiencias interactivas, como en los videojuegos.

Ing: MULTIMEDIA
Fr: MULTIMÉDIA
Al: MULTIMEDIA
It: MULTIMEDIA

Diseño: GEORGINA MALAGARRIGA; **Compañía:** GEORGINA MALAGARRIGA, www.gmalagarriga.net

arial
arial negrita

VERDANA
VERDANA NEGRITA

NEGRITA

Tipo en el que las **letras** tienen un trazo más grueso que la versión ordinaria del mismo tipo. Las aplicaciones de autoedición suelen ofrecer una herramienta que "cambia" a negrita, haciendo más grueso el trazo del tipo que se está utilizando. El tipo True bold está diseñado para que sea proporcional al resto de "miembros" del mismo tipo, lo que permite que al imprimirse tenga un parecido mayor.

Ing: BOLD/BOLDFACE
Fr: GRAS, CARACTÈRES GRAS
Al: FETT (SCHRIFTEN)
It: GRASSETTO

Minion Pro

Minion Pro Oblicua

Myriad Pro

Myriad Pro Oblicua

1234567890

1267712455605768883

NÚMEROS DE CAJA ALTA

Conjuntos de números con la misma altura (o casi) de las letras de *caja alta* de un **tipo de letra**. Son caracteres de anchura constante que descansan sobre la línea de base, por lo que son especialmente aptos para ser utilizados en tablas. Véase: **números elzevirianos**.

Ing: LINING NUMERALS/FIGURES
Fr: CHIFFRES ARABES
Al: MAJUSKELZIFFERN
(TABELLENZIFFERN)
It: NUMERI E LETTERE DI ALLINEAMENTO

NÚMEROS ELZEVIRIANOS

Conjunto de números de proporciones comparables a las letras de *caja baja* de un **tipo de letra**. Al igual que en el caso de las **versalitas**, los números elzevirianos suelen usarse dentro de una línea de tipo debido a que son menos llamativos que los **números de caja alta**.

Ing: OLD-STYLE NUMERALS/FIGURES
Fr: CHIFFRES SUSPENDUS
Al: MEDIÄVALZIFFERN
It: NUMERI E LETTERE IN STILE ANTICO

OBLICUA

Tipo **sans serif** inclinada hacia la derecha, formada por letras muy parecidas al tipo de letra ordinario en el que se basan. La **cursiva** también se inclina hacia la derecha, pero su trazo está totalmente transformado y suele ser muy diferente de los tipos ordinarios en los que se basa.

Ing: OBLIQUE
Fr: OBLIQUE
Al: SCHRÄG
It: CARATTERI OBLIQUE

A B C D E F G H I J K L M N O **P** Q R S T U V W X Y Z

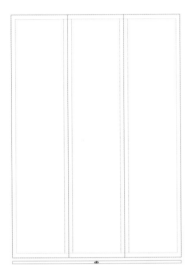

PÁGINA MAESTRA

Plantilla que emplean las aplicaciones de maquetación de páginas para asegurar la colocación óptima de la **cuadrícula**, **columnas** de texto, números de página y otros elementos de **maquetación**, en un documento. Se pueden utilizar diferentes páginas maestras para un mismo documento, según el estilo o maquetación de cada sección. Cuando se usan páginas maestras, la numeración de páginas se realiza de forma automática.

Ing: MASTER PAGE
Fr: PAGE TYPE
Al: MUSTERSEITE
It: PAGINA MASTRO

PAGINACIÓN

Numeración de las páginas que indican su correcta secuencia en un libro u otra publicación. También puede utilizarse para referirse al número total de páginas de una publicación. Actualmente ha adquirido un nuevo significado: la manera de organizar la información en las páginas web. Los *blogs*, por ejemplo, pueden paginarse de manera que únicamente se vea el primer párrafo de una publicación en la página principal, o de manera que se vean únicamente los diez primeros comentarios a dicha publicación. Véase: **imposición**.

Ing: PAGINATION
Fr: PAGINATION
Al: PAGINIERUNG
It: IMPAGINAZIONE

Diseño: Rubengarcia-Castro.com 2009; **Compañía:** RubenGarcia-Castro, www.rubengarcia-castro.com

PÁGINAS ENFRENTADAS

Páginas izquierda y derecha en una doble página. Existen aplicaciones de maquetación como el Adobe InDesign que permiten crear documentos en formato de página única o en páginas enfrentadas. Véase: **recto/verso**.

Ing: FACING PAGES
Fr: PAGES EN REGARD
Al: DOPPELSEITEN
It: PAGINE AFFIANCATE

Diseño: Bendita Gloria (Alba Rosell + Santi Fuster); **Compañía:** Bendita Gloria, www.benditagloria.com

A B C D E F G H I J K L M N O **P** Q R S T U V W X Y Z

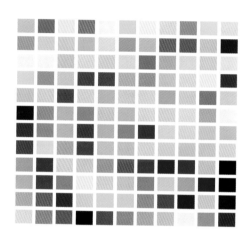

PÁGINAS FINALES

Sección de un libro que sigue al texto principal, como apéndices, bibliografías, glosarios, notas, etc. También denominadas *páginas referenciales*. Véase: **páginas preliminares**.

Ing: END MATTER
Fr: PARTIES ANNEXES
Al: ANHANG
It: PAGINE FINALI

Diseño: Max-o-matic; **Texts:** Tomás Astelarra;
Compañía: Max-o-matic, www. maxomatic.net

PÁGINAS PRELIMINARES

Parte de un libro que precede al texto principal, como la portada, *frontispicio* (ilustración o grabado en la página opuesta a la portada), tabla de contenidos, listados de números y tablas, prólogo, etc. Véase: **páginas finales**.

Ing: FRONT MATTER
Fr: PAGES LIMINAIRES
Al: TITELEI
It: PAGINE INIZIALI

Diseño: Max-o-matic, Photo of Meli-k; **Compañía:**
Max-o-matic, www. maxomatic.net

PÁGINAS REFERENCIALES
Véase: **páginas finales**.

PALETA DE COLORES

Conjunto de colores definidos por un medio concreto, como la paleta de 216 colores seguros para usar en web, o por un diseñador o artista, para un proyecto específico. Las paletas de color a medida suelen crearse utilizando las relaciones de la **rueda de colores**.

Ing: COLOR PALETTE
Fr: PALETTE DES COULEURS
Al: FARBPALETTE
It: PALETTE DI COLORI

Arial

Helvetica

Impact

Verdana

Geneva

Tahoma

Century Gothic

Pica

Puntos

PALO SECO

Tipos de letras sin **serifa**, los pequeños remates que adornan los rasgos principales de los caracteres. También llamadas *sans serif*. En comparación con los tipos de letra con serifas, los de palo seco tienen un menor contraste entre los rasgos finos y gruesos, lo que mejora la **legibilidad** de un **tipo** para ser leído en la pantalla de un ordenador.

Ing: SANS SERIF
Fr: CARACTÈRES SANS EMPATTEMENTS
Al: SERIFENLOS
It: CARATTERI SENZA GRAZIE

PAPEL ESTUCADO O CUCHÉ
Véase: **revestimiento acuoso**.

PARTICIÓN SILÁBICA
Véase: *H&J*.

PICA

Unidad de medida tipográfica absoluta, equivalente a 12 **puntos**. Seis picas americanas equivalen a 0,9936 pulgadas, mientras que seis picas *PostScript* equivalen a una pulgada. Un *espacio de pica* tiene una anchura de ⅙ de pulgada.

Ing: PICA
Fr: POINT PICA
Al: PICA
It: PICA

PICTOGRAMA

Icono o **símbolo** utilizado de manera que su significado se entiende por encima de barreras lingüísticas o culturales. Los pictogramas inteligentes forman parte de un sistema estandarizado de pictogramas, regido por muchas convenciones y pautas como cuando se crea una colección completa para unos Juegos Olímpicos o en el caso de las señales de tráfico reconocidas mundialmente. Las señales de recogida de maletas que se usan en los aeropuertos no son más que iconos hasta que se colocan dentro del contexto de un aeropuerto u otra terminal de viaje. Ese mismo icono se podría utilizar, por ejemplo, en un sitio web en el que se vendan maletas. En este caso, aunque su significado como icono sería el mismo, su significado como pictograma sería diferente.

Ing: PICTOGRAM
Fr: PICTOGRAMME
Al: PIKTOGRAMM
It: PITTOGRAMMA

Diseño: Damià Rotger Miró, Andreu Moragues, Laura Lerycke. Editorial Rotger; **Compañía:** Dúctil, www.ductilct.com

ABCDEFGHIJKLMNO **P** QRSTUVWXYZ

ACUARIO DEL HOTEL ATLANTIS, DUBAI, 17:00H.

PIE DE FOTO

Texto breve utilizado para describir o explicar una fotografía, ilustración, cuadro o cualquier otro elemento visual. Suelen estar situadas por encima, por debajo o a un lado del material gráfico, separados del **cuerpo de texto**. Véase: **llamada**.

Ing: CAPTION
Fr: LÉGENDE
Al: BILDUNTERSCHRIFT
It: DIDASCALIA

PÍXEL

Elemento básico utilizado por diversos dispositivos digitales para representar imágenes. El nombre píxel proviene de la combinación de las palabras *picture* (imagen) y *element* (elemento). Los píxeles se ordenan en una cuadrícula bidimensional en la que cada píxel es una muestra del punto correspondiente en la imagen original. La **resolución** de imagen es una característica de la densidad de la cuadrícula. Para los dispositivos que utilizan el sistema de color **RGB**, el color de cada píxel corresponde a los valores numéricos del rojo, verde y azul, asignados a cada uno de ellos.

Ing: PIXEL
Fr: PIXEL
Al: PIXEL (BILDPUNKT)
It: PIXEL

Diseño: Francisco Úbeda Llorente;
Compañía: Francisco Úbeda Llorente,
franciscoubeda.llorente@gmail.com

PLEGADO EN ACORDEÓN

Doblado de una hoja de papel en dos o más pliegues alternos, de manera que cada uno de los *paneles* (de los que hay seis o más) se dobla en dirección contraria a los paneles adyacentes. Dos pliegues realizados de esta manera dan como resultado un acordeón de seis paneles (o seis páginas), es decir, tres paneles en cada lado de la hoja; tres pliegues crean un acordeón de ocho paneles, etc. También denominado *concertina*.

Ing: ACCORDION FOLD
Fr: PLI ACCORDÉON
Al: LEPORELLO
It: PIEGHEVOLE A FISARMONICA

Diseño: Fernando Masselli; **Compañía:** Subcoolture, www.subcoolture.com

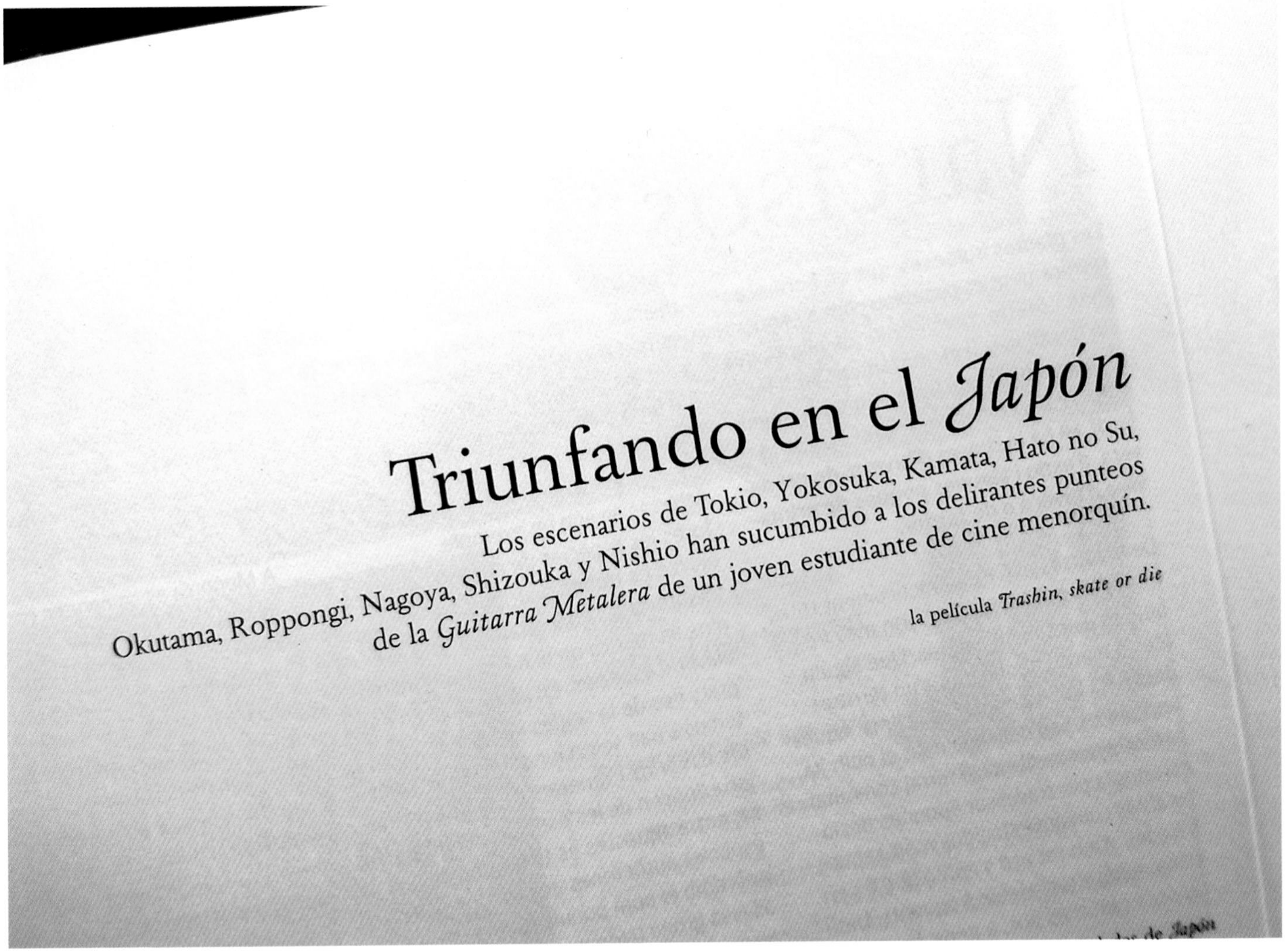

Triunfando en el *Japón*

Los escenarios de Tokio, Yokosuka, Kamata, Hato no Su, Okutama, Roppongi, Nagoya, Shizouka y Nishio han sucumbido a los delirantes punteos de la *Guitarra Metalera* de un joven estudiante de cine menorquín.

la película Trashin, skate or die

PLIEGO

Conjunto de páginas impresas por ambos lados de una gran hoja de papel que, una vez dobladas y cortadas, seguirán el orden y secuencia correctos para la **encuadernación**. Véase: **imposición**.

Ing: SIGNATURE
Fr: CAHIER
Al: BOGENMONTAGE
It: SEGNATURA

Diseño: Damià Rotger Miró; **Compañía:** Dúctil, www.ductilct.com

A B C D E F G H I J K L M N O **P** Q R S T U V W X Y Z

Tahoma
Futura

POSTERIZACIÓN

Efecto que se produce cuando la gama de colores (o grises) disponible no es suficiente para reproducir, tanto en pantalla como impresa, una imagen que contiene áreas de cambios graduales de tono. Esto sucede, por ejemplo, cuando una imagen se convierte a un GIF de 256 colores para utilizarse como gráfico web simple. La posterización también puede realizarse a propósito, utilizando un *software* de edición de imágenes para convertir tonos continuos en un número limitado de campos de color, creando efectos visuales interesantes, parecidos a los que se pueden ver en los pósters tradicionales.

Ing: POSTERIZATION
Fr: POSTERISATION
Al: POSTERISATION
It: POSTERIZZAZIONE

POSTMODERNISMO

Reacción contra el dogmatismo del **Modernismo**. Cobró forma durante la década de 1960 y alcanzó importancia internacional en la década de 1980. Allí donde los modernistas habían rechazado el pasado, los postmodernistas aplaudían los estilos históricos y sus tendencias decorativas, reinterpretando y combinándolas de manera inesperada y juguetona. Entre las características visuales se encuentra el mayor **interletraje** en los tipos, la ubicación de elementos aparentemente al azar, *collages* complicados, **paletas de colores** pastel, etc.

Ing: POST-MODERNISM
Fr: POSTMODERNISME
Al: POSTMODERNE
It: POST-MODERNISMO

Diseño: Damià Rotger Miró; **Compañía:** Dúctil, www.ductilct.com

PROCESO DE COLORES
Véase: **CMYK** y **cuatricomía**.

PROPORCIONAL

Tipo de letra en el que la anchura de cada carácter es única, a diferencia de los tipos de letra **monoespaciados**, en los que todos los caracteres tienen la misma anchura.

Ing: PROPORTIONAL
Fr: CARACTÈRES À CHASSE VARIABLE
Al: PROPORTIONALSCHRIFT
It: PROPORZIONALE

A B C D E F G H I J K L M N O **P** Q R S T U V W X Y Z

8 pto
10 pto
12 pto
14 pto

18 pto

24 pto

36 pto

48 pto

PRUEBA

Versión preliminar de un libro, informe, folleto o documento a publicar. Las pruebas tienen varios usos, desde la edición y corrección hasta la promoción, como cuando se envían a los críticos antes de su publicación. Tradicionalmente eran páginas sin encuadernar ni recortar, pero actualmente se utilizan las pruebas electrónicas. Cuando aún se utilizaban moldes de metal para los **tipos**, la composición se realizaba en bandejas metálicas antes de pasarse a la imprenta. Estas bandejas se llamaban *galeras* y las impresiones se llamaban *galeradas*, término que aún se utiliza para las primeras pruebas. Las *pruebas finales* se utilizan para confirmar detalles, como el color, antes de la impresión.

Ing: PROOF
Fr: ÉPREUVES
Al: KORREKTURABZUG
It: BOZZA/E

Diseño: Rubengarcia-Castro.com 2009; **Compañía:** RubenGarcia-Castro, www.rubengarcia-castro.com

PRUEBA DE GALERADAS
Véase: **prueba**.

PUNTO/TAMAÑO DE PUNTO

En **tipografía**, unidad absoluta de medida. Un punto americano equivale a 0,0138 pulgadas; un punto *PostScript* equivale a 0,0139 pulgadas. El tamaño de punto se refiere al tamaño del **tipo**, medido en puntos. Sin embargo, a pesar de que el punto sea una medida absoluta, el tamaño real de un tipo para un tamaño de punto concreto varía según el tipo de letra. Esto sucede porque el tamaño de punto, al principio, no estaba determinado por el tamaño de los caracteres sino por el de los bloques metálicos en los que éstos se fundían. En los tipos digitales, la relación entre tamaño de punto y tamaño de carácter es aún menos directa. Véase: **pica**.

Ing: POINT/POINT SIZE
Fr: CORPS
Al: PUNKT/PUNKTGRÖSSE
It: PUNTO/I/DIMENSIONI DEL PUNTO

PUNTO FOCAL

Elemento del diseño de una **maqueta** que atrae en primer lugar la atención del espectador; el área desde la que parte la línea de orientación. El punto focal puede crearse a través del **color**, la **escala** y la **composición**. En publicidad es conveniente que exista un punto focal único e inequívoco.

Ing: FOCAL POINT
Fr: POINT CENTRAL
Al: FOKUS
It: PUNTO FOCALE

Diseño: José Jimenez Valladares; Valladares Diseño y Comunicación; **Compañía:** Valladares Diseño y Comunicación, www.valladaresdc.net

A B C D E F G H I J K L M N O **P Q R** S T U V W X Y Z

"Imagínese a un hombre sentado en el sofá favorito de su casa. Debajo tiene una bomba a punto de estallar. Él lo ignora, pero el público lo sabe. Esto es el suspense".

Alfred Hitchcock (1899-1980) Director de cine británico.

" Imagínese a un hombre sentado en el sofá favorito de su casa. Debajo tiene una bomba a punto de estallar. Él lo ignora, pero el público lo sabe. Esto es el suspense".

Alfred Hitchcock (1899-1980) Director de cine británico.

puntuación

PUNTOS SUSPENSIVOS

Signo de puntuación formado por tres puntos seguidos, utilizado para indicar que se ha omitido una parte del texto, cuando se utiliza una parte de una cita directa en lugar de la cita entera, por ejemplo, o cuando el texto está incompleto (al final de una palabra, cuando discurso queda en suspenso). Cada tipo tiene su propio carácter de puntos suspensivos, y es mejor usar el carácter que tres puntos seguidos, ya que así se evita su separación en un **salto de línea**. Sin embargo, la única manera de conseguir un espaciado preciso es utilizando los puntos. Se escriben pegados a la palabra que precede y separados por un espacio de la palabra siguiente.

Ing: ELLIPSIS
Fr: POINTS DE SUSPENSION
Al: ELLIPSE (AUSLASSUNGSPUNKTE)
It: PUNTI DI SOSPENSIONE

PUNTUACIÓN VOLADA

Signos de puntuación situados ligeramente por encima del bloque de tipo, para mejorar la alineación visual. Las **comillas** y los **bolos** de apertura se colocan de manera que se inclinan hacia el margen izquierdo, mientras que los signos de cierre se colocan fuera, en el margen derecho. Las comillas voladas requieren un tratamiento muy delicado, ya que el objetivo es crear una tipografía limpia, no resaltar elementos concretos. Los caracteres que no son de puntuación a veces también se colocan más allá del límite del bloque de tipo para mejorar la alineación visual, como en el caso de las marcas de notas al pie o citas. En este caso se llaman *caracteres volados*.

Ing: HANGING PUNCTUATION
Fr: PONCTUATION MARGINALE
Al: SATZKANTENAUSGLEICH
It: PUNTEGGIATURA ESTERNA

RAYA

Trazo horizontal del tamaño de un **cuadratín** que se utiliza para crear una pausa o inciso en una línea de texto y para resaltar una frase explicativa. En español, si se usan dos rayas (de apertura y cierre), se colocan pegadas a la primera y última palabra y separadas por un espacio de la palabra precedente y siguiente. Véase: **semirraya** y **guión**.

Ing: EM DASH
Fr: TIRET CADRATIN
Al: Geviertstrich
It: LINEETTA EM

RECORTAR

Cortar una fotografía o cualquier tipo de material gráfico por medios
digitales o mecánicos, eliminando las partes no deseadas de sus
extremos. El recorte se realiza para enmarcar de forma precisa los
contenidos de una fotografía, o para ajustar el tamaño y proporción
de una imagen al espacio asignado para ella dentro de una **maqueta**.
Las líneas que se utilizan para encuadrar el material gráfico que debe
recortarse se llaman *marcas de corte*

Ing: CROP
Fr: RECADRER
Al: AUSSCHNITT
It: CROP

Baskerville

Garamon

Times New Roman

RECTO/VERSO

Término utilizado para describir las páginas a la derecha y la izquierda en una **doble página**. La derecha es el *recto* y la izquierda es el *verso*. En el sentido estricto, sin embargo, el término se refiere a las caras opuestas de una misma página, siendo el *recto* la parte frontal y el *verso* la posterior.

Ing: RECTO/VERSO
Fr: RECTO VERSO
Al: RECHTE/LINKE SEITE (VORDER-/ RÜCKSEITE)
It: RECTO/VERSO

Diseño: Max-o-matic; **Texts:** Tomás Astelarra;
Compañía: Max-o-matic, www. maxomatic.net

REDONDA

Tipo de letra con **serifas** cuyos orígenes se remontan a la Italia del siglo XV. El término redonda, o romana, también se usa para describir la versión ordinaria de un tipo de letra, con o sin serifas, para distinguirla de la **negrita** o **cursiva** del mismo tipo.

Ing: ROMAN TYPE
Fr: CARACTÈRES ROMAINS
Al: ANTIQUA
It: CARATTERI ROMAN

REGISTRO

Superposición exacta de todas las capas de tinta de un trabajo de impresión. En principio, cada aplicación sucesiva de tinta se superpone a la aplicación previa, por lo que los diferentes colores se solapan o se encuentran exactamente donde lo tienen que hacer. En la realidad, sin embargo, pueden producirse variaciones debido al movimiento del papel o a problemas de la impresora. Se dice entonces que están *fuera de registro*. Los problemas de registro se pueden solucionar mediante el **reventado** o la **sobreimpresión**.

Ing: REGISTRATION
Fr: REPÉRAGE
Al: REGISTERHALTIGKEIT
It: REGISTRO

Diseño: Diego Feijóo; **Compañía:** Studio Diego Feijóo, www.dfeijoo.com

RELACIÓN FIGURA-FONDO

Aspecto de la percepción visual basada en la relación entre una forma, como una figura, objeto, forma geométrica o **letra** y su entorno: una forma solo es distinguible del fondo cuando son diferentes. Gracias a una minuciosa manipulación de esta relación inherente, los diseñadores son capaces de crear efectos visuales increíbles partiendo de las formas más básicas. Esto es especialmente importante en el diseño de logos, en donde deben expresarse muchos contenidos en una marca sencilla y de fácil identificación. Las relaciones figura-fondo estables suelen tener un punto focal de fácil identificación y un aspecto armonioso, mientras que las relaciones ambiguas confunden al espectador. Utilizadas de manera adecuada, estas relaciones pueden resultar muy útiles. Véase: **espacio positivo** y **espacio negativo**.

Ing: FIGURE-GROUND
Fr: DESSIN EN GRISÉ
Al: FORMFLÄCHENGESTALTUNG
It: FIGURA-SFONDO

Diseño: Subcoolture, in collaboration with AA Records;
Compañía: Subcoolture, www.subcoolture.com

RESMA

Conjunto de 500 páginas de un papel de una determinada calidad en su *tamaño básico*. Aunque existen muchas medidas estándar de páginas, el tamaño básico viene determinado únicamente por la calidad del papel. En EE.UU., el tamaño básico del papel de escritura, el de cuentas y el de carta es de de 17 x 22 pulgadas; el papel de cubiertas tiene un tamaño básico de 20 x 26 pulgadas. El gramaje es el peso de una resma de papel. En EE.UU., el *gramaje* se expresa en libras mediante el símbolo #. Como el gramaje varía en función del tamaño básico del papel, dos papeles de calidad diferente con el mismo gramaje pueden ser diferentes en cuanto a espesor y peso. Un papel de escritura 28# tiene casi el mismo espesor que un papel fino de 70#. El espesor de una hoja de papel es su *calibre*. Los papeles con valores de calibre bajos también tendrán menos peso que los de calibre alto. El término *volumen específico* se utiliza para cuantificar el calibre de un papel en relación con su peso.

Ing: REAM
Fr: RAME
Al: RIES
It: RISMA

RESOLUCIÓN

Calidad relativa de una imagen digital según el número de muestras por unidades de medida. Los diferentes términos que se utilizan para expresar la resolución muchas veces se utilizan de manera intercambiable. **PPP**, o *puntos por pulgada*, es la medida relativa de la calidad de un dispositivo de impresión. Las impresoras de 300 ppp pueden imprimir 300 puntos alineados en el espacio de una pulgada. **PPI**, o *píxeles por pulgada* (*pixels per inch*, en inglés), se utiliza para cuantificar la resolución de un monitor o pantalla digital. **LPI**, o *líneas por pulgada* (*lines per inch*, en inglés), es una medida de frecuencia de **medios tonos**. Aunque las líneas sean filas de puntos diminutos, aparecen como líneas cuando se imprimen. Cuanto mayor sea la frecuencia de una trama, más detallada será la imagen impresa. Los periódicos utilizan tramas de 65-86 lpi, las revistas ilustradas suelen usar tramas de 133-150 lpi. Los libros de arte utilizan tramas más finas, de hasta 300 lpi.

Ing: RESOLUTION
Fr: RÉSOLUTION
Al: AUFLÖSUNG
It: RISOLUZIONE

A B C D E F G H I J K L M N O P Q **R** S T U V W X Y Z

REVENTADO

Técnica empleada para evitar huecos entre áreas de colores cuando el registro no es correcto. Si, por ejemplo, se imprimiera un tipo color magenta contra un fondo de cian puro, lo que quedara fuera de registro sería un hueco entre el tipo y el fondo, y se vería el papel de debajo. El reventado es una línea de color muy fina, en este caso una combinación de magenta y cian, colocada alrededor del objeto para evitar los huecos. Hay diversos tipos de reventados, cada uno adecuado a una situación de impresión concreta. Los más adecuados para aplicar reventados son los impresores. Véase: **registro**.

Ing: TRAPPING
Fr: GROSSI-MAIGRI
Al: ÜBERFÜLLUNG
It: TRAPPING

REVESTIMIENTO ACUOSO

Capa de base acuosa aplicada a una hoja de papel en su totalidad después de la impresión para producir un lustre general (brillante o mate) y proteger la tinta de humedad y ralladuras. Los papeles sin revestimiento absorben la tinta, por lo que el aspecto de las imágenes impresas se difumina, mientras que los papeles con revestimiento impiden la absorción de la tinta, lo que permite que las imágenes permanezcan nítidas. Los revestimientos acuosos se usan sobre todo en aquellos materiales de impresión que sufren un mayor uso, como las revistas o folletos. Existen otros tipos de revestimientos, como los **barnices**.

Ing: AQUEOUS COATING
Fr: PELLICULAGE AQUEUX
Al: DRUCKLACK
It: RIVESTIMENTO AD ACQUA

Diseño: Ana Varela y Elena Rodríguez. Cover image from Ryuji Nakamura Architects; **Compañía:** Pasajes Diseño, www.pasajesdiseno.com

REVESTIMIENTO ULTRAVIOLETA

Proceso de aplicación de un polímero líquido a un papel, en el momento de la impresión o justo después, y posterior secado mediante luz ultravioleta. En comparación con los **revestimientos acuosos**, los ultravioleta (o UV) ofrecen una mayor protección contra rascadas o daños producidos por su manipulación, aunque se agrietan con facilidad. Este tipo de revestimientos se aplican a zonas específicas de trabajos de impresión, como *máscaras* de barniz, o como *camas*, si se cubre toda la página. Véase: **barniz**.

Ing: ULTRAVIOLET COATING
Fr: VERNIS UV
Al: UV-LACK
It: FINITURA A ULTRAVIOLETTI

Diseño: F33, www.f33.es

A B C D E F G H I J K L M N O P Q **R** S T U V W X Y Z

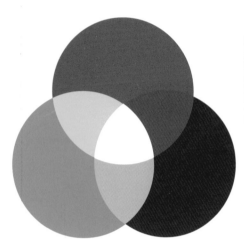

RGB

Sigla inglesa de rojo, verde y azul (*red*, *green*, *blue*), los colores usados para mostrar gráficos en los monitores o dispositivos digitales. El rojo, el verde y el azul son los llamados *colores primarios aditivos*, y combinados en la misma proporción forman el blanco. Corresponden a los tres receptores de luz del ojo humano. Véase: **CMYK**.

Ing: RGB
Fr: RVB
Al: RGB
It: RGB

Diseño: Donna S. Atwood, www.atwooddesign.com

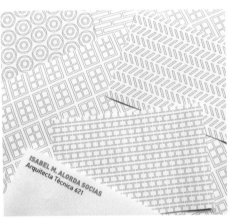

RITMO

Repetición visual creada mediante modelos estructurales subyacentes situados dentro y entre varios elementos de diseño, como el **tipo**, las **líneas** y las formas. Una única línea de tipo, por ejemplo, puede tener un ritmo propio debido a los trazados verticales creados mediante un interletraje cuidadoso. Los pósters o las portadas de libros suelen utilizar modelos geométricos para crear un ritmo estable sobre el que colocar elementos sorpresa. A mayor escala, las **cuadrículas** se pueden utilizar para crear un ritmo suave por toda una publicación larga, llevando al lector por ella.

Ing: RHYTHM
Fr: RYTHME
Al: RHYTHMUS
It: RITMO

Diseño: Damià Rotger Miró. Editorial Rotger;
Compañía: Dúctil, www.ductilct.com

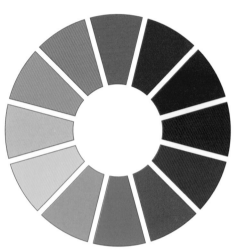

RUEDA DE COLORES

Espectro de colores representados en forma de segmentos de un círculo. La rueda de colores más común, utilizada para la mezcla de pigmentos, está formada por los **colores primarios** rojo, amarillo y azul, situados de forma equitativa en la circunferencia. El rojo, el amarillo y el azul son colores puros que no se pueden crear combinando otros colores. Sin embargo, su mezcla en diferentes proporciones puede proporcionar el resto de colores de la rueda. Existen otras ruedas de colores que muestran relaciones similares dentro de otros sistemas de color, como el modelo **RGB**, utilizado para visualizar gráficos en pantalla. Véase: **colores análogos**, **colores complementarios**, **colores primarios**, **colores secundarios** y **colores terciarios**.

Ing: COLOR WHEEL
Fr: ROUE CHROMATIQUE
Al: FARBKREIS
It: RUOTA DEI COLORI

Diseño: Donna S. Atwood, www.atwooddesign.com

A B C D E F G H I J K L M N O P Q R **S** T U V W X Y Z

No se nos otorgará la libertad externa más que en la medida
exacta en que hayamos sabido, en un momento determinado,
desarrollar nuestra libertad interna.

Ghandi

No se nos otorgará
la libertad externa más
que en la medida
exacta en que hayamos
sabido, en un momento
determinado,
desarrollar nuestra
libertad interna.

Ghandi

Estoy pensando en el verano, y me
acuerdo de ti, y de la casa de la playa.

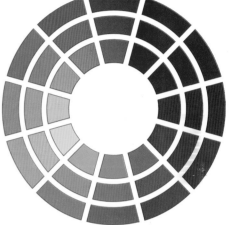

SALTO DE LÍNEA

Lugar en el que se acaba una línea de **tipo**,
para continuar en la siguiente línea. Las aplicaciones de maquetación realizan saltos de
línea después de un espacio entre palabras o
de un **guión**, **raya** o **semirraya**, aunque estos
ajustes automáticos pueden modificarse.
Para crear un salto de línea también se puede
utilizar un *retorno de carro*, empezando una
nueva línea de tipo sin necesidad de empezar
un nuevo párrafo (que tiene unas características específicas, como la *sangría*). Véase:
H&J y **ajuste de texto**.

Ing: LINE BREAK
Fr: SAUT DE LIGNE
Al: ZEILENUMBRUCH
It: INTERRUZIONE DI LINEA

SANGRÍA

Ajuste realizado en los márgenes de una o
más líneas de tipo. Se utiliza para marcar el
inicio de un párrafo nuevo, en el que se deja
un espacio al principio de la primera línea
mayor que en las líneas sucesivas. La *sangría
francesa* se utiliza para aumentar los márgenes de todas las líneas de un párrafo excepto
la primera. Los *recorridos* se pueden utilizar
para alterar los márgenes derecho o izquierdo
de muchas líneas de tipo, por ejemplo para
ajustarlas alrededor de una ilustración o fotografía. También se utiliza una *sangría en un
punto o carácter* para ajustar los márgenes a
un punto o carácter específico de una línea
de tipo previa.

Ing: INDENT
Fr: COMPOSITION EN ALINÉA
Al: ZEILENEINZUG
It: RIENTRO

SATURACIÓN

Pureza de un color en relación con la cantidad de gris que contiene. Los **matices** puros
están completamente saturados y son vivos.
Al disminuir los niveles de saturación, el color
se apaga a pesar de mantener el mismo matiz.
Se puede desaturar añadiendo gris a un matiz
o mezclándolo con una pequeña proporción
de su **complementario** (creando *tonos*).
También denominada *croma*. Véase: **color**.

Ing: SATURATION
Fr: SATURATION
Al: SÄTTIGUNG
It: SATURAZIONE

Diseño: Donna S. Atwood, www.atwooddesign.com

A B C D E F G H I J K L M N O P Q R **S** T U V W X Y Z

Garamond

Courier

Baskerville

Times

Palatino

Rockwell

Century

SCRIPT TYPE

Tipo de letra que imita la escritura a mano. Aunque proporciona a los textos un toque personal y elegante, hay que usarlo con moderación y únicamente dentro de un contexto adecuado, como por ejemplo en invitaciones y comunicados. Los textos largos escritos con este tipo de letra pueden aburrir al lector.

Ing: SCRIPT TYPE
Fr: CURSIVE
Al: SCHREIBSCHRIFT
It: CARATTERI INFORMALI

Diseño: Damià Rotger Miró; **Compañía:** Dúctil, www.ductilct.com

SEMIRRAYA

Trazo horizontal de la anchura de medio cuadratín. Véase: **raya** y **guión**.

Ing: EN DASH
Fr: TIRET DEMI-CADRATIN
Al: DIVIS
It: LINEETTA EN

SERIFA

Pequeño remate en el extremo del rasgo principal de un carácter. Las serifas ayudan a leer los distintos tipos, sobre todo en tamaños pequeños, en parte porque permiten que el ojo distinga con facilidad una letra de la siguiente. Las serifas se originaron en la antigua Roma, aunque los detalles del origen son tema de debate: hay quien sugiere que se originaron con los picapedreros, que las utilizaban para "limpiar" los trazos de los tipos cincelados, mientras que otros sugieren que fueron adornos creados por los pinceles utilizados para delimitar las letras antes de su tallado. Véase: **sans serif**.

Ing: SERIF
Fr: EMPATTEMENT
Al: SERIFE
It: CARATTERI CON GRAZIE

SERIGRAFÍA

Proceso de impresión en el que la tinta se hace pasar a través de una malla fina a la superficie del material de impresión, como papel o tela. Para determinar las áreas de la superficie que recibirán la tinta se utiliza una plantilla, que puede realizarse en otro material o sellando las partes de la malla. El uso más común de la serigrafía es la producción de ropa, aunque también se utiliza para imprimir sobre superficies irregulares.

Ing: SCREEN PRINTING
Fr: SÉRIGRAPHIE
Al: SIEBDRUCK
It: SERIGRAFIA

Diseño: Luis Princep Fabra; **Compañía:** DEFERE, www.defere.com

A B C D E F G H I J K L M N O P Q R **S** T U V W X Y Z

Miona a a *a* *a* a

ABCDEFGHIJKLM
NOPQRSTUVWXYZ
abcdefghijklmnopqrst
uvwxyz.fifl";-?¿$&*·§¶»
áàâäåñç@! (0123456789}
ćıćtchffgíıþıĨıtŝıste᷎a

Fabules	*rechenc*	*Entijans*
Webule	noîþtem	Rancord
Categorias	ģuitarró	Fatks 0,87
Armales	*Quantis*	*& xispa*
Reģistrar	*Pertshongs*	a unfen
hechos 24	**manehu**	*Zonhints*
Mercant	Zancontes	*Rimbaut*
Johnesem	Vonters	wendelin
...baheuf	*Bionic*	*matbinwe*

SET EXPERTO

Conjunto de caracteres tipográficos no ordinarios, como **versalitas**, **números elzevirianos**, **ligaduras**, etc., de una fuente específica. Los set expertos, indispensables para la tipografía elegante, solían venderse separados de las fuentes básicas, pero actualmente se incluyen dentro de las fuentes digitales *OpenType*. También denominado *fuentes alternativas*.

Ing: EXPERT SET
Fr: CARACTÈRES ÉTENDUS
Al: EXPERTENSATZ
It: EXPERT SET

Diseño: Damià Rotger Miró; **Compañía:** Dúctil, www.ductilct.com

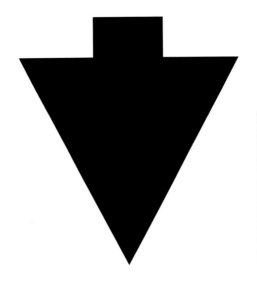

SÍMBOLO

Signo gráfico cuya representación es diferente de su significado. En muchas culturas, por ejemplo, la ilustración de un corazón, sobre todo si es rojo, simboliza el afecto y el amor. El signo no representa al amor, de hecho ni siquiera es un corazón real. Pero como su significado es universal, sirve como elemento de comunicación. De igual manera, una cruz roja lleva una carga de significado que puede ser entendida en casi todas las lenguas, superando las barreras culturales, pero esto sucede porque los usuarios del signo han acordado su significado. Véase: **icono** y **pictograma**.

Ing: SYMBOL
Fr: SYMBOLE
Al: SYMBOL
It: SIMBOLO

SIMETRÍA

Distribución regular de los elementos a lo largo de un eje, que puede estar orientado vertical u horizontalmente. Las maquetas simétricas se organizan de manera que los elementos se distribuyen de manera más o menos regular de arriba abajo, o de izquierda a derecha, por lo que suelen ser más conservadores, proporcionando una mayor estabilidad que en las maquetas asimétricas. Véase **asimetría**, **equilibrio**, y **línea de orientación**.

Ing: SYMMETRY
Fr: SYMÉTRIE
Al: SYMMETRIE
It: SIMMETRIA

Diseño: Maja Denzer; **Compañía:** Gestaltica, www.gestaltica.de

A B C D E F G H I J K L M N O P Q R **S** T U V W X Y Z

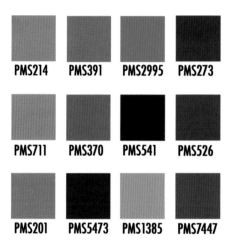

PMS214 PMS391 PMS2995 PMS273

PMS711 PMS370 PMS541 PMS526

PMS201 PMS5473 PMS1385 PMS7447

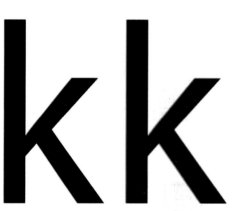

SISTEMA DE AJUSTE DEL COLOR

Variedad de referencias estándar utilizadas para la especificación precisa del **color**, que suelen presentarse en forma de cartas o muestras de colores con diferentes designaciones numéricas. Los diseñadores utilizan estas designaciones para asegurar que los colores usados en un proyecto se "traduzcan" correctamente en la fase de impresión. Para conseguir un ajuste de color preciso es necesario conocer el sistema que utiliza el dispositivo de impresión.

Ing: COLOR-MATCHING SYSTEM
Fr: SYSTÈME D'ASSORTIMENT DES COULEURS
Al: FARBKENNZEICHNUNGSSYSTEM
It: SISTEMA DI COMBINAZIONE DEI COLORI

SISTEMA DE EQUIPARACIÓN DE PANTONE (PMS)
Véase: **sistema de ajuste del color**.

SOBREIMPRESIÓN

Mezcla de tintas impresas, una encima de otra, de manera que se crea un nuevo color. En la mayoría de los casos, cuando dos elementos del diseño se solapan sólo se imprime el color del elemento superior, ya que su color sobresale de todo lo que hay debajo. Por otra parte, cuando la sobreimpresión ya está hecha, los dos colores, o más, de la tinta, se combinan para formar otro color.

Ing: OVERPRINTING
Fr: SURIMPRESSION
Al: ÜBERDRUCKEN
It: SOVRASTAMPA

Diseño: Damià Rotger Miró, Andreu Moragues, Laura Lerycke. Editorial Rotger; **Compañía:** Dúctil, www.ductilct.com

SOLAPAMIENTO/ANTISOLAPAMIENTO

El fenómeno de solapamiento se produce cuando la **resolución** de una imagen de **mapa de bits** es menor que la del dispositivo utilizado para su visualización o impresión. Una imagen con una resolución de 72 *muestras por pulgada* (spi), por ejemplo, mostrará solapamiento cuando se imprima a tamaño completo a 300 puntos por pulgada (**ppp**), lo que producirá un efecto escalado. El antisolapamiento es la técnica que utilizan los software de edición de imagen digital para minimizar la distorsión que se produce a causa del solapamiento. Esto se consigue difuminando ligeramente la imagen, suavizando los bordes cortantes del escalado. Aunque en el proceso de antisolapamiento se pierde calidad, es preferible al solapamiento. Véase: **Resolución**.

Ing: ALIASING, ANTI-ALIASING
Fr: CRÉNELAGE, ANTICRÉNELAGE
Al: ALIAS EFFEKT, ANTIALIASING
It: ALIASING/ANTI-ALIASING

A B C D E F G H I J K L M N O P Q R **S** T U V W X Y Z

$Agua \rightarrow H_2O$

distintas edades del espacio, la interpretación de la arquitectura y acabando con una reflexión por la historia moderna de la arquitectura. La gran mayoría de ejemplos que aparece en el libro se refiere a obra pública o religiosa.

Analizando brevemente la obra construida en Menorca durante los últimos veinte años, las más significativas también siguen estas pautas, con un compromiso

SUBÍNDICE

Carácter de tamaño menor que el texto principal, normalmente colocado sobre la línea de base. Se utiliza en notación matemática y fórmulas científicas. Los subíndices creados a partir de versiones en escala de caracteres estándar tendrán un peso menor que los tipos del resto de texto, lo que puede distraer la atención del lector. Por esta razón, los tipógrafos y diseñadores prefieren utilizar fuentes especiales para los subíndices.

Ing: SUBSCRIPT
Fr: INDICE
Al: TIEFGESTELLTE SCHRIFTZEICHEN
It: PEDICE/I

SUBTÍTULO

Título de menor nivel que se utiliza para romper un texto largo en diferentes secciones, mostrando su estructura y **jerarquía**. La **composición** de los subtítulos de una publicación (tamaño, **color**, **tipo de letra** y ubicación) debería reflejar el grado de similitud o diferencia entre un nivel y el "superior" o "inferior" a él. Por ejemplo, si los *subtítulos de nivel A* se utilizan para nombres de ciudades principales y los *subtítulos de nivel B* se usan para las categorías de datos censales, es mejor que sean diferentes.

Ing: SUBHEAD
Fr: INTERTITRE
Al: UNTERTITEL
It: SOTTOTITOLO

Diseño: Damià Rotger Miró. Editorial Rotger; **Compañía:** Dúctil, www.ductilct.com

SUMARIO

Nota extraída de un artículo o texto, situada fuera del contexto original (aunque normalmente en la misma página) y compuesta de tal manera que atrae la atención del lector. A veces se componen en un **tipo de letra** mayor, o incluso diferente, del utilizado en el **cuerpo de texto**. Se puede diferenciar aún más mediante el color, los adornos, **bordes**, etc.

Ing: PULL QUOTE
Fr: EXERGUE
Al: HERVORGEHOBENES ZITAT
It: CITAZIONE ESTERNA

Diseño: Damià Rotger Miró; **Compañía:** Dúctil, www.ductilct.com

$$A^2 + B^2 = C^2$$

A1 594 x 841 mm		A2 420 x 594 mm	
		A3 297 x 420 mm	A4 210 x 297 mm
		A5 148 x 210 mm	A6 105 x 148 mm
			A7 / A8

A0 841 x 1189 mm

SUPERÍNDICE

Caracteres de de escala específica, más pequeños que el texto principal. La ubicación de los superíndices depende de su finalidad. Cuando son números que indican notas al pie o el numerador de una fracción, los supe-ríndices se alinean en la parte superior de la *línea ascendente*. En expresiones matemá-ticas o científicas la alineación es central. También se utilizan letras de *caja baja* como superíndices. En inglés, los *ordinales* utiliza-dos para las fechas (4th of July) se pueden expresar como superíndices (4th), aunque lo más correcto es expresarlo con letras de caja baja ordinarias.

Ing: SUPERSCRIPT
Fr: EXPOSANT
Al: HOCHGESTELLTE SCHRIFTZEICHEN
It: APICE/I

SURREALISMO

Movimiento artístico europeo (1920-1930) que plasmaba la intuición, los sueños y el inconsciente mediante yuxtaposiciones sorprendentes o inquietantes, ilusiones ópticas y violaciones de las leyes físicas. Los diseñadores gráficos se inspiraron tanto en las técnicas surrealistas como en la experi-mentación de la representación del espacio tridimensional.

Ing: SURREALISM
Fr: SURRÉALISME
Al: SURREALISMUS
It: SURREALISMO

Diseño: Antonio Guzmán; **Compañía:** Domodo estudio, www.domodoestudio.com

TAMAÑO DE HOJA

En EE.UU., los tamaños de hoja estándar parten de la medida de 8½ x 11 pulgadas, de manera que se pueden fabricar hojas con una cantidad mínima de material de desecho. Una hoja de 23 x 25 pulgadas se puede usar para crear un pliego de 16 páginas de 8½ x 11 pulgadas después del corte. En el resto del mundo, la Organización Internacional para la Estandarización (ISO) establece tamaños de página en metros cuadrados.

Ing: SHEET SIZES
Fr: FORMAT DE FEUILLE
Al: BOGENGRÖßEN
It: FORMATI DEI FOGLI

TAMAÑO DE PAPEL
Véase: **tamaño de hojas**.

A B C D E F G H I J K L M N O P Q R S **T** U V W X Y Z

TEXTO O TIPO CENTRADO

Líneas sucesivas de tipo alineadas de manera
que el punto medio de cada línea se sitúa
siguiendo una misma línea de referencia. Es
el utilizado en tarjetas de visita, invitaciones
y otros materiales con poco texto, ya que
requiere un patrón de lectura poco natural.
Véase: **alineación**.

Ing: CENTERED TYPE/TEXT
Fr: TEXTE CENTRÉ
Al: MITTELACHSSATZ
It: TESTO/CARATTERI CENTRATI

Diseño: Alex Aráez; **Compañía:** Alex Aráez,
www.therwx.com

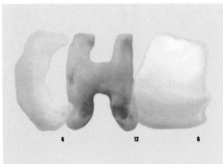

TEXTURA

Calidad táctil de algunos elementos de
diseño o una **maqueta**. A pesar de que el
término se utiliza sobre todo para describir
atributos tridimensionales, como la superficie del papel, también se puede usar para
describir esas mismas calidades en obras
de diseño bidimensionales. Por ejemplo,
existen diferentes modelos y gradientes
que proporcionan una sensación de textura,
sobre todo cuando se colocan en **contraste**
con elementos lisos y uniformes. Algunas
técnicas de impresión, como la xilografía,
también proporcionan textura. Incluso una
página de tipos, con sus **ritmos** verticales y
horizontales, tiene una cierta textura según la
composición del **tipo**. Cuando esta textura es
regular dentro de una página o maqueta, el
tipo tiene lo que los tipógrafos llaman "buen
color" tipográfico.

Ing: TEXTURE
Fr: TEXTURE
Al: STRUKTUR
It: TEXTURE

Diseño: Marieke Bielas; **Compañía:** Marieke Bielas,
www.contemporaryobject.net

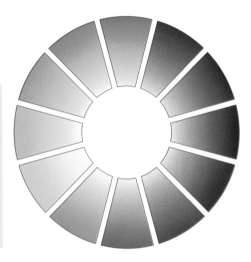

TINTE

Color creado añadiendo blanco a un matiz,
es decir, variando su **brillo**. También se
puede oscurecer un color, matizándolo en
negro. Este término se utiliza también para
expresar la densidad de puntos de las *tramas
de medio tono* usadas para la cuatricromía. Si
la trama de cian está cubierta por un 60% de
puntos se dice que tiene un tinte del 60%.

Ing: TINT
Fr: COULEUR DE FOND
Al: TÖNUNG
It: TINTA

Diseño: Donna S. Atwood, www.atwooddesign.com

A B C D E F G H I J K L M N O P Q R S **T** U V W X Y Z

GUAY
COOL
TRENDY
CHACHI

ABCDEFGHIJKLMNÑOPQRSTUVWXYZ

TIPO

Conjunto de caracteres ordenados de manera que pueden ser leídos tanto impresos como en pantalla. También se usa en referencia a las **fuentes** utilizadas para crear tipos, como en la frase: "Los *tipos* metálicos se guardaban en cajas…" Véase: **composición tipográfica** y **tipografía**.

Ing: TYPE
Fr: CARACTÈRES
Al: SCHRIFT
It: SEQUENZA DI CARATTERI

Diseño: Subcoolture Typeworks; **Compañía:** Subcoolture, www.subcoolture.com

ABCDEFGHIJKLMN
ÑOPQRSTUVWXYZ
abcdefghijklmnñop
qrstuvwxyz
1234567890
!$%&/()=?¿*¢¨ —:;,
.—´+`¡\@#´][

TIPO DE LETRA

Conjunto de caracteres que comparte características de diseño, como el *peso del trazado*, las proporciones, la presencia o ausencia de **serifas**, etc. Un tipo de letra está compuesto por letras (a menudo en *caja alta y caja baja*), números y un gran número de símbolos (tipográficos, matemáticos, etc.) A menudo se confunden los términos *tipo de letra* y **fuente**. El *tipo de letra* define el diseño general de los caracteres mientras que las *fuentes* son los medios de producción, que pueden ser mecánicos, fotomecánicos o digitales.

Ing: TYPEFACE
Fr: POLICE
Al: SCHRIFTTYPE
It: CARATTERE/I

Diseño: Subcoolture Typeworks; **Compañía:** Subcoolture, www.subcoolture.com

TIPO EN NEGATIVO

Tipo creado mediante la aplicación de tinta a las zonas de alrededor e interior de un carácter en lugar de sobre los trazos normales. Así, el tipo resultante es del color del papel utilizado, no de la tinta. Se puede conseguir el mismo efecto en los monitores de ordenador utilizando el mismo **color** de tipo y de fondo, y poniendo el tipo contra un campo de otro color. La anchura de los tipos de colores claros parece disminuir cuando se coloca contra un fondo oscuro, por lo que debe utilizarse un **tipo de letra** más grande y grueso para mantener la **legibilidad**.

Ing: REVERSE/REVERSE OUT
Fr: INVERSION
Al: NEGATIVE SCHRIFT
It: REVERSE/REVERSE OUT

Diseño: Luis Manteiga; **Compañía:** Luis Manteiga, luismanteiga@hotmail.com

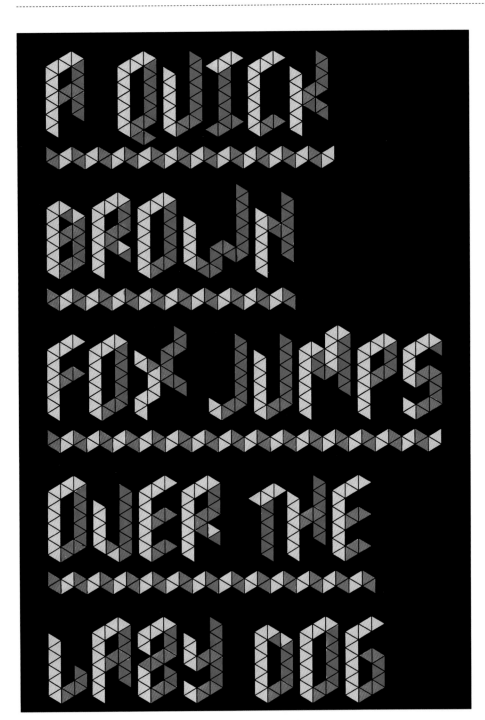

TIPOGRAFÍA

Arte y ciencia de la **composición tipográfica**. Los tipógrafos deben tener en cuenta un gran número de aspectos, desde lo general, como la **legibilidad** de un texto, hasta el más mínimo detalle, como el *kerning*. Aunque las tecnologías digitales facilitan el trabajo, los tipógrafos deben seguir fijándose en todos los detalles como cuando se usaban tipos metálicos o la *fototipia*.

Ing: TYPOGRAPHY
Fr: TYPOGRAPHIE
Al: TYPOGRAFIE
It: TIPOGRAFIA

Diseño: Bendita Gloria (Alba Rosell + Santi Fuster);
Compañía: Bendita Gloria, www.benditagloria.com

A B C D E F G H I J K L M N O P Q R S **T** U V W X Y Z

VIENTOS DE OPOLE. Música para gatos

TIPO TITULAR

Composición de **tipo** un punto mayor que el resto de un texto para distinguirlo del texto principal, como las que se utilizan en títulos y **titulares**.

Ing: DISPLAY TYPE
Fr: CARACTÈRES DE TITRE
Al: AUSZEICHNUNGSSCHRIFT
It: CARATTERI DI VISUALIZZAZIONE

Diseño: Performed by Lorenzo Petrantoni & Subcoolture; **Compañía:** Subcoolture, www.subcoolture.com

TITULAR

Término que suele asociarse al periodismo y la publicidad, utilizado para describir un texto muy breve que aparece antes del **cuerpo del texto**, con información sobre su contenido. Al crear el marco del texto, suelen escribirse en un tamaño mayor o con **tipografía** diferente a la utilizada para el cuerpo. En los titulares, sobre todo en periódicos, se utilizan **mayúsculas** o una combinación de mayúsculas y **versalitas**.

Ing: HEADLINE
Fr: CHAPEAU
Al: SCHLAGZEILE
It: TITOLO

Diseño: Max-o-matic; **Compañía:** Max-o-matic, www. maxomatic.net

TÍTULO

Recurso tipográfico para dividir un texto largo en sus principales secciones, como los capítulos en un libro o las secciones de un folleto o informe. Suelen expresarse en **mayúsculas** o mediante una combinación de mayúsculas y **versalitas**, a menudo en **negrita**. Los **subtítulos** se utilizan para dividir aún más un texto según su estructura organizativa.

Ing: HEADING
Fr: TITRE
Al: ÜBERSCHRIFT
It: TESTATINA

Diseño: Max-o-matic, Music: Vientos de Opole; **Compañía:** Max-o-matic, www. maxomatic.net

A B C D E F G H I J K L M N O P Q R S **T** U V W X Y Z

Tracking = 0

Una ciudad es un área urbana con alta densidad de población en la que predominan fundamentalmente la industria y los servicios. Se diferencia de otras entidades urbanas por diversos criterios, entre los que se incluyen población, densidad poblacional o estatuto legal, aunque su distinción varía entre países. La población de una ciudad puede variar entre unas pocas centenas de habitantes hasta una decena de millones de habitantes.

Tracking = 20

Una ciudad es un área urbana con alta densidad de población en la que predominan fundamentalmente la industria y los servicios. Se diferencia de otras entidades urbanas por diversos criterios, entre los que se incluyen población, densidad poblacional o estatuto legal, aunque su distinción varía entre países. La población de una ciudad puede variar entre unas pocas centenas de habitantes hasta una decena de millones de habitantes.

TRACKING

Medida del ajuste de una línea de tipo. Al aumentarlo, se amplía el espaciado general del tipo, acrecentando los espacios entre caracteres. Si se disminuye el *tracking* se produce el efecto contrario. El **interletraje** se refiere al espaciado entre caracteres en general mientras que el *tracking* cuantifica ese espacio.

Ing: TRACKING
Fr: APPROCHE DE GROUPE
Al: SPERREN
It: TRACKING

TRAZADO

Serie de curvas de Bézier o **vectores**, utilizadas por algunos *software* de diseño gráfico para describir las formas de varios elementos de diseño, como el tipo. Al ser vectores, los trazados pueden hacerse mucho más grandes sin afectar a la **resolución**. Los trazados definidos por el usuario suelen utilizarse para "cortar" una parte de una foto original y colocarla en otra, como cuando se añade una persona a una foto con Adobe Photoshop®.

Ing: PATH
Fr: CHEMIN
Al: PFAD
It: PERCORSO/I

Diseño: Paz Tornero; **Compañía:** Paz Tornero, www.paz.tornero.com

TRITONO
Véase: **bitono**.

TROQUELADO

Proceso mediante el cual se realizan cortes precisos sobre una hoja de papel impresa. Estos cortes pueden ser funcionales, como los de las carpetas con separadores o el sistema de lengüeta y ranura para embalajes, o decorativos, como en el caso de las ventanas utilizadas para mostrar imágenes o en el tratamiento de bordes. A veces se combina la funcionalidad y la decoración. Véase: **troquelado de medio corte** y **corte láser**.

Ing: DIE CUT
Fr: DÉCOUPE
Al: STANZSCHNITT
It: FUSTELLA

Diseño: Bendita Gloria (Alba Rosell + Santi Fuster); **Compañía:** Bendita Gloria, www.benditagloria.com

A B C D E F G H I J K L M N O P Q R S **T** U **V** W X Y Z

TROQUELADO DE MEDIO CORTE

Tipo de **troquelado** utilizado para pegatinas y calcomanías. El corte se realiza sobre el papel impreso sin llegar hasta el papel protector, permitiendo que las pegatinas o calcomanías puedan separarse de él.

Ing: KISS DIE CUT
Fr: DÉCOUPE PAR EFFLEUREMENT
Al: ANSTANZUNG
It: ADESIVO CON FUSTELLA

VALOR
Véase: **brillo**.

A B C D E F G H I J K L M N O P Q R S T U **V** W X Y Z

precio total con IVA

precio total con IVA

VERSALITA

Letras de caja alta de proporciones y grosor compatibles con las letras de caja baja de un **tipo de letra**. Se usan con las mismas funciones que los **números de caja alta**: porque son menos llamativos. Si se tiene que escribir un acrónimo dentro de una frase, el uso de mayúsculas sería una distracción. Otra ventaja de las versalitas es que sus proporciones proporcionan una mejor **legibilidad** incluso en pequeño tamaño.

Ing: SMALL CAPITALS/CAPS
Fr: PETITES CAPITALES
Al: KAPITÄLCHEN
It: MAIUSCOLETTI

VERSO
Véase: **recto/verso**.

VICTORIANO

Estilo arquitectónico decorativo, ostentoso, que apareció en Inglaterra y se hizo muy popular tanto en Europa como en EE.UU. entre 1820-1900. Toma su nombre de la Reina Victoria de Inglaterra. Este estilo fue la respuesta a la Revolución Industrial y al exceso que supuso el cambio de la producción artesana a la producción masiva. Los avances tecnológicos superaron las técnicas de diseñadores y tipógrafos y como resultado apareció una mezcla caótica de estilos de diferentes períodos. Durante la primera mitad de la época victoriana se mezclaban tipos desproporcionados de trazos gruesos, llamados *Fat Face*, con ilustraciones toscas y, dentro de una misma **maqueta**, se usaban **tipos** de estilos y tamaños diferentes, dando una sensación de agobio. Al final de este periodo empezó a usarse un estilo más claro y sofisticado.

Ing: VICTORIAN
Fr: STYLE VICTORIEN
Al: VIKTORIANISCHER STIL
It: STILE VITTORIANO

Diseño: Karen Hatzigeorgion; **Compañía:** Karen Hatzigeorgion, www.karenswhimsy.com

La viuda negra americana (***Latrodectus mactans***) es una araña araneomorfa, la más grande de la familia Theridiidae. También se la conoce como araña del lino o cuyucha (en Argentina), araña del trigo o araña de poto colorado (en Chile) y araña capulina en México.

VIUDA

Línea final de un párrafo demasiado corta, a veces formada únicamente por una palabra, que crea la sensación de un espacio entre párrafos que en realidad no existe. Al igual que con las **huérfanas**, las viudas se pueden evitar mediante varias técnicas, como el **interletraje** y la **partición silábica**. Véase: **H&J** y **ajuste de texto**.

Ing: WIDOW
Fr: VEUVE
Al: WITWE
It: VEDOVA

INDEX OF TERMS

English

Français

Deutsch

Italiano

Español